25 NOVEMBER 1917—4 MARCH 1918

ONE HUNDRED RED DAYS

A Personal Chronicle of The Bolshevik Revolution

BY EDGAR SISSON

SPECIAL REPRESENTATIVE OF
PRESIDENT WILSON IN RUSSIA

NEW HAVEN
YALE UNIVERSITY PRESS
LONDON · HUMPHREY MILFORD · OXFORD UNIVERSITY PRESS
1931

TO

DIXIE LADD SISSON

MY DEAR WIFE, WHO BORE THE STRAIN OF MY RUSSIAN DAYS
WITHOUT THE EXCITEMENT THAT LIGHTENED THEM FOR ME,
THIS BOOK OF THEIR RECORD IS LOVINGLY DEDICATED

The Enemies of Peace

I HAVE waited twelve years to assure myself that time would develop two conclusions reached through observation of the Bolshevik Revolution in Russia in 1917 and 1918.

The first was that there could be no peace in the world while the masters of one nation warred upon all other nations by fanning within them every attack upon their forms of government and every flame of dissension, whether economic, racial, or religious.

The second was that the leaders of the Russian adventure were doomed to die by violence, but that their movement—unless overthrown from within by revolt in consequence of famine or of reckless oppression, or from without because of mistaken effort for the military conquest of any of their western neighbors—would endure until the peasants became coherently conscious of their power and by pressure, either slow and continuous or centered in a single mighty impact, realized an intensely individualistic, small-landholding state, in the vernacular of the Bolsheviks themselves, a *petit-bourgeois* state.

A third possibility, that of military overturn of the leaders by the emergence of an able and ambitious chieftain, has of course been always inherent in the situation. Yet should such an event occur, it might only record a shift of power; or it might be transitional, either toward breakdown of Bolshevism and substitution of personal dictatorship and monarchy or toward new fury for World Revolution and military advance. The phenomenon, to this date, has not appeared; nor should its arrival more than temporarily deflect the course of the deeper-seated, broader-based peasant impulse. Under some form of government agreeable to them, the peasants, I am confident, ultimately will possess Russia.

Meantime there has been no peace. For twelve years Russian

Bolshevism has waged the war of World Revolution against all nationalistic governments, using the combined armament of advertising slogans and of mob incitement; posing itself against nationalistic defense in the hope of weakening the weak and of gaining, among the strong, the tolerance of good, peace-loving folk; preaching within national boundaries a gospel of hate for man toward man and of civil war—the merciless class war in comparison with which mere national war becomes civilized and bearable. In the lands of the strong the gains have been meagerly disproportionate to the effort, and will be as long as justice rules and opportunity for the individual prevails. As an object lesson to show the nations what conditions to avoid among their peoples in order to prevent the growth of the germs in a fertile soil, Bolshevism has indeed its uses. For Bolshevism as a tenet will starve to death in a happy land.

Realistically, however, the scene has another side. Russian Bolshevism is not the sort that waits for a propitious day. It aims, aggressively, to force the day. Its appeal is not to majorities but to minorities. Its reliance is force, guns in the hands of the disaffected. No less than Islam in the days when Mohammed exhorted and slew, it is militant. Aware, too, of its inability to keep its Russian supporters everlastingly on the emotional plane where they will stand sacrificial toil and deprivation, its leaders are obliged always to set millenniums on the hills ahead. When the particular hill is climbed and the particular millennium is not there, another has to be set up quickly. It is an exhausting process for leaders as well as followers. Lenin said in January, 1918, that the socialistic conquest of Russia should be complete in a few months, and that then the progressive World Revolution would begin. It must be said for him that he never reiterated that mistake of prophecy, while from it his successors learned the advantage of stretching time as far as they were able. Yet they must still place a definite goal. Hence the current visualization of the Five Year Plan for the winning of the economic victory in Russia. So a crisis, whether of joy or sorrow, will come in

Russia when the period of that plan approaches its last days, either attained or unattainable, omening plenty or famine. And whatever happens in Russia will have import for the world outside.

For many years the Bolsheviks have believed that the best road toward the World Revolution lay eastward into Asia. There, however, they have had, as elsewhere, more defeats than successes. Asia continues, nevertheless, to invite their presence by its continual turmoils and cleavages.

Once only has Russian Bolshevism trusted openly to arms and carried them beyond its borders against a western nation. When the Poles and the French turned back Trotsky's Red Army from the gates of Warsaw in 1920, it is not improbable that they set in history the date of the beginning of the ebb of western Bolshevism. We shall know presently.

Doom already has come to those who led the Russian Bolshevik Revolution. Of those whom I saw in the active executive rôles in 1917–18, Uritsky, Vorovsky, and Volodarsky died by assassination; Sverdlov died suddenly; Lenin, all his forces consumed as by fire, died in his bed, having survived two attempts at assassination, his shoulder bearing the scar of a deflected bullet; Dzerzhinsky, the killer in the deferred and awful Red Terror, died in 1926, an emaciated, fear-haunted wraith; and Ioffe killed himself.

Trotsky, Karakhan, Lunacharsky, Zinoviev, Dybenko, Kamenev, Chicherin, Bukharin, and Radek, of the original group, remain alive—unless Dybenko has died in the obscurity which engulfed him after he was deposed as Navy Commissar. Of them all, however, only Karakhan has active political office or power in this autumn of 1930. Trotsky, again a writing man, is an exile in Turkey, the doors of Russia and all other European countries closed equally against him. Chicherin, invalided, has been superseded in the Foreign Office by Litvinov, who does date far back, but whose post was outside of Russia in 1917–18. Lunacharsky was removed from his office of Minister of Education in 1929. Zinoviev was ousted with

Trotsky and humbled himself to make an underling's terms with Stalin. Kamenev is Trotsky's brother-in-law and shared his fall. Radek is a cynical, witty adventurer, who gambled and lost. Karakhan, the suave, after eclipse due to failure to dominate the Chinese Nationalist movement for Bolshevism, reappeared again in 1929, owing to his useful knowledge of Asia, but Stalin holds him in check. Bukharin is a stubborn doctrinaire, close to Lenin in the latter's lifetime, gradually demoted since, and publicly threatened on October 28, 1929, with "Bolshevik rigor" if he did not cease opposition to Stalin. He thereupon recanted.

Stalin is not the newer figure he is supposed to be. In justice he could be called a member of the inner body of power from the first, although it was not until January, 1918, that he became visible.

The English of Stalin is Steel, and as the name was self-chosen as a party alias or *nom de guerre* by this dour Georgian, born Djugashvili, it explains a good deal about the man and his ambitions, which are measureless.

Will he become a new Tsar, a Red War-Maker, or an overthrown leader?

All these possibilities are in him.

Bolshevism overthrew Democracy and became a despotism. After these repressive years, Democracy again becomes the best foeman of Bolshevism, since it offers freedom. As Russia has neither free speech nor free press, the difficulty—on which the Bolsheviks rely defensively—is the lack of a rostrum on which to cry a popular party program. The appeal itself is simple. The piercing of the censorship and secret police cordons for its distribution within Russia the Bolsheviks believe to be impossible. Perhaps so. Yet a compact party organization would try. It might overthrow Stalin and Bolshevism together if it could strew among the peasants the promise that it would give them ownership titles to the lands they occupy and till only at the will of a government which, now threatening and now mollifying, persists in dispossessing them in favor of vast national farm units where they are to become state laborers, the new serfs of Bolshevism. Such a party could perpetuate itself, after its first victory, by keeping that promise.

E. S.

New York City,
    January, 1931.

CONTENTS

ERRATUM

For Kuhlman *passim* read Kühlmann

LIST OF ILLUSTRATIONS

BEFORE THE HUNDRED DAYS

CHAPTER I

Orders from President Wilson.
Breaking into Russia.

1.

PRESIDENT Woodrow Wilson ordered me, on Tuesday, October 23, 1917, to go to Russia. I sailed from New York on Saturday, October 27, and reached Petrograd on November 25.

My letters of introduction were to Premier Kerensky and the members of his cabinet; my powers were wide and were increased by the control of funds. The men to whom the letters were written were fugitives when I got to Petrograd, overthrown by the Bolsheviks on November 7. But opportunity remained for disseminating the war and the peace aims of President Wilson throughout Russia and into Germany, and for feeding into Germany the facts of America's steadily growing war power. So I stayed in Russia to utilize this chance, coming among the Bolsheviks on the eighteenth day of their Revolution and leaving them on the one hundred and eighteenth day, they on that day in full possession of their sorry Brest-Litovsk Peace with Germany.

My mission was to organize for operation the practicable portion of the recommendations of the Root Commission, concerning the diffusion of information of American purpose and effort, to participate in all movements to support Russian morale, and from the Russian base to do whatever was possible to weaken German morale.

The plan was a composite of the administrative experience of the Committee on Public Information in the months of its domestic operation, of the suggestions of the Root Commission, and of the views of the President.

The Root Commission, headed by the veteran statesman and famous orator, Elihu Root, was sent to Russia following our entry into the War not only to give visible and oral proof of the sympathy of the American people and its Government for the democratic Provisional Government which had been recognized by the United States as the successor of the former Tsarist Government, but also to learn what were the Russian needs and what help could be given to an Ally.

The Report of the Commission on its return made recommendations of large scope covering financial and technical and welfare assistance. Some of this aid could be, and was, quickly given. The American Red Cross sent a medical and welfare unit into Russia. Railroad experts, directed by John F. Stevens, a noted engineer, attacked the complicated transport problem. Y.M.C.A. groups that were ready, just before we were drawn into the War, to go into Germany to give neutral service at war prison camps, were diverted into Russia.

Sections of the Root Report upon these subjects, except that of the Y.M.C.A., which was dealt with under the heading of army morale, were not brought into the area of the Committee on Public Information. The President, however, referred to the Chairman of the Committee, for study and report back to him, the recommendations of the Commission relating to news service, periodicals, pamphlets, advertising, film distribution, public speakers, establishment of government centers, and army morale apart from its military phases.

The Commission in drawing its Report had implied that administration of the proposed installations should be under the State Department, which in practice would be under the Embassy in Russia, with oversight from the Secretary of State.

As the President had created the Committee on Public Information as the instrument "for the business of mobilizing the mind of the world so far as American participation in the war was concerned,"[1] he delegated administration to the Committee instead of the State Department.

The Committee on Public Information was a division of the Executive Department. Its members were the Secretaries of War, Navy, and State, and George Creel, who was Chairman. In May, 1917, a few weeks after the Committee was formed, I became, by appointment of Mr. Creel, Associate Chairman.

The first labors of the Committee were national, within the country solely, but even before the Root recommendations were

[1] Quoted from the address of Secretary of War Newton D. Baker, member of the Committee, at a dinner given to Chairman Creel of the Committee in Washington, Nov. 29, 1918.

referred to the organization it was recognized that the time
had come for the extension of the service both to the capitals
of our Allies and to the neutral countries abutting on the Central
Empires. The Committee already had received the approval
of the President for the twin tenets of all foreign presentation
of the American cause.

They were:

For the Central Empires (through infiltration from neutral
and Allied countries): Fact news tending cumulatively to
demonstrate the inevitability of defeat from the oncoming military
and economic power of the United States. If the enemy
scoffed or denied, so much the better, since the eventual disclosure
would be that the leaders had deceived their own
people, intensifying then the loss of national morale. The General
Staff of the Army selected for committee broadcast the
military truths that would disconcert the enemy.

For the rest of the world, Allies and neutrals: Diversified
evidence of the unselfish aims of the United States, and promulgation
of its war and peace aims.

The instruments of the campaigns were to be the cable, the
wireless, the printing press, the mail, and the films.

In many particulars the specific suggestions of the Root
Commission conformed with the Committee's outline for foreign
countries. Some, however, were too vague, and some unpractical.
Chairman Creel analyzed the Report carefully and
we discussed the various proposals. We had found that for the
quick building of a gigantic advertising enterprise, section had
to be added to section, and that too much of set plans hampered
instead of helped. We had learned, too, that the best results
came from restricted and businesslike expenditure of money.
Every dollar had to do its work.

The Commission recommendations were on the basis of a
grant of $5,500,000, not in itself a big sum in a day of war
credits advanced in the billions, yet a vast amount when expressed
in terms of printing, circulation, cables, wireless, service,
office cost, and travel. Figures have to be grasped relatively.
The final accounting of the Committee on Public
Information in 1919 showed a total appropriation of $6,850,-
000 against which the Committee had a credit for earnings of
$2,825,670 from films and expositions; and it returned $2,-
385,397 to the Treasury of the United States. The whole cost

to the Government for its war-day mouthpiece was $4,464,-602.[2] Of this sum the expense of the Foreign Section, of which I became General Director on my return from Russia in the spring of 1918, was $1,723,960, for operative centers in sixteen countries.

Since other nations have said that America's presentation of its cause was unparalleled and have assumed that limitless expenditure of money was the reason, the citation of figures has validity.

The Russian estimates, when we saw them, danced before our eyes.

The recommendations, on a year's budget, were:

1. The establishment of a modern news service to furnish news to all periodicals in Russia . . . . . $ 285,000
2. Printing and distribution of pamphlets and leaflets 500,000
3. A film service 255,000
4. Color poster advertising 211,000
5. Employment of 500 Russian orators to influence public opinion 405,000
6. Headquarters in Petrograd 51,000
7. Subsidies to Russian agencies such as $10,000 to the *Soldiers' Newspaper* 250,000
8. An emergency fund for increased service 250,000

TOTAL $2,207,000

9. To strengthen the morale of the army, the employment of 700 secretaries and the erection of 200 buildings 3,305,000

TOTAL $5,512,000

Chairman Creel's memorandum to the President advised a news service on a scale double that of the commission estimate, a film service at the commission estimate, and the allotment of $10,000 to the *Soldiers' Newspaper*, and disapproved the other projects. He suggested an allotment of $810,000, not to include the cost of whatever more moderate program the Y.M.C.A. itself might adopt. Subsidies to newspapers were viewed as improper. Though the *Soldiers' Newspaper* was excepted, it did not receive funds as its career ended in Novem-

[2] Report of the Committee on Public Information to Congress, June, 1919.

ber, 1917. Of the use of Russian speakers, Creel commented: "Who is to select 500 speakers? How are they to be trained? How is double dealing to be guarded against? In order to determine the effectiveness of the campaign and see that the 500 were not betraying the bureau, a large force of inspectors would have to be created."

The President approved the Creel summary, and instructed him to prepare to organize in accordance. Ultimately no set total of Russian allotment was made, it being decided to transfer funds in units of $250,000, as I might call for them. In one respect only was Creel in error on the usefulness of media in Russia. He did not think that leaflets and pamphlets were of value. I found the contrary to be true, and also added a new device, the wall poster. Had the service gone on uninterruptedly for a year the cost would have been in the vicinity of $1,000,000.

The choice of organizer became the question as soon as the Russian division was decreed. Staff, it was argued, could be assembled in Russia from different governmental offices. I had no idea of myself for the post. My work during the summer had been the building of machinery for the domestic distribution of the Committee's news service and handling the printing and distribution of the Committee's series of Red, White, and Blue Books. By autumn the news section was staffed and functioning and the problem of mass printing had been solved by taking over the presses of catalogue printing companies in New York. The Committee was now geared solely for diffusion, having avoided the bogey of censorship by outlining a volunteer system under which the newspapers censored themselves. Without being quite conscious of the condition, so full of details could a day crowd itself, I was ready for other effort; and so may have been chosen. I do not know. Others were up for consideration.

The President and Creel were in consultation, and no decision was reached over the week-end.

Then on Monday afternoon Creel came restlessly into my office, one hand rumpling his thick black hair, and his lips moving. These were signs of concentration with him—he was phrasing his thoughts.

"I have an appointment for you with the President tomorrow afternoon," he said abruptly. "I'll go over with you."

"On the carpet?" I questioned. "For what?"

"He is apt to ask you to go to Russia? Can you go?"

Nor did Creel ever tell me more directly that I was his selection, and that he had secured the President's assent.

But could I go? My wife had come to Washington with our daughter and son and fitted out a new home for us. My sturdy young daughter was in the local Red Cross ambulance corps, my wife about to join, my son in high school. Although transplanted, they had found new and useful interests. Now they would have to winter alone, and thriftily—for I was not a dollar-a-year man, but a person paying war taxes on last year's civilian salary and eating into nominal reserves to eke out government pay.

My wife should take part in any decision to be made, I told Creel. We left it so.

In the evening, hesitatingly, I told my wife what had happened, concluding unconvincingly that it might be possible to make the journey in three weeks, complete the organization in another three weeks—for it was not thought that I would have to remain to operate—and return in another three weeks. I knew better. So did she.

"If the President asks you," she said finally, "you must go. When will they want you to start?"

"At once, if at all," I said. "Perhaps I'll not be asked."

"No," she said. "You are going. I feel it."

Creel and I went to the White House the next afternoon. By my greeting from the President I saw that my assumption of a preliminary interview was wrong. I had been called before him to receive going-away orders. I looked sideways at Creel. He was smiling. I hid my feelings under as stoic a pose as possible. Except as an intelligence who would have the responsibility of voicing him, I was in the President's regard an impersonal factor. I concentrated on listening.

We were all standing, and at the beginning of the talk the President walked back and forth, three or four paces, treading deliberately. Finally, he stood still, continuing to speak in short, conversational sentences. The gist of his talk was the necessity of making understandable to a newborn democracy the fellow feeling of our own older state, our friendliness, our unselfishness toward Russia, and our desire of helpfulness. The war aspects, he seemed confident, would take care of themselves if a bond were forged between the Russian and the American people. Of details of what I was to do he said nothing. Principles with him were the essential. Operation he delegated. Sometimes I have wondered whether he did not believe that if the principles were right they would operate themselves. Yet that quality of mind is the attribute of great leaders, the source of their dominion.

The President's physical state that afternoon was of the best. The arduous months of war had not worn him down. His face, indeed, was setting in sterner lines than of old, but became singularly kind when he smiled. He had pleasant, journey-speeding words for me in parting.

A final note of guidance came from him before I left Washington:

24 Oct., 1917.

MY DEAR MR. SISSON:

Mr. Creel informs me that you are leaving for Russia at once. In our conversation of yesterday I tried to make clear my views as to the nature and extent of any manifestation of our interest in the Russian struggle, and I know you will be guided by them in everything you say or do.

We want nothing for ourselves and this very unselfishness carries with it an obligation of open dealing. Wherever the fundamental principles of Russian freedom are at stake we stand ready to render such aid as lies in our power, but I want this helpfulness based upon request and not upon offer. Guard particularly against any effect of officious intrusion or meddling and try to express the disinterested friendship that is our sole impulse.

It is a distinct service that you are privileged to render your country and the whole democratic movement, and I know that this will serve at once as reward and inspiration.

Sincerely yours,
WOODROW WILSON.

MR. EDGAR G. SISSON
Committee on Public Information, Washington, D. C.

When the President talked with us and when he wrote this note, it was the belief of the three of us that I was going as a friend to a friendly country. A new republic, apparently, was being born, patterned on representative and constitutional lines. The word Bolshevik scarce had been heard in the whole country, and its political significance was understood only by a few persons of foreign background and by some American Socialists. A brief effort at a Bolshevik uprising in Petrograd had, indeed, attracted attention in July, but the outbreak was quelled swiftly and the leaders had been in hiding since. I had no reason to believe that Bolshevism was even a cloud on the Russian horizon when I left Washington. Yet the Bolshevik overturn in Russia was only thirteen days distant.

On Tuesday evening, following the interview with the President, John R. Mott and Cyrus W. McCormick, representing the Y.M.C.A., came to Creel's office to give me messages to their forces in Russia, and for informal discussion with Creel and me. It was decided that a Y.M.C.A. leader should follow me as soon as possible and work in alliance with me. I was to bear that word to the different sectional leaders. There was to be a steady expansion of the Y.M.C.A. army service, though not to the degree contemplated by the Root Commission. Creel was to participate in the arrangements.

My preparations for a start were made quietly. A treasury allotment was placed to my order in a New York bank, which arranged for cable transfer to its Petrograd correspondent bank. Progress bade fair to be as orderly as that. The Navy Department told me I would have passage on the *New York*, famous as a fast scout and dispatch boat in the Spanish-American War, and in its old age again in war-dispatch service. By late afternoon Wednesday I was ready to close my desk.

As I was about to leave I had a caller, an old friend, Julian Street, traveler, writer, and humorist. One glance at him, and I saw he was in the dumps. Under a little prodding he admitted that the gloom of the War had got him. All he could do, he said, was to write a few foolish pieces or swing his hat in the cheer section. What he needed, I thought, was a bit of chatter to relieve drabness. So I took him home to dinner, telephoning my wife to avoid the Russian topic.

The dinner was good for us all. After Julian had groaned over the state of the world and the War, he became his entertaining self, and we were brightened together. The conversation went on finally to magazine matters, and he asked me if I had any idea when I would return to the editorship of *Cosmopolitan Magazine*. I told him I thought never, as I had during

THE WHITE HOUSE
WASHINGTON

24 October, 1917

My dear Mr. Sisson:

Mr. Creel informs me that you are leaving for Russia at once. In our conversation of yesterday I tried to make clear my views as to the nature and extent of any manifestation of our interest in the Russian struggle, and I know that you will be guided by them in everything that you say or do.

We want nothing for ourselves and this very unselfishness carries with it an obligation of open-dealing. Wherever the fundamental principles of Russian freedom are at stake, we stand ready to render such aid as lies in our power, but I want this helpfulness based upon request and not upon offer. Guard particularly against any effect of officious intrusion or meddling, and try to express the disinterested friendship that is our sole impulse.

It is

-2-

It is a distinct service that you are privileged to render your country and the whole democratic movement, and I know that this will serve at once as reward and inspiration.

Sincerely yours,

Woodrow Wilson

Mr. Edgar G. Sisson,
Committee on Public Information,
Washington, D. C.

the day informed the business manager of the magazine that since the War promised to be indefinite, there was no use holding the post longer for me. I had been on leave of absence without salary since May.

"Well, if the War goes on indefinitely as you seem to think, what are you going to do next?" he questioned, glum once more.

"I am going to Russia," I said. He dropped his coffee spoon.

"When?" he asked.

"I'm starting tonight," I replied.

"My God!" he exclaimed. Life had become interesting to him again.

He rode to the station with the family party.

Outfitting in New York for a Russian winter appeared a difficulty to me. Not one, however, for my wife. She knew what to do. Nothing but fur or leather will keep a zero wind from biting through, but I was too slight to bear the weight of a fur coat. My wife searched until she found a cloth coat lined with soft and almost weightless fur, with a high fur-lined collar. It kept me comfortable all winter, although there were stretches of days when the thermometer stayed between twenty-two and thirty degrees below zero. Light woolen underwear, overshoes high enough to buckle over trouser bottoms, fur-lined gloves, and sweaters completed the basic purchases. As it was the Russian habit to take off overshoes every time one entered either house or office, I sometimes unclasped and re-clasped those shoes twenty times a day. No wonder the Russians wore slip-ons. Yet the latter were designed for clean streets, for snow banks stripped the loose shoes from the feet. As street cleaning was included early in the Bolshevik discard of utilities and amenities, I was to be glad that I had wading shoes.

I went aboard the *New York* on Saturday morning, October 27. She lay in dock below Twenty-third Street, her trim lines distorted, foreshortened, and fractured by a pastel *camouflage*. Creel came from Washington to see me off.

There were only a score of civilian first-cabin passengers on board, nearly all of these, too, in government service, ours or the Allies'. Of the military and naval balance, ninety-odd, most were army engineer officers and junior naval officers going to join Admiral Sims's destroyer unit.

Among the passengers was Capt. Sir William Wiseman, the slight, cool, and canny man whom I knew to be David Lloyd George's confidential messenger between London and Washington. Captain Wiseman knew also that I was on mission from President Wilson, and my destination. In London he speeded up requests to the British Government for transportation onward. On board ship he was an amusing companion. Invalided after passing through the hell of the defensive fighting of Kitchener's proud-named Contemptibles, he glossed satire over reality and so kept life palatable. He was wearied, too, of all slogans, including that of Democracy. "I would be willing," he said, "to pass the rest of my life on a desert island, if I were sure that there I would never hear the word again." On this sentiment he and I disagreed whimsically, not only because I had more faith in the course of a solid-boned democracy than I had in the edicts of any class, but because I felt that as an implement of offense in the war against Germany, Democracy, given diffusion, was a prime reliance.

We voyaged serenely, little inconvenienced either by the darkened decks at night, or by the zigzagging maneuvers of the ship in the submarine zone. The most beautiful sight on a submarine-infested sea, I am sure, is the one we saw the next Saturday afternoon. Three destroyers came over the horizon line and in a few minutes we could make out the American flags flying over them. They were up to us speedily, and took up our course, one on each side and the third, at higher speed, darting around irregularly. The escort remained with us until Monday morning when, off the Welsh coast, we passed into the lines of the British patrols. On Monday evening, November 5, we docked at Liverpool.

The clutter of Liverpool did not carry with it the atmosphere of war change. But London in mid-afternoon next day was different. There were no waiting taxicabs at the station and no porters. I left my baggage on the platform and went out on the street to hunt a taxi, a job that took fifteen minutes and six blocks of walking.

Quarters were waiting for me at the Savoy, an embassy courtesy I appreciated the more when I discovered that the hotels were crowded with officers on leave. Late that afternoon I reported at the American Embassy, then at 4 Grosvenor

Gardens, near Buckingham Palace. There I found a welcome from Secretary Crosby of the embassy staff. He said that a request would go at once to the Admiralty for transportation to Norway, and that an appointment had been made for a call on Ambassador Page next day.

When I did meet the Ambassador he was cordial, asked me many questions about the state of affairs at Washington, and offered me every help of the embassy staff. The Embassy had become a center of war activities, and was soon to be doubly and triply expanded. The courier service for all Europe was to be handled from there, the shore offices of the navy were there, and war-trade controls were to be located there.

But if Walter Hines Page had been alone, the United States could have had no better symbol of itself in Great Britain than he. There were gloomy times when the British people turned to this southern gentleman as to a prophet of hope. They had courage but they needed cheer, and cheer he gave. They felt that he put the American people at their back.

He gave his life not to one but to two countries, and when the War was over came home to die. If there could be any tragedy about such a career it was that of the sensitive, imaginative writing-man. A master of expression, he was precise and fluent in the relation of his views and feelings. The record of both, I knew, was considered of unceasing value at Washington. Yet it would have required a secretariat there to have replied to all of his correspondence. The State Department was undermanned in the war period, and the Executive Department, and the President overburdened with daily labor. In communications to ambassadors the cable superseded the letter and to Ambassador Page the cable seemed curt and lacking in mannered grace. I sought to ease the situation a little by an account of the stress everywhere at Washington. Mr. Page then appeared in good health, a vigorous, gracious personality. Six months later, when I saw him next, signs of weariness, if not illness, were visible.

My stay in London might be short or long. I gave myself to observation. London was thronged with soldiers on leave and the industry of the city seemed to be for their entertainment. The theaters, given over for the most part to revues, were crowded nightly, and while the streets were in darkness except for occasional lights masked above and throwing dim rays downward, the heavy traffic poured along them with little confusion. The Hyde Park commons were occupied with anti-aircraft equipment; otherwise the defenses of the city were not visible.

At the Savoy Hotel an orchestra of American darky banjo players was performing in the lounge, and winning acclaim. Jazz, as such, had not arrived, though its forerunner was on the scene. There was no dinner dancing, however. One could enter the dining-room in the evening in street clothes, although the dinner jacket was common among those not in uniform. Even after three years of war London was changing its social ways as slowly as possible. Women were smoking cigarettes at dinner tables and in the lounge. As a measure of the habits of the America of 1917, the prevalence of women smokers in England struck me as odd.

Of the evening lounge-room picture, I wrote:

A gorgeous scene, with the somber pushed away. Uniformed officers predominate among the men, many wearing wound stripes, the others home on lively leave. And uniforms of all sorts: the Highland tartan, sometimes kilted, sometimes (ugly to my eye) trousered; the splendid chain epaulets of the Guards; the wings of the flyers; boots and spurs; puttees and riding crops; the blue of the Navy, our own as well as the British; and not infrequently the trim cut of our own infantry, as natty as the nattiest when set off by a good figure and the Sam Brown belt. The age of the British officers impressed me often by its contrasts, for the men of fifty and the boys of twenty were equally noticeable. It is evident that England has mustered her strength to the full of her man power.

The tax, too, upon food resources was apparent. At the end of three days, I noted:

I am accustomed already to my one slice of brown bread at a meal. Sugar one lump (large) or two (small). Sufficient meat, drink in plenty. Butter enough. Very little fruit. England, I should say, has food for its necessities and none to spare. If there is starvation anywhere, it is kept from sight. Germany's chance of starving England does not look any better than its chance of destroying London with air bombs.

What I set down, had I but known, was food luxury. I was to do without butter and with little sugar for the next five months.

In spare daytime I walked the streets to touch the populace. No lights of merriment there. No one smiled. My spirits went down. I feared the consequences of new disasters, if they came. I was next to be in London when the disasters had come, when the contingency of the abandonment of Boulogne and the north of France was being faced, when British armies had melted away in the most terrorizing defeat of the War. Yet the British head was up, the British spirit was swelling: it was as if the nation trod to the beat of an ancestral warrior chant. Odd folk, the British, and hard to lick! Grouchy with nothing worse than a cold dull winter ahead, uplifted when they stood at bay!

2.

Vague word of a strange new Russian disturbance called Bolshevik began to permeate London. Petrograd became silent. Accounts from points outside Russia were murky and contradictory. There were rumors that Kerensky had fled and rumors that he had placed himself at the head of a loyal army outside of Petrograd and was returning to crush the rebellious city. The American Embassy was no better informed than others. Though deeply concerned I could learn nothing dependable anywhere. When Washington heard that Kerensky had fallen, would I be recalled? No message came to me. Therefore it was meant that I should go on—which was what I wanted to do.

The Bolsheviks have recorded their Revolution as dating officially from November 7 of the Western Calendar, which is October 25 of the Russian Old Style Calendar that continued to be the calendar of Russia until February 1, 1918, when by decree the Western Calendar was adopted. Not for ten days did they begin to have confidence in their hold on Petrograd; and Moscow still held out against them. So it was not surprising that the world outside could get few facts. I hoped the curtain would stay down until I could get behind it. The journey delay fretted me.

The Embassy doubted whether I could get beyond Stockholm. Mail was being bagged for Scandinavia and Russia in the first trip to be made by courier, inaugurating that service.

The expectation was for indefinite delay in Sweden until the Russian frontier should open. It was now closed. Well, Stockholm was a good distance off. I could worry about frontiers when I got there. The courier and I would travel together. I took leave of Ambassador Page on Friday, November 9, packed, and waited.

The starting summons came at nine o'clock Saturday night. An hour later, the courier and I, sharing two compartments with the mail, were speeding on a dispatch train for Aberdeen, the port of crossing. The courier was First Sergeant Joseph Franklin of the U.S. Marines. Though he also had come to England on the *New York*, our first acquaintance was when we looked each other over under the light in the compartment, knowing we were going to be companions on what probably would be a tough trip. The odds were all with him. I was disclosed as a short eye-glassed person of neutral hue; but the whole square cut of him was pleasing to me. A frank and sturdy personality, I thought. I never was to change that view. In his own belief too old for the officer's commission offered him, he had welcomed assignment to embassy service abroad. He bore marks of wounds from the Spanish-American War, the Philippine insurrection, and the Boxer campaign.

The sun was rising as we alighted at Aberdeen, a rugged little stone city. In an hour's time we were aboard a yacht-like dispatch boat steaming toward the breakwater. Outside the harbor a destroyer fell in on each side and the dash across the North Sea for Bergen, Norway, was on—without any excitement. We did not zigzag, trusting to speed. The dispatch boat was nearly as fast as the destroyers. By late afternoon we were steaming up the winding fiord into Bergen Harbor.

With delays both at Bergen and at Christiania, where the American Minister, Albert Schmedeman, had been able to add only slightly to information of what was going on in Russia, a final tedious railroad journey of sixteen hours brought us into Stockholm on November 16.

What I heard from Minister Ira Morris was the worst—there was no entrance into Russia. The Bolsheviks were succeeding to the mastery of Petrograd. Only the young cadets of the Military School had put up a real fight against them, according to reports. The Russian army in Finland had joined the Reds. That had immediate meaning to me, for seven hundred miles of Finland from the head of the Gulf of Bothnia lay between Torneo, the frontier gate, and Petrograd. Nearly the same distance, of course, was between Stockholm and Haparanda, the Swedish town opposite Torneo, but for the journey to Haparanda the question was only one of time and orderly travel. Beyond, who could tell?

At the moment, it was plain, no one could. Franklin was ordered by Mr. Morris to remain at Stockholm. The Minister also pointed out to me that Stockholm was not lacking in desirable qualities as a residence, and that it should suit me as a working base. My instructions, however, were to go to Petrograd, and only the President, who gave them, could change them. He did not. Hence the snowy pavements of Stockholm burned my feet.

Patience was necessary for a day or so, however, and I took stock of the condition of the country. It was bad. Soft coal was selling at approximately $100 a ton. There had been little gasoline in Norway. There was none in Sweden. I wrote:

There is no tea or coffee in Sweden. Bread is rationed and my bread card is my most valued possession. The bread is black and soggy. Have not had any pure white bread since I left the Atlantic boat. In London it was part wheat; here no wheat. Butter, a trifle, once a day only. Sugar, one lump, at breakfast only. Meat and potatoes in plenty as yet but prices have mounted until the poor in the cities must be having a hard time. In the country it probably is better. Sweden has sold all it has to Germany and now is paying the price. . . . Minister Morris asked me to lunch with him today, which I did at the palace he rents from the King's second son. Mr. Morris has occupied the place for two years, the Prince is happy in the income, and the people (with whom he is popular) seem glad that the American Minister should have helped him out by leasing the palace. It is like a sumptuous American house, with pleasant grounds, a cheery outlook on the sun-side, where the sun-parlor (a feature of all Swedish houses) is the general family gathering room. The winter sun is travelling along so near the horizon that it seems always about to set. But the result is that on a sunny day the rays come into one room all day long. Mrs. Morris was a pleasant hostess, we had a good lunch (though no white bread) and cups of real coffee afterwards. The coffee came from London in one of Franklin's bags. Four small size pancakes served with strawberry preserves won my appetite the most. There was a tiny bit of butter to each person.

Money was abundant in Sweden, for Germany was a paying customer. So Sweden was overtempted in the selling of its food supplies and discovered it could not dine upon money. It was natural that the Allies looked coldly upon efforts to import provisions into Sweden, aware that any surplus would find its way into Germany. Sweden's geographical position made import difficult in any event. Norway, nearer to England and friendlier, fared better. At the worst, too, Norway always had fish and potatoes.

Affairs engrossed me again. I ran across a man who came calling at the Legation on the rumor that someone there was planning to attempt the Russian frontier. The caller was Captain Pirie of the British army, and of Gary, Indiana, U.S.A. Of the engineering staff of the United States Steel Company, but Canadian born, he had given up his job and gone to war, to find that his specialized training pursued him. In France he had charge of a plant for the reconditioning of artillery. Kerensky had asked England for an expert to establish similar works in Russia. England had sent him. British diplomats had detained him at Stockholm when the frontier closed. His work, he felt, would be delayed. That the guns he hoped to repair would not speak again in the World War none of us guessed. His papers were still held, but he was ready to go on without them. This course, I was sure, would not do, yet Captain Pirie was distinctly the man I wanted with me, particularly if Franklin had to be left behind.

My impression was that Pirie's papers would be released as soon as the American Legation sent official word that men of its own were going to try to get through. A plan of action was the first need. Up to this time—the eighteenth—no message from Torneo had come through Haparanda, on the Swedish side. Contact with Torneo was requisite. So the two of us agreed that Pirie should leave at once for Haparanda. As the town was in Sweden he would not need his passports. One of my tasks would be to bring them on to him. I either could wait report from him or start without it. Pirie left Stockholm for

Haparanda the next day—a more than twenty-four-hour journey.

As a matter of fact I did not intend to wait until I should have a report from Pirie. I knew from Minister Morris that when the frontiers were closed, which I judged to have been on November 8 or 9, a young *attaché* of the Petrograd Embassy, Lieut. A. L. Kliefoth, had been at Torneo as passport control officer. If I knew anything of his ilk, he was still there. I had told Captain Pirie to try to get in touch with him, and to tell him to expect me at Haparanda any day, with a likelihood that a courier with mail would be with me. As it happened Kliefoth got over to Haparanda before Pirie got there and wired that the border was still closed. The message, instead of depressing me, cheered me a lot, for if an American government man could get across the border in one direction, it implied that one could get across in the other.

I told the Minister I was going to Haparanda on the twenty-first, and argued that he should let Franklin take the mail at least that far, that the border was bound to open eventually, that when it did the mail ought to be at the entrance door, and that the probabilities were that the Russian Embassy badly needed the supplies contained in the heavier sacks. The Minister assented.

Then I asked him to inform the British that American mail was going out, that we understood Captain Pirie was at Haparanda and would be glad to take his papers to him. I had them in my pocket that afternoon.

Many mail bags were left at Stockholm—and more were added. The pile loaded on the Haparanda express was bigger than ever. Franklin was jubilant at the prospect of movement. The weather was cold, below freezing, but the train was as comfortable as any American train.

We reached Haparanda in the forenoon of November 22. I stepped off the car to take the handclasp not only of Captain Pirie but also of Lieutenant Kliefoth. They made a contrast— Kliefoth an arctic figure of furs, and tall and lean; Pirie trimly uniformed for not so cold a climate, and short and lean. For greeting to Pirie I put his papers in his hand. Of Kliefoth I asked our prospects.

Not a train had moved from Torneo, he said, yet there were

rumors every hour, had been for days. The best he knew was the report that the local Red Commissar was going to Petrograd. If he went, he would have to go by train. Ergo a train would have to go if he went. Our aim would be to be aboard. Could we, then, get to Torneo? The Swedes, it appeared, did not feel called upon to stop Americans or English if they wished to pass out of Sweden, while the Bolshevik control, new come to unknown powers, intended to do what it pleased to Russians and did not know what to do to foreigners. Hence, by Russian formula, it did nothing. Let the foreigners take care of the doing.

They had. Kliefoth and an English consular agent were running the control office in so far as foreigners were concerned, stamping papers and telling deputy commissars where to sign. The stream so far had been one way—refugees, going out.

Of Kliefoth, an account: A graduate of the University of Wisconsin, versed in several languages, he had trained himself to familiarity with all the schisms and patters of the so-called class conscious revolutionary groups. I believe he was the only person in government service to have knowledge in early 1917 of what Leninism was, certainly the only one who gave any indications of foreseeing how Lenin's brew would work toward disintegrating Russia if Lenin could be projected into the country.

He heard in the spring of 1917 that Germany had given Lenin passage through Germany from Switzerland, learned that Lenin had come to Stockholm, watched for his appearance at Torneo, uncovered him there, and Zinoviev, and their suite; obliged them to admit their identity, and induced the Russian control officers to refuse them entrance pending report to Petrograd. The Provisional Government, impractically faithful to its idealistic stand that Russia welcomed the return of all former exiles, ordered them to be let in, to its own destruction. In the same wise the Provisional Government brought Trotsky upon itself by requesting the British to free that homeward-bound worthy from Halifax arrest. The Russian Bolshevik Revolution may be compared to a game of consequences.

Kliefoth remained at Torneo until December, when permission to function longer was refused by the Bolsheviks; returned then to Petrograd; remained long in Russia, traversing it under cover from end to end, and for years later was in the Russian Division of the State Department at Washington. In 1930 he was First Secretary of the American Embassy at Berlin.

On the morning of my meeting with him, I knew him only as the person who could aid Franklin and Pirie and me to get into Finland, which was then Russian territory. Did he think we could risk the mail? Fortunately he had the knowledge most useful concerning embassy mail.

"There will be shoes everyone will need," he said, "and probably a lot of Christmas packages. You would be robbed if it was guessed that there was food also. But the courier looks husky. Might as well try to get the load through."

Franklin was certain no one was going to take his mail bags away from him. "Wish I was armed," he added. We laughed at him, and soon he laughed at himself. There was not a weapon in the party. Captain Pirie's side arms were packed away in his baggage, protected from search by diplomatic seal. Neither Franklin nor I carried a pistol, even under seal. Arms were banned at all borders.

We set about the movement toward Finland. Haparanda was a straggling town on one side of a stream, or possibly the arm of a bay. Torneo was a cluster of snow-mantled, indifferent buildings on the other side. Kliefoth got together a string of sledges, and while the mail was loading we got our passports stamped for exit from Sweden. Then the caravan drove off, took the road to the ice-bound water, crossed on the ice and trailed into Torneo, which for our purposes was the barn-like structure containing waiting-rooms, customs offices, restaurant, and railroad station. For refugees, of which there were scores, it also constituted living quarters. Kliefoth, however, had a comfortable, porcelain-stove-heated room with one of the Swedish families in the town.

The big waiting-room overflowed, and many were Russians, including several army officers who still wore their good looking epaulets. At this remote point the Bolsheviks, few numerically, still were doubtful of their ability to hold on and were not forcing any issue. Reports from Petrograd were wholly at odds. A smiling officer, speaking Oxford English, told me that the fuss would be over in a few days and the Reds put down, and that he was waiting philosophically. Fatalistically would have been a better phrasing. He was the Russian spirit of his class—talking, expecting others to act. I hope he got into Sweden soon, sprinting on a dark night. The Reds were saying also that the end was near. The sailors and the Letts, they said, had Petrograd under foot. Moscow, they claimed, would fall soon. They were right, yet not confident.

The Commissar was a sailor of the fleet, sent to take Torneo with the aid of Russian soldiers, a passive adventure. He now wanted to get back to the center of things. He was a rough young fellow, looking more farm-boy than sailor, a thick navy jacket his only sign of uniform or of authority. He eyed us from a distance, whether shyly or sulkily we could not tell.

We learned that cars and an engine were being assembled for a train. So we hurried through our glasses of tea and bowls of cabbage soup and tackled the technicalities of entrance, for, while we were in Torneo, we were not in official Russia, which was on the other side of a door.

No one else had expressed a desire to enter since the Russian *coup d'état* and we had the welcome of first comers at the door. Surely, we could come in, but without guaranties. Was a train to go? It could not be said. In counterquestion, were we carrying guns and ammunition in the sealed sacks? No, we were not. Why did we desire to come into Russia? And where were we going? Kliefoth grinned and interrupted to explain our satisfactory status and to indicate the places where our papers should be stamped. The stamps were affixed. We were in Russian Finland.

An engine backed several carriages onto a sidetrack. It might be our train. Could we put our goods aboard? No, decidedly no. There was nothing to do but loaf around the station, talk to refugees, pay a visit to Kliefoth's quarters, and consider shelter for the night.

Suddenly about five o'clock there was excited movement in the control office, and the rushing around of guards. We investigated. It was not mere turmoil. The train was to go out—that night—soon—in an hour's time—maybe. We assumed we had permission to go on it. No one interfered as the four of us dragged sacks through the snow and threw them into three adjoining compartments of a big passenger car. Then two of us collected what food we could, chiefly bread and tea. If the cars had the service of even a dust-woman we could get hot water. At the worst we might get it from the locomotive. For the rest we would have to trust to foraging at train halts.

In the darkness we said goodbye to Kliefoth, reluctant to leave him alone on the edge of the Arctic. We were off on the last long leg to Petrograd—the evening of November 22. We had a car to ourselves and other cars could we have used them. Aside from the train crew, which did include a dust-woman, the only other persons aboard were the Commissar and two of his guards. The official stared gloomily at us when we met in the corridors. He took our proffered cigarettes without reluctance, however, and mellowed under them, though not to graciousness.

We seemed to crawl down Finland, once or twice halting for several hours, and sometimes brought to short stops by failing steam. The engine was a wood-burner. Yet as we ran with no schedule of passenger stops, paying no attention to towns save for water and fuel needs and the appetite compulsions of the Commissar—which coincided fairly well with our own—we ate up the distance persistently. We got meat balls and more bread at the eating stations and we made our own tea. The seats were long and we slept well, our overcoats for covering. The cold was rather bad as the train was unheated. But we were approaching a goal and did not mind a little hardship. Finland made little impression upon me except that the northern part was snow-carpeted grass and farm land and that industrial signs increased southward on the second day, in a more timbered country. I had been told of lakes, but water ice and land ice looked much the same. For me, real acquaintance with Finland waited until the next March.

Late on Saturday afternoon we heard that we were likely to reach Petrograd during the night. Viborg was passed and eventually Terioki, the last town in Finland. Some time after midnight we were at Beloöstrov, the actual border of old Russia. Finland might be a province of Russia, but an extra barrier of entrance to Russia was provided at Beloöstrov. The inspections at this control station soon were to become notorious for their rigors, for Beloöstrov was the neck of the bottle of the only western escape route from Russia that winter and the Bolsheviks grasped it tighter and tighter. As incomers, our papers were given a curious examination. There was some discussion about the mail, but it is not unlikely that our commissar companion was here our friend. Being so near Petrograd, he was impatient of delay, and had no hesitation in expressing his feelings. He had a way with him. The inspectors expedited everything.

We entered the Finland station in Petrograd at three o'clock Sunday morning, November 25. Captain Pirie was the first Englishman to pass from Scandinavia to Petrograd after the Bolshevik Revolution. Sergeant Franklin and I were the first two Americans to enter Petrograd after the Revolution. We had come from London in fourteen and a half days, from New York in twenty-eight days.

ONE HUNDRED RED DAYS

CHAPTER II

November 25, 1917. Inside the Gates of Red Petrograd.

W E had hoped that the Embassy had received a telegraph message sent from Torneo or might be watching for the first train from North Finland. No one,
however, was in the big, dim station to meet Franklin and me.
An officer in British uniform came forward smartly to ask if
one of us was Captain Pirie.

"Thought you might come through on the first train down,"
he said to the Captain after they had saluted each other. "Rotten trip, what?" To which Captain Pirie agreed.

"I have a car here," said the friendly visitant, including us
all in his remark. "You chaps better come along."

So it seemed to us. With his assistance we parleyed for a
locked room in the station, got some sleepy soldiers to move
the mail within, and with a personal bag apiece we climbed
into the big, open motor car. The top was down, giving the
effect of a natty sleigh on wheels. Over the driver's seat flew
the British flag with a spotlight trained so the emblem would
show in the night.

"The city is quiet," explained our escort. "The Bolsheviks
have control. We may hear shots, but they will mean nothing.
Patrols fire into the air to keep their fingers warm or just for
deviltry."

He was exactly right. Intermittent shooting in the winter
nights never meant anything. We came to regard silent nights
as more ominous. We crossed the Neva on the Alexandrovsky
bridge and kept near the river until we skirted the Winter
Palace, which sprawled an unlighted, deserted pile, illy defined
under the cloudy sky. The lights edging the plaza beyond
served only to throw the hulk into deeper shadow. Under the
lights at intervals were small patrol groups of soldiers, long-
coated, muffled figures. Medley-attired workmen occupied
some of the posts. The soldiers carried bayoneted guns; the
jacketed Red Guards did not bother with bayonets. Wood

fires burned at the posts and the sentinels huddled close. The night was not wintry cold but below freezing.

As our car advanced patrol members moved into the street, but at sight of our illuminated flag turned negligently away. We swung into the Nevsky Prospect, and passed, I was told, over the Moika and then the Catharine canal. I had said I believed rooms were in readiness for me at the Hotel d'Europe, so we turned off the Nevsky Prospect into the Michaelovsky and drew up before the hotel. But the frightened night clerk inside said he knew nothing about arrangements and that it would make no difference anyway, as the Bolshevik orders were that no new guests were to be taken into the hotel. He begged us nervously to leave at once.

This was disappointment for two tired men. Our hospitable British friend came to our aid with the suggestion that he would drop Captain Pirie at his quarters, and then go seriously at the business of hotel hunting for us. We reached Captain Pirie's place and parted from him warmly. I never saw him again. He remained in Russia for several weeks trying to carry out his impossible orders, and then, I heard, returned to the army in France.

After repulses at several hotels, our escort concluded that the best hope was to seek shelter from the Bolshevik command, which had taken over the Astoria Hotel.

The foyer of the hotel looked like a camp-ground. We trod among sleeping soldiers, a guard ahead of us, until we found a sleepy commandant. A few sentences in Russian passed between him and the English officer. The commandant nodded his head and gave an order to the guard. "It's all right," said the Englishman. "They'll give you a room. I'll be moving on." We thanked him. The guard showed us a room containing a bedstead without a mattress. In a corner, however, was a pile of folded blankets. We spread some of them on the floor, pulled others over us and went to sleep. Four o'clock was past.

Six hours later Franklin and I separated, our immediate roads to lie far apart, though he sought me out on the two occasions he was afterward in Petrograd, and in the spring picked me up protectingly in Scandinavia to take me back to London. The next day he was on his way to Jassy, in Rumania.

In separate one-horse, one-passenger sledges, secured by the use of signs and penciled numerals, we went different routes from the hotel, he to the railroad station and I to the Embassy. There my first request was for men and sleighs to be sent to him.

Ambassador David R. Francis had been informed by Washington that I was *en route*, but my arrival was unexpected. Messages Minister Morris had sent from Stockholm and telegrams I had started at Torneo were delivered together the next week. One surprise more or less meant little to the Ambassador, however, after the excitements of the fortnight. In spite of his years, too, he had retained his native energy, seasoned just now with an angry disdain for Bolsheviks. Of a sanguine temperament, he had placed his faith in the stability of the Kerensky Government. Chaos had come instead. He had reason for the depth of his present feelings.

Of the Petrograd situation he remarked, at our first meeting soon after we had exchanged greetings, that he "never would talk to a damned Bolshevik." Circumstances were to compel him to change his mind about talking, though never to lessen his abhorrence of Bolsheviks and all their works. His situation was different from mine. I knew I would have to talk to them.

Not all of my early experiences with the Ambassador were pleasant, the fault of conditions, but we were to bridge both differences and mistakes before they had done damage and to work reliantly together.

His personality was not an unknown quantity to me. Years before as a Chicago newspaper reporter I had gone to St. Louis to cover the opening of the St. Louis World's Exposition, of which he was General Director. A big, blonde, prepossessing man in his prime, he had weathered into a statelier likeness of his earlier self. One would expect to address him as Mr. Ambassador or as Governor. Both titles, too, belonged to him, for he had been Governor of Missouri. He had a preference for the earlier, familiar title and "Governor" was the usual address to him around the Embassy.

He wanted to know more about my orders than he had been able to glean from his official dispatches, which appeared to have been vague. My own account was equally unsatisfactory. How could it have been otherwise? The situation was equivocal without blame to either of us. I was not sent to work under him and was independent of him, in powers and in funds. War, not I, was the intruder.

Our national diplomacy until a few months before had been keyed only for peace. Ambassadors sent for pleasant duties remained to face the strange equations of war. They did very well, but expansions and functional additions, bringing in new executives subject to headships at Washington other than diplomatic, tended to create a twilight zone of divided authority. These invasions into the diplomatic zone were necessary—war-trade boards and various specialized commissions —but an ambassador would not be human if he did not feel that he should be in chief command of all the governmental units in the country where he is the titled representative of his Government. If another war should come, it would be better, I think, to supersede the ambassadors to allied countries with commissioners-general charged with the coördination of every political, economic, and welfare activity of our Government in those zones. If an ambassador to any country happened to be the best man for commissioner-general, he could be appointed.

That morning, however, I was less interested in the functions of ambassadors than in learning what had been happening in Russia in the last fortnight, and what it seemed to portend. All that I could conceive at the moment was that if the Bolshevik effort at peace with Germany was successful, the chances of useful coöperation with the new Russian masters probably were negligible. But if the projected peace met obstacles, what then? This question had been on my mind ever since I left Stockholm, and particularly after I had talked with Kliefoth at Torneo. Could one work with the Bolsheviks against Germany? Or put impulse on them to work against Germany? Kliefoth had believed not. I had curiosity to find out.

I relate this state of mind because of its bearing on the future. Without it I would not have been able to make the presentation throughout Russia of President Wilson's campaign of ideas against Germany; without it I might have been less inclined in the first two months to credit with sincerity the Bolshevik attitude in the day-to-day maneuvers in one of the oddest minglings of hippodrome, double crossing, and the matching of wits against force that history can show. The scale as far as it concerns me may balance. Anyway, I will not seek to judge, but to try to treat myself, in quotation and in action on the scene, as objectively as if I were a third person.

To summarize the hour of entrance into Russia: I had come without bias against Russians of any sort, degree, or politics. I was there for three purposes: to be helpful to Russia in any practical way that might develop; to place before Russians the American viewpoint on the waging and the ending of the War; to inaugurate from Russia an additional American campaign to lower German morale. These aims were military, the United States being at war with Germany. But in pursuing them there was the desire and the hope of bringing to the Russian people an understanding of the United States that would form a tie after the War was finished.

I had come to the Embassy directly to get into official communication with my fellows, yet without intention of establishing myself there, although the Ambassador kindly offered office quarters in the building. The sledge trip, however, had shown the distance from the center of the city, and I concluded to defer a decision. The Embassy was at Fuhrstatskaya 34, in the Liteinaya section about a mile and a half from the business area. All distances in Petrograd were difficult during the winter owing to the handicap of uncared-for streets. No dependence could be placed on tram cars; motor cars stalled in snow banks, and sleighs crawled, slipped, and teetered over icy hummocks. Smolny Institute, the Bolshevik center, where Lenin and Trotsky and the balance of the working machinery of the Red control were housed, was on the same side of the city as the Embassy, some distance beyond, and reached more easily by a different route from the city. The Foreign Office, except for Trotsky's quarters, was near the Winter Palace, and the State Bank and other important Bolshevik offices were in the city itself. What a time-spending travel-weariness a day in Petrograd could be!

The Embassy building itself was a two-story and cupola structure that had more outward appearance of warehouse than residence. Through its walls of solid masonry, double-leafed doors to coach width gave entrance to an inclosed court from which stairways ran to offices and living-rooms on the floors above. A bay-window in the Ambassador's office offered him a view up and down a street in which there was little movement in the dreary months ahead. His personal suite was toward the rear of the building. The Embassy from this time until late February was in effect a prison for the Ambassador. He seldom went beyond its walls.

I left the Ambassador to pass into the hospitable hands of Butler Wright, Counselor of the Embassy, who took me away to lunch. He and his wife had a little apartment near by and had been comfortable until the disturbances came. Now there were troubles of food buying, rumors that soon only the proletarians would be fed, and household torment generally. Mrs. Wright, a capable and attractive woman, was regarding the outlook calmly and saying she wanted to stay with her husband. He was anxious, nevertheless, to have her return to the United States before matters grew worse, as he believed they would. She did leave soon. Butler Wright remained, to participate in many matters where I was concerned, and in late February to accompany the Ambassador into inner Russia. Adroit and able, his later advancement to Under-Secretaryship of State, and then to ministerial rank abroad, was not surprising.

He had represented the Embassy in its relations with the different agencies, British and French, which had attempted to sway public opinion in the final months of the Kerensky *régime*. He had a sad story to tell. The British news agency, Cosmos, had disintegrated and he anticipated it would be closed by the Bolsheviks. It was, a few weeks later. The French had under-cover tactics of their own, for which the Counselor had no esteem.

Resident Americans in Petrograd, advised by the Counselor, had formed an organization, raised funds among themselves, and done what they could to issue straightforward accounts of what the United States was doing in the War and for Russia. Frederic A. Corse, representative of the New York Life Insurance Company, with seventeen years of experience in Russian living, headed this committee and was all that was left of it when I arrived. He had skirmished stubbornly, putting out clear and forcible statements, though lacking means and machinery to give them effective circulation. The Embassy itself had no funds for use in any effort to make public opinion. Properly so, I thought. The rôle of embassies, I believe, is to be the formal voice of government to government. Under this definition there is no place for an embassy in the domain of unrecognized rulers.

Such American funds as were in Russia until my coming were largely in the hands of the Red Cross for its welfare work, now also threatened. The Red Cross unit, which had entered in July, was now in command of William Boyce Thompson, who had succeeded the original chief, Dr. Frank Billings, and had been given the title of Colonel in the Red Cross. Known hitherto as a copper multimillionaire, he was welcomed into the expanded Red Cross organization of war time, and had contributed extensively to its funds. Before I left Washington George Creel told me that Thompson also had given $1,000,-000 to the Russian Government for welfare work since his arrival in the country. At that distance the hue of splendor attached itself to the story of the gift. I bore a letter to Colonel Thompson and looked to him as an ally.

So, on my return to the Embassy with Butler Wright, I was glad to get the message that an officer of the Red Cross was waiting with an invitation to visit the commander that evening. On the heels of the word came the deputy who brought it. He was introduced as Maj. Raymond Robins.

Until I heard his name I had not known he was a Red Cross man or in Petrograd. Yet I knew much about him. He had come to Chicago several years before and gained attention as a wealthy settlement worker. He had mined a comfortable fortune, it was said, in the Alaskan gold fields. He had an exhorter's quality of oratory and a liking for forensic politics. These were possessions which tended to get the owner of them into the columns of newspapers, and as an executive of the *Chicago Tribune* I became familiar with his name and activities.

Then a year or so later a turn of fate directed his sister, the novelist Elizabeth Robins, into the circle of my acquaintances. She was writing a novel which I bought for serialization in *Cosmopolitan Magazine*, of which I had become editor, and at a stage of its progress I went to Florida to talk with her about the book. So I saw the house where she and her brother Raymond were born and heard the story of their childhood. The year of the Big Freeze was disastrous to the orange plantation and to the family. In a little while the children were orphans. Different relatives took them. The girl, the elder, was gently cared for, and reared in the East and in England. She had a minor gift for the stage and a larger one for writing. She made a place for herself.

The boy was taken west. In his 'teens he had become a hard-rock miner in the Rocky Mountain country. Then he began the reading of law in San Francisco. From there Alaska of the gold rush was a natural goal. In the Alaska period, besides making his sizeable stake, he had his great emotional experience. Lost in a wilderness of snow and in peril of cold and hunger, he, like Socrates and Paul, saw a vision, or, what is as much to the point, believed he saw one. Before his eyes a skeleton ice-bound bush appeared in angelic likeness. Beyond the token of the bush lay the road to shelter. He became now a rough and ready evangelist. On this scene came his sister, hunting for him. She took him to London, and he was to tell me later that there he walked the streets in mental pain, seeking for a way to express himself. Chicago received him presently.

The man who entered rushingly and greeted me with a military salute, wore a Red Cross uniform and was short and dark. For his height his shoulders were of unusual width. The face was severe, the expression intent, and the eyes deep-set.

We soon were chatting about my trip. He explained that rooms were waiting for me at the Hotel d'Europe but that I was not looked for so soon. He had come in a Red Cross car and shortly I was on my way with him.

Neither on the morning trip to the Embassy with a Russian *izvozchik* (driver) or on my motor car return did I get any deep imprint of Petrograd from the part I saw. In the morning I had been too busy keeping my seat in the sleigh, in the afternoon wintry darkness was near. I did, however, have more the feeling that I was in a western European than a Russian city —that is, a Russian city as I expected it to be. The larger structures were solid four- and six-story box-like apartments and business blocks, and the smaller were two- and three-story buildings with shops below and living-rooms above.

Blank walls, slitted with doorways, were frequent—and these were the busiest, noisiest walls in Petrograd, the billboards from which the city read its newspapers and the placards of the edicts and the proclamations of its rulers. Those walls interested me from the first.

The Nevsky Prospect struck me as a clutter, not a fair conclusion as to vista, for the golden spires of the Admiralty building were not visible in the murky distance toward the Neva, and I passed the park inclosing the Alexander Palace without giving it attention. The bronze steeds leaping at the corners of the bridge over the Fontanka canal did attract me, however. Wild horses and wild men—quite symbolic of the city of the hour!

The Hotel d'Europe occupied most of one side of the short Michaelovsky, a block running from the Nevsky to the Michaelovsky Park. It must have been an excellent hotel in prewar days, and strove still to be. I was taken to a comfortable room, in what I glimpsed as a spacious suite on the second floor of the hotel, reached by a broad flight of stairs. The suite, I learned, was that of Colonel Thompson.

Except for changes of linen I had not been out of my clothes since I left the Swedish frontier, and of the last thirty-six hours I had not slept five. Yet, though dirty, I did not feel tired. No more meetings with anyone until I was bathed and freshly dressed. So it was nearly dinner time when I went into Colonel Thompson's living-room.

As I entered, a short, round man lifted himself from a cushioned chair by a big fireplace and came toward me, with genial greeting. As soon as possible I bowed him back to his seat, for he looked ill. Sitting, he clasped chubby hands across an expansive front.

Hardly had I expressed my pleasure at finding him active on the scene when he told me he was leaving Russia at once. I was sorry, but aware that I had no knowledge of circumstances. I waited until I should be made acquainted with them. I knew from that moment that I would be in Russia indefinitely.

Members of his own staff may have explained Colonel Thompson better than I could. They said that it was his habit when defeated in an adventure of finance to leave the salvaging to subordinates and to seek other arenas. He may have applied the same method here. It can be said of him that he went down with Kerensky. If Kerensky had succeeded, the American financier would have had a position of after-war prestige in

Russia. He himself wrote after his return to the United States, "I was in touch with Kerensky day by day."

He had been, and that relationship was an understandable part of his present embarrassment. There was, however, no danger in it. Lenin and Trotsky, playing the card of invitation to all the war governments to participate in a general peace conference, might insult the representatives of the institutions of the Allies, but would not harm them. Moreover, Colonel Thompson already was aware that he would be treated with toleration, whatever flicking his pride might get.

Raymond Robins had been closely concerned with Colonel Thompson in his association with Kerensky and was due to share in any ill-effects. The two, Robins explained to me soon, argued the matter out, concluded that as their party was out and another party in, it would be better to make their peace and a Red Cross peace with the new elements before worse happened. Robins went to Smolny and came away with assurances that the Red Cross, depending upon its behavior, would not be molested. This may have been Robins' first meeting with Trotsky. I do not know. He did not meet Lenin until many weeks after my arrival.

In the essence, what Colonel Thompson had lost was not safety or the right to remain in Petrograd, but usefulness, and that was his own opinion.

Doubtless it was as well that, sitting this evening in his big living-room, I lacked knowledge of the realities of his Russian adventure. Possession of it might only have added more confusion to the prevailing ferment. At that hour no one in Russia, individual or group, foreigners or Russians, Bolsheviks or their enemies, knew what a day would bring. Thompson was going. I was coming. Of instinct my thoughts went on past him to the members of his staff, the men who were to stay.

It was evident at a glance around the room that, importantly, they comprised three—Robins, who would succeed to command, Allen Wardwell, and Thomas D. Thacher. There was a fourth of equal rank, who attended more to the personal needs of Colonel Thompson and departed with him. Two others, William Webster and Heywood Hardy, looked after much detail. After Colonel Thompson left, Robins became a Lieutenant Colonel and Wardwell and Thacher were raised to the rank of Major.

They made an odd trio. Thacher and Wardwell were New Yorkers of different molds. Thacher was a young lawyer with the habits of a business man, downright in speech. I always knew where he stood and liked him accordingly. In after-war years he marched his stocky body and stubborn jaw to a seat on the Federal Bench. In 1930 he resigned to accept political appointment as Solicitor-General of the United States. Allen Wardwell was a tall fellow, lithe, mannered, with a knack of smiling and lording his way through. Our name for him was the Grand Duke, and one night when we installed him in one of the Tsar's private cars and saw him off at the railroad station for a vigil at Archangel, where supplies were stalled, we christened him the Bolshevik Grand Duke. The title clung while he remained in Russia. They were two fine men, not always able to understand or to grapple with their fervid superior officer.

Before I retired to my room, it had been agreed that I would take Colonel Thompson's headquarters on his departure, set for three days ahead. The Red Cross offices, rooms for personnel, and the miscellaneous supply depot of the organization were on upper floors of the hotel.

Late that night I began a skeletonized Log which I kept for the next hundred days in Russia and for an ensuing month in Finland. I started the memory reminder to assure accuracy of dates, depending upon clipped phrases to bring back the picture of a day or the contour of an episode. Sometimes, too, I used indirect references and occasionally symbols, for it was needful that the notations should have innocuous look if my person should be searched. They were written on thin, loose sheets, carried in a pocket billfold. For reference and for the checking of events the record became increasingly important. By the method of its entry, five minutes a night at my portable typewriter was enough to keep it in order. The opening entry will illustrate:

November 25—Arrived 3 in morning. Pirie's car. Astoria hotel. Impressions night ride. Winter Palace. Street camp-fires. Embassy at 11. Francis. His remarks. Butler Wright and lunch. Arrival Robins. See Thompson. Evening with him.

My first day in Petrograd was ended.

November 26—November 27, 1917. Foreshadowing the Strategy of Lenin. The Dauntless Spiridonova. The Russian Adventures of Col. W. B. Thompson.

1.

ON the following day, Monday, the Ambassador surveyed the situation for my benefit, and there was no cheer in the outlook. For the moment the single assured fact was that of break-down. The Ambassador still hoped, however, that the Bolshevik seizure would be limited to areas adjacent to Petrograd and Moscow, and he was not ready to recommend to Washington that an embargo be placed upon Russian credits and supplies. That action, too, when it did come, was initiated at Washington. The Ambassador, in his sympathy for the Russian people and in his desire that supplies of clothing and necessities already in Pacific transit be delivered to them, believed that an open door might be kept through Siberia.

Yet if supplies were uninterrupted, how were they to be diverted from Bolshevik hands? In no way, as far as anyone could see. The Red Cross had a different view. It was willing that Bolsheviks should share in its supplies—milk and medicines on hand. The hitch in that benevolent theory, as shown later, was that the Bolsheviks had no notion of sharing with any except Bolsheviks.

Even in the early stage of debate on principle it was evident that there was a rift between the Embassy and the Red Cross, though neither was interfering with the actions of the other. The only injunction that the Ambassador laid was that the Red Cross in whatever contact it had with Bolshevik officialdom must avoid committing the Embassy to any seeming sanction of the new *régime*. I sought not to form any opinion on what I trusted would be a passing difference of opinion between the two American institutions, though it occurred to me that the actions of none of us would be apt to have any real bearing on the affirmative side of a question of formal recognition of the Bolsheviks as heads of a government. If the Ambassador should advise recognition, Washington would consider thoughtfully and at this stage of the war undoubtedly consult with its Allies. Even with the Ambassador's support, recognition was not conceivable, and without it the issue would not come up for consideration. Therefore contacts with Bolsheviks did not seem to me an important matter, then or afterward.

The evening found me enjoying a Thanksgiving dinner at the Hotel d'Europe, though the day was not Thanksgiving. Colonel Thompson, however, would be gone before Thursday, turkeys had been found, and the feast was set. Of the fare I wrote: "Turkeys, two for nine people, all Red Cross men except me, a sauce near to cranberries, fried potatoes, baked apples, and coffee. Not so bad for Petrograd in Revolution."

It was a night for tales. Conversation went up and down the table in lively fashion. Different versions of Kerensky's escape were related, agreeing only in their conclusion—he had gotten safely away. There were surmises that he would be heard from next with Alexeiev in the Cossack country. The Bolsheviks maintained, some weeks later, that he returned to Petrograd prior to the Constituent Assembly. Kerensky himself is the only worth-while authority on his wanderings. Russia rarely has failed to provide burrows for fugitives. Several of his ministers, however, less agile than he, failed to go to ground in time and were lodged in the fortress prison of SS. Peter and Paul.

Colonel Thompson himself came in for good-natured banter at the figure he had made one night recently in the Tsar's box at the Opera. There had been, it appeared, great stir in the audience when the rotund American took his seat in the box, and cries of welcome to the "American Tsar." Colonel Thompson protested that he had not known where he was being ushered, and once posted in the box he did not care to retreat.

My second day in Petrograd had been placid and pleasant.

The third day began with a visit to the Embassy, where I learned that a courier was about to start for Stockholm and that I had just time to write a home-bound letter. In that letter, saved for my files, were the following sections:

There are no menaces that I can find. Bolsheviks are not terrible at close range. The city is orderly. There is food and the probability of its continuance. This to reassure.

The atmosphere here, of course, is electric. The city stands at a crisis in future history. The curtain, however, does not lift. When it does, not impossibly it may be on more stability than the outside world suspects. My impression, perhaps momentary, is that the Bolsheviks cannot make the peace they want, even by their utmost efforts. If not, Russia must stay in the war for the simple reason that it cannot get out. Somehow, too, the likelihood of strenuous effort for separate peace seems remote. And the chance of Germany being poisoned by Revolution does not seem so impossible to me here as it did in Washington. The Russians are sending leaflets into the German lines telling the soldiers to seize the German Government as they have seized theirs. This does not look as if the Russian peace movement were German controlled even if it may have had the pestiferous aid of German money as it grew.

Of our own work there is nothing left but the wreckage and it is too early to appraise the salvage or start a new structure. Americans, to some degree, are getting out of Russia. The Allied diplomacy, including our own, is helping to make their stay untenable, but I have hopes of a general change that will halt the Embassies of the Powers in their present policy of playing the German game. You can't move the people of a nation by bluffing and if the people of Russia are in power, the error will have later —or present—penalty. An attitude of sitting still and waiting to see if it is the people of the nation who are speaking would have been better. And I think this is now being realized.

The soldiers, millions on millions of armed men, are the answer. If they go Bolshevik, and they seem to be going, Bolshevism is in for an indefinite stay, provided only that it can feed Petrograd and the cities.

Moscow is Bolshevik. Had dinner last night (Colonel Thompson's Thanksgiving celebration) with two of the Red Cross men who were in the besieged National Hotel for a week—shells of shrapnel dropping on the hotel, machine-gunfire of the Cadets coming down one street, and of the Bolsheviks up the right-angled street. The Kremlin, continuously bombarded, was just beyond. The Kremlin was damaged but not badly. David McGowan, vice-consul, came up from the Moscow consulate three days ago. They were shut up in the consulate for a week, among them Arthur Bullard, who is ill of an abscess in the ear. He is

better, I understand, and I expect to see him in Petrograd this
week. If he cannot come I will go to Moscow.

Error was included in the opinionative part of the letter.
The reflection was that of a sincere, onlooking stranger. The
theory of the Allied diplomacy was sounder than my own but
in matters of action was more uncertain and wavering than I
then considered it to be.

It was not the people of Russia who had come to power but
a compact, schooled bloc of demagogues, some of them aliens,
heading cohorts of disciplined thousands rather than of ten
thousands, armed with the slogans to win a war-wearied, battered people: "Peace for the Soldier; Land for the Peasant;
Bread for the Laborer; the Property of the Rich for the Poor."

There was no stalwart middle class to intervene. At the last
the Bolshevik phalanx seized the seats of government, believing
truly that the advertising campaign of slogans would keep the
nerveless masses from rising against them. Once in power they
soon possessed the military means of staying there, regardless
of the feeling of the masses. In reality bottom-side had become
top-side. Power had changed hands but power itself was unchanged. The same imperial motor cars coursed recklessly
through the streets. Ostentation still rode within, priding itself
now upon its uncouthness. New tyrannical rulers had arrived,
a sneering, joyous crew except when they intoned a solemn
public ritual. Who, they proclaimed hilariously, was there to
throw them out? Not the soldiers, if they could toss away their
guns and go back to the villages. Not the peasants, if they got
the land. Lenin himself paraphrased the attitude when at a depressing later hour he stated sourly that they might be dead,
but that if they were there was no one to bury them.

The fact was that they were the rulers of the heart of Russia. In viewing them, the War, in the muck of which they had
thriven and come to noxious flower, remained the complication. The War also was a fact. The injury if not the ruin of the
Allies loomed in a separate peace with Germany. That peace
was not yet accomplished and still could be opposed. A united
plan among the representatives of the Allies would have been
something, might not have been hopeless of advantage, might
have made more of an attempt to safeguard the armistice to

prevent the complete transfer of the German eastern armies to the western front, might have kept up enough of a play to have obliged Germany to have retained more of its forces in the eastern area throughout the winter and spring, might have done all this even if confident the while that the Russian and the German leaders were playing a farce between them.

This projection is not one of mere optimism. I know how Lenin grabbed at instruments offered him—including those in my hand—when he could use them to offset a German move. He was playing a game, seeking tactical advantage, intent only upon saving enough of Russia to give him an area for a doctrinaire experiment, despising those who had nourished him or would nourish him, willing to run with the quarry or chase with the pack and to lead the one to destruction or to throw the other off the scent if thereby he might hurry the day of a class war, owning that he looked on ethics as a weakness of the *bourgeoisie* and as lure by which to trick them, delighting in falsity to multitudinous enemies—Lenin, the sly *muzhik!* I believe that his realest desire was to destroy the universe. I believe that he hated humanity. He could organize and he could build, but I believe that he meant to destroy even the edifices he reared. His doctrine of the Continuous Revolution implied no less.

In the important hour, however, there neither was a united plan, or any knowledge of Lenin. Lacking the latter, any plan of general contact might, of course, have come to wry disaster. He did so enjoy fooling the serious!

As for myself, I was to make my contacts, hold a rôle in the drama until the Bolsheviks earned their own penalty of the terrible German peace of Brest-Litovsk in March. Then I got myself out of Russia and six weeks later, in London, having come by deduction to the conclusion that it was the Bolshevik purpose, under German compulsion, to imprison all Allied nationals remaining in Russia, I ordered the American members of the force under my jurisdiction to leave Russia, knowing that in their wake must come all other American officials. In August and September, Englishmen and Frenchmen went to Russian jails. Not Americans. All but one was safe, and he, my good friend Consul Roger Tredwell of Petrograd, suffered only temporary misadventure in distant Tiflis. So I made atonement for my part in 1917 in keeping Americans within the Bolshevik domain. But how I was cursed from afar by the unwillingly rescued during the early summer of 1918, while in Washington I held grimly to my aim and induced the State Department to keep hands off. The sentiment was different when the gates clanged down.

2.

CHAIKOVSKY, leader of the peasants until the Bolshevik hour, came to the hotel on November 27 to take farewell of Colonel Thompson, and I met him and talked with him. He was downcast and weeping. The desertion of the peasants still was incomprehensible to him. In one sentence he said they surely would call him back to leadership, in the next he condemned them to perdition for treachery.

Taller than ordinary men, his gaunt slenderness added to his appearance of height. His white beard, long but not thick, was never at rest, fluttering across his chest as he gestured and moved about. Very frail and old he seemed. In a few weeks or months, I reflected as I watched him, he would be dead, another leader broken on the wheel of change. I underreckoned the vitality in him, as I did in other Russians in the first days. Afterward I grew wiser. It is the Russian habit to rise from deathbeds and live another twenty years. Chaikovsky, the next summer and autumn and early winter, headed a government which though limited in territory was while it lasted a particular Bolshevik thorn—the Government of Archangel on the Arctic coast. Thence, on the final withdrawal of Allied forces, he proceeded safely to western Europe.

I wrote in the Log that night that Chaikovsky had been overthrown by a "woman." Such was my casual reference to Spiridonova, rare Puritan figure of the Revolution, who looked like a little old-maid school teacher of a past generation, who was firebrand and fanatic, who turned at last to fight the Bolsheviks and to go to prison under them as she had done under the Tsar. As yet I had not seen her or heard of her except from Chaikovsky's lips, so treated her as a lay figure.

A woman other than his victorious rival concerned Chaikovsky even more. He spoke regretfully of Mme Breshkovskaya, who he feared was in danger of arrest. They had worked shoulder to shoulder throughout the summer, the two most picturesque figures of the Kerensky *régime*, the erect, silver-bearded man and the short, broad-faced, benign woman, so often seen together in public places that they were linked as "The Grandfather and the Grandmother of the Revolution." For his own fate he was without fear. Even deposed, he was reverenced by the peasants in the remote villages. The Bolsheviks would not risk physical torment to one who had been an idol. Instead they lifted him from his pedestal, set him down in the streets, and dismissed him from their attention. He would have suffered less from martyrdom. Breshkovskaya, it seemed to us, was in no more danger than he, and for the same reasons.

She was not to be saved, however, from the embarrassment of an attack made jointly upon her and upon the Red Cross. Fortunately for Colonel Thompson's feelings, the onset did not come until he was outside of Russia. To dispose of the united circumstances they are treated here.

The attack was begun by one Vladimir Bakrylov, a former secretary of Mme Breshkovskaya, in the form of a letter of recantation appearing in the newspaper *Znamia Truda* ("The Banner of Labor") in its issue of November 24 Russian Old Style, December 7 Western Calendar. The letter, headed "My Conscience Bids Me Speak Out," related that the writer witnessed Mme Breshkovskaya's efforts to get funds for the publication of books for the masses, saw how disappointed she was with the Moscow capitalists who would not help her, came with her to Petrograd; it proceeded, according to translation made for the Red Cross files:

The first thing that struck me was that Mme Breshkovskaya and Kerensky's secretary, D. Sosskiss, are concocting some sort of business with a group of Americans from the Red Cross. Breshkovskaya explained to me that Russia ought not to remain unassisted. She said that the Americans are giving her two millions of dollars and are helping in many ways. She told further that she is starting in conjunction with Sosskiss a committee for civil instruction. Its purposes include the organization of a press of its own, the use of cinemas, the sending of a staff of lecturers into the provinces, etc. On the same day Mr. Sosskiss brought Mr. Robins and two other Americans. After a short talk in English one of the gentlemen handed Mme Breshkovskaya two packets of notes of 50,000 rubles each and said in Russian, "Here is the money for expenses at your personal disposal." Then he asked whether the appeal to the American nation had been prepared, and the appeal, being ready, was handed to him.*

When the Americans left Mr. Sosskiss announced that the balance had already been deposited in a bank, and he made Mme Breshkovskaya sign on the spot a cheque for R. 100,000. On the same day Breshkovskaya gave 200,000 rubles to S. L. Maslov, who soon became Minister of Agriculture, for the paper *Zemlia y Volia* in Moscow on the condition that this publication of the local committee of the S.R. [Social Revolutionary] party should pass to a joint-committee of four—Breshkovskaya, Maslov, Orlov and one other.

I understood from the further talk between Breshkovskaya and Sosskiss that the *Volia Naroda* is going to pass under the control of the committee on civil instruction.

The Petrograd cinemas began to show the well known film, "The Ruin of a Nation," made by an American firm and intended as a warning. Pitirim Sorokin, who had proclaimed the ruin of the Russian nation in the Democratic Council, published in *Volia Naroda*—N. 121, Oct. 17—an historical paper under the same title, "The Ruin of a Nation" and this would-be "socialist" presented to the Russian readers the same prospects for Russia as were shown in the film.

On September 10 a meeting was held in Teneshev Hall under the auspices of Sosskiss and the Red Cross. Mr. Robins delivered a lecture and Mme Breshkovskaya came to the meeting. She made a speech to an American audience, including the American Ambassador, Mr. Francis—and one of our company declared to Mme Breshkovskaya afterwards that the speech was humiliating to hear from a Russian. The next day after the meeting with the Americans, Mme Breshkovskaya told me that her appeal had been cabled to President Wilson and her autobiography had been sent likewise to America, and that the two cables had cost the Americans 3000 rubles.

An order was given shortly afterwards to Vassily Kiriakov to organize the publication of the paper *Narodnaya Pravda* ["The People's Truth"]. The first number came off the press but was not published. It had such a violently reactionary tendency, caricaturing Chernov, Lenin and others that even Mme Breshkovskaya

---

* The Breshkovskaya Appeal, September, 1917, which aroused sympathy in the United States.

and Sosskiss protested and asked for revision. In its improved form the paper continued to appear up to the very last days.

On seeing all these abominations I said to Mme Breshkovskaya that I refuse to continue to work with her, and I left her.

So had a scared Russian made his own peace with new masters. What had been respected and favored by authority had overnight become counter-revolutionary.

The whilom secretary named two million dollars as the "American" gift, a mixing-up of rubles and dollars as other circumstances showed. Two million rubles in pre-war valuation, the Russian concept of value, would be one million dollars.

With Mme Breshkovskaya and her efforts to aid her beloved Russia I had and continue to have the fullest sympathy. Money to her was a medium for educating and uplifting her people. Her notion of party newspapers was good and she put the control in the proper place, a committee of the party, the old Social Revolutionaries, the party in whose membership she had opposed Russian autocracy all her days. The operating money, however, should have been solely Russian money. The offer of American money to Kerensky and to her, however generously meant by the individual, was a mistake, in my opinion, since the action could not help but involve the American Red Cross, which the donor represented.

The subsidizing of newspapers never has had American favor and in varying time scandal has been its certain aftermath, even as it was here, where excellence of motive counted for nothing.

Colonel Thompson himself received consideration from the Bolsheviks to the extent that accusations were against "American capitalists," "unscrupulous business men," and the "Allied purse." The first effect of the printing of the Bakrylov letter was the appearance in the Bolshevik semiofficial newspaper, the *Pravda* ("Truth"), of a slapping paragraph, in translation as follows:

THE SOCIALIST REVOLUTIONARY OBORONTZY KEPT ON THE MONEY OF AMERICAN BANKERS

In the *Znamia Truda* (No. 80) a monstrous exposure has been published from the secretary of the famous "Grandmother,"

Breshkovskaya. It now turns out that the fore-mentioned Grand-mother and the whole brave crowd of the Socialist Revolutionary Oborontzy (Defensive Organization) is on the pay list of the Morgans. This is not Revolution any longer; this is simply pros-titution. And these political prostitutes who have been selling the Russian people and even their Revolutionary past to the Allied purse have dared to accuse the Bolsheviks of getting German money. Forsooth, one could not have sunk any lower. On the bottom of the stenching pit the traitors of Socialism are wres-tling. In tomorrow's issue we shall reproduce the letter from the *Znamia Truda.*

The next morning, December 8, the *Izvestia* ("News"), the official publication of the Bolshevik party, proceeded more solemnly with the castigation, in translation as follows:

HEROES OF THE COUNTER REVOLUTION

The *Volia Naroda* ["Will of the People"] people are proud to have Mme Breshkovskaya, "the Grandmother of the Russian Revolution" in their group but in yesterday's *Znamia Truda* we find a killing revelation of the activities of the honorable "Grand-mother." The revelation is made by her private secretary, Com-rade V. Bakrylov. Mme Breshkovskaya used to speak with much eloquence on "the land for the peasants." Her paper declared its program to be "the land for the peasants," but ONLY by a vote of the Constituent Assembly. Well, and what do we hear now? We learn that Mme Breshkovskaya had received on her return from Siberia 100,000 rubles from the Moscow capitalists for her publications on the condition of insistence on the settling of the land question by the Constituent Assembly. Half of that money was passed to her by the people's socialist party.

Together with the secretary of Kerensky, Mr. Sosskiss, she en-tered into dealings with the American capitalists. She addressed humiliating appeals to American imperialists, imploring them to supply her with money for her publications and she has sent with the very same purpose her autobiography to Wilson. She made a speech in the presence of the American Ambassador and to an audience of foreigners and even her friends qualified the speech as humiliating for a Russian to listen to. The result was that she was given two millions and a hundred thousand rubles for her use. In return unscrupulous American business men had a portion of their hopes realized. Thanks to the "Grandmother's" effort the

Russian masses were poisoned in the cinemas by a vulgar American film "The Ruin of a Nation," and the comrade of Mme Breshkovskaya, Mr. Sorokine, published in the *Volia Naroda* a paper headed "The Ruin of a Nation."

When the Government of the Soviets was established in Russia, the *Volia Naroda*, Mme Breshkovskaya's paper, opened a campaign against it. Her politics are and were those of a paid agent of Moscow merchants and American capitalists. There is no need of comment, as the saying is.

Apart from topical content, there was in this editorial much material for study of Bolshevik technique of defense and attack. It was to be borne in mind, too, that the matter, in spite of masks of vituperation and solemnity, was not regarded seriously by the Bolsheviks. They were having cynical sport with the Americans and with poor Mme Breshkovskaya, who did not emerge from hiding. The *Volia Naroda* on December 8, unable to communicate with her, printed, as translated, the following:

REGARDING AN UNWORTHY ATTACK

In yesterday's issue of the *Znamia Truda*, the organ of the Socialist Revolutionary extremists, a Letter to the Editor has been published under the heading "My Conscience Bids Me Speak Out." In this letter, Mr. Bakrylov, former private secretary to Mme Breshkovskaya, the author of ultra-patriotic appeals to the soldiers, and of pamphlets on the war, the land, etc., suddenly turning into an extremist makes an unworthy attempt to dishonor Mme Breshkovskaya. He makes the basest insinuations in reference to financial means placed by her American friends at the disposal of the Grandmother and the committee for civil instruction. Mme Breshkovskaya is out of town for the present but we will do our utmost to enable her to give in one of the next issues of our newspaper her answer to the unworthy attack of Mr. Bakrylov. The Editors.

I have no record that Mme Breshkovskaya replied additionally in her own name. She remained quietly in Petrograd until December 20, when I saw and talked with her in her retreat. She left Petrograd either that night or the following day. There was scarce a doubt that the Bolsheviks knew where she was, sneeringly but perhaps not ungallantly protected her, and winked to each other when she slipped past their guards.

There was mettle in the man Sorokin, whom Bakrylov also attacked. In the *Volia Naroda* he came back fighting, thus:

Mr. Bakrylov, who has suddenly transformed himself into a radical from his previous shape of a patriot, devotes the following lines to me in his slovenly article, in which he is trying to discredit E. K. Breshko-Breshkovskaya. [Mr. Sorokin quoted the paragraph referring to himself in the Bakrylov letter.]

Anent this statement I consider it necessary to note the following: If Mr. Bakrylov imputes by his statement that I am in sympathy with the film "The Loss of a Nation," then I declare candidly that I consider this film very valuable and very useful, and would be extremely glad if someone could spread this and similar films all over Russia. Should, however, Mr. Bakrylov, by drawing a parallel between the film and my article which has nothing in common with the film except the title, insinuate something else, any commercial reasons in particular, then I would ask him to have the courage to formulate his thought clearly in order that I may bring him before a court of arbitration as a dirty liar.

The challenge went unanswered. Besides, and very soon, there were no courts of arbitration. Sorokin had the snappy last word in the newspaper controversy.

No public announcement was made concerning the disposition of whatever balance of the original fund remained in bank when the Bolsheviks succeeded to power.

For David Sosskiss, Kerensky's secretary, who represented the Premier much in the same way that the then Major Robins represented Colonel Thompson, the favored English spelling of the name was David Soskice. He escaped to England. He was a veteran member of the Social Revolutionary party and Kerensky appointed him to his post at the request of the right (conservative) wing of the party. His son, Victor Soskice, who had been with his father in Russia, came to the United States in 1918, and on July 30 of that year he made a detailed statement in reference to the Thompson fund to Herbert L. Carpenter, chairman of the executive committee of the American League to Aid and Coöperate with Russia, an organization of which Colonel Thompson was a vice-president. Mr. Carpenter sent a copy of the statement to me, with a covering letter.

Victor Soskice, for himself and his father, stated:

Shortly after the arrival of Col. Thompson in Petrograd he met Kerensky and after some investigation agreed to give $1,-000,000 for war work and the Provisional Government. Kerensky sent Col. Thompson to his secretary, David Soskice. After due arrangement, David Soskice organized the Committee on Public Education in the name of the "Grandmother" [Breshkovskaya]. The committee consisted of five members—the "Grandmother," Chaikovsky, Argunov, Soskice, and Miakhotin.

The committee organized twenty newspapers and gave subsidies to about sixty more. This work was an educational campaign to combat the Germans and Bolsheviki and their propaganda. The committee organized schools, pictures and lectures among the soldiers. Col. Thompson and Major Robins promised that when more money was necessary that Col. Thompson would get the capitalists of America and that Major Robins would get the labor forces of America to raise $3,000,000 a month to carry on the work. To this committee Major Robins was known as a representative of American labor. He had two documents with him, one signed by Mrs. Robins, representing a Women's Union of Chicago, and the other some large Chicago Labor Union.

This work by Col. Thompson and Major Robins was very much appreciated by the Russians but the later action in turning to the Bolsheviki was considered as treachery. If Col. Thompson had stuck to the "Grandmother" he would have been looked upon as a Lafayette but no good Russians would again receive or trust Thompson or Robins. Col. Thompson told the Russians that their Revolution (i.e. the March, 1917 Revolution) had turned him from the capitalists and that he was for the people in the future. When the Bolsheviki came into power Raymond Robins stopped lecturing and took charge of distribution of milk and supplies for Petrograd and the Rumanian front.

Robins should not have been blamed for not lecturing further against the Bolsheviks after they came into power. Mr. Soskice's references to milk distribution and the Rumanian supplies were pertinent though indefinite. Later chapters of this book will be concerned with the subjects. I suspected, too, that a portion of the grandiose campaign could be regarded in the Russian sense, that is, as something accomplished when the plan had been put neatly on paper. There had not been sufficient time to do so much. Big projects, however, had begun and had been advancing. In their light I understood the less Colonel Thompson's advocacy of the Bolsheviks after he returned to the United States.

What his second set of views were he himself recorded in interview, letter, and speech.

While I still was in Russia there appeared in the *Washington Post,* and doubtless in other newspapers, the following dispatch, which was clipped and kept for me:

GIVES BOLSHEVIKI A MILLION
W. B. THOMPSON, RED CROSS DONOR, BELIEVES PARTY MISREPRESENTED.

New York, Feb. 2 [1918]. William B. Thompson, who was in Petrograd from July until November last, has made a personal contribution of $1,000,000 to the Bolsheviki for the purpose of spreading their doctrine in Germany and Austria.

Mr. Thompson had an opportunity to study Russian conditions as head of the American Red Cross Mission, expenses of which also were largely defrayed by his personal contributions. He believes that the Bolsheviki constitute the greatest power against Pro-Germanism in Russia and that their propaganda has been undermining the militarist regimes of the Central Empires.

Mr. Thompson deprecates American criticism of the Bolsheviki. He believes they have been misrepresented and has made the financial contribution to the cause in the belief that it will be money well spent for the future of Russia as well as for the Allied cause.

On the scene in Petrograd at the date of the dispatch I heard no statement that Colonel Thompson had given a new million dollars to the Bolsheviks, or any million. Considered as a gesture of renunciation, it would show his conviction that the Bolsheviks were in the possession of the unexpended balance of the Kerensky-Breshkovskaya fund. He could hope, if he wished, that they might expend it against Germany.

One of Colonel Thompson's speeches was made in Denver. On January 25 he sent a letter to my wife in Washington, inclosing the text of that speech. One section of it was:

I have returned to this country with some very strong ideas regarding Russia and the duty of the United States and the Allies to that stirring and somewhat erratic young democracy. I come from a people now generally known as the Bolsheviki, who just now are extremely unpopular in the American press. They are held up as assistant Germans and are being denounced for having deserted the Allies.—I am afraid the American people are slow to realize one of the greatest facts of the war at this time. The Bolsheviki at the present time are a tremendous factor in making the Central Powers of Europe realize that they can never win the war: that they will be forced to a basis of a reasonable and a lasting peace.—The example and efforts of the Russian democracy are setting the Central Empires on fire.—Democratic Russia in my opinion, will never make a separate peace with Germany.

The German-Bolshevik peace was made a month after the speaker registered his opinion.

The address contained also this passage:

I can easily see how Maria Spiridonova, now a leading figure in Russian life, believes that freedom is to be realized by a Government of working men alone. The Russian Revolution released this young woman now only in her thirties from fifteen years solitary confinement in a Siberian prison.

If Spiridonova believed in November, 1917, that freedom was to be found under the Bolsheviks, it was possible at the end of seven months to measure her disillusion exactly. For this dauntless young woman came nearer in July, 1918, to overthrowing the Bolsheviks with invective than ever Alexeiev, Kaledin, Kolchak, Wrangel, or Denikin were to do with arms. On July 4 she rose in the All-Soviet Congress at Moscow, faced Lenin and Trotsky and Count Mirbach, the German Ambassador, and challenged them all three, and the Bolshevik cohorts, to combat. The Associated Press correspondent (either "A.P." Smith or Yarros, both of whom were with me during the winter), who heard her and remained in Russia long enough to witness the consequences of her words, was not able to get a dispatch through the Russian censorship, but when in the American exodus from Russia he reached Stockholm on September 8, he cabled the epic account:

Maria Spiridonova probably was the most powerful leader in the establishment of the Bolshevik power. As the recognized spokesman of the peasants, forming 85 per cent of the Russian population, she swung the peasant strength into line and persuaded the Social Revolutionaries of the Left to join the Bolsheviki.

On July 4, eight months later, she delivered a startling speech of defiance to German oppression which resulted in the assassination of Count von Mirbach, German Ambassador to Russia, and announced that the Social Revolutionaries of the Left would make bitter war on the Bolsheviki. Several prominent officials have been slain since Spiridonova's declaration, and now Nikolai Lenin, idol of the Bolsheviki, lies badly wounded by the shots fired by a Russian woman, Dora Kaplan, a Social Revolutionist, who said she placed her life in jeopardy to save Russia and believed this could be realized only through the Constituent Convention.

Mlle Spiridonova and Mlle Kaplan are educated women, the former a teacher, the latter a medical student. They are both about thirty years old. Mlle Spiridonova did not favor the Brest-Litovsk Peace, but accepted it as inevitable and kept the peasant organizations in line until she learned that the Bolshevist Government was preparing to turn over millions of yards of cloth to the Germans. She denounced this in the press.

Then Admiral Stchastny,* who saved the Baltic Fleet for Russia, was executed without trial on the charge of being implicated in a Counter-Revolutionary plot. Mlle Spiridonova always opposed capital punishment and denounced this act.

Premier Lenin's policy of dividing the peasants into poor and rich classes and urging the poor to plunder from the rich was also offensive to Mlle Spiridonova.

The cumulative evidence of submission to the German demands fired Spiridonova to revolt, and her challenge to the Bolshevist leaders in the All-Russian Soviet Congress of July 4 will never be forgotten by the great audience which filled the Grand Opera House of Moscow.

"You may have a majority in this Congress," she shouted, "but you have not a majority of the workmen of Russia with you and you have not ten per cent of the peasants."

Mlle Spiridonova then explained that there were not ten per cent of the peasants who did not have property, and she declared she would "never help these loafers to rob their thrifty neighbors."

She announced to the Bolsheviki that she would fight if they

* Execution of Admiral Stchastny, at the demand of Trotsky. Appendix, pp. 433–444.

wanted fight and if necessary would take revolver and bomb in hand and lead the peasants against oppression.

She shook her fist at the box occupied by representatives of the German Embassy and declared Russia would never submit itself to become a German colony.

Mlle Spiridonova's speech practically broke up the Congress. Premier Lenin and Minister of War Trotsky were ineffective in their attempts to refute her charges. Lenin, who had seemed to be a tower of strength in the All-Russian Congress four months before had lost all his fire.

Two days later Count Mirbach was dead. Gen. Hermann von Eichhorn, the German commander in the Ukraine, was killed at Kiev by another group incited by the same speech. Moses Uritsky, Chairman of the Petrograd Commission for the Suppression of Counter-Revolution, was shot to death at Petrograd. In a few days more Lenin was shot by Dora Kaplan. The bullet was deflected by the shoulder bone and he recovered, though the shock must be counted as a factor in shortening his life.

There were uprisings in many sections of the country and Bolshevism reeled from the blows of a woman. Central organization was lacking, nevertheless, and the rebellion was broken piecemeal. Spiridonova was hunted down and imprisoned. The Bolsheviks, however, feared to execute her, and several weeks later, believing her helpless, released her. Again in January, 1919, she was arrested for planning a new revolt, and intermittently was in prison and out until 1921, when she was allowed to retire into obscurity. Emma Goldman, the American anarchist, who also failed to find in Russia the liberty she expected and who after escape from the rigors of Communism became its vivid critic, found Spiridonova in 1920 living as an "outlaw" in a Moscow retreat, an invalid from the harshness of her terms in jail. New arrest soon ensued. Miss Goldman kept track of her for a year longer and recorded astonishment that she still lived.

Unless Colonel Thompson chanced to see Spiridonova and others of the later Bolshevik leaders in the late summer when they were private and for the most part subterranean agitators, he never saw them. His experience with Bolsheviks as rulers was limited to the interval between November 7, the beginning day of their Revolution and November 28, when he departed from Russia. His conversion to their support was unexplained. It never was my purpose, however, to judge the man himself. He was generous and he had imagination. To my great regret he died (June 27, 1930) while this chapter was being written. The importance of the lessons of his adventures in Russia concerns not the individual but the organization he commanded. A strong man, he bent the American Red Cross in Russia to political use. That he was invited to do so by the Russian Provisional Government and that he spent his own money were extenuating circumstances and otherwise immaterial to the issue. The American Red Cross is restricted to the function of being a welfare institution; it is for the helping of peoples, not causes, whether at home or abroad. That the American Red Cross did fall into pitfalls in Russia in the World War is, I believe, a moderate statement, permitting the conclusion that, having been seen, the same snares can be the easier avoided if ever war again sends the organization to far places.

CHAPTER IV

November 27—November 29, 1917. Lenin and Trotsky,
Agitators. Preliminary Armistice with Germany.
General Judson to the Front.

1.

WHEN I entered Russia, the preliminary armistice
with Germany had not come. While there was no
fighting, the formal situation still was that of war.
The Bolsheviks were going through the phase of making peace
proposals to all belligerent nations. The response of the Allies
could be, and had been, discounted, but even Germany had
not accepted. There were insults of words the Germans would
have to swallow along with the provender on the peace platter.
Might not German pride take offense, even at the last minute?
I had yet to learn how little on this front Germany weighed
pride against utility, and how assured was its method of dealing with Bolsheviks—to nurse them when they were helpful to
Germany, to shake them roughly when they cut perverse and
impish capers, and punch them on the jaws when they became
actually troublesome. The Bolshevik leaders were indeed out of
control to the extent of their cynical daring from the moment
they began to taste the fruits of their Russian conquest, but
there never was a moment when the Germans were not able to
measure that daring, and master it if need be. Force major!
Both the Germans and the Bolsheviks understood the doctrine
perfectly.

We discussed at the Embassy the morning of November 27
Lenin and Trotsky's earlier call to the German soldiers on the
eastern front to make a revolution of their own. There was no
copy of the handbill at the Embassy but the Bolsheviks were
talking about the tract. Some time later I got hold of a cluster
of the sheets and kept them. They were written in the German
language. Incidentally the Germans protested against the im-
polite venture and confiscated bundles of the literature wherever they could find them along the front. The Bolsheviks,
however, were expert at propaganda infiltration. The voices of
Lenin and Trotsky were at least heard.

The translation of the circular, as made in the News Bureau office in Petrograd, lacked literary finish but was accurate in substance:

TO THE GERMAN SOLDIERS!

SOLDIERS, BRETHREN!

On October 25 (Old Style) the Workers and Soldiers of St. Petersburg have overthrown the imperialist Government of Kerensky and have placed the entire Government organization at the disposal of the Workers, Soldiers and Peasants' Soviets. The new Government has been confirmed by the All-Russian convention of Workers and Soldiers' Soviets. The programme which this Government began at once to carry into effect comprises: the offer of an immediate conclusion of a democratic peace, already submitted to all belligerent nations and their Governments; the passing, without payment, of the entire acreage of field and forest land of the country to the peasants and field workers for their use; and the realization of the labor control of manufacture and industry. These tasks already have been accomplished in part or completely for the benefit of the workers and peasants. We, the undersigned, have been charged by the Government to preside over the Council of People's Commissars and to manage the foreign affairs of the country, respectively.

Our Government, the Provisional Workers and Peasants' Government addressed on October 26th (Old Style) a peace proposal to the Governments and nations of all belligerent countries, insisting upon the earliest possible cessation of hostilities on all fronts and upon the immediate opening of peace negotiations for the restoration of a just democratic peace without annexations and contributions.

We took all necessary measures and also shall not fail to use in future all means to acquaint all belligerent Governments and nations with the complete text of our peace offer. Supplementary to this peace offer we consider it our duty to address you in particular as the representatives of a nation heading a coalition which on a wide front is waging war against Russia.

Soldiers, Brethren! We are asking you to help us, with the exertion of all forces, in this struggle for an immediate peace and for Socialism, as only Socialism can secure for the labor classes of all countries a just and permanent peace and can heal all wounds struck at humanity by the present war, the most disgraceful of all wars.

Brethren, German Soldiers! The shining example of your com-

An die deutschen Soldaten!

Soldaten, Brüder!

Am 25-ten Oktober (alten Stils) haben die St. Petersburger Arbeiter und Soldaten die imperialistische Regierung Kerensky's gestürzt und die ganze Staatsgewalt zur Verfügung der Arbeiter-, Soldaten- und Bauern-Räte gestellt. Die neue Regierung ist unter dem Namen des VOLKSKOMMISSÄRENRATES durch den Kongress der Arbeiter- und Soldaten-Räte aller Reussen bestätigt worden. Das Programm, dessen Ausführung die obengenannte Regierung unverzüglich angebahnt hat, besteht aus dem Angebot eines sofortigen demokratischen Friedensschlusses, das bereits den sämmtlichen kriegsbeteiligten Nationen und ihren Regierungen unterbreitet worden ist, aus der unentgeltlichen Übergabe der ganzen Acker-, Felder- und Wälderfläche des Landes in den Gebrauch der Bauern und Landarbeiter, und aus der Verwirklichung der Arbeiterkontrolle im Gewerbe und in der Industrieerzeugung. All dieser Aufgaben hat sich die neue Regierung der Arbeiter- und Bauernbevölkerung gegenüber schon teilweise oder vollständig entledigt. Uns, die Unterzeichneten beauftragte die Regierung mit dem Vorsitz im Volkskommissärenrate und mit der Leitung der auswärtigen Geschäfte des Staates.

Unsere Regierung, die provisorische Arbeiter- und Bauern-Regierung, wendete s'ch am 26-ten Oktober d. J. mit einem Friedensvorschlag an die Regierungen und Völker aller kriegführenden Mächte, bestehend auf dringendster Einstellung der Feindseligkeiten an sämmtlichen Fronten und unmittelbarer Einleitung der Friedensverhandlungen zwecks Wiederherstellung eines gerechten demokratischen Friedens ohne Annexionen und Kriegsentschädigung.

Wir ergriffen alle Massnahmen und keine werden wir auch künftig unausgenutzt lassen, um über den vollen Text unseres Friedensangebotes alle die kriegführenden Regierungen und Völker in Kenntnis zu setzen. Zur Ergänzung des erwähnten Friedensvorschlags erachten wir es als unsere Pflicht, uns speziell an euch zu wenden, als an die Vertreter einer Nation, die an der Spitze der Koalition steht, welche gegen Russland auf einer ausgedehnten Front den Krieg führt.

Soldaten, Brüder! Wir ersuchen euch, uns in diesem Kampfe für den sofortigen Frieden und den Sozialismus mit Anstrengung aller Kräfte beizustehen, da dieser letztere allein dem Arbeiterstande aller Länder, einen gerechten und dauerhaften Frieden sichern kann und alle die Wunden heilen, die der Menschheit der gegenwärtige und frevelhafteste aller Kriege geschlagen hat.

FIRST AGITATIONAL APPEAL BY LENIN
REVOLUTIONARY

Brüder deutsche Soldaten! Das grosse Beispiel eures Kameraden, Karl Liebknechts, des ansehnlichsten Führers des internationalen Sozialismus, der beharrliche und langwierige Kampf, den ihr gegen den Krieg mit der Herausgebung von Zeitungen und Flugblättern, mit zahlreichen Demonstrationen und Streiken geführt habt, der Kampf, für welchen eure Regierung Hunderte und Tausende eurer Kameraden ins Gefängniss geworfen hat, endlich der heldenmütige Aufstand eurer Matrosen der Flotte bürgen uns dafür, dass innerhalb breiter Massen des Arbeiterstandes eurer Nation die Fertigkeit für einen entscheidenden Kampf für den Frieden schon gereift ist.

Brüder, leistet uns Hilfe! Wenn ihr es tut, dann kann nicht einmal der geringste Zweifel darüber bestehen, dass die Friedenssache, wenigstens auf dem Kontinente Europas, in paar Tagen die Oberhand ergreift, dass der schnellste und gerechteste Friede verbürgt wird und der Anschluss an einen solchen Frieden seitens auch der übrigen kriegführenden Mächte am schmerzlosesten vor sich geht.

Wenn ihr uns bei unserer Aufgabe behilflich sein werdet, die Einigung der Arbeiter mit den Bauern und den allmählichen Übergang zum Sozialismus in Russland zu bewerk-stelligen, bei der Aufgabe, die für Russland allein unheimliche Schwierigkeiten darbietet, dann werden eure Organisationsfähigkeit, eure Erfahrung, eure Vorbereitung zur Bildung der Arbeiter-Massenorganisationen uns den Übergang zum Sozialismus unfehlbar sichern.

Eilt uns zu Hilfe! Im Namen der Arbeiter- und Bauern-Regierung haften wir dafür, dass unsere Soldaten keinen einzigen Schritt nach vorwärts machen werden, wenn ihr entschlossen die Friedensfahne in die Hände nehmt auch falls der Kampf für den Frieden innerhalb eures Landes einen Teil eurer Streitkräfte von unserer Front abzöge.

Genug des Blutvergiessens!
Hoch lebe der Friede!
Hoch lebe der brüderliche Verband der Arbeiter aller Länder!
Hoch lebe die Internazionale sozialistische Revolution!

Der Vorsitzende des Volkskommissärenrates,
Wladimir Uljanow (Ljenjin).

Der Volkskommissär des Äussern,
Leo Trotzky.

AND TROTSKY TO GERMAN SOLDIERS FOR
HELP, NOVEMBER 1917

rade, Karl Liebknecht, the most eminent leader of international Socialism; the stubborn and untiring struggle which you have launched against the war by means of numerous demonstrations and strikes; the struggle which has moved your Government to throw hundreds of thousands of your comrades into prison, and finally the heroic uprising of your navy, are sufficient guarantee to us that the readiness for a decisive struggle for peace has ripened already among the large masses of your nation.

Brethren, help us! If you will do so, then not the slightest doubt can obtain that the cause of peace, at least on the continent of Europe, will get the upper hand within a few days; that the earliest and most equitable peace will be safe-guarded; and that the accession of the other nations to such a peace will be consequent.

If you will help us in our task of uniting the workers with the peasants and of promoting the progressive transition of Russia to Socialism, which is a task of tremendous difficulties in Russia, then the transition to Socialism will be secured inevitably through your capacity for organization, your experience and your practice of forming mass organizations of labor.

Don't be slow in helping us! In the name of the Workers and Peasants' Government we pledge that our soldiers will not advance a single step forward if you will take resolutely the banner of Peace into your hands, even if the peace struggle within your country should take part of your fighting forces from our front.

Enough bloodshed!

Long live Peace!

Long live the fraternal partnership of the workers of all lands!

Long live the Internationalist Socialist Revolution!

President of the Council of People's Commissar:

VLADIMIR ULIANOV (LENIN).

People's Commissar for Foreign Affairs:

LEO TROTSKY.

The ingenious paragraph in this appeal of slogans was that in which the writers sought to sow in the minds of the German soldiers at the front the belief that the German navy was in revolt, and that national and industrial morale was breaking down in their rear. The Germans detested this form of Bolshevik maneuvering. There were later instances of Germans on duty with the War Prisoner Commission in Petrograd who became so confused by the flaring reports of outbreaks in Berlin that they telegraphed asking what truth there was in them. They were promptly reassured.

Excitement, I was to learn, was apt to reserve its liveliest efforts for the late night hours. This night, November 27, was a beginning. Armistice suddenly was rumored, just a street word at first, with nothing to give it credence. The first messengers brought back the report that no official announcements had been made, which was a negative admission, and by midnight we were aware that the initial armistice either was established or imminent. Confirmation did not come publicly until the next day. The preliminary armistice went into effect at four o'clock in the afternoon of November 27.

Krylenko, the little Commissar who now signed himself "Generalissimo," hastened to dispatch to Petrograd the orders he had issued in connection with the event:

4.15 P.M. Our emissaries have returned with an official answer from the German Commander-in-chief, expressing his willingness to open negotiations for an armistice on all fronts. The next meeting of the representatives from both sides has been arranged for Nov. 19/Dec. 2. Those who would suppress this order or should prevent its publication shall be tried by a Revolutionary Court of the local Regimental Committees without any regard to the usual formalities. I order that firing and fraternization on the entire front cease immediately. [Note by the Editor of *Pravda*—Undoubtedly this refers only to attempts at unorganized fraternization.] Increased vigilance is now necessary against the enemy. Military operation is to be opened only in case that such has been undertaken by the enemy. Everybody is to remain in his place. Only the strong will realize his purpose. Long live an early peace.   GENERALISSIMO KRYLENKO.

On the subject of fraternization Krylenko must have known what he was forbidding.

Krylenko preceded the 4.15 order with his Army Order No. 2, which led to the death of General Dukhonin less than a week later:

The emissaries detailed by me have passed into the German lines in the region of the 5th Army. The enemy has promised an answer by 8 P.M. November 27th (New Style). Comrades, peace is near, it depends now upon you. Hold out staunchly these last days, exert all your forces, and in spite of hunger and deprivations defend the front. Success is dependent upon your revolutionary stubbornness. Stigmatize with contempt the deceitful and hypocritical appeals of the gang of Generals which has entrenched itself at Headquarters, and of their bourgeois and pseudosocialist agents who for eight months have been imposing upon the Russian nation with deceitful promises of an early peace, and have brought immeasurable misfortunes upon the country by causing hunger and exhaustion in the army through their gratuitous and criminal attempts to oppose the authority of the Government created by the All-Russian Convention of Soviets.

I discharge General Cheremisov from his post of Commander of the Northern front. He disobeyed the order to appear before me. Comrade Posern, the Commissar of the Northern front will take command until a new appointment is made. Shubin, the Commissar of the former Government is to be placed under arrest owing to his refusal to surrender his post. General Boldyreff has been arrested and turned over to the Court because of non-compliance with a military order. The Commander of the 27th Corps is discharged owing to his refusal to report to me in person. The Corps is to accept a Commander selected by the Commissar of the Corps and the Corps Committee.

The former Generalissimo Dukhonin who through his obstinate refusal to obey the orders removing him from his post and his criminal action in driving the country into a new civil war is declared an enemy of the nation.

All persons supporting Dukhonin, irrespective of their social or party standing and without regard to their past are to be arrested, the arrests to be made by persons specially empowered by me for this task.

General Manikovsky is instructed to issue a corresponding order about the changes in Army posts, and such changes are to be noted accordingly in their Service lists.

The italics of the Dukhonin paragraph were mine. In the light of Krylenko's order the slaughter of General Dukhonin, at Mogilev on December 3, was not surprising. On November 28 General Cheremisov was brought a prisoner to the fortress of SS. Peter and Paul.

In an extra edition on Wednesday, November 28, the evening *Pravda* gave this official detail of the experiences of Krylenko's delegation carrying the armistice proffer:

The emissaries of Krylenko, returning to Dvinsk at 2 P.M., Nov. 27, have given an account of their mission.

Their offer to open parleys for an armistice on all fronts was immediately transmitted to Divisional Headquarters and thence to the Headquarters of the Commander-in-Chief of the Eastern Front, Prince Rupprecht, and to the Generalissimo of the German armies.

The emissaries were then taken by automobile at 6.20 P.M., November 26, to the Headquarters of the Divisional Commander, General Hofmeister, who received them "in full dress field uniform, decorated with the highest German orders and other insignia, surrounded by Staff officers."

General Hofmeister told them that an answer to their proposal [of armistice] could be expected within 24 hours. But at 7.50 P.M. Nov. 26 the first answer was received from the German Supreme Army Command, authorizing General Hofmeister and the emissaries to arrange for the details of the next meeting of the representatives of the belligerent countries. It expressed also a willingness to open negotiations on the principles set forth by us in the authorization given them in writing by Krylenko.

At 12.20 A.M. Nov. 27, a statement was given to the emissaries under General Hofmeister's signature containing the following provisions: (1) Categorical consent for the immediate opening of armistice parleys, which the Commander-in-Chief of the Eastern front is vested with power to conduct. (2) The placing of a special train at the disposal of the representatives of the belligerent countries who are to participate in the negotiations. (3) Establishment of a direct telegraphic communication between the emissaries and the supreme Russian authority, the Council of People's Commissaries. The meeting place shall be the Headquarters of the Commander of the German Eastern front, which is on Russian territory in the town of Brest-Litovsk. Time of meeting—December 1, 12 noon, Middle European Time.

The Germans wasted not even minutes in grabbing the precious Russian gift. At 6.20 o'clock General "Hofmeister" (General Hoffman, in the naming he had in these first Russian dispatches) said that a reply would be given in a day's time. He had communicated the report of the Russians' arrival to Prince Rupprecht, and the latter had telegraphed the news to the German Supreme Army Command behind the distant western front. Action there was prompt. At 7.50 General

"Hofmeister" at the east had in hand the authorization from the west. Twenty minutes after midnight he delivered his own signed papers to the Russians.

The text of the order he received from Prince Rupprecht, relaying the instructions of the German Supreme Army Command, was:

1. The Commander-in-chief of the German Eastern front is authorised by the German Supreme Army Command to conduct negotiations with the Russian Generalissimo.

2. In the event the Russian Generalissimo consents to negotiate with the Commander-in-chief of the German Eastern front he is requested to detail a delegation, vested with the necessary power in writing to the Headquarters of the Commander-in-Chief of the Eastern front.

3. The Commander-in-Chief of the German Eastern front will also detail a delegation, vested with special power.

4. The date and the place for the meeting of both delegations can be determined at the discretion of the Russian Generalissimo. A preliminary notification of the German Commander-in-Chief of the Eastern front is necessary in order that arrangements can be made for a special train. The sector of the front which is to be crossed by the Russian delegation must also be indicated.

5. The Commander-in-Chief of the German Eastern front will furnish the necessary technical facilities for communication by direct wire between the delegation and the Russian Supreme Army Command. It is also permissible to bring a wireless installation.

Commander-in-Chief of the German Eastern Front.

(Rupprecht—unnamed)

The town of Brest-Litovsk was headquarters for the Commander in Chief of the eastern front. No one then knew that Brest-Litovsk also was to be the scene of the later formal peace conference.

Two days later Trotsky, in his capacity of Minister of Foreign Affairs, went through the form of advising the diplomatic representatives of the Allied Powers of action already taken, and asking to be informed if any of them desired to participate in the negotiations. He followed the diplomatic usage of sending a communication to each Embassy, his first use of a method so polite. The epistle, however, was brusquely written:

PEOPLE'S COMMISSAR
       FOR   *For the Information of the Diplomatic*
FOREIGN AFFAIRS   *Representatives of the Countries*
Nov. 17/30, 1917   *Allied to Russia.*
PETROGRAD

In response to the formal proposal of the Council of People's
Commissars for an opening of negotiations for an immediate
armistice on all fronts with the object of concluding a democratic
peace without annexations and contributions, which would accord to all nations the right to determine independently their own
destinies, the German Supreme Army Command has expressed
its consent to the proposal. All documents and statements containing data pertaining to this proposal have been published by
me in the *Izvestia* of the Central Executive Committee.

Military operations on the Russian front have been suspended.
Preliminary negotiations will be opened on Nov. 19/Dec. 2. The
Council of People's Commissars considers now, as it did heretofore that the simultaneous conduct of negotiations by all Allies
is necessary for the purpose of accomplishing the earliest possible armistice on all fronts, and for safe-guarding a general
democratic peace.

The Allied Governments and their representatives in Russia
are asked for the favor of a reply as to whether they desire to
participate in the negotiations, which will open on Dec. 2, at
5. P.M.

      People's Commissar for Foreign Affairs, L. TROTSKY.

Trotsky received from the embassies the only reply he could
have anticipated—the negative of silence.

Prior to the sending of the missive, Trotsky and Lenin had
joined in a more flamboyant announcement of their intentions
to the world at large, this appeal being among the "data" referred to in Trotsky's letter to the ambassadors. The joint
proclamation, appearing Nov. 28, was:

TO THE NATIONS OF THE BELLIGERENT
COUNTRIES

In answer to our offer of an immediate armistice on all fronts
with the object of concluding a democratic peace, without annexations and contributions, with guarantee for all nations to
determine autonomously their own destinies, the German Com-

mander-in-Chief has expressed his willingness to conduct peace negotiations. The Generalissimo of the Russian republic has requested that the opening of negotiations for the armistice be deferred for five days in order to allow us the time for us to ask the Allied Governments once more if they will not define their attitude in the matter of peace negotiations. By mutual agreement war operations have been suspended on the Russian front. It is understood, of course, that there shall be no transfer of troops on either side during these five days.

The decisive step has been taken. The triumphant revolution of the peasants and workers of Russia has set up squarely the issue of peace. The period of vacillations, procrastinations and bureaucratic agreements is over. All governments, all classes, all parties of all belligerent countries must answer unreservedly the question: Are they prepared to unite with us in negotiations for an immediate armistice and general peace—on Dec. 1? Yes or No! It will depend upon the answer to this question whether the toilers of the factories and fields will be spared a new winter campaign with all its terrors and mishaps, or whether Europe will continue to shed its blood.

We, the Council of People's Commissars, are addressing this question to the Governments of our Allies: France, Great Britain, Italy, the United States, Belgium, Serbia, Rumania, Japan and China. We are asking them, in the face of their own nations, in the face of the entire world: Are they ready with us to open peace negotiations on Dec. 1?

We, the Council of People's Commissars, are addressing our appeal to the Allied nations, and, pre-eminently, to the toiling masses: Are they prepared to continue this meaningless and aimless slaughter, going blindly along the road which leads to the perdition of the entire European culture? We demand that the labor parties of the Allied countries give an immediate answer to our question: Do they want peace negotiations to open on Dec. 1?

The issue has been set up squarely. Soldiers, Proletarians, Workers, Peasants: Do you want to take with us a decisive step for the peace of the nations? It must be an honest understanding, guaranteeing to each nation the freedom of economic and cultural development. Such a peace can be concluded only if the revolutionary masses will wage a direct and courageous struggle against all imperialistic projects and territorial aspirations.

The Revolution of the Peasants and Workers already has proclaimed its peace programme. We have published the secret treaties of the Czar and the bourgeoisie with the Allies, and have announced that these treaties are not binding upon the Russian nation. We propose to all nations to conclude openly a new treaty based on the principles of co-operation and common friendship.

Our offer has been answered by the official and the semi-official representatives of the ruling classes of the Allied countries with a refusal to recognize the Soviet Government, and with a refusal to enter into an agreement with it in regard to peace negotiations.

The Government of the triumphant Revolution does not stand in need of the recognition of the professional representatives of the Capitalist diplomacy. And we address ourselves to the nations: Does the reactionary diplomacy express their thoughts and longings? Are the nations willing to allow diplomacy to ignore the great perspective of peace opened by the Russian Revolution?

An answer to these questions must be given immediately, and not in words but in actions. The Russian army and the Russian nation can not and will not wait any longer. On Dec. 1 we shall open general peace negotiations. If the Allied nations do not send their representatives we shall conduct the negotiations alone. We want general peace. But should the *bourgeoisie* of the Allied countries force us to conclude a separate peace, the responsibility for it will lie entirely upon its shoulders.

Soldiers, Workers and Peasants of France, England, Italy, the United States, Belgium and Serbia! On Dec. 1 negotiations will be opened. We are waiting for your representatives. Act! Do not lose a single hour's time! Down with the winter campaign! Down with War! Long live peace and the brotherhood of nations!

Commissar for Foreign Affairs, L. TROTSKY.

President of the Council of People's Commissars, V. ULIANOV (N. LENIN).

This message was an avowal that Trotsky and Lenin intended to sign a separate peace with Germany. For purposes of domestic politics it was an apology in advance of action, an effort to shift blame and responsibility from their nearby selves to distant and nebulous ogres, the *bourgeoisie* of far-away lands. The manifesto contained not a hint of appeal to German elements of unrest, no call to the toilers of Germany to "participate in the negotiations," no intimation that the authors had been making earlier pretence of rousing the German soldiers to a companion revolution.

Separate devices had been used in the two proclamations,

though for the same end—increase of Bolshevik prestige and
strength in Russia. The appearance of incitement of German
soldiers, which Germany could fend off harmlessly, conveyed
also to the Allied world an impression of the possibility that
the Bolsheviks might become foes of the Germans. It tended
to make the Allies hesitant of outright action against the Bolsheviks, and to give the latter the breathing period they
needed. The second proclamation added to the stature of the
Bolsheviks in Russia by the studied insolence of such phrases
as "the Government of the triumphant Revolution does not
stand in need of the recognition of the professional representatives of the Capitalist diplomacy" and "We address ourselves
to the nations." Lenin and Trotsky had "sassed" the world and
to Russia the world began to look smaller. Yet as palliative, intended to make easier the task of the Bolshevik leaders in keeping power after they should sign a separate peace, the second
proclamation was most significant.

There were the words, plain enough: "Should the *bourgeoisie* of the Allied countries force us to conclude a separate
peace, the responsibility for it will lie entirely upon its shoulders."

This once, and so soon, Lenin and Trotsky did ingenuously
show their hand. Nor does this view preclude a recognition of
the real quarrel soon to break out between the Bolsheviks and
the Germans over the division of Russia.

If the Allies had accepted that letter as final sign of intent,
and from that day had built upon the basis that Russia was
to be looked upon as an economic ally of Germany and treated
accordingly, the War might have been easier if not sooner
won.

The manifesto, however, did not receive much attention
around the embassies. On the surface it was just another announcement of what already was known—that armistice consideration was to begin. The ray of truthful light soon was
dispersed among confusing shadows, its meaning and its value
unseen.

2.

Upon Colonel Thompson's departure I took over his suite of
rooms as headquarters. The place, as time passed, became an

American hall. Until the latter days of February the doors may be said to have been always open during the working day, which was a mingling of day and night. The hours between three in the morning and ten in the forenoon were the only ones for which I claimed a degree of privacy. From ten o'clock at night to three o'clock in the morning was the favorite time for the gathering of groups. More things happened, also, between those hours than in other divisions of the twenty-four, and for news of what did happen this was the clearing-house. The Bolshevik hierarchy, too, was membered with night owls. There was so little daylight anyway that the twisting of the hours made no difference. Light soon was uncertain at ten o'clock in the morning and on cloudy days was fading shortly after two o'clock in the afternoon.

When I had more organization and could establish a routine, my habit was to move until late afternoon between my offices and places where I had business engagements, pass the evenings at Bolshevik gatherings, public entertainments, or at the Embassy, and aim to be home by midnight. My presence or absence made no difference at the center. If I was late someone else could act as host.

What a medley of humankind passed in and out of the doors of the apartment that winter! Military *attachés*, consulate and embassy men, my own staff men, American and English newspapermen, Red Cross men, visiting professors and experts in the few remaining weeks that Russia remained accessible to the rest of Europe, Petrograd Americans, Russian Bolsheviks, American Bolsheviks, Russian patriots, Russian adventurers, watchers who were eyes and ears for Smolny, and at least one German officer! A compounding that was diverse, diverting, stimulating!

The fireplace room was big enough so that a dozen or more persons did not crowd it. The naming came from the fireplace, a cord-width hearth cutting the inner corner of the room. Entering one found one's self facing the fireplace, and on its side of the room. The mantel was high and the structure of the heater ran higher still, two-thirds of the way to the ceiling, the back being bricked or tiled for radiation. Otherwise the appearance was that of any other honest open fireplace. So efficient was it that I never used the tiled stove in my sleeping room beyond. By piling the hearth high with wood before going to bed there was likelihood of finding coals enough left to rekindle new wood in the morning. Sometimes of course the fire did go out, and then I built it anew, learning the Russian method of lighting from above instead of below, stripping bark from the birch-like wood for shavings. Perhaps with wood less tindery the method might not work.

The room itself scaled to the fireplace. Even a library sized table did not get in one's way. The windows were high, with heavy inner draw curtains, in hue a dusky Italian rose, agreeably warm. This color, too, was the key to the furnishings of the room, carried out in table drape, the rugs, and the upholstery of the comfortable chairs. In Russia, color is an antidote to climate. I always felt cheered when I came into the room.

There was a bedroom on each side of the living-room, and beyond, toward the Nevsky, another big room which the Red Cross retained, nominally as a breakfast-room and a library. It had no heating facilities, however, and was not used after sharp cold weather began. Instead I had a portable table set up in my living-room and invited Robins, Thacher, Wardwell, Hardy, and Webster to breakfast there in front of the fireplace. I was the gainer, for the Red Cross had its own supply of compote—fruits of many kinds canned in natural juices with little or no sweetening. Breakfasts for awhile were uniform—compote, coffee with condensed milk, one lump of sugar, and brown bread. If one had the patience to toast the bread over the fire, one could. After a few trials one did not. In a little while the coffee was taken without sugar, there being none left, and without condensed milk, there being children in Petrograd who needed it more than we. Black coffee became so natural a beverage that for a year or more after I came out of Russia I drank coffee no other way. Other meals of the day were taken in a side dining-room on the first floor of the hotel.

The apartment had only one inconvenience—the bathroom was off the entrance hall and it had an uncertain lock. Anyone coming in from outside and opening the first door, was as apt to find himself in the bathroom as in the living-room, depending upon whether the turn was to right or left. The only way to bathe without expecting intrusion was to lock the outside door, which was not often locked in the hours callers might come. So I bathed either after three o'clock in the morning, or sleepily at nine on awakening. For the latter practice there was a second handicap—the tub had a tricky and cumbersome self-heating water attachment, difficult for a sleepy person to operate. The bath sometimes had to be a quick plunge into cold water. But there had to be a bath. Rigid living was the only chance of health. Typhoid already was epidemic in Petrograd, typhus present and increasing, and other infectious diseases in the ascendant. The Neva water was bad. After my third day in Petrograd I did not drink raw water, or use it for the brushing of my teeth. That was where the samovar became useful, boiling the water for tea and drinking both. All the Americans I knew followed the same regimen. Of tea and coffee we drank heavily.

The matter of habitation settled, the business of the day, November 28, was to discover the situation of the government funds transmitted, ahead of my arrival, to the Bank of the Azov-Don. I found the director of the bank, Witold Czamanski, a worried man, and before he was through talking, I was sharing his worry. He did not believe that either he or the bank was going to last long. The Bolsheviks had not yet seized the banks; they merely had said they would get around to that action when they had more time. The threat stopped all normal banking business.

There was a quarter of a million dollars of United States Treasury money to my order in that bank and I wanted the use of it. The director said he had 1,750,000 rubles to my credit, the exchange having been at the rate of seven rubles to the dollar, which I thought a regrettable loss in exchange. The transfer evidently had been made the week of my departure from New York, when the ruble had pre-Bolshevik rating. I had expected to find not less than 2,000,000 rubles in the account and had hoped for 2,500,000. That night I cabled to hold the second allotment of $250,000 in New York. As a summary of finances, eventually I only transferred $50,000 of the New York balance, and that in dollars to the Moscow consulate. After nearly eight months of heavy printing and circulation operations there still remained of the two funds upward of $20,000 for the Bolsheviks to seize. That amount (in 1930) they still have. My personal expenses amounted to less than $5,000, including transportation from Washington and back. I started from Washington with $3,000 and accounted for $2,000 to my credit fund.

Director Czamanski gave me a bank statement and an ornate check book, with the warning that he could not cash my checks. Did he think the situation would change? Yes, he thought so, probably for the worse. Of course, if for the better, he would honor checks as soon as possible. I did not intend to lose the money, but for the problem of keeping it I needed a better financial head than mine, and one familiar with Russian banks.

The National City Bank of New York had a branch in Petrograd. So I went directly to the English Quay along the Neva, where the offices were, and sought out the manager, Stephens, who proved to be a slender chap in his early thirties, kindly, nervy, resourceful. We pulled up chairs in front of his wide windows, surveyed the frozen Neva and the spire of SS. Peter and Paul on the opposite bank, and considered.

"Remember one thing," he said presently. "One can get most anything in Russia if one keeps after it. First refusals are an invitation to argument. The one that can talk the longer wears the other down. Keep on talking."

On that advice I talked myself into every place I wanted to go while I was in Petrograd, by it I got everything I needed.

Stephens admitted, however, that the bank troubles were real and that he probably would be closed up with the rest.

"Though I believe," he added, "that I can hang on longer than the others." Events were to prove him right.

The logic of the situation, he argued, was that the Bolsheviks, if or when they seized the banks, would merge them all with the Russian State Bank. Therefore, in his opinion, the best chance of safety for the fund was to get it into that bank before it was seized in another bank. Acquiring the use of the money thereafter would be my job, likely a tough one, though with time afforded for tackling it. The immediate step, we agreed, was to get custody of the fund away from the Bank of the Azov-Don. In the next few days we had other meetings and the outcome was a draft upon the Bank of the Azov-Don for the entire amount, for redeposit in the National City Bank as United States government money. We figured that the Bolsheviks would hesitate to stop such an operation. Then, subtracting a check for a working amount within Stephens' ability to cash, we redeposited the balance in the Russian State Bank itself.

3.

WHILE I busied myself with a day of detail, difficulties for all official American groups were developing in consequence of the armistice outlook. Logically they centered about the American Military Mission and its head, Brig. Gen. W. V. Judson, who also was the Military *Attaché* of the Embassy. I had met him at the Embassy, a formal rite. From this time on, however, needs in common threw us together.

All the Allied military men in Petrograd had been hardly less than frantic from the start of Bolshevik success. They saw the prospect and the peril of the removal of the German army from the eastern to the western line. It is reasonable to assume that some of the military *attachés* and heads of military missions sought to get from their Governments permission to try to have a hand in the preparation of the technical points of the armistice, if there should be one, to the extent at least of arguing for the insertion of strict clauses to restrain the unhindered movement of troops away from the German line. Whatever their appeals, the Governments one and all took the political view that military advice had a flavor of recognition, and either advised against it or sent no instructions. Washington took its place in the latter class.

General Judson and Ambassador Francis found themselves in disagreement. General Judson wanted to act, even if he failed. The Ambassador felt that action would result in failure, and perhaps in insult. It was another instance of a twilight zone of authority. The argument was friendly, and the Ambassador decided the course of events by telling General Judson that he would be suited if the General took such steps as he deemed to come within the duties of Chief of the Military Mission.

The immediate result was to place General Judson in the forefront of the Petrograd picture. He had no rivals among the Allies. They held to their silence. In his elected rôle, General Judson wrote as early as November 25 a letter which he addressed to the "Chief of the Russian General Staff," a person he did not name, not knowing who he was. General Dukhonin still claimed to be functioning at Staff Headquarters at Mogilev. Krylenko was calling himself Generalissimo. There is no doubt, however, where the letter ultimately went. Trotsky got it at Smolny. The communication was:

12/25 November, 1917.

To the Chief of the Russian General Staff,
Petrograd.

Excellency:

There has been brought to my attention the following press communication from the United States:

The American Government has announced that no shipments of military supplies and provisions to Russia will be effected until the situation of this country will be established. The Government before permitting the export of American products wants to know into whose hands they will get in Russia. The exports to Russia will be resumed only after the formation of a steady government which can be recognized by the United States, but if the Bolsheviks will remain in power and will put through their program of making peace with Germany, the present embargo on exports to Russia will remain in force. The credits to the Provisional Russian Government reach to the present day 325 million dollars, of which 191 millions have already been appropriated. The larger part of this money has already been spent for the purchase of supplies, which are ready for loading. The ships allotted by America for the carrying of this freight are ready for sailing but do not receive permission to leave the ports and they will be refused coal.

It occurs to me that it is but fair to convey to Your Excellency the circumstance that neither I nor the American Ambassador has as yet received from the United States of America instructions or information similar to that contained in the press report above quoted. Nevertheless it seems but fair to express to Your Excellency the opinion that the press report correctly states the attitude of the Government of the United States. We are in daily expectation of receiving information similar to that conveyed by the above-mentioned press report.

Before sending you this communication I have submitted it to the American Ambassador who concurs in the expressions in it.

I avail myself of this opportunity to renew to Your Excellency the assurance of my high consideration.

(Signed) W. V. JUDSON.
Brig. Gen. U.S. Army, Amer. Military Attaché,
Chief of American Military Mission to Russia.

If General Judson's motive in sending the letter was to open a door of communication, the first effect seemed to be that he had locked the door against himself. The Bolsheviks, already enraged by the news report, were angered further by the official concession of its probable truth, and their newspapers launched a hate campaign against Americans in general. For material in this they also received aid from another American officer, Lieutenant Colonel Kerth, the official observer at Mogilev Staff Headquarters, though his innocent action was in the course of duty. Other Allied military representatives had sent a joint letter to General Dukhonin protesting against an armistice with the Germans. Colonel Kerth did not join in this, writing separately:

Your Excellency: In accordance with instructions from my Government, transmitted to me by the U. S. Ambassador in Petrograd, I beg to inform you that, the Republic of the United States being allied with Russia in the present war which is essentially a war of democracy against autocracy, the United States firmly and energetically protests against any separate truce that may be concluded with Germany. I request a written acknowledgment.

When Colonel Kerth came later to Petrograd he told me that he acted under instructions from the Ambassador, as set forth. The instructions, too, were proper. Ambassador Francis could have sent no other for communication to General Dukhonin, who desired, needed, and appreciated the approving help of his Allies. No one was more against the armistice than General Dukhonin. Unhappily he was a beaten man, his cause lost, ordered removed from his command, outlawed the very day the note was written. Between them, General Judson, the Ambassador, and Colonel Kerth had slapped the Bolsheviks on both cheeks, almost on successive days. The Kerth note was sent on November 27.

Yet General Judson's letter writing did open up for him a channel of communication to Trotsky since, in order to lessen the ill-humor roused by the first letter, the author wrote a second letter, as follows:

14/27 November, 1917.

To the Chief of the Russian General Staff,
Petrograd.

EXCELLENCY: Referring to my letter of 12/25 November, 1917, relating to a quotation from American press reports, I desire to say that nothing therein should be construed as indicating that my Government has or may be expected to express preference for the success in Russia of any one political party or element over another. Americans have the greatest sympathy for the whole Russian people in the complex situation in which they find themselves and do not wish to interfere except helpfully in the solution of any Russian problem. Their sympathy extends to all sections of the Russian people. Their representatives here are now informed that no important fraction of the Russian people desires an immediate separate peace or armistice. And it is certainly within the rights of Russia, in the position in which she now finds herself, to bring up the question of a general peace.

There is no reason why the attitude of her Allies toward Russia or toward any important elements in Russia should be upon anything but a most friendly foundation.

I desire to avail myself of this occasion to renew to your Excellency the assurance of my high consideration.

(*Signed*) W. V. JUDSON.
Brigadier General, U.S. Army, American Military Attaché,
Chief of American Military Mission to Russia.

A modicum of mystery attached to the assertion in the letter that American representatives had been informed "that no important fraction of the Russian people desires an immediate separate peace or armistice." No such formal statement had come from the Bolsheviks to American representatives nor did General Judson intend the sentence as a numerical reflection upon the Bolsheviks. By this time, however, informal word was being scattered among the Americans that armistice terms and later peace conference would be slow and stormy. General Judson could have built hope upon the calculated hint. Nevertheless, the news of preliminary armistice came the evening of the day he wrote and sent his second letter.

Twenty-four hours later we knew that the second letter as

well as the first had gone to Trotsky and were told, indirectly though certainly, that the General was welcome to continue communication if he desired, either by letter or in person. The possibilities afforded by such an entry were discussed that Wednesday evening. There was, however, a lapse of two days before developments were positive, and as they were inter-woven with a speech of Trotsky's they will have relation to-gether, in the next chapter.

Thursday, the twenty-ninth, was Thanksgiving Day though none was celebrated that year in the United States, as we learned afterward. Nor did we have much to be thankful for save health and enough to eat. The food conditions of the moment were not bad, although there were reports of a coming shortage of bread, and it was said that waiting lines in front of the food shops were longer. It seemed more important to me that the composition of the lines had changed. Formerly it was the servants who went to the markets early in the morning. Now it was the mistresses. Furs were their symbol.

At the hotel, milk, cream, and butter had gone from the menu before my arrival. I never saw a beefsteak in Russia. Veal was the prevailing meat, varied by the tasteless flesh of a grouse-like bird from the plains, cold storage kept. Beet soup was a certainty both at lunch and dinner. There were neither eggs nor cereals. Cabbage stew, a later resource, was not yet frequent at the hotel. In the people's eating places it was encountered as a matter of course, sometimes with a chunk of meat in it, more often not.

In the evening Arthur Bullard arrived from Moscow, com-ing at my request to take a post beside me. I meant to build the news service around him. We were friends of not so long an acquaintance, thrown together closely for the first time in the spring of 1917, when he had joined the Committee on Public Information long enough to write in conjunction with Ernest Poole the widest distributed of the Committee's pub-lications, the Red, White, and Blue Book, *How the War Came to America*. That work completed he left the service of the Committee.

Having witnessed the unsuccessful Russian attempt at revo-lution in 1905, he was desirous of studying the new effort of the Russians at self-government, and at the same time wished to be useful to his country. Appointment for him was sought through the State Department, Chairman Creel writing to the President, who gave his approval in May in a letter to Secretary Lansing. Plans must have been changed, however, since Bullard left for Moscow in June without government connection, as he wrote to Colonel House, on June 18, 1917, "I will be going, therefore, entirely unofficially, which is from my point of view the most desirable. I will be glad to write to you from time to time." Soon after he reached Moscow he became a volunteer worker at the consulate, helping Consul Madden Summers to present to the Moscow public as much of a picture of American institutions as possible, meanwhile maintaining himself by magazine writing.

As part of a plan of education he began the preparation of a series of "Letters to a Russian Friend," a primer of American principles of self-government. Consul Summers could ill spare Bullard. My need, however, was greater; and Bullard already knew by cable from Creel, by my arrangement before leaving the United States, that he was drafted. Him and his "Letters" I took over together, and on completion the series was strewn far over Russia.

When Bullard walked into the room I feared he was a sick man. Since the Washington days he had grown a poet's beard, scraggy and graying; and he was wrapped like an invalid. He had been threatened with mastoiditis. He smiled, however, and said he would be all right in an easy chair, with tea within reach. He did perk up quickly.

All that winter he never was too sick to do a day's work or to meet an emergency, although he could rarely go abroad of evenings, nursing himself then to new strength in front of the fire. I put him up in the spare room in my suite. Returning to Moscow for a short interval, he then was in Petrograd from late December until middle March. The subsequent epic of his journey round the world from one side of Russia to get in at the other has relation in a concluding chapter of this book.

CHAPTER V

November 30—December 1, 1917. Meeting with Tseretelli in His Retreat. Encounter of Trotsky and General Judson. Trotsky's Circus Moderne Speech.

1.

IN his place of retreat I went on November 30 to visit Tseretelli, the only one of Kerensky's former ministers not under arrest or in flight from Petrograd. Only one Russian I ever met impressed me as his equal in courage and none as his superior in intelligence. Nor do I imply the bravery of remaining in hiding in Petrograd at this time. His great hour was to come when he dared and baited the Bolsheviks at the single session of the Constituent Assembly.

Yet when I sought him I believed I was going to see a dying man. His state of ill-health was supposed to be the barrier between him and arrest, for his whereabouts could have been discovered by the Bolsheviks. Perhaps he also was judged by them to be too much of the stuff of which dangerous martyrs are made. He lived unmolested in a comfortable apartment, not venturing into the street, though receiving not a few callers.

Sasha Kropotkin took me to him and acted as interpreter. Sasha (Sonia) Kropotkin, the Princess Kropotkin of today, who was in the United States in 1927–28, was the daughter of Prince Peter Kropotkin, the aristocratic philosophical anarchist of an older day. Of him and his wrath against the Bolsheviks as the enemies of Russia, presently. Sasha might have been taken as easily for English as Russian, consequent on speech and manners acquired in up-bringing in England. She was married to a young Russian by the name of Lebedev, who became an efficient member of my staff. Sasha herself was a spirited, good-looking, dark-haired girl, and one of the best of interpreters. Other duties, however, soon occupied her and this was the only occasion on which she acted as interpreter for me.

A Georgian by birth, Tseretelli was dark of hair and eyes, and in health must have been a graceful, eye-attracting figure. Fire he retained even in illness. Too weak to sit erect, he lounged on a pillowed couch. Although supposed to be in a late stage of an emaciating disease, he smoked one long Russian cigarette after another, pressing the tube end of each new light with two motions of his hands, in the Russian fashion. The fingers were long and painfully thin. He coughed frequently. I wondered then if his cigarette smoking was not the cause of his coughing. Russian tobacco, while much esteemed, smokes acridly. Not only did Tseretelli recover but won his way back to Georgia, was at the forefront of repeated Georgian efforts to rid itself of the Soviet yoke, and in 1928 came into western Europe to present such a case against Bolshevik terrorism that he won the support of Henderson and the English Labor party.

On this afternoon in 1917, seeing in me an American of official connections, he considered that he had an opportunity to proclaim that all the Allies, America included, could share the blame for what now had happened in Russia. The refusal to give encouragement to the project of a socialistic conference outside of Russia, at Stockholm, he declared to have been a political error of the first order. What Kerensky had needed to retain power, he argued, was enough outside support to convince war-wearied Russia that he was making in conjunction with the Allies an effort for Peace.

Given that, he said that the Russian army, or a sufficient part of it, could have been kept indefinitely on the front line as a menace, even if it never made another aggressive campaign. When the Allies refused to sanction the Stockholm meeting, they denied to Kerensky, in his opinion, not only the forensic advantages of the gathering but also prepared the Russian soil for the Bolshevik program of a separate peace, a program which Kerensky was left to face weaponless.

If this were not bad enough, he blamed the continental Allies—carefully excluding the United States—for weakening Kerensky in a positive, palsying way by seeking to have Kornilov made a military dictator. This project he considered to have been fostered by military foreigners lacking in political sense, and ignorant of the Russian mind. So the last of the vital energies of Kerensky's government had been exhausted in putting down a military uprising, not done without recourse to the Soviets of the city, although in these Councils of Workmen the Bolsheviks still were a minority factor. But when the Bolsheviks bored into the Soviets until they could seize control of them, they were in a position to pull the props from under Kerensky. At the last, said Tseretelli, Kerensky was a head without a body.

I asked Tseretelli how Kerensky, had he been supported in the way indicated, could have progressed stably without imperiling the Allies. His face lighted.

The Constituent Assembly was to have met in a few weeks [he said]. The Bolsheviks hurried their outbreak so that they would be in Petrograd and Moscow before the Assembly could meet. Now they may never let it meet. The Assembly not only would have established Russia's permanent government, but would have supported a Kerensky program of effort toward peace by general negotiation and refusal to consider a separate peace.

I ventured the inquiry as to whether the Bolsheviks might not have been able, given more time for campaign, to control the Constituent Assembly, an elective body.

Tseretelli lifted himself from the couch in excitement and protested that the Bolsheviks could not win the Constituent Assembly elections even now that they were in power unless they should prevent the elections by force of arms, which he was confident they dared not do.

"The Russian voice will be heard," he declared fervently. "I will sit in the Constituent Assembly."

He was right. Even after deferring the meeting of the Constituent Assembly until January, the Bolsheviks were in the voting minority in the Assembly, in spite, too, of the fact that the Kadets (Constitutional Democrats) did not send their elected delegates, fearing massacre. Tseretelli did sit in the Assembly, and spoke valiantly; but at the day's end a Bolshevik armed guard dissolved the Assembly as Cromwell did Parliament.

I left Tseretelli regretfully, fearing to tire him too much. In the years since whenever I have thought of Russia at any length, his cameo-graven face has taken form before me.

2.

CONFERENCE was held at the Embassy in the afternoon, for

important debate. Those present were the Ambassador, Counselor Wright, General Judson and one of his aides, and Raymond Robins. I was a late comer, and the atmosphere already had been considerably stirred.

General Judson had advanced the purpose of calling on Trotsky the following day to urge the strictness of non-troop-transfer clauses in the temporary armistice. The Ambassador was opposed to sanctioning the meeting. It was evident that much of the ground had been covered by General Judson and the Ambassador in previous conversations. Again General Judson's double post of Military *Attaché* and head of the Military Mission proved a convenience. General Judson argued that public comment would attach only to the latter rôle, which was the one he would take. At the same time he insisted that if he went, it must be with the Ambassador's assent. The Ambassador did assent.

General Judson went to Smolny Institute the next day, was received by Trotsky, who was expecting him, and through interpreters the robust soldier and the crafty politician conversed to mutual satisfaction. General Judson thought he got the assurances he went after, and Trotsky knew how he could use the visit to his own and Bolshevik advantage.

The Russian formal account of the visit, as published in the official newspaper, the *Izvestia*, on December 2, and prepared by Trotsky himself, was comprehensive on all subjects except one. It contained not the slightest reference to the topic of troop transfers that General Judson went to discuss. Trotsky, however, supplied that detail in his speech the same night at the Circus Moderne, so General Judson was content with the statement, which was:

THE CHIEF OF THE MILITARY MISSION CALLED ON THE NEW COMMISSAR FOR FOREIGN AFFAIRS

Yesterday, December 1, General Judson, Chief of the American Military Mission paid a visit to Comrade Trotsky at Smolny. The General pointed out that at the present time it is not possible for him to speak in the name of the American Government, as the Soviet Government has not yet been recognized. He came in order to open relations, to ascertain certain circumstances and to dispel misunderstandings. General Judson asked whether the new Government desires to end the War conjointly with the Allies, who, according to the General, scarcely will be able to participate in the negotiations on December 2. Comrade Trotsky explained to the General in a few words the policy of the Soviet Government in its struggle for a general peace. The fact on which the People's Commissar for Foreign Affairs laid special stress was the complete publicity of all negotiations. The Allies can follow each stage of the peace negotiations, and consequently can appear in them at one of their subsequent stages.

General Judson asked for permission to transmit this answer to his Government and concluded: "The time of protests and threats against the Soviet Government is over, if there was such a time."

General Judson asked whether the People's Commissar insists upon explanations being given in reference to incidents which have taken place—statements of protest from the officials of the American Military Mission. Comrade Trotsky replied that the formal aspect of the matter was immaterial and can be considered as settled by the statement of the General that the "time for threats and protests against the Soviet Government is over."

The statement was condescending and subtly uncomplimentary in spite of surface politeness.

General Judson's plea for armistice stipulations that the German troops be held on the line was concluded with a warning that the Russians beware of German trickery, to which Trotsky replied, as he stated in his public address: "When General Judson told me that one has to be careful with the Germans as they are a very crafty people, I told him we are stronger because we do not want to delude anybody."

This was the assurance that General Judson got. The clause forbidding troop transfer did get into the terms of the armistice. It was not inserted, however, until December 15, owing to dilatory tactics and postponements of the sittings of the preliminary conference, as will be shown, and it then read: "The parties to the agreement undertake not to effect strategic military troop transfers from the Baltic–Black Sea front, excepting those which had already begun when the agreement was signed."

The delayed stipulation told its own story. For thirteen days (from December 2) the German Commanders had been free to withdraw troops as they desired.

3.

I saw and heard Trotsky for the first time at the Circus Moderne meeting of the evening; and he gave a good performance. His appearance in that scene was itself theatrical, for the arena had been a people's rostrum since the summer. It was just the kind of place for Trotsky to come to play the rôle of a Minister of Government reporting his doings to the common folk.

The scene itself was memorable for its smoky color. Torches and swinging lanterns gave a wavering, meager light. With my interpreter at my elbow I climbed a tortuous, ladder-like stairway in the rear of the stadium and came out in a gallery from which I could overlook audience and platform. The tableau was lurid. Smoke from the torches rose in widening spirals and floated cloud-like between the higher galleries and the stage.

Trotsky already was speaking and seemed a fitting part of the setting. His likeness to the traditional conception of Mephistopheles could not have been accidental. The tuft of chin beard, the schooled mustache, the high-brushed black hair were too easily suggestive. Even the glasses did not mar the illusion, for they centered the eyes. In an air line Trotsky was in good eye-range of me, and his face was in the light.

Trotsky was an orator and beyond that he was playwright and actor, contriving drama, and skilfully impelling his audiences to the moods he desired. His speech this night was important strategy, despite its fluffy formlessness. It was delivered with the hale heartiness of the Circus Moderne manner.

They told me at some caucus conference [he said bluffly], that I should not use the language of the Circus Moderne. Comrades, I am using the same language whether addressing you or speaking in the Ministry of Foreign Affairs with the Germans or the Allies.

The tickled audience cheered him. A few minutes later he tailored General Judson's visit to his own pattern, with this introduction:

If we are told that our diplomacy is not in accordance with customary rules, this is true. There never was such diplomacy be-

fore, playing with open cards, and it has produced its effect upon
the Allied Embassies. During the first days of the existence of
the Government the Chief of the American Military Mission like
other Allied representatives protested against an armistice, and
threatened us with grave consequences. After I announced that
no foreign agents here have a right to influence Dukhonin and
that grave consequences threaten them and not us if they should
incite to civil war, General Judson called upon me.

Content with this slash, he proceeded then to give a more
moderate account of the call almost in the language of his
statement in the *Izvestia*. After swinging away from the topic
long enough to tell how he was baiting England with the threat
of retaliation on their own nationals in Russia unless two Bolsheviks then unknown, Chicherin and Petrov, were released
from prison and given safe-conduct out of England, he turned
to an optimistic consideration of the projected armistice, and
thereby once more to General Judson.

The demand will be made [he said], that during the armistice the
Germans do not transfer any troops to the western theatre of
war, as Russia could not consent that the armistice should be
utilized to crush England and France. Germany will not dare to
refuse, as every German soldier will understand that we demand
an honest armistice. Then Germany will not be allowed to force
her will on Courland and Lithuania and we shall not stand before
Germany like a defeated country. The soldiers and workers of a
nation who after the trials of the war could take the power into
their own hands cannot consider themselves defeated. Real victories are not being won in the trenches but in the struggle with
oppressors of the people. The interests of the Russian working
people coincide with the interests of the working people of other
countries.

When General Judson told me that one has to be careful with
the Germans as they are a very crafty people, I told him we
are stronger because we do not want to delude anybody.

The German and Austrian Governments are afraid of the day
of peace because for them, the originators of the war, it will be
judgment day. The peace conference will become a tribunal,
where we shall be the accusers. We shall of course defend also the
integrity of the territory of the Russian Revolution. [And he
concluded] This is your program, born in the Circus Moderne.

A simple, guileless man was Trotsky if the armistice section of this speech were mirror of him.

Yet for his blunt declaration that the Germans and the Austrians were the originators of the War he may be forgiven even guile.

The interpreter who poured the speech into my ears was Rosenberg, a translator of the Red Cross staff, a frock-coated, clerkly-appearing young Polish Jew, well educated, acute, and cynical. I heard a few years later that he became a Bolshevik official in the Asiatic service. At this time he leaned in the Bolshevik direction, though free of ironic comment on the party doings. Bolsheviks, he said, had organization and luck. The next day he wrote me a full translation of the speech, and prefaced it with his own analysis of the method of the Bolshevik up-turn, a performance so intelligent that I quote a substantial portion:

The real propaganda work against the Provisional Government and against Kerensky was underground work among the organized proletariat, while the brooding dissatisfaction among the soldiers of the Petrograd garrison did the rest. Finally the garrison was confronted with the choice either of being sent into the trenches or of resisting the order and of overthrowing the Provisional Government. In the frame of mind the soldiers were in the latter proved more to their taste.

The Government of Kerensky, attacked by the "Black Hundred" which in reality counts many thousands in Russia; tolerated by the regular Bourgeoisie "until the Constituent Assembly"; and lukewarmly supported by the leaders of the Revolutionary Democracy who had moved their quarters from the Soviets to the Pre-Parliament at the Marinsky Palace, seemed to have evaporated into the air when Petrograd was occupied by the troops of the garrison acting under orders of the Military Revolutionary Committee of the Petrograd Soviet. This evaporation coincided with the convocation of the All-Russian Convention of Soviets in Petrograd, in which the Bolsheviks had a clear majority.

When the Bolshevik leaders came before the Convention announcing that the Kerensky Government was overthrown, and that the Convention was now the source of the supreme power of the country, the majority of the Convention had no objections to raise, while the Ministers and Social Revolutionists withdrew from the Convention and their leaders tried in despair to get to the Winter Palace in order to protect with their own bodies their colleagues in the Kerensky cabinet, who were being beleaguered at the Winter Palace. The soldiers, however, did not allow them to throw themselves between the firing lines, and history may not even record this act of intended self-sacrifice.

The Ministers were brought safely to SS. Peter and Paul, but the town was full of reports of the lynching of cadets and the raping of the women soldiers who had defended the Winter Palace. When Petrograd learned, therefore, that Kerensky with Cossacks stood not far outside the gates of the city, the men in the Nevsky felt that deserved punishment soon would be meted out to the insolent usurpers of the Government.

But Kerensky failed when the Cossacks learned that the Army (at the front) was not going to send any re-enforcements. The Cossacks said they did not want to shed any more blood. Afterwards the Cossack Ataman Kaledin (to the South) seemed to be the best equipped to play the rôle of liberator, but the railroad men refused to transport his troops, and other factors intervening, he missed his chance.

From the moment that the Bolshevik leaders constituted themselves as the Council of People's Commissaries, they drafted manifestoes decreeing to their faithful people all they wanted, viz: land, bread, and peace. With land it was comparatively easy: the peasants' committees were invited to seize the property of the landed proprietors—they would have done it even without authorization wherever they could. Kronstadt sailors were sent out into the country to get bread for Petrograd. Most important of all, an armistice was proposed to all belligerent nations.

Yet the new Government seemed to be obstructed in all quarters. The Revolutionary Democracy turned away from it with abhorrence and formed Safety and Salvation Committees; the *bourgeoisie* looked on in disgust—to them the Bolsheviks were only criminals and traitors. It seemed to be a parody of Government. But it survived as it succeeded a Government which it was possible to simply brush away. There had been no centralization of power (in the Kerensky Government) and the Bolsheviks accelerated the process of decentralization by installing the Soviets as the only local Government authorities, ruling by their grace. The process of decomposition received also a stimulus (from the country at large), the Ukraine, the Caucasus and Siberia declaring themselves autonomous.

It appears now that the indirect recognition by the German

Government has made the Allied Governments recede from their contemptuous attitude toward the Smolny Government, and the German answer to General Krylenko seems to have been the last stabilizing factor of the tottering structure of the new Government. Trotsky's speech therefore was marked by distinct self-confidence which did not fail to communicate itself to his audience.

Apart from its clean-cut commentary here was disclosure of Kerensky's early escape from the beset Winter Palace and of his success in reaching and gathering the Cossack troops immediately outside the city, and of his failure to induce them to attack. Shown also was the total unwillingness of the Petrograd citizenry to take guns and fight for themselves.

CHAPTER VI

*December 2—December 3, 1917. Intervention
and Its Fruits.*

GENERAL JUDSON'S trip to Smolny got me into the
thick of the disputes centering around the Ambassador. Judgment told me to stay neutral. In the din I
forgot to listen. A month later I would have been stone deaf
to turmoil or persuasion. The men who besought me, however,
were of longer experience than I in Russia, and were sober and
earnest. They knew I could reach the President and they
wanted him to view a situation.

General Judson wanted White House attention brought to
the reports he was forwarding to his military superiors at
Washington. He wanted sanction for the steps he had taken
and desired to take. DeWitt C. Poole of the consular staff at
Moscow, sent by Consul Summers, reported that the Consul
needed embassy permission for business and routine dealings
with the local Soviet authorities, a consent denied him. Unanimity extended to the embassy staff itself, where it was felt
that the Ambassador should be instructed from Washington
that routine contacts with the existing rulers would not imply
government recognition of them. The Red Cross view was that
of General Judson, while Arthur Bullard based his concurrence on support of Consul Summers.

The discussions took up the better part of two days. In outcome, I agreed to cable a summary of opinion to Chairman
George Creel of the Committee on Public Information, with
the request that he lay it before the President.

Before a message could be sent, however, it was necessary to
contrive a way of cabling it without using the embassy code
room and also without putting it on the open wire for the
Bolsheviks to read. For this difficulty, Bullard, who knew a
good deal about codes, made the ingenious suggestion that we
take a familiar Department code, give it a twist to throw decoders off the track, and cable the coded message to the State
Department for delivery to Creel. To get the key twist to
Creel was a remaining puzzle. For that maneuver I chanced

the open cable with the cryptic message to Commander Hoff, the cable censor at New York (not naming him as such): "Inform Creel subtract three hundred. Sisson Compub." The Bolsheviks might not suspect that the instruction referred to code, and if they did and were attempting to decode all the numerous cipher messages in transit they would have difficulty in locating the right dispatch. We covered even the address to the State Department, and likewise that of a short separate message to the Department in one of its own codes asking that Creel be told to use the Consular Red code in decoding. Although I could imagine the irritation at the State Department on the discovery that the Red code would not unlock the long message, I was determined that Creel should have the first reading of the communication and decide whether to lay it before the President.

The State Department got the dispatch, could not decode it, and refused to pass it to Creel. I was prepared for that also, and when I replied with a formal protest, the dispatch was turned over to Creel. The spat had one good effect. Up to that time the State Department had taken the attitude that other administrative departments were not free, except in emergencies, to use their code facilities. From this time on we, in Russia at least, were invited to use them.

In consequence of all the to-do, Creel did not have the troublesome message until December 14. He took it to the President.

Expanded from skeleton form, the first section of the dispatch was:

The actual Russian situation is disturbing. It is my duty and yours to see that the facts are laid before the President clearly and as soon as possible. The statement is the result of rigid though rapid investigation, not of impressions. Have conferred with Embassy staff, heads Military and Red Cross Missions, and Consular officers. Submit hard facts, unavoidable, unyielding, and joint conclusions therefrom.

Russia is out of the War. She can not be counted on as a fighting factor. There is no possibility of a war party gaining power. If new Revolutionary army is organized it will be in indefinite future and more likely to be used for internal than external war. Refer to General Judson's report on condition of Russian army.

This should be no surprise to Allied Governments, for Tseretelli of Kerensky's former cabinet tells me that several months ago he told British and American Ambassadors that Kerensky could not hold power unless he advanced peace program. Pressure of Allied diplomacy forced Kerensky to hide facts from Russia and the world.

Bolsheviks played peace card, combined with popular land program, and swept the country. Even if they fail on the administrative side and are forced out, any new party to gain support must accept their formula, "Peace and Land."

Phraseology of Armistice agreement and of future negotiations is of enormous importance. Armistice should be technically guarded, no transfer of troops to other fronts, no exchange of prisoners, no re-establishment of trade relations and other points of immense military interest, to assure at least a benevolent rather than a German neutrality in the event of a separate peace. Obviously logical deduction for us is importance of practical contact between our official representatives and those in actual power here so that these points may be treated in conference as friendlily as possible. Formal recognition not involved. The question need not now be considered.

Found Ambassador without policy except anger at Bolsheviks, unamenable to arguments or entreaties of his official advisers, military and civil, and General Judson very anxious to meet Trotsky for conference on terms of armistice. My own work hopelessly involved in this situation. Can hope to accomplish nothing if there is open break between the Embassy and de facto government. Risked using what pressure I could muster, helped to secure from Ambassador wavering consent to a single conference between Judson and Trotsky. Judson has reported to Washington the satisfactory results of his conference. Trotsky referred to the conference in a public meeting I attended. [Trotsky's armistice comment from his speech and his reference to General Judson's words about crafty Germans were inserted at this point.] These sentiments were applauded by audience and Bolshevik leaders are publicly pledged to insist on an honest armistice and to resume war if negotiations fail. This is summary of argument for immediate establishment of working, informal contact with de facto power by official representatives, and I recommend such instructions.

The cable closed with the suggestion that the Embassy be placed in the hands of a *chargé d'affaires*, who by seniority would have been Butler Wright, and the Ambassador be summoned home by way of Japan to report upon the revolution he had witnessed. Thereby his counsel would be valuable in Washington, the high office of Ambassador would not be exposed to the possibilities of insult inherent in an equivocal position in an unrecognized country, and the actions of lesser titled officers in the country could not take on any hue of implied recognition by the American Government.

The procedure outlined in the message was sound enough. In regard to Embassy, Great Britain took an identical view in a short time, summoning Sir George Buchanan for conference and leaving *Chargé* Lindley to front the Bolsheviks.

Only: I had no business to take the burden of the battles of others. The error was particular since my own enterprises were not launched.

I got my deserts quickly enough once the message was under the eyes of the President. It was not difficult to imagine, even before I knew, that there was a scene in which Chairman Creel and Secretary Lansing faced each other hotly, brought to an end by the President's curt order that I should be reproved for meddling. Certainly, from Secretary Lansing's outlook, the ritual of the State Department had been given unceremonious treatment.

Creel obeyed orders and on December 16, I received the rebuke: "Cable received and properly referred. President insists that you avoid political entanglements and personal matters."

To this were appended caustic inquiries of Creel's own about the status of my operations, winding up with the prod: "Consult Ambassador about widest distribution of President's message sent him by Reuter's from London. Spare no expense to get it all over Russia."

The cable was sent me through the Embassy, so I knew that Creel had fought for me, lost the bout, and been obliged to censure me publicly.

Yet this is the oddity of turbulence. So much may happen in brief space that the occurrences, the victories, or the disasters a fortnight gone, three days by, or even a few hours fled, have lost all pertinence.

The delay in the transit of the first message had won me

immunity. When the reply cable came, the Ambassador and I were on terms of working amity in which General Judson was included, my organization was shaped and welding fast, and the jibe about the President's message was pointless, since it had been in my hands ten days, already had had wire distribution, and the presses then were turning for its mass placard and pamphlet distribution. The speech itself was that of the President before Congress on December 4, calling for a declaration of war against Austria.

Creel's cable drew from me the only letter I wrote him while I was in Russia, other communication being by cable. Abridged in business detail the contents were:

December 17, 1917. Have given Professor Ross of Wisconsin University, who is leaving today for Madison, a note to you. (Letter of introduction.) Know you will want to talk to him, and likely the President also. Am not saying that I agree or disagree with him, but he has gone out after facts, is a laboratory and you can delve in him as you see fit. He will visualize Russia sliced through from Finland to Turkestan, and a close-up of Petrograd as a last view. He and I spent yesterday at the shop-run government munition plant at Sestoretsk—simplified spelling. We saw how the employes run the plant, the weakness of some of its practice, the strength of some of its idealism.

What Ross did not know was that the seeming interpreter and I were there for the added purpose of telling the Red Guard manager of the plant and head of its shop committee, that six miles away from him was the only present gate of large shipment smuggling into Germany, and that his guards, on the information we could give him of car numbers could confiscate in the next few days nearly a hundred cars of lead and machine oil at the Finnish frontier border. We had told him our faith that there could be no successful Revolution in Germany until preceded by military defeat. Now we agreed that the increase of Germany's military strength would be disastrous to the idealism of both sides. So the guards will be multiplied and I hope to hear speedily of seizures. The plant needs machine oil, anyway.

The German bribe offered for this smuggling was one million rubles. It was offered inadvertently to the right place for us and the wrong one for Germany. Sunday midnight when I took the first copy of the full armistice to General Judson he showed me a cable he had sent begging Washington for permission to ar-

range informally with the Government for American co-operation
at this smuggling point. He probably will not get it. For this one
occasion, however, some luck and some action have stopped the
hole. Should it have been done despite the official censure I found
waiting for me in cable form when I got back at nine o'clock
last night? I believe so, I believe George Creel would have done
it had he been here.

And the only price was friendly contact with an earnest,
though very likely mistaken, young idealist. I expect he will be
smashed in a few months, for he has the almost impossible task
of satisfying 6500 wage workers at an industry which already,
owing to army demobilization, is not capable of supporting half
that number. But I am glad to have known him. His name is
Rostchek and he got his training in organization as a walking
delegate—Boston, New York, Philadelphia, Chicago and Texas—
ten years in America always battling against capital, with no
contact with America's real democracy. It dawns on me that a
different decade at home might have written a different history
for the Russian October of 1917.

If this last line fighting is meddling in politics then I am a
meddler. Which may mean much or little to you, according to
what regard you may have for my judgment. The fact simply is
that to outward publicity I have added internal intelligence. I
have not bribed, I have not gone to Trotsky but am working im-
personally behind a screen. The intelligence service is the only
channel General Judson has into Smolny. And when you consider
that with the melting of the Russian army what other areas are
left for military information you can judge what is the need and
decide what orders for continuance or discontinuance you care
to give.

My only comment on the Embassy situation is that I gave you
the truth. It is for others to use or disregard.

On the informative side I told you that Russia was beaten and
now would fight no more. Any other war will be a new war. I
indicated civil war as the only continuing war. It is here. In the
interval before this reaches you events will show whether I am
right or wrong in regarding the present status as that of frank
combat between a proletarian Commune and the *bourgeoisie*. The
principles of democracy are not on either side. Officially the
Commune was established on Friday, December 14, in Petrograd.
The Communal decrees for the seizure by the state of leased city
property are out and in partial operation here and at Moscow.
Rent paying to landlords is forbidden and obligated to the State.

The peasants have seized land—the estates they formerly tilled—but the land division has not generally begun. Peasants owning land are excepted. Factories can operate as union shops under private ownership if they keep up the output, etc.—otherwise the State takes and has taken them. The movement, you see, is too fast, leaving all else aside.

The practical effect, as it concerns us most, is in relation to internal cleavage. If the Germans in getting a could-be permanent armistice from the Bolsheviks have got all they want from a Government otherwise threatening to them, then it may very well be that their machinations henceforth will be in favor of the useful minority of the propertied. The Kadets are talking now of the advantages of any "order." For the moment they look to the Cossacks and the Rada of the Ukraine. The Bolsheviks proclaim that this attitude of sympathy and aid make the Kadets of the north responsible for the Bolshevik blood shed in the south. You will perceive the road the argument follows. So far the executions are rhetorical, for the Bolsheviks are still too strong to require The Terror.

They will let the Constituent Assembly meet when they can control it.

Printing of President's message being done in Petrograd by government printing office—half million in two page news sheet, half million in pamphlet. Heading "Americansky President Wilson—Democratic Peace!" Not an American head-line form but it gets over what we want. Committee on Public Information imprint. Delivery both in Petrograd and Moscow.

Hart (Y.M.C.A.) is not here, though you say he left November 15. His organization was scattered when the army exodus from the one-time front began, but I gathered with the executive committee at Moscow and induced it to send men back for a survey of the after-scene, to ascertain if the Bolsheviks carried out their announced intention of sending in relief troops to patrol line during armistice period. If Hart will let me, I can use several of his young men, but I have not wanted to further disorganize a shattered body.

Stopped writing to get report from the courier with whom I came through (Franklin), who had just arrived from Jassy. He says that the Russian army is gone from the flanks of the Rumanians, a scramble homewards. He saw the Rumanian Queen (Marie) with Minister Vopicka while he was waiting for delivery of packet to him. She was crying, saying that her army could not fight unsupported, and had to accept armistice.

Breshkovskaya and Chaikovsky are in deepest retreat, the former in hiding, the latter deposed from the Peasants' society and his place taken by a woman Bolshevik. Bolsheviks suppress with force the opposition they do not like—newspapers, persons, movements.

Never any bodily danger for Americans, however. The Moscow Bolsheviks stopped a machine gun while Summers crossed the street in front of it. After which it resumed.

The letter did not reach Creel for nearly a month and in the interim various cables had passed and larger happenings had still further minimized the episode. I expected no new reference. Yet Creel did reply to the letter, by cable, January 21, 1918: "Cabled you as I did in order to satisfy opposition and not at all as a rebuke. Have communicated irregularly because I wanted you to have a free hand, using your own judgment. God bless you."

The message contained also some business fragments, among them a sentence that connected accidentally with the letter of December 17. It was: "Have Bullard and Gumberg identified (for signature) at National City Bank."

The significance was to the second name, that of Alexander Gumberg, one of the least proclaimed, in the nature of his associations one of the most contradictory, and at times one of the most powerful of the odd figures of the Revolution. He was my interpreter at Sestoretsk. He was friend and sometimes messenger of Trotsky. The record made by the cable is that Gumberg was on my pay roll. He was, and being fearful of Bolshevik money, whatever his feeling for Bolshevik tenets, he wished to be paid in dollars, on which he did not draw while he stayed in Russia, collecting his back salary after he returned to the United States.

He was a New York Jew with melancholy eyes, sensitive features, and a mind crammed with resources. He had known Trotsky when the latter was on the *Novy Mir*, a small Bolshevik newspaper, in New York City, and after the March Revolution he proceeded to Russia by way of Siberia. Whatever his touch with Trotsky during the summer he did not associate himself with him or the Bolsheviks, acting as interpreter and handy man for American groups. I found him attached in that capacity to the Red Cross and gradually annexed him.

From the moment the Bolsheviks were in, his friendship with Trotsky was of practical use. Raymond Robins continued also to have a call upon his services. So Gumberg served two masters, and which he served the better I did not know, or care. He satisfied me in all I ever asked of him, and I was content with his Trotsky friendship. If any wardship of me went with it so much the better. On matters which I desired to trust to Gumberg I gave him full confidence. On matters which I did not, it was up to my wits to keep them from him. I never used him in any enterprise against the Bolsheviks.

He took care to return to livable America, reëntering without objection of mine as nominal secretary to Raymond Robins in the early summer of 1918. I let him come to see me one night afterward in a New York hotel, sat him down alongside me, told him that he was so close to Trotsky that he ought to have absorbed knowledge of the elaborate game of the winter, that I sought no admissions from him, had no threats for him, but would expect him, in Russian as well as American idiom, to "keep out of politics" while the war lasted. That pledge he smilingly gave. I hope he kept it, and never made any effort to find out if he did. A mighty man in Russia, he was powerless in America.

The smuggling clue referred to in the letter came from Trotsky, likewise the kindred information received by General Judson. The bribe offer was not to Trotsky but was supposed to be to train routers, handlers, and custom guards, and to an unnamed commissar. The report could have been invented, even, to dramatize the matter to General Judson and to me. The smuggling attempt, nevertheless, was real. Rostchek got his machine oil.

Time disclosed that the original cable, despite the storm raised by its reception, did much of the work it was intended to do at Washington. And before the winter was over I had avowed to the Ambassador my responsibility for the dispatch and my reason for sending it. The measure of the man was that I could do so.

It befell, therefore, that when in the spring, after I was out of Russia, Raymond Robins went to the Ambassador with the

tale that he had stood out against the "Sisson cable," he made
a mistake. For Arthur Bullard did then what I had not done—
told the Ambassador what Robins' participations had been.
Bullard cabled me from Vologda (it was then May) in private
code which the State Department now readily delivered:

Robins has told Ambassador of famous cable and pretends to
have opposed it. Francis cross-questioned me as to others involved. I told him nothing except truth of Robins' rôle. He now
is in Moscow playing with Lenin. Anderson arrived from Jassy
looking for his scalp.

Anderson was Col. H. W. Anderson, commander of the
American Red Cross unit to Rumania. Of him and the source
of his emotions, the chapter on "The Kalpashnikov Case" will
tell, as the wheel of events turns.

The last conversation of all on the cable topic was between
the Ambassador and me, sitting companionably in his rooms
in Paris in the winter of 1919. There the Ambassador might
have picked another bone with me, for he had objected to my
purpose of getting Americans out of Russia in the summer of
1918, leading as it did to his own departure. But instead of
complaining, he agreed that it was well for him that he had
been obliged to go to England, where long illness had been
relieved by a surgical operation. He told me that he wanted
only two things—to see the President and to go home. Both
desires, it occurred to me, could be met together. So it was arranged that he should return to the United States on the
steamship *George Washington*, going back with the President
on the occasion when he made his intermediate trip home from
the Peace Conference. On the decks of the vessel the two tired
men talked at ease. Once later in New York I saw the Ambassador and he told me how courteously the President had
received him and chatted with him. He was failing then. In
1926 he died.

CHAPTER VII

December 4—December 6, 1917. The "Lynching" of General Dukhonin. Radek the Jester. The Dragging Armistice.

1.

A SUMMARY, in retrospect, of varied events of five days: In the list of Bolsheviks reported elected to the future Constituent Assembly appeared on November 29 the names of Lenin, Zinoviev, Trotsky, Kamenev, Kollontai, and Djugashvili. All were familiar names except the last, that of the person who in time was to supersede all the others. For Djugashvili was Joseph Stalin, and this his first naming for public place. When he appeared next, in connection with the arrangements for the Brest-Litovsk Peace Conference, and at the All-Russian Convention, it was under his party name of Stalin.

On the evening of December 1 the Soviet delegation to the preliminary armistice conference left Petrograd for the front. Its membership comprised Karakhan as secretary, Sokolnikov, Kamenev, Mme Bitzenko, Mestislavsky, an official of the Peasants' convention, and two officers of the General Staff, Colonel Shishkin and Colonel Stanislavsky.

Trotsky made public announcement on December 1 that Count Czernin, Austrian Foreign Minister, had sent the Soviets a wireless message "expressing the willingness of the Austro-Hungarian Government to open negotiations for an immediate armistice and general peace proposed by the Russian Government" and stating that it "will send its delegates to participate in the negotiations scheduled for December 2."

On December 3 all but one of the *"bourgeois"* newspapers were closed. The Opposition Right Socialist newspapers were allowed under sufferance, but frequent issues were confiscated. Within a day or so, advertising was decreed a government monopoly.

For two days there was silence concerning the progress of the armistice arrangements. The interval, however, was loud with the echoes of the barbarous murder of General Dukhonin, the deposed Russian Commander in Chief.

Outlawed by Krylenko's decree, his headquarters at Mogilev surrounded by hostile troops, he surrendered and as a prisoner he was slain—hauled from a railroad car by Bolshevik soldiers and tossed on their bayonets as a body of schoolboys would toss a fellow on a blanket.

Krylenko made formal proclamation of the "lynching," which, incidentally, is a term naturalized into the Russian language.

The *Izvestia*, on December 4, published the proclamation:

Comrades! I have taken possession of Mogilev at the head of Revolutionary troops. Surrounded, the Stavka surrendered without resistance.

I cannot pass over in silence the deplorable lynching of the former Generalissimo, Dukhonin. The popular hatred had reached its culmination point. In spite of all attempts to save him, he was taken out of a railroad car at the Mogilev station and killed. The escape of General Kornilov preceding the surrender of the Stavka was the cause of the outrage.

Comrades! I cannot tolerate blots on the escutcheon of the Revolution and such actions must be repudiated in the sternest manner. Be worthy of your new-won liberty! Do not sully and dishonor the people's rule! The Revolutionary people must be stern in struggle but merciful in victory.

Comrades! By the fall of the Stavka the struggle for peace will gain new momentum. In the name of the Revolution and of Liberty I appeal to you to preserve Revolutionary organization and discipline. Long live the Government of the Soviets of Workers, Soldiers and Peasants Deputies.

KRYLENKO, *Generalissimo.*

So, the deed accomplished, Krylenko repudiated the blame.

But for a while he kept closer to Petrograd than to his armies. There were reports that his train had been fired on as it moved along the front. Sentiment was not yet all one way in the armies. By all except the Bolsheviks the slaughter of Dukhonin was viewed with horror, both as fact and omen. The first assassination of the Bolshevik *régime* had been recorded.

December 4 and 5 were for me planning and observation

days. Much was included—search for office space for a translating and news unit, and survey of channels into which cable
news could be fed when it should begin to arrive from the
United States. Amid the humdrum, however, was interest and
diversion.

While I was trying to find out what remnants of *Vestnik*, the
former Russian news agency, were left, I ran into Radek at
the offices of the Petrograd Telegraph Agency. I am not sure
but that Russia without Radek sometimes would have palled
on me, detonations and all! But here was a right merry scala-
wag, taking neither himself nor his companions seriously in
matters of tongue. With a pen in his hand he could write solemn bombast with the best of them and volley the slogans for
the crowd to catch; tossing the pen aside he swaggered gaily
for the gasconader he was.

Into the room he came with a clatter and clop. Good reason! He was wearing knee boots several sizes too large for his
thin shanks. Russian boots, be it not forgotten, are worn tight,
fitting ankle so snugly that the feat of getting into and out of
them is one of patient adroitness. Above the ankle they may be
loose and crinkly. This pair had been cobbled for an ampler
man. Black shining marvels they had been in their prime,
though now they were dull and splashed. Above the boots was
a rail-like figure topped by a lined and impish face, unshaven
for several days and a-bristle. Trousers were tucked into the
top of the boots and overhung like the plus fours of later days.
The upper body was covered by a double-breasted corduroy
jacket, above which was glimpsed the buttoned collar of a Russian blouse, largely hidden by a colored scarf looped around
the neck. The man wore a Cossack cap, serving to elongate the
peaked face. He looked a wayfarer. His years were doubtful,
somewhere in the thirties, taking some youth from lively manner and quick-moving eyes. Until we were introduced I did not
know whether he was messenger or official.

He no less than I, it developed, was taking stock. He was to
have supervision of the *Pravda*, the secondary official Bolshevik
publication, and was finding out about telegraph service, of
which he also was one of the overlords. Potentially the machinery about us was good. On the desks before us were sets of
telephone instruments in direct connection with Moscow. News

bulletins could be flashed instantly—had the sets been working. They had not been put in order since the Moscow battles. They were, of course, to be repaired quickly. Radek thought they might be working in another day. Several weeks later, however, their condition was the same. I found that a service of our own couriers between our Moscow and Petrograd offices was faster than the wires ever came to be.

At the time of our meeting, Radek's Russian was a lame affair, his main reliances being Polish and German, and I was amused at the notion that we were both foreigners. When I had this view interpreted to him, he laughed and aped his own manner of making a speech in Russian. I understood how he got his meanings over, for he had the arts of a pantomimist. At that, I do not recall that he made a public speech in Russian throughout the winter. When the Russians desired to bait the Germans at the prisoner-exchange and trade parley held later at Petrograd, contemporary with the Peace Conference at Brest-Litovsk, he was an early spokesman because of his facility in German.

From the first my intercourse with Radek was on an airy plane. I thought he liked the release given by dropping one form of pose to take another. At no moment did he cease to be an actor. We drifted on longer acquaintance into a form of jibing debate, a curious give and take procedure, carried on with interpreters, staged sometimes on benches overlooking a dull public meeting. He picked up some English and my ear got attuned to more German. In polyglot we conversed a little directly.

America was a place of never failing interest to him and for contrast to Russia I liked it as a theme. Almost immediately after we met in the telegraph and telephone room he asked me what the prospects of proletarian revolution were in the United States. He should have been insulted by my gleeful attitude toward the inquiry, but was not, so I could conclude that he was poking fun at me. However, when I had straightened my face, I told him that Bolshevik seeds would find no soil in the United States, and that he and the whole crew of leaders could break their hearts in the effort to sow. "Besides," I added, "you will be laughed to death."

"Why would Americans laugh?" he asked.

"Because Americans hate to be bored," I retorted. "They would guy you because you are bores, and then forget all about you."

I had to explain the meaning of guying. He seemed to like the word, and said he wished me to know that he was considerable of a guyer himself. Perhaps these few sentences established the basis of our continuing relationship.

At another meeting he asked me pointedly if I would dare to let him write for me if I had a publication and he were in New York. I replied that it was not a question of daring but of refusing to be fed on by a parasite. "The trouble with you fellows," I told him, "is that you want your opponents to support you in luxury while you try to stick knives in their backs. I wouldn't invite a wrecker into my house though I might defy him to try to tear the house down."

At another time I told him that Samuel Gompers, not Karl Marx, was the real apostle of labor, bringing it rewards instead of prophesying its degradation, preaching production and high wages instead of sabotage and starvation. American labor, too, I declared was profiting from the War as well as fighting in it, making a mockery of his doctrinaire tenets.

Thereupon he switched the topic to the chances of "making a Revolution" in Germany, where at least we were on more sympathetic ground. Radek alone of all the Bolshevik leaders I am inclined to credit with unchanging sincerity in the position of hostility to Germany. There was something personal about his hatred, due possibly to treatment he had received in Germany. I am not too positive, since he was aware of all the complex maneuverings, but even at their height he made sardonic comments on the major directors, as will appear, and in the party councils of February in the short-lived German war on the Bolsheviks he fought stubbornly for continued warfare instead of surrender.

He was the chief propagandist against Germany, conducting for that purpose a separate publication, the well-named *Die Fackel* ("The Torch"), printed solely for distribution along and inside the German line. His printing operations with *Die Fackel* and mine with President Wilson's messages and pamphlet material combined to keep one of the largest of the Petrograd printing plants running at capacity from middle

December to latter February. Our sharing of the plant was accidental but fortunate. Stacks of the Fourteen Point Speech and stacks of *Die Fackel* were loaded together in car-lots and circulated together through the spaces on the whilom German front.

The upshot of the first meeting with Radek was an arrangement for feeding American cable news into the Russian wire network of newspaper service. The project remained theoretical until I could get dispatches started from New York. They began to come through on December 24.

The succeeding day was occupied with a survey of telegraph offices, the State Bank and the Petrograd telephone building, the last less for any technical reason than because it had been a scene of battle. A passage in a home letter, written December 17, related the visit:

Presumably you read of the efforts made by the Yunkers (young military cadets) to overturn the Bolsheviks just a few days after they seized Petrograd. I heard that hundreds of them were killed. Also that the women's Death Battalion was mistreated cruelly. The fact is that there was amazingly little killing in the Petrograd combats. I have talked in detail with the members of a group of spectators caught in a court near the telephone building and forced under fire to witness the armored car episode there. The car moved up and down the street by the telephone building, spitting machine gun bullets to keep the sailors off the street. In the court were a hundred pedestrians, taken by surprise. A part of the fire came their way and one person was killed and several injured. Suddenly the machine stalled and the sailors rushed it in the face of fire, surrounded it, opened the door and bayoneted the three cadets operating the gun. The chauffeur called out that he had been forced to run the car and had stalled it on purpose. He was not injured and was allowed to go.

A second armored car got out of control and backed into the river in another part of the city. I am inclined to believe that only two cars were out. Several cadets were killed in the telephone building. When all had surrendered they were kept prisoners for a few days and then turned loose. As for the Death Battalion, it was taken to its quarters, given over to Bolshevik women, who sent out for women's clothing, ordered the women to change into skirts and sent them home. The uniforms were kept as the only hostages.

The sights in the telephone building gave me a sick feeling, though not from anything that had to do with gore. I saw machinery in the hands of the ignorant, loafers where workers had been. The place was no more than a camp, guards lounging and smoking, groups of uncouth "committeemen" chattering or moving aimlessly about, food and drink littering the vacant desks. This was more than stoppage. It was a breaking-down, a sign of what was about to happen to all of the normal services of city life except those necessary to day-to-day governmental activities.

The State Bank, for example, was an exception. When its clerical forces struck as a protest against Bolshevism, they were taken back to work with bayonets at their back. The money plant must keep on functioning. On this date the banks had not yet been nationalized, although the State Bank had a new head, the yellow-haired Piatakov, who was introduced to me as an "economist." I smiled afterward at memory of the word, yet it was apropos, for one must know a lot about the normal working of an apparatus before one puts it to abnormal use.

We may credit post-war German inflation, reaching its acme in the destruction of the value of the mark, to the Russian model, the State Bank, in its inflation of the ruble, based quite frankly on Lenin's notion of depriving money of its function as a medium of exchange. The labor hour was to take its place as a unit. On the progress to oblivion the inflated money was to perform the useful counter-revolutionary purpose of making paupers of the *bourgeois* and all thrifty money savers, and of erasing all internal debts.

In midwinter the government presses were turning out so many notes that the officials writing the signatures could not keep abreast of the grist. So the notes were issued without signatures. Inflation, however, did not begin immediately, and the early indications were that the rulers were trying to support the ruble inside of Russia. Its fall in the international market they could not control. Money was exceedingly valuable to them in the beginning. On November 30 the Council of People's Commissars required of the State Bank the first short-term forced loan to the amount of five million rubles. There would have been no sense in making this loan valueless until the time approached for its repayment. The currency of course was wholly fiat. The gold reserve now existed only as treasure in possession of the Bolsheviks.

2.

THE armistice situation, meantime, continued cloudy. The proceedings were dilatory, both sides sparring for advantage, delay itself being an advantage to the Germans.

In Petrograd there was tense impatience. It is probable that in this week the Bolsheviks were in worse state than at any time since they seized power. They had gambled on peace and while it might be coming, slowly, the march of hunger was faster. I heard military men say that a stout regiment of soldiers could have cleared Petrograd of Bolsheviks in twelve hours' time. What a regiment would have done with the city afterward, I opined, was another matter. For the Bolsheviks, Petrograd was a rostrum from which to advertise themselves. For a military victor without political plan Petrograd was just a city to feed. The Bolsheviks were weak, yet all others were weaker.

Meeting on December 2 to hear the premises of each other's proposals, formal sessions of the armistice body were postponed from day to day while the delegates sought in private conversations to lay the groundwork for public agreement. The Bolsheviks had sent a political group with two lesser officers as military advisers. The delegation of the Central Empires was military and knew exactly what it wanted. The Bolsheviks continued to maintain that they were seeking an armistice on all fronts. The Germans retorted coldly that they were empowered to consider only the terms of armistice on the Russian front.

By December 5, Petrograd was filled with conflicting reports: armistice terms were settled and there would be an immediate peace conference; armistice terms were not settled and the Russian delegation was returning; hostilities had ceased, but without formal armistice; hostilities were about to be resumed.

As usual, the actual developments were in the medley, once they could be identified. The Conference had been postponed for a week, with cessation of hostilities assured from December 7 to December 17. (Hostilities, with hardly less formality, had ceased on November 27.) The Russian delegation was returning, but Secretary Karakhan was left behind as a representative. Troop movements were permitted in the very clause that was advanced as leaving the subject undecided. Face-saving had become the order of the day.

An official statement was issued from Smolny under the heading, "Government Communiqué on the Progress of the Armistice Pour-Parlers":

Nov. 22/Dec. 5. Representatives of Germany, Austro-Hungary, Turkey and Bulgaria are present at the conference. Hindenburg and Holtzendorff have charged the Commander-in-Chief of the Eastern front with the conduct of the negotiations, and he has commissioned his Chief-of-Staff Gen. Hoffman to represent him. The other delegates have similar authority from the Supreme Army Command. The delegation of the enemies is entirely military.

Our delegates began by making declarations about the war aims, for the furtherance of which the armistice was offered. The delegates of our opponents remarked that this was a matter for statesmen while they were only military men authorised to speak about the military terms of the armistice. Therefore they could not add anything to the statements of Czernin and Kuhlman, which are known to us.

Our delegates recorded this evasive statement and made the proposal that all belligerent countries, including Germany and her Allies, should offer an opportunity to the belligerent countries not represented at the conference to participate in the consideration of armistice terms for all fronts. The opposing delegation again replied evasively, stating that it did not have adequate power to decide this proposal. We suggested that the representatives ask their Governments to give them authority. This suggestion was accepted but up to 4 A.M. Nov. 22/Dec. 5 no further information has been given to the Russian delegation.

Our representatives submitted a plan for an armistice on all fronts, drawn up by our military experts. The main features of this offer were (1) Interdiction of troop transfers from our front to the front of our Allies, and (2) Evacuation of the Mohnsund Islands by the Germans.

The opponents submitted their project for an armistice on the line of the Baltic Sea to the Black Sea. The German proposal is now being considered by our military experts. In the morning the negotiations will be continued.

The first item of the conditions submitted by our opponents was the duration of the armistice, which had been originally proposed by them as fourteen days, beginning Dec. 8. As a result of negotiation the time was extended 28 days with the provision that it should be automatically prolonged in the event that no notice should be given 7 days prior to its expiration and to take effect on Dec. 10 should our delegation leave Brest-Litovsk tomorrow. Prior to the beginning of the official truce there shall be cessation of military operations.

With this communication the Bolsheviks retreated from their pretense of seeking to have the armistice negotiations comprehend other fronts than their own front. Later the same day Lenin in addressing a Navy Convention avowed a halt in the deliberations at the front and placed the onus on the question of transfer of troops. He said, "When the Germans gave an evasive answer to our demand not to transfer troops to the Western and Italian fronts, we interrupted the negotiations and shall resume them some time later."

For this statement he had later advice from Brest-Litovsk than appeared in the *communiqué*. The session there had reopened at noon and at the suggestion of the Russians, readily concurred in by General Hoffman, had adjourned until December 12, "owing to the difference in the armistice offers." Before the session rose, however, an agreement tantamount to practical armistice was signed: the pact for cessation of hostilities, the dates differing from those in the early-morning *communiqué*. The point left open was that of transfer of troops, as the Germans desired, and even this issue was phrased nearly in the form it took eleven days later.

The official *Izvestia* published the clauses of the agreement, December 7, as follows:

The following document for the cessation of hostilities was signed on Dec. 5 in Brest Litovsk between the representatives of the Russian Generalissimo on the one hand and the representatives of Germany, Austro-Hungary, Bulgaria and Turkey on the other:

1. The cessation of hostilities takes effect Dec. 7, 1917 at 12 noon and continues until Dec. 17, 1917, 12 noon (2 P.M. Russian time).
2. Both parties to the agreement reserve the right to resume military operations on three days' notice.
   (a) The cessation of military activities extends over all land and air forces of the countries entering into this agreement—be-

tween the Black and the Baltic seas, likewise to the Russo-
Turkish front in Asia.

(b) Naval air forces are restricted to flights over sea and are
prohibited from flying over land.

(c) The German land forces on the Mohnsund islands are included in the terms of the agreement for the cessation of
hostilities.

(d) The van-guard fortifications are to be taken as the demarcation line for both parties wherever there is a continuous line
of fortifications. The demarcation line is a line between and
paralleling both lines of trenches. The space between both
lines of trenches is defined as neutral territory. On the Asiatic front the demarcation line is to be determined by agreement between the Commanders-in-Chief of both parties.

3. Both parties undertake to issue a definite order interdicting the
crossing of the demarcation line.

4. For the duration of the cessation of hostilities only such transfers
of army units, *of divisional strength and larger, as have been ordered prior to Dec. 5 can take place.*

5. All partial armistice agreements concluded between individual army
units become ineffective.

Under Clause 4 the Germans could move their entire army
in regimental units, and "by divisions and larger" if the order
had been given prior to December 5. The italics are mine.

The *Izvestia* reported further, "The Russian delegation has
left for Petrograd, L. Karakhan remaining at Brest as its representative."

The Russians had gotten nothing and given everything even
in this first stage of peace parleying. And in Petrograd began
at once the releasing of German and Austrian prisoners of war.
Soon they were loosed in the camps throughout the land.

Both "parties" may have undertaken to issue an order interdicting the crossing of the demarcation line, but that was as
far as the Russians got. Even the Germans intended it should
apply only to Russians coming through. The line was a sieve,
either way.

Lenin and Trotsky thought the week between meetings a
good time to show that they were not harmless. Their earlier
circular to German soldiers was printed in greater quantities
and given new impetus to circulation. General Hoffman protested to Karakhan that the action of distributing the circular
to German soldiers was an "unwarranted interference in the
internal affairs of Germany, placing in jeopardy the success-

ful continuation of the negotiations and evincing a lack of knowledge of the real state of affairs in Germany."

Karakhan quoted himself as replying that "the exact text of the Proclamation was unknown to the Secretary of the Delegation and he can only say that the Russian Government has not so far undertaken any obligation toward the German Government except that of living up to the terms of the agreement for the cessation of hostilities."

Thus the suave Secretary played his supplemental part, hinting that the Bolsheviks already felt they had been roughly used, and were retorting in kind. The Germans cut new rods and put them in stronger pickle.

CHAPTER VIII

*December 6—December 12, 1917. Voices of Wilson and
Kerensky. The Smolny Scene. Moscow the Desolate.
The Wrath of Prince Kropotkin.*

1.

PRESIDENT WILSON'S voice, calling upon Congress
on December 4 for a declaration of war against Austria,
penetrated the Russian barrier on the evening of December 6. Fragmentary extracts of the speech were telegraphed
from Stockholm, and then the entire address began to come
into the Embassy on direct sending from London. Fortunately
enough of a translator force had been assembled to begin to
handle the speech at once, though we still lacked satisfactory
offices. Rooms for the time being had been taken at the Hotel
France. The newspapers, however, would not print the speech
entire, the Bolshevik *Izvestia* and *Pravda* because the call for
"Peace by Victory" was especially displeasing in the hour they
were trying to make "Peace by Defeat," and because the President's references to Russia were against them. The anti-Bolshevik papers lacked both space and courage. The news effect
of the address, nevertheless, was not lost. The Bolsheviks circulated and hammered in the effective points of the address
by their very attacks, and all the papers, with full text at
hand, made such various comments as pleased them.

Yet I was disappointed. The Bolsheviks might not like the
speech but I wanted Russians in general to read it. I determined upon a billboard placard display or effort toward it
until I might be halted. The opportunity was a test, anyway,
and if successful a dress-rehearsal of organization to insure
speed and precision in subsequent performances. To my surprise I found myself nearly encircled with doubt and opposition as soon as I told my purpose. Even the Embassy suggested
that in Bolshevik view the action might look like a challenge,
while the Red Cross opinion was that the plan was imprac-
ticable and that if I attempted it I would be stopped, to the
damage of the Red Cross and American endeavor in general.

But what American endeavor except this was of consequence? I couldn't see any. Bullard, who knew Russia even if I did not, agreed with me that the attempt had a chance of success. Neither of us could see any harm in trying. My own organization, I concluded, was all that need count.

Seeking out the Commissariat in charge of printing plants, I asked permission for the use of any idle or part time plant. I said I wanted it for American news work, specifying no particular printing, emphasizing only that here was a chance for the Soviets to open paying jobs to unemployed printers and pressmen. I had the money, I said, and permission to use it. The last statement stretched the facts, although I believed I could make it true, as I thought it extremely unlikely that the Government would refuse to let me pay money to its own workmen. Gumberg was with me and from official to official we talked our way. We came away with a plant promised. It was indeed available to us within a week.

Moscow printing was the next essential. I wanted to meet Consul Summers and get an impression of the city, although I knew my stay must be brief. Leaving Bullard to prepare the President's message for the printer and to continue the business arrangements for the plant itself, I made plans to start for Moscow on the night of December 8, taking with me the finished Russian translation of the Wilson speech.

In the meantime the Bolsheviks had reached an official attitude on President Wilson's stand and disclosed it in the *Izvestia* on December 8. There were in the speech, as far as Russia was concerned, three salient points, the general assertion of determination to win the war, and two comments on Russia, both uncomplimentary to the Bolsheviks. Of the three points, the *Izvestia* editorial quoted two, the second being aimed against Bolshevism. The *Izvestia* editorial of December 8:

THE ALLIED GOVERNMENTS AND THE PEACE DEALINGS

We tried to prove in an article yesterday that the English, the French, and the American Governments, the same as the German Government, are all of them interested in the continuation of the war and are willing to go on with it for years. The speech of President Wilson, published today and the declaration of the French Ambassador Noulens prove how right we were in our anticipations.

The great "peace-maker," President Wilson, spoke very like Noulens. In his speech on war aims before Congress Wilson made the following declaration:

Our object is, of course, to win the war; and we shall not slacken or suffer ourselves to be diverted until it is won.

Touching on the formula, "No annexations, no contributions, no punitive indemnities" Wilson said:

Just because this crude formula expresses the instinctive judgment as to the right of plain men everywhere it has been made diligent use of by the masters of German intrigue to lead the people of Russia astray—and the people of every other country their agents could reach, in order that a premature peace might be brought about before autocracy has been taught its final and convincing lesson, and the people of the world put in control of their own destinies. But the fact that a wrong use has been made of a just idea is no reason why a right use should not be made of it. . . . Let it be said again that autocracy must first be shown the utter futility of its claims to power or leadership in the modern world. . . . Not until that has been done can Right be set up as arbiter and peace-maker among the nations. But when that has been done . . . we shall be free to base peace on generosity and justice, to the exclusion of all selfish claims to advantage even on the part of the victors.

We hear in these words the same tune, "war to the victorious end." We are perfectly sure that all the Krupps, Thyssens, Erhardts, Skodas and the rest of the German and Austrian "gun kings" are delighted to listen to such speeches; and that all the militarists in Germany as well as the Hohenzollerns and Hapsburgs are overjoyed to be able to put the responsibility for the continuation of the war on the shoulders of the enemies of Germany. But the joy of the German Chancellors and French Premiers will not last long. The powerful appeal of the Russian proletarian masses will soon be heard all over the world and the awakened masses will force their Governments to advance toward armistice and peace.

A paragraph as outwardly naïve as the last would seem to qualify Bolsheviks as the romantics of the ages yet there was cunning in the advice to Germany to take the position that responsibility for the continuation of the war be charged henceforth to the Allies. There was, too, one omission in the quotation from Wilson's speech—the sharp-edged sentence: "It is impossible to apply any standard of justice so long as such forces are unchecked and undefeated, as the present masters of Germany command." The insertion changed the context to quite a degree, making the reading: "Let it be said again that autocracy must first be shown the utter futility of its claims to power or leadership in the modern world. It is impossible to apply any standard of justice so long as such forces are unchecked and undefeated, as the present masters of Germany command. Not until that has been done can Right be set up as arbiter and peace-maker among the nations."

The Russian section of the speech passed by without Bolshevik comment was:

German rulers have been able to upset the peace of the world only because the German people were not suffered under their tutelage to share the comradeship of the other peoples of the world either in thought or in purpose. They were allowed to have no opinion of their own which might be set up as a rule of conduct for those who exercised authority over them. . . .

All these things have been true from the very beginning of this stupendous war; and I cannot help thinking that if they had been made plain at the very outset the sympathy and enthusiasm of the Russian people might have been once for all enlisted on the side of the Allies, suspicion and distrust swept away, and a real and lasting union of purpose effected. Had they believed these things at the very moment of their Revolution and had they been confirmed in that belief since, the sad reverses which have recently marked the progress of their affairs toward an ordered and stable government of free men might have been avoided. The Russian people have been poisoned by the very same falsehoods that have kept the German people in the dark, and the poison has been administered by the very same hands. The only possible antidote is the truth. It cannot be uttered too plainly or too often.

These were sentiments to be kept visually before Russians. The President's words read to me like orders from home.

It was a week of thrusts for the Bolsheviks, from Germans, showing that they intended to give the orders; from President Wilson, increasing the scope of America's war, and hardening the resolve not alone of his own people but of the nations of the

Allies; and even of a slashing jab from the supposedly negligible Kerensky. From his hiding place Kerensky wrote a philippic, of date November 21, and sent a messenger to Petrograd with a copy for the newspaper *Dielo Naroda* ("The People's Cause"), which took a risk and published it on December 5, estimating shrewdly that the Bolsheviks might not care to advertise Kerensky additionally by closing the paper. The guess was good.

Kerensky wrote to the Russian people:

Come to your senses! Is it possible you do not realize that your credulity has been abused, and that you have been shamelessly duped! You have been promised peace with the Germans in three days and now the traitors are imploring it. But all of Russia has been flooded with blood. Nicholas II can proudly raise his head, for it is true that never during his rule did such horrors happen. The guardsmen of Leo Trotsky have surpassed them.

You have been promised bread but terrible famine already has begun and our children soon will understand who is exterminating them.

You have been promised the kingdom of liberty, the rule of the working people. Where is that liberty? It has been disgraced. A set of rascals and traitors is strangling liberty, betraying the Revolution and ruining our country. Come to your senses, all who have a conscience left, who remain human beings!

Be real citizens, do not destroy with your own hands both the country and the Revolution for which you have struggled throughout eight months! Forsake the maniacs and the traitors! Return to the nation, and to the service of the country and of the Revolution!

I am telling you that! I, Kerensky, that Kerensky whom your leaders have glorified as a "counter-Revolutionist" and "Kornilovist," but whom the Kornilovists wanted to surrender into the hands of the deserter Dybenko and those who are with him.

For eight months, by the will of the Revolution and of Democracy, I guarded the liberty of the nation and the future happiness of the toiling masses. With the support of the best men of the country I have brought you to the very doors of the Constituent Assembly.

Now that the violence and the horrors of lawlessness are the only rule, now that you have the dictatorship of Lenin and of Trotsky, now it is clear for even the blind to see that when I was in power there was real liberty and democracy.

Come to your senses, lest it be too late, and our country perish! Hunger and unemployment will destroy the happiness of your families! You will writhe under the yoke of slavery! Come to your senses!

November 8 (Old Style) 21 (New Style).

A. KERENSKY.

Bitter true and prophetic words! They did hearten his followers and give stubbornness to the movement demanding that the Bolsheviks let the Constituent Assembly meet. The Bolsheviks let the winds blow and continued systematically to disarm all the citizenry not their own active adherents. Words might sting but force would rule.

One of the signs of the disturbed feelings of the Bolsheviks anent the general state of their affairs was a step taken in the line of their conception of an attack on "Allied morale." The action was the publication in the *Pravda* (either of December 5 or 6) of a seeming decree nullifying all foreign debts. It read:

1. All Government loans, concluded abroad, are nullified. The application also is to all Agrarian Bank and Railroad loans concluded abroad under Government guarantee.

2. Payments of interest and payments on principal of the loans referred to in Clause One are discontinued.

3. All bonds of internal Government loans and of loans issued with Government guarantee, held abroad at the time of the publication of this decree are cancelled.

The pseudo-decree of repudiation was not signed. Nor did it appear in the official *Izvestia*. Its use in the *Pravda*, a semi-official newspaper was a threat, or perhaps it could be called a promise. Hearing of it abroad, greedy *bourgeois* investors were to be supposed to put the well-known and potent money pressure on their Governments and force them to come begging for a place in the Russian peace negotiations! Foreign debts were not repudiated until February 3, 1918.

2.

HAVING heard there was to be a meeting of the Petrograd garrison, I went to Smolny Institute on the evening prior to my departure for Moscow. The occasion may have been my introduction to Smolny. It will serve in any event for my first impression of the Bolshevik citadel. Smolny had been a girls' school, endowed by royalty.

What I found was external fortress and internal capitol. The building was low, extensive, with a central edifice and flanking wings, a church in one of them, approached from a plaza which was also a street car terminal. Broad steps led up a pillared entrance. Machine guns were posted on the sides above the steps, and at other places of vantage. Several pieces of larger artillery also were placed so as to command the square. Canvas coverings were thrown carelessly over some of the heavier guns and some were snow covered. Red Guards armed with rifles, and without uniform, patrolled the plaza front of the buildings. Gun crews were not in sight, though I was told that they were scattered inside within call.

Strolling workmen and many sailors, the former with rifles and the latter with holstered pistols, were plentiful in the halls inside. The Guards had a fancy for looping their cartridge belts from shoulder to waist. The sailors for the most part wore their belts under their jackets, but even with them habiliments seemed to be a matter of individual taste. Sentinels scrutinized the papers of all seeking entrance. At that time I did not have a personal pass and was an escorted visitor.

Once through the doors and in the long, transverse hall, I thought I was in the rotunda of a pamphlet publishing house. Tables and counters piled high with tracts were along the back walls of the hall and down the corridors, most of them in charge of short-haired, active, and chattering girls. The place was as noisy as a college building between recitation hours. The floor was slimy with drippings from incoming feet, there being no overshoe custodian at the door, almost the only exception to the rule I ever found in Petrograd. In some of the office sections on the floors above, however, one did remove overshoes. The pamphlet girls wore cloaks but went with uncovered heads.

The sight of the masses of printed matter removed from my mind any lingering notion that ideas in Russia were not spread by the printing press. Here was proof that where the Bolsheviks placed dependence others might also. The factories, I also was to find, were links in the system for the circulation of the party literature. The printing, too, was good, in spite of the coarseness of much of the paper. Some of the pamphlets were bound in coated paper. Of sheet material there were quantities. Altogether an interesting exhibit of the advertising proclivities of Bolshevism.

Trotsky's office on an upper floor was the most accessible of the offices of the leaders. That night I only passed curiously by the doorway of the suite. A sentinel was on duty outside. Lenin's center was far away in a wing, with a cordon of guards intervening. At this time the machinery of rule at Smolny included telegraphic offices, the editorial offices of the *Izvestia*, committee quarters, assembly rooms for the Council of Commissars and the Central Executive Committee, individual offices for the majority of the commissars, staff offices, and meeting halls for the Petrograd Soviet and other bodies. The many recitation halls and study rooms of the seminary fitted conveniently to their new uses.

The so-called garrison meeting that I came to witness turned out to be a committee conference and not a mass affair. However, I was not turned away. No one seemed to pay any attention to me or to my interpreter. In one room possibly forty persons were milling around a table on which maps and papers were spread, and at one end of which stood a speaker. The gathering was a mixture of unmilitary looking soldiers and civilian workmen.

No one wore the insignia of an officer, yet I gathered presently that here was Podvoisky, the Bolshevik Minister of War; and representatives from the different regiments in barracks, and Red Guard spokesmen. I presumed that the discussion might be about the defense of the city, but it was on a topic that interested them more, the keeping of order, their own kind of order in the main, with much mention of counter-revolutionaries.

Yet there was discussion also of the necessity of repressing "hooliganism." The term, too, meant exactly what it would mean in America. Tough gangs were forming for pillage. Wine-shops were mentioned, and drunkenness. The period when this subject of looting became serious was not yet at hand, and the meeting seemed to me dull, trivial, and unsoldierlike. All this it doubtless was, although the get-together represented a molding process. Podvoisky seemed an indeterminate kind of man, and his manner less that of a leader than of a committeeman, urging his fellows to speak their mind. He had, however, more energy than he then disclosed, and both Trotsky and Lenin relied on him. I stayed until midnight and when I left the meeting showed no signs of breaking up.

3.

I STARTED for Moscow on Saturday night, December 8, and reached there the afternoon of the next day—a dragged-out journey due to station waits. No one seemed to be in a hurry. Not expecting so much delay I had not taken any food with me, so had to forage for breakfast at a village station. All I could get was a loaf of soggy brown bread, which had been slashed with a knife for an opening into which sliced salt cucumbers had been stuffed. I had appetite enough, however, to munch the fare both for breakfast and lunch.

Dining with Consul-General and Mrs. Summers that evening I was recompensed for previous fasting. Sipping the after-dinner coffee and chatting with my host and hostess, outer chaos seemed far away. But we could push it aside only momentarily, for very close it had pressed upon these two. Consul Summers knew Russia better than any American in government service, I believe better than any American in Russia. He had served in the country for years, and married there, his wife a woman of culture and broad sympathies. I could have expected her to show anger, for she had lost her moderate possessions in the last turn of the Revolution. Her acceptance, however, was calm, and her grief was for the people, treading toward starvation.

Famine, said Summers, certain famine, faced Russia in two years' time. I said I had seen figures in Petrograd showing a vast storage of grain in the harvest regions. The figures were very likely right, he said, and then took a map of Russia and showed me how the railroads ran, and where the grain areas were. They did not match, too many of the roads planned for military strategy, too few for economic purpose. The stored grain, he said, would deteriorate and much of it rot where it was because the railroad system also had so broken down that transport would be slight. Such grain as could be gotten out would be used too quickly.

The trouble, he indicated, was in the harvests ahead, a lesser sowing, a lesser reaping, the eating of seed wheat, a progressive increase of limiting conditions the following year, and in the after year the famine. He foretold it as it happened.

We were witnessing, he said, the disintegration not so much of Russia as of Russia's modern movement. The country, he surmised, had been set back fifty if not one hundred years. The breakage and disruption of machinery, he called it, and I found that in this disaster he included the developing purpose of the Bolsheviks to smash the peasants' coöperative organizations. For the Russian peasants he had much esteem, not only as tillers of land but as city merchants and manufacturers, and cited many Moscow instances of peasant initiative and success. In the end, he was sure the peasants would control Russia, but when he came to the question of years he shook his head. He had lived long enough in Russia to know its oriental valuation of time.

Since ruin and Bolshevism were synonymous to him, I wondered if I had not been misinformed on his views of business contact with the ruling crowd. I had not been. Reality, he said, could not be dodged. As long as American representatives remained in the country, they would have to have relations with the officials of the country. In his case, it was a day-to-day matter. First there were American citizens to be gotten out of the country. He meant business folks and travelers. As for himself, after they were gone there remained the duty of looking after American property as best he might. The large-scale American exodus was about completed in the days of my visit, the last trainload going Siberia-ward in that interval. Many individuals, however, remained. In the nationalization of property were included great American factories, although Americans would not yet accept the decrees as final. It could be truthfully said that the Consul was concerned in the action of every American then in Moscow, appealed to by someone at every hour of the day.

Beyond that, I asked him, what did he think there was to do? "Fight the Germans," he said tersely, "and sow as many seeds of American democracy into the Russian soil as we can. They'll grow up to beat tyranny."

There was encouragement, and I needed it. In the afternoon

hours I had learned that two of my reliances were gone. The wireless, upon which I had depended for news service more than upon the cable, was smashed, equipment torn apart and aërials down. And the great printing plant of the newspaper *Russkoe Slovo* ("The Russian Word"), with resources fitted to every project in my list, where I had assurances of coöperation, had been seized by the Bolsheviks and the publication suspended. It still would be possible to do much printing in Moscow, but the heavier operations would have to remain in Petrograd. I cabled Washington not to attempt a Moscow service, and to cable direct to Petrograd. The message did not get through.

Moscow in fact at that moment was a wrecked city, unrepaired from its civil war.

Of this aspect in my home letter of December 17, I wrote:

Moscow, where I was a week ago, saw the real tragedy. The National Hotel, where I stayed, had stood mid-way between the two lines of cannon fire. It got off easy but its ground floor windows on one street were shot away and bullet holes were sprayed around its panes on every floor. The Kremlin is just a block away. The Nicholas gate is ruined—the proud ikon titled with the inscription that Napoleon's effort to blow up the gate as he departed had failed to disturb its sacred serenity, is not left to exult anew. A Bolshevik shell smashed it and ironically left the title unharmed.

A few yards outside the gate, along the stern brick wall, are buried in a huddled grave three hundred of the Red Guard. Probably five hundred of the White Guard were killed. They were buried by their families. I did not have time to get a pass to go inside the Kremlin, but some of its buildings, I know, were badly pounded.

A mile back, toward a wide boulevard, is the place where the Bolshevik cannon stood, and against which the Kremlin defenders directed their fire. In one apartment building in the line of fire thirty or more persons burned to death. Another apartment house of New York up-town size was demolished but without loss of life.

The battle lasted a week, during which time the yellow streaked inhabitants for whom a small body of young soldiers was giving up life never came to their aid. So the Bolshevik wave, itself a thing of courage, rolled over the defenders. "As cowardly as a Moscow *bourgeois*" is now a by-phrase in Russia.

The grave-trench along the Kremlin walls had not been sealed, merely planked over for the winter. Tiers of red-painted wooden coffins within were said to reach nearly to the flooring. In one area of the trench were the uncoffined bodies, some of them unidentified. The populace trod the boards as they would a sidewalk.

The city seemed not so much stoical as dazed. Only trade in provisions continued. Mercantile industry was stilled. Street after street showed shuttered windows. Both the National and the Metropole hotels were nearly vacant. The most optimistic person I met was an American business and banking scout for a New York bank. For some reason he thought the opportunity excellent for acquiring "future prospects." A few weeks later he passed through Petrograd homeward bound, convinced at last that Russia was no place for investment. The days were gray and snowy, the Moscow river frozen over. In a twilight hour I went to the river side of the Kremlin to visualize the contour of its walls. Chill and dreariness. Petrograd was snug and lively by comparison.

I had promised Madame Lebedev that I would call on her father, Prince Kropotkin, to see if the aged man and his wife were comfortable. I found the *savant* and erstwhile revolutionary in a cold though otherwise livable suite of rooms in one of the beehive blocks of flat buildings. He was not in want, he said, but lonely and distressed, grieving for the downfall of his country. He looked to be a man of seventy-five or thereabouts, far yet from being drained of vigor. A short plump figure of a patriarch, he strode up and down the room stroking a full, white, and well-kept beard. He was nearly bald, with white, shaggy eyebrows.

The next fifteen minutes were clamorous with his denunciation of the Bolsheviks. A master of English invective, he spared them in no detail, calling them aliens, enemies of Russia, robbers, and gangsters, set upon looting and destruction.

They have deluded simple minds! [he shouted]. The peace they offer will be paid for with Russia's heart. The land they have been given will go untilled. This is a country of children, ignorant, impulsive, without discipline. It has become the prey of demagogues, discarding the teachers who would have led it along the slow, safe way. I am too old to lead any longer and I am without that form of ambition, but I returned to Russia to observe, to share in the new bounty of liberty offered by the downfall of Czarism, to be warmed by home fires. There was hope during the summer. The war was bad. I am the enemy of war, but this surrender is no way to end it. The Constituent Assembly was to meet. It could have built the framework of enduring Government.

I was unfamiliar with his written works, believed him to be an individualist who was so opposed to the tenets of government that he was reputed a philosophical anarchist, and had heard that he had been witness if not participant in the Paris Commune, yet here he was talking as a conservative constructionist. I made a reference to the Paris Commune, asking him if he thought this might not be Lenin's model.

The French Revolution is more his pattern [he replied]. Or if not his, it is Trotsky's. Lenin, if he outlasts the Hundred Days of the Paris Commune, will bleat about it. [He did indeed.] But Lenin is not comparable to any revolutionary figure of history. Revolutionaries have had ideals. Lenin has none. He is a mad man, an immolator, wishful of burning, and slaughter and sacrificings. Things called good and things called evil are equally meaningless to him. He is willing to betray Russia as an experiment.

He told off Trotsky, Zinoviev, and their group in a curt, harsh phrase. Russians, he thought, were foolish to give them opportunity.

He did not expect to live, he said sadly, to see a better day.

His wife, who seemed frailer than he, joined in the conversation occasionally, and wished to know as much as possible about her daughter. I told her that Mr. Lebedev, her son-in-law, would be stationed at Moscow, which gave her hope that the family might be together soon. Some time during the winter Mme Lebedev herself did go to Moscow, and in the spring she removed her parents into the country, remaining with them until Prince Kropotkin died, a few years later. He refused to recognize the existence of the Bolshevik rulers. They left him in peace, an exile in his own land.

When I parted from the fine old couple I had the feeling

that I never would see them again. I never did. Nor did I return again to Moscow, though I had purposed to do so frequently.

With organization work quickly advanced, thanks to the competence of Consul Summers and his staff, I was ready to start back for Petrograd the night of December 11. My leave-taking with Consul Summers was almost casual, so confident was I of seeing him again in a few weeks. He was of the rugged type, and in the prime of life. I thought he would shed hard weather if ever a man could. Yet he died at his post, too worn by overwork to rally from a sudden attack of pneumonia. That was, however, after I had left Russia. So he was another of those I met once, was drawn to, and saw no more.

The train for Petrograd as usual was late, and DeWitt Poole, who had come with me to the station, suggested that we have tea in the restaurant and study the crowds. We sat for nearly two hours over our tea glasses, viewing a whirling scene. The travel mania was scourging Russia. Money had cheapened and railroad fares had not been raised. It was cheaper to keep moving from town to town than to stay in one place. Restlessness, too, stimulated movement. From as far away as Turkestan and the Caucasus, the hordes moved in toward the cities. Moscow was the vortex, but once in it the victims were whirled around until soon they spun away to Petrograd. There, however, the nomads found no sustenance, for Petrograd was the hardest city in Russia to feed, and throughout the winter the exodus always was greater than the inrush. Back to Moscow flowed the human stream, thence somewhere else, and on again, and again.

Townsman, peasant, and tribesman, each bore his goods with him in disorderly packages. Knotted kerchiefs served the women as light traveling bags, and quilts and blankets looped from the corners were containers of the heavier duffle. Grain bags were not uncommon luggage holders among the men. No goods were checked. Passengers and belongings went together.

Boots were the only apparel of the men to receive the attention of neatness. More than knee high and sometimes reaching the thighs, they were the expression of their owners' pride. Countrywomen, too, ambled past wearing boots with colored tops. The women wore many petticoats, the outer ones at least of many hues, all bright. The panorama was agreeable, the throng good-natured. In the jam to board the train I was crushed breathless by smiling folks. Clinging to my single bag I finally was shot to the platform by the mass impetus behind.

Inside I had better luck, for two large men entered the compartment with me, and they closed the doors on the many who would have followed them in, grinning at those who hammered the glass. The corridor was packed immediately with standing passengers and through the windows I could see men mounting to the roof of the car. We were a traveling hive. The car would have been second class in other days. Now it was for all classes. Being for day travel, the compartment did not have berth shelves, and the two long seats did sleeping duty for the three of us. My two tall companions, both Russians, one a peasant and one a soldier, addressed me as "Gospodin," the Russian equivalent for "Mister," and I could only reply with a smile and the word "Amerikansky" to show my lack of language. Cigarettes they accepted happily.

They were going to leave one seat to me and sleep together on the other but by signs I explained that I was small, and that, with heads at different ends, a better arrangement would be for one of them to share a place with me. Their joint width was too much for one seat. The one who was slightly narrower than the other bedded down with me. The process was simple, just rolling tighter into our overcoats and lying down. My feet came only to his chest but his reached my ears, and once or twice during the night tapped my head. However, we slept sounder than might be expected. In the morning we ate a common fare, bread and meat balls, each having brought along a portion. The bigger of the two also forced his way out at a way station and came back with tea for three. The trip from Moscow to Petrograd took sixteen hours.

In the evening, at Petrograd, I went to the ballet at the Marinsky Theater, witnessing wonderful dancing and hearing fine music. The audience was of the people, a mottled array, yet its comprehension and enthusiasm was that of connoisseurs. Shadings which I missed entirely seemed definite in its ears, judging from applause. How much tradition decided favor, I had no means of knowing and my Russian and Russian-American companions were equally ignorant.

Revolution did not halt the ballets either in Petrograd or Moscow. The performances became to a degree state presentations made by the companies themselves. The public was admitted at so low a price, however, that no funds remained for costume replacements, so that stage shabbiness increased. The players, too, had a thin time. Yet their public merriment lightened life not a little. Aware of this, the Bolsheviks distributed tickets liberally among the workers and urged attendance.

The night was that of December 12. While I had been away the armistice delegation had gone again to Brest-Litovsk, leaving Petrograd the evening of December 10. No new word had returned.

Also on December 10, the Revolutionary Military Committee, in sequence of the meeting I had attended December 7, had issued an order prohibiting the further manufacture of alcohol and alcoholic drinks. Wine stores were not closed at that time, the first prohibition being aimed at vodka. Stealing of wine and "bootlegging" were heavily penalized. The wine cellar at the Winter Palace was flooded with water to keep a mob from looting the vintages.

Arrests of the leaders of the Kadet (Constitutional Democratic) party were ordered by the Council of People's Commissars the night of December 11, and the decree was formally promulgated the next day. The Countess Panina, former Deputy-Minister of Public Welfare, was arrested by Red Guards at her home the day before the edict was issued and taken to Smolny for examination. She was charged with returning the Ministry funds to the State Bank so that the People's Commissars found empty safes in the Ministry. This was subterfuge, for a fund in the State Bank also could be taken by edict. The arrest was assault on the Kadet party and was followed at once by the Bolshevik demand that all Kadets be excluded from the Constituent Assembly under threat of dissolution of that body, which now was trying daily to meet at the Tauride Palace and daily being cleared from the building.

More importantly still, the members of the Central Committee of the Kadets, Shingarev and Kokoshkin, former Kerensky ministers, were arrested on December 12. They were asked whether they recognized the authority of the People's Commissars. They replied that they were elected members of the Constituent Assembly and immune to arrest. They were taken to the prison of SS. Peter and Paul, their death march begun.

CHAPTER IX

December 13—December 20, 1917. Petrograd Upside Down. Permanent Armistice and a Flamboyant Trotsky. "Babushka."

1.

AWAITING me on my return from Moscow was a delayed message from Chairman Creel of the Committee on Public Information sent in cipher through the State Department on December 3, before receipt of my trouble-making message of the same date, and delivered to me by the Embassy. It read:

Creel for Sisson. Drive ahead full speed. Coördinate all American agencies in Petrograd and Moscow and start aggressive campaign. Use press, billboards, placards and every possible medium to answer lies against America. Make plain our high motives and absolute devotion to democratic ideals. Deny that supplies are going to be stopped and state America's eagerness to help. Have Breshkovskaya and others issue statements and translate pamphlets. Engage speakers and halls. Urge Red Cross and Y.M.C.A. to fullest effort. Cable Hart, Stockholm, to send motion pictures and give necessary details. Sending thousand words daily from Sayville via Eiffel Tower to Bullard at Moscow. Try to have *Vestnik* get service at Petrograd. All members your family are well and happy.

(*Signed*) LANSING.

Some aspects of the cable were amusing, though natural—Creel thought I was in a free country. Whatever its exuberance, it settled affairs for me at the Embassy, for it was a plain order to coördinate every American agency in Russia, transmitted through the State Department, therefore having its indorsement. When I called next on the Ambassador all the odd barriers of officialdom were down, and an unbroken unity began right then. But word from my family was what pleased me most in the message—the first I had had.

Fortunately the tardiness of the cable had not mattered. As I listed the practical ventures, I had discounted them all. The

Y.M.C.A. situation had come to a head at Moscow, where I had called together the executives for conference. So I cabled prompt reply:

Ask Mott to cable his headquarters Moscow that Hart is coming with instructions and approximately when due. Boys have not heard from him directly for months. Force is sticking at my request and part has gone back for new survey army front line conditions. No active hut work immediately possible. Peasants' coöperative association which was erecting huts has been disrupted forcibly by present Government. For your information, the Grandmother is in hiding. *Russkoe Slovo* was closed by Government Tuesday. This Government forcibly suppresses opposition. Therefore public meeting and protest side of your program cannot be carried out. News side can, and is being soundly organized. Encouragingly, danger of separate peace or early peace lessens. No improvement, however, in Russia as external fighting factor.

A portion of error here on the peace outlook, and correctness on the time element. The talking tactics of both sides gave assurance of long-drawn-out peace parleys, and the permanent armistice itself was not yet fixed. I did not refer to the wireless breakdown at Moscow, trusting to the warning message sent from Moscow. Failure of its receipt cost me delay and further messages before I could get news cable service installed to Petrograd.

The Y.M.C.A. men never did hear from their commanding officer. I began soon to use parts of their organization.

My Log for the next four days had this variety:

Dec. 13—People's Court. Narodny Dom.
Dec. 14—Peter and Paul. Ross at night.
Dec. 15—Soviet meeting and Trotsky. Opera Narodny Dom. Contrast. Trip through town. Shooting.
Dec. 16—Drunkenness and wine-shop looting. Bad outlook. Armistice.

Among the institutions at once erased by the Bolsheviks were the law courts—wiped away with the casualness with which a boy would brush his sleeve across a slate. Later the rulers were to employ their own system of courts as an arm of warfare against "counter-revolutionaries" with the army commander of the moment, Krylenko, as chief prosecutor and often chief judge. Just now "the people" were invited to hold court themselves. It was seen to, also, that they did. I was invited to attend a session and went.

A crowd of the streets filled a large but stuffy room—probably a former courtroom, for there was at one end a platform bearing a long table. A workman rose and called upon the body to choose a few judges. He, of course, was named for one, and after some hubbub a soldier and a woman seemed to have the more voices favoring them, and moved forward to the dais. The spectators all were considered a part of the court.

I wrote of the scene in added detail:

A woman of the wealthy class was brought in, charged with dismissing a servant without notice and calling her a thief. The presiding commissar (the first workman who had gone through the motions of creating a volunteer court) asked the servant if she felt insulted at being called a thief, or if she preferred to rest her charge on violation by the mistress of the rule of the servants' union. The servant passed the insult and made the union charge. After a cross-examination with all participating, a little volunteer jury went out and put the verdict into form. It was that the mistress should pay the servant a month's wage and a month's keep and be "called down" by the commissar for breaking the law of the labor union. I was relieved, for I feared she was to be imprisoned for defiance.

The mistress, an upstanding matron, had stood her ground on the witness stand, declaring that she had dismissed the servant for theft. She was not allowed to call witnesses of her own.

The Narodny Dom (The People's House) which I visited the same day was a great barn of an edifice, the hall of which might have been used for anything from a dance festival to a military drill arena—a Madison Square Garden of crude sort and outfitting. It was of long existence. Concerts and opera were of occasional performance there. On a wintry afternoon, without people about, the aspect was one of dreariness, and my stay was short.

An opportunity to see the inside of SS. Peter and Paul prison without becoming a permanent resident came my way Friday, December 14, and I seized it. Crossing the Neva, we

passed into a large courtyard or park through a fortified gate
in the inclosing outer wall. Heavy guns, snow covered and
rusting, were all about the grounds, and the outlook everywhere
was disorderly. Groups of soldiers were loafing about, off duty
and without guns or military appearance. Even the prison
itself seemed without outside patrols. The entrance, however,
was guarded. The sentinel, after a glance at our papers,
directed a soldier to take us to the commandant's office, or so
we thought.

We found ourselves in a square, bare room, the anteroom of
the guard, into which a man looking like another of the private
soldiers came a few minutes later, said he was the commandant
for the day, and jovially asked us whom we wanted to see.
Though I knew the identity of many prisoners there, including
Tereshchenko of Kerensky's ministry, to whom I had brought
a letter of introduction, I did not care to talk to any of them
in their prison surroundings. A bit of a walk about was our
only desire, we said.

I had expected the prison would be filled. It seemed, in the
sections we saw, to be sparsely tenanted. The stony place was
cold, and grim enough, although the commandant was at pains
to indicate, whether truly or not I did not then know, that the
rule of the place was not as harsh as of old. He said prisoners
had been allowed to vote in the elections for the Constituent
Assembly, that they were permitted to have books and writing
materials, and to buy provisions if they did not like the prison
fare. Muffled men were reading in some of the cells. In the cold
I did not see how anyone could hold a pen in the hand. On inquiry I found that prisoners had been given the privilege of
voting. The vote for the Constituent Assembly was the last
popular vote taken in Russia, none but proletarians having
the voting franchise since. No felons were within Peter and
Paul. All were political prisoners—opponents of Bolshevism.

In addition to the prison, the fortress was the site of the
Arsenal, a military museum, and of the Cathedral of SS. Peter
and Paul, the Westminster of Russia. The Arsenal we did not
visit—there were enough ruins of World War artillery parked
outside to take away any taste for relics of older history. The
Cathedral, closed to the public, swung open to the order of the
commandant, who himself was the guide. Reports had been

prevalent that the tombs of the Tsars had been rifled. He wished to show us that they stood intact.

They did, their golden wreaths glittering in the bare, dignified, unfriendly expanse of the Cathedral, the one splendor of which, the needle spire, as gilded as the Admiralty steeples, and higher than they, was reared for the world outside the walls, best seen from the opposite bank of the Neva. The Cathedral was domed and pillared, and in architecture indefinite.

We faced, on entering, the altar far away at the other end of the nave. Rather more than halfway down, by a pillar, stood the Tsar's throne. The tombs for the most part were between the throne and the altar, within the aisles to right and left. The tomb of Peter the Great lay at the extreme right of one standing by the throne and facing the altar, to his left in order those of Catherine I and of Elizabeth I. The resting place of Catherine II was in the rear, nearer the altar. Among the monarchs buried in the opposite aisle were Paul I, Alexander I, and Nicholas I. Alexander II and Alexander III were buried apart, in the left aisle not far from the mid-line of the edifice. Nicholas II had indicated that his body was to lie beside that of his father.

Gossip said that the treasure of ornaments and jewels within the tombs was equal to that of the gold without. Other gossip proclaimed that the gold without was gilt and was skeptical of treasure within. While I was in Russia the Bolsheviks did not seem interested in either report. They did maintain that historical possessions were to be protected. The art treasures of The Hermitage were guarded scrupulously, and in general the palaces. Only the Winter Palace suffered from the mob.

The huge key clanked in the lock and, not unreverently, we left the seat of the dead. Ill days had come to the city that Peter the Great had built and named. From Peter the builder to Lenin the leveler less than two hundred years! So short the history of Russia.

In the evening of that day I received a caller whose interest was all in the new Russia—Professor Edward A. Ross of the University of Wisconsin, just arrived in Petrograd from a journey from the south of Russia. He had begun his travels before the Bolshevik Revolution, had encountered the outbreak in mid-Russia, and had been so intent on his own theory of what Russia needed that he listed Bolshevism as a temporary phenomenon until he was at its center. He admitted that he was bewildered by the new developments and said he would be cautious in forming an opinion of their meaning. He was not shaken, however, in his own tenet, which was that the enduring governmental solution for Russia was a federated state—"The United States of Russia" he named it. Hours or days or years naturally meant little from this scientific viewpoint; and I admired his studious detachment and capacity for discounting the prevailing excitements.

Already he had drafted one article, of which the subdivisions were: "What Is a Federal Union?"; "The Adaptability of the Federal System"; "The Blessings of the Federal System"; and "Why Russia Needs the Federal System." The essay was logical, textbookish, and remote—neglecting only one factor, that of troublesome mankind, always a bother to doctrinaires. In his Russia to be federated so neatly, Professor Ross included Finland, Estonia, Latvia, Lithuania, and Russian Poland.

He himself I thought more interesting than his orderly writing. A towering fellow, several inches above six feet and built in proportion, he was a fine exhibit of an American in Petrograd. I would have been delighted to have had him stay indefinitely. He was due, however, in his lecture chair at Madison in a few weeks. He wanted to cram himself with Petrograd and be on his way. War was an intrusion on his habits. He hoped it would soon end.

During the evening of his first call, news of the armistice session began to drift in. The first of the resumed meetings had been held, it became known, on the morning of December 13. The chief question at issue, agreeing with forecasts, was that of troop transfer. The declaration was that no decision was reached, either then or at a later sitting. Agreement for the exchange of invalid prisoners was made, however, and the important decision reached that questions of trade resumption between Germany and Russia, and of prisoner exchange, would be considered apart from the peace conference to follow the armistice, and that the meeting place of the commission for this purpose would be Petrograd. It was apparent that the armistice was near.

We could accept it as certain the next morning, the fifteenth, when the *Izvestia* published the following telegram from Secretary Karakhan:

Brest-Litovsk. People's Commissar Trotsky: After a lengthy discussion of the question, necessitating an adjournment for reference to the Governments of the negotiating parties, the delegations of Germany, Austro-Hungary, Bulgaria, and Turkey consented to the acceptance of the provision stipulating the nontransferability of troops from the Eastern to the Western front. The exact text of the accepted proposal reads:
"The parties to the agreement undertake not to effect any strategic military troop transfers from the Baltic-Black Sea front excepting those which had already begun when the agreement was signed."
Consider it necessary to publish this announcement immediately in Russia and abroad. L. Karakhan.

But even when we knew the worst, understood that this meant that the door had not been closed until the orders for transfer had been given, and that the work of the armistice negotiators was finished, the formal announcement of armistice continued to be deferred—through that day and the next.

Conditions, too, in Petrograd seemed to be approaching violence. The undercurrent of feeling against the Bolsheviks was ugly and they realized the fact. They tightened military control and began to threaten. Outside events, and apart from the armistice advance, were having their influence in the city. General Kaledin and his Cossack army, to which had flocked army officers and various troop units hostile to Bolshevism, were becoming a military menace from the Don. In the Ukraine the Rada, the legislative assembly in control, was rearing its head and preparing for armed defense at Kiev. It is fairness to record that the Bolshevik leaders faced their situation without outward sign of wavering.

A meeting of the Petrograd Soviet to consider local difficulties was called for the afternoon and evening of December 15. Of it I wrote on December 17:

I heard there was an important meeting of the Petrograd Soviet and having acquired a pass to Smolny a week ago, I drove out and believe I was the only American in the assemblage of 1000 delegates representing the half million workers of Petrograd.

Trotsky spoke a gentle little piece telling "the *bourgeoisie*" that safety for them lay in ceasing to trouble if they would avoid The Terror. A threat, I took it, which he hoped would work in place of a real Terror. Then to stamp out an outbreak of looting of wine store-houses the city was put in charge of a "Commissar of Drunkenness" with authority to call for troops and declare martial law if necessary. As I left Smolny bicycle couriers were going to the barracks and before I crossed the town soldiers in motor trucks and Cossacks on horse-back were out in patrols. The three regiments of Cossacks in Petrograd are Bolshevik, at least at present. There was shooting all night but the town was clear in the morning and I heard of no casualties.

Then I went to the opera "Lakme" at the People's House (Narodny Dom)—and a fine performance. Have been to one other theatrical performance, the Russian ballet in its own home. Packed houses, fervid enthusiasm. A city of dramatic contrasts, ready any hour.

Paragraphs from this home letter, though approaching the tenor of a part of my letter to George Creel, serve further to illuminate the days. I wrote only four letters home while I was in Russia, communication being possible only through couriers and the embassy pouch. Only one other of them was of length. So from the letter of December 17, finally:

I have said there was no present peril for the *bourgeois*, members of the middle class, but it is evident that if they are found supporting by money or sympathy the Cossack and Ukraine movements in the South and if Bolshevik life is lost there in quantity, the lives of Kadets, the Constitutional Democrats of the middle class, will be in danger in Petrograd and Moscow, as counter-revolutionaries.

A courier goes tomorrow, my old friend Franklin, just back from Jassy in Rumania. He saw the Russian army break up and go home. He saw the Queen of Rumania, weeping, and heard her say that the Rumanian army, unsupported, could do nothing but sign an armistice. There is rumor that the Rumanian army headed independently for the Ukraine to fight against Bolshevik Russia, but I have my doubts.

I think it more than likely that the court in a month's time will be allowed to go back to Bucharest. It is within reason that Germany would prefer the rule of the present court rather than risk the chance of revolution by changing dynasties. I think it will be some time before Germany supports another Revolution. The one she helped light in Russia is burning her fingers right now, though she will get from Russia the peace she sought. For Russia will fight no more externally this time. Disorganized and beaten, what energies she has left are now locked in the strife of civil war. Her armies have been deserting the front for weeks. The last, biggest exodus began a week ago, and while I will not know certainly for three or four days, I doubt if any but the thinnest line of patrols is left anywhere, and know that long stretches are marked only by the deserted trenches and shelter huts and the rusting artillery.

"Peace and Land!"—that's what the Russian workmen and peasants want, and when the Bolsheviks came along with that program they all turned Bolshevik. Germany in its own good time may deny them the one and take the other, but that, too, is another day. . . .

Power has been transferred from one class to another and is being held by a majority militantly carrying bayonets. No pacifism here. Every Comrade (*Tovarishch*) is a soldier and if he doesn't carry a gun he knows where one is. The Red Guards are armed and un-uniformed workmen. They can shoot, and do, but are not disorderly except for a purpose. They hold the cities. From Petrograd they went to fight Kerensky's soldiers. The soldiers ran away. The Red Guard did not. From Petrograd they have gone to fight Kaledin and his Cossacks, and, numbers anywhere near equal, I back the Red Guards to win. Soldiers and sailors, workmen and peasants—these comprise the Soviets (Councils), a local Soviet to each city, a general Council for the nation. For the present it is class solidarity, and if the peasants, and the soldiers, who are mostly peasants, get enough land it will continue solid until it is broken down by armed force. Unless Germany supplies that force there is none in Greater Russia or Siberia to face it. I mean that literally—men armed with guns. And if it is beaten solidly and not by inner dissension it will die fighting and shedding blood.

You see this body already has taken what it wants, and the issue is that of dispossessing it.

The letter showed that, despite the unrest both on the surface and below, I did not believe the Bolsheviks were in danger of being kicked out. Nor did I, although my private notes, in which I did not need to soothe a family that believed I was in frightful surroundings, were franker.

Listening to Trotsky on Saturday night at Smolny and trying to think in terms of his own mind, I had surmised that his aim was to use the excuse of drunken rioting to cloak new severity against party opponents. What more natural than to claim that conspirators were at the bottom of disorder?

Sitting not more than twenty feet from Trotsky and studying his lively face, watchful of the reactions of his listeners, I got the feeling that he was inciting them to a rôle which it was desired they should play of their own seeming initiative. I left the meeting before it was over, for other speakers were to follow, including the shock-haired Zinoviev, head of the Petrograd Soviet. Yet troop movements already were in progress. Everything was in accord with a plan arranged not by the Petrograd Soviet but by the Central Council.

The step was martial law for Petrograd, a "state of siege" in Bolshevik parlance, dating officially from the sixteenth, coincident with the signing of the armistice, in effect the night that Trotsky spoke, although the decree was not published until December 19. Sunday was a taut day. Many persons were abroad, all of one class. Well-dressed Russians kept off the streets. We heard reports of disturbances, although only one came near, and that was made to order.

Across the street from the Hotel d'Europe in the afternoon a party of Red Guards ostentatiously raided a wine storehouse in one of the basements. The place was locked and without custodian. The Guards smashed the door, ran a fire-hose down and attached a pump. Soon the snowy gutters ran with liquor, the stream growing wider as bottles were brought up and shattered, and kegs rolled out and emptied. *Izvozchiks* came running from the neighboring cab-stands and, heedless of the booting they got from the Guards, threw themselves full length on the snow to drink from the rivulet. My windows overlooked the scene and those present in the rooms enjoyed the sportive event. So Petrograd experienced the phenomena of Prohibition before the United States came to know them.

2.

A copy of the signed armistice was brought to me late in the evening of December 16. Except for the period it set for peace conference, twenty-eight days, with a provision for automatic extension of armistice unless denounced by either side, there was no unfamiliar material in the distasteful agreement. The real meaning of such stipulations as that for a German-Russian Commission to deal with economic relations and prisoner exchange was not of course to be accurately plumbed. In the main, however, we who studied the pact could conceive that we understood its possibilities. The clause relating to troop movements was as Karakhan had reported it.

Leaving the hotel at midnight I drove to the Military Mission, which was on the Fuhrstatskaya not far from the Embassy, and roused General Judson from bed to read the document. Although warned by the events of the two days preceding, he was shocked at the completeness of the military disaster to the Allies.

"German troops of two fronts massed now on one front—the Western!" he exclaimed. "The Russians have been tricked, as I told Trotsky they would be."

There was trickery somewhere.

We agreed to keep up a good front of our own. Harassment of the Germans still was possible. Armistices did not always lead to peace. The Germans could not take the offensive in the West until the spring. The Bolsheviks at the moment itself were faced with the problem of overawing Russian hostility to the terms of the armistice, hinting already of punitive peace terms to come.

A Petrograd garrison meeting of December 19 was the flower of the seed sown by Trotsky's speech, though Zinoviev was this time the stage manager. All the looting and the inciting to drunkenness, according to the reports made by various excited investigators, was the outgrowth of conspiracy against the Revolution nursed by the Kadets in alliance with the "Black Hundred." Only vigilance and the sacrificial energy of the defenders of the Revolution, it was proclaimed from the platform, had unmasked the evil enterprise. The moral tone of the gathering was high. Abstinence and stern sobriety were preached by earnest exhorters. Except for occasional flings at religion as a capitalistic soporific and as a staff of property, the atmosphere was that of a revival meeting. The "State of Siege of Petrograd" came under the head of resolutions approved by the meeting.

Many activities, it developed, could be restrained in the name of the suppression of drunkenness. The declaration of martial law as put out by "The Committee for the Combating of Pogroms," a specially formed subcommittee of the Central Executive Committee, read:

1. The City of Petrograd is declared to be in a state of siege.

2. Meetings and gatherings on the streets and squares are prohibited.

3. Attempts to loot wine stores, wine cellars, factories, shops or private apartments will be answered by machine-gun fire.

4. House committees, door-keepers, and guards are held responsible for the maintenance of strict order in the houses, courts and streets. House-gates and street-doors shall be closed at 9 P.M. and opened at 7 A.M. After 9 P.M. residents of the house are to be allowed to leave only at the discretion of the House Committee.

5. Persons charged with distributing, selling, or purchasing any alcoholic drinks, or with infringement of clauses 2 and 4 will be immediately arrested and subjected to the severest punishment.

Blagonravov, a lank, lip-curling personage whom I was to see at close range in a few days, was made Commissar-in-charge of the warfare on "drunkenness" and this appointment gave the game away. For Blagonravov had been in command at the Tauride Palace with the special duty of harrying the elected members of the Constituent Assembly as they sought daily to enter the palace with a view of calling the body into session. It was against these Right Social Revolutionaries, and against the Kadets that the ban upon public assemblage was laid. So the Bolsheviks killed two birds with one stone. For its residents Petrograd became a tight city. Our own freedom of movement, however, met no interference. We went about as usual, early and late, and save for the plaints of downcast Russians would not have realized the rigor of their curfew existence.

Trotsky, once the city campaign was launched, paid no more attention to it. He had larger matters on his hands.

With the armistice signed, he became truculent toward the former Allies of Russia and toward the Kiev Government in Russia. He warned the French Ambassador, Noulens, to withdraw French officers from the Ukraine, or, if they remained, to order them to cease coöperating with the forces of the anti-

Bolshevik Rada. Noulens replied that French officers in Russia were ordered not to interfere in internal politics, a general instruction that applied to the officers at Kiev, who, however, he explained, were attached not to the Military Mission to Russia but to the Mission to Rumania. The French officers stayed in the Ukraine. Noulens was not molested. Trotsky, however, claimed that the contact with the French Embassy, which included an interview with a representative of the Ambassador, gave *de facto* recognition to the Bolshevik *régime*.

Great Britain also drew a threat, to which the British Ambassador made no reply. The United States, for the hour, was excepted.

To the Rada, the governing legislative body at Kiev, Trotsky sent what the Bolshevik press described as an ultimatum. Complaint was not made against the Ukraine for stating itself to be independent of Russia. That course had been encouraged. The rub was that the classes opposed to Bolshevism were in power, and were willing to fight to stay there. As the Bolsheviks expressed it, "The counter-revolutionary hope is in Kiev." From Kiev came prompt response—the demand that the Bolsheviks recognize "the rights of the Ukrainian People's Republic and cease interference with its affairs."

It was war from the start, and neither Lenin nor Trotsky hesitated. In the first place they did not have to wage it themselves, depending upon incitation of the proletariat in the Ukraine to seize Kiev as they had seized Moscow and Petrograd. In the second place, if they did not bring about the overthrow of the Rada they would be in a poor place in bargaining with Germany for peace. What Germany would do they did not doubt. Germany would make a separate peace with the Ukraine if it could, and would prefer to do so. In giving their support to the Rada, this is the point that both France and England overlooked. The two Allied countries gave funds and military counsel, all apparently without assurances of what the Ukrainians would do on the issue of peace with Germany. The Germans seem to have known all along what they would do. The Bolsheviks read their own fears and hoped for quick overturn of the Rada.

Trotsky found time also to proclaim to "The Suffering People of Europe" that armistice with Germany had been made and that a peace conference was about to begin between Germany and Russia.

We have shown to all nations the way to an open understanding on the basis of the recognition of the right of every nation, large or small, advanced or backward, to determine freely its own destiny. We do not conceal from anybody that we do not consider the present capitalistic governments capable of concluding a democratic peace. Only the revolutionary struggle of the proletarian masses against the present governments can accelerate such a peace in Europe.

Entering into negotiations with the present governments, which are permeated on both sides with imperialistic tendencies, the Council of People's Commissars does not deviate from the road of social revolution. The struggle for a genuine democratic peace of the nations is still to come. The first stage of the struggle finds, everywhere except in Russia, the old monarchic and capitalistic governments in power. They bear the responsibility for the present war and have not yet rendered to their deceived nations an accounting for the blood shed and the wealth squandered.

We are forced to open negotiations with these existing governments. Likewise the monarchic and reactionary governments of the Central Powers are forced to treat with the representatives of the Soviets' Government because the Russian people have confronted them with the fact of a Workers and Peasants Government in Russia. During the peace negotiations the Soviet Government will pursue a two-fold task. First, it will aim to bring about the earliest possible conclusion of the disgraceful and criminal slaughter which is ruining Europe. Second, it will attempt to help the labor class of all countries, with every power at its disposal, to overthrow the rule of capitalism and to take possession of the machinery of governments.

To the Socialists of all countries and preëminently to the Socialists of Germany it must be clear that irreconcilable antagonism exists between the peace program of the Workers and Peasants of Russia and the program of the capitalists, landowners and military leaders of Germany. If these programs clash then peace is impossible, for the Russian people did not break the rule of the monarchy and the *bourgeoisie* of its own country to fall before the monarchs and capitalists of other countries. Peace can only be hastened, realized and safeguarded if Germany and her allies hear the firm voice of the working people. The German, Austro-Hungarian, Bulgarian and Turkish workers must combat the imperialistic program of their ruling classes with their own revolutionary program.

Armistice has been concluded on one front only. Our delegation has secured as one of the armistice conditions, after long struggle, the agreement of the Central Powers not to transfer troops to other fronts. The Rumanian army has been included in the armistice against the will of the Rumanian Government. But on the French, Italian and remaining fronts war still continues. The capitalistic governments are afraid of peace; they are trying to postpone the hour of their final bankruptcy. Under phrases of eternal justice and the future partnership of nations the capitalistic rulers of these countries are shrouding the base and egotistic motives of exploiters. They do not want an armistice. But you proletarians of France, Italy, England, Belgium and Serbia—you, our brothers in suffering and struggle, do you want peace with us, an honest, democratic peace of the nations? Those who are telling you that such a peace can be secured only through victory are deceiving you. They have been unable to give you victory in forty-two months of war, nor any evidence that they will, should the war last for years. Should victory, moreover, prove possible for one country or another, it would signify only new domination of the strong over the weak, and would sow the seeds of new wars.

The liberation of Belgium, Serbia, Rumania, Poland, the Ukraine, Greece, Persia and Armenia cannot be achieved through the victorious imperialists of one of the groups of the powers, but only through the victorious struggle of the revolutionary workers of all belligerent and neutral countries against all imperialists.

We, the Council of People's Commissars, clothed with the authority of the Russian workers, peasants, soldiers, sailors, widows and orphans, we appeal to you for a common effort to halt the war on all fronts. Let the news of the armistice at Brest-Litovsk sound like an alarm bell in the ears of the soldiers and workmen of all belligerent countries.

Down with the war! Down with the originators of the war! The Governments resisting peace must be swept away, like the Governments which are veiling pretences of annexations in orations about peace. The Workers and Soldiers must take the cause of peace out of the criminal hands of the *bourgeoisie* and into their own hands. We have the right to demand this from you because we have done it in our own country. It is the only way for your and for our own salvation. Close your ranks, proletarians of all countries, under the banner of peace and social Revolution.

I have quoted the cry almost entire, omitting only a little preliminary verbiage and occasional duplication. One could read into it about what one desired. The Germans could take the threat of revolutionary incitement and overbalance it with the practical fruits of present armistice and prospective peace. Those who knew that the Russian and the German terms so far voiced were indeed "irreconcilable" had Trotsky's promise, whatever its value, that Russia would not retreat from its terms, an indication that war could be renewed. Realists might read that Russia was going into peace conference without other arm than the threat of revolution-making in Germany, and was shouting its weakness to high heaven either in hope of miraculous aid or as excuse for expectant surrender. I took my place in the second group, not from faith, but because that was the line of continuing attack upon Germany.

In his proclamation Trotsky aligned his principles of a peace of defeat against the Wilson principles of a peace of victory. The opposing views had companion presentation to the Russian populace.

For several days I had been trying to get a posting company to cover the billboards of Petrograd with President Wilson's "Peace with Victory" speech, which already was being distributed in handbills through the street crowds. The eye-attracting quality of the billboards was more desirable, however, and I had need of the hand sheets for shipment to other places. The vexatious delay in posting was due to the fear of the contractors in the business. Explaining that they were listed as *bourgeois* and speculators, they dreaded arrest should the Bolsheviks take offense at the posters. They insisted upon a Bolshevik permit, for which I had no intention of asking, as the request would give an excuse for delaying, if not halting, the project.

The sight of the street crowds of idle soldiers finally gave me an idea. I asked a posting contractor if he would superintend the job if soldiers were provided for the posting. He saw the point—there was protection for him. A word around the barracks did the rest. The honest soldiery desired rubles even to the extent of working for them. It may be that billsheets never went on Petrograd walls so fast. Certainly the speed and the scope of the posting was pleasant to me. The entire speech went on the boards, two sheets pasted side by side, or one above the other.

In a day's time Wilson's name and words were to be seen and read on every street in Petrograd. Taking care not to plaster-over Bolshevik decrees and posters, we smothered everything else on the walls. Nor did the Bolsheviks try to nullify the exhibit by new posting. The speech had a good fortnight of display before it was gradually overspread, and many bills still were up when we supplanted them in January with the Fourteen Points Speech.

The bills began to go up the morning of the twenty-first, serving thereby to lighten a blow delivered from another quarter, the subject of the next chapter.

3.

WITH the arrangements for the posting of the speech off my mind, I was free to pay a visit—several times planned and deferred—to the fugitive Mme Breshkovskaya, "Babushka," the "Grandmother." The time, too, was now or never, as she was about to be smuggled out of Petrograd. Robins and I went together, he to say farewell, I to meet her for the first, and only, time. We found her in the apartment of a dependable friend in an accessible residence section. She was sitting in a chair, a shawl wrapped around her shoulders and her hands in her lap in the folds of the shawl. The apartment, as usual, had little or no heat. She looked old and ill and cold. We begged her not to rise.

Her reception of Robins, I thought, was as chilly as the room, and he hastened to tell her that his attitude of seeming friendliness to the Bolsheviks was only realistic politics. The sight of her forlornness did indeed touch all his sympathies and for the present she was mollified by his kindness, though at a later time she wrote a bitter article charging him with desertion of her cause and of Russia. Now our concern, however, was with her safety, and the plans for her flight to Moscow were discussed. Very simple they were.

As a muffled old peasant woman she had eluded Tsarist police and so would she elude Bolshevik Red Guards. The journey mattered little; the cause gave her grief. She had come to Petrograd in hope. She was leaving it in despair. We knew, too, that we would add to her sorrow if we gave any hint that the Bolsheviks were minded rather to speed her departure than to retard her. There was the matter of exit-passes for her and her friend, made out in commonplace peasant names. The papers were given to her.

She wanted to talk at length, my coming being a new interest. I answered her questions as best I could. She sought cheer for the future and there was little to give. I begged her to forswear an ungrateful country and go to her friends in the United States as soon as a way could be opened for her to escape. She shook her head, saying she would keep on fighting to make Russia free, and would live until she could die in a free Russia. I hope she may. To this day she has not ceased fighting. She did in time flee from Russia. Prague gave her haven.

At parting she insisted on rising to her feet. She shook hands with us gravely and we bowed low, wishing her cheer, harbor, and better days. We moved toward the door, but on impulse I turned back. She was standing with her arms at her sides, her fingers pressed into the palms of her hands, tears on her cheeks. I took her in my arms, laid her head on my shoulder, and held her close. The comforting seemed to be what she needed, for she smiled and clung to me. Then I kissed her and hurried away.

CHAPTER X

*December 20—December 23, 1917. The Kalpashnikov
Case and Its Consequences.*

1.

IT was apparent to American observers in this period between accepted armistice and the opening of the peace
conference that the Bolshevik leaders were searching for
excuses for verbal challenges to the ambassadors of the countries formerly the Allies of Russia. The political utility of such
a course was obvious, serving to divert the attention of the
public from the difficulties the party faced in consequence of
having agreed to attempt a single-handed peace.

If the Russian people could be made to believe that their
unhappy condition of the present and the evil aspect of the
future was a responsibility of the Allies, the Bolsheviks were
the gainers. If they could not be made to believe it, they might
be confused by the dust of accusations thrown into the air. At
the least the body of Bolshevik followers could be heartened
by clamor against "Foreign Imperialists" and their representatives on the scene. Finally there was the advantage of
threatening the Embassies with penalty for any action that
could be interpreted as hostile to the Bolsheviks.

Trotsky, as Foreign Minister, was the natural leader of the
campaign. If we Americans needed warning we got it when
Trotsky tilted against Noulens, the French Ambassador. We
felt, however, that we already were on guard. Though aware
that the silence of Ambassador Francis was resented even more
than that of Sir George Buchanan, the British Ambassador,
we were confident that Trotsky could not attack without concrete material, and that we were giving him none.

We underestimated his ingenuity and overestimated our
immunity from error. In the Kalpashnikov case he got his
weapon, a poor, twisted thing good only for one thrust; only
an irritant to the American Embassy in finality, but nearly
fatal to Kalpashnikov, and for its hour a danger to all Allied
nationals in Petrograd.

Andrew Kalpashnikov was a Russian officer then in the service of the American Red Cross unit for Rumania. In the pre-war period he had been an *attaché* of the Russian Embassy in Washington. In 1917 he was again in the United States in behalf of the Russian Red Cross to raise money for its ambulance equipment and to buy the ambulances. On his return journey it was his misfortune to be at Halifax when Trotsky was arrested there by the British and to be asked by English officials to act as an interpreter in their questioning of the prisoner. Kalpashnikov therefore was known to Trotsky and in a fashion not apt to commend him to the now Foreign Minister.

Kalpashnikov had the ambulances shipped across the Pacific, across Siberia, and got them at Petrograd. Before the Russian Red Cross could put them into service, the Bolshevik Revolution came. The Russian front for which they were intended ceased to be. Kalpashnikov, by authority, at once disposed of the cars to Col. H. W. Anderson, head of the American Red Cross in Rumania, and he himself was attached to Colonel Anderson's staff. After consultation with Colonel Anderson at Jassy, Rumania, he returned to Petrograd to carry out the orders he had received to ship the trainload of cars through Russia to Jassy. The disaster to the Rumanian army, following the Russian defection, did not change Colonel Anderson's determination that he wanted the cars. Through the Embassy at Petrograd he transmitted telegraph orders to Kalpashnikov, who already had loaded his train.

Suddenly, on the eve of his departure, Kalpashnikov was arrested on Trotsky's orders—the midnight of December 20; and on the evening of the ensuing day, Friday, December 21, Trotsky delivered a violent speech in the Alexandrovsky Theater charging that Ambassador Francis at Petrograd and Colonel Anderson at Jassy had plotted to send the ambulances to the anti-Bolshevik army at Rostov-on-Don commanded by General Kaledin. He had arrested Kalpashnikov, he stated, as the active agent of the conspiracy.

As alleged proof Trotsky read a message Colonel Anderson had sent to the Embassy for delivery to Kalpashnikov, and in which Rostov-on-Don was named as destination. The telegram had been sent at a time when Colonel Anderson was considering routes for his own retreat from Rumania, and had been nullified in a succeeding wire six days later, restoring the order for direct shipment. Trotsky did not read or refer to the vetoing message.

Trotsky did not send a direct communication to Ambassador Francis either before or after his public tirade, letting the matter be one of newspaper exploitation. The Ambassador, therefore, was enabled to make his reply through the same channel. He printed the complete set of three telegrams received from Colonel Anderson, showing between them an aspect of routine and an absence of intrigue. The inflated attack against the Ambassador collapsed.

But Kalpashnikov was lost the moment Trotsky's attention was directed to him. The personal motive was shown in the *Izvestia* of December 25, under the heading, "Who is Col. Kalpashnikov?"

Col. Kalpashnikov-Kamak was attached to the Russian Embassy in Washington under Nicholas II. Col. Kalpashnikov came from New York to Russia on the same steamer with Comrade Trotsky, who was arrested by the English gendarmes at Halifax, Canada. Col. Kalpashnikov courteously offered his services to these gendarmes and helped them to interrogate Comrade Trotsky.

There was nothing of the cavalier about Trotsky. He was vindictive.

Kalpashnikov was kept in prison until May, 1918, first in the fortress of SS. Peter and Paul and afterward in the worse surroundings of Dzerzhinsky's prison for victims of his Extraordinary Commission against Counter-Revolutionaries, not then known as the *Cheka*. He never had a trial. Uritsky, head of the Petrograd Terrorist commission, who finally released him, told him, Kalpashnikov wrote in his book, *A Prisoner of Trotsky's*, that he had voted for his arrest "and that of those foreigners who would not recognize the Bolshevik Government," adding, "your arrest was to be the first step in this direction and if the Government had listened to me the Americans with whom you worked would have been arrested and shot."

Trotsky, however, had no intention of shooting any foreigners, whatever the desires of subordinates. Kalpashnikov had been the scapegoat.

For an affair in which only one man was a victim the Kalpashnikov case has had singular vitality. This has been due in part to the fact that Kalpashnikov proved to be a hard-fighting man. He set down the circumstances, as he saw them, in a book, and Ambassador Francis wrote for it a preface out of the ordinary. Raymond Robins prepared a *dossier* of material for his Red Cross superiors at home. And while I was *en route* to the United States the next spring I was interviewed by a staff representative of the Red Cross in a manner to indicate that Colonel Anderson also had made report and that the two accounts were being weighed. The latter's communication I did not see. Colonel Robins gave me a copy of his report. The only active rôle I took was in relation to the defense of the Ambassador. It kept me close to the scene once developments started. At the Embassy the disturbing issue was less what Trotsky did than how he got the chance to do it.

An initial circumstance favoring both blunders and mischief-making, was that there was dissension between the two American Red Cross units, the one in Petrograd and the one in Rumania. The fate of war, it can be said as directly, had ended the missions to Allies upon which each unit had been sent. Russia was no longer an Ally; Rumania was an Ally smashed. Each unit, without new orders from home, was striving to find something to do, and each got in the other's way. The Russian unit, too, from the beginning of the *régime* of Colonel Thompson, had directed its energies into political as well as welfare work, with helpful intent and encouragement enough from the Kerensky Government in its day but with embarrassing implications of being outside its field when the enemies of Kerensky came to power. Thereafter its existence was by favor of the Bolsheviks. Such a condition risked misfortune and humiliation. The Red Cross unit in Rumania now was attached to a broken force, the remainders of which were hostile to the Bolsheviks and, even in disarray, feared by them. The unit in Rumania, moreover, had no practicable way out of the country except through Russia, and Petrograd was its supply base. Close and sympathetic coöperation between the two branches of the organization was imperative for the well-being of the isolated Rumanian unit.

These factors warrant an examination of the details of the Kalpashnikov case and account for its longevity.

It fell to the lot of Major Robert Griswold Perkins of the

staff of Colonel Anderson to have the first visible rôle in the miscued performance. The Major had no such intention. Misadventure chose to walk at his elbow.

He arrived in Petrograd from Jassy on Sunday, December 16, and I met him that day in the Red Cross dining-room at the Hotel d'Europe, his interest for me lying in what he could tell me about the army disaster in Rumania. He was a small, active man, anxious to finish up Petrograd detail, for he was homeward bound, *via* Siberia. He darted around for a day or so, and then on Tuesday he was gone. I heard rumors that he had quarreled with Robins and Wardwell, regarded the spat as a Red Cross family matter, and kept well away. He had this good luck—he made his exit safely.

Not until Friday morning did the explosion come. We heard then that Kalpashnikov had been arrested during the night, and that the charges against him were based on embassy communications and upon letters he and Major Perkins had written to Colonel Anderson at Jassy. Of the contents of the letters the Embassy knew nothing. Its own actions seemed so incapable of distortion that the Ambassador and Counselor Butler Wright decided upon a course of frankness—to seek to demonstrate to Trotsky privately and at once that there was no basis to any charge against the Embassy, and so prevent a public accusation. News of Kalpashnikov's arrest had not yet been printed and was not during the day.

Means for unofficial communication existed in Robins' access to Trotsky for Red Cross purposes. Accordingly it was decided to supply Trotsky with true copies of Colonel Anderson's trio of messages to the Embassy to explain any purported or partial messages he might have. Robins, who had brought the news of the arrest to the Embassy, was again called into the conference and given an authorization, as follows:

EMBASSY OF THE UNITED STATES OF AMERICA.
Petrograd Dec. 8/21, 1917

Colonel Raymond Robins,
Acting Chairman American Red Cross
  Mission to Russia,
Petrograd.

DEAR COLONEL ROBINS:

Pursuant to our conversation today I beg to enclose herewith copies of three telegrams from Col. Anderson of the American

Red Cross Mission to Roumania, two of which are addressed to Col. Kalpaschnikoff through the medium of this Embassy and one to the Embassy itself; copies of which were delivered to the American Red Cross Mission to Russia for Col. Kalpaschnikoff on December 14, 1917.

Further pursuant to our understanding you may state to the appropriate persons that you are authorized to speak for the American Embassy in this connection in order to correct any misapprehension that may have arisen. You are also authorized to state that Colonel Kalpaschnikoff when he approached the Embassy relative to the shipment of these motor cars was told that the shipment of the cars must be arranged by him with the parties in control in Petrograd. You will recall that you heard at the Embassy this morning that no money whatever had ever been advanced to Colonel Kalpaschnikoff for this or any other purpose.

Trusting that this may serve your purpose in clearing up the misunderstanding, I am, my dear Colonel Robins,

> Very truly yours,
> For the Ambassador
> (*Signed*) J. BUTLER WRIGHT,
> *Counsellor of the Embassy.*

This was a lastingly important document to Robins, for it legitimized conference relations with Trotsky, and later provided him with a defense against Kalpashnikov's insinuation, made to Ambassador Francis, that Robins turned over to Trotsky prior to Friday a copy of the telegram upon which Trotsky based the arrest. This telegram was supposed to have been found on Kalpashnikov when he was taken into custody. He asserted afterward to Ambassador Francis that the raiders did not find the message on him or in his flat; that, on his release, he found it still safely hidden.

As Robins took the embassy letter, and the telegrams attached, to Trotsky in the afternoon before the speech was delivered, the Embassy itself could have provided an unscrupulous Trotsky with the prime instrument of his strategy. In this case Robins, however much tricked by Trotsky, was cleared of Kalpashnikov's insinuation. Counselor Wright's letter disclosed, too, that copies of the telegrams had been sent to American Red Cross headquarters on December 14 for delivery to Kalpashnikov, who, on his testimony, did not receive them until a day later. If Trotsky had spies in the Red Cross offices, they had their opportunity.

The insincerity of Trotsky, in any event, stood forth naked. He had all three telegrams before he made his speech, used only the one that served his inflammatory purpose, and knew that he had no grounds for attack on the Ambassador.

The text of the three telegrams, the first and third from embassy files, the second—to show its Bolshevik use—in re-translation from the Russian, verified by the Embassy and included in Robins' record:

American Embassy, Petrograd. Following from Anderson: "Jassy, Dec. 5th. 568. Please see my number 569 today which is for Col. Kalpaschnikoff. Please supply him for the purposes stated therein necessary funds up to 100,000 rubles and draw on American Red Cross, Henry P. Davison Chairman, with this telegram attached to cover. It is most urgent that this matter be done at once so please assist Kalpaschnikoff in the matter in every way possible." American Minister.

The mischief-maker, No. 569, with its newspaper heading, from the *Izvestia* of December 22:

Telegram of the Chief of the American Red Cross Mission to Roumania, Colonel Anderson, to Colonel Kalpaschnikoff.

December 5, 1917.

Provide for the possibility of dispatching all automobiles assembled or non-assembled to Rostov-on-Don with the first available train. Try to convoy them to Rostov personally. Colonel Verblunsky is asking you to take his wife with you. I held him back here for the time being. Please apply all possible instrumentalities to carry this immediately into effect and wire me. If you need money apply to the American Ambassador who will advance you up to 100,000 rubles on the account of the Red Cross. Inform me by telegraph. I shall have ready for you further instructions in Rostov, or shall meet you there.

(*Signed*) ANDERSON.

The order voiding above message:

American Embassy, Petrograd. 575. Following signed Anderson for Kalpaschnikoff. "Jassy, Dec. 11. Perkins and Verblunsky left for Petrograd tenth. In view changed conditions here disregard my 569 Dec. 5. Have motors ready for shipment on arrival

Perkins who carries instructions. Spend necessary funds up to 50,000 rubles and move them promptly. See Robins about other supplies mentioned my 559 Nov. 28, and act on Perkins advice as to further purchase." Vopicka, American Minister.

The telegrams were sent for Colonel Anderson by the American Minister, Vopicka, at Jassy, the first to the Petrograd Embassy direct, the second and third to Kalpashnikov, *via* the Embassy. Colonel Kalpashnikov did not ask for funds, being aware probably that the Embassy could not supply them in the manner suggested. Machinery for such easy transfer of credit had been shattered.

By itself the message naming Rostov-on-Don as destination was suspicious in Bolshevik ears. Kaledin and his Cossacks were at Rostov-on-Don, and rallying around them was an army that threatened the Bolsheviks seriously. The interpretation could be that the commandant of the American Red Cross unit in Rumania was moving to join Kaledin.

Yet Trotsky was aware that such an interpretation was wrong, not only from the countermanding order but also from an explanation in Major Perkins' letter to Colonel Anderson, already in his possession. Major Perkins had referred to Colonel Anderson's plan, which was for a long trek by way of Rostov-on-Don into Asia Minor to join the British army in Mesopotamia. Not a good plan, one almost if not quite impossible of physical accomplishment, and one abandoned as soon as it had a sensible survey. Yet the vagaries of the beleaguered are understandable. Once in February, after we also were encompassed, I sought to map an escape by way of Afghanistan into India.

The best way out of Rumania was up to Kiev and Moscow and thence Siberia-ward or Finland-ward. The new instructions Major Perkins brought were to ship to Jassy in preparation for a motor journey back to Kiev should train service cease presently. No provender of sensation in this program.

But a sensation can be manufactured.

In the fitting surroundings of the Alexandrovsky Theater Trotsky raised the curtain Friday evening on his piece, himself the hero, Kalpashnikov and the Ambassador as twin villains, and Robins praised and put forward in the rôle of one "correct with regard to us in all his dealings."

Robins sent a stenographer to the meeting, using the report thus obtained in his own records, which I have used for this account.

Spoke Trotsky, in this version:

Last night we discovered documents showing that agents of the United States were implicated in the Kaledin plot; documents which are of international significance, and which were found on a Col. Kalpashnikov, detailed to convoy a train of the American Red Cross to Jassy. This officer is undoubtedly connected with the Kornilov Staff. The officer stated that he has received a certificate from Colonel Robins.

To avoid all misunderstandings I want to state that Colonel Robins has been loyal and correct with regard to us in all his dealings, and everything we know about him excludes the possibility that he was in any way implicated in the story.

Colonel Robins came to me two weeks ago to make arrangements that a Red Cross train for Jassy should proceed without any obstacles being laid in its way. Of course we extended all cooperation. Then we were advised that the automobiles might not get to the Rumanian front, but to the Russian internal front, and very possibly to Kaledin, on the Don. I then addressed a letter to Colonel Robins.* (The letter was read.)

We found a letter of Kalpashnikov's addressed to Colonel Anderson, Chief of the American Red Cross Mission to Rumania:

At least ten days prior to the arrival of Major Perkins here I had 35 cars entirely fitted up and ready for shipment. . . . Knowing that the American Red Cross Mission to Russia has also sent some supplies I went to the Hotel d'Europe and proposed to take some of their cars. From this time on all our misfortunes began and if we should be blocked up here altogether then to Colonel Robins and his assistant our gratitude will be due to them for having prevented, by all legitimate and illegitimate means, the Rumanian Mission from getting the automobiles.

(Trotsky's comment): Until his arrest we did not know he was against Col. Robins.

At first I was informed that Wardwell had formed a regular train taking upon himself all responsibility for delivery; when I was told that no special formalities were required. I was informed that the

---

* Robins did not include a copy of this letter in his prepared record. Apparently it was not printed in the newspapers. Search of the *Izvestia* and the *Pravda* did not disclose it. However, if I had asked Robins for a copy at the time, he might have given it to me. I did not then notice the omission. E.S.

American Red Cross Mission wants to be fair and honest with regard to Smolny, and to the Bolsheviks, who gave them a special "Laissez Passer."

(Trotsky's comment): Robins probably told him that the train could go only to Jassy.

I was extremely surprised to hear all this. . . . The next day . . . Major Wardwell

(Trotsky's comment): Probably another member of the Mission.

began to question me as though I was some criminal capable of embarking on all kinds of questionable things. He wanted to find out from me the names and the general description of my assistants and chauffeurs. When I asked him right out what the strange conversation signified, he told me that Col. Robins suspects me of the desire of joining, with the automobiles, troops fighting against the Bolsheviks.

(Trotsky's comment): He, Robins, an official person, suspected that the American Red Cross would be mixed up in a dirty story, and had guessed, by smell or otherwise, what kind of a type Kalpashnikov is. And that's why Kalpashnikov wrote that the Hotel d'Europe, where there are no Bolsheviks, is dangerous.

I announced to him immediately that instead of thirty-five Russian chauffeurs I would send only eight mechanics.

(Trotsky's comment): Thanks to Col. Robins, Kalpashnikov was ready to throw off a number of mechanics from the train.

Your telegrams have probably been delayed somewhere as I received them only a day ahead of the arrival of Major Perkins. Considering the present state of affairs, Major Perkins decided to send you only ten Fords and one Talbot motor-truck, and to make the rest ready for shipment as soon as the horizon would clear up.

Robins in an intensely disagreeable conversation told Perkins that he wasn't going to send his automobiles because this contravenes the desires of Smolny, and attempted to convince him that Col. Verblunsky is on the verge of being arrested by the Bolsheviks and that I myself am in his, Robins' opinion, a suspicious person. He informed him of a few more details referring to me with animosity as if to a dangerous counter-revolutionist.

(Trotsky's comment): Within the last ten days I stated to all representatives of the Allied Embassies that all officers with the Rada or Kaledin are to be recalled, as they are accredited to the Russian Government, and that all who would not comply with this request would be treated like ordinary counter-revolutionists.

I consider Col. Robins as a man who has been playing a false game and acting not only against me, but also against the interests of the American Mission to Rumania in an entirely ungentlemanly and revolting way, and when Perkins asked for the straight evidence against me neither Robins or Wardwell could say anything except "We are suspecting—We must be honest in regard to Smolny."

Formally the Bolsheviks didn't know even about the existence of my automobiles and if they issued to me a certificate for the safety this was only due to a paper from the Embassy representing this.

(Trotsky's comment): Ambassador Francis asked us for a document, and Smolny, in its naïve way, failed to suspect anything.

Through Robins' interference the whole thing can be spoiled. He is a malicious enemy of America, and I have hopes of defeating our enemies. I worked very hard since I came back here and I did not expect such surprises.

(Note by stenographer): Trotsky produces a certificate* signed by Ambassador Francis, dated November 13th, and adds ironically that in an Ambassador's document there can be no disloyalty. He reads the text which certifies that seventy-two ambulances and eight Red Cross cars, purchased by money collected by voluntary contributions in the United States are to be sent to Rumania, and asks for the extension of all courtesies and coöperation to Kalpashnikov.

(Trotsky's comment): I regret to have to announce that all the coöperation and courtesy we could extend to him so far was to put him under arrest.

(Note by stenographer): The next document read by Trotsky was the telegram addressed by Col. Anderson to Kalpashnikov: "Dec. 5, 1917. Provide for the possibility of dispatching all automobiles assembled or non-assembled to Rostov-on-Don with the first available train. Try to convoy them to Rostov personally. . . ." etc.

---

* I insert the text of this purely formal certificate: "United States Embassy, Petrograd, November 13, 1917. This is to certify that seventy-two ambulances and eight light trucks of Ford and Talbot make are destined for the American Red Cross Mission to Rumania. These automobiles were brought from America where they were purchased by funds supplied by voluntary contribution, thanks to the activities of Colonel Andrew Kalpashnikov, who is now in charge of them. I would appreciate it if all those to whom this document may be presented will extend to Colonel Kalpashnikov all courtesies and co-operation, as he is in charge of the transport of these automobiles from Petrograd to Jassy. David R. Francis, American Ambassador."

Trotsky continued in a voice which gradually swelled with indignation:

There is here a contradiction between alleged ambulances, certified by the American Embassy, and the instructions of Anderson to send them to Rostov where Kalpashnikov would receive further instructions how to act! There are here threads uncovered going from Kalpashnikov to Anderson, and probably quite by chance— [with a falsetto voice]—from Anderson to Francis! This Sir Francis will have to break his golden silence which has remained unbroken since the Revolution. He has written that silence is golden and evidently belongs to the diplomatic school of Bismarck, but these documents will force him to unloose his eloquence against the calumnies which are being set up against him. They think that we are so weak that we must swallow all such affronts. For us, revolutionary dignity is of foremost importance. We have taught this to the British Embassy and we shall prove it to all who think they can tread with impunity on our toes. Such things as a donation of two million dollars to Breshko-Breshkovskaya for the propagation of ultra-patriotic literature—as the bribing of a Russian Colonel to help Kaledin—shall not repeat themselves! Let them understand that from the moment that they interfere in our internal strife they cease to be diplomatic representatives—they are private counter-Revolutionist adventurers and the heavy hand of the Revolution will fall upon their heads! [*Applause.*]

The *bourgeoisie* cannot accomplish everything with dollars. We shall either perish or maintain our honor against German and Allied Imperialists. The Russian soldiers will know henceforth that among Kaledin's supporters are men who are hirelings of the United States militarism. The *bourgeois* conscience compels them to line themselves with those who are up in arms against the proletariat! But as long as we live; as long as red revolutionary blood flows in our veins we shall not tolerate that our revolutionary dignity be impugned from any quarter!

The demagogic outburst could be laughed at for theatricalism. Soberly looked at, however, its intent was sinister—the whipping up of mob anger against the Ambassador.

In the speech Trotsky used the larger part of Kalpashnikov's letter, omitting some paragraphs containing uncomplimentary references to Bolsheviks.* The letter was written

* For full text of Colonel Kalpashnikov's letter, see Appendix, pp. 449–451.

in English. Both it and the letter of Major Perkins, which Trotsky did not read into his speech, were translated into Russian and printed officially in the *Izvestia,* from which they were re-translated into English. Except for oddities of literal translation back and forth the versions were regarded as giving substantially the meaning of the writers. The Embassy so accepted them, and Robins used the translations in his report.

Major Perkins wrote his letter to Colonel Anderson on December 17, and after he had quarreled with Colonel Robins, added a long postscript. A portion of the letter was given to description of his trip, personal matters, and to freight lists. The immediately pertinent sections were:

December 17, 1917. Dear Col. Anderson: Since my arrival I have had many conversations of various character and, taking into consideration the public terms of the armistice I decided to alter all plans. It stands to reason that at present it is difficult to travel to Rostov, Kiev or Odessa because of military engagements going on there. On the other hand I think there will be a cessation of hostilities during which much may be accomplished. The train is quite loaded up and was to leave when I arrived.

It is clear that there must be sufficient automobiles for distribution according to the note I left with you, but on the other hand it is clear that you need several automobiles for your personal use. Therefore we are sending you one Talbot motor truck, one Ford, nine light Ford motor-trucks, with two assistants and twelve Russian chauffeurs who can be entirely depended upon. Besides, two soldiers as guards for the train and couriers between Petrograd and yourself. Each automobile will have a reservoir for gasoline, and there also will be a reservoir with a capacity of 210 gallons, 175 kilos of butter and sufficient automobile grease for traveling around the world.

Thus I think you will be well enough equipped and will have a sufficient stock of gasoline to transport your contingent to Kiev. While in Kiev you will find more gasoline should it be necessary to go further (by motor). It seems to me that all your plans will be realized. You will be kept posted as far as possible regarding the delivery of the automobiles, which will probably begin soon after the arrival of the courier who will bring this letter. (Note: The indication here is that the Bolsheviks secured the letter by arresting the courier. E.S.) It would be difficult to guard the automobiles from our friends here, and this no doubt will leave a group (part) which could be transferred if need be, without explanations to any place.

At all events when the soldiers are returning from the front and the whole pot is boiling I do not advise you to travel with the mixed crowd which is down there with you, especially because you are not menaced with any danger in Jassy.

Besides automobiles there are still here two kinds of goods, those purchased by the Rumanians with their own funds, and those purchased with funds loaned them by the Red Cross. This property belongs to the Rumanians and the only question to decide is whether to ship the goods in the name of the Red Cross or whether to give them to the Rumanians to manage themselves as well as they can. I think that all must be finished with glory and everything possible done for the civil population before we leave there. We have now a good reputation there and having a pledge that there will be no profit on the goods furnished by the Red Cross I believe that all will be well.

I am writing in the apartment of the Verblunskys, who are very kind to me.

The last paragraph showed that Major Perkins did not use the office facilities of the Red Cross, giving no chance for a spy there to get either letter or copy; increasing the sign that Trotsky got the letter by arresting the courier.

The letter showed that Colonel Anderson's arrangements aimed at the safe evacuation of his unit from Rumania as soon as a final distribution of supplies to the stricken civilian population should be completed. Where safety lay was the puzzling question.

The break with Robins, ensuing in a few hours' time, was disclosed in the postscript, quoted complete except for a paragraph of personalities.

Postscript Dec. 18: Since I wrote the letter many things have happened and I shall attempt to explain them.

When I came here the armistice terms were known, as stated in the preceding letter and I advised to leave (delay) the matter of transporting the automobiles, for reasons already stated by me. After the armistice was read through by me and I thought it all over a bit, I thought of another plan.

Next day I went again to the Hotel d'Europe and found them in a great excitement, and Robins was very energetic. It appears that they have entered into an agreement with the existing government for the passing of the train, and decided all of a sudden that it is dangerous to transport automobiles even in small numbers. Wardwell stated that Kalpashnikov was quite unable to ship anything and came to him for assistance, and that the train could be only shipped thanks to their personal efforts.

Kalpashnikov says that this is a manifest lie, and that their statement about any assistance is a mere invention. This, in short, is the essence of the matter from both sides. Also, Robins was very much dissatisfied with my proposal not to send the train immediately, but on the next day he assumed the attitude that it would be dangerous to ship any number of automobiles and refused to give any definite explanations. It is evident that they are trying to preserve good relations with the existing government and are afraid that it is the intention of co-workers to seize the entire train as soon as it crosses the frontier and to go with it to known or unknown places. They apparently are trying to interfere with either of the two persons—Col. Kalpashnikov and Verblunsky—because when I stated that they do not intend to accompany the train at present, they (Robins and Wardwell) were almost ready to reconsider everything. They also discussed the number of Russian chauffeurs and suggested to get along with a smaller number. I gave them purposely to understand what I needed them (the chauffeurs) for, and insisted besides that forty-five Rumanians can protect the train against ten Russians.

I insisted further that the selection of the personnel of the train was our business and not theirs. Robins stated that if anything should disappear from this train the chances of getting passes for other trains would be very small. Finally he stated that under no circumstances could the automobiles be shipped with this train. After that he left the room abruptly and discourteously. Wardwell tried to explain but I received the impression that he is to an extent between two fires.

I also learned from him privately that there is an order for the arrest of one of our friends. It seems to me that if one has such information regarding a member of the mission it would be more than courtesy to inform him of it. Evidently they don't want to have anything to do with these men because they consider them as reactionaries. Considering all this precautionary measures were taken, but all this is very disagreeable and I cannot understand such an attitude.

By this time Robins returned and stated that the information came over the telephone that the train cannot leave because of political changes in the South. I regret that I risked telling him it was in vain that he did come out with this earlier which would have prevented his brusque conduct.

(Note: The Russian translator tied this sentence into a knot. The evident meaning is: "I regret that I risked telling him it was too bad that he did not come out with this earlier instead of acting so brusquely." E.S.)

He replied that he was sorry that I am of such an opinion, and that all he has stated regarding shipments to Rumania remains unaltered, and left again. We are trying now to arrange the shipment of the train independently of them and I hope that we shall not stand in need of having to deal with them.

With the assistance of Kalpashnikov who is very efficient I got a ticket at the last minute and think of leaving via Siberia tonight. I sent a telegram to you and cabled home. Francis was very kind and helped me as much as he could. . . .

In conclusion I desire to express my gratitude for the assistance, kindness and hospitality of Col. Verblunsky, without whose assistance the journey to Petrograd would have been difficult.

R. G. P.

Major Perkins left that night. Verblunsky, who was Kalpashnikov's assistant, fled in time. An implication in the letter was that Perkins also warned Kalpashnikov. The statement was made by Major Perkins that Colonel Robins knew on Monday, December 17, that an order was in process for the arrest either of Kalpashnikov or Verblunsky. The arrest of Kalpashnikov was not made until Thursday midnight.

A "Memorandum of Interviews with Major Perkins" was prepared by the staff of the Petrograd Red Cross unit on the very day of the Major's departure. It contained no reference to knowledge or warning of the impending arrests. As a whole it recorded the pull and haul between the Red Cross units in Russia and Rumania. It placed blame for wavering upon Major Perkins, and dealt charily with the final stormy interview between the representatives. The statement was impersonal, ending with the indorsement: "Dec. 18, 1917. To the extent of my knowledge the foregoing statement is correct. (Signed) Raymond Robins, Thomas D. Thacher, Allen Wardwell."

According to the Memorandum, Major Perkins' attitude on his arrival was that no supplies should be sent to Rumania.

Major Perkins stated [the Memorandum set forth] that Rumania was out of the war and that the American Red Cross could render no further relief. Col. Robins asked Major Perkins if he had definite instructions from Col. Anderson to this effect, and Major Perkins replied that he had. Col. Robins then stated that the train would be held.

This train was one that Colonel Robins was preparing to send and was unconnected, at the beginning, with Kalpashnikov's train of motor cars. A later discussion—the same day, Sunday—dealt with the motor cars.

The Memorandum continued:

Major Perkins (then) positively stated that in view of the fact that all fighting had ceased there would be no need whatsoever for any motor cars in Rumania.—It was definitely decided not to ship any motor cars. In the course of the discussion Major Perkins stated that Col. Anderson was planning to leave Rumania and move his entire unit to the British front in Mesopotamia; that the plan discussed before he left Jassy involved the sending of Col. Kalpashnikov's motor cars to Rostov-on-Don, but that in view of the disorders in Rostov he would advise against shipping any motor cars to Rostov at the present time.

The Petrograd men stated their contentment with the motor-car decision but argued for the dispatch of the general supply train, they recorded. Major Perkins, they also entered, asked for a night in which to consider the question.

The climax came Monday, and it was dissension.

The Memorandum proceeded:

The next day, Monday Dec. 17, Major Perkins called on Majors Wardwell and Thacher, stated that he had decided that the supplies purchased by the Rumanian Government should go forward and that he desired that about twelve motor cars should also be transported. A tentative conclusion was reached but upon communication with Col. Robins the latter stated to Majors Wardwell and Thacher that the situation in the Ukraine was most critical, that an open break between the de facto Russian Government and the Ukrainian Rada was quite probable, and that in view of this situation he regarded it as impossible to ship with the other supplies any motor cars whatever. . . .

Major Perkins immediately insisted upon the moving of these cars.—Major Wardwell explained to Major Perkins that in the

judgment of Col. Robins and himself the attempt to transport
motor cars through the Ukraine would seriously endanger the
transportation of other supplies; that the only question was
whether the motor cars should be transported with the Red Cross
train, and that the Russian Mission would not attempt to prevent
Col. Kalpashnikov from transporting his cars to Rumania as
had been originally planned by Col. Anderson, that the Russian
Mission had merely offered to assist Col. Kalpashnikov when it
became evident that Col. Kalpashnikov was unwilling to assume
the responsibility for the transportation of his cars under present
conditions.

Major Perkins nevertheless urged the movement of the motor
cars, and at this point Major Wardwell said the matter ought
to be taken up with Col. Robins, and thereupon asked Col. Robins
to come in.

On Col. Robins' arrival he advised that the situation in the
Ukraine would not permit the shipment of the automobiles.

Major Perkins objected and criticized the conduct of the Russian Mission, charging that it had continuously blocked the
efforts of the Rumanian Mission to render relief in Rumania. He
said that when the Russian Mission had not blocked it had interfered with and delayed their plans and that if it had not been
for the Russian Mission the motor cars would have already been
in Rumania; that he was expressing not only his own opinion but
the opinion of Col. Anderson; that we had treated the Rumanian
Mission as a mere appendage of the Russian Mission.

Col. Robins simply stated to Major Perkins that he was sorry
that was his feeling, that he could not agree with him and that
nevertheless the motor cars could not be moved.

Col. Robins then left the room and within ten minutes thereafter received direct instructions from the Russian de facto Government that the transportation of the entire train was refused
because a definite break between the Ukrainian Rada and the
Russian de facto Government had occurred. Col. Robins immediately advised Major Perkins of these instructions.

On the following day, Tuesday, Dec. 18, Col. Robins had an
interview with representatives of the Russian de facto Government as the result of which he received written instructions authorizing the dispatch of the train of cars containing clothing
and other materials for civilian relief, but that no motor cars
could be transported.*

* For full Memorandum see Appendix, pp. 452–455.

The discrepancies between the accounts of Major Perkins and of the Memorandum were the concern of the American Red Cross organization. The menace from the rivalry and ill-feeling between the two Red Cross groups, however, had no such limitation. It flowed outward against the American Ambassador at Petrograd. It advantaged none save Trotsky.

Refutation of "calumny"—and none knew better than he that calumny it was—Trotsky had called for from Ambassador Francis. Refutation he should have, for instinct told us once we had analyzed the drama of Trotsky's speech that disclaimer by the Ambassador would end the attack upon him. Moreover, Trotsky had shown the way to reply. He had not made a diplomatic onset in the rôle of Foreign Minister but an oratorical and newspaper sally. So he could be answered through the newspapers and no official situation created.

As for the Red Cross it would have to take care of itself. The Ambassador's statement ought to help Kalpashnikov but his fate, unless his life was endangered, also was secondary. For him we sought and gained assurance that he would not be shot. Indefinite imprisonment was likely. Guilt or innocence did not weigh in regard to him. Trotsky had stigmatized him. Trotsky would hold him. Action otherwise would be confession of the trick scheme.

Butler Wright and I aided the Ambassador in preparing his statement and between the embassy staff and mine we made a fairly rapid job of a Russian translation and the rechecking of it. The broadside against the Embassy was published Saturday morning and afternoon. The Ambassador's answer was printed Sunday morning.

The statement opened with a summary of the various allegations made both by Trotsky and the newspapers and continued with denials in category. All the telegrams were printed, showing the annulment of the Rostov order. Letters between Colonel Anderson and the Ambassador were included. There was no milk of conspiracy in the correspondence.

The Ambassador proceeded:

The charge or insinuation that I was aiding Kaledin or any other of the numerous and varied factions in Russia is absolutely without foundation and my statement to this effect should be sufficient to convince all of its truth.

The charge that these motor cars are intended for the use of General Kaledin is preposterous and impugns the good faith of the official representatives of a Government known to be actuated by the most friendly motives toward the Russian people. I trust it will be very difficult to convince the Russian people that America does not feel friendly to Russia and that her people do not cherish an earnest and sincere sympathy for the people of this country in the difficulties that confront them. Many substantial evidences of such sentiment have been given since the Revolution of March last. Only yesterday a delegation called at this Embassy and presented a floral offering as an expression of the effort I am making to have one million pairs of boots and shoes shipped from America for the members of the Railway Union and their wives and children.

As far as the Ambassador was concerned the episode had its conclusion in the following paragraph in the official *Izvestia* of December 26:

Attention of the American Ambassador.

Answering the statement of the American Ambassador, which was printed in No. 249 of the *Izvestia*, we can declare the following:

Our charges are not devoid of "all foundation" and the Ambassador's affirmations do not convince us.

We do not know whether the shipment of automobiles to Rostov instead of Jassy would relieve suffering of humanity.

Telegram 575 does not cancel 569. This is confirmed by the letters of Messrs. Perkins and Kalpashnikov.

Nobody has any doubts that the American people assume a friendly attitude toward the Russian people; but it is not a question of the American people but of actions of some representatives of the American Government, whom we have become accustomed to distinguish from the American people.

A farewell not gracious but harmless! The Ambassador was extricated without breaking his "official golden silence." As a Minister of Government Trotsky had failed to develop his first gain as orator into a success of official contact with the American Government. Yet to save a bigger man than Kalpashnikov, the Ambassador and all foreign diplomats would have to go officially a few weeks later to Lenin himself—and Rumania still would be the cause. Rumania inexorably, under the German pressure against the two conquered nations of Russia and Rumania, was woven into the major events ensuing.

2.

AMBASSADOR FRANCIS waited until 1920 for his final say in regard both to Robins and Kalpashnikov, writing then the Foreword for the latter's book, *A Prisoner of Trotsky's*.[1] The Ambassador wrote:

On or about Dec. 10, 1917, I received a telegram from Col. Anderson at Jassy, sent through the American Minister at the Rumanian capital in the code of the diplomatic service. The telegram was a request from Col. Anderson to advance to Kalpashnikov 100,000 rubles and draw on the Red Cross organization in America for whatever portion of the 100,000 rubles Kalpashnikov requested. There was another telegram addressed to Kalpashnikov in care of the American Embassy, saying he should bring his automobiles to Rostov-on-Don. This telegram, which was also in code, was deciphered at the American Embassy and a paraphrase thereof sent to the headquarters of the American Red Cross Mission to Russia, which were located in the Hotel d'Europe. Kalpashnikov did not call at the American Embassy until several days after said telegram was received; I asked him if he had received the telegram and upon his replying in the negative, ordered that a copy of the paraphrase be given to him. Only two copies of this paraphrase were ever made. The original is in the files of the American Embassy—which have been moved to the State Department at Washington—one copy was delivered to the American Red Cross Mission to Russia, of which Raymond Robins was at that time the chief, and the other copy was given to Kalpashnikov.

On the morning of Dec. 20, 1917, Kalpashnikov was brought to the American Embassy by the Naval Attaché, Captain Crosley. He told me he had loaded his automobiles on a special train and had a permit from the Soviet Government to transport them through to Jassy, Col. Anderson having changed his instructions from Rostov-on-Don to Jassy, and that he would not require any money. After giving Kalpashnikov a letter stating that he was in charge of motor ambulances for the use of the American Red Cross Mission to Rumania, I bade him good-by, cautioning him, however, not to attempt to move his automobiles and ambulances out of Petrograd without a permit from the Soviet Government,

[1] *A Prisoner of Trotsky's* (New York: Doubleday, Page & Company, 1920).

which he assured me he had secured. I met him the same afternoon at a tea in the apartment of Mrs. Crosley, wife of the Naval Attaché. He told me he would start his special train containing all of the ambulances loaded thereon for Jassy the next morning at eight o'clock.

The next morning about ten o'clock Raymond Robins came to the American Embassy and informed me that Kalpashnikov was imprisoned in the St. Peter and St. Paul Fortress, and that his apartment had been searched. I asked Robins why Kalpashnikov had been arrested. He replied he did not know. Whereupon I requested him to go to the Smolny Institute, headquarters of the Soviet Government, and demand his release. Robins, who was *persona grata* with the Soviet Government, promised me to do so. He returned to the Embassy the same afternoon or the following morning and informed me that Trotsky had unearthed a plot showing Kalpashnikov's connection with Kaledin who was commanding the forces in south Russia opposed to the Soviet Government. The Petrograd papers on the next or the second morning contained an account of Trotsky's address at a meeting the evening before for which word had been sent out claiming Trotsky would expose a plot against the Soviet Government in which the American Ambassador was the main figure.

Trotsky read in this speech an exact copy of the paraphrase of the Kalpashnikov telegram from Anderson, of which I had given Kalpashnikov a copy, and also my letter commending Kalpashnikov, and claimed these to be evidence that the American Ambassador was organizing a reactionary movement for the overthrow of the Soviet Government. He concluded this speech by saying: "At last the American Ambassador must break his 'golden silence.' In fact he is not an ambassador but an adventurer and the heavy hand of the revolution must deal with him."

I made a statement setting forth the above narrated facts. It was published in the Petrograd papers the following day.

I remained in Petrograd more than two months after this occurrence, and then went to Vologda, where I remained five or six months. Before leaving Petrograd I requested Robins time and again to secure the release of Kalpashnikov and his invariable reply was to the effect that he was doing all he could to effect his release. Robins was recalled about May 15, a few days before the untimely death of Consul-General Madden Summers, whose obsequies I journeyed from Vologda to Moscow to attend.

The first week of the following month which was June, I visited Petrograd and while there Kalpashnikov, who had been released, called upon me. He was greatly changed in appearance and told me that his five months' imprisonment, from which he had been released the week before, if I remember aright—had undermined his constitution and afflicted him with rheumatism. He, furthermore, in answer to my questions, told me that he had never been arraigned for trial, that the damp cells of St. Peter and St. Paul Fortress had not only jeopardized his life and destroyed his health but were so trying that if he had not thought it cowardly he would have made away with himself.

I recalled the telegram sent in the diplomatic code in care of the American Embassy and told him that he should have destroyed his paraphrase of this telegram, because the finding of it in his apartment not only was the cause of his arrest and imprisonment, but had given me a great deal of trouble, as Trotsky had read it word for word, had endeavored to incite his auditors against me, and had threatened me with the counter revolution commission.

Whereupon Kalpashnikov said that when he returned to his apartment with his copy of Col. Anderson's message, he had placed it in a secret compartment of his desk where he had found it since his release. I was very much astounded at this statement, and had him repeat it.

I conclude, therefore, that if Kalpashnikov was not mistaken, Robins or one of his attachés must have given to Trotsky the verbatim copy which he read in the speech charging the American Ambassador with being in a plot to overthrow the Soviet Government.

I have made diligent inquiry from every source at my command concerning Kalpashnikov and cheerfully testify to his character.—I have written this foreword through a desire to do all in my power to aid a patriotic and intelligent Russian, who has served his country well, and is not despairing of his people eventually ridding Russia of Bolshevism, which is not only a disgrace to any country it dominates but is antagonistic to all organized government everywhere and an enemy to society itself.

And he signed his name: "David R. Francis."

CHAPTER XI

December 23—December 29, 1917. The Turbulent Christmas Week. Scrutiny of a Russian "Victory." War Film and Peace Title.

1.

THE Red Cross train to Rumania, without motor ambulances, did not move in accord with the optimistic report of its sponsor. The assertion of permit given on December 18 was accurate, though not enduring. Trotsky had no intention of letting any train move before his show was over. The train was stalled throughout the week.

On Sunday midnight, too, the twenty-third, came a visitation that threatened cancellation of the permit. Blagonravov, the martial law Commissar of Petrograd, brought his guards to Red Cross headquarters and made the announcement that the train was officially "arrested." I rarely entered this office, which was on an upper floor, but was there this evening, having had word that new excitement was due. During the day I had visited, with Robins, the huge warehouses where the Rumanian supplies were stored. No wonder the Rumanians wanted them. There was outfitting there for an army or for a civilian multitude. How much of the contents of the depots ever reached Rumania I do not know. Warehouses, however, were not Blagonravov's concern for the night.

Kalpashnikov, who was taken into custody by Blagonravov personally, wrote that his caller arrived in the splendor of a seal overcoat. No such sartorial Blagonravov stalked in upon us, but a person wearing the long, rough ulster of a private soldier. The only difference between him and his pair of guards was that they carried rifles and he did not. In light of what Uritsky told Kalpashnikov we may have been in a danger we did not suspect, though at the time we thought of the scene as farcical, as I believe it was. Robins was disturbed at the prospect of losing the train, a shock he had not anticipated. Yet he parleyed shrewdly for a day's continuation of the state of delay until he could make another appeal to Trotsky. The matter, as usual, was not quite in the open, Blagonravov voicing pretexts about doubtful persons among the train guards, civil war perils, and what not.

Every person in the room—and the group included either Wardwell or Thacher or both, Robins, and Gumberg—was accustomed to the jibing style of Bolshevik conversational encounter, and soon the guards were the only solemn-faced persons present. Blagonravov, who could be evil in manner—I saw him so at the Constituent Assembly—could also act the dry satirist, and with relish. He enjoyed the opportunity to confront American officials, and said so, without realizing that the remark was admission of feeling of inferiority. He was jovially invited to search the train—that probably had been ten times done—to search the offices, to do anything except scatter the assembled train. He shrugged his shoulders, laughed, accepted a cigarette, smoked it, and went away in much better humor than he came. He had not lifted the interdict but had agreed to take no further steps until he received new orders.

The command he got from Trotsky the next day, after Robins went to Smolny again, was to lift the ban against the train, which pulled out Christmas Eve—and did get through to Jassy.

Earlier on the Sunday evening of Blagonravov's call I met, of intent, a German who had ensconced himself at Smolny. The occasion was dinner with Roger Simmons, an expert of the American Forestry service, who in the kinder days of the Kerensky *régime* had been invited to make a survey of Siberian forestry resources. He was marking time now in Petrograd. As a semiofficial his presence had not passed without attention and I was not surprised when he told me he was making the acquaintance of a person who had entrée at Smolny. I suggested that he play along politely to see what happened. So when he asked me to dine with him and a German known to him as Professor Kunz, I accepted.

The trio of us had an agreeable evening, the professor sparring for information, and in turn yielding a little. When I chanced to mention New Jersey as my home, he said he had lived formerly in Plainfield. Assuming that I considered him a fellow American, I asked him flatly what he, an American citizen, was doing among the Bolsheviks at Smolny. He muttered something about not having taken out his second papers, and said he was an "economist" studying the "Russian experiment," and that the Smolny authorities were kind enough to give him every facility for research. That was my first hearing of the phrase "Russian experiment," used then as now as an entering wedge of formula to gain a tolerant hearing for Bolshevik presentment. Professor Kunz was a thickset man in his fifties, bearded, melancholy. I fancy he deemed his inquiry in our direction sterile, for he did not seek our company again.

The first news cable dispatches from the Committee on Public Information came through on December 24, marking the installation of an automatic incoming news service. One of the first paragraphs to reach print dealt with the severe treatment of Russian prisoners in Germany, the report of the neutral Spanish Embassy. In addition to giving the cable service to the Petrograd News Agency for distribution to the Press, the American News Bureau transmitted copies, for their daily information, to the Embassy, the Military Mission, and the Consulate. It already was supplying all but the Red Cross, which had its own translating force, with daily summaries of the contents of the Russian press. The news organization was now well housed at 4 Gorokhovaya, a central location. I bought the equipment of a departing English business concern, down to the blotters on the desk and the force was in a day after the purchase, greatly to its happiness, as it had been working in cramped quarters.

Creel sent me a cable on December 21, received three days later:

What about sending Russians from here to speak and write? Any number fine men eager to go at own expense representing every class.

I could imagine of what such an infusion desiring safe-conduct through the war zones would largely consist, and I cabled negatively. Anti-Bolsheviks would be risking their lives; of the others there were too many already in Russia.

Some time later, in middle January, Creel cabled again, on a variant of the idea of speakers:

Gompers has a proposition to send thirty American Labor Leaders to Russia with similar delegations from France and England. Cable your opinion. Also great pressure to send Russians from here.

Then I cabled:

Best thing Gompers can do is to arrange series trade conventions to endorse Wilson Peace Terms and cable us resolution after resolution. Labor deputation useless. American labor leaders regarded by Bolsheviks as exponents capitalistic system and against proletariat. American aims would be lost in haze of controversy. Too many Russian talkers here now. Do not add more.

Neither delegations nor Russians were sent.

Christmas was a Russian day just like any other, for the Russian Christmas was under the old calendar, thirteen days later. Americans, however, insisted on celebration. The Ambassador kept open house. I had a little tree placed on a table in my rooms, got together a collection of Russian toys—balls within balls, boxes within boxes, and the like, all gayly colored—and gave a tea in my rooms, and in the evening Stephens of the National City Bank was host at the crowning festivity—a dinner and dance in his apartment adjacent to the bank, the food tables in the big reception room of the bank itself.

Each one, provided with platter, cutlery, and napkin, was a self-server. There were too many present to be seated at table—nearly a hundred, every American in Petrograd, and none to be there more than a few weeks longer. Nearly half of those present were women, the wives of *attachés* from the Embassy and of the few civilians left, a scattering of unmarried women from the different households, and a few adventurous travelers not yet gone. If the style of their evening wear was six months behind New York, who could tell?

And such food—white bread, cake, and pie! We hadn't tasted the like of it for weeks. The Embassy had sent the bank manager a portion of its precious white flour and sugar as its contribution to the *fête*. Everyone made a business of eating. The Ambassador came and as a forager was the equal of any. We acclaimed the smiling Stephens as a true patriot. In the light of the gay scene the cheerless outer background seemed far away. Yet bleak Petrograd forced its way in before the evening was over.

Of the incident, in a later letter, I wrote, after describing the party:

As usual the Bolsheviks furnished the unusual in the way of excitement. They descended upon the festival at one o'clock in the morning, and women hurriedly hid their jewels in their bosoms. It was an accident, however, and not a raid. A youngster went to bring his best girl to the party and stumbled into the wrong apartment, disturbing a nest of Red Guards. They thought he was a counter-revolutionist, arrested him and took him to Smolny. There, some hours later, they were told to take him to the bank. A little explanation in Russian and a considerable quantity of food satisfied them and they turned him loose. I am sorry to say that I had gone back to the hotel earlier and missed the episode. The hotel itself is pulled for some conspirator or other every few nights, but that is all in a day's routine. When the Red Guards hold the stairway we go up the elevator.

2.

IN the concentration of activities around the Embassy during the period Trotsky was baiting the Ambassador, the beginning of the Peace Conference at Brest-Litovsk was, for several days, almost unnoticed.

The official day for the first sitting was December 22, and the early proceedings were cautious and restrained while the delegations felt each other out. Trotsky did not go to Brest-Litovsk, the delegation being headed nominally by Kamenev, his brother-in-law. Karakhan remained as secretary. Adolph Ioffe divided headship with Kamenev. Professor Pokrovsky also was a member of the delegation. Its powers were limited, its rôle for the time being to be a voice to speak for Lenin and Trotsky and an ear to hear for them.

The voice spoke the Russian proposals and recess was allowed for reply. What the ear heard then was pleasant enough until it came under analysis. The Central Powers agreed readily, in principle, to conduct the negotiations on the basis of Russian terms, to "accede," as Count Czernin of Austria put it at the second session, the night of December 25, "to the view point of the Russian delegation, which is condemning the continuation of the war for the sake of pure conquests. The delegations of the quadruple alliance are prepared to immediately conclude general peace without forcible annexations and without contributions."

Czernin apparently was chosen as spokesman because his telegram of the same tenor prior to the armistice had been praised by Trotsky and Lenin, and because Germany desired to have Austria at the forefront of the negotiations. Prince Leopold of Bavaria had opened the conference with an address of greeting. Von Kuhlman, the German Secretary of State for Foreign Affairs, had been made presiding officer. General Hoffman was the German military adviser.

Czernin went on to particularize:

Taking these principles for a basis:

1. It is not the intention of the quadruple alliance to annex forcibly the territories occupied during the war.

2. It is not the intention of the quadruple alliance to deprive of political independence the nations which have lost their independence during the war.

3. The question of national groups having no political independence cannot in the opinion of the quadruple alliance be solved internationally. The question must be decided by each state in conjunction with its nationalities.

4. Likewise the safe guarding of the rights of minorities constitutes an essential part of the right of self-determination.

5. The quadruple alliance has emphasized repeatedly the possibility not only of the restitution of war expenditures but of the restitution of the losses caused by the war. In accordance with this understanding each of the belligerent nations would be reimbursed for the expenditures made for its subjects who have become prisoners of war and for losses caused in its own territory by civilian subjects of the enemy in violation of international law. The creation of a special fund proposed by the Russian Government for these purposes could be discussed only in the contingency that the other belligerent nations become parties to the negotiations within a stated time.

6. Of the four allied powers only Germany is the possessor of colonies. On behalf of the German delegation it can be stated, in agreement with the Russian proposals: The return of the German colonial possessions seized during the war constitutes an essential part of the German demands, which Germany could not

renounce under any circumstances. Taking into consideration the nature of the German colonial possessions the realization of the right of self-determination in the forms proposed by the Russian delegation appears at the present time practically impossible.

And he added, softly:

The anticipations of the Russian delegation could be realized only if all nations in a state of belligerency, without exceptions and reservations, would within an adequate length of time undertake in the strictest sense to live up to terms equal for all nations. Naturally the powers of the quadruple alliance, now negotiating with Russia, could not bind themselves by such terms in a one-sided way, having no guarantee that the Allies of Russia will recognize and carry out these terms honestly and without reservations in regard to the quadruple alliance.

It is to be presumed that Czernin sat down smiling. This account of the statement of the terms of the Central Powers was the one made officially at Petrograd and is used because on the basis of it the Bolsheviks claimed a diplomatic victory—for a few days. In its issue of December 27 the *Pravda* carried an editorial headed "Our Victory."

The Central Powers had answered categorically these proposals of the Bolsheviks:

1. No forcible incorporations of territories occupied during the war to be tolerated. The armies occupying these territories to be withdrawn from them in the shortest space of time.

2. The political independence of those nationalities deprived of this independence during the war to be restored.

3. The national groups which had no political independence are to receive the guarantee of solving freely through a referendum the question of their allegiance to any state or of their political independence.

4. As regards territories inhabited by several nationalities, the rights of the minorities are to be safeguarded by a special law guaranteeing them cultural-national independence, and, if possible, administrative autonomy.

5. None of the belligerent countries is bound to pay another belligerent contributions. As regards the so-called military expenditures the contributions already levied are to be returned. As far as the restitution of losses sustained by private persons

through the war, it is to be made from a special fund created by proportionate payments from all belligerent countries.

6. Colonial questions to be decided in compliance with principles set forth in Clauses 1, 2, 3 and 4. Supplementary to these clauses the Russian delegation proposes that the parties represented at the Conference recognize that any indirect restrictions upon the freedom of weaker nations, such as economic boycott, economic subjugation of one country by another through an imposed commercial treaty, separate Customs' agreements restricting the freedom of commerce of another country, or maritime blockade which does not serve immediate military purpose, must be repudiated.

Not even Bolshevik casuistry could long hide from its own or the general public the realistic meaning of the German-Austrian reply.

Russia had been offered nothing—unless all belligerents joined in the Peace Conference. Germany would not withdraw its troops from Russian territory—unless Germany got back colonies held not by Russia but by England and France. Germany would not consider granting self-determination to its colonies in any case and would not grant self-determination elsewhere before it had the colonies back.

Germany would collect an indemnity from Russia under the guise of prisoner cost and of damages for sabotage and for incited strikes and revolutionary efforts.

And of terms for a separate peace with Russia not an inkling!

Politely hiding a Gargantuan mirth, Germans and Austrians had offered the Russians a stone instead of bread. How Lenin must have writhed in his Smolny lair to be treated as negligible when he had come to a seat of power! To see, too, that very seat threatened!

Nor could the stone be cast back. The Bolsheviks themselves had masked their bid for separate peace under an appeal for an armistice for all belligerents, a peace conference where all belligerents should sit. Now they were told to go get the other belligerents in or accept the status of a conquered nation.

Yet it is my opinion that the Bolsheviks were not so much surprised at the enunciation of the terms as by the later dawning knowledge that the Germans meant them. They were prepared for one more call for a peace conference to include all fronts, and they hoped for German mildness toward them when the issue resolved itself to a separate peace. Lenin and Trotsky trusted that Russia in large part would be left to them. Moreover, I think they would have had a chance if they had been able to show control of Russia.

Occurrences between the first peace session at Brest-Litovsk, December 22, and the second, December 25, had served to harden the German attitude. The representative of the Ukrainian Rada suddenly withdrew from the Conference in the interval, and after his departure the Rada sent a telegram refusing to recognize a treaty in which the Ukraine would be unrepresented. The Rada, winning in the field in the military conflict with the Bolsheviks, and not lacking German encouragement, had decided to play its own hand. How the action embarrassed and weakened the Bolsheviks was disclosed ultimately in the *Izvestia* of January 1, in an analysis credited to Pavlovich, a member of the peace delegation. In his view:

The Germans do not want to be confronted with a non-recognition of their peace-treaty by any portion of Russia. They apparently are not prepared to make serious concessions without knowing what they have to expect from the Don and the Ukraine. The degree of their readiness to make concessions stood in direct relation to the news they were receiving from Russia. In the progress of the Brest negotiations one can mark two periods: prior and subsequent to the receipt of a telegram from the Ukrainian Rada announcing its refusal to recognize any treaty in which it did not participate. The telegram was a complete surprise to the Russian delegation as Nicholas Lubinsky, a representative of the Rada, had been participating in the negotiations in an advisory capacity. The day before the receipt of the telegram Lubinsky left. The tone of the representatives of the Central Powers changed sharply after the telegram came.

The excuse of time for further invitation to England, France, and the United States to join the Peace Conference, was acceptable to both sides as grounds for adjournment. In Petrograd, Trotsky announced deferment of the Conference until January 8. The Germans insisted later that the ten-day interval expired January 4, and made some point of continued

Russian delay. Trotsky held to the assertion of Russian success at Brest-Litovsk until New Year's Day.

He issued, in the interval, a proclamation addressed "to the peoples and governments of the Allied countries," in which besides reiterating much he had said in connection with the armistice, he stated:

Peace negotiations, now being conducted at Brest-Litovsk between the delegation of the Russian Republic and the delegations of the Central Powers have been adjourned until December 26/ January 8 to give the Allies the last opportunity to take part in the further negotiations, and in this manner safeguard themselves against the consequences of a separate peace between Russia and the enemy countries.—Ten days separate us from the renewal of the peace negotiations. Russia does not bind herself in these negotiations to the consent of the Allied Governments. If they continue to sabotage the cause of general peace, the Russian delegation in any case will continue the negotiations. A separate peace signed by Russia would no doubt be a hard blow to the Allied countries; but to foresee the inevitable results of a separate peace is the task not only of Russia but of all the Allied countries.— Addressing the governments with this last opportunity to participate in the peace negotiations we at the same time promise our complete support to the laboring classes of any country which will rise against their national imperialists.

To aid him in his program of world solicitation he besought Germany to transfer the sessions of the Peace Conference from Brest-Litovsk to Stockholm, and got a short refusal. Germany was better content with Brest-Litovsk on Russian territory. In a campaign for general peace it had lost whatever interest it ever had had, for Germany foresaw a victor's peace over the Allies consequent on a conqueror's peace over Russia. The business to which Germany addressed itself in the ten days was the grooming of the Rada for the rôle of seeking its own separate peace when the Conference should reconvene.

The last paragraph in Trotsky's proclamation may be connected not unreasonably with the decree of December 26, setting aside 2,000,000 rubles for revolutionary propaganda abroad, and with the seizure of the banks and of the contents of private safety-deposit boxes on December 27.

The text of the decree allotting funds to be devoted to disturbances in Allied and neutral countries follows:

The Soviet Government, standing on the principles of the international solidarity of the proletariat and fraternity of the working peoples of all countries; believing that the struggle against war and imperialism can be successful only on an international scale, the Council of People's Commissars deems it necessary to come with all accessible means to the assistance of the left international wing of the labor movement of all countries, quite independent of whether these countries are in a state of belligerency against or in alliance with Russia, or whether they preserve neutrality. For the advancement of these purposes the Council of People's Commissars resolves to assign Rubles 2,000,000 to the needs of the international revolutionary movement, to be placed at the disposal of the foreign representatives of the Commissariat for Foreign Affairs. President of the C.P.C. Vl. Ulianov (Lenin). People's Commissar for Foreign Affairs, L. Trotsky.

For this sort of incendiary enterprise real and not fiat money was necessary, and in the name of nationalization Lenin and Trotsky stripped not only bank vaults but the safety-deposit boxes of individuals. The wholesale raid was without warning and was timed to an hour. Squads of soldiers and sailors marched into every bank at eleven o'clock on Thursday morning. Bank directors as a rule were arrested, although the custody was nominal where they were obedient, as their clerical services were required. Public orders were issued for the owners of deposit boxes to present themselves with their keys within three days and open the boxes. When they came a commissar was judge of what of the contents they could retain. When they did not appear the boxes were opened—with master keys or with chisels. The funds of the banks largely were transferred to the State Bank.

The report of the confiscation, made to the Executive Committee of the Council of Commissars by Sokolnikov, the Commissar charged with its execution, showed the opportunistic nature of the proceeding.

"We cannot pass at once," he said, "a decree thoroughly defining the principles of the merger of the private banks with the State Bank into a single Bank of the Russian Republic.

We can give only a general line of the measures to be taken."

The first of these, he continued, related to

the new millionaires, who during the war have become rich on speculations. They did not dare to deposit their gains in current accounts and have protected them through steel safes, watched over by hired bank guards. There we shall find gold in coins and bullion. The owner of the safe will have to be present when it is opened, and his failure to appear will signify that the contents of the safe are too compromising. The contents of the safes of those who prefer to stay away will become national property.

It was implied that where individual bank accounts were in order they would be transferred to the State Bank and could be checked against, subject to government countersigning of each check.

Lenin rose in the same committee meeting, December 28, to state bluntly that one of the purposes of nationalizing the banks at the moment chosen was "to stop the criminal activities against us."

The Bolsheviks had indeed not only gained gold for their own world propaganda, but they believed they had taken the gold which their adversaries in Russia intended to use against them. Their maxim was: "Without money, an enemy is helpless."

In this week, too, Baron Keyserling and Count Mirbach settled themselves in Petrograd with an extensive German Mission to begin the economic conferences which were as important as the peace sessions themselves, the aims being the resumption of trade relations and a commercial treaty. It is significant that the Petrograd conclave was not interrupted by the various rifts at Brest-Litovsk until the armistice was denounced in February, and that following the final Russian surrender in March, Count Mirbach became the first German Ambassador to the Soviets. While Trotsky and General Hoffman were at Brest, Mirbach and Lenin were at Petrograd.

Count Mirbach came to the Hotel d'Europe and took a suite of rooms a few doors from mine, opening on the same corridor. The German delegation sat at the Grand Hotel, where most of its members were housed.

The bank situation, when it became acute, concerned me

more than either arriving Germans or the status of the Peace Conference. I had not attempted to draw against my account since it had been placed in the State Bank, the cash supply obtained from the National City Bank having been sufficient. Had I known of the impending bank maneuver, I would have moved earlier, for I was due in a few days more to make considerable payments to the printing plant. With the closure a fact, I dared not let time pass without securing a recognized status.

The instruments, however, were within reach. I got the Committee at the government printing plant to make not only a requisition on me for the current amount due but to include in it a liberal estimate for a future period. The manager, who was Committee Chairman, quickly got my point that I did not want to dicker with the bank every week. Then armed with this document and with a formally drawn estimate of a quota necessary for my own organization, I sought out Menzhinsky, the Minister of Finance, and asked for an order on the State Bank to cash my check. The situation itself was eloquent, for what I had was the request of one institution of the Government— the printing plant—upon the government Treasury for pay roll and maintenance needs. The drawing of the papers took one day. Arrangements for an interview with Menzhinsky occupied Friday morning, but he gave his assent to the plan as soon as he understood, and was willing to be jocular at the notion that the American Government was paying the wages of Soviet government printers. Then he had to draw papers and put impressive stamps on them, and I spent most of the afternoon in his offices. He had what might be described as "downtown" offices, neat and businesslike, in comparison to the haphazard array at Smolny.

At the bank next day Piatakov, after a glance at my sheaf of papers courteously passed me on to the countingroom, where clerks quite literally were counting out money, or the bills that were called money, each using the abacus as an adding machine, and quite frequently chanting the sums as they flipped the perforated wooden disks up and down the wires. I tried without any luck at all to understand their method of using the abacus. The place itself was more like a warehouse than a bank, though, when my turn came, I took my stand in front of a cashier's window. I bore away a portfolio filled with bills of the old issue, having stipulated that I was to receive neither Kerensky notes nor those of the new printing. All were paper, with the same reserve or lack of it behind them, but I had found that the older issues had more buying power and were taken eagerly by those who could get them. In the end, to whoever hoarded them, they became under inflation as trifling in value as their successors. With the amount of cash about me I did not feel at ease until I had the portfolio stowed in the steel chest of Thacher, the Red Cross treasurer.

3.

A PLEASANT interlude of the week, Friday night, was the public presentation of an American film which we had titled, *All for Peace*. Of the extensive film program I had hoped to employ this was to be the sole picture, two shipments of films being overtaken by disaster *en route* to me. Machinery for their distribution was ready, had they arrived.

A few days after my arrival in Russia, a quiet young man reported to me. He was Guy Croswell Smith, who, at the request of the State Department, had brought over two assembled pictures and a miscellaneous collection of reels in the early autumn. One picture had been shown at Moscow and was ready for performance at Petrograd when the Bolshevik Revolution came. His operations were stopped by Bolshevik order, and the picture prints in the theater lost. Yet he was ready to make a new attempt.

Attaching him to my staff, I set him hunting for office quarters capable of use as a film exchange, and in a few days he found space in a building on the Kazansky Square, by the Cathedral. He fitted it out. Thereafter we had a morning ritual. He would come into my room after breakfast, report what he had done the day before—carpenter's shelving up, arrangement made for Moscow handling, or wiring in, as case might be—and ask me sadly if I had news of the film. In time I did get news—bad news. Hart of the Y.M.C.A. was to have convoyed a shipment. He did not get beyond Sweden. Herman Bernstein, newspaper man, was to have brought a quota. He got into Petrograd in March, after the Brest-Litovsk Peace, leaving the films behind the barrier of Red and White war in

Finland. In the spring Smith and I found the bulk of the two lots in Stockholm. Why the shipments were not turned over to government couriers at London, or even Stockholm as I several times requested, I never learned. Until February 1, they could have been brought in thus.

Even in December, however, I had begun to doubt whether outside support of any kind ever would come. So I asked Smith to consider what could be done by extemporization. He had in his limited collection a set of films which we called the "Uncle Sam Immigrant" picture. The theme of it was a youngster's climb up the ladder in a free country, with the included text that the price of liberty was the willingness to defend it. The immigrant boy and the native son marched away together when America went to war. The film was replete with American scenes, among them the tall buildings of New York. The Statue of Liberty was not overlooked. A news picture of the summer procession at Washington, with President Wilson leading the recruits, had, with proper musical setting, possibilities as a curtain raiser. I told Smith to get up the best show he could, and wondered how far the Bolsheviks would let us go.

The title we wanted was *All for Peace through War*. This proved to be a step too far, as I determined by cautious procedure. In a formal way I never asked anything of Smolny in reference to the film, going ahead as if interference was not to be anticipated, leasing a theater and beginning to prepare promotional matter. In the progress of the latter, however, I got a friendly hint that the war note was attracting attention in unfavorable quarters. A printer, it seemed, thought he had best make a report to committee superiors about a rough proof he had seen. Another printer thought he had best tell me. Ostentatiously I killed the old proof and substituted new copy—*All for Peace*. It was peace campaign week anyway, and the new title was short, brisk, and a curiosity rouser.

Smith, who was so shy and soft spoken that he gave no appearance of the showman's genius within him, did a promotion job that would have gotten him applause on Broadway. He practiced in Petrograd what New York did not adopt generally until after the war—the introductory run of a film at a single theater in the country's metropolis. In fact, does not New York itself owe the idea to the method by which the Committee on Public Information featured its war films in the city? Have the music and the scenic settings "Roxy" gave those films been forgotten? And when did the popularity of "Roxy" begin?

The Nevsky was Smith's Broadway and he posted it with advertising, while the exterior of the theater was gay with bunting and American flags. A big orchestra was secured to give an operatic effect, and the leader was supplied with the score of "The Star Spangled Banner" for overture. The Ambassador came and sat in a box. The embassy staff came, and General Judson and the officers of the Military Mission in uniform. Admission was set at a nominal price, with liberal arrangements for request tickets. The presentation was a popular success. We ran the film a fortnight at the theater and then sent copies traveling. In spite of chaos it reached far places and still was heard from the next summer.

The New York section of the Smolny crowd—which was a numerous section—came in numbers to see the home scenes in the film. It always seemed to me that those who had experienced America while young never were quite able to submerge themselves in Bolshevism, whatever their effort. And how glad I was to have them in Smolny! Their accented English was heard in every corridor. I used to say that I needed an interpreter less in Smolny than in any building in Petrograd.

Arthur Ransome, English labor paper correspondent, called on me the midnight after I left the film performance and we amused ourselves by guessing at what might happen in the next day or so. Both of us were puzzled by inactivity at Brest-Litovsk since the first interchange of communications, and the absence of offer of terms of separate peace to Russia. Ransome had a catch phrase, "Watch Trotsky!" When he used it I gave ear for he had unusual channels of information. He used it now, although claiming to have no reason better than the feelings in his bones.

Ransome himself was one of the odd personages clustered in Petrograd. An Englishman of the six-footer, lounging sort, red-mustached and pipe-smoking, he was rather unctuously a radical. He knew Russia well, speaking the language after a fashion of his own, gutturals elided, and claiming admiration for the roughness and dirt of Russian villages, scene of his summer-time rovings. He was noted locally for an encounter with the British Ambassador, Sir George Buchanan, in which the Ambassador, glimpsing him in passing had turned and shouted, "I hope to live to see you hanged!" receiving in answer the quip, "Your head first, Sir George!"

"I meant his official head," was Ransome's grinning explanation to me one night. "It will be falling soon."

Sir George Buchanan, owing to ill health, did resign some time after his departure from Russia. He left Petrograd the first week in January.

For a while I thought Ransome was being camouflaged as a revolutionist and very likely was an operative of the British Intelligence service. When British officials were in a tight place a few weeks later over the Bolshevik demand for right of passage of their spokesmen to England, I noticed that he gave his countrymen aid. The Red tinge to him, however, may have been real, or romantic. In his writings he continued to take the rôle of a Bolshevik apologist. He had friends in many places in Smolny, and even then was attentive to Trotsky's young secretary, Eugenia Petrovna Sholopina, whom we called "The Big Girl," because she was a big girl. A cable the following summer told of their marriage, and by now they should be a comfortable *bourgeois* pair, Bolshevism exciting only as a romantic memory.

In spite of Ransome's omen Saturday passed without further outburst from Trotsky than his appeal and threat to the Allies. There was no surprise in that.

CHAPTER XII

*December 29, 1917—January 1, 1918. Peace Parade and
War Clamor. Trotsky Maneuvers for New Position.*

1.

IN his public proclamation for the ears of the Allies, Trotsky had urged the proletarians of all countries to demand
of their Governments that they sue for peace. So what
more fitting than a demonstration by the Petrograd working
populace that it desired the Bolshevik rulers to proceed with
their own peace, thus overawing internal opposition. Peace
Parade day was Sunday, December 30, and was prepared for
elaborately. Yet even as the marchers trod the streets, their
leaders were being dealt such a blow of punitive peace terms
by Germany that the peace cry of Sunday was followed by war
clamor of Monday. This was the surprise for us, an agreeable
one. The extent of Trotsky's surprise was a matter to be considered in relation to circumstances.

First in order, the parade.

Preparations for it were made noisily, with orders given
for every Bolshevik supporter to be in the line of march. Inti-
mations were given that "counter-revolutionaries could be expected to try to break up the procession" and warnings were
added that if they did try they would receive the "justice due
to all enemies of the people." As Petrograd was then under
martial law, held by an army and patrolled by Red Guards, the
idea of interference with the parade was comical. The incitement, however, was guaranty that the marchers would be many
and their spirits high.

We looked forward to a lively day and arranged accordingly. The messenger who went to Trotsky's office to get right-
of-way passes brought back word that Eugenia Petrovna
Sholopina wanted to see the parade without getting her feet
wet. Anyone knowing her was bound to sympathize with her,
for her tiny feet were the big girl's pride. She encased them in
high-heeled and expensive shoes and refused to conceal them
under the usual slip-on goloshes. Others might walk the ice
but where Eugenia Petrovna went, she rode. An invitation

went to her to do her riding this day under an American flag, and she accepted, sending back word that she would be an interpreter. This was humor, for she spoke only a few words of English. Her presence in the car, however, insured us of favors an interpreter could not have won with words. Alexis, the chauffeur, when he saw her enter the motor, straightened up with an air which said that with her in the car, he would drive through Red Guards as if he had Trotsky and Lenin behind him. And he did.

As other guests in the car I took "A.P." Smith of the Associated Press, Stephens, the bank manager, and a real interpreter. In letter, a few days later, I wrote of the parade, its scene, sequel, and meaning:

The Peace Parade was held Sunday, December 30, just one day before Germany's action in regard to Lithuania and Courland spoiled that particular expectation of immediate peace. One hundred thousand workers, by conservative estimate, marched in that parade. Vehicles were ordered off the streets. The cars did not run. The procession contained all sorts of workers and fighters, from the women who sweep the streets to the Cossacks who have been known to sweep them also—with bullets.

Mostly they marched in silence but when they passed the graves of the martyrs of the First Revolution—on Mars Field—they all sang the burial hymn. They carried thousands of red banners, inscribed with mottoes, as a rule lauding the Soviets, the People's Rule, the Workers, etc., together with many abusing the *bourgeoisie*. One said, "No Separate Peace with Kaiser Wilhelm—No Alliance with Capitalistic Nations." The universal slap in the face. It was the only German reference on a banner.

Our bold chauffeur, proud of a potent pass, broke through that parade four times. Once he halted a regiment while he crossed. Another time he drove into a crowd of thousands of onlookers at the densest point on the Nevsky. The crowd closed in. The parade marshals cursed. But it was easier to clear a way ahead than backward. So the way was cleared. Twice we paralleled the whole parade in the five hours of its passage. We drove to the place of review on Mars Field itself. We took more than tourist liberties with the parade and it did not mind. I am not sure that it even noticed, so intent was it about its own business. But the Petrograd wealthy did not come upon the streets while the parade was there. It might have been safe but they did not think so.

I saw only two motor cars on the parade streets during the day. One was a German military car containing German officers. The other was the car in which we rode. The Germans were from the prisoner-exchange and trade commission sent to Petrograd under the terms of the armistice.

Incidentally the events of the next few days made the Germans actual prisoners in Petrograd, though their guard is spoken of as a courtesy guard. They have been insulted and verbally slapped in the city where they thought they would be welcomed, and are at this moment the most worried persons in Petrograd. Yet to-morrow they may be back in grace, depending as Germany yields the point of Polish and Lithuanian self-definition. I think the Bolsheviks will *will* to fight, for their principle of Revolution against the Polish *bourgeois* is involved, but they cannot fight successfully if Germany invades. This they admit, but are confident that Germany cannot bring an army against them now that German soldiers know that Russia is not fighting for territory. I have not the same amount of confidence. . . .

The trouble is that the Bolsheviks can be forced, both by Germany, and from within. The morning after the Bolsheviks proclaimed that Germany had betrayed them and that they must fight for their proletarian Revolution, all the anti-Bolshevik papers sang one song and have been singing it ever since: "The Bolsheviks promised Peace. They failed. Now we must get PEACE through our party (Social Revolutionary, etc.) and the Constituent Assembly. The Allies would not recognize the Bolsheviks because they did not represent all Russia. But they will recognize the Assembly and then we will get general PEACE."

All for peace, you see, and more for politics, no more dependable for the Allies than the Bolsheviks, and nowhere near so willing to fight. I am confident at least of this: If any class in Russia will fight Germany it will be the Bolsheviks, though the class is just as willing to "revolute" against capitalistic us, as it regards us, as it would be against militaristic Germany. And if a pacifist ever refers to "Russian Pacifists" laugh heartily, thinking of these truculent huskies with guns in their hands and an itching willingness to use them. Some ready boys they are but they are not peaceful ever.

So the letter told that the climax of the Peace Parade was eruption of new war feeling in the next twenty-four hours. How much of a surprise was it to the Smolny leaders to learn that the next logical step Germany would take, following the manner of its reply of December 25 to the Russian terms, would be to refuse to apply the principles of Russian Bolshevik self-determination to Russian Poland, Lithuania, Courland, and Latvia? How long had they known that Russia was to be deprived of these territories? Was the unhappy development known to them and held back in order that paeans of victory be sung first to rouse the emotions of the people, trusting that at fever heat they could be turned as easily to war as to peace? Or had the leaders been misled by overconfidence?

In taking the view that Trotsky was not self-deceived during the week I am crediting him with the intelligence I believe to be his. Judging him by his public announcements he would appear to be a guileless, trusting soul. As an example of seeming childlike faith, witness the following, from a speech he delivered on December 27 before the Central Executive Committee of the Soviets:

The German, Austrian, Turkish, and Hungarian *bourgeoisies* have already decided to return what they seized during this war, but ask us not to demand the nullifications of the despoliations of former wars. Although our enemies, who predicted that the German diplomacy would refuse to deal with us, consider the German offer as a tremendous and quite unexpected success of our diplomacy, we have not receded from our former demands for complete self-determination of the nationalities, and reparation for all historical injustices perpetrated up to now. We shall not recede —even by an inch.

This speech pleaded for him as an innocent in the hands of the wicked—a view, however, that would have to be conditioned upon the assumption of his inability to read correctly the meaning of Germany's first reply.

What Germany did next was too plain to be misread by anybody. If one is to accept the view that the trusting were tricked, Trotsky did not get the news of disaster until late December 31, when I did—from his office. For this was the official form in which the matter was made generally public the following day, January 1. Said the *Pravda:*

Late last night we received from the press bureau of the Commissariat for Foreign Affairs the information that the German delegation in Brest-Litovsk has submitted to the Russian delegation a document giving a more complete picture of the German peace terms. This document shows protruding the greedy paw of German despoiling imperialism.

The German Government expresses its conviction that in "Poland, Lithuania, Courland, part of Estonia and Livonia, the masses already have expressed their will, have self-determined themselves and have expressed a desire for State independence."

The German Government recognizes this expression of the will of the Polish, Lithuanian, and Lettish people, and this terminates the matter.

Such "self-determination" of nationalities is a flagrant and unheard of mockery of the principle of self-determination.

The Russian delegation was quite right in replying that it does not recognize such an expression of popular will at a time when the country is occupied by foreign troops; when this martial domination is strangling the entire country; when hundreds of thousands have been forcibly exiled and when the whip of the conqueror is ruling the land. It is enough to recall what the German authorities have done in Poland to know that the will of the Polish nation has not yet found expression.

The German Government conceives that "self-determination" is to be nothing but a reflection of the will of German imperialism.

The Russian Revolution will not agree with a peace with imperialism at the price of the suppression of the nations—in whatever form imperialism may attempt to evade the watch-word of "self-determination of nationalities." In the struggle for its future the Russian Revolution must fight for the complete freedom of self-determination of nationalities as a basic principle of a democratic peace.

Germany had calmly erected new governments on Russian soil, subtracting the territory from the domain of the Bolsheviks, using the Bolshevik formula of "self-determination" of government by sectional areas of Russia, with this pronounced difference—they had permitted the propertied classes instead of Bolshevik workmen to have the rule. A blow painful indeed to Bolshevik pride!

The question as to how long Trotsky had known the blow was coming was not answered. His announcement gave no clue. The Peace Conference had not sat since December 26, when adjournment had been taken until the second week in January.

Members of the Russian delegation still were at Brest-Litovsk as individuals. In Trotsky's announcement there was no intimation that they were called together as a body to receive a German document. Yet it was stated that the delegation not only received one but replied in dissent to it. Such a course could not possibly have been taken without consultation with Trotsky and Lenin at Petrograd. The mildest of deductions would make them aware of the German challenge before they loosed their Peace Parade.

Whether or not the two were surprised into what began to look like an approach to new war, the Allied observers were as surprised as they were pleased.

I entered in my log for December 31: "Peace break—word at five o'clock." This was many hours before the public was aware of the changed aspect. At the Embassy the word was received with joy. Here was something to work on. The Ambassador cabled the information to Washington.

Wanting more news, I hunted up Radek that night. He was walking on air, breathing war of arms and propaganda. The Bolsheviks would fight, he said, because they would perish if they did not. He said, too, that he had been baiting the German Commissioners at the trade and prisoner conference in Petrograd, and from his words I surmised that he had come fresh from that arena. He had flung in their teeth, he said, their crimes in Poland—exile of Polish laborers for forced work in Germany, starvation of the populace, levies of moneys and goods—and had proclaimed that they would have to reckon with the principle of self-determination. His speech, by his own account, was altogether insulting.

Many months afterward, in a transcript of the telegrams sent from Petrograd to Berlin by the German Mission I found a paragraph in one of Count Mirbach's reports verifying the tenor of Radek's tale.

Wired Count Mirbach:

"The Pole, Radek, made severe attacks on the German Government, mentioning the Reichstag debates."

According to Mirbach, the demand voiced by Radek was for the unconditional return to Russia of all Russian prisoners held in Germany. It was refused despite Radek's threat that the action would lead the Central Council to break off the negotiations. The nature of Radek's "attacks" on the German Government was not specified. The Polish theme was one Radek would be likely to use.

Allowing for picturesque exaggeration, Radek must have said many things that the German Commissioners did not like to hear, for they protested to Smolny against his attitude. He concluded, he said, by telling them that "for their protection when they went abroad hereafter" they would be accompanied by Russian escorts. The guards certainly were imposed, and the German delegates complained against them presently to their representatives at Brest-Litovsk, where there was return talk of setting guards over the Russian conferees. The incident faded away, however, and so did the guards.

Radek was loquacious, also, about his German agitational paper, *The Torch*. He had troubles of organization, had to do too much writing himself, and wanted the publication to be running smoothly soon, as he was to go with Trotsky to Brest-Litovsk when the peace sessions resumed. Channels for the distribution of his revolutionary sheet in Germany were opening, he said, adding boastfully that his torch would light a fire there. If channels were opening for him, I figured they would be useful for me as well. The manager at my printing plant—and Radek's—would know more about the detail of those channels than Radek himself.

At midnight came a rumor that the Bolsheviks were to repudiate the Russian debt at once. In view of the nearer German crisis, the time seemed unfitting for new threats. We doubted the report, which was premature.

We watched the scarred year of 1917 go out and greeted, according to our temperaments, the untried, undoubtedly fateful year of 1918. We were far from home, in a dark and riven land. In that moment of thoughtful pause I was not light-hearted.

2.

THE New Year began at high pressure. A meeting was held at the Embassy in the morning between the representatives of all American bodies in Petrograd to outline a plan for emergencies up to the point of what could happen if the Germans denounced the armistice and thrust an army toward Petrograd.

There could be only one outcome to rapid invasion. Petrograd would fall. If it did we wanted no American Ambassador captured. The Ambassador at first was for staying and sitting under the flag. We convinced him, however, that the useful place for him would be wherever the Bolsheviks picked a new capital—if they lasted long enough to make a choice. Where the Ambassador went, General Judson perforce must go. The rest of us could fend best for ourselves. We agreed that no immediate decision was necessary, that we should wait upon Bolshevik developments, which were encouraging in their menace of war, even if that war had to be fought on a new line far in the interior of Russia. We resolved that under no circumstances would we leave Russia.

Like most men of action, the Ambassador was exhilarated by the prospect of having something positive to do. He began to plan a request for the movement of supplies to what he trusted would become again a fighting Russia; and that afternoon in fine fettle he received New Year's callers at the Embassy.

I left the Embassy to go to Smolny to attend the meeting of the Central Council called for afternoon and evening. With a pair of interpreters I planted myself close to the platform, an interpreter at each ear. Both were good interpreters and neither liked the other. I told them to keep the speeches going in monotone sentences and relaxed myself to become a receiving machine. In the weeks I had learned the trick of releasing my body in order to get mental concentration. To much of Russian oratory I listened with closed eyes.

Trotsky brushed me as he passed to the rostrum. His hands moved nervously. He was under strain. He had staged a scene where others were to speak the important preliminary lines, and the effect could not be foretold. As the meeting went, so would go Bolshevism—and it might be down. For this assembly was called to weigh war and peace—to weigh and not to push the balance too far in either direction, a delicate business. Yet a safety valve had to be provided the party before the course of the delegation to the next session of the Peace Conference could be charted. The army itself was to be heard, its delegates at hand.

The meeting was the most moving of any I attended in Russia—not the equal in tense drama of the Constituent Assembly nor in colorful scene of the January Soviet Congress, but the only assembly in which I heard the terse eloquence of simple men, reciting terrible facts. The hue of the gathering was gray, unrelieved. Perhaps eight hundred persons were present in the dreary, ill-lit hall. The rostrum was low, probably a school teacher's platform in other days. Soldiers in long uniform coats and sailors in jackets were grouped in front of it and at the sides. The soldiers were representatives of the different armies at the former front, hurried to Petrograd to report to the Central Council on the state of the armies for defense.

Lenin was not present. With Trotsky sat Kamenev, summoned from Brest-Litovsk to speak for the Peace Delegation. With his well-trimmed brown beard and eyeglasses, Kamenev had the look of a teacher or a doctor rather than an agitator and politician. He was the first speaker.

He made his report in an explanatory and, I thought, an apologetic way, stressing the "early successes" and trying to color the later reverse with some hope. The question of the time of the German statement of its intentions for Poland, Lithuania, and Latvia, could not be entirely overlooked. "The reply that was given to this declaration," he said, "was announced three hours after its receipt and not three days, as has been stated."

Telegraphic consultation between the Brest-Litovsk delegation and Smolny headquarters in three hours was physically impossible. He was not frank.

He explained truly that the German purpose in keeping troops in Poland and Lithuania was to prevent the effort at Bolshevik revolution.

"The Germans," he said, "are guided by considerations of a pure class character."

And with a flourish he asked rhetorically, "Is the great Russian Revolution to cede to the German Imperialists the right of supervision over the workmen, soldiers and peasants of Poland and Lithuania or will it assume the position of uncompromising repudiation of such encroachments?"

He asserted the willingness of Soviet Russia to assent to either autonomy or independence for Russian Poland, Lithuania, and Latvia—provided the Bolshevik "workers, soldiers and peasants" overthrew the propertied in those provinces and took the rule.

Before Trotsky spoke, the delegates from the army and the navy were asked what the forces could do in "battle for the Revolution" if war returned. Some of the men who answered were fine looking, upstanding fellows. The fire of fanaticism burned in them all. The appalling painting they limned together was of a broken, scattered front, men staying in spots, sometimes hordes of them, milling like cattle in a storm, or starving in their huts. Artillery horses were dying for lack of hay and grain, the artillery itself abandoned.

Yet they would return to the line and fight—if the country would organize behind them and feed them; send them clothing and ammunition; send new regiments from the city garrisons to relieve the weariest. Quite pitifully it was shown that an army is a composite of fighting men at the front and of supply organizations at the rear. The first act, almost, of Lenin and Trotsky, had been to destroy the Coöperatives, the people's organization which had fed and clothed the army. So they had hamstrung the fighting forces.

Bielinsky, the gaunt, grizzled delegate of the First Army, standing forth in spattered, frayed long-coat and gesturing with clumsy, red-chapped hands, greeted "Revolutionary Petrograd and the Fleet" with solemn restraint and told his hearers the stark truth that the First Army, "thanks to the breaking down of the food supply system," was tired, ready for demobilization, and asking to be relieved by fresh troops from the rear. Halting hostile murmurs with an upraised arm, he described his section of the front, or what had been the front. The artillery could not be hauled back to safety because the horses had starved to death. Men were dying faster than in battle. Desertions were many and would be increased except that the men believed they had better chance of succor if they held together. He said whimsically that they had become accustomed to their huts as to home. It was plain indeed that he spoke not of an army but of a mass of needy campers. He had come to Petrograd to beg for succor.

He would return nevertheless to urge the army to prepare for new struggle. He pledged the army to support of the Soviets "whatever the result of the peace negotiations" if he could go back with the promise that food would be shipped and "so convoyed that it reached the First Army." He was the second delegate to speak.

The first was an orator, Yaresevsky of the Twelfth Army, who largely asserted that his army would continue to "uphold the power of the Soviets as it had from the beginning," but said that before it could fight it might have to turn its face inward to Russia to "destroy those who are keeping the army from receiving food and military supplies." This sounded like a threat against the Central Council although he meant, as it appeared, "the enemies of the Revolution."

Delegates followed from the Fifth, Second, Third, Fourth, Seventh, Eighth, and Ninth armies. Their stories were nearly alike in their accounts of disintegration, though food conditions were not so bad outside of the northern area. Along the whole front not one heavy gun was fit for service, and it was evident that when the delegates spoke of the front they did not refer to trench lines and outposts but to cantonments well in the rear of the fortified lines. An army of the enemy could come marching on about as it pleased, clearing the way with light field artillery.

When the army reports were in, the voice of the navy was heard from Baranov, a sailor, who bore the long title, "President of the All-Russian Navy Convention." The navy had no food troubles, for the sailors foraged for themselves. The first to be faced with the likelihood of short rations, they overcame the threat in an original and effective way. Recruited from the peasantry, they knew there was plenty of food in the villages. So they went for it and got it. Forage parties of five, three, and two traveled hundreds of miles regularly, took their guns along, and came back with butter, eggs, bread, and meat, requisitioning a railroad car, or bringing the produce in the compartments of the passenger trains.

So Baranov was well fed, lusty, and peppery with fighting ardor. He proclaimed that the navy was ready to fight "to the last man" for "the principles of the Revolution." I did not desire to underrate this turbulent lad, for he advanced the best practical military thought of the session. "The army," he said, "confessed that it was without artillery. Well, what of it? The navy has big guns, men to fire them, and ammunition for firing. This is winter. The Germans can't come through on a wide front. They will follow the railroads. The navy will mount its guns on railroad cars, go with our army to meet them and blow them off the face of the earth."

The sailor got the cheers he was after.

When the Germans did advance in February, no navy guns confronted them.

Trotsky took the welter of addresses and argued smoothly that the answer to German "perfidy" would be the sight of Russia's readiness to fight. He promised the armies their supplies, shook his fist at the German "imperialists," and expressed a faith that the German soldier would not fight in Russia for territorial conquests. My thought as I listened was that he was expecting the threat of breaking off the German negotiations to aid him in continuing them. Yet he had raised a storm and it might blow when he sought to still it. In the French Revolution the people rose in war against the foreign invader. Might not the Russian people do the same?

The meeting adopted a resolution, calculated to be useful to Trotsky when he himself went to face the German delegates, containing not the least threat of war, leaving him free to advance the menace if he desired. Incidentally, the Germans never recognized that the negotiations were imperiled at this stage of affairs. The salient paragraphs of the resolution were:

Having heard the report of the Peace Delegation the Joint Meeting of the Executive Committee of the Soviet Council, the Petrograd Soviet and the Demobilization Conference decides:

The first statement made by the representatives of the quadruple Alliance recognized in principle the conclusion of peace without annexations or contributions. This created the basis for further negotiations regarding a general democratic peace.

In this announcement, however, the representatives of the German Government refused to recognize the right of self-definition to oppressed nationalities seized prior to 1914 or to colonies. This limitation, which was immediately noted by the Russian delegation, showed that the ruling classes of Germany, under guise of making concessions to the idea of democratic peace, were misrepresenting the idea and construing it in the meaning of the old annexationist policy.

The further statement of the Austro-German delegation declar-

ing the practical terms of peace in the East, still further mis-
represents the idea of a just democratic peace.

The sense of this statement is that the Austro-German Governments refuse to give a guarantee to remove their troops from
the occupied parts of Poland, Lithuania, Courland, Livonia and
Estonia. The free expression of the will of the inhabitants of
the occupied regions is impossible while foreign troops remain.
The declaration of the German delegation that the will of the
people of these regions already has been expressed is an absolute
falsehood. The evidence which the German Government may submit could only certify the desires of privileged groups, not the
popular masses of these territories.

We announce:

The Russian Revolution remains true to its international
policy. We stand for the real self-definition of Poland, Lithuania,
and Courland. We will never recognize as just the impulsion of
foreign will upon any people.

The Joint Meeting insists that the further peace negotiations
be conducted in a neutral country and instructs the Council of
People's Commissars to take all possible measures to that end.

The resolution admitted that the ill news of Germany's intentions was forecast in the first reply the delegation of the
Central Empires made to the statement of Russian terms. So
early jubilation and later long-faced mourning both were
devices.

I returned from the meeting to report at the Embassy that
war feeling was being born, whatever Trotsky intended to do
with it, but that there was no imminence of a drastic course
apt to induce Germany to denounce the armistice, nor any intent on Russia's part to denounce it. The outlook, I said, was
for much talk and delayed action. The hostile attitude en-
gendered was for us to take advantage of, if we could.

In my log that night, of Trotsky I wrote: "His plan of
'ready to fight'; my thought that thereby he still hoped to
avoid fighting."

He was arming himself for speeches, not battles.

CHAPTER XIII

January 2—January 9, 1918. Russian Holidays,
Lull and Playtime.

CALM would not be expected at this time. Calm came. The Russian holiday season was near at hand, and in spite of distress and revolution people began to prepare for it, Christmas Eve being due to fall on Sunday, January 6. Whatever else the Bolsheviks could do they were helpless before Russian holiday habits.

Until the next meeting of the Peace Conference, January 8, there could not be even peace or war debate. The German Commission in Petrograd got what was left of political attention. Some newspaper comment on mystery around this conclave got under Trotsky's skin, and he had himself officially interviewed to recite that the Commission was in Petrograd, under the provisions of the armistice, to deal with questions concerning the exchange of war prisoners.

This was true and yet not all. Germany did not send its Keyserlings and Mirbachs to do clerical work. The Commission also had political, military, and naval sections. It was charged with demarcation problems on the White Sea, and with naval issues. The question of much borderland railroad control was in its realm. The transcript of its daily dispatches to Berlin disclosed it as a busybody, in fields, however, which were legitimate. As far as I could determine, the German Commission in Petrograd was more harassed than harassing.

The proximity of Mirbach and Lenin for purposes of personal communication could be regarded as a fact equal in importance to the presence of the routine Commission. From the Commission, after the brief interval of the February war, Mirbach stepped, full fledged, to the crucial duties of German Ambassador to Russia and pulled the levers that sent Germany the supplies she needed most from Russia.

Trotsky also claimed publicly that he had been asked by Sir George Buchanan, the British Ambassador, for passports for himself and the members of the British Military Mission, and that he had replied that he would not comply unless England

gave identical privileges to diplomatic representatives of the
Soviet going to or through England. He said that the *attaché*,
Captain Smith, who brought the request, expressed the opinion
his Government could not accede, but that an hour later the
officer telephoned that the Ambassador gave the guaranty.
While Sir George departed in peace, Great Britain did not
reciprocate in diplomatic courtesy in the months ensuing, or
in fact have to meet the issue. Persons sent by the Soviet to test
the promise, if one was made, somehow seemed to lose their way
in Sweden or Norway. Trotsky's interview with himself appeared on January 2, in the *Izvestia*.

A chance visit to Smolny that day gave me a sight of Karakhan, in Petrograd for the Central Council meeting and for
new contact before returning to Brest-Litovsk to continue to
serve as secretary to the Bolshevik delegation. He was not then
regarded as one of the strong men, although he already had a
reputation for adroitness. Less outwardly rough than Stalin,
he yet hid an oriental craft under affectation of crude address
to fellow workers. He did not have the appearance of one who
ever had worked with his hands. His name can also be given
the Germanic spelling Karachan; his initial was L, for Leo
or Leon.

A cable of January 3 has its fitting place in the next chapter.

President Wilson was the subject of attack in the semiofficial
Pravda on January 4, slurring editorial reference being made
to him as a "Quaker-minded person who yet served the interests of the munition makers and Wall Street." As sign that we
did not intend to sit silent under assault, also as a test of the
willingness of the *Pravda* to keep a promise made to me by
Radek that it would open its columns for reply to its own articles, I asked Arthur Bullard to prepare a counter-statement,
which he did. The next day the article was translated and taken
to Axelrod, the editor of *Pravda*. The paper did not publish
daily during the holiday week. In the first issue afterward,
however, the statement was printed. From it, quotation of a
few paragraphs:

Your readers are told that "Mr. Wilson serves the interests of
the American Munition industry" and protects "the cynical interests of the New York Stock Exchange."

The American Socialists would be the first to smile at the suggestion that Mr. Wilson was the spokesman of the great capitalists. The opposition of the Socialists to Mr. Wilson has been based on the accusation that he represents—as he himself professes—the petite bourgeoisie. Certainly Mr. Wilson is not a Socialist. If he were he would not be President of the United States. The great majority of the American people are not "class conscious proletarians" nor are they big capitalists. They are simple people, who are neither very rich or very poor. Mr. Wilson has won their confidence in internal affairs because he has led them to one victory after another. And, as he has been the champion of this middle class of simple people in domestic matters, so he is their spokesman in international affairs.

Not the most bitter of Mr. Wilson's critics in the American Socialist party accuses him of Imperialism. His record makes such a charge absurd.

Since the entrance of the United States into the war the munition makers have found their profits cut from all sides, by price fixation, by heavy taxation, by the legalization of Labor Union standards.

Money supplies to foreigners were cut off on January 5, as a further effort to keep funds from being employed against the rulers. The action was supplementary to the seizure of the deposits of Russians in the banks. At the time the blow was believed to be aimed chiefly at the French. The German Commission in Petrograd, as the transcript of its reports to Berlin afterward disclosed, protested against the application of the act to Germans and was assured that the prohibition would be employed with discretion. Exceptions, in fact, were numerous and no acute difficulties were rumored. From the moment of the bank seizures it had been the part of wisdom to acquire reserves of cash. The American Embassy considered itself sufficiently prepared for economical operation. I had enough funds outside of bank for several weeks.

Trotsky, heading the Peace Delegation for the first time, left for Brest-Litovsk on the night of January 5. With him as delegates went Ioffe, Kamenev, Mme Bitzenko, and Pokrovsky. Karakhan had preceded the group by a day or so. Radek went along with the title of an "adviser," not sitting as a delegate. The staff was extensive.

General Judson found himself free on January 6 to begin

preparations for return to the United States. His request for relief was of long standing, though the outlook had been that he would remain for a considerable period as his successor, Colonel Ruggles, had not been heard from in many weeks, his whereabouts a matter of doubt. Out of Siberia, however, by slow stages, came Colonel Ruggles, with credentials as Military *Attaché*. Apparently also he succeeded to the assets of the Military Commission, which comprised a lease on a palace for residence, and no duties. General Judson was to report to Washington. Major Kerth, who had been the observer at the headquarters of the Russian General Staff, had been promoted to a colonelcy and had not been ordered home. Colonel Ruggles ordered him back to Mogilev, where there was no Russian General Staff, although Generalissimo Krylenko put the word *Stavka* above his letters and his telegraphic orders.

To Colonel Ruggles, however, a soldier built on straight lines—shoulders, head, nose, lips, and jaw—the place for an observer was with the Russian Command, whether there was an army or not. So Colonel Kerth went to find General Krylenko and to report that he was the first of the foreign observers officially attached to study Bolshevik military tactics. Krylenko, however, was a fly-by-night and Kerth never caught up with him, being back in Petrograd shortly. Colonel Ruggles, who had wanted to go to France, who found himself instead in Russia, cursed glumly and set about to find what his duties were. They were not many. A soldier of the line, condemned to fret in idleness, answering now and then the summons of the Ambassador! I felt sorry for him.

To celebrate the Russian Christmas Eve there was a group dinner in the apartment of Mrs. Walter Farwell of Chicago, who had added Russian experience to Serbian adventure. In Serbia she had acted as newspaper correspondent. In Petrograd she had used her surplus energy in supervising an orphanage. Now to our personal regret, and also somewhat to our relief at the Embassy, as we were urging the departure of all American women from Petrograd, she was about to leave to join her husband in Paris.

Consul Tredwell had given her a dinner the night before. She was hostess this evening to the same party, with the addition of two of her Russian friends as guests—Adam and Eve.

By an oversight I never jotted down the Russian names of the delightful pair who moved among us answering to the address their romance had given them. I was the more remiss, since Adam went with me to the Russian border in March and deftly smoothed my exit into Finland. They were pets of Mrs. Farwell's, and may owe their titled identity to her.

Both were soldiers. Eve had marched with her man, not as a member of any Death Battalion but as a soldier of the regiment. He fell, desperately wounded, in a pistol and bayonet *mêlée*. She killed the attacking German, fought over her husband's body until a counterassault saved them both, and then brought the wounded man off the field. She, too, was bullet marked, though not disabled. In the hospital she nursed Adam and won him back to life. Now they had each other again, two happy children. He was big and blonde, with a sheaf of yellow hair. She was dark and lithe, nearly as tall as he. They were proper mates.

Though they had served in the ranks they were not of the people, being of the professional and bureaucratic class. Adam spoke English and French, and Eve was learning English fast, gliding on pantomime when a word failed her. They were musicians and artists, with that multiplicity of talent noticeable in Russians when they have talent at all.

They fascinated us with their explanation of Russia and Russians. Rhythm, they maintained, was the key to land and race, life moving by beat, differing in individuals yet with a tendency toward mass unison, clamorous discords sounding irregularly. Carrying the parallel farther they insisted that each house and room had a beat of its own, and that one could not be happy in a house out of tune with the individual. We were dining in a soft gray room, and someone argued that it could not fit all our personalities, and won the retort that this was a neutral room, welcoming all.

Eliminating masonry and wood, my own inclination, with moderate reservations, is to accept the view of Adam and Eve. Themselves emotionally primeval, they mirrored a robust people not far traveled from barbaric youth. Sound and measured beat are conveyors of emotional impulses. The Russians have perceptions of rhythm long dimmed if not lost to older races. Our forefathers could read the signs of a wilderness. We cannot. The Russians are more emotionally receptive than we. They never have restrained themselves. We have generations of restraint behind us. I make no deduction of mysticism. Quite the contrary, for the conclusion, I think, is that the Russian people are exceptional instruments for master composers to play upon.

I have a friend, steeped in classicism, who claims that music is the lowest of the arts. He resents it because it is a force unregulated by reason. The better way, I take it, is to accept it as such a force, knowing what music will make people weep and what music will make them dance, or fight, or run away. The military general staffs of the nations should have departments of music strategy to study and classify the emotional rhythms of each race and country. The enduring ruler of Russia will have an orchestral as well as a gun-bearing army.

Aside from our own playtime doings the day was so lacking in events that I logged the feeling of a false quietness:

Russian Christmas Eve calm. Surface only. Have an impression that this play is about over and bill about to change. Probably wrong, this being Russia.

The tag comment was fortunate. The players were not to change; only, new sequences were nearer.

Of the Russian Christmas day, January 7, I wrote in a home letter:

The Russian Christmas began on Sunday evening (Christmas Eve) and lasted three days. Similarly New Year's, next Monday will last three days. Even Smolny, seat of the Bolsheviks, has been closed. Little things like revolutions do not interfere. When Russia pleasures, it just pleasures. Eating, apparently is the chief recreation, and the home the shrine. The Christmas tree is as plentiful in Petrograd as in New York.

On Christmas Day I went in the late afternoon to the Refuge conducted for children by the Americans here. A Russian nurse was in charge. There was a tree with candles on it. The children, tots of three to girls of fifteen, sang and recited. It was a scene that might have been found in New York or Chicago, except for the marvelous amount of language that welled forth from beings so small. A little rascal of three—Kerensky they call him, for they say he looks like the late departed—delivered himself of more Russian than I ever will learn. I am shamed. The Ambassador was there, and among the Americans present was Mrs. Walter Farwell of Chicago. She is a bright, lively person, and energetic. She has been running this Refuge as a side issue, but is leaving this week.

During the holidays not even a newspaper has been issued, and the street cars do not run. Christmas night a party of us dined on cold meats in my rooms. For two nights the hotel did not serve dinner. Holiday, you perceive, means a resting time for all working Russians, waiters and cooks included.

Such of our work as was not performed by Russians went on as usual. And some political events insisted on happening. There is no way of telling from one day to the next whether the one may not be the day of our enforced and rapid going, so we go ahead on the principle that Americans are to stay in Russia always. A little while will tell, at least, whether we have to pay further attention to this phase. The balance cannot be kept much longer. I have a good deal of real confidence that the tip will be in the right direction, but in the last two weeks I have seen days when the arrest of every American in Russia, including the Ambassador, has been near a fact. In each instance, however, we have been able to influence the debate, and have emerged with more mass strength and solidarity of our own. Also we have fared better than the British and the French. The British Ambassador has gone, worn out, and with him the head of the British Military Mission. Individuals of the French have been ordered out and they are still in a tight place.

The situation is that day by day the Bolsheviks become more angered at being ignored by the world upon which they wage class war. Their general method is that of a suitor who slaps a pretty girl, and then says, "Kiss me, darling!"

Yet when it comes to getting permission to have specific things done by their officials, the Bolsheviks are decently human. I have been able to do the things I set out to do.

On Tuesday evening, the quiet continuing, a party of us went to the Marinsky Theater to the ballet. The bill was *The Little Hunch-Back Horse*—the performance excellent, the audience motley.

Active warfare between the Soviet and the Rada subsided during the holiday week, and efforts at armistice were in progress. The Bolshevik aim was to make at least a temporary alliance with the Ukrainians in order that a common front might be presented at the Peace Conference. Trotsky was depending much upon the success of this maneuver. The Ukrainians were willing enough to talk but were as anxious for delay as the Bolsheviks were for speed. They cared little for unity of purpose at Brest-Litovsk. The outlook was against any lasting agreement between Soviet and Rada. The former, too, continued to spread revolutionary propaganda intensively in the Ukraine.

The news from Brest-Litovsk was that Kuhlman had censured the Russian delegation for delaying the sessions from January 4 to January 8 and again had cold-shouldered the Russian plea for the transfer of meeting-place to Stockholm.

Jerome Davis, a Y.M.C.A. man, brought me on the night of January 8 a report of a visit of inspection to the Northern army. He said that, dressed as a Russian soldier and in the company of Russians, he had been able to penetrate the German lines without difficulty, and that the German officers and men declared that there was peace with Russia already because Russia had no army. Russians were halted when they came to the German lines, he said, but generally were allowed to pass through. German prisoners escaping from Russia were filtering across. The Russians were camping along the front, as a body of men if not an army. Querying the representatives of the regiments, he said he found among them a willingness to aid in the distribution of American printed material attacking the German rulers and appealing to the German people. The military lines, they said, would not keep them from reaching German soldiers.

That was good news and in keeping with other reports. I told Davis I would call on his group and the base supply organization of the Y.M.C.A. to aid in army and in prisoner camp distribution.

Lenin appeared suddenly on January 9 before the Army Demobilization Committee, which had been at work in Petrograd for a week or more, and suggested its adjournment until the skies cleared at Brest-Litovsk. The word from there was that the day had been stormy.

The lull was over.

CHAPTER XIV

*January 10—January 13, 1918. The Fourteen
Points Speech.*

1.

WHEN the threat of "Peace Break" came on December 31, I began to search in mind for ways it could be made a factor of pressure against Germany on American behalf; and at the end of three days concluded that at least the hopeful situation of dissension between the Bolsheviks and the Germans could be encouraged best by the voice of President Wilson. Keeping my own counsel, I called for that voice.

To avoid the delay of coding and decoding, I put the message on the open cable, confident that the contents would expedite it through both the Bolshevik and the British censorships. It made, in fact, record passage to Washington. The cable:

Creel, Compub, Washington.

January 3—If President will re-state anti-imperialistic war aims and democratic peace requisites of America thousand words or less, short almost placard paragraphs, short sentences, I can get it fed into Germany in great quantities in German translation, and can utilize Russian version potently in army and everywhere.

Excerpts from previous statements will not serve. Need is for internal evidence that President is thinking of the Russian and German common folk in their situation of this moment and that he is talking to them.

Can handle German translation and printing here.

Obvious of course to you that disclosure German trickery against Russia in peace negotiations promises to immensely open up our opportunities for publicity and helpfulness.

The cable continued then with business details, requests for film equipment and additional personnel, neither of which had practical outcome, material and escort being unable to get through to Russia.

Words, however, may pass under the sea and through the air. Creel, I was to learn long afterward, went at once to the White House with the appeal, all his own force behind it. The time was opportune. A speech of Lloyd George's had given another reason that the President soon should enunciate his Peace terms, their substance already ripened in his reflective mind. My appeal very likely had an effect in shaping and simplifying the external form of the "Fourteen Points," decided the moment of their expression, and led the President to address to the Russian people the general introduction to the concrete Peace terms. He spoke as if to them, his text the Brest-Litovsk Peace Conference.

From Creel I received on January 10 the cable that a "wonderful three thousand words are going to you today," with the personal tonic, "Congratulations on great work—Go the limit." The cable presumably had left Washington the night of January 8, following the delivery of the President's speech before Congress. The speech itself was coming in when I got Creel's word.

The activities ensuing summarized thus, in the Log.

Jan. 10—(Thursday) President's Peace terms. Tumult at 4 Gorokhovaya. Smolny and Petrograd Telegraph Agency. The sardonic smile. Night portion but message still incomplete.

Jan. 11—At it again. Last of message comes. Lenin and message to Brest-Litovsk. Poster plans.

Jan. 12—Money grouch. Pravda grouch. Robins grouch. Some day for grouches. But German text to printer and Poster text and presses start.

Jan. 13—Posters up.

Besides cabling an account of progress to Creel, I included longer description on January 13, in a serial letter I was writing to my wife, the chapters to be forwarded together on the next trip of a courier outward, always an indefinite date. I wrote:

Three days of tumult, but happy work in the fine cause of the President's mighty message of January 8. I had the feeling in the early hours of Thursday morning that a new brew was mixing. It so happened that the outlook was so peaceful and the machine running so easily that I had mapped the day as the only purely pleasurable one since my arrival in Russia. In the morning I intended to shop for a birthday present for Mildred,* and in the afternoon had accepted an invitation to share a box at the opera of "Boris Godunov." That left the evening for work if it developed. The Russian day, let me enlighten you, ends at 2 o'clock in the morning. I've done a good day's work from six o'clock on many a time.

But in this case the beginning was at 10 o'clock in the morning when a friend who was translating the morning papers for me read a paragraph from Stockholm referring casually to the fact that President Wilson had made a speech before Congress. That was all, but I grabbed for my over-shoes, over-coat, and cap. I knew that the meaning was that a cable was on its way to me somewhere, and right at that second I had the suspicion that it was hung up at the Embassy—which is a mile and a half from the hotel. I drove first to our Compub office, 4 Gorokhovaya, picked up Bullard there, and went on to the Embassy.

I found that the message had got in, addressed to me, at midnight, and that the error had been made, first of not notifying me, and second of breaking the seals and starting to make Embassy copies for its different uses. If the thing had not been serious it would have been humorous as an exemplification of the red-tape habit. No damage of unrepairable nature had been done, fortunately, as several portions of the message had not come. Still it made a delay of several hours in starting translation.

I did not blame the Ambassador for wanting to see the message, but we agreed that he would have it just as soon for his purposes if I sent him a copy of the transcript. For the rest of the day the telegrams were sent to my office unopened. For days I had expected that messages would be coming direct to the Gorokhovaya but it took another cable to get them finally directed there.

Some vital parts of the message were strangely delayed, either in England or in Russia itself. One last bit of a hundred words did not get here until Friday morning. Translation, however, could begin at once, and two teams of translators and typists were set at it in our offices, one team doing Russian and the other German. Three of us worked at parts of the cable transcription simultaneously. I have not pounded a typewriter so fast since old newspaper days.

By six o'clock the translation of all parts of the text we had was done into Russian, and I started with several sets and an in-

* My daughter.

terpreter for Smolny, bent on shooting that much of it to the Russian Peace Commission sitting in Poland at Brest-Litovsk inside the German lines. I wanted it to begin to get in its work as anti-German ammunition where I knew it would do the most good. I did not expect the Bolsheviks to welcome aid. They didn't. They smiled at me and asked what new caper of the Imperialistic American Government was this.

Alexander Gumberg, interpreting for me, may have told them that they were a lot of children and that it was time to stop playing and grow up, but I do not think he did. He did, however, by his own original methods impress upon one or another of them that their destinies depended upon their ability to be sincere toward sincerity. The satisfactory outcome was that the message started by courier within an hour's time for Trotsky at Brest-Litovsk. The trouble was that Lenin as well as Trotsky was out of the city, and little people left in charge. I make one exception— Trotsky's secretary, the big girl. She sees things quick and far, and she got the courier herself.

The translation of the full message was finished early the next afternoon, and with that, Col. Raymond Robins of the Red Cross, Gumberg and I went again to Smolny.

This time Lenin was back, and we were able to get direct to him. It did not take one minute to convince him that the full message should go to Trotsky by direct wire. He grabbed the copy and sprinted for the telegraph office himself. We were told afterward that it began to go in five minutes, all other messages side-tracked.

It was the first time either Robins or I had met Lenin, for until now, while I have worked all through Smolny, attending Soviet and garrison meetings, and have had channels running to every seat of power, I have camouflaged as a newspaper man, and have kept out of any situation that could have been interpreted as giving the government recognition that Washington did not desire to give. Even on this occasion I went only as the head of the American Press Bureau.

Lenin, in appearance, might be the *bourgeois* mayor of a French town—short, sparsely bearded, a bronze man in hair and whiskers, small, shrewd eyes, round of face, smiling and genial when he desires to be. And this time he did. But he is the Wildest of the Wild men of Russia, with the gift of being an organizer of wild men. He sits in the deepest back room at Smolny and spins.

He welcomed the message as an unexpected but not undeserved staff, but he did not let us forget for a moment that he regarded it as coming not from a fellow thinker but from a just and tolerant class opponent. It will be a mistake for any one to believe that our political democracy can merge with this industrial democracy. The latter will seek revolution against capital until it conquers or is conquered.

But on the specific matter of general peace Lenin saw the potency of the speech and accepted its help. "It is a great step ahead toward the peace of the world," he said—and in English, which he speaks very well. He was as joyous as a boy over the President's humanly understanding words to Russia, and his recognition of the honesty of Bolshevik purpose.

"Yet I have been called a German spy," he said, and smiled and threw up the palms of his hands.

His only criticism was on the colonial clause, which is the only weak clause in the message. When he went unerringly for it, I knew that he had the gift for finding the cracks in any armor. But he wasn't fanatic and took the practical view that the word "equitable" could be turned in Bolshevik direction no less than in an Imperial direction.

Yet at the last he ran true to Bolshevik form (Bolshevik means more), for he said, "This is all very well as far as it goes, but why not formal recognition, and when?" That is the Bolshevik idea—ask more and more until you get it all.

Robins went away after we left Lenin, and then I sought the Smolny press bureau to start the real job of getting the full text into the government papers. One of them, the lesser, the *Pravda* ("Truth"), is pronouncedly anti-American, and while it took the copy, did not print it in full and was both unfair and unintelligent in its editorial comment. The big one the *Izvestia* ("News"), which circulates free to all the Soviet headquarters throughout Russia, and as a selling newspaper has the biggest circulation in Petrograd, not only took it, but allowed us to black face the passages we desired—all clauses relating to Russia—and printed a comment that this was sincerely meant recognition of the idealism of the Soviets, and a present aid of invaluable consequence. The appearance in the *Izvestia* alone guarantees that every Russian soldier will get the message, for the *Izvestia* is read aloud to soldiers who do not read.

Other papers printed such sections of the speech as fitted their political purposes. The anti-government papers, for instance, carefully left out all the good references to Russia, because they were good also for the Bolsheviks. Such is the newspaper method of Russia. The formula is, "Lie about your enemies."

But all Petrograd is getting the speech. Already 100,000 poster copies of the speech are printed, and although this (the 13th) was Sunday and New Year's Eve, 30,000 are on the walls of Petrograd, posted there since noon—on the third day since the message entered the town, and the second since it got here completely. It cost money, for the presses had to run on double-pay overtime Saturday night to make the delivery. But the results are worth it. Not even money will get work tomorrow, New Year's day.

On Tuesday the posting will be finished. I am re-setting in hand-bill form for a distribution of 300,000 on streets, in theaters and public places, and that distribution should be completed by Friday night. A German version of one million copies will go to press Tuesday night. The Y.M.C.A. volunteered the distribution of this number of German copies along the lines, and while I have seen signs of quitting on the fullness of the job, I am going to drive them through. The volunteering was done enthusiastically and at no urging from me, for my best German plans are elsewhere. They have the men, the facilities, and I am putting up the money for extra costs. They will work, I am quite sure.

Sent a man to Moscow last night with Russian copy for printing posters there, and as the office there is ready with its plan, both the poster and the street distribution should be completed there also in five or six days. Will print about a million and a half copies there, 800,000 of them for Y.M.C.A. in Russian. Will print Polish and Ukrainian pamphlets there, also the permanent pamphlet form for mailing list distribution.

The deepest German drive, aside from what Trotsky may do in the way of gunnery at Brest-Litovsk, will be in the Bolshevik propagandist organ for Germany, called *The Torch*. It is printed in about three quarter of a million daily gobs and fed to German soldiers by Russian soldiers and by various contrived mediums. Its aim is German Revolution. It is the chief cause of the German yell against Russian literary efforts behind and across German lines. We have the promise of its use Wednesday morning. Perhaps I write too soon, but I have reason for confidence.

Nor was my confidence misplaced.

On the Russian version of the speech, too, I placed prominently a subhead crediting the *Izvestia* with the first printing of the original text. It had the effect of an order to the Bolshevik organizations and armies to help to circulate the posters, and as an order it was obeyed. No proclamation of Lenin's or

АМЕРИКАНСКІЯ УСЛОВІЯ

ОБЩАГО МИРА.

ДЕКЛАРАЦІЯ

Президента ВИЛЬСОНА.

(Напечатанныя въ № 263 „Извѣстій Центр. Исп. Ком. Совѣтовъ Крестьянск., Рабоч. и Солдатск. Депут." и „Петроградск. Сов. Раб. и Солд. Депутат.").

Рѣчь президента Вильсона въ конгрессѣ, 26-го декабря (8 января 1918 года).

Снова, какъ это дѣлалось уже нѣсколько разъ раньше, представители Центральныхъ Имперій выразили желаніе обсудить цѣли войны и возможныя основы общаго мира. Въ Брестъ-Литовскѣ происходили переговоры между представителями Центральныхъ Державъ, на которыя было привлечено вниманіе всѣхъ возможныхъ въ цѣляхъ выясненія возможности превратить эти переговоры въ общую конференцію для разработки условій мира и окончательнаго соглашенія. Русскіе представители предлагали не только вполнѣ точно изложеніе тѣхъ принциповъ, на которыхъ они были бы согласны заключить миръ, но и столь же точную программу конкретнаго осуществленія этихъ принциповъ. Представители Центральныхъ Державъ, со своей стороны, предложили схему соглашенія хотя и менѣе точную, но которая, какъ казалось, поддавалась либеральному толкованію, пока въ ней не была прибавлена ихъ спеціальная программа, содержавшая эти практическія условія.

Эта программа не заключала въ себѣ никакихъ уступокъ, ни по отношенію къ принципу русскаго суверенитета, ни по отношенію къ предоставленнымъ оккупаціямъ народовъ, о будущей судьбѣ которыхъ она трактовала. Она сводилась къ краткихъ словахъ, къ тому, что Центральныя Имперіи должны удержать за собою каждую пядь занятой ихъ войсками территоріи, каждую провинцію, каждый городъ, каждый выгодный пунктъ, въ качествѣ постояннаго прибавленія ихъ территоріи и ихъ могущества.

Благоразуміе требуетъ предположить, что предложеніе сначала общіе принципы соглашенія были внушены болѣе либеральными государственными дѣятелями Германіи и Австріи, людьми, которые начали проникаться силой мыслей и цѣлей своихъ собственныхъ народовъ, въ то время какъ конкретныя условія соглашенія исходили отъ военныхъ властей; они имѣли только обѣ одномъ, о выгодѣ и сохраненіи добытаго. Переговоры были прерваны. Русскіе представители истовыми искренно и твердо. Они не могутъ обсуждать такихъ предложеній завоеванія и господства.

Весь этотъ инцидентъ представляется весьма знаменательнымъ. Отъ такъ очень создаетъ. Съ кѣмъ въ сущности имѣютъ дѣло Русскіе представители? Отъ имени кого говорятъ представители Центральныхъ Имперій? Выступаютъ ли они отъ имени большинства своихъ парламентовъ, или отъ имени партійнаго меньшинства, того имперіалистскаго и милитаристскаго меньшинства, которое до сихъ поръ господствовало во всей ихъ политикѣ и подчиняло своему контролю турецкія дѣла, а также тѣ балканскія государства, которыя разлаглась вынужденными обязались изъ совмѣстныхъ этой войной?

Русскіе представители настаивали весьма справедливо, весьма разумно и въ соотвѣтствіи съ истиннымъ духомъ современной демократіи на томъ, чтобы совѣщанія съ германскими и турецкими государственными дѣятелями происходили при открытыхъ, а не закрытыхъ дверяхъ; и дѣйствительно, согласно ихъ желанію, весь міръ внимательно вниманіе совѣщаніямъ. Кому же мы однако внимали? Тѣмъ ли, которые выражаютъ духъ и извѣстія резолюцій, принятой германскихъ рейхстагомъ отъ 9 іюля, духъ и намѣренія либеральныхъ лидеровъ и партій Германіи, или тѣмъ, которые сопротивляются и отвергаютъ этотъ духъ и панфиеизмъ и настаиваютъ на навязаніи и подчиненіи? Или мы внимаемъ въ дѣйствительности общимъ этихъ сторонамъ, находящимся въ непримиримомъ, открытомъ и собственномъ противорѣчіи нежели собой? Это весьма серьезные и знаменательные вопросы. Отъ отвѣта на нихъ зависитъ миръ для человѣчества.

Но каковъ бы ни былъ результатъ переговоровъ въ Брестъ-Литовскѣ, каковы бы ни были рѣшенія, принятыя совѣщаніемъ представителей Центральныхъ Имперій, они снова попытались окрашивать миръ съ цѣлями ихъ войны и снова предлагали своимъ противникамъ, о чемъ заключались ихъ цѣли и какого рода соглашенію они признали бы справедливымъ и удовлетворительнымъ.

Нѣтъ никакой основательной причины не принять это предложеніе и не отвѣтить на вопросъ съ полною откровенностью. Мы не доходимся его поставить. Мы и много разъ излагали нашу мысль и много разъ передъ всемъ человѣчествомъ, и не только въ общихъ выраженіяхъ, но всякій разъ съ достаточной опредѣленностью, чтобы сдѣлать очевиднымъ, какого рода окончательныя условія соглашенія должны быть достигнуты. На прошлой недѣлѣ г. Ллойдъ-Джорджъ съ выдающимся откровенностью — и съ величайшимъ подъемомъ выступилъ съ рѣчью отъ имени народа и правительства Великобританіи.

Среди противниковъ Центральныхъ Имперій нѣтъ никакихъ разногласій, никакой неопредѣленности въ принципіальныхъ вопросахъ, никакая неточность въ подробностяхъ. Только на эту Германію и ея союзниковъ падаетъ вина за тайную дипломатію, за отсутствіе честности и искренности, за нежеланіе выступить съ опредѣленными заявленіями о цѣляхъ войны. Отъ этого опредѣленія зависитъ вопросъ о жизни и смерти. Ни одинъ государственный дѣятель, малѣйшимъ образомъ сознающій свою отвѣтственность, не вправѣ длить ужасъ кровопролитія и трату богатства, если онъ окончательно не убѣждёнъ, что цѣли, ради которыхъ приносятся эти жизненныя жертвы, являются неразрывными частями истинной жизни общества и что народъ, отъ имени котораго онъ говоритъ, считаетъ эти цѣли правыми и категорическими, подобно тому, какъ это предполагается имъ самимъ.

Еще одинъ голосъ взываетъ къ опредѣленію этихъ принциповъ и цѣлей войны, — голосъ, который, какъ мнѣ кажется, болѣе волнуетъ и приковываетъ вниманіе, чѣмъ какой-либо другой изъ многочисленныхъ голосовъ, потрясающихъ теперь человѣчество. Я говорю о голосѣ русскаго народа. Народъ этотъ, казалось-бы, повергнутъ и совершенно безпомощенъ передъ суровымъ могуществомъ Германіи, которое до сихъ поръ не знало колебаній и жалости. Могущество этого народа повидимому сокрушено.

И тѣмъ не менѣе его духъ непреклоненъ. Онъ не желаетъ уступить ни въ принципѣ, ни въ надеждѣ. Его представленіе о цѣли, что являются правыми, гуманными и благородными, шириотъ взглядовъ, душевныхъ благородствомъ и сочувствіе съ къ человѣчеству, что должно вызвать восхищеніе со стороны всякаго друга человѣчества; и русскіе отказались войти „а соглашательство въ вопросѣ и ихъ идеалахъ, или измѣнить другимъ дабы спастись самимъ. Они обращаются къ намъ, спрашивая, чего мы желаемъ и въ чемъ наши цѣли и стремленія отличаются отъ ихъ собственныхъ цѣлей и мнѣній — и я полагаю, что это исчерпывающей простотой.

Вправѣ ли они къ этому ихъ нынѣшнимъ лидеры, или нѣтъ, ни мы глубоко имъ и надѣемся найти пути представленія намъ возможность оказать поддержку русскому народу въ достиженіи его величайшихъ упованій и свободу и мира и рядовъ.

Наше желаніе и наше цѣль въ томъ, чтобы мирные переговоры, когда они начнутся, были совершенно откровенны и не велись въ будущемъ, на основаніи не могло быть хищнаго никакихъ тайнахъ. Эрей завоеваній и явнаго прошлаго; точно такіе и время тайныхъ соглашеній, при благодати которыхъ хищный интересъ нѣкоторыхъ правительствъ, и благодаря которымъ въ любой моментъ могъ быть нарушенъ миръ человѣчества.

PRESIDENT WILSON'S FOURTEEN POINTS IN RUSSIAN

First page of a two-page poster displayed on Petrograd billboards, carrying a line showing that it had been printed in the newspaper *Izvestia*. The same form was used for handbill distribution on the streets. The heading reads: "American Conditions of General Peace.—Declaration of President Wilson."

Trotsky's ever got a wider or a faster distribution throughout Russia or along its borders than President Wilson's Fourteen Points Speech.

In its different handbill, poster, and pamphlet forms the printed issues of the speech totaled 3,463,000 copies issued from Petrograd and Moscow presses, and this sum took no account of the millions of distribution through the *Izvestia* and other newspapers, nor of handbills printed at Odessa, Tiflis, Kiev, Chita, Omsk, and Ekaterinburg, where the text of the speech was telegraphed to American Consuls and to representatives (in several places) of the International Harvester Company, and in each place circulated in quantity. The American Consul at Vladivostok received text of the address by direct cable from the United States. The entire circulation in Russia and Siberia otherwise—whether by wire or in printed form— was from the Committee on Public Information (Compub), Petrograd.

Of the one million copies of the speech printed in German— entirely apart from the printing in *The Torch*—I wrote in 1920 in a report published in George Creel's book, *How We Advertised America:*

Of this quantity 300,000 were put across the northern line and 200,000 similarly at the central and the southern front. Half a million copies went to German prison camps in Russia, for the reason that these prisoners were soon to return to Germany.

It would have been more accurate to have said German cantonments than prison camps, although the Germans still were in nominal custody, pending formalities for their transfer. Like the Russian soldiers, the tendency of the German bodies was to remain where they were sheltered, although the lack of Russian discipline encouraged much restless moving about.

The distribution of the German edition was done by an organization of soldier package carriers formerly in the service of the Y.M.C.A. and secured from that body, becoming a part of our machinery of diffusion. In February when the German army advanced into Russia, the package men worked along the line scattering German and Hungarian versions of President Wilson's later speech of February 11 in territories about to be occupied by the Germans. The head of this organization was B. Morgernstern, a sturdy personage, and able. Jerome Davis, when he found the Y.M.C.A. itself could not function as he had hoped, brought Morgernstern to me.

With the Y.M.C.A. itself I did not find lasting fault. The comment in my letter, written in heat, was too severe. The disruption of personnel became inevitable with the breaking up of Russia, and was accelerated by the inability of the officials outside of Russia to send a leader to the contingent. The most energetic men in the group at once volunteered for work with the consulates or with my organization. Crawford Wheeler, at Petrograd, held a part of the force staunchly together. A. M. Waldo became Vice-Consul in Finland. Malcolm Davis, one of the best men in our own organization, came from the Y.M.C.A. The two Davises, Jerome and Malcolm, were not related.

The story of one contingent of the Russian division of the Y.M.C.A. was unusual. While the larger body came direct from the United States after the March Revolution, the first section entered from western Europe. Members of it, before the United States entered the War, had volunteered for war-relief work as neutrals at prison camps in the countries of the belligerents. They were men who happened not to want to join the armed forces of any other country than their own, but they did want to get into action. None of them was a regular Y.M.C.A. secretary. Even in Russia those in this group were concerned less with Y.M.C.A. service than with the War Prisoners' Aid which had been set up on a basis of reciprocal agreement between the Allies and the Central Powers. Some had volunteered in December, 1916, to do work for English and French prisoners of war in Germany and Austria, sailed from the United States in January, 1917, and were in Denmark when diplomatic relations between the United States and Germany were broken off. The Allied Governments held conferences and this group was requested to go to Russia and carry on the War Prisoners' Aid there until it could be turned over to neutrals. This had to be done because all the agreements were on a reciprocal basis and if the work in England, France, and Russia was allowed to fall to the ground, work for all Allied and American prisoners in Germany would likewise collapse and many of the prisoners starve. These men did carry on until Dutch, Scandinavian, and Swiss volunteers arrived to

Amerikanische Bedingungen des allgemeinen Friedens.

Botschaft des Präsidenten Wilson.

Abgedruckt in Nr. 263 der „Iswjestia" des Zentralausschusses der Arbeiter-, Soldaten- und Bauerndelegiertenräte.

Die Rede des Präsidenten Wilson zum Amerikanischen Kongreß vom 8. Januar 1918.

Noch einmal, wie es schon wiederholt geschehen ist, haben die Bevollmächtigten der Mittel-Mächte ihren Wunsch, die Kriegsziele und die wahrscheinlichen Grundlagen eines allgemeinen Friedens zu erörtern, kund getan. In Brest-Litowsk wurden Unterhandlungen mit den Vertretern der Mittelmächte gepflegt, zu denen die Aufmerksamkeit aller kriegführenden Mächte geleitet wurde, um festzustellen, ob es möglich sein würde, diese Unterhandlungen zu einer allgemeinen Konferenz zwecks der Bestimmung der Kriegsziele und der Beendigung des Krieges auszudehnen. Die Russischen Vertreter legten nicht nur eine vollständig bestimmte Darlegung der Grundsätze vor, auf Grund deren sie willens sein würden den Krieg zu beschließen, sie unterbreiteten auch eine im gleichen Maße bestimmte programmatische Auseinandersetzung der realen Anwendung dieser Grundsätze. Die Vertreter der Mittelmächte unterbreiteten ihrerseits Abrisse einer Verständigung, die durch eine geringere Bestimmtheit gekennzeichnet, einer denkbaren Auslegung standzuhalten schienen, bis eine konkrete Auseinandersetzung ihrer realen Ziele hinzugefügt würde.

Diese Auseinandersetzung enthielt gar keine Zugeständnisse, weder für die Souveränität Rußlands, noch für die Wünsche der Bevölkerung, deren Schal es sein sollte, und, in einem Wort, sie bedeutete, daß die Mittelmächte jeden Fußbreit des Gebietes, das ihre bewaffneten Kräfte besetzt hatten, — jede Provinz, jede Stadt, jeden Punkt von jedweder Bedeutung — als einen wertvollen Zuwachs in ihrem Gebiete und ihrem Machtbereich zurückhalten würden.

Die Voraussetzung ist folgerichtig, daß die allgemeinen Grundsätze einer Kriegslösung, die sie anfangs vorschlugen, von der überaus gesinnten Staatsmännern Deutschlands und Österreich-Ungarns ihren Ursprung nahmen, den Männern, die die Frucht der Gedanken und Ziele ihrer eigenen Völker zu fühlen begannen, während die konkreten Bedingungen der tatsächlichen Lösung von den Heerführern, deren Gedanken darauf beschränkt sind und zurückhalten, worauf sie ihre Hand gelegt haben, ausgingen. Die Unterhandlungen wurden abgebrochen.

Die Russischen Vertreter waren aufrichtig und handelten in vollem Ernst. Vorschläge, die aus Eroberungsgeist und Herrsucht entspringen, können nicht ihre Betrachtung verdienen.

Der ganze Vorfall ist im höchsten Maße lehrreichend. Er ist auch im gleichen Maße verblüffend. Mit wem unterhandeln eigentlich die Russischen Vertreter? In wessen Namen sprechen die Vertreter der Mittelmächte? Sprechen sie für die entsprechenden Parlamentsmehrheiten, oder sprechen sie etwa im Namen jener Parteiminderheit, jener militaristischen und imperialistischen Minderheit, die bisher für jene ganze Politik beherrscht, und die Angelegenheiten der Türkei und der Balkanstaaten, die sich verpflichtet hielten, sich ihnen in diesem Kriege anzuschließen, gelenkt hat.

Die Russischen Vertreter haben in gänzlich gerechtfertigter Weise und im wahren Geiste der modernen Demokratie darauf bestanden, daß jene Besprechungen mit den Vertretern des Vierverbandes vor offenen, und nicht vor geschlossenen Türen gehalten werden sollen, so daß die ganze Welt ein Zuhörer wurde, wie es auch ihren Wünschen entsprach.

Wessen Stimme haben wir also vernommen? Etwa die Stimme derer, die dem Geiste und den Absichten der Reichstagsresolution vom 9. Juli 1917 Ausdruck gaben, dem Geiste und den Absichten der freisinnigen Parteiführer Deutschlands, oder war es die Stimme derer, die diesem Geiste und diesen Absichten Widerstand leisten, sie verächtlich herausfordern, und ihrerseits auf Eroberungen und Unterdrückungen bestehen? Oder mag es gar sein, daß wir beide Stimmen vernehmen, die unversöhnt und in offenen und hoffnungslosen Widerspruch einander gegenüberstehen? Dies sind sehr ernste und bedeutungsvolle Fragen. Von ihrer Beantwortung hängt der Weltfriede ab.

Hindenk, was auch das Ergebnis der Unterhandlungen in Brest-Litowsk sein mag, und welchen Abschluß die in den Äußerungen ihrer Ziele finden mögen, sie haben wiederum es versucht die Welt mit ihren Kriegszielen bekanntzumachen, und wiederum haben sie ihre Gegner herausgefordert, ihre Ziele auseinanderzusetzen und bekanntzumachen, was sie als eine gerechte und befriedigende Kriegslösung betrachten.

Ich kenne keinen gewichtigen Grund, weshalb diese Herausforderung nicht die Antwort erhalten sollte, und zwar die Antwort, die durch Hochmaß der Aufrichtigkeit ausgezeichnet sein muß. Wir haben jedoch auf diese Herausforderung gewartet. Nicht einmal, nein, zu wiederholten Malen haben wir unseren ganzen Gedanken- und Zielkreis vor der Welt dargelegt, und jedes Mal mit zureichender Bestimmtheit um es klarzumachen, welche realen Bedingungen für eine Kriegslösung daraus mit Notwendigkeit hervorgehen müssen. Herr Lloyd George hat im Laufe der letzten Woche mit bewundernswerter Aufrichtigkeit und in einem bewundernswertem Geiste, für das Volk und für die Regierung Großbritanniens gesprochen.

Es herrscht keine Verwirrung in den Ratschlüssen der Gegner der Mittelmächte, keine Unsicherheit in den Grundsätzen, keine Unbestimmtheit in den Einzelheiten ihrer Anwendung. Auf Seiten Deutschlands und seiner Verbündeten allein finden wir Heimlichkeit in den Ratschlägen, nur sie entbehren furchtlose Aufrichtigkeit, nur sie haben es unterlassen eine genaue Darlegung der Kriegsziele zu geben. Diese Schlußfolgerungen hängen von diesen Erklärungen ab. Kein Staatsmann, dem wenigstens die geringste Vorstellung von seiner Verantwortlichkeit vor Augen steht, sollte dieses tragische und erschütternde Blutvergießen und Fortwährung materieller Güter auch nur für einen Augenblick länger dulden, wenn er nicht abseits dessen gewiß ist, daß die Entzwecke, derenhalber solche Welten geführt werden, lebenswichtiger und unentbehrlicher Bestandteil des Lebensinhalts der menschlichen Gesellschaft bilden, und daß sie auch in der Schätzung des Volkes, in dessen Namen er spricht, also gemein und kategorisch bindend erscheinen.

Außerdies, höre ich eine Stimme, die diese Bestimmungen der Grundsätze und Ziele heischt, die aufwühlender und machtvoller klingt, denn irgend eine andere unter den vielen rührenden Stimmen, die in der erregten Weltunrust erhalten. Dies ist die Stimme des Russischen Volkes, das, wie es scheinen mag, niedergedrückt und bloße listlos vor der eigenen Macht steht, entblößt daselbst, die sich bloß aber erwiesen sich und kein Mitleid kannte.

Seine Macht, die Macht des Russischen Volkes, scheint zertrümmert.

Und doch ist seine Seele nicht unterdränig. Es weicht weder in Grundsätzen, noch in Handlungen zurück. Sein Begriff von Gerechtigkeit und davon was sich mit der Würde der Menschheit verträgt und was so ehrenhaft annehmbar kann, wurde mit einer solchen Offenheit, Gesichtsweite, geistigem Coolmut und allumfassenden menschlichen Verstehen dargestellt, daß es die bewundernde Verstehen eines jeden Freundes der Menschheit hervorrufen muß. Das Russische Volk hat es von jeder gewiesen die Reinheit seiner Ideale zu trüben, oder gar andere im Stiche zu lassen, seiner eigenen Sicherheit halber. Sein Stimme kündigt auf die Ziele seiner Wünsche, und auch worin unsere Ziele und unsere Auffassungen sich von der seinigen unterscheidet, — wenn solch ein Unterschied überhaupt besteht. In glaube darum, daß es Wunsch des Volkes der Vereinigten Staaten ist, mit der äußersten Schlichtheit und Offenheit Antwort zu stehen.

Mögen es seine gegenwärtigen Führer auch glauben oder nicht, es ist unser innig gehaltener Wunsch und Hoffnung, daß irgend eine Möglichkeit offengelegt werden möge, die uns das Vorrecht geben würde, dem Russischen Volke in der Erreichung seiner höchsten Hoffnungen von Freiheit und geordnetem Frieden Beistand zu leisten.

Unsere Wünsche und unsere Ziele werden darauf hinauslaufen, daß die Werke des Friedens von ihrem Anfang an gänzlich offenkundig seien, und daß sie von nun an keine geheimen Uebereinkommen irgend welcher Beschaffenheit bedingen sollen. Die Tage der Eroberungen und Machterweiterungen sind vorüber. Uebergangen sind auch die Tage der Geheimverträge, die im Interesse einzelner Regierungen geschlossen wurden und imstande waren in einem unvorhergesehenen Augenblick den Weltfrieden zu stürzen.

Dieser glückliche Umstand, der sich jetzt jedem Menschen, der im öffentlichen Leben steht und dessen Gedanken nicht mehr in einem Zeitalter verweilen, das tot und verflossen ist, offenbart, ermöglicht es für jede Nation, deren Ziele mit Gerechtigkeit und dem Weltfrieden im Einklang stehen, jede Welt, zu irgend einer anderen Zeit, die Endzwecke, die sie im Auge hat, zu bekennen.

Wir haben an diesem Kriege teilgenommen, weil Rechtsverletzungen vorgefallen sind, die uns bis aus Lebensmark gingen, und das Leben unseres eigenen Volkes unmöglich machen würden, wenn wir ihnen nicht Einhalt geböten und die Welt ein für alle Mal gegen ihre Wiederholung sichern würden.

PRESIDENT WILSON'S FOURTEEN POINTS IN GERMAN

First page of a two-page poster and handbill, as printed at Petrograd for distribution among German war prisoners and along the German army front in Russia.

replace them, after which they reported themselves at the American Embassy in Petrograd, registered for war enlistment if they were within the years, and considered themselves out of the Y.M.C.A. ranks.

By this time, however, the Bolshevik Revolution had come, to return them to the United States was difficult, also there was other work for them to do in Russia. The Embassy was short-handed in clerical and code-room force, the Consulate at Moscow in need of assistants, and I had use for all those who could write or had skill in foreign languages. I asked the Embassy to send such men to me. Perceiving the urgency they volunteered readily, several of the younger men, however, asking for limited service and early return to the United States. Two of them, Malcolm Davis and William Adams Brown, Jr., having in the course of duty gotten as far east as Peking in the summer of 1918, cabled me at Washington for permission to come home and enlist. The orders they received instead were to go to Harbin in Manchuria. Davis was in the party that had left the United States for Denmark in January, 1917.

2.

My meeting with Lenin, on January 11, I described in my letter as it was. He pleased me because he did what I wanted him to do, the more so because he did it quickly. For that occasion my mind had only one focus—the end sought. Achieving it, I was satisfied.

In early retrospect of the meeting, I perceived, however, that none of my distrust of Lenin was lessened, although my respect for his ability had increased. On Robins the effect was different. Some fire in him was lighted. Lenin, too, must have observed something malleable in him. Mischief came of the contact between the two. Robins had wanted to come with me. With Trotsky away he felt hampered by the lack of channel to the top. The opportunity, in fact, seemed excellent. He was able to broach to Lenin plans that he had for food distribution, and Lenin was agreeably attentive and approving.

Doubtless, too, if the men had not met then, they would have done so presently. But almost immediately afterward I wished we had not gone together. For, in a day's time, we were acridly debating Lenin; while the break between us was delayed, it had its beginning then. As I turned over the incidents of the session with Lenin a lower stratum of my mind began to send its message upward. When it broke through I found myself repeating Lenin's sentence, "Yet I have been called a German spy!" Without incentive from us he had spoken from inner compulsion. We had heard the voice of his brooding. The subject was one he hugged to himself, however unwillingly.

None of this feeling did I put in my letter, as I had suggested to my wife that the letter be shown to George Creel—and he might show it to others. A letter was no place for analyzing a mental problem. But Robins knew my conclusions and resented their expression. Lenin, he contended, spoke from hurt innocence.

If ever a man had a hard shell it was Lenin. I could not conceive a tenderness of covering. I could imagine, instead, that as a dictator he felt his prestige subject to injury from imputations of servile dealings and that, confronted by two innocents like Robins and me, he had used the chance to get us to proclaim a denial for him. Where Robins saw a sensitive person I saw a calculating one.

If Lenin had not used the outright words, "German spy," I never would have used them in reference to him. They are only popular catchwords. But they enshrined themselves in the brain of this maker of catch phrases. That is their significance.

I can imagine the bitter well of that mind of Lenin's and dare to venture that the thoughts rising through it were:

Germany thinks me its tool and servant because I used German help and German money to make a revolution in Russia. Now I will use Russian help and Russian money to try to make a revolution in Germany. If I fail I still will have much of Russia as a laboratory for my leveling experiments and as the seat for efforts toward World Revolution. I bow always to major force and only to major force. When I must obey I will obey. When I can rebel I will rebel. I am the Great Destroyer. I use all weapons—enemies, rascals, riff-raff, sentimentalists—all. Yet they call me a German spy! Bah!

The only agreement that Robins and I could reach was to drop Lenin as a topic between us. I noted the dispute in the

Log, January 12, as "Robins grouch." We shared it equally. Other reasons for bad temper developed, too, during the day. The heavy expense of the handling of the President's speech warned me of the need of drawing more funds from the State Bank soon, a tiresome and perhaps difficult action. Also, the treatment given the speech in the *Pravda* had been cynical. But, as I ended the record of the day, the poster presses were starting and the text of the German translation had gone to the printer.

3.

NOT while I was in Russia nor until the War was over was my telegram of January 3 connected with the Fourteen Points Speech. Neither Creel nor I referred to the episode after my return to Washington in May, 1918.

In June, 1920, The League of Free Nations Association published a volume entitled *Russian-American Relations, 1917–1920,* the editors of which had been enabled in a manner apparent to me but without my consent or that of the Government, to get hold of some of the cables I had sent on the open wire, among them the telegram of January 3. The comment, in a spirit of unfair and brutal hostility to President Wilson, these being the days of his crucifixion by his own people, ran:

In the light of the cable dispatches from Mr. Sisson, President Wilson would seem to have written the Fourteen Points speech on the advice of the Publicity Department of the United States Government for pure publicity purposes in Russia and Germany. For the dispatches reveal an eagerness on the part of Sisson in Russia to popularize the war with the Russian common people, and a decision on his part, apparently concurred in at Washington, that this could be accomplished only by such an address as the President delivered on January 8, 1918.

Three years later, in 1923, in San Francisco, George Creel made the public statement, in the San Francisco *Call* of May 19, that he had taken my cable to the President, the Fourteen Points Speech resulting.

In 1927 one of the editors of *The World's Work* wrote me, asking an account of the circumstances, which I gave, asking

him, however, not to use the material in the way he had projected. He had intended to cite the instance as one of publicity.
Assenting courteously to my desire, he refrained from publication. I wrote:

I am a little bewildered at the view of me from the standpoint
of another. It never has occurred to me that I used "the technique
of a publicity man" during the war. I never have been a publicity man, you see.

I did use, however, everything that I knew about the working
of the human mass mind and about exploding emotional impulses
upon and within that mass.

As for Woodrow Wilson's Fourteen Points Speech, if I were to
state that I suggested the formula for it, knew what that formula
would be, or what the effect of it was to be upon the nations, I
would appear as ridiculous as the would-be historian of whom
Philip Guedalla tells, who began his narrative by putting into
the mouth of a General the words: "Men, do your duty! The eyes
of the world are on you who are about to fight the first battle of
the Hundred Years' War!"

The fact is, historical, spiritual, or what you will, that once or
twice in a century there comes along a man able to express his
own great thoughts with such grace, clarity, and simplicity that
they are heard and cherished by the folk of all the world—of every
plane of life and of every race.

Woodrow Wilson had, supremely, this quality of universality.
I often have wondered if Americans knew this, as assuredly the
rest of the world does. I know it because whatever he said could
be turned into other languages, any other language, without losing any of its content, whether of charm, of force, or of idea.

Such a leader knows not only what to say but when to say it.

What happened, judging by my Petrograd records, by the
text of the January 8th speech itself,* and by a statement made

* Text extracts from President Wilson's Fourteen Point Peace Program
Speech, delivered January 8, 1918:

Parleys have been in progress at Brest-Litovsk between Russian representatives and representatives of the Central Powers to which the attention of all
the belligerents has been invited for the purpose of ascertaining whether it
may be possible to extend these parleys into a general conference with regard
to terms of peace and settlement.
The Russian representatives presented not only a perfectly definite statement of the principles upon which they would be willing to conclude peace
but also an equally definite program of the concrete application of those
principles. The representatives of the Central Powers, on their part, presented
a settlement, which if much less definite, seemed susceptible of liberal inter-

by George Creel subsequent to the war, was that my cry of need in Russia for a restatement of our aims of War, a statement of our terms of Peace, reached Washington at the time the President was deliberating upon the subject matter of a speech of that scope.

That the speech was hastened by my cable appears likely; that some of the fashion of the appeal to the Russian and the German people was a consequence, is probable; and that the primer-like arrangement of the Program of Peace (the Fourteen Points) was the use of a mechanical form suggested in the cable, is more than presumable.

But I am aware of these things, in the main, only from circumstance. Up to this time I have not discussed the matter or commented upon it. While the war lasted Mr. Creel and I, whenever we were together, were too driven by the things that remained to be done to be concerned with the things that had been done.

pretation until their specific program of practical terms was added. That program proposed no concessions at all either to the sovereignty of Russia or to the preferences of the populations with whose fortunes it dealt, but meant, in a word, that the Central Empires were to keep every foot of territory their armed forces had occupied—every province, every city, every point of vantage—as a permanent addition to their territories and their power.

It is a reasonable conjecture that the general principles of settlement which they at first suggested originated with the more liberal statesmen of Germany and Austria, the men who have begun to feel the force of their own people's thought and purpose, while the concrete terms of actual settlement came from the military leaders who have no thought but to keep what they have got. The negotiations have been broken off. [Note: An error. The Russians threatened to break the negotiations; the Germans paid no attention. The Embassy reported the situation correctly to Washington. The dispatches evidently were delayed in arrival. E. S.] The Russian representatives were sincere and in earnest. They cannot entertain such proposals of conquest and domination. . . .

But, whatever the results of the parleys at Brest-Litovsk, whatever the confusions of counsel and of purpose in the utterances of the spokesmen of the Central Empires, they have again attempted to acquaint the world with their objects in the war and have again challenged their adversaries to say what their objects are and what sort of settlement they would deem just and satisfactory. There is no good reason why that challenge should not be responded to, and responded to with the utmost candor. We did not wait for it. Not once but again and again we have laid our whole thought and purpose before the world, not in general terms only, but each time with sufficient definition to make it clear what sort of definite terms of settlement must necessarily spring out of them. . . .

There is no confusion of counsel among the adversaries of the Central Powers, no uncertainty of principle, no vagueness of detail. The only secrecy of counsel, the only lack of fearless frankness, the only failure to make definite statements of the objects of the war, lies with Germany and her Allies. The issues of life and death hang upon these definitions. . . .

There is, moreover, a voice calling for these definitions of principle and of purpose, which is, it seems to me, more thrilling and more compelling than any of the many moving voices with which the troubled air of the world is filled. It is the voice of the Russian people. They are prostrate and all but

At this point I inserted the request cable of January 3, and gave a *résumé* of the circulation the speech received, continuing:

As far as Russia was concerned there was not much immediate military utility in this distribution. The military utility was against Germany, our first heavy and organized attack upon her morale. But for Russia, although shattered, still remained the question of the future, which in Russia is more a matter of years than of days, of decades more than of years, and of peasants more than of Bolsheviks.

To illustrate. In 1924, Dr. William T. Ellis, traveler and writer, returned to Swarthmore, Pennsylvania, and was interviewed by the *New York Times* (Feb. 6, 1924). I clipped and kept the interview and here in part it is:

Apparently none of us who has been writing during the past seven years has been able to make clear to stay-at-home America the unique and marvelous place the name and central ideas of President Wilson

helpless, it would seem, before the grim power of Germany, which has hitherto known no relenting and no pity. Their power, apparently, is shattered. And yet their soul is not subservient. They will not yield either in principle or in action. Their conception of what is right, of what is humane and honorable for them to accept, has been stated with a frankness, a largeness of view, a generosity of spirit, and a universal human sympathy which must challenge the admiration of every friend of mankind; and they have refused to compound their ideals or desert others that they themselves may be safe.

They call to us to say what it is that we desire; in what, if anything, our purpose and our spirit differ from theirs; and I believe that the people of the United States would wish me to respond, with utter simplicity and frankness. Whether their present leaders believe it or not, it is our heartfelt desire and hope that some way may be opened whereby we may be privileged to assist the people of Russia to attain their utmost hope of liberty and ordered peace. . . .

We entered this war because violations of right had occurred which touched us to the quick and made the life of our own people impossible unless they were corrected and the world secure once for all against their recurrence.

What we demand in this war, therefore, is nothing peculiar to ourselves. It is that the world be made fit and safe to live in; and particularly that it be made safe for every peace-loving nation which, like our own, wishes to live its own life, determine its own institutions, be assured of justice and fair dealing by the other peoples of the world as against force and selfish aggression. All the peoples of the world are in effect partners in this interest, and for our own part we see very clearly that unless justice be done to others it will not be done to us.

The program of the world's peace, therefore, is our program; and that program, the only possible program, as we see it, is this:

1. Open covenants of peace, openly arrived at, after which there shall be no private international understandings of any kind but diplomacy shall proceed always frankly and in the public view.
2. Absolute freedom of navigation upon the seas, outside territorial waters, alike in peace and in war, except as the seas may be closed in whole or

Американскій Президентъ

ВИЛЬСОНЪ

и

ДЕМОКРАТИЧЕСКІЙ МИРЪ.

Американск. Бюро Печати.—Вашингтонъ,
Русскій отдѣлъ, Большой Чернышевскій, 6, Москва.

PRESIDENT WILSON'S FOURTEEN POINTS IN FOLDER FORM

Title-page of folder containing the Fourteen Points Speech, as printed in Moscow for street distribution. The heading reads: "American President Wilson and Democratic Peace."

have come to hold in the minds of the masses of Asia and Africa as well as Europe.

It may sound like an exaggeration to say so, but I think it is true that no other mortal man has ever obtained so nearly absolutely universal fame as President Wilson. Often I have pondered the subject while in lands far outside the currents of civilized life—for the illiterate millions of Asia and other backward countries must be considered in summing up really universal fame. At best, fame is little more than a local celebrity. Shakespeare's name and Caesar's and Alexander's are unknown to two-thirds of the human race. Even contemporary military figures like Foch and the Kaiser had only a relatively limited circle of fame.

But because of his magic appeal to the deepest sensibilities of all human life, which were given the wings of the morning by the unprecedented propaganda of the Allies, the Wilson principles quickly spread to the uttermost parts of the earth. There the innate vitality of the ideals caused them to take root and grow. As no other wholly human man has ever done before Woodrow Wilson voiced the basic instincts and desires of the race.

In my travels throughout Russia I found that the Wilson name and

in part by international action for the enforcement of international covenants.

3. The removal, as far as possible, of all economic barriers and the establishment of an equality of trade conditions among all the nations consenting to the peace and associating themselves for its maintenance.

4. Adequate guarantees given and taken that national armaments will be reduced to the lowest point consistent with domestic safety.

5. A free, open minded, and absolutely impartial adjustment of all colonial claims, based upon a strict observance of the principle that in determining all such questions of sovereignty the interests of the populations concerned must have equal weight with the equitable claims of the government whose title is to be determined.

6. The evacuation of all Russian territory and such a settlement of all questions affecting Russia as will secure the best and freest co-operation of all the other nations of the world in obtaining for her an unhampered and unembarrassed opportunity for the independent determination of her own political development and national policy and assure her of a sincere welcome into the society of free nations under institutions of her own choosing; and, more than a welcome, assistance also of every kind that she may need and may herself desire. The treatment accorded Russia by her sister nations in the months to come will be the acid test of their good will, of their comprehension of her needs as distinguished from their own interests, and of their intelligent and unselfish sympathy.

7. Belgium, the whole world will agree, must be evacuated and restored, without any attempt to limit the sovereignty which she enjoys in common with all other free nations. No other single act will serve as this will serve to restore confidence among the nations in the laws which they themselves have set and determined for the government of their relations with one another. Without this healing act the whole structure and validity of international law is forever impaired.

8. All French territory should be freed and the invaded portions restored, and the wrong done to France by Prussia in 1871 in the matter of

aims had become the slogan of the peasants. Nowhere was the influence of the Wilson ideas more amazing than in Japan and China.

The Committee on Public Information distributed all of the Wilson war speeches in Japan and China. In Europe they were translated into every European language except the Finnish. The Croatian, Magyar, Serbian, and Czech tongues were included.

I may add that in my day I have encountered only one towering intellect. It was that of Woodrow Wilson.

The reason that America's diffusion of its war and peace aims was pervasive beyond that of all other nations was because those aims were not of opportunistic artifice but of belief.

Alsace-Lorraine, which has unsettled the peace of the world for nearly fifty years, should be righted, in order that peace may once more be made secure in the interests of all.

9. A readjustment of the frontiers of Italy should be effected along clearly recognizable lines of nationality.

10. The peoples of Austria-Hungary, whose place among the nations we wish to see safe-guarded and assured, should be accorded the freest opportunity of autonomous development.

11. Roumania, Serbia, and Montenegro should be evacuated; occupied territories restored; Serbia accorded access to the sea; and the relations of the several Balkan states to one another determined by friendly counsel along historically established lines of allegiance and nationality; and international guarantees of the political and economic independence and territorial integrity of the several Balkan states should be entered into.

12. The Turkish portions of the present Ottoman Empire should be assured a secure sovereignty, but the other nationalities which are now under Turkish rule should be assured an undoubted security of life and an absolutely unmolested opportunity of autonomous development, and the Dardanelles should be permanently opened as a free passage to the ships and commerce of all nations under international guarantees.

13. An independent Polish state should be erected which should include the territories inhabited by indisputably Polish populations, which should be assured a free and secure access to the sea, and whose political and economic independence and territorial integrity should be guaranteed by international covenant.

14. A general association of nations must be formed under specific covenants for the purpose of affording mutual guarantees of political independence and territorial integrity to great and small states alike.

CHAPTER XV

January 13—January 15, 1918. The Rumanian Affair.

1.

IT was my lot to view the eruptive "Rumanian Affair" from every angle. The name was given by common consent to a series of events beginning, as far as the public could perceive, with the arrest of the Rumanian Ambassador, M. Diamandi, in Petrograd on January 13, and ending, on his part, with a fortuitous escape into Sweden from Torneo in Finland—nearly a thousand miles from Petrograd—in February, weeks afterward, his suite left behind in Finland. The enactment as a whole was against Rumania, an effort to force that country into the Russo-German Peace Conference at Brest-Litovsk. Diamandi bore the brunt because he was the Ambassador of Rumania stranded by the Bolshevik Revolution in a land now become inimical to his own, with an alliance denounced. The presence of Rumania's gold reserve in Russia, sent there for safe-keeping in the early days of the War, was a factor of importance in the situation. Diamandi's arrest was prelude to Bolshevik seizure of the gold.

Much of this knowledge I had not gained when I played a light-hearted rôle amid the curtain-raising events. So presentation has two parts—the first, objective and visual of the scene as it was unrolled under Bolshevik management; and the second, subjective and realistic, the result of research and analysis. Words written at the time of the action, either by me or by others, make the body of the combined account.

For introduction, entries from my Log:

Jan. 13—New Year's Eve, Russian. Midnight sensation—Rumanian Ambassador pinched.

Jan. 14—Rumanian episode boils. Diplomats meet and prepare notes. Behind the scenes. Four o'clock—going out or staying in? Part of the versatile Gumberg. Comedy conclusion. Cards with Ambassador Francis in the evening. Again midnight word—that Rumanian is to be released.

Jan. 15—He was released.

Jan. 28—Ten hours notice for Diamandi (to leave Russia). Ambassador asks help for extension. Try but fail.

The narration advanced, from the concluding paragraph in my serial letter of January 13:

Was called from typewriter to telephone just now to get the nightly bit of the unexpected. It was news that the Rumanian Ambassador has been pinched and put in Peter and Paul. As yet have no details. There is nothing sacred about Ambassadors in this land, but this is violation of traditional immunity and makes a serious situation. However, everything here has an equal chance of being comedy or tragedy. This may turn to comedy in the morning.

From the next chapter of the letter, dated January 15, the eve of courier departure with the mail:

The arrest of the Rumanian Ambassador turned to comedy, though not without some stage managing I was near enough to see. The Rumanian was arrested because a Russian army is being starved by the Rumanian army which is so stationed as to cut off Russian supplies. Also Russian commissars have been shot by the Rumanians. Yet both armies are supposed to be under the same armistice with the Austro-Germans. The chief Rumanian in Russia was the minister at Petrograd. So the Russians took him. It was a ferocious violation of diplomatic privilege and a world challenge.

Every Ambassador saw himself stripped of world immunity. They moved some. By noon (Monday, January 14) they had drawn up and signed a note of protest. The first draft contained the sentence that if the Rumanian was not released they would all call for passports at once; but Francis, knowing that the President did not want the United States to cut its relations with Russia, kicked hard and wisely. So the final form was protest but not ultimatum.

Then up to Smolny went the whole nineteen in their motor cars. The way was prepared for their coming in more ways than they knew. An intermediary not at all diplomatic—a man close to me —had gone during the forenoon to Lenin to tell him that if he wished to make Russia helpless before Germany and destroy his own party all he would have to do would be to keep the Rumanian in jail, but that if he had hopes for the future the best practical politics would be to release the man.

At the same time he was asked if he would like to talk to our Ambassador and hear a formal protest. He wrote a note of assent. Then when the surprise party of 19 was decided on, it became necessary to acquaint Lenin with the change of plan and make sure of his presence at the hour. This job was done by telephone from my room and as usual the telephone refused for fifteen minutes to work at all. But the word came in time and the doors were open when the diplomats reached Smolny. It certainly was recognition that the Bolshevik Government had an official call from the representatives of the countries that refuse to concede its existence.

It was a pleasant party. The callers, most of them, agreed to protest against Germany's starvation plan, and Lenin agreed to turn the Rumanian loose. Which he did at 9 o'clock today.

The Ambassador was spokesman and came forth saying that he thought Lenin an "agreeable, friendly person." I do not think so, but I would sooner see the Ambassador on easy terms with a government that has to be dealt with every day in some way or other than to have him take his old stand that he would be "damned if he ever would talk to a Bolshevik."

The objective narration may be completed with the explanation that the "intermediary" who first went to Lenin was the resourceful Alexander Gumberg, thereafter to be known among us as the "International Ambassador." He went on instructions, with knowledge and consent of the Ambassador, who, with all of us, realized that instant protest must be made. If the Council of Ambassadors had not reached the same decision we would have acted independently. We feared less that the Council would not act than that it would not act with the promptness required. We believed that a delay of a few hours, or inaction, would imperil the American and the French Ambassadors and the *Chargé* of the British Embassy, and were certain that a bit of dignified by-play would relieve the pressure.

We were both right and wrong. If the Allied Ambassadors had sat sullenly they would have invited later insults and violence. But the Rumanian Ambassador was the immediate and special quarry, as events were to show. The Rumanian gold reserve was seized at the Kremlin in Moscow on January 26.

Two days later Diamandi and his staff were ordered to leave Russia in ten hours' time. He sent a plea to Ambassador Francis to intervene for delay, and the Ambassador asked me to aid. The iciness with which the request was met at Smolny warned me of futility. I advised the Ambassador of the uselessness of further intercession, lest he be embarrassed by a refusal made direct to him. Diamandi, his personnel and his goods, were loaded upon a train and thrust into Finland.

2.

A WEEK after Diamandi's exit, a letter averred to have been written by Adolph Ioffe of the Bolshevik peace delegation at Brest-Litovsk to the Central Council at Petrograd, came temporarily into the possession of Ambassador Francis, who was so roused by it that he urged me to undertake an inquiry to verify or disprove the disquieting contents. The letter purported to be one of instructions emanating from Trotsky for the sending of agitators to break down the Rumanian army and referred to a telegraphic proposal from Trotsky that the Rumanian Ambassador be arrested in Petrograd. Trotsky had been instigated to that course, according to the letter, by General Hoffman. This paragraph, sinister in import to the Allies as well as to Rumania, read:

It is greatly in the interests of the German and Austrian delegations that complete harmony should prevail on the entire Russian front, seeing that in this event the German and Austrian chief command will propose to Rumania their terms of peace, and will be in a position to take up their operations on the Western front on a very large scale. At the same time General Hoffman in the course of a conversation with Comrade Trotsky twice hinted at the necessity of immediately beginning these war operations. When Comrade Trotsky declared that the Council had no means of influencing the Rumanian staff, General Hoffman pointed out the necessity of sending trustworthy agents to the Rumanian army, and the possibility of arresting the Rumanian Mission in Petrograd.

The date of the letter* was December 31 (Old Style), January 13 (Western Calendar). Diamandi was arrested on

---

* Document No. 37A, "The German-Bolshevik Conspiracy," Appendix, p. 478.

January 13. The letter mentioned earlier telegraphic communication to that end.

The steps of the inquiry thereupon begun will have relation in later chapters, concern here being for information bearing upon the Rumanian Affair. I soon was participating in the surveillance of the wires between Brest-Litovsk and Smolny, and had transcripts of the January messages from the opening of that month's session. This was material that did not enter into the report I made to the Government in May, 1918, as the larger part of it had not then had written translation. The wire overlooking, both of the Brest-Litovsk Conference and the War Prisoner Commission in Petrograd, was done in union with the British Military Intelligence unit in Petrograd.

On my return to Washington I sent the telegraphic mountain, which included tedious articles for the Bolshevik newspapers as well as the personal and official dispatches in which I was interested, to U.S. Military Intelligence for translation. When text and translation came back, I was too busy with other matters to take the time for study. So the government report was long published, the War over, and I back in private life, before I began to hunt through the mass for the pieces to round out the Rumanian episode. I found them, lacking in the end only the text of Trotsky's first telegram, for which there was sequential disclosure of receipt.

On the night of January 13, the date of Diamandi's arrest, Podvoisky, the Commissar for War, wired from Petrograd to Trotsky at Brest-Litovsk:

"Your proposition with regard to Rumania was carried out. Podvoisky." [U.S. Military Intelligence translation.]

There was exactness of time and circumstance about the next message, from Petrograd to Brest-Litovsk on January 14:

The following to Trotsky: Today at 4 P.M. the whole diplomatic corps in the capital, with the American Ambassador at the head, appeared at Smolny requesting that the Rumanian Ambassador be released. We, stating the circumstances of the case, promised to hasten the investigation. At eight o'clock the American Ambassador communicated that if the Rumanian Ambassador is released he, the American Ambassador, would file a protest against the actions of the Rumanian command and will qualify (explain) the arrest of the Rumanian Ambassador as a protest on the part of the Russian Government against the non-admissible course of actions by the Rumanians. After such a statement on the part of the American Ambassador we considered it possible to state that a way is found; that in view of that the Rumanian Ambassador can be released, holding the Rumanian command responsible. I am waiting for a reply. I am speaking by direction of the People's Commissar, Stalin. (Note: Stalin, at Smolny, was in charge of official communications between Smolny and Brest-Litovsk. A subordinate was at the instrument.)

Trotsky, replying, from the Brest-Litovsk end of the direct wire:

I agree with your statement that the American Embassy took upon itself a definite share for the Rumanian command. A conditional release on the given conditions appears fully adequate. I advise you to summon Rakovsky and Boujor for the conference on Rumanian affairs. Energetic action on their part is necessary. If Rakovsky had considered it possible to take a "battle" stand against his government in the matter of peace his coming here would have been advisable. [U.S. Military Intelligence translation, Executive Division, G.S.]

Trotsky asked, the same day: "If Lenin received a letter by the Lettish courier and whether he is satisfied with the plan proposed in that letter," adding: "The question is highly important." The plan would refer not to Diamandi's arrest, already accomplished, but to the project of sending agitators to the Rumanian army, the larger concern of the Ioffe letter.

On January 15 Stalin wired to Trotsky: "Letter by courier not yet received."

The Ioffe letter contained the sentence: "This report is being sent by special courier." The tardiness of couriers, beset by poor travel conditions, was a usual occurrence.

Lenin disclosed on January 17, in the following fashion in a wire to Trotsky, that he was not acting independently in the Rumanian maneuver, and that in the crisis he waited for word from Trotsky:

Received reply from Rumanian Prime Minister to the ultimatum to the Rumanian Government: "Diamandi, Rumanian Minister, Petrograd—I have just received a telegram headed 'Ultimatum of the Soviet of People's Commissar,' signed by several Commissars. The measures taken by the Rumanian authorities are not of an unfavorable nature in respect to the Russian army. The purpose of these measures is to avoid armed conflicts on Rumanian territory and also disorderly moving which could have resulted in plunder and destruction. The statements regarding the 49th Division are nothing but pure invention. The Rumanian army does not confiscate the fodder, but on the other hand supplies the Russian army with all kinds of products from its own reserve supply. The Rumanian authorities did not take any part whatever in the arrest of the military. Austrian officers appearing beyond the line of the wire fencing were sent to the enemy advance posts, although, according to the agreements of the armistice, we had the right to detain them. Prime Minister Bratiano."

I would like to know your opinion on this reply immediately. Lenin. [U.S. Military Intelligence translation.]

The "ultimatum" to which Lenin referred was sent by wireless on January 14 and was a violent measure, practically a declaration of war, based on the flimsiest of pretexts:

ULTIMATUM OF THE C.P.C. TO THE RUMANIAN GOVERNMENT.

The Chief of the 49th Revolutionary Division has filed with us a protest against the conduct of the Rumanian authorities. In addition to disregarding the elective system of the Russian army they refuse to enter into agreement with our elected military chiefs and with the soldier committees, and they are seizing the forage stocks of our troops. As a result of this the horses in the 49th Division remain without forage.

The transfer of regiments is being stopped by the Rumanians by armed force. One of the regiments of the 49th Division, namely the 194th, Troitzko-Serge regiment, was surrounded by the Rumanians, the supply of provisions was cut off, and the regiment disarmed and led to the rear. The Rumanian authorities have arrested the elective committee of the regiment and the Austrian officers invited as guests of the staff of the 195th regiment.

The Council of People's Commissars demands of the Rumanian Government the release of those arrested and the punishment of those who made the arrests; and a guarantee from the Rumanian authorities that there will be no repetition of the illegal and disorderly actions.

The failure to receive an answer to this demand within 24 hours will be considered by us as a new rupture and we shall take then the most energetic military measures. (Signed) The President of the C.P.C., Ulianov (Lenin); Krylenko, Generalissimo; Podvoisky, People's Commissar for War.

The "ultimatum" was a public announcement, printed in the *Izvestia*.

No wonder Lenin did not know how to answer the protest of the Rumanian Government. Bratiano had made a simple reply to an invented accusation. The Russian threat had been blustering and clumsy. Lenin showed no deftness here. He had shrieked that he was angry because the Rumanians would not let Austrian officers go about their mission of breaking down Russian and Rumanian armies.

I found no record that Trotsky gave any helpful assistance of opinion as to what to do, and doubt if he responded by wire. On January 16 he had been summoned urgently to return to Petrograd, Lenin wiring; "Request you to call an intermission to leave for Petrograd." It had become obvious that consultation on many matters was necessary between the two. The All-Russian Soviet was to meet in a week. Report of the Peace Conference was due before that body. The Rumanian matter was itself troublesome.

Trotsky did not acknowledge the instruction promptly and Stalin asked querulously on the seventeenth why he had not. Trotsky answered that there would be a reply presently, and did not send one until the eighteenth, when he wired: "Tomorrow at 10 P.M. I leave for Petrograd. Will arrive on the 7th (January 20, Western Calendar). The other members of the delegation remain in Brest-Litovsk to continue negotiations. Trotsky." [All wire quotations U.S. Military Intelligence translations.]

In the same week at Petrograd I had become aware that Bolshevik agents, including Rakovsky who later was to become a Bolshevik diplomat to western European post-war conferences, had been sent to try to break the morale of the Rumanian army. On Rakovsky's return later in the month I talked with him about his venture, which was unsuccessful and rather trivial. Thus far I had accepted the contention that the Rumanians were harassing the Russians.

When Trotsky did come from Brest-Litovsk he remained in Petrograd a week, speaking in the interval before the All-

Russian Congress, leaving again for Brest-Litovsk on January 27.

The Rumanians continued obdurate. While Trotsky was in Petrograd he went before the Council and secured its assent on January 26 to a proclamation severing diplomatic relations with Rumania, decreeing the deportation of the Ambassador and all official Rumanians, and giving authority for the segregation of the Rumanian gold reserve "to be preserved as the property of the Rumanian people and kept inaccessible to the Rumanian oligarchy."

After Trotsky returned to Brest the record of the execution of the last order was telegraphed to him:

Memorandum to the Commissar for Foreign Affairs, Trotsky: Protocol—In pursuance of the order of the Commissar for Foreign Affairs L. Trotsky, I have seized the funds of the National Rumanian bank in regard to which the following protocol has been drawn up: "Moscow, Jan. 13 (Jan. 26, New Style)—I, the undersigned commandant of the Moscow Kremlin, Ivan Petrovich Petriakov, in consequence of the order of the People's Commissar for Foreign Affairs, L. Trotsky, in the presence of the director of the Moscow office of the Imperial Bank, T. I. Popov; a director of the same office, N. V. Veniaminov; and an assistant director of the Imperial Bank, V. I. Iakovlev, have affixed on the doors of the reserve store-house in the Kremlin, under the armory building, same being under the management of the Moscow office of the Imperial Bank, in which according to protocols in the Moscow office there are deposited funds of the Rumanian National Bank, the stamp of the Commandant of the city of Moscow—not the damaged stamp formerly affixed by the former director of the Moscow office of the Imperial Bank, V. I. Kovalnitsky and two of the above mentioned officials of the bank.

"Acting in accordance with the instruction of the commander of the armies of the Moscow military district and the People's Commissar L. Trotsky-Bronstein, I invited the Rumanian Consul General in Moscow, Citizen P. G. Geren, to assist in the drawing-up of the protocol. He, however, refused to come to the premises of the store-house, but gave his assent to the placing of the stamp on the doors of the store-house, and the original was signed by the Commandant of the Kremlin. Ivan Petriakov; director of the office of the Imperial Bank, T. Popov; director of the same office, N. Veniaminov, and the assistant director of the Imperial Bank, V. Iakovlev. In agreement with the original, Adjutant Commander of the Kremlin." Supplement: The guard is worthy. Do not worry. Salutations. Petriakov. [U.S. Military Intelligence translation.]

Even amid the troubles of the Peace Conference, then nearing climax, Trotsky did not lose interest in the Rumanian Ambassador. On February 4 he asked from Brest-Litovsk:

"Have measures been taken for the deportation of the Rumanian Embassy?" adding, "I understand that the Rumanian King is now in Austria. According to the German newspapers we have in Moscow not the Rumanian national fund but the gold fund of the Rumanian National Bank."

The distinction, if any, between the national and the bank fund was unknown to me. No other reference appeared.

Not receiving immediate reply to his question about Diamandi, Trotsky telegraphed again, "Has the deportation of the Rumanian Ambassador and the Military Mission from Petrograd been executed, and did anything happen?" [U.S. Military Intelligence translation.]

Reply to the inquiries was sent the evening of February 4 by Chicherin, lately become Assistant Foreign Minister:

Chicherin in Petrograd: "Please tell Trotsky it is very important for me, Chicherin, to have a talk with him. Please call Trotsky to the instrument."

Trotsky could not be reached.

Chicherin: "Hand Mr. Trotsky a note, then—at once. The sending out of the Rumanian Embassy and Military Mission from Petrograd has taken place, but beyond Tammerfors the party fell into the region of civil war. We have no word from Torneo from Svetlitsky who went with them. Friday we had a telegram from Torneo from Balabanova, but Balabanova has not arrived (here) up to this time. Evidently she is being held some place. Platten went away with Zalkind and Kamenev. Thanks to the help of the Red Guard they took the steamer that goes to Stockholm from Abo. Mr. Shaplen, correspondent American United Press, showed a telegram that the interview with Trotsky was received." [U.S. Military Intelligence translation.]

In his second message Trotsky had also asked:

"Did Kamenev leave for France? When will Zalkind depart?"

Zalkind had been Trotsky's assistant in the Foreign Office until succeeded by Chicherin and deputized with Kamenev for anti-Allied agitation abroad. Both did leave but could not get beyond Sweden. Platten was a Swiss Bolshevik, an intimate of Lenin's, now homeward bound after long stay in Petrograd. Balabanova was a famous continental and Russian woman revolutionist, in-coming after a stay in Sweden. Joseph Shaplen, the United Press correspondent, had interviewed Trotsky for the United Press on January 27 and presumably now had informed Chicherin that his dispatch was received in the United States.

"Did anything happen?" Trotsky had asked.

What did he expect to happen? What, too, was the meaning of Chicherin's reference to the Commissar Svetlitsky "who went with" Diamandi?

The record of telegraph conversations between Brest-Litovsk and Smolny had nothing more to add. There was no more news of Diamandi until the Peace Conference was over. Nor did Bolsheviks anywhere gain more information for a considerable time. What they heard then was that Svetlitsky was dead and Diamandi was alive. Had they expected the fates of the two men to be reversed?

In Petrograd we heard in latter February that Svetlitsky had been killed in Finland. In March, I followed a part of Diamandi's route through Finland, and came up with the members of his staff and their families at Bjorneborg. Guranesco, the Secretary of the legation, joined our American party. I heard the Rumanian story up to that point. When the Rumanian train approached an area where civil war was breaking out between the Reds, or Finnish Bolsheviks, and the Whites, or Finnish anti-Bolsheviks, the Ambassador decided to leave his suite at Tammerfors and, with Svetlitsky, to push on for Torneo. The internal warfare was still desultory, with no part of the country in the complete control of the Whites, who, however, were coalescing in the north. The Reds still held Torneo. No word came back from Diamandi to his group.

The train carrying him and Svetlitsky got through, however, to Torneo. But the Whites, unknown to the latter, had captured the town the day before. Svetlitsky was shot.

When I reached Torneo I was told by the border control

officer of the Whites that Svetlitsky, searched after arrest, was found to be carrying an order, addressed to Timofeiev, the Local Commissar of the Reds, for the execution of Diamandi at the border. For that reason, it was explained, Svetlitsky was given the death penalty, although it was argued in his behalf that he might not have known the contents of the note he was carrying. Svetlitsky was an important person among the Bolsheviks, regarded as close to Trotsky.

Final link in the chain of circumstances came to me in the autumn of 1918 when I was informed that a Czech officer, Captain Zedwic, in the service of the Whites ordered the shooting of the Russian, because, he told my informant, "I found a note on him signed by Trotsky ordering him to shoot Diamandi. The order was not as blunt as that but stated that Diamandi 'should be done away with.' "*

From first to last Trotsky appeared as the director of the onset against Rumania, Russia's nearest Ally in the Great War, and against Diamandi, the official representative of that neighbor nation—seeking the extermination of both.

---

* My informant was Joseph Shaplen, representative in Russia of the United Press Association. After his return to the United States, he wrote me on September 24, 1918:

"On my way from Stockholm to Christiana, July 26, I made the acquaintance of a Czecho-Slovak officer who was acting as commander of the anti-Bolshevik forces in Torneo during the civil war in Finland. He informed me that he was the man who ordered Svetlitsky shot. The information was given in reply to my question whether he knew Svetlitsky. When I asked him why he ordered him shot, he said; 'Because I found a note on him signed by Trotsky ordering him to shoot Diamandi. The order was not as blunt as that but stated that Diamandi "should be done away with." '

"The officer's name was Captain Z—. I cannot permit the publication of his name as that may interfere with whatever work he may be contemplating in the future. I am prepared to furnish you his full name if necessary. He served with General Mannerheim, but quit Finland when the Germans occupied it."

At my request Mr. Shaplen sent me the officer's name on my promise not to use it then except in case of an emergency. None arose, and the two letters were filed. After twelve years the reasons for the original precautions have passed.

CHAPTER XVI

*January 15—January 19, 1918. The Birth and Death
of the Constituent Assembly.*

1.

QUIET of holidays and the excitement of the first arrest
of the Rumanian Ambassador alike were pushed aside
by the approach of the Constituent Assembly which
at last was to be allowed to meet. The date was set for January 18, and the outcome was to be forecast in no way except
that it would be trouble in one form or another.

Rancor of Bolsheviks against all foemen was increased by an
attempt, made on January 15, to assassinate Lenin. It failed
narrowly. Four bullets struck the automobile in which he was
riding. His companion in the car, Platten, the Swiss Bolshevik, was acclaimed, when the circumstances became known,
as Lenin's preserver. At the sound of the first shot he pressed
down Lenin's head with the palm of his hand. The second bullet
grazed the finger of the hand. The other shots lodged in the
framework of the car. The assailants never were discovered.
The Bolsheviks capitalized the attack by placing blame upon
supporters of the Constituent Assembly. The leaders of that
movement denied it indignantly.

The Bolsheviks had paraded as the year ended. Now their
opponents purposed to parade from the center of the city and
from the Field of Mars to the Tauride Palace, where the Assembly was to sit. The Bolsheviks had been masters of the
streets of the city and their marchers went unmolested. They
still were masters. Would they let their foes have free use of
the streets?

We believed not, from the signs we saw. The machine guns
at Smolny were cleaned. Machine guns were installed at the
Tauride Palace. The street by the telephone building, nerve
center of the city, was blockaded for defense. Against what?
It was not conceivable that in Petrograd were anti-Bolshevik
forces which would face guns and an army. The Bolsheviks
were safe enough in a military way; and if there were onsets

it was more reasonable to suppose that they rather than the Assembly acclaimers would be the aggressors. Yet the Bolsheviks had agreed to let the Assembly meet and had not denied the streets to the paraders.

They had decreed, however, that the parades should not approach the Tauride Palace; and it was to the doors of the Tauride that the parades were announced to go. The signs, we agreed as we heard reports and talked the situation over in my rooms the night of the sixteenth, were for clash. Colonel Kerth, who was present, gave us a lecture on the military tactics of city fighting. We prepared to be onlookers, both of the parades and the Assembly.

The whole design of the present session-call of the Constituent Assembly left me cold, admirable as was the original design of the body. For practical purposes the Bolsheviks destroyed the Assembly when they staged their Revolution of force, and they timed their outbreak with that intention. The Constitutional Democrats (Kadets), the balancing party of the middle class, were eliminated from the Constituent Assembly by that fact of proletarian revolution. What remained was contesting parties of Socialists. That fact enhanced the bitterness that overhung the gathering, for the gulf between the educational and peaceful policies of the Right Social Revolutionaries and the force doctrine and immediate class war intention of the Bolsheviks was unbridgeable, and at the same time it subtracted from the body nearly all possibility of constructive effort. Circumstances tended, too, to lead the opponents of Bolshevism to adopt the politically popular parts of the Bolshevik program—particularly that of peace. Chernov, the present leader of the Right Social Revolutionaries, was vigorous, but under the realities of the moment was crying for peace as loudly as the Bolsheviks.

The campaign cry, indeed, had been that the Bolsheviks, having sought and failed to gain peace, must now give way to the Constituent Assembly, which would seek a general peace among the belligerents in the name of the whole Russian nation.

A digest of the resolutions to be presented by the Social Revolutionaries to the Assembly already had been made public as a part of their campaign. The statement was:

The country needs peace. By promising to give it immediately the Bolsheviks have lured the worn-out soldiers. But they did not give peace. They only opened the front to the enemy and brought upon the country the menace of a new, distressing war. They seek to avert the popular wrath by loud and hypocritical phrases about a sacred war, which prostrate Russia, deprived of her army by their very efforts, shall wage against the entire world.

Our party will adopt urgent measures both to save Russia from a new war and from that political and economical enslavement and the surrender of Russia to the mercy of the victors prepared by the Bolsheviks. By separate armistice and separate peace parleys the Bolsheviks have impaired the relations with the Allies and left Russia alone in the struggle. By opening the front and by destroying industry, the Bolsheviks surrender defenseless Russia into the power of its enemies.

The aggregate of these causes makes a peace at the expense of Russia—dooming it to miserable vegetation.

It is not possible for the Bolsheviks to cut the knot tied by them. Within the country they must wage a civil war and try to establish themselves by terrorism. Outside Russia they are only reckoned with by the Central Powers and only there to the extent that they serve as tools for Germany's imperialist aspirations at the expense of Russia. The Bolsheviks have surrendered already to the enemy Government to which they applied over the heads of Democracy.

Only the Constituent Assembly, the only body which has the authority to speak in the name of Russia and which is recognized by all Governments, can free our country and achieve a general democratic peace.

The party of Social Revolution will propose immediately to the Constituent Assembly to choose a delegation with plenipotentiary powers to begin negotiations for the terms of a general democratic peace, acceptable to all belligerent countries, a peace without victors and without vanquished.

But while these negotiations progress all those who are weary and whose spirit has broken must be freed from the hardships of military service. We must give a deserved rest to those worn out by three years of war. They have fulfilled their duty to the country. In order, however, that the country should not remain defenseless during the war, and to deprive the enemy of temptation to break off the negotiations and to strike a final blow at the country for the purpose of dictating peace terms, the Social Revolutionary party will immediately undertake the reformation of the army on the basis of volunteer service leaving those who do not uselessly burden the front to defend the borders and the people's Revolution. All volunteers and their families will be worthily supported. Support also will be given to all those who have suffered in defense of the country.

A clause of the resolutions themselves created a federal republic. Another clause abolished the private ownership of land; provided for the nationalization of mines, oil wells, railroads, and water power and for State control over industries; provided for the reorganization and State control of banking; provided that interest on the war loans be raised by the taxation of the wealthy classes; and provided for an eight-hour employment day, a minimum wage law, for social insurance, and for measures against unemployment.

In conclusion appeal was made to the country to offer resistance to the "enemies of the people."

The program was practical only if there was strength to offer resistance. In an Assembly meeting under the guns of its opponents there was no such strength. Either a feeble pose or a bloody repulse was the likelihood. I expected to witness heroism and a disaster. That the session should be in Petrograd instead of in an anti-Bolshevik area in inner Russia appeared to me to be itself fatal.

The notion prevailed, however, that wider national influence would come from action in Petrograd. On this basis, too, was the Bolshevik claim that there was Assembly purpose of seizing the city. Rumor, of course, was busy. Two regiments were said to be ready to declare themselves for the Assembly. There was even report that the Germans were friendly to the body. Count Mirbach was said to be counseling its leaders. This was not to be credited with any reasonableness unless as a hint to the Bolsheviks to hasten to conclusion the existing peace parleys. Although they might be approached by German emissaries, men of the caliber of Tseretelli could be trusted to recognize the shallow guile. That point bothered me little. The hopelessness of the session was the thing apparent.

I expressed my own feelings by logging: "Jan. 17—Eve of battle or collapse of a bluff, which?"

On this same eve of the Assembly and its public demonstration, the Petrograd Soviet and the Extraordinary Commission for Combating Counter-Revolution both issued warnings to the populace—and in terms of threat. The Petrograd Council declared in resolution:

The parties of the counter-revolution have arranged a demonstration January 5 (January 18, New Style) against the Council of Workers', Peasants' and Soldiers' Deputies. This will be a demonstration against the Workers' October Revolution, against the claims to land, peace, workers' control, nationalization of the banks. This will be a demonstration of the enemies of the people, a demonstration of the friends of Kaledin, Kornilov.

Under the watchword, "All power to the Constituent Assembly" is hidden the watchword, "Down with the Soviets." This will be a demonstration of the strikers, the *bourgeoisie*, the servers of the *bourgeoisie*, who are hiding themselves under the name of the Right Social Revolutionaries.

The Petrograd Council decrees:

On January 5 (January 18) all the workers remain at their usual work. All the regiments remain in their barracks. Only those armed companies will appear on the streets which will be called for that purpose by the organs of the Council.

The Petrograd Council charges the Commissar Blagonravov to take all measures to the effect that on January 5 (January 18) order should prevail on the streets of Petrograd.

The occupation of any public institution whatsoever by the counter-revolutionary demonstrators will not be allowed and will be met with unsparing resistance. The Petrograd Council gives to the Petrograd military authorities the widest powers in this respect. The Petrograd Council calls on all the district councils to be vigilant and to mobilize.

The Extraordinary Commission made proclamation:

The Extraordinary Commission for the protection of Petrograd is in possession of information that counter-revolutionaries of all shades, united for the struggle with the Soviet authorities, have scheduled their demonstration for January 18—the day of the opening of the Constituent Assembly. It has also become known that the leaders of these counter-revolutionary plots are Filonenko, Savinkov, and Kerensky, who have arrived in Petrograd from the Don, from Kaledin.

The Extraordinary Commission has taken appropriate measures for the maintenance of strict revolutionary order in the capital. Making this public to all citizens of Petrograd, the Extraordinary Commission calls their attention to the following:

(1) Petrograd is under martial law and all attempts at pogroms will be suppressed by armed force.

(2) Any insubordination to the orders of the authorities will be met with reprisals.

(3) Any attempt of groups of counter-revolutionists to enter the district of the Tauride Palace will be stopped by armed force.

(4) Comrades and citizens loyal to the authority of the Workers' and Peasants' Soviets are called upon to support everywhere the maintenance of the strictest order and not to participate in demonstrations, meetings, and street disorders in order that they may not suffer accidentally should it prove necessary to use armed force against the counter-revolutionists.

In the face of these orders for their destruction thousands of the supporters of the Constituent Assembly gathered at chosen points on Friday morning to challenge force by the visible protest of marching ranks, their faith in their rightness, and in nonresistance. They were heroic and pitiful.

The Cossacks were out, galloping up and down the Nevsky, when I started afoot in the early morning of January 18 for the Foreign Office for necessary passes. They ringed, too, the plaza before the Winter Palace.

In the whole Foreign Office I found only two persons, Rosa Radek, the wife of Radek, and Sholopina, the big girl, and they not in the office section but in a magnificent apartment set aside in other days as the private suite of the minister. They were huddled in furs eating a breakfast of bread and tea on a table set up in an entry, although in a salon next birch wood was laid for a fire in a grate. Ransome, my companion, and I laughed at them for being cold when they might easily have been warm but they shrugged their shoulders.

They had not found kindling, they said, and it was too much effort to seek it. So, knowing the ways of the Russian white wood which I have called birch, I walked over, tore off some of the loose bark, put it above, not under, the sticks, and touched a match to the oily stuff. The wood went cheerfully about the business of burning. And after she had drunk her tea, Sholopina wrote the passes, good for way through parade patrols, through the sailor barrier to the Tauride, through Uritsky's or

Blagonravov's minions, as the case might be, at the doors of the Tauride itself. Rosa Radek, a plump, comely woman, said she thought we would have a dull day. As for herself, the fire being lighted, she intended to do her day's writing alongside it. Like her husband she was contributor both to the *Pravda* and *The Torch*.

Walking back to the hotel, I took sledge to get a view of the parades before going to the Tauride Palace.

The processions were allowed to assemble unopposed. How many lines formed in different parts of the city I did not know. Three I placed and I heard of others. One gathered in the plaza by the Winter Palace. One raised its standards in the Field of Mars. One sought to come across the Neva to the Liteiny on the Alexandrovsky Bridge. All were to converge at the Tauride Palace.

The first parade from the Winter Palace was passing along the Nevsky in very good order when I saw it. I drove along the line for several blocks. As many women as men were in the double column. Banners on which the most common inscription was "All Power to the Constituent Assembly" were borne at the van. The marchers might have been the middle-class citizens of any continental city or of New York or Chicago. Only their terrible soberness set them apart from their kind all over the world. Until deprived of occupation they had been teachers and lawyers, clerks and business men, engineers and builders, government functionaries and technicians. Among them, they represented most of the city's culture, most of its individual mental initiative. Their dress was neat and poor. The ornate were not here.

The walks of the Nevsky were crowded with onlookers, hostile, most of them, smiling laborers out to see a show. They jeered but did not attack; and I got the impression that the Bolsheviks had decided to protect the paraders and divert the lines peacefully in the wide areas adjacent to the Tauride Palace. The reality was that no trouble was desired in the center of the city. The policing there was intrusted less to the infantry soldiers and the sailors than to the cavalry Cossacks.

Retracing the route to the Michaelovsky I was driven toward the Field of Mars. On the way I heard shots but could not tell from what quarter they came. At the Field I came upon a scene of confusion, though not of battle. A procession, I was informed, had moved in the direction of the Summer Garden, intending to pass the bridge over the Fontanka canal and so reach the Liteiny Prospect. Report had come back that this parade had been broken. One of its marshals, standing in a crowd near where the martyrs of the March Revolution were buried, was telling excitedly of the disaster. He had run far.

The distance, however, by short cut was not so great. The driver ran his horse and in a few minutes I was on the Liteiny, in the wreck of the procession, or rather of two processions, the one I had left on the Nevsky and the one that had started from Mars Field. The latter, coming upon the Liteiny just about the time the former was halted, broke up, I think, more from panic than attack. The head of the first procession had come squarely against the Bolshevik bulwark several blocks ahead at the corner of the Liteiny and the Shpalernaya, where a right turn was to have been made to the Tauride.

The Bolshevik patrols scattered this van and the whole procession rolled back on itself through the length of the Liteiny. Yet our sledges (one followed mine) were engulfed in no *mêlée*. For a moment or two I thought we had missed the scene. Then I perceived that the street was thickly peopled but not at its center. Much snow had fallen lately and was piled in great heaps along the curbs. Behind the snow banks and in the door and area ways were the remnants of the parade. Seeing that we were not soldiers the routed members crawled into view or peeped over the top of the snow piles. Over the *débris* of their fallen and broken banners we glided. No bodies of dead or wounded were anywhere in sight, though men shouted to us that there had been slaughter near.

Blood certainly was shed. We moved back and forth on the Liteiny and into the side streets where the flight had continued. The blocks on both sides of the Fuhrstatskaya were in disarray. The snow in the Liteiny and for a considerable distance in the Fuhrstatskaya was bloodstained in many places. Some of the paraders claimed there had been shooting from the roofs. Lettish soldiers came running from somewhere and soon established a patrol along the Liteiny. They were greeted with cries, "Murderers of the People!" They paid no attention and went briskly about—pulling persons from the snow, helping them to their feet, and ordering them to move out of the neighborhood. In reply to question a soldier in charge of the squads nearest said that his men had done no shooting.

The Bolsheviks later laid the blame for all killings of the day upon provocators as the most convenient of counter-revolutionary ogres, although they admitted there was shooting where the vans of parades were dispersed.

The Embassy was further down the Fuhrstatskaya and, leaving the vanished parade, we went there before proceeding to the Tauride Palace. I had thought the Ambassador might care to witness the opening of the Constituent Assembly. However, he judged that his presence would be inadvisable.

2.

GETTING into the Constituent Assembly was a matter of parley. Our passes opened a way through the close-drawn sailor cordons in the streets and about the Tauride Park, and through the palace guards themselves. Inside the building, however, we encountered a point of etiquette. We were not provided with credentials from the Constituent Assembly itself. The Bolshevik deputy commissars in lengthy conversations said they did not mind what we did, but that they were there to "protect" the Constituent Assembly, not to say who could enter it. So we dug into our pockets for some paper bearing an embassy seal, nice and red. Finding one, we marched to the entrance of the visitors' gallery, pronounced the word "*Diplomatique,*" showed the seal, and were ushered with much courtesy to a trio of boxes set aside for foreign diplomats. Several Frenchmen and Englishmen in uniform had preceded us but the boxes were commodious, and there were chairs on the gallery rail for our small party.

The arrangement of the chamber was formal and colorful. The seats for the four hundred odd delegates were planned much as in our legislative halls, chairs, some with desks in front, aligned in fan-like formation away from the presidium, which in the Russian manner included not only a rostrum but also seating space for the members of the steering committee and for important personages. Galleries nearly encircled the auditorium and even ran above the presidium. The chairs all were upholstered in red leather, and the decorative scheme of the hall was in red and gold. Illumination was soft and shadowless. The place was fitting for a Parliament.

The seats were sparsely occupied, the presidium was vacant, and the opening of the session not in early prospect. The likeness to a civilian body meeting for debate and quiet action ended with the survey of the document-piled desks and the clusters of dignified but restless delegates.

The Constituent Assembly was to meet within a ring of steel. Armed guards were all about us—sailors with pistols in their belts and rifles on their shoulders, soldiers with rifles and with cartridge belts strapped outside their overcoats, sleeve banded deputy commissars with pistols at side. The galleries held scarce a score of visitors, and yet resounded to the tramp of feet. A line of guards stood or walked in the connecting corridor, and in every box, including our own, was a pair of sailors or soldiers. The ushers, even those on the assembly floor, were armed men.

The wait was tedious. We had entered a few minutes before one o'clock. Three o'clock passed without sign of beginning. A light breakfast had not been followed by lunch. Hunger sent us searching for food. Sure enough there was a tearoom in the building and we found it better populated than the session floor. Tea only, however, was being served—no soup or bread. We drank tall tumblers of tea and went back to our seats, and this time we were none too soon. The presidium was filling. Two major groups were apparent there, on different sides of the ample platform, the committee of the Right Social Revolutionaries and their allies on one side, and of the Bolsheviks and their minor party adherents on the other. Members of the Central Council of the Soviets were there, and presently we made out Lenin among them, in the rear of the presidium, under the gallery. His lieutenants slipped back to him for counsel occasionally during the day but at no time during the day or night did he participate in debate or approach the rostrum.

We wondered what his appearance meant. Did the Bolsheviks have hope of a majority in the Constituent Assembly itself? Were they nearing the national victory of controlling that body? That, naturally, had been their aim in successively postponing the sitting of the body, in putting their own candidates up for election as delegates, in eliminating the Kadets from the lists of candidates. If they had thus won a majority they would be accused of cheating in the count at the polls and of riding over the will of the voters, but notwithstanding would have increased the semblance of legal control. None of the preliminary figures, however, indicated that the Bolsheviks had a majority in the Assembly. Estimates had been as extreme as two to one votes against them on a test.

Shown to be in a minority, would they seize the Constituent Assembly by force and use it as their own instrument, or would they destroy it out of hand? They had threatened destruction. The day of answer had come.

In the turbulent minutes following four o'clock it seemed as if the Bolsheviks had won initial parliamentary control. By Russian precedent the oldest member present calls a meeting to order. When all the delegates had taken their seats and the chair of the presiding officer was vacant, an old man, Shvetsov, rose from a place among the Right Social Revolutionaries and advanced toward the platform. Until then there had been silence. Uproar suddenly broke out among the Bolshevik delegates, stamping, shouting, hissing. The Social Revolutionaries responded by rising and applauding. The old man reached the chair and faced the delegates, but in the clamor his voice could not be heard. Several Bolsheviks on the platform tried to pull him from his place, but he lifted their hands away and continued to stand silently. The din increased.

Uritsky, the commandant of the Tauride, stepped forward but did not speak. Past him from the rear of the presidium came Sverdlov, a member of the Central Executive Committee. He walked in front of the old man, rang the bell, and abruptly called the meeting to order. At sight of him the Bolsheviks stilled their outbreak so that his voice was heard. The opposition, bewildered, dropped into its seats. Sverdlov had made himself the temporary chairman by typical Lenin strategy. It looked as if the Bolsheviks were going to have their own way in everything.

In the speech which was his right as temporary chairman Sverdlov read the Declaration of Rights of the Bolsheviks, and they cheered every clause; and at its conclusion they rose and sang "The International," a socialist hymn to which the Social Revolutionaries also had to give lip service. The Bolsheviks had staged themselves magnificently, maneuvering with a solidarity in contrast to the wavering leadership of the Social Revolutionaries.

The real grapple for the permanent chairmanship remained, and for this the Bolsheviks had reserved a flourish. They put forward as their candidate not a member of their own party and not a man but the slender, flaming Spiridonova, the woman leader of the peasants, member of the Social Revolutionary party of the Left. Crafty politics, surely, not only for the day but for the morrow. Who knows how much the compliment may have influenced Spiridonova when the following week in the All-Russian Soviet she led the peasants and her party definitely into the Bolshevik ranks?

The Right Social Revolutionaries nominated Chernov, their leader. The vote was by ball, a weary business of distribution, collection, and placing of the balls in glass vessels. By the accompanying noise Spiridonova would have been judged the victor, but the count spoke decisively for Chernov. He had 244 votes and Spiridonova 153. Surprisingly the Bolsheviks accepted the defeat without new tumult. The session took up an orderly progress.

Chernov's address when he took the chair was largely an exposition of the Social Revolutionary Declaration, nowise new. His attack upon the Bolshevik program was energetic, but his emphasis that the Constituent Assembly could get peace where the Bolsheviks had failed was not calculated to rouse any enthusiasm in me. Bukharin, the doctrinaire of the Bolsheviks, in his reply to Chernov stripped Bolshevism down to what it is when he asserted bluntly that it was more than nationalization of industry—that it was the dictatorship of an armed proletariat over all other classes, and that the party declaration provided that the middle and propertied classes should be disarmed.

While Chernov was speaking the Bolsheviks lolled in their seats, taking their cue from Lenin, who stretched himself full length on a settee on the presidium, and pretended to sleep. In my notes I jotted "A goat-getting stunt," and such it was, although Lenin may have had a restful nap as well.

When Bukharin started to talk the party men leaned eagerly forward as if intent on every word, applauding frequently.

The tactics changed when the dark Tseretelli rose for counter-reply. Here was a hated challenger and a moving orator. Out of two months' hiding he had come, staking his liberty on his rights to attend the legislative body to which he had been elected. I had seen him couch-ridden and pallid. Now he had arisen in strength to smite his enemies. The notes I took did not do his speech justice although they set forth the lawyer's argument upon which the Social Revolutionaries counted most—the principle that the acts of the Soviet already had recognized the Constituent Assembly.

From argument he passed to invective, arraigning the Bolsheviks for their sins against the nation and the people. His sentences cracked like whip-lashes and cut as deep. Either by order or because of the spell of his oratory he was not interrupted after he began to speak. He was hooted when first he appeared on the platform, then won silence as an orator will. His voice was clear and musical. He spoke for less than ten minutes, and in six weeks the Bolsheviks were not through answering him.

To no other hostile speech did they ever pay such attention. In a meeting of the Petrograd Soviet the next day Zinoviev worked himself into a rage against Tseretelli, and the Bolshevik newspapers kept up lengthy bombardment. Yet Tseretelli's outright statements were few and simple. He said that the Bolsheviks were miserable failures, that they were wrecking Russia, that their peace was conquest from without and civil war from within, and that they did not have the slightest idea of the meaning of creative socialism. And these opinions he put into language any Russian could understand.

The proof of this was the action of the sailor in our box. He cursed in monotone and several times raised his rifle threateningly. I doubt if he really meant to fire, and enough were near to prevent him, but he was tempted. One of us got the eye of his superior, lest accident happen, and had the emotional one removed. In the box next, shortly before, another sailor had amused himself by sighting at Chernov along the gun barrel, grinning the while. A passing commissar, smiling also, motioned him to lower the gun.

It was seven o'clock in the evening when Chernov was elected Chairman and eleven o'clock when Tseretelli was safely off the rostrum. My stomach was empty and my head bowed down with oratory. Party caucuses were in prospect, with recess or adjournment likely. If I had been told that the Constituent Assembly would be dissolved at one o'clock, I would have tightened my belt and stayed on, and then would have seen little that was recognizable as a moment of death. The Assembly in truth did not know that it was dead until after the event.

As prologue to the notes of the day and night, I made Log entry: "Jan. 18—(Friday) Collapse. Tonight's report six dead, thirty-four injured—probably underestimated."

From Vaskov, one of the Bolshevik delegates with whom I was acquainted, I got in the morning the story of the final hour of the Constituent Assembly.

After caucus at midnight the Bolshevik members did not return to the Assembly. Vaskov said that the caucus, after deciding to bolt the Assembly, sent their allies of the Left Social Revolutionaries back into the session for the purpose of completing the record. A delegate of the Left, after the Assembly was recalled to order, moved an indorsement of the Bolshevik stand at the Brest-Litovsk Peace Conference. This the Right Social Revolutionaries voted down and the announcement of the vote was the signal for the Lefts to rise and march out of the chamber.

A deputy commissar, representing Uritsky, thereupon walked up to Chernov, presiding, and told him curtly that the Assembly did not now exist and that the soldiers and sailors had no further duty to guard it. I asked Vaskov, who with other Bolsheviks had crowded around the doors near the rostrum, what the Commissar had said and he replied that the soldier spoke jerkily, without finishing sentences, but that he got this approximate meaning: "We soldiers and sailors were sent here to guard the Constituent Assembly. There isn't any Assembly now. You are just a lot of private persons, and what you say doesn't matter. We are through protecting you."

Chernov refused to recognize the interruption and motion was made to draft an appeal to the country for support of the Constituent Assembly and the Right Social Revolutionary program. The motion was passed, appointment of the drafting committee provided for, and adjournment taken until the next afternoon.

By this time there was little parliamentary semblance to the scene. Soldiers and sailors were shouting threateningly to the delegates to go home. Chernov was retorting and trying to keep order. Vaskov said that the Bolshevik delegates hurriedly advanced between Chernov and the noisy guards, got the Social Revolutionaries together, and flanked them as they showed them a way to safety. Many of the Bolsheviks had friends among the Social Revolutionaries. They had roused a storm against them but did not want them slain.

The sailors intended massacre, either inside the chamber or at the exit gates of the Tauride. Vaskov was of a group that argued with the sailor guards at the gates to keep them from killing. Escort of Bolshevik fellow members was kept around the Social Revolutionaries until they were well away from the Tauride. Not a member of the Assembly was harmed. Even Tseretelli got safely away. Chivalry for a moment raised its head.

Further record of the peril in which the Social Revolutionaries stood was made by the telegraphic report of Arosiev, a Bolshevik delegate, to the conference body at Brest-Litovsk: "We had to restrain the sailors from dispersing the remains of the Constituent Assembly." [U.S. Military Intelligence translation.]

My logged observation was: "Evidence that pogrom of Right S.R.'s narrowly avoided. Indications that purpose of sailors was volley fire into seats in early hour of morning." And to notes of Vaskov's account, I added: "Piecing together night. Figures 30 dead and 100 wounded." Reference was to casualties of the parade of the eighteenth.

The Constituent Assembly had passed, its life one day. The decree of dispersal was drawn at Smolny the morning of the nineteenth. I knew of it by ten o'clock. The Social Revolutionaries heard of it during the day or were advised. They made no effort to meet again. I went through the Tauride district under guard during the evening, finding the streets occupied only by patrols and the body of the Tauride Palace dark.

The city muttered over the street killings of the preceding day and was gloomily passive. The atmosphere at Smolny was cheerful.

CHAPTER XVII

January 20—January 22, 1918. The Dawn
of the Red Terror.

THE newspaper *Dielo Naroda* ("The People's Cause") made a brave showing on January 20 by declaring that a state of civil war existed. Hostile action against the Bolsheviks generally was followed by the closure of a newspaper but this defiance was allowed to pass unnoticed. The staffs of two other newspapers, the *Dien* ("The Day") and the *Volia Naroda* ("The People's Will"), were arrested on January 17 for lesser deeds, and the plant of the former closed. The *Dielo Naroda* was allowed to appear until the Bolshevik capital was moved to Moscow. The determination had been reached, however, to suppress more or less casually all of the opposition Socialist press. The *bourgeois* press was crushed early.

The *Dielo Naroda* voiced also the appeal of the Social Revolutionaries to the country, issuing it as the action of the Assembly. Only two Bolsheviks, a soldier and a Red Guard, the newspaper contended, had been among the victims of the shootings of January 18, these in its opinion killed by the fire of their comrades. The *Izvestia*, for the Bolsheviks, was clamoring that the violence was provocatory. For its own reasons, however, the *Izvestia* continued to belittle the total of deaths—only eight dead, all told, it insisted.

Then purple atrocity came along to overshadow the street killings. Shingarev and Kokoshkin, former Ministers of the Kerensky Government, were shot in their sick-beds at the Marinsky Hospital in the early morning of January 20. I got the first news of the crime when I heard report of it made at the meeting of the Petrograd Soviet at Smolny on the night of that day. First the report and then prompt introduction of a resolution for inquiry and for the punishment of the murderers! A claim at once that this also was a provocator killing by men "dressed as Red Guards and sailors"! Yet all the circumstances bespoke an ordered assassination.

As a preliminary the two men, who had been prisoners in the

fortress of SS. Peter and Paul since November, were removed
to the Marinsky Hospital, and new guards were placed over
them. The illness of the victims was the excuse for transfer.
Ruffians made unopposed entrance into the hospital and killed
them. Many of the details were in my possession by midnight
of January 20, but public accounts for a day or so were of
the briefest. The following relation was written by a French
investigator and appeared on January 22 in *The Combat*, an
occasional publication printed in French:

The former Minister of Finance, A. I. Shingarev, and the former
Minister F. F. Kokoshkin, arrested in November among the number of members of the Commission for the Constituent Assembly,
were assassinated during the night of January 6 (January 19
New Style) in the Marie Hospital, where they had been transferred owing to the state of their health.

MM. Kokoshkin and Shingarev were brought from the fortress
of Peter and Paul at 7 o'clock in the evening and placed in a section of a ward. The doctor who received them remembers these
words spoken by M. Shingarev: "I have a presentiment that I
will be killed tonight. While we were being transferred here we
heard the Red Guards discussing among themselves the best way
of getting rid of us. They said they would throw us into the Neva
except that there were too many people around."

As soon as the Red Guard retired, the sick men, very feeble
from the *régime* of the fortress, took immediately to their beds.

Toward 1 o'clock in the morning a detachment of Red Guards
appeared at the hospital. These men, after having stated to the
guard that they were sent to make a survey of the condition of
the prisoners, entered the court. They gave the same explanation
to the concierge of building in which the prisoners were. They
entered without opposition and were directed to the third floor.
M. Kokoshkin was already asleep. M. Shingarev was reading.
Everything happened then in a moment. Two men seized the
hospital nursing sister, who tried to bar their way, and held their
revolvers to her head while the rest of the band accomplished the
sinister mission with which they had been charged.

Three revolver bullets were fired into the bodies of each of the
sick men. M. Kokoshkin, hit in the head, the chest, and the ab-
domen, was instantly killed. M. Shingarev, shot in the mouth and
twice in the body, lived for an hour and a half without recovering
consciousness.

Their crime accomplished, the assassins took their leave. The bodies repose in the mortuary of the hospital beside the victims of January 5 (January 18).

After the Petrograd Soviet made its inquiry, two hospital Red Guards, Kulikov and Baskov, were arrested ostentatiously for suspicious connection with the murders, but I never heard rumor of the arrest or punishment of the assailants themselves. Kulikov, held for a while in SS. Peter and Paul, was in a cell near Kalpashnikov, who recorded this conversation:[1]

Kalpashnikov: Why did the Bolsheviki arrest you and have you imprisoned in the fortress?

Kulikov: This is a misunderstanding.

Smolny made an official statement about your arrest and announced your coming trial.

Kulikov: This is again a misunderstanding. I am not a murderer but one who believes that Bolshevism is striving for the good of the oppressed soldier, and I took service in the Red Army because I felt I could be useful in drilling the citizens and making them into good soldiers.

All this has nothing to do with the death of your victims.

Kulikov: I have a lot of friends at Smolny. I used to go there nearly every day. A few days ago one of my influential friends at Smolny summoned me for an important political conference.

(Note: Earlier he had said, "I am an educated man who knows what he is doing.")

He explained to me that some of the weak-willed comrades were undermining the prestige of the party by wanting to be lenient to the big *bourgeois*, and that such a policy would give courage to the counter-revolutionists to lift their head again. He told me they had obtained the right to transfer some of the ministers to private hospitals and that this would mean their ultimate release.

Your friend wanted to get rid of them simply.

Kulikov: Perhaps. But in any case Comrade Dybenko and his sailors were determined not to let the *bourgeois* get the better of them and asked me to take a company of my Red Guards to guard the hospital and follow every movement of their enemies.

You guarded them badly, because if you tell the truth, it would not have been possible for strange sailors to come and kill them without your knowledge.

Kulikov: What you say is not fair.

Why?

Kulikov: Because we had agreed with the comrades that should

[1] *A Prisoner of Trotsky's,* pp. 141–143.

there be any danger of their falling into the hands of the counter-revolutionists, sailors would come to transfer the ministers to a safe place, kill them if necessary but not let them fall into other hands.

To shoot them was a strange way to transfer them.

Kulikov: Not at all. It was not my fault. Late in the evening when I was having tea, two sailors came to me with a paper from my friend which asked me to show them deputies Kokoshkin and Shingarev because they were to reënforce the watch that night and, in the morning, if further orders were received, they were to take them away to a safer place. The paper was all right and I sent Baskov, the chief sergeant, to show them the rooms of the deputies, and fully expected them to come back in a few minutes and talk the matter over. When I heard shots it was too late.

Why did you not arrest the two murderers?

Kulikov: It was too late. I was stopped on my way up the staircase by other armed sailors, who pointed their revolvers at me and, when I protested, told me I had no right to prevent them from carrying out orders received at headquarters.

What did you do next?

Kulikov: I went to headquarters and reported about everything. I was indignant at being involved in such a nasty piece of work, but they told me not to worry because everything was so well organized that no one would have to bear the responsibility for what they called, "this good riddance."

Why are you now in the fortress?

Kulikov: The next day I was called back to headquarters where my friend informed me that this stupid piece of work had created more trouble than they expected and something had to be done to calm the public.

What did they do?

Kulikov: A statement, as you know, was published, and I was asked to go to the inquiry commission—my friend told me that if I were kept there a few days it would not last long—but that is quite different from being sent here with Baskov. I find the joke very bad and have advised my friends.

What are you going to do next?

Kulikov: You need not worry. I shall not remain here very long.

The fruits of Kulikov's arrest were at least more than an Inquiry Commission of the Petrograd Soviet expected them to be.

So the Red Terror dawned. Its beginning can be dated historically from the three days, January 18, January 19, and January 20, 1918, and Shingarev and Kokoshkin were the first official victims. Other brave and little-known persons died as martyrs earlier than they, some of them in this three-day period itself, but these two former civil servants were killed to put terror into the consciousness of the multitude, which is the purpose of Red Terrors. General Dukhonin was cruelly slain, and his death was viewed with horror, but his death was the product of the Bolshevik Revolution's initial violence. An organized practice may be traced from the era of the scotching of the Constituent Assembly. The Extraordinary Commission, it should not be forgotten, was charged with the "suppression of disorder in Petrograd" on January 18, the day of parade, when killings began.

At the Soviet meeting of the twentieth, at which Zinoviev presided, more attention was given to "washing up" the party actions touching the Constituent Assembly than to the assassination of the two ministers. The decree dispersing the Assembly was approved without debate. Then Zinoviev launched into a tirade against Tseretelli. This oration directed to the party and not to the public was significant of the fearsome quality in Tseretelli's arraignment of Bolshevism as a failure. Zinoviev made no reply of argument—he merely declared Tseretelli a *bourgeois*, and a counter-revolutionary enemy, and invoked the class war against all opponents of Bolshevism.

The reports heard by the Soviet concerning the disruption of the parades were trifling and cynical. The Right Social Revolutionaries had hired men, according to the light explanation of speakers, to shoot their fellows so that innocent Bolsheviks would get a bad name. Nothing more than that. The listeners applauded. One officer who reported was a comedian and it was impossible not to laugh with him. He had been in command of the bridge over the Neva leading to the Liteiny (the Alexandrovsky Bridge) and he swore that none of the people were killed there. He broke up the parade, he said, by firing into the air, and then described how the paraders ran, he gesticulating, grimacing, and hopping around the platform like a rabbit. Finally, with a long face, he said he had a confession to make—that he had not shot a soldier and a sailor whom he believed to be masquerading. He could have made his report all over again had he desired, so much pleasure did the session take from his recital.

From the Soviet meeting I went to a late tea at the Ambassador's, the first diversion in three days. "Some contrast," I inscribed in my Log, and indeed it was, and a pleasant one. Yet one sign about the Embassy bespoke the uneasiness of the outer city. The building was guarded within by several of the marine couriers, answer of the Ambassador to a rumor that Russian guards were to be installed without. Two or three of the couriers had come in from Stockholm a few days apart, and the Ambassador had decided to hold them until the city settled into more peace. The men were unarmed, but husky specimens. Franklin was not among them.

It is my recollection that Russian soldiers did take post presently for a day or so, and that we were assured that they were designed as real and not Marinsky Hospital protection, but one way or the other, the incident was not lasting. Some of the couriers were doomed to a long stay in Russia, one only of them going out the week following over the Finland route, soon to be closed.

Came two days of comparative interlude.

General Judson, who had found travel arrangements difficult, now was going. When he made a farewell call, January 22, I asked him to take word of me to Creel and to my wife. The day was so lacking in turmoil that I logged: "Too peaceful. Somebody must be planting dynamite somewhere."

Even that entry did not bring an explosion. The days, however, were not without significant events.

The draft of the Resolution for the "Repudiation of State Debts," although it was not to be promulgated until February 3, was taking final form. The draft went before the Council of Commissars on January 13, and we knew presently that it had been approved and that the final decision, delay, veto, or enactment, lay with the Central Executive Committee of the Council. On January 16 the draft was dragged out as had been done once before to threaten the Allies with a consequence of non-recognition of the Brest-Litovsk Conference. Having failed either as threat or lure an early use as penalty became a certainty. The contents of the draft were in fact those of the Decree of February 3.

In the document all foreign loans were canceled "unreservedly and without any qualifications." All internal state loans in excess of ten thousand rubles were canceled, except short-term obligations and treasury bonds. Payment of interest on the excepted obligations was abrogated. Coöperative societies owning government securities were promised a degree of compensation to be determined later by the Supreme National Economic Council. Citizens of "small means" owning bonds under ten thousand rubles might exchange for a Soviet loan. A declared "inviolability" of savings deposits was not intended to protect the *bourgeoisie*. A clause annulled savings "which have not been acquired through work," the local Soviet of a community to be the judging body.

The decree was made retroactive to December 14, 1917, and December interest coupons declared valueless.

Two lesser confiscations, each in the week beginning January 20, were those of the properties and equipment of the Russian Red Cross and of the Union of Cities.

Into the Bolshevik maw flowed the fluid and property wealth of an artificially desolated nation.

The completeness of the disintegration of the army was made apparent during the week by the unintended publication of a telegram sent by General Bonch-Bruevich, Chief of Staff, to his superior, Krylenko. General Bonch-Bruevich was an officer retained because a few technical soldiers were judged indispensable. General Bonch-Bruevich made terse report of survey of the Russian potentialities of defense:

Entire lack of authority. Many portions of the front have been divested of troops. On the Western front there remain only 160 men per verst. No reserve troops are replacing the comrades in the trenches. A stupendous number of trained officers were removed during the elections. The present officers are inexperienced. The staffs and other institutions will soon cease their work automatically as there is nobody who could do it. There are no members of the General Staff. The conditions of work in the staffs are terrible. The training and order among the troops are insignificant. Complete economical disorganization. No military order. An abundance of deserters. Orders are not being obeyed. Those on leave of absence do not return. In many places the connection between the troops has been lost. Scarcely any horses left.

The fortified entrenchments are being destroyed. Barbed wire entanglements being removed to facilitate fraternization and trading. Impossible to withstand a pressure from the enemy's army. Only salvation of the army lies in a retreat behind natural boundary lines.

Trotsky was enraged at the publicity given the dispatch, which apparently was issued as a matter of routine.

Another misadventure in their own Bolshevik press, nearly simultaneous, was the reprinting of an interview given out in Stockholm by von Lucius, German Ambassador to Sweden and former Counselor of the German Embassy at Petrograd. The diplomat in abrupt and undiplomatic language expressed thus his view of the German-Russian situation:

The Russian Bolsheviks have interpreted erroneously our readiness to facilitate the task of concluding peace. They began to conduct themselves in a distinctly provoking way, dictating terms to us like victors to the vanquished. In other words, they have been decreeing them as they are doing at home. Of course Germany could not consent to such an attitude toward herself. If the Bolsheviks will remain stubborn we will have to use more weighty arguments, and to show them our power, so much the more so as Russia from a military viewpoint is at present a non-entity.

So Trotsky, back from Brest-Litovsk with little to show his public for his fortnight of oratory abroad, and no desire to explain his part in such matters as the Rumanian Affair, was reduced to the level of writing in the *Izvestia* on January 22:

The significance of the Brest negotiations consists in the fact that they tore off the hypocritical cloak from German imperialism and exposed the cruel actuality of territorial and capitalistic annexation. The Brest negotiations have created complete lucidity. More cannot be expected from them.

While his words were warning of surrender to come, they also betrayed depression of mind. He had expected more. To have the weakness of the army rubbed in and a harsh German threat printed in a Bolshevik paper was most annoying.

But if he was low, he was not in the depths for a long stay. He was his gaudy self at the All-Russian Congress in another day or two.

CHAPTER XVIII

January 23—January 28, 1918. The Ringmasters of the All-Russian Soviet.

1.

IN name the Third All-Russian Soviet, the congress of awed delegates and smart leaders installed in the Tauride Palace on Wednesday, January 23, 1918, was the First All-Russian Soviet in panoply and in power. No parliament house had sheltered its predecessors, nor had many districts of Russia been represented by other than stray and often alien agitators. So this assemblage was planned as fête and lure to the peasants of Russia. Men and women of the soil to whom Petrograd had been only a mystic name were ushered from afar to the capital, and there welcomed and treated as superior beings. Circus and ceremonial was the All-Russian Soviet, as picturesque a gathering as the world might have. Every peasant costume known to Russia was on its floors.

Within the body, and around it, plied a frictionless machinery. Lenin was a party boss. He prepared the spontaneous. Spiridonova was to lead the peasants and the Left Social Revolutionaries into the Bolshevik ranks with fanfare and speech, and the upsurgence was to have the look of irrepressible impulse. Trotsky's oratory was to gloss the defeat at the Peace Conference, Lenin's was to be assertive of confidence and of power.

The Tauride Palace had its own rôle in the creation of impressions. Here the Constituent Assembly had died. Here was proper seat for the display of new-risen dominion. Red flags draped pillars and galleries and rostrum. Seating arrangements had been changed in the auditorium by the removal of desks and replacement with close-set lines of chairs. Room was given for eleven hundred delegates.

The opening session was one of celebration—of band-playing, of the singing of the "International" and the "Marseillaise," and of formal greetings of delegations from near and far places. Trotsky presided.

The participants were entertaining, in the main, to each other but watching was dull work. There was no gallery of on-looking visitors because nearly all in attendance were delegates or, like the peasants, expectant delegates. Consequently only a fringe of the more restless delegates and a few groups of official observers made use of the ample gallery space. So one might hang over the rail in the arc of the gallery above the presidium and look down on the speaker or stroll to one side and have a view across the front of the rostrum.

In such positions of vantage I watched the scene and from them I witnessed the most disagreeable feature of the day. Two Americans and one foreigner of considerable residence in America presumed to bring the greetings of the United States to this body of International Revolution, thereby taking its cause as their own. This was time of war, and the two Americans were bearers of passports of the United States, issued under their oaths of loyalty to their country, the protection of which they claimed.

These men were Albert Rhys Williams and John Reed. The alien of the trio was Reinstein, an agitator who had been in the United States long enough to learn the English language. He was fluent on his feet. Fortunately neither of the Americans had any ability as a public speaker and they made a stammering, sorry show of themselves. Their remarks were quoted by the official *Izvestia*.*

* The *Izvestia* reported in its issue of January 11 (Old Style), January 24 (New Style):

In the name of the American democracy Comrade Williams greets the Congress.

Comrade Williams says that he is the representative of the proletariat highly developed in the capitalistic sense, but an exceedingly conservative proletariat. And therefore he has come here not to teach the Russian comrades anything, but in order to state how Russia's lessons are being received beyond the Ocean and in order to learn from the Russian van-guard proletariat.

"From Russia," says Comrade Williams, "I shall take with me two lessons never to be forgotten. The first lesson is that I have become convinced that when the proletariat seriously decides to take up their self-liberation the *bourgeoisie* must come to nought as there is no such force which could resist an onslaught from the representatives of labor. The second lesson is that the forms of the present *bourgeois* parliamentarism are passing out and that there is room in life only for the parliament which you have advanced in the process of your revolutionary fight—the Councils of the Workers', Soldiers' and Peasants' Deputies.

"This form of parliamentarism will also be adopted by us when the American proletariat will resolve upon a revolutionary fight and will wage war against its *bourgeoisie*. For now it is clear that revolution is the only method

What Reinstein did was of interest to me only in that he had assumed to voice America. Williams I had not sought to influence—he could answer to his own conscience. But Reed had promised me not to make this very appearance, and for his own sake I had hoped he would not put himself forward. A few nights before he had far overstepped the bounds of privileged action by doing Bolshevik patrol duty in front of the Foreign Office, a silly and florid performance. Hearing what he had done I had a talk with him and told him that he should have experience enough to know that he was being used by the Bolsheviks for advertising purposes. He said he was

by means of which they can free themselves. Hurrah for Revolutionary Russia! Hurrah for the International Revolution! Hurrah for the power of the Councils of Workers', Soldiers' and Peasants' Deputies."

Comrade Reinstein:

"Comrades! In America the *bourgeoisie* is preparing something like the Liebknecht affair. There the imperialistic soldiery has entered into an active fight against everything that is connected with the progressive movement of the masses, against everything that fights militarism. By the application of violence they have closed the American revolutionary periodical, *The Masses*. Present with us is one of the editors of this periodical, Comrade John Reed, who has been prosecuted by the American Imperialists. He is being accused of agitating against the army levy and of organizing sedition in the American army. He is under the threat of forty years' imprisonment in the prisons of 'free America.'

"Comrade Reed has decided to immediately return to America in order to present himself in the court of the *bourgeois* imperialists despite the danger threatening him. We trust that, in case Comrade Reed is thrown into prison by the American executioners, hands will be found at last—like the hands of Trotsky, who has opened the doors of Russian prisons—to free the American captives."

The appearance of Comrade Reed is met by stormy applause.

The representative of the American Socialists declares that, leaving for the country of inveterate reaction and where capitalism rules, he is deeply satisfied in the knowledge that the victory of the proletariat in one of the most powerful countries is not a dream, but reality. Only six weeks ago the *bourgeoisie* laughed at the revolution, derided the power of the Councils, called the rebellious people bandits. But later on it saw the power, strength and invincibility of the revolutionary movement, which, it appeared, could not be broken down by any acts of cruelty and repressions.

Comrade Reed, observing the whole course of revolutionary creative work, has become convinced that behind the crumbling foundations of capitalism, two types of quite new and powerful organizations have been established— the Councils and the factory committees.

Comrade Reed promises, when returning to the conservative country of the ruling imperialists, to tell the American proletariat about everything that is happening in revolutionary Russia, and he is deeply convinced that this will call forth an echo amongst the oppressed and exploited masses.

Reed was a cautious promiser. There were no charges against him in the United States, else he would not have had his protective passport. Relieved of military service on the ground of physical debility, he had come to Russia in the Kerensky period as a magazine writer.

sorry, that he was only looking for writing color and that he would be more careful.

Handsome and spoiled, I am afraid that Jack Reed never quite grew up. Nor was he at the end of his errors. He left Russia soon afterward with so much rumor circulating as to what he was to do upon his return to the United States that it seemed advisable that he should be received at home with some care. He was delayed so long in Sweden that I reached the United States not long after he did. In the State Department at Washington I found waiting for me his papers, which had been taken into custody on his arrival. Among them was his commission as Soviet Consul at New York City.

The Bolsheviks victimized him, of course, in giving him the useless document. They were counting on the newspaper attention they would get if he sought to claim the nonexistent post, and hoping for him a jail martyrdom. There was no furor, however. Reed, like the writing man he was, wanted his literary material, which was returned to him. The Government kept the consular commission. Poor, brilliant, unhappy Reed! His destiny marked him for return to Russia, swift illness and death in an unsanitary city, and burial by the Red Kremlin!

2.

Trotsky's first speech before the Congress, following the rites of introduction, was purposely devoid of the sensational, a general and a reasoned apology for delay in the dawn of any millennium. He emphasized that Russian capital was so little organized that it had no creative machinery to turn over after seizure and that the double problem lay in the taking over of capital and in the creating of going-on machinery. What he said was true. Russia was the least fitted of any large European country for the socialistic experiment the Bolsheviks claimed they were making. Saying that they were going to operate the machines of capital and of industry they had seized a country which had neither.

While the delegates to the Congress desired above all to hear report of what had been going on at the Peace Conference at Brest-Litovsk, the account of negotiations with the Germans was the one that the leaders wished to delay as long as possible. They had nothing good to report and they had a reason for delay. Thursday they let the convention mark time by giving it chance to abuse the late Constituent Assembly. They were waiting for the diversion of public and Congressional interest to a Bolshevik upturn in the Ukraine, at least to a pledged effort at it, with hope for its success.

My attention was attracted to the situation early Thursday by the rumor that Germany had made a secret peace with the Ukraine and was about to get food supplies from the country. The Bolsheviks were circulating the report. Rapid inquiry showed that the purpose was equally to disclose a real peril in the shadow of which they stood, and to declare that they meant to overthrow the Rada at Kiev before it could make a separate peace with Germany.

There was more activity in the corridors of the Tauride Palace that afternoon than in the Congress. Various groups were giving and receiving information that included both chaff and wheat. Here I encountered the Rumanian Rakovsky, as yet regarded only as a Rumanian agitator readier of words than of deeds. He was full of a design to signal for a revolution in Rumania on the day Kiev fell, and it was his remark that sent me hunting for the source of the statement concerning Kiev. His authority was the best—the word was being scattered officially. Aware of the Bolshevik practice of forecasting certain of their movements, I was confident that a determined attempt was in preparation. I made Log entry: "Jan. 24—Information of Bolshevik intent to attempt overthrow of Rada in three days. Record for future comparison."

Rumanian success I was more inclined to doubt, although Rakovsky was free with his plans for sending additional agitators, and was reporting success from those already sent. I had other reports, however, that many agitators had fled, one from a person who had brought back a vivid account of his own flight. This frank young man was Joe Gumberg of New York and Petrograd, brother of the interpreter, Alexander Gumberg.

Joe, who had turned Bolshevik, his brother said, because he was too lazy to work, had no intention of lopping off the years of his life unnecessarily. Ordered to the area of the Rumanian army, he went, knowing that food was plentiful in that part of the country and hoping that the Rumanians liked to fraternize. He was a genial fellow, liking nothing better than conversation—except food.

According to his account he found himself detrained in a cold and an unfriendly land. He heard that there were troops in a certain quarter and toward them he went. A sentry let him come close enough for converse and Joe opened up with a flattering patter, good, he felt sure, for food and bed. The sentry, however, gave him an up-and-down glare, muttered something that Joe thought might have meant "Another one of them!" and called for the guard. When businesslike soldiers began to advance toward him, Joe, as he put the matter, "took it on the run." He wasn't sure whether the sounds he heard behind him were shots in the air or just explosive laughter. No more agitating among Rumanian soldiers for him. He made his way back to safe Petrograd and reported that the fierce Rumanians had threatened his life and that he had escaped from them. For the latter feat he was given a better post. He was made a judge.

Joe Gumberg is Zorin, who showed the English novelist, H. G. Wells, around Russia and told him about Bolshevism. Wells named Zorin as a goodly example of the young leaders coming along.

3.

LENIN made two formal speeches before the Congress, and several extemporaneous appearances. In debate on the subject of socialistic cleavage he dominated the session of January 25, making his set speech in the evening. It was announced that the peace subject would be taken up the next day.

Lenin maintained that he was not an orator. The contention was part of his pose. He was not an actor like Trotsky but he was a speaker who got and held his hearers. Sometimes he spoke conversationally, sometimes he roared with wide open mouth. Occasionally he turned his back to the Congress and talked to the members of the presidium behind him. Lenin was a brown man. He glinted under the bright lights.

The opening passage of his speech took my fancy. It was a comparison of Bolshevik endurance of rule with that of the Paris Commune. The imaginative flight may not have been one that the peasant portion of his auditors understood, but I could realize its appeal to him and the doctrinaire group. He exulted that he and his followers had outlasted the so-called "Hundred Days" of the Paris Commune. Prince Kropotkin was justified as prophet. Two months and ten days Lenin set as the historical limit of the Commune's mastery of Paris. Two months and fifteen days, he proclaimed, the rule of the dictatorship of the proletariat already had lasted in Russia.

After he had gotten into the body of his speech and I was tired of hearing the droning translation, I left the gallery back of him and went down to the floor of the Congress. The space in front of him was tight with standing listeners but I edged slowly through them until I stood directly before him, looking up at him. From that angle he was a leering, animated gargoyle. Frequently his face set in lines of animal ferocity. As I had left my interpreters in the gallery, I did not know what he was saying. So I studied those around me to judge effect. Mostly they were peasants or persons in workmen's garb—the latter not a sure sign of the wearer's status in life— with a scattering of older men who looked like needy teachers, these the intellectuals and the doctrinaires of the party. Lenin roused them all to a pitch which sometimes seemed to be of fury. When I came to read the speech I understood why.

Quotations from his speech, following, are not in full, although omissions have been confined to lesser illustrative and duller doctrinaire paragraphs:

Comrades, in the name of the Council of People's Commissars I come to report to you the activities of the two months and fifteen days which have passed since the formation of the Soviet Government in Russia. Two months and fifteen days! Five days longer than workmen ever have ruled over an entire country and over the exploiters and capitalists—five days longer than the rule of the workmen in the Paris Commune of 1871.

We must remember this first rule of the workman and compare it with the Soviet power which had its beginning on October 25/ November 7. From this comparison of the former and the present dictatorship we can see what gigantic progress has been made by the international labor movement, and also the immeasurably more advantageous circumstances under which the Soviet power is progressing in Russia in spite of the complexity of conditions and in spite of war and disorganization.

Having held out for two months and ten days, the workmen of Paris, who for the first time created a Commune, perished under the bullets of the French Cadets, the Mensheviks, and the Social-Revolutionary Kaledinists. The French workmen had to make appalling sacrifices for the first experience of a workmen's government, the meaning of which was not comprehended by the vast majority of the French peasantry. We are better placed because the Russian soldiers, workmen and peasants knew how to create an apparatus—the Soviet Government—which informed the entire world of their methods of struggle. The workmen of Paris had no organization machinery, while we had at once the support of the Soviet authorities. Therefore we never have doubted that the Soviet power has the sympathy and the most ardent and devoted support of the majority of the masses, and that therefore the Soviet power is invincible.

Skeptics have shouted that the power of the proletariat alone could not maintain itself in Russia. As if anybody among the Bolsheviks or those close to them would forget for a moment that in Russia only that power can perpetuate itself that is able to merge the labor class, the majority of peasants and all working and exploited classes into one integral force directed against the landowners and the *bourgeoisie!*

This his bidding for the support of Spiridonova and the peasants. He continued:

We have never doubted that only the union of the workmen and the poorest peasants can embrace in Russia the majority of the population and secure a solid support for government authority. We have succeeded in a few weeks in surmounting all obstacles and in creating government authority on the basis of this solid union. . . .

As soon as the peasants came to a clear realization of the issue the thing came true. The peasants' Soviets and their conventions have shown that when it comes to choosing between an alliance with the *bourgeoisie* or with the working people, they will follow the party which expresses the genuine aspirations and interests of the peasantry, the party of the Left Social Revolution.

Comrades, there is not a socialist who does not realize the manifest truth that between the socialism to be and the capitalism that has been must intervene a prolonged and more or less difficult period of the dictatorship of the proletariat and that this period in its forms will largely depend upon the prevalence of large or small property, small or large culture. It is a matter of course that the transition to socialism in a small country like Estonia, where everybody is literate and which is composed of large estates, cannot resemble the transition to socialism in a country like Russia, which is preëminently *petit-bourgeois*. Every intelligent socialist will say that socialism cannot be forced upon the peasants, and that only the force of example and the acquisition of experience by the peasantry can be relied upon. The Russian peasantry is confronted with the problem of finding the best transitory form of socialism.

The contrasting illustration of Estonia was a shrewd stroke. Germany was demanding control of Estonia and the government it would set up there would be that of the landed proprietors. Lenin was preparing his Russian followers to view equably the loss of the province. Again he directed himself to the topic of coalition with the peasants, and with the expansion of this text reached the class war.

The alliance which we concluded with the Left Social Revolutionists is created on a solid basis and is being solidified not by days but by hours. If we apprehended at first in the Council of People's Commissars that party strife might impede the work, I can state now as the result of two months' experience of joint work that on the majority of questions we are able to reach a unanimous conclusion. We know that only experience can guide the peasants in the development of their relations with the towns and the villages.

On the other hand the experience of civil war demonstrates explicitly to the representatives of the peasants that there is no way to socialism other than by a dictatorship of the proletariat and by the ruthless suppression of the rule of the exploiters. Comrades, every time we dwell on this subject exclamations of "Dictator!" come to my ears. Yet "when we were socialists" all recognized the dictatorship of the proletariat. Socialists wrote about it in their programs. . . . Opposition to it now is Utopian prejudice, which has long ago been shattered in theory, and which it is our task now to shatter in practice.

To conceive socialism as a thing which socialists will present on a plate in a ready-made gown is not permissible. This will never come to pass. Not a single question of class struggle has been solved yet in history through other means than force. Force! When used on behalf of the exploited working masses against exploiters—we are for the use of force! [Burst of applause.] We are not concerned in the least with the moans of those who consciously or unconsciously are on the side of the *bourgeoisie*, and so frightened by it, so oppressed by its rule that, looking now at this unprecedented class struggle they become confused, break out into tears, forgetting all their premises and demanding from us the impossible—that we socialists should without struggle against exploiters, without breaking their resistance, attain full victory.

This is why the October Revolution has launched that systematic and unflinching struggle for breaking the resistance of the exploiters. However difficult it may be they must reconcile themselves to the thought that the exploiting classes will rule no more, that henceforth the plain *muzhik* will order and that they will obey him. However this may displease them they will have to submit.

This is why civil war has now broken out in Russia. Against us is the watch-word "Let civil war perish!" I heard this from the representatives of the right wing of the so-called Constituent Assembly. "Let civil war perish!" What does this mean? With whom is civil war being waged? With Kornilov, Kerensky, Riabushinsky, who are spending millions to bribe the penniless and the officials; with those sabotagers who are anyway consciously or unconsciously taking these bribes. Among the latter, no doubt there are people of limited mental development who cannot imagine that it is possible and necessary to demolish the former *bourgeois* structure to the very foundations and to begin the building upon its fragments of an entirely new socialistic society. . . .

When these people talk to us about civil war we reply with a smile. The class struggle does not come accidentally to its last stage. It is not an accident when the exploited take power into its own hands in order to finally destroy its class enemy, the *bourgeoisie*, and to sweep off the face of the land of Russia not only the officials but the landowners. . . .

This is why, comrades, we answer all reproaches and charges of dictatorship, civil war, terrorism—though we are still quite far away from real terrorism—by saying that we are stronger than our enemies. The nationalization of the banks and the confiscation of property will suffice to make them subservient. We have the Soviets. Yes, the first government in the world to speak openly of civil war is the government of workmen, peasants and soldiers. Yes, we have begun and are waging a war against exploiters. The more plainly we say it the sooner the war will end.

I do not think, comrades, that you will succeed soon in achiev-

ing victory in this struggle, but in the course of two months we
have achieved a good deal. We have lived through the attempt of
Kerensky against the Soviet power and the complete break-down
of that attempt. [The effort of the Constituent Assembly.] We
have lived through the contest with the Ukrainian Kerenskys.
There the struggle has not ended but anybody who hears the
truthful reports made by representatives of the Soviet knows that
the *bourgeois* elements of the Ukrainian Rada are eking out their
last days. We also infer from the manifest evidence of the Peasants' Conventions that the cause of Kaledin is hopeless and that
the working masses are against him.

This is why looking at the front of civil war in Russia we can
say with complete certainty: Here the victory of the Soviet power
is complete and completely secured. The victory of the Soviet
power has been achieved through its realization from the very
outset of the general teachings of socialism. This is why the old
army, the army of barrack drill, has gone into the past. It has
been given to demolishment and not one stone of its foundation
remains.—In its stead we will create a socialist Red Army. It has
been said about Russia that she cannot fight because she will have
no officers. Yes, these Red Guards technically are worth nothing,
but if these people received some training they would be an invincible army. For the first time in history elements have entered
the army who are guided by the purpose of liberating the exploited. When the work begun by us is completed the Russian
Soviet Republic will be invincible.

The German observers in the gallery must have had difficulty
in hiding their elation over the confession of Russia's utter
defenselessness at the moment. Having described the razing
of the military institution, Lenin returned to the topic of
civil dismemberment.

The course taken by the Soviet power with regard to the army
was taken by it also with regard to another more complicated
and refined instrument of the ruling classes—the *bourgeois* court
which was a ruthless tool for the oppression of the exploited. We
at once gave the court up to destruction. Let them cry out that
we did not reform the old court. By demolishing it we cleared
the road for a real people's court.

So he came to the usual peroration of slogans. He had
exalted ruin, heralded terror, sung the paean of a people's
immolation.

4.

SPIRIDONOVA led her peasants into the All-Russian Soviet on January 26, a ceremonial entrance since they had been in bodily presence from the first day. Now, however, they were accredited as four hundred new delegates. Spiridonova made a short, impassioned speech in which she avowed her faith in the outcome of the union of her party of the Left Social Revolutionaries and the peasants with the Bolsheviks. She was as much afire as usual and as a speaker was a pleasant surprise, no shrill shrieker but of clear and modulated voice of a carrying quality that reached all parts of the chamber. She did not shrink from the honors given her, accepting the tribute with a poise untouched with arrogance. Fanatic she undoubtedly was, but of metal singularly fine.

Trotsky shared with her the forefront of the day and more of its time. With the peasants inducted into the Congress the matter of the Brest-Litovsk Peace Conference could not be longer deferred. Trotsky spoke at great length and with attention to the niceties of oratory.

Both in this speech and in the one of the following day he slashed out in all directions, hoping to make an impression somewhere, upon the Germans most of all. He was mustering his forces for a last parley with Germany. If he could awe Kuhlman and Czernin a little with the report their observers would make of the big scenes of the Congress, and if a Bolshevik victory at Kiev would startle them a little, he believed that he and his delegation would not be as negligible as it had been. But he could not afford to be too optimistic. He must prepare his listeners for anything that might happen.

So in the address he proceeded to argue that if Russia was forced to make a separate peace the blame was not upon the makers but upon the Allies—his December line of talk. He said:

For six weeks we have kept on advising the Allies about each step we have taken and have asked them to join us. We have done everything in our power. If we have been impelled to enter into separate peace negotiations the guilt of it falls entirely upon the Western Imperialists.—We know that we have enough enemies. Rumanian troops, maintained by French money are shoot-

ing at two of our divisions near Galatz with British cannon. We
have replied by seizing the entire gold reserve of Rumania,
amounting to about one and a half billions [of gold rubles], and
by sending out of Russia all agents of the Rumanian Embassy.*
Wilson and Kuhlman and Lloyd George and Clemenceau all are
prosecuting the same aims.

Then he went to particular attack on Germany for breaking
its early promise of peace without annexations and contributions, and setting up governments of its own military control
in Poland, Courland, and Latvia. He said that apart from
these indefinite occupations of territory the indemnities Germany demanded from Russia in the way of goods and money
would reach the total of four billion rubles if not twice that
sum. He asserted that Russia would not accept these punitive
terms. For escape he placed his faith on revolutionary menace
within Germany and Austria, and on Bolshevik success in the
Ukraine. The trickery used on all sides in the Ukraine he ex-
pounded lucidly, foreseeing every move, as the future shaped
itself, except the one move that Germany finally used against
him—that of making peace in early February with a nonexistent government, and of establishing a government under garrison protection. Double-crossing in the Ukraine appears,
indeed, to have been universal, and Trotsky's account of such
of it as he knew has its place in international history. He declared:

We know that the Ukrainian delegation had several secret sessions with the German and Austrian delegations. We informed
the Ukrainians that we would conduct all our negotiations with
the Quadruple Alliance in the presence of their delegation and
we asked the same procedure from them. We received a reply that
the delegation would ask instructions from the Rada, but no further answer ever was given us. The weakness of the Ukrainian
Rada has kept it from pursuing an independent and an open and
honest policy. History will show that the Rada played a malicious
trick on those who have supported them because of their hostility to us. We are aware of what cynical support has been given
to the Rada by the Embassies and the Missions of our Allies. We
know that English gold and French officers and the heavy artil-

* The deportation order was not executed until January 28.

lery of both these countries have been sent to the Ukraine. But the Rada has followed the course of those *bourgeois* governments of small Balkan states who took bribes at the same time from Russia and from Austria-Hungary. While Albert Thomas of France is expressing the hope that the stoutness of the Ukraine on the Eastern front will be the preserver of France on the Western, the Kiev Rada already has begun separate and secret negotiations with Germany. Such also was the intended rôle of the Constituent Assembly which some days ago aspired to power here.

At least we in Petrograd, wrestling with the Bolsheviks for advantage, mistrusting them, seeking to use them as revolutionary factors against Germany, in danger of being used by them to their own ends, knew that we were in contact with power—with increasing power. The British and the French in the Ukraine always were amid instability and placed undue reliance upon it.*

* Just a year later, in the last week of January, 1919, returning from a mission to Prague, I had occasion to travel from Vienna to Trieste. The military train was provided for an American and a British group and in command of the latter was Captain Gerald H. L. FitzWilliams. Chatting over tea and jam we learned that each had spent the previous winter in Russia, he at Kiev. The next day the conversation was resumed, and when I left him I wrote down at once the following account:

Jan. 27 (1919). During the morning I had a long chat with Captain FitzWilliams following the clew of his evening-before comment that Professor Masaryk had travelled out of Russia with him through Siberia last March and April. Again accident of travel has helped me in piecing out the whole Russian picture of the winter of 1918. For Capt. FitzWilliams is the British officer who was working with the French in the Ukraine in the early winter in the clumsy and no-wise well considered plan of buying the aid of the Kiev Rada. Of course the Rada took the money—and then took a bigger bribe from Germany and "stayed put." The British and French should have let the Germans buy first.

The double-cross was obvious to us in Petrograd. I surmised it last winter before the victims guessed what was being done to them. It was a farce and the Bolsheviks took cynical advantage and played it as such in their publications. I asked Captain FitzWilliams how much the French and the British paid out. He replied indirectly that they did not pay out as much as the total of funds at their disposal. "I had heard," I said, "that twenty million rubles was the amount." "It was much more than that," he said. Therefore I guess more than 50,000,000 rubles.

I asked the Captain what his opinion now was as to the wisdom of the effort. He replied philosophically: "The plan failed, so it has to be called bad. If it had succeeded it would have been called good." A terse epitome. Later he added thoughtfully, "We were tricked—double-crossed as you say." I had used the expression.

But even failure did not daunt him. After Muraviev, the Bolshevik military leader, took Kiev, he tried by conversation, funds and promises to detach Muraviev from his German connection and the German-Bolshevik orders he received from Petrograd. Again he thought he had succeeded. Muraviev had

Trotsky concluded his speech by making promises that were contrary—to complete the demobilization of the army and to continue to oppose the German peace terms. In manner rather than in words he implied that he had a reserve card to play. It might be, of course, news of the capture of Kiev. The word about was that the event was only a few hours off. Which meant that the fighting already had gone far in Bolshevik favor.

On Sunday afternoon, January 27, while the All-Russian Soviet was in session, came the definite information that Ukrainian Rada was dissolved, its leaders resigned, that Kiev was occupied and that a delegation of Ukrainian Bolsheviks would start at once for the Peace Conference at Brest-Litovsk. I could write, "On schedule" in my Log.

Not until evening did Trotsky mount the rostrum to make full use of the news from Kiev. The day before he had been truculent toward opponents and explanatory toward the assembly. Now he was increasingly threatening against the former and jubilant before the latter. Taunt of the Social-Rights outside the Soviet that he intended to make a "rotten peace" had rasped him. "There cannot be a rotten, disgraceful peace," he shouted. "There can only be an unfortunate peace. Men who have suffered for three and a half years in the trenches can bear no more."

reached the point of checking up the men upon whom "he could rely" in starting warfare against Germany. But Germany smelled the rat this time and without taking the pains to buy him back stirred up a Rumanian-Bessarabian fuss and Muraviev posted off to save this fertile territory to Russia or to his "tradeable" part of Russia.

Then Muraviev went openly to market on his own account, levying a fine of ten million rubles on Odessa and instructing that it be paid to his personal account. The last time Captain FitzWilliams saw him he was raging about Odessa with a motor car and an armed escort of sailors. His coup had gone at least partly wrong. A part of his army had deserted him, accusing him of feathering his own nest and forgetting his brigand bands. Later there came a report of his death but Captain FitzWilliams figures he might have given that out himself for protection. Before going to Odessa Captain FitzWilliams had participated in the Czech conferences as to the way out, and strongly advised Vladivostok as against Archangel. Then from Odessa, after wrestling two railroad cars from the reluctant Muraviev, he went to Moscow, picked up Masaryk and some English nurses, and started around the world for the United States and England.

Odd as was this meeting of participants in the Russian drama, it was not odder than the presence of Karl Radek in Vienna in the few days I was there. Czech associates of mine traced him to his hiding place but I concluded that if the Austrian authorities wanted him they could get him themselves without our help, and called off the chase.

But when his listeners were deciding in amazement that he was about to announce that Russia would take any peace, he pivoted abruptly:

Late tonight we are leaving for Brest-Litovsk under much more favorable circumstances than formerly. We are in a position to tell Kuhlman that the military quarantine through which he intends to guard the Courland land-owners from the blessings of the Revolution, is ineffective. Nor shall we meet there the representatives of the Rada as the Central Executive Committee of the Soviets of Ukrainia has recognized the Council of People's Commissars as being solely vested with the full authority of conducting peace negotiations. We shall be able to draw additional strength from the events at Kiev. We shall be able to say that civil war does not weaken but rather strengthen us, and that an identical civil war strengthening our position has broken out in Austria.

Then between the two extremes of his utterances he placed these cryptic sentences:

Taking into consideration all the circumstances we do not make here any solemn avowal. We take no oaths but we promise you to fight together with you for a democratic peace. We shall struggle with them and they will not be able to face us with the threat of an offensive as there can be no certainty among them that the German soldiers will agree to go on an offensive. We shall unfalteringly continue the demobilization of the army, for we are continuing the formation of a Red Guard.

Contradictory we thought the speech and not a little mysterious. No two persons who heard it could agree on its meaning, and all were flicked by some part of it. In portions of it he repeated former attacks on the Allies, including this time even the American Red Cross in echo of the Kalpashnikov case. The French he had booted, claiming they had sought his aid in fanning the revolutionary flame in Germany and that he had told them he wanted no help from them. At that instant I was glad that I had gone ahead without asking consent. By this time distribution of the Fourteen Points Speech by package-men at the borders was to be complemented by carload shipments. While he was speaking I was notified that the first car was safely away at six o'clock.

Among the notes of the day I wrote the question: "Will German advance into Russia, particularly Petrograd, be risked?"

The impression made by both speeches that Trotsky had something up his sleeve was well based and became more visible the next day, although kept out of print and public speech. In the day's Log of January 28 I wrote that the "novel plan of Brest action" was "non-resistance, demobilization of army, organization of revolutionary army in the rear," and added, "Recall that in neither speech Trotsky told what he would do; wait and see."

This the genesis in Petrograd, before Trotsky returned to Brest-Litovsk, of the famous "No War, No Peace" declaration with which Trotsky walked out of the Peace Conference on February 10 and left Russia open to the German army.

The fact answer to my question of January 27 was: The German army advanced into Russia and upon Petrograd.

5.

IN legislation the most important action of the All-Russian Soviet was the adoption of a plan of federal organization, the resolution for which was offered by Stalin, and accepted without debate. Under its terms:

(1) The Russian Socialistic Soviet Republic is founded on the basis of a voluntary union of Russian nations, as a federation of the Soviet Republics of these nations.

(2) The supreme organ of power within the federation boundaries is the All-Russian Convention of the Soviets of Workmen's, Soldiers' and Peasants' deputies, summoned at not longer interval than three months.

(3) The All-Russian Convention elects the All-Russian Central Executive Committee. During the periods between the Conventions the Central Executive Committee is the supreme power.

(4) The Government of the Federation, the Council of People's Commissars, is elected and dismissed, entirely or in part, by the All-Russian Convention of the Soviets, or by the All-Russian Central Executive Committee.

(5) The manner in which the separate Soviet Republics will take part in the federal government and the limits of the federal and the regional units of the Russian Republic will be determined by the All-Russian Central Executive Committee and by the different Central Executive Committees of these Republics.

(6) All local affairs are to be settled by the local Soviets. The superior Soviets reserve the right of regulating the relations between the lower Soviets.

Stalin was powerful even then, although the document itself was believed to be the handiwork of Lenin.

The All-Russian Convention, or Congress, elected a slated Central Executive Committee, heard a long and pedagogic but not exciting speech from Lenin, and adjourned in the early morning hours of February 1.

CHAPTER XIX

January 28—February 3, 1918. Trotsky's "Pedagogical Demonstration." Lenin's "Looters." Radek's "Sly Muzhik." Zorin as Palace Guide.

1.

WHILE the All-Russian Congress was sitting, the Central Executive Council also was unremitting in its labors. Trotsky appeared before it to secure the order for the confiscation of the Rumanian gold reserve, and before it he also outlined his "novel," or as he himself called it, his "pedagogical demonstration," expressing it in the form, "We shall stop the war without signing the Peace Treaty." He got the plan indorsed, although not without disagreement and debate.

In a preliminary draft of this chapter, I wrote, "Trotsky and Lenin may have been in opposition, though it is more than likely that Lenin had given consent to Trotsky's proposal, not because he believed in it, but because he was willing to let the enthusiastic Trotsky test out his pet idea."

Later, in Trotsky's book, *Lenin*,[1] I found his own admission that this was so. He wrote that he made the first proposal by letter to Lenin while he was at Brest-Litovsk prior to his return for the Congress and received reply that they would talk the matter over later in Petrograd. Trotsky recorded that he suspected from the noncommittal response that Lenin did not agree. When they met for discussion Lenin said that the only result of the attitude would be a quick invasion of Russia by picked German troops, and asked Trotsky what he would do then. Trotsky wrote that he replied that they would be forced to sign a peace treaty, it being clear to everyone that they had no other way out. In that fashion also, he contended, as he explained, a decisive blow would be struck "at the legend that we are in league with the Hohenzollerns behind the scenes." He had stated earlier in his account that this was the reason for the "demonstration":

As is well known, even in Germany among the Social Democratic

[1] Published by Minton, Balch & Co., 1925.

Opposition, there were stubborn rumors current that the Bolsheviki were bought by the German Government and that what was going on in Brest-Litovsk was merely a comedy with the rôles allotted in advance. This version must be more credited in France and England. It was my opinion, cost what it might, before the signing of peace we must give the workmen of Europe a clear proof of the deadly enmity between us and Governmental Germany.

If one accepts this self-given explanation of the Trotsky plan of "No Peace, No War!" for a Peace Conference conclusion, the "cost" that Trotsky was willing to have paid for controverting a "legend" was German invasion of Russia, with contingent loss of Russian life and with certain loss of more Russian territory as penalty for sure defeat.

The record so written would be that of an obsessional fear of the "legend" and the sharing of the fear by Lenin, since, according to Trotsky, he assented to the plan at that argument.

The reasoning of the pair, if this was their reasoning as Trotsky said, was illogical, and so proved by reality. No one in 1918 reached any of the conclusions Trotsky in 1925 said were meant to be reached. Trotsky's opponents in 1918 viewed his action as advantageous to Germany, and the Bolsheviks conceded this to be so by submission to new and harder German terms. The "workmen of Europe" failed to deduce the meaning he said he desired. In Petrograd, in circles where he would have considered it useful to have his later interpretation put currently upon his action, I heard no like echo, nor came upon record of any. The device, "cost what it might" and whatever its purpose, collapsed expensively upon itself and upon its avowed creator.

When Trotsky wrote his *post facto* account, the "legend" still was bruited, and Trotsky's concern about it was shown to be unlessened.

My inclination, also *post facto*, is to accept his version and to demerit him as shallower and less intelligent than I sometimes have thought him to be. The device was poor, even for his declared aim. He himself admitted that the motives behind it were egotistic and cruel. A nation was to pay lest his own esteem be hurt.

If, as he related, he advanced his argument to Lenin, he was met, he wrote, with the further question by Lenin:

"But you will not support the solution of a revolutionary war?"

To which Trotsky said he answered: "Under no circumstances."

With that, he said Lenin was satisfied to let him go ahead, although voicing the fear that after renewal of German attack there might be no time to sign the treaty. Pallid support it was as far as Lenin was concerned, but enough to gain Trotsky the assent of the Central Executive Committee.

Lenin was willing at any time during latter January and February to make peace with Germany on any terms—if he had to. He was, however, not as much disturbed about the possibilities of a peace break as those of his henchmen who thought that everything depended upon instant peace. He simply did not think the moment urgent, aware that one can always surrender. Trotsky was right, from all collateral circumstance, when he said that Lenin's only worry was lest the time to make surrender was denied.

Lenin made no concealment of his attitude in regard to the War, stating at Smolny in an address on February 5, before agitators he was sending into the provinces against the *bourgeoisie:*

"The external war is ended or nearing its end. The matter is settled. We are now at the beginning of internal war."

Careless of the War, willing to leave either fighting or peace pose to Trotsky as long as no harm to his plans came of the play, he was in a hurry to get on with the job of leveling Russia.

"The *bourgeoisie* has hidden its loot in chests," he cried. "The people must drag it out. Loot what has been looted."

The last slogan of these "instructions to agitators" sank deep into popular memory and was destined to have political consequences. "When the poor have taken and grown richer, what then?" asked a logical peasant of Lenin several months later. To which Lenin, also logical, replied, "Let the poorest peasants take from the richer." He was illustrating his doctrine of the "continuing revolution" in a way the simplest could understand. The peasants understood. Spiridonova, their leader, understood. The incident of repartee was a realistic factor among the events that led Spiridonova to withdraw support from Lenin and attack Bolshevism in midsummer, 1918.

Reflection of one Bolshevik party meeting where Trotsky led his followers to victory was disclosed in the study of the telegraphic dispatches between Brest-Litovsk and Smolny. Radek and Bronsky were in converse. The latter was a member of the Economic Council, a lieutenant of Lenin's, and shared with Stalin the duty of contact with the Brest-Litovsk delegation.

The conversation—veiled though at times transparent—took place about eleven o'clock on the night of January 28. Trotsky had made his final speech at the All-Russian Convention the night before, and then had started after midnight for Brest. Radek, from Brest, was seeking information of what was going on in Petrograd and Kiev, and was repaying with flippant but cautionary observations of his own.

Identical translations were made by the British Intelligence Service in Petrograd and the American Intelligence Service in Washington. The former, however, included in parentheses some of the ideas of a commentator, to which I added indicated notations of mine. The transcript:

15/28th. Jan. 1918. Conversation on direct wire between Radek (Brest-Litovsk) and Bronsky (Petrograd).

Radek at the apparatus asks Bronsky to speak.

Bronsky: "The party of Gregoriev have won. Our people are greatly disturbed. Trotsky and Gregoriev won at the meeting. The Moscow people were not present at the meeting of the fraction. Trotsky left today. The Central Rada is defeated and has handed in its resignation. The supply of provisions is improving. What do you want to know?"

[My note: Gregoriev may be Gregory Zinoviev, who was considered to be in agreement with Trotsky. Fraction is the Russian term for a sectional party meeting. The English word faction is not its equivalent.]

Radek: "Does Antid Oto (Antonov?)* think to sell his book (?) to the editor (Monarchist party?) at a cheap price?"

---

* There is no longer any mystery about the identity of Antid Oto. The pseudonym or pen name was one used by Trotsky in his earlier days. I have left the manuscript text unchanged, however, to illustrate the progress of in-

Bronsky: "No, not cheap but—"

[My note: Antonov was the ambitious Bolshevik Commissar who was the superior of the military commandant Muraviev in the campaign against Kiev. That Antid Oto was Antonov can be only a guess. The British commentator surmised that the "editor" was the "monarchist party," showing that he believed the reference was to status of matters in the Ukraine. The inference could be another anti-Bolshevik group or the Germans directly.]

Radek: "What are the relations between Krupsky (?) and the editor?"

Bronsky: "Very near. I do not understand his relations with Antid Oto (Antonov?)."

Radek: "What is the actual position of Kiev? Has Kiev been taken and if so has it been taken by our troops or by the local forces?"

Bronsky: "Kiev was taken by local forces. Our people are in the new Kiev Rada. I await your further question."

Radek: "Do you know the names of the leaders?"

Bronsky: "No."

Radek: "Are there any connections between Kiev and Petrograd or Kharkov or between the Kiev new Rada and the Kharkov Central Executive Committee?"

Bronsky: "I do not know. The question will be decided shortly but they will probably join us."

Radek: "If you get any information please telegraph to us at once and also in detail abroad. How does the sly muzhik [My note: Lenin] want to arrange the matter? How does the muzhik think to sell the horse? (Russia?) Will it be soon or will we have to wait?"

[My note: The British commentator supplied the name of Trotsky, where I have inserted the name of Lenin for the excellent reason that Lenin was often referred to at Smolny as "the muzhik." His slyness, too, was a by-word. He was meant.]

Bronsky: "We will have to wait a little."

quiry since 1918, when a British Intelligence officer queried the name of Antonov as a possibility; and since 1929 when I wrote in separate note, "That Antid Oto was Antonov can only be a guess." A year later a Russian student who read the manuscript recognized the name as a property of Trotsky's. Then Trotsky himself in his book, *My Life,* wrote that he had once used the name as signature, adapting it from the Italian word, *antidoto,* or antidote.

Bronsky and Radek, therefore, in their wire conversation were discussing whether Lenin, "the sly muzhik," or Trotsky, "Antid Oto," would be successful traders, in what, and to whom. Separate rôles in activities were indicated. There were two scenes, Petrograd and Brest-Litovsk.

Radek: "I am not asking for your advice, as I do not deal in horses myself. But what does the sly muzhik think?"

Bronsky: "He thinks to sell soon. He is a sly customer."

Radek: "Have you told the muzhik that one need not sign the contract at the notary's nor alter anything?"

Bronsky: "Have not told him anything nor has he asked anything."

Radek: "Tell the husband of the beautiful Ellen (Krylenko?) that one must clear away all articles which are lying at the fence (front?) or they may be sold or fall into the hands of a passer by (Ukrainians, Poles, or German?) who may take them with them."

Bronsky: "I have understood you."

Radek: "One must hide further in the shed [Note: Russia] and take the most energetic steps in this matter. If you do not act yourselves but rely on your seniors you will have your skins pulled off."

Bronsky: "What is happening at your end?"

Radek: "I have a heap of good news which I am now going to transmit to the agency by telegraph. Tomorrow I will send an article to the *Pravda*. Hold Max's head. Do not let him be frightened and make him print it. The article is of a conciliatory nature. [My note: That is—more than usually violent.] I am against soft measures in the question. Communicate to Zalkind at once: I want a government urgent telegram to be sent to my brother requesting the address of my parents at Lodz. My brother's address is Abramovich, Moscow, Lialin Pereulok, No. 20 or 22. Of course I do not need this for myself. Do not forget to telegraph to my brother Zalkind's address so that he can answer. The answer is to be communicated to me at once by direct wire. I have not received *Voelkerfriede* for a whole week. Send them daily. Have you understood everything?"

Bronsky: "Yes, everything. Goodnight."

Radek: "Show this to Peter Ivanovich." (?)

Radek's advice to the Petrograd and army leaders to get all military equipment away from the front and into the interior of Russia was plain. The conversation was in the cynical Radek style. Not a seller of "horses" himself, the traffic of the traders amused the adventurer. The suggestion that the peace "contract" need not be signed was in accord with Trotsky's plan, which Trotsky had discussed with members of the delegation, according to his statement, while he was with them at Brest.[2]

2 Leon Trotsky, *Lenin*, p. 106.

The policy schism between Trotsky and some of the followers of Lenin, if not Lenin himself, was not to be taken too seriously. In crisis Lenin would be obeyed. The party debate, from my own knowledge of the currents in motion at the time, would concern not only Trotsky's peace plan but also the virility of the revolutionary efforts in Germany and Austria. Lenin had no confidence in the success of the strikes, although he was willing to stir them up. Trotsky either had some confidence or declared he had.

2.

So agog was Petrograd with the activities of the Congress, speeches of Lenin and Trotsky, and the outbreak in Kiev, that a beginning civil war in Finland received so little attention from Americans, British, and French as to astound them presently with the realization that they were being shut off from western Europe.

Finland had been a province of Russia. When I passed through it toward Petrograd, Russian troops were in every town. Their presence made the Bolshevik revolution in Finland an easy matter. In the week of the Congress, however, the troops were suddenly withdrawn, in accord, Trotsky explained, with the Russian policy of permitting the self-definition of all racial groups within Russia, or of allowing independence if it was the Finnish desire. The order was not given until Trotsky returned from Brest-Litovsk.

A project of proletarian dictatorship was launched to synchronize with the withdrawal of the troops, in the hope that Finland would not follow in the wake of the Ukraine and the Baltic provinces and come under the control of its *bourgeois* class. But without those troops, themselves Bolshevik, the chances of proletarian success were lessened almost to the point of hopelessness. If Trotsky and Lenin had been deeply concerned for the fate of the Finnish Bolsheviks they should have kept their troops there a while longer. By withdrawing them, they abandoned their associates, whatever their words might be. Lenin's determination to demobilize the Russian army, a movement resumed after the subsidence of the first brief war clamor of early January, stood in the way of support. So also did the German demand for the removal of Russian troops from Finland, already put forward at Brest-Litovsk as a peace treaty proviso.

The difference between Russia and Finland was that the Finnish *bourgeois* were unlike the Russian *bourgeois:* they matched the Bolsheviks in ferocity and gave back blow for blow. On Sunday night, January 27, the Central Council of the Finnish Bolsheviks issued a manifesto proclaiming a workmen's revolution and the overthrow of the *"bourgeois* Senate," which until then had maintained some semblance of authority. On Monday a general strike began in Helsingfors, and the Red Guards occupied the government buildings and expelled or arrested the members of the Senate. The cities in the south came, in the main, under Bolshevik domination, although not without hard fighting. The country regions and much of the north of Finland remained unsubdued. Civil war was lit. In three weeks two armies faced each other on a battle line drawn across Finland, centering on Tammerfors, which was held by the Reds. Long before that time we were watching the war with forebodings as to its effect on our lot. The bridge behind us was cut.

3.

OCCURRENCES of the last three days of January were varied, with emotional accent on incoming accounts of revolutionary unrest in Vienna and Berlin, and physical meaning in the signs of food shortage due to the stoppage of the flow of grain from the Ukraine.

This was a period when hope rose in Petrograd that revolution was beginning in Vienna, where the younger Bolsheviks had replaced older and more cautious leaders, and that Germany would be shaken by rioting declared to be in progress in Kiel and Hamburg, with the backing of a three-day strike in Berlin. The reports came rosily from Brest-Litovsk and more moderately from neutral Stockholm.

In successive days I logged impressions of the latter phenomena:

Jan. 30—Study growth indications seriousness three days' revolt in Vienna.

Jan. 31—News from Berlin, via Brest and Stockholm, three days' strike Berlin, Danzig, Kiel and Hamburg docks. Is it the beginning of the blow-up?

It was not.

The next day I placed more importance on a nearer matter, entering as opening note: "Feb. 1—Less food. Petrograd bad way. Some food looting."

Famine, when it starts, goes apace. After only a few days of alarm, between the effects of hoarding and the failure of new supply, the city gave evidence that the inhabitants were hungry. The lines before the bakeries doubled and tripled, and formed long before dawn. Their resemblance to long, loose queues gave them their name—queues they were called. Hoodlums, quiet for three weeks, looted unguarded shops. Added guards quieted the disturbances. Hoarders were threatened. Nothing good could happen to the population.

On my own part, with news and distributing organization complete and running evenly, I began to think of leaving Russia in a fortnight, trusting that film, the final element in my projects, would arrive in the interval. Creel had already asked me if I was returning when the distribution of the Fourteen Points Speech was concluded, and I had replied that I was not yet ready but hoped to be in a few weeks. The doubtful point was the state of Arthur Bullard's health. I intended, if he continued to grow stronger, to place him in charge when I left, and desired to have the way smooth in front of him.

Sallying around the different American centers to see how matters were, I called on Colonels Kerth and Ruggles on January 29 and found they had nothing to do and were chafing under it. Kerth was hoping to leave for France soon, and was the more cheerful of the two. At the Embassy, the Ambassador was being tormented by a new device. The Bolsheviks were permitting their lawless underlings, the anarchists, to threaten that he would have to answer to them if the United States Government did not release colleagues from American jails and permit them to come to Russia. When the abuse was called to the attention of Zalkind, then in his last days as assistant Foreign Commissar, he politely regretted his inability to control the anarchists. Something had to be done, so from a different quarter we started a back-fire on the anarchists, alleging that in another field they were violating Bolshevik decrees, and presently they were so busy extricating themselves that they left the Ambassador alone.

Zalkind was more persistent in a warfare of his own, serving notice on the Ambassador that unless visas were given to governmental Russians desiring to go to the United States, the Soviet would refuse visas to Americans wishing to leave Russia. This was part of a campaign against the British and the French, intended to enable Zalkind and other agitators to leave Russia. A policy of inaction was adopted by the Ambassador. The Finnish war kept the issue from coming to a crisis. Zalkind, not getting a reply to his letter, vented his feelings harmlessly by sending under cover of the Foreign Office a copy of new resolutions, adopted at a public meeting, calling for the release of Mooney from California prison. He said he thought the Ambassador "ought to have" the paper. The Ambassador thought otherwise. He was looking upon himself as immured, so in the evening I returned to play bridge with him and officers from the Mission.

Colonel Kerth came to my rooms the next evening, January 30, and drew me aside from a group to explain that he had brought a caller, waiting at the entry. He said the man had come to the Military Mission with the story that he was a Prussian officer, who had deserted from the German army because President Wilson's Fourteen Points Speech had convinced him that Germany was in the wrong—as naïve as that.

"Did you ever hear of a deserting Prussian officer?" I asked Colonel Kerth.

"Never," replied the smiling colonel. "His story's good, though. You will want to hear it."

I did not, believing that the visitor's assignment was to make a tour of different American headquarters. He was there, however. So, in an inner room, I heard the story.

Mayer, the German said his name was, a lieutenant. He begged to be excused from naming his unit. He was a good-looking chap about thirty years old who might have passed for a colonial Englishman in London and an American in New York, of an accent more American than English. Well dressed in a civilian suit, he bore himself stiffly as a military man will who has been long in uniform. He was an officer, Colonel Kerth agreed.

When I could do so with politeness, I asked him what he wanted. He said he wished to be sent to the United States to lecture against German militarism. A question as to why brought his account of himself.

He said he had been stationed with an outpost company, and that with no war in front of him he had taken to reading, his fare reaching eventually the address of President Wilson. He insisted upon his conversion to the President's stand. Action with him, he said, followed belief. A few days later, he continued, he wrapped himself in a cloak and walked east into Russia through the vanishing Russian front until he came to a railroad, thence by train to Dvinsk and on to Petrograd, no one questioning him, and his German serving well enough for language.

I asked him how he got his civilian suit, and he replied that he had bought it in Petrograd. Clothes were among the things unattainable in Petrograd. His suit fitted. I surmised that the length of his walk had been from the hotel of the German Mission or from a palace where the overflow of the group was housed. Although amused, I was not complimented by the German notion of our obtuseness.

"Have you been in America before?" I asked.

It gained a volley of reply—indeed yes, several years in St. Louis, Chicago, and New York, and the naming of many well-known families of his acquaintance. He was not lying—he knew the United States.

Time perhaps would disclose more of the game, so I suggested to Kerth that he take his guest away. Kerth put him up for a day at the Military Mission, a safe lodging and an arid one for a spy. Kerth reported the man a pleasant companion except when he became heated in his contention of conversion to American aims. We chose a plan of separation from him. Kerth took him to the center of Petrograd, told him we would be unable to send him to the United States, and that the time had come for parting. They smiled at each other, saluted, and the visitor went nonchalantly down the street.

4.

ONE afternoon of the early part of the week included a visit to an office the active woman Bolshevik leader, Madame Kollontai, was opening in preparation for a city campaign for the feeding of children. I came away with doubt of her intention to feed babies who were not in institutions or in the homes of Bolshevik parents, although the milk was to come from the American Red Cross.

This point I discussed with Colonel Robins, who claimed the distribution would not be thus limited. Major Thacher, whom he named as his representative, made sincere effort to have the milk divided among all hungry children, regardless of class, but I could not see that he had power to carry out his desire.

The American Red Cross, by action of Colonel Robins, gave the milk, four hundred thousand tins of the condensed product, to a Commission formed of representatives of the People's Commissariat for Social Help, Mme Kollontai delegated; the American Red Cross, Major Thacher delegated; and the district Soviets and their Central Board of Food Supply.

For its distribution the following regulations were adopted, and announced by the Government:

1. The Commission is to distribute the milk according to the direction of the District Soviets of Workmen and Soldiers, and in accordance with regulations adopted by the Commission.

2. The first to be satisfied are the needs of all institutions working for children under three years of age.

3. The second to be satisfied are the needs of children of poor parents: i.e.—those not provided for by the institutions.

4. The remaining milk is to be distributed at the discretion of the District Soviets to the children of the poorest among other categories.

5. The milk is to be given to the institutions on the written order of the District Soviets.

6. To the institutions the milk is to be delivered on these orders direct from the stores of the American Red Cross.

7. To the groups enumerated in 3 and 4 the distribution will be from places established by the District Soviets.

8. The milk is to be delivered to all children comprised in groups enumerated under 2, 3, and 4, only on the authorization of special cards of the Commission. These cards will be delivered by the Commission to the District Soviets in accordance with their needs. (Details of checking the use of the cards follow). The special card is to bear the name and address. The District Soviets, delivering these cards, fill them up and register the number of the card, the name, the address and all other information in a special book, which is kept by the Soviets.

Children could get through the regulations to the milk only by the favor of the district Soviets. Russians are kind to children and could the hungry children have presented themselves they would have been fed, but the regulations were so drawn as to deter, if not prevent, middle-class and anti-Bolshevik parents from applying for milk for their children. The Soviets took acclaim to themselves for feeding the children of Petrograd. There was need of feeding. Any use of the milk to that end was better than none at all. Cut off from sources of food supply by encircling civil war, the February hunger of Petrograd was beginning.

Mail day, the last for me, was January 31. The increase of the Finnish troubles was warning that the railroad might be closed any day. The courier who got in reported that he had been obliged to use a sledge between two stations held by opposing forces, both sides allowing him to pass. He wished to start back immediately. I got together packages of newspapers and translations with which I did not wish to be hampered later, and wrote a short letter saying that I hoped to be following in ten days time. The courier brought a letter my wife had written Thanksgiving Day. I carried it in my pocket until the envelope wore thin. To my disappointment the courier brought no films, or word of them. It was the last chance, I feared. I regretted I had not sent men from Petrograd to get the pictures.

Of the Peace Conference itself there was little news, so little that the Bolsheviks themselves appeared to be disturbed. Nor did this condition change for several days.

On February 1 a decree was published ordering the formation of a Red Army, to be the fighting arm of Revolution. A fund of 20,000,000 rubles was set aside for initial organization. Soldiers were to be paid 50 rubles a month. Volunteers were called for. For the present, however, the affair was one of paper only. No enlistment stations were opened. Red Guards constituted the existing nucleus. Demobilization of the army was hastened.

John Reed's appointment to the chimerical post of Consul to New York having been announced on January 31, I sought to have it withdrawn, sending Gumberg to see if he could side-track it at Smolny. He made a report of accomplishment, and perhaps a truthful one, for Petrov, who just about this time took, under Chicherin, the post in the Foreign Office that Zalkind was giving up, told me a few days later that the Reed selection had been canceled. Reed left Russia in a supposedly dejected state of mind, paying me a parting call in which he blamed me for getting him deposed. Not until he was in Sweden did I put two or three pieces of contradictory detail together and conclude that a scene had been played to pull the wool over my eyes in order that he might reënter the United States without search of his papers. Time remained for action.

5.

CHANCE for diversion came on Sunday evening, February 3, and I accepted it gladly. Zorin gave an invitation for a sight-seeing trip through the Neva-side palace of the Grand Duke Nicholas. Efforts to get a group to go along were a failure. Only Thacher was curious for the experience. The pair of us and the two Gumbergs made the party.

For Zorin it was opportunity for happy display, since he was sitting as judge of a people's court in the grand ducal halls. The palace and its contents had been confiscated. We took sledges across the Neva to the palace gates and were welcomed there by grinning Red Guards, pleased that night-time dulness was broken. Of the outside of the palace I got little impression, except that of size, but the interior was not only luxurious but comfortable in a livable modern way. The baronial elements of banquet hall and elaborate decorations were not intrusive. Electric elevators ran between the floors, and in some respects the arrangements were those of a fashionable apartment house. Apparently the palace had risen in a recent decade.

The draperies and the upholstering in the hall and in the salon and rooms adjacent were of the Napoleon bee design, brocade-like fabrics of rose hue on which the bees were worked in gilt or gold thread. The parquet floors had been stripped of their rugs, and some of the chairs had been moved to a pine board dais in the hall to become seats for the new judges. Vandals, however, had not been allowed to enter. Treasures were all about. The Grand Duke's writing-room, corresponding to the business room to be found in continental residences, was undisturbed, the heavy and ornate desk dusted and set for use. To one side of this spacious room, near a window overlooking the Neva, was a cabinet in which the Grand Duke had kept a collection of pistols, knives, and some military mementos. What historical significance the grouping had was not apparent; some of the weapons were modern and none ancient. On one end of a shelf stood a businesslike looking bomb. Zorin suggested that it might be the relic of a would-be assassin's unsuccessful venture.

The hall could now be called the Red Hall. At the far end a platform had been roughly carpentered and at the front had been erected a judicial bench behind which a trio of judges might sit. Zorin took his seat at the center, and frowned as he said he frowned when doing his stint of bench duty. No robes, he said, but in attire as he stood, generally cap and overcoat, too. The palace was not well heated, although fires enough were kept to prevent deterioration of the contents. The judicial bench was draped with red flags, and others hung about the room.

Taking the elevator we rose to the floor containing the private suites of the Grand Duke and his family. The rooms might have been those of persons who had stepped out for the evening. Even the disarray was that of costumes thrown over chairs or laid out on beds.

A committee, Zorin explained, was listing the contents of the palace, and had been working during the day in that room, which was the bedroom of the Grand Duke. Several complete uniforms were before us, with headgear and epaulets for each. The Grand Duke, for so large and tall a man, had an unusually small head. The military bonnets were too small for any head among us except mine, and I, wearing a six and three-quarters size hat, found them roomy.

Spread out on a table were many holiday gifts of friendly, intimate, and costly kind. Nearly all had a religious significance, as if bestowed on Easter, Christmas, or a Saint's Day. Easter Eggs predominated, although they were not of the kind familiar to the children of the West. Rather they were jewel boxes of solid gold, opening to hollows in which diamonds and pearls might have nested. Many too were of egg within egg, the tiny one at the center able to contain a single jewel.

A few of the gifts represented labor rather than price, among them a work-bag of hundreds of patches of a design, or lack of it, that would have done honor to a New England crazy quilt. And inside, in a feminine hand, was a letter which, translated, read: "Do not laugh at this work of my hands. If it gives you pleasure, it will give me endless joy." There was no signature.

The intrinsic value of the gifts was great. The jeweled orders of the Grand Duke, too, were heaped upon a dresser. The room alone would have been treasure trove for looters. I asked if robbery was feared, what with the influx of the public into the courtroom daily. Guards, Zorin said, blocked the remainder of the palace from casual access, adding that the guards themselves were carefully picked. Robbery from confiscated properties was indeed an unheard-of thing, perhaps because death was the published penalty.

Nothing about the palace as far as we had gone had suggested either the *outré* or the medieval, and we would have left unenlightened had not one of the caretakers, an old peasant woman, insisted that we follow her. She wished to show us something strange, she said. Zorin, as curious as any of us, led us behind her up a stairway to a story of the building apparently not reached by the elevators. At the head of the stairway was an alcove in which were two niches occupied by icons.

Running her hand along the base of one of them the peasant woman touched a spring and a concealed door opened toward her, showing dark space behind. Motioning us to wait, the woman entered and in a moment returned with a bundle of candles which she lighted and passed among us. She led us then into a large room with arched walls rising to a low dome, and left us in the center while she lighted other candles in brackets on the walls. The hall outside was electric lighted but this room had not been wired. In the full light we saw that the walls and dome were covered with crudely drawn, highly colored pictures of biblical scenes as familiar to us as if we had been turning the pages of a Sunday-school leaflet.

We had entered the Grand Duke's prayer-room, to which, the peasant woman said, he often retired for hours at a time. Our wonder that he did not suffocate at his devotions disappeared when we noticed that the smoke of the candles rose toward the dome and was carried away in the draft. Somewhere above was a ventilation system, although the room seemed to be windowless.

When we voiced the opinion that the Grand Duke was a very pious man, the peasant woman smiled enigmatically and walked behind one of several pillars along the sides of the room. Keeping behind her we perceived that there was an opening in the thick wall beyond the pillar, doorless, and not masked. Climbing a few stone steps we stood in a bare, stone-walled circular chamber not more than nine or ten feet in diameter. Up from the floor, a few feet from our place of entrance, rose an iron railing much like a park fence or the guard to a well.

When we came to the railing and thrust our candles ahead of us we supposed at first that we were looking down into a pit. Soon, however, as the light increased we perceived that we stood at the head of spiral stairs winding down into depths of masonry, a handrail following the stairs. Taking turns we climbed down far enough to see that the secret way led to the lower stories, if not to street level. With a few questions to the peasant woman, mystery vanished.

The circular stairway was from the top of the building to a basement exit on the bank of the Neva. The Grand Duke could retire to the prayer-room and by the use of the stairway and a waiting boat on the Neva, leave the palace for hours, and return the same way without attracting attention to his absence. As Grand Duke Nicholas had a puritanical reputation, his own use of the secret way enabled him at least to escape from boresome guests without hurting their feelings by open flight.

Guards henceforth were posted not only at the palace gates but at the hidden portal on the Neva bank. The peasant woman got her tip and thanks for merry entertainment.

CHAPTER XX

*February 3—February 12, 1918. A Matter of Inquiry.
The Curtain of Silence. The Gossipy Chicherin. Daze
of "No Peace, No War!"*

1.

IT was not written that I should follow my purpose of early
home-going. Two months of Russia and Finland lay before
me. On the morning of February 5 the Ambassador sent
word asking if I could come to the Embassy at once.

When I reached him he said he was troubled about an occurrence of the night before—a visit from a well-known Russian, Eugene Semenov, one of the editors and the signing
leader writer of the newspaper *Vecherneë Vremya* ("The Evening Times"), now suppressed. Mr. Semenov had placed in
his hands the Ioffe letter (which figured in the Rumanian Affair), and had provided both photographic copy and translation. After the translation had been checked and the photograph verified as that of the letter, Mr. Semenov had retained
the letter, stating that it would have to be returned to the Bolshevik files at Smolny from which it came. The material was
put before me.

Under ordinary circumstances I would not have been greatly
attentive, but in the preceding three days a sequence of happenings had made me uneasy. On February 2, Robins had
brought me an English version of a set of documents which, if
true, showed that Lenin, Trotsky, Zinoviev, Lunacharsky,
Furstenberg-Ganetsky (Hanecki), and several others of the
Bolshevik leaders, had been the accredited and financed agents
of Germany at the moment of their entrance into Russia, and
the manner of the financing. The papers did not show German
connection after the Revolution, none bearing later date than
October, 1917. Not more than a clue in themselves, and soon
to become a part of background, the importance of the circulars lay not a little in the mental effect upon the pair of us
who studied them. Robins, against his own desires, had brought
to me a paper secured by chance. Why? Because he dared not

do otherwise—the responsibility was too heavy to bear alone. If neither of us had known much about the Bolshevik organization, we would have felt either little concerned or unable to make any worth-while inquiry. The fact was that we knew the Bolsheviks so well that we did not possess these excuses for inaction. Should the two of us agree, however, that reasons of policy bade us be inattentive, the chances of other American investigation would be slight. It may have been that Robins expected I would counsel that the bother be discarded. He argued at once for rejection.

The matter was altogether too circumstantial for such a course, it seemed to me. Proof or disproof appeared possible. When he told of a tentative appointment he had made for the evening, I asked him to keep it, particularly as he refused to name his informant. Some hours later he made quite a rite of the visit, coming to my rooms and leaving his keys with me, in the contingency that he did not return. He came back for the keys at one o'clock in the morning, safe and tight-lipped. He had seen his man, he said, had gotten nothing, and knew of nothing more to do. I may add that the person he visited was not Eugene Semenov, who testified that he never saw Robins but once and that in a public place where Robins was talking to Ambassador Francis. On the night visit Robins again declined to give me what, if any, fact leads he had.

The material, however, was more widely scattered in Petrograd than he knew, and on February 4 another English copy was delivered to me at our Gorokhovaya office, and I also found a Russian language copy in the possession of the dragoman at the Embassy. Organized distribution was apparent. In my later government report* this set of circulars was printed as an "Appendix to the Report," put there for record. It was the only part of the contents of the Report that Robins ever saw or knew about. I asked his help for further inquiry and he refused it.

This was the situation at the morning conversation with the Ambassador, facing me with data that, if true, implied the continuation of a German-Bolshevik bond after the Revolution, having at least the status that impulsion came from the German side and had an effect on Bolshevik action, variable

* "The German-Bolshevik Conspiracy," Appendix, pp. 484–486.

though it might be. What the relations between the German militarists and the Russian peace agitators might have been prior to the Bolshevik Revolution was of the past; what the relations were between two ruling Governments was of the realistic, war present. The horrid point, both to the Ambassador and to me, was that the communication before us presented Trotsky as conniving at precise military advantage for Germany against the Allies, against the United States. General Hoffman, according to the letter* "twice had hinted" to Trotsky the "necessity of immediately beginning German operations on the Western front on a very large scale." A peremptory demand, so stated, for an early Russian peace.

The best argument against the value of the letter was that the Bolsheviks had not made peace; appeared in that week of February to be nearer war than peace. Moreover an attitude of middle January might not have remained constant. The latter view I was willing to advance, although I perceived the matter could not be dismissed.

The Ambassador begged me to undertake a thorough investigation, saying that he was without facilities. I did not care to make a quick promise, nor did I wish just then to meet Semenov, outlining the questions I wanted asked if he returned to the Ambassador. Then I told the Ambassador about the earlier circulars of specific accusation against the Bolshevik leaders, saying that I thought they might have been sent into Petrograd from the headquarters of General Alexeiev or General Kaledin. This was not quite a guess on my part, for the circulars, making no pretense at being anything but typed or mimeographed copies, obviously would emanate from an anti-Bolshevik center. I learned soon that was their source.

We agreed that there was one thing we could do both about the circulars and the Ioffe letter, and that was to notify Washington. I set about making an analysis of the set of circulars and of the Ioffe letter and we cabled the text of both, and the notations, to the State Department in cipher on February 9. Prompt instruction came back to make every investigation within our power. From that time I began to sever myself from my own organization lest it be involved in what I might

* Document 37A, "The German-Bolshevik Conspiracy," Appendix, p. 478.

have to do. Besides, I wanted the machine I had built to test itself with lessened overlooking.

One of my first actions, following the first talk with the Ambassador, was to put myself in touch with the British Intelligence Service. The head of it, E. T. Boyce, had a Robins of his own on his hands, Bruce Lockhart, who called himself a commissioner and was playing with the Bolsheviks in a serio-comic diplomatic rôle, without the approval, as far as anyone could learn, of his own Embassy. Some department of the British Government, however, had sent him. Boyce was so disgusted with Lockhart that at first he thought I came from Robins to further some maneuver of Lockhart's, as he had heard that the two were working together. When I freed his mind of that doubt, he accepted me as an ally.

We found we had knowledge and instruments that complemented each other's forces. I knew Smolny and the Bolshevik leaders in a way he did not, their names, rôles, and party identities. He was equipped with mechanical facilities I did not have. For three weeks he had been in daily receipt from a Russian military and naval group of the telegraph dispatches passing between Smolny and its peace delegation at Brest-Litovsk, and between the German War Prisoner Commission at Petrograd and Berlin. I assumed a proportionate share of the expense of this enterprise, gaining the back files and the quota thenceforth, though too late to advantage me in the current overlooking of the last days of the Brest-Litovsk Conference. Surveillance of the telegraph wires at Smolny was maintained after the session closed. Detailed Petrograd translations of Brest-Litovsk material were confined to salients like Radek's talk with Bronsky and to matters of British diplomatic concern in reference to the Bolshevik effort to send agitators to England. Much commentary passed by word of mouth, and not having men of my own in the translating force I did not get a major value out of the file until I had it translated in the United States. Unfortunately, too, the Germans of the Commission in Petrograd—covered also—used, when they wished to tell Berlin whatever they considered of most importance, a numeral code which the experts never were able to crack. Nevertheless I had amusement at the German account of troubles over lack of soap and food in Petrograd, and gained valuable information of the scope of their labors. One thing the Germans did from Petrograd was to demand control of Murmansk on the Arctic coast—potentially a marine base for a part of the year. The Allies spoiled this plan. One day I read in the dispatches a mathematical "proof" that the Americans could not send an army of numerical threat across the Atlantic in three years. The Germans were great wire gossips.

Taking Boyce into my confidence in regard to the Ioffe letter at the Embassy, I was rewarded by learning that he credited Semenov as dependable and intelligently hostile to the Bolsheviks, and believed him to be in touch with the wire group, with the personnel of which Boyce himself maintained an indirect contact. The inquiry centering about Semenov I deferred temporarily for separate action, handling him for another week through the Embassy, to which he brought two or three more letters of declared Bolshevik origin, one of them of later date than the Ioffe letter.

Most cables of this period went to the State Department and not to Creel, although on February 13 I gave him opportunity to learn at Washington whatever details he desired, cabling him in code:

Have made a digest for Ambassador which went through in last three days. In spite of contradictions to present developments it cannot be disregarded as measuring instrument and should have rigid investigation. Study it. For myself, I lean to conclusion that after January 12 Germany's grasping attitude disclosed itself as finally unyielding except at sacrifice of a Revolution, the unexpected success of which had given enlarged ideas to the leaders. The real Bolshevik sincerity lies in international revolutionism. I find it impossible to believe therefore that present bitterness is not real and apt to be lasting. The Ukrainian situation illustrates, too, the German method of disruption by dealing with many factions at the same time. In fact this mess seems to me to be simplified by its very contradictions.

For the Ambassador, at a later date, February 22, after I had begun to make organized use of Semenov and his group, I wrote a dispatch, which he sent, in which Robins' rôle was related:

Secretary of State. February 22. Following statement to me by

Sisson on points raised in your message: "Photograph of letter signed Ioffe is in possession of the Ambassador and was secured by him. Purported originals of documents preceding Ioffe letter [Note: Circulars in digest of February 9] were seen by Raymond Robins who from brief look surmised they were copies. His faith in Bolshevik leaders was such that he declined to utilize the material which thereupon was taken back by persons who offered it. He has not named, for reasons that seem proper to him, this source and that particular collection has not re-appeared. Shortly, however, other sets admittedly copies appeared at different Embassies and at one other place [Note: My office]. Robins also turned over to me the English translation of set he had seen. These sets, except the last, trace to a group not working for money. [Note: The Alexeiev group.] It is stated that many of the documents were collected outside of Russia—Rotterdam, Copenhagen, and Stockholm. Originals may never have been in Russian secret service archives. I do not expect much from hunt for [their] originals.

"Their content authenticity is being proved by later documents of which photographs are being taken. Have evidence that the working compact between the People's Commissariat and Germany, especially against the United States, was in existence as late as January 14. [Note: Reference was to a German proposal that disassembled submarines be shipped by rail through Russia for re-assembling at a Siberian port for use in the Pacific ocean.] Referring to last inquiry, revolutionary propaganda was worked by the Bolsheviks against Germany but never the policy of agents-destructors. Germany simply took the revolutionary risk at the beginning, confident that it would burn others but not itself. Probably the time it realized it was apt to be scorched was the signal for it to double cross the Bolsheviks with the Ukraine deal. Mutual double crossing at some date is apparent. If cable communication remains open will send text of the later documents." [Signature] Francis.

In asking for detail the State Department had included a request for a view on Bolshevik revolutionary activity in Germany.

When that message went steady progress was being made upon the problem which the Ambassador and I had set ourselves, which was this:

On the working theory that compacts did exist between the Bolsheviks and the German command at the outset of the Bolshevik

Revolution, do they continue in force, and are German orders being obeyed?

A negative reply to the question of present and military moment would tend to disprove the premise. An affirmative outcome would prove the premise as well.

2.

THE early days of February in Petrograd, apart from my own worries, were oddly without event other than nearing famine, an external condition brought by absence of news either from Brest-Litovsk or from Kiev, a situation which continued to wait explanation. Under those circumstances those about me turned to the meager pleasures possible.

A performance of the ballet *The Sleeping Beauty* at the Marinsky Theater the evening of February 6 was enjoyable. Consul Tredwell gave the party and in an intermission we went behind the scenes. There the members of the company grouped around us to tell a story of hardship. The theater like everything else had been nationalized, which meant that it had been deprived of its revenues and the players put upon a pittance of wage. Entrance prices had been so lowered that the performances were almost a gift to the proletarian public, which thronged nightly. There was gaiety on the stage and sorrow and hunger behind the curtain. Rich costumes, in spite of care of needle, were going the way of unreplaced outfitting. Under their paint the faces of the players were thin and lined, though the unremitting spirit of all artists burned within them while they worked before the public.

They asked us if there was not a way of getting them to America, which they pictured—and with no exaggeration under the circumstances—as the players' heaven. We could only disabuse them of hope, though we encouraged them to hold to their determination, and to come when the bars of war were lowered. None who became acquainted that winter with the Russian stage ever doubted its American vogue if the finer representatives of it could be transported to New York. I was informed continually, however, that the greater stars were in Moscow, not in Petrograd, though Petrograd sometimes was credited with superiority of ensemble performances, due to the nurturing of the Imperial Ballet.

A bad time with Robins was starting for me, though I did not yet give up hope of changing his attitude. In a precautionary way, however, I already had cut him off from knowledge of my actions and the Ambassador had promised me a like secrecy. Bullard and Robins and I being alone in my rooms the late night of February 7, I made an effort to talk out our differences of opinion before Bullard, who was serenely reasonable in debate. Robins sensed my purpose at the first word and left the rooms, the first of two occasions on which he did this. At any rate I wanted the play of another mind than my own on the whole matter up to then, and laid it before Bullard, being not greatly surprised when for reasons opposite to those of Robins, he advised inaction. He distrusted the Bolsheviks but feared the inquiry would imperil our other work, as indeed it might.

In the morning, nevertheless, he came to me, said that he had spent most of the night thinking, and that duty had grown larger every minute. The risks seemed to him unlessened, as any misstep would bring closure of news and printing sections, but in the face of them, the inquiry, in his opinion, ought not to be abandoned. I told him that I intended soon to place him in charge of all committee work in Russia, and that as far as possible I would conduct any investigation independently. Yet before I was through I required him by my side on several occasions. Of the others of my organization I called only upon Malcolm Davis for occasional translation and upon Guy Croswell Smith for photography.

Robins, too, came in to apologize for his bad manners of the night before, although he continued to decline to enter into a three-cornered discussion. I concluded that he felt the odds would be two to one against him, and bided a time when he would have more support. His better temper I took as a good sign.

I made a call upon Petrov at the Foreign Office that afternoon to find out if Zalkind were about and if Petrov still thought of returning to England. On both these topics he was noncommittal, from which I deduced that Zalkind was on the way to Stockholm and that he was not so sure of his own trip. He gave me a good greeting, however, and wanted to talk about everything American. If only Russia could get American engineering and business help, so that the Soviet could learn to run its nationalistic enterprises! To my dry comment that the business of war rather occupied the United States for the moment, he replied optimistically that the War would soon be over. Would I help him in what ways I could? I let him run on in his glib, thick English until he made a modest request for copies of several American engineering and economic journals. He didn't explain what use he had for them in the Foreign Office, but I promised to send for them, and did so, cabling, "Send Peter Petrov, Foreign Office, fifty copies each best technical journals in variety industrial lines." It is possible that in time they reached him. When I sought him again three weeks later it was to ask and secure from him papers according safety of exit from Petrograd to all Americans then remaining. The good-humored relationship earlier established was of prime value then.

Treasures at the Embassy lured us that week more than ever before. They were those of food and drink. The Log of February 8 had entry: "A real dinner, white bread, wine, cookies—paying by toil." I had dined at the Embassy before attacking the task of digest of next day's long cable. Most of us, by this time, had reached a state of sugar hunger, something not adequately explainable to those who never have experienced it and a life memory to those who have. Sugarless food, regardless of quantity, finally does not meet the body's craving for sweets. The pangs are present every waking hour. For a time after there was no more sugar I was able to get a solid mixture of compressed honey and honeycomb. An inch square section of this, eaten twice a day, lessened the misery. The supply of palliative went in wake of the sugar. The Embassy was the only haven left. The Ambassador had a reserve supply of American white flour and of American whiskey, although he was not much better off for sugar than the rest of us. We found that a drink of whiskey sent the sugar haunt scurrying away, not to return for hours. A drink at ten o'clock at night might mean immunity until noon next day.

The Ambassador was a careful doler, sharing, however, with the utmost fairness, warning that the stock was getting lower. The final courier of the last day of January, happily, brought a new supply from far-off St. Louis, replenishment from the old man's thoughtful sons. Not till the old stock was gone and mourned did the Ambassador tell gleefully about the new. A welcoming drink and a good dinner following was mighty cheer.

3.

OBSERVERS were not the only ones puzzled by the practical absence of news from Brest-Litovsk following the return of Trotsky to the Conference. A curtain of silence shrouded the negotiations. Assertions made at Smolny that the Bolsheviks themselves did not know what was happening were received skeptically. Yet they were true as I learned when I came to read the dispatches that passed between Smolny and Brest-Litovsk. On February 4 Stalin at Smolny called Secretary Karakhan to the direct wire and stood by while he wrote and sent this peremptory message:

Comrade Karakhan: we fail to understand your four days' silence. Of course you understand that reports from Brest are doubly important to us, yet Brest remains silent. There is something kept secret in Brest. Either Brest is playing a comedy, or the officials sitting in Brest. Once again we request that you inform us as to affairs in Brest. I have something interesting to communicate about Finland and the Ukraine, but will do that only in case I receive news of the peace negotiations. I am standing at the instrument. Speak.

Karakhan, replying:

Sorry that we could not communicate with you. This is due, solely as the Germans assure us, to the wires being out of order. I sent you a wireless message as to the course of the negotiations and sent you this morning, by courier, detailed information. We fear that the first reports did not reach you—I sent by courier stenographic reports of all the five meetings which were held during that time. In the process of negotiations the most essential is the recognition of the Kiev Rada by the other side. I have communicated that by wireless so as not to repeat.

Stalin, in a rage:

We did not receive your wireless message. The recognition of which Rada are you speaking about? The Kiev Rada has been overthrown already two days ago and is replaced by the Kharkov Rada. How could you have permitted the recognition of a delegation to an "empty place"? I communicated with you two days ago. Did you get my communication?

Karakhan did not answer the last question, but shoved the text of the lost wireless message upon the wire. Stalin in speaking of the overthrow of the Rada two days ago did not mean the first capture of Kiev which had taken place nearly a week before and was known to Trotsky before he left for Brest-Litovsk, but to the political supersedence of the Kiev Rada by the Kharkov Rada. Of the military situation at Kiev, which included reverses, he was not then well informed. In this message from Karakhan was the first news of Germany's maneuver in continuing to treat for peace with the delegation of the dispersed Rada. Stalin naturally was shocked.

The former wireless message of February 2, now sent as a telegram, continued with the disagreeable details:

We in Brest-Litovsk appear to be completely cut off. The wire is completely out of order, reason not known to us. Yesterday the delegation of the Kiev Rada presented a statement by which the Ukraine declares itself a separate Republic, not desirous of entering the Russian Federation. The Austro-German delegation immediately recognized the sovereignty of the Ukrainian Republic . . . although we informed them of the new elements in the question: first, the complete overthrow of the Rada; second, the creation of the Federal Republic at the Third Congress of the Soviets. The behavior of the delegations of the Central Empires can be understood only in this sense—that in view of internal conditions they must achieve some sort of success, even though purely external. We said that irrespective even of the "state's rights" position of the Ukraine as a composite part of the Russian Federation, the fact remains unaltered that the Ukraine is not territorially separated from Russia, and consequently no agreement with the Ukraine can be valid without recognition by the Russian delegation. To this indisputable declaration the opponents did not reply but they continue—this is quite apparent—negotiations with the Rada. [Translation by American Military Intelligence, Executive Division G.S.]

There was the Ukrainian double-cross that Germany handed to the Russian Bolsheviks, and the date of it, February 1, 1918, culmination of Ukrainian peace treaty to come eight days later, February 9.

The double fact that the wireless message did not get through and that simultaneously the telegraph wires were stilled for several days, did not bespeak an accident. The facilities of transmission were in German territory.

Although communication, once restored, was not broken again, Smolny continued toward the outer world the silence for which it had blamed its peace delegation. Until February 11, Petrograd had no public intimation of crisis in the peace negotiations.

It was known, however, that the control of Kiev had fluctuated after the first seizure of Kiev by the Bolsheviks, that for a few days they had lost the city again but most certainly had taken it securely with Muraviev's army not later than February 9. Aware of the extent of the forces moving against the city we had discounted—too much so—the outcome of the contest after the Bolsheviks got their first foothold in the city. We underrated the tenacity and the valor of the middle classes of the city. They rose and retook the city—although in vain, save that as "Bloody Kiev," the capital of the Ukraine was to be entered in the annals of the Bolshevik Revolution. An army had reconquered them and Kiev was an actual Bolshevik city when the Germans signed formal peace with representatives of a parliament which no longer had a country.

4.

In the Log for February 10 was the entry:

Bronsky's plan for raw product monopoly to the United States. Whose idea? Lenin wants Robins to feed Petrograd and Moscow from China.

The question was rhetorical. I knew when I wrote that the idea was Lenin's and considered that its purpose was to try to befuddle the United States in the name of humanity and of industrial opportunity in the hope thereby of breaking the Asiatic blockade established by China and the Allies. The move was weak, but in intent hostile to the Allies and favorable to Germany. To send food or supplies to Russia if it made a separate peace would amount to sending the equivalent to Germany itself, since Germany would be able to draw upon the produce of Russia, become a friendly nation.

More about the project I learned when I conned subsequently a long and gossipy message from Chicherin, at Petrograd, to Trotsky, at Brest-Litovsk, in which he explained not only this plan but also the challenge of naming Petrov for a mission to England, and the light in which Robins was viewed by Lenin and Chicherin. A part of the message was in reply to comment made by Trotsky in a telegram February 4. Said Chicherin:

With reference to the Allies the situation is evidently favorable. Separate peace will not cause a rupture. England has reconciled herself to this in advance. The recognition of us is a matter of the near future.

England and America are playing up to us separately. A few days ago there appeared a so-called head of a Commercial Mission, Lockhart, with a letter from Litvinov [Note: At Stockholm or Christiania] stating that the bearer is an honest man who indeed fully sympathizes with us. Indeed he is a subtle alert Englishman, expresses very liberal views, runs down his Government. He is a type of the diplomat of the new school. At present he is not an official representative but de facto he is an envoy, having been sent by the War Cabinet. After our recognition he will obtain an official position with us. He promises all kinds of favors from England.

The situation has been defined concerning the following: (1) Petrov's Mission; (2) The incident with China.

On receipt of the news of a revolution in Berlin we, together with Lenin, decided to immediately send Zalkind to Switzerland and Petrov to England on behalf of the People's Commissars. This became known and Lockhart came to me and explained that if we should not spoil the situation our recognition is a question of the near future, but something would have to be ceded on our part. He said that no Government would tolerate intervention in its personal affairs. If we are going to raise the British people, if our agents in England will attempt to cause strikes, England will not tolerate this. It proved later that this had reference to Petrov's Mission. Concerning the latter especially, Lockhart said that his appointment would be difficult for England to swallow,* and should he be arrested in England or not be allowed to land, we probably would reply by reprisals and thus the whole situation would be spoilt. He begged that we should postpone this matter

* Petrov was deported from England in December preceding.

for ten or twelve days. Simultaneously Ransome tried to persuade Petrov not to go to England. His journey in case of a conflict could put the question of a Revolution in England on edge and would be exceedingly risky.

We discussed this question and decided that our strength was in attack and that whatever would happen would be the worse for Lloyd-George & Co., and the Revolution would be the gainer. We sent Petrov's passport to be *viséd*. Lockhart came running to us. I arranged for an interview with Petrov. Lockhart stated that the question had been referred for decision to London. We said that Russia represented a part in the world revolutionary movement and that in this was its strength. We and our comrades in England would proclaim that this is not a concrete organization of strikes. We explained the aim of Petrov's mission: that is, the clearing up of misunderstandings between the two nations. He will appeal to all organs of the British nation. This has also been sent by radio.

Lockhart stated that he was very well impressed and promised to telegraph advising that the *visa* should be granted. We await further developments. He stated that according to English information the German troops on the eastern front were so badly affected by our propaganda that no second course of barrack *régime* could cure them. He said that our method of fighting militarism was most effective. We listened to this and laughed up our sleeves.

Concerning China's prohibition of transit of goods we have received a telegram from the Horvat that this was done in accordance with the demands of the Allies. The Secretary of the Chinese Legation explained to me that China was not free. Lockhart promised decisive steps for the removal of this embargo. He doubted the guilt of England and explained the measure by China's fear that food stuffs would fall into the hands of the Germans.

At the same time Robins appeared and luridly depicted the friendly feeling of America and stated that it was probable that America would recognize us in the near future. He said that America did not participate in the decision concerning the embargo in Manchuria. He promised that America would use all its influence to have the embargo removed.

Yesterday I telegraphed to you concerning the question of Khasaovich's journey with a view to elucidating the question of national minorities; and about the American journalist Shaplen who interviewed you in Brest. Please telegraph.

[Note: This inquiry, I think, was mixed up on the telegraph wire and should have read "who wished to interview you at Brest." The correspondent of the United Press, Joseph Shaplen, interviewed Trotsky in Petrograd January 27, and I think did try to get permission to go to Brest-Litovsk. As that place was inside the German lines, the project did not look feasible. I have no record that Shaplen succeeded.]

The Left Social Revolutionary, Axel, is going to New York. He offers his services as Consul; gives as reference Lenin and Spiridonova, but Lenin seems to know him very little.*

Concerning Kamenev and Zalkind we have information from Poznansky, who was with them, that they got aboard a steamer at Abo. We have no further news. The Rumanian Mission is in the north of Finland. For the moment the White Guards reign there.

Your proposition concerning a note to Japan arrived rather late as we already had made a similar statement to the Secretary of the Japanese Legation. He produced a verbatim report of Motono's speech. In it we do not find the aggressive views. He assures us that the two Japanese war ships will soon leave Vladivostok.

[Note: Trotsky wired Chicherin on February 4: "In view of the fact that the Japanese Government threatens to take further steps in Vladivostok I would consider it advisable to draw up a short note showing that no one is threatened by any danger in Vladivostok because order reigns there; and that besides Japan there are many other countries interested, particularly the United States, and that by taking military steps and making declarations Japan threatens to bring on an extreme complication in the condition of affairs in the Far East—a complication which will inevitably, injuriously, affect not only the interests of Russia but also the interests of other nations, especially the United States. A copy of a note of this sort should, in my opinion, be communicated to the American Embassy. Prepare the plan of the note and confer with Lenin in regard to the matter." But that particular note was not written.]

Chicherin continued his grist of home news for his chief:

The Swedish Government has approached us to find out how we would look upon the arrival of a war vessel with two ships and an

---

* Here was record that John Reed was separated from his consulship at least for a time, although it is possible that the indication was merely that Chicherin was not yet familiar with the earlier appointment.

ice-breaker for the removal of Swedes from Finland. After consulting Dybenko we replied that this would not be tolerated. Nevertheless in a secretly intercepted wire from Stockholm to the British Embassy we find the following: "We are glad to inform of the despatch of the armed vessel *Svenizund* with two passenger steamers and ice-breaker for the transport of Scandinavian citizens. We have information that Mentuoloto is mined, but we hope to embark them in Abo."

Vorovsky [at Stockholm] is very nervous because of the lies in the press. We westerners* know that they are used to lying there. This of course must be counteracted. In the press section the work of translation and printing is moving along at a snail's pace. Reforms must be undertaken. Part of the employes are dead souls.

Chicherin then revealed that Petrov's mission was an offensive sally only. He stated:

Petrov has now been appointed chief director for English propaganda. He will be going away temporarily only. He has started the work of re-organization and has arranged for daily telegraphic communications to Litvinov and Vorovsky of latest news and several decrees. He will introduce life into the business.

A nervous, lively epistle from a nervous, lively person! Chicherin, a dancing shadow of a man, was diplomacy's gift to the Communists. Gone Bolshevik after sound schooling in the diplomatic service of Imperial Russia, he knew his way about. Had his training been manual rather than mental he would have been a juggler. His traits were impish. Language was his tool. "Lurid!"—one word to epitomize Robins! And, of the solemn Lockhart, complimenting the cynic band on its "effective method of fighting German militarism," the tag, "We listened and laughed up our sleeves!"

The translation of Chicherin's report of his stewardship, as I have used it, was made by the British Military Intelligence unit at Petrograd, and was in the possession of E. T. Boyce not long after Trotsky had mulled the contents. Petrov's chances of getting to England were slight after that, even had the Finnish war not raised effective barrier against the intended journey. The information that the Bolsheviks not only had intercepted telegrams entering the British Embassy but

---

* Chicherin's description of himself as familiar with western Europe.

were able to decode the cipher dispatches was taken philosophically. The only protection possible was the constant
changing of code. Captain Crosley, our Naval *Attaché*, was
thrown into a seaman's voluble rage one day by having one of
his own code messages returned to him nicely decoded. The
jest did us a good turn, however, for afterward we switched
codes fast enough to give nervous prostration to Bolsheviks
assigned to wrestle with them.

5.

THE news from Brest was out Monday, February 11. Trotsky
had received an ultimatum of peace terms from the Central
Empires, had not signed, had replied with declaration that the
Russian position was "No peace and no war," and had left
the Conference. Petrograd did not comprehend and was dazed.

There was hot debate in my rooms that night, Robins,
Thacher, Bullard, and news association correspondents present. The text was, "Had Trotsky opened Russia to the Germans, or had he not?" The majority opinion was that he had
left Russia defenseless. Robins was the only one to argue that
Trotsky had made a brilliant stroke, whether the outcome was
peace or war.

The action itself did not come to most of us as a shock, for
we had known the outlines of the plan since January 28, when
I logged: "Fuller disclosure [of Trotsky plan]—non-resistance, demobilization of army, organization revolutionary army
in the rear." Order of demobilization of army was included in
Trotsky's farewell presentment at Brest.

Realization, however, had a different atmosphere than conjecture. A state of war between Russia and Germany in itself
was satisfactory if it hampered Germany, but a war that would
be only a march would not be much of a harassment to the
Central Empires. What of a revolutionary army? None at all
in the vicinity of Petrograd. Muraviev and Antonov had the
fighting forces in the Ukraine, and would need them there.
Alexeiev and Kaledin on the Don had to be faced with the rest
of a fit army. And back of all, the question whether the Bolsheviks meant to fight or to hippodrome—an issue upon which
I was becoming daily more convinced that hippodrome was the
intent.

The outsiders of the visitors left and I determined to force the discussion upon this very point, Robins now having Thacher of his own organization with him, to counterbalance the presence of Bullard. I told Robins that I desired to take up a situation that had been private between us. He angrily refused the opportunity, and when I said I would not accept that attitude any longer he rose and left the room, ordering Thacher to accompany him. That was our last conversation.

Late that night I wrote, at once lightly and seriously, and sent the note to his room:

Dear Colonel: How's your mad? As I never had any, and never was more surprised in my life than by yours, I would like to mollify the panther. If a real good word fight will soothe him, I am ready for that, too. Haven't any favors to ask. Am posted on intervening events. If you will appoint time and place for combat, am at your service.

He came to breakfast the next morning and did not speak. I made no further advance. Our meals after that were apart. We did not meet again—in Russia or afterward.

Rumor that day, the twelfth, was that Lenin had annulled Trotsky's order of army demobilization. Later in the day it was officially denied. Lenin, nevertheless, had practically canceled the order by instructing Commissars to hold it in abeyance pending further instructions, adding, "We cannot give you the peace terms as actual peace has not been concluded yet."

In the afternoon I called on Colonel Kerth at the Military Mission to wish him good luck, having heard that he was starting the next day to try to break out through Finland to France. He was to travel with his outfit in one grain sack, so he could go afoot if need be, sack on back. Railroads between north and south of Finland were cut or in opposing hands. I logged, "Wonder if the rest of us are trapped."

Colonel Kerth got through, the last American to dare successfully the Finnish route between that date and late March. He had a hard time, according to later rumor, being caught in the ice on a boat between Abo and Stockholm. We never heard directly from him.

Petrograd, for days, did not understand realistically that the Peace Conference had come to nothing, its oblivion due partly to the fact that the Bolshevik press teemed on February 12, 13, 14, and 15 with the accounts of earlier sessions of the Conference, containing much debate and little action, and all the talk on both sides designed for public consumption. Couriers—not the telegraph—had brought the minutes of many of these open sessions. So a dust cloud was in the air, and the drama of "No Peace, No War!" failed of distinctive presentation, to Trotsky's disappointment. Trotsky was reported to be on his way back to Petrograd. He arrived and made a speech on the fourteenth.

The members of the German Commission in Petrograd packed their bags.

CHAPTER XXI

February 9 (Retrospect)—February 13, 1918. Tragedy at Kiev Is Farce at Brest-Litovsk.

THE curtain of silence was vain. The telegraph records penetrated it and delineated the back-scene. With their aid one afterward could sit beyond it at will and through them the public performance visible at the time became lucid. The relation of events can be from both positions—front and rear.

Kiev was the prize for which the Bolsheviks battled and the Germans intrigued—Kiev and the food-bins of the Ukraine. To win, the Germans were willing to flout the Bolsheviks, thinking the risk slight and not worth a concession. To win, they were willing to make a paper peace with titular representatives of the Rada, a parliament in flight, and to use armies to force the acceptance of the paper upon the Bolsheviks.

Although Kiev, first taken by interior insurrection on January 27 and lost by counterattack on January 30 and 31, was recaptured on February 3 and control consolidated in the days following, the frantic Trotsky did not get reliable news until February 9, the day the Germans signed "Peace" with the Ukrainian delegates. Petrograd was not better informed.

The dispatches of Muraviev served further to confuse Trotsky, who complained bitterly that Muraviev never dated his messages. One such, which from its neighborhood to other dispatches appeared to have been received on February 3, was particularly ominous:

To Stavka, High Command: In the name of the Revolution and the People's Commissar Antonov I demand the immediate dispatch to the Ukraine front, Nikotova, by order of the People's Commissar Antonov, infantry, artillery, and a railroad battalion. Condition serious. Muraviev. [American Military Intelligence translation.]

The Germans were telling Trotsky the Rada was again in power. He denied and doubted his own words. He did not receive the first circumstantial, formal report of the fall of the city. The Bolshevik press in Petrograd did not have the account until February 9, and its publication was a day later. That official report follows, its value being its Bolshevik perspective:

The Kiev Rada has fallen. The power is in the hands of the Soviets. Kiev has been finally taken by our troops.

The course of events in Kiev was the following. While our troops were marching upon Kiev, the workmen and soldiers there had already risen against the Rada. Firstly, success was with them, but then the troops of Petlura, although defeated near Kruty on January 17 (January 30, New Style), blew up the bridges, checked our advance toward Kiev and descended upon the forces in insurrection.

By overpowering forces of cadets and soldiers, the Arsenal was taken. The Revolutionary Military Committee, which was arrested there, was shot in a body, including the members of the Central Executive Committee, and Assistant People's Commissar, Gorovitz, of the Soviet of the Workmen and Soldiers of the Ukraine. Three hundred men were shot in the Arsenal.

The terrorism of the counter-revolution was indescribable. They shot all workmen, and under this definition came everyone who was horny-handed or was dressed in a worker's overall. More than 1500 men were shot altogether. At last, the Soviet troops, headed by the Commander-in-Chief of the Ukrainian Republic, Kotzubinsky, forced their way into Kiev January 21 (February 3, New Style), united with the besieged comrades, and after a fight occupied the station, the Lavra, the Arsenal, the Fortress, and the Palace.

The Kiev workmen showed in mass heroic enthusiasm. We did not have arms enough to supply all the fighters. Five hundred workmen, who remained unshot and were liberated from the Fortress joined the battle immediately. I am sorry to state that of the (Revolutionary) Ukrainian regiments, those of Bogdan and Shevchenko succumbed nearly in full. But it is holy blood, a sacrifice of redemption in the cause of the liberation of the workers of the Ukraine.

Step by step the counter-revolutionaries were dislodged by artillery and by bayonets. The detachment of Muraviev greatly assisted in the struggle. Muraviev's armored train captured the blinded train of the Rada. [Note: The train in which many members of the Rada were attempting to flee.]

The counter-revolutionaries fought obstinately. In their ranks

French and English, as well as Kiev monks, and Rumanian officers were fighting. French aviators threw bombs from airplanes.
Our artillery bombarded the central streets, where the counter-
revolutionaries held out for a long time under fire. The Town
Municipality attempted to act as an intermediary, but our representatives demanded an unconditional surrender of arms, and
the delivery of the directors of the counter-revolutionary insurrection.

At last Kiev was taken. The capital of the Ukraine has become Red Kiev. The Soviet power in the Ukraine is taking a more
firm stand and is now definitely crushing the insurrection of the
bourgeoisie. . . .

It may be said with every conviction now that the adventure
of the Kiev Rada of the small *bourgeoisie* is ended. (Signed) The
People's Commissar, Skrypnik. [Published in the *Pravda,* Bolshevik official organ.]

An eyewitness telegraphed: "The town is awful to look at.
The vicinity of the Kievo-Pechersk Lavra is in flames. Gangs
of hooligans are robbing the shops and flats."

The "firm stand" against the *bourgeoisie* reported by the
Commissar was reprisal. Our private advices told us the middle
and officer classes of Kiev were eliminated by slaughter.

When a year later I met the British officer, Capt. Gerald
H. L. FitzWilliams, who had been in Kiev during the battles,
I asked him what he knew about the killings on both sides. He
said that the French did not take part in the fighting, nor he
or his English companions. I wrote then:

He (Captain FitzWilliams) was in Kiev when it was partially
taken, lost, and then retaken by the Bolsheviks in early February—as we both recall, though without our notes. He walked
the streets in his English uniform, unmolested and in only the
casual danger of shrapnel or misdirected rifle fire, while 27,000
persons were killed in Kiev.

When the Bolsheviks finally got in to stay they killed 2700
Russian officers—after all fighting had ceased. They shot them
down in the street, searched them out in their houses, shot them
in squads, and singly. The representatives of outside nations
hurried to Muraviev and begged him to stop the slaughter. He
said it was done without his orders, and, at the protest, did stop
it. The Metropolitan was murdered, but perhaps that was private
vengeance done under the cloak of general disorder. Nearly

10,000 of those opposing the Bolsheviks were killed in the last two days of battle. This does not include the officers hunted down later. The Bolsheviks lost even more heavily in battle, as they were attacking, but their losses were over a period. I asked:

"Did not the Reds take the inner city and the Rada building itself when they first attacked?"

"Yes, and were thrown out."

"With heavy slaughter?"

"Yes."

The Reds at Petrograd gave the alleged execution of Reds in Kiev in this first struggle as excuse for the vengeance taken later on the officers. Captain FitzWilliams said there were no executions of Red prisoners and that the Red losses were only those in battle.

The fact that Commissar Skrypnik admitted that the Red forces found and released 500 Red prisoners was self-given evidence against his charge of wholesale execution of prisoners by the Rada army.

Yet this was incontrovertible: Thousands of Russians died in Kiev, and other Russians killed them! Red baptism of Red Kiev! Burnt offerings on the altar of a god who demanded the human sacrifices of civil war, fraternal war! If history decides that Lenin was a madman, it will be charitable, and—it may be—judicious.

The killings at Kiev and the capture of the city were politically useless to Trotsky at Brest-Litovsk.

On February 9, in chagrin at his lack of information, he sent an identical telegram to Chicherin, Lenin, and Stalin following a wire which had stated simply that Kiev had fallen:

Is it possible that one cannot definitely establish who is now in authority in Kiev? The delegation of the Rada in Brest has been showing to Czernin telegrams from the president of the general secretariat, Golubovsky, from Kiev, dated February 5, New Style. What does that mean? Verify immediately. If we receive a true and verified communication from you before five o'clock that Kiev is in the hands of the authorities of the Council, it may have a great significance in the negotiations. Trotsky. [American Military Intelligence translation.]

But by the time Trotsky received verification it was too late. The shock was registered mechanically. During the evening of the ninth the wire to Petrograd was being occupied by transmission from Brest-Litovsk of the dull account of a Danish syndicalist movement for newspaper use when Karakhan rushed to the instrument and called for Stalin to come to the Smolny end. He wrote:

I can report news, in all probability correct, that the Ukraine has tonight signed peace with Germany, Austro-Hungary, and Turkey. That is, with everybody. That's very fine. Will we sign sometime soon or not? Why do we wait—what else are we to wait for?

Operator at Brest-Litovsk: "At this point Comrade Karakhan must leave."

Operator at Petrograd: "Comrade Stalin is here."

Operator at Brest-Litovsk: "At the apparatus is Comrade Ioffe."

Ioffe, continuing:

Several days ago I wrote Lenin in detail, also sent a wireless message. I surmised that the Germans were preparing a business with the Ukrainians. At the same time the Germans reported the capture and arrest of Krylenko by the Poles and the victory of the Rada.

Stalin cut Ioffe off, and put news of the official status of Kiev on the wire for Karakhan and Trotsky:

In Kiev inquire (direct) of the Commander-in-Chief, and in Kharkov of the national secretary of the Ukraine republic. Officially, up to February 8 the whole of Kiev with the exception of the Pechersky section was in the hands of the council. The remaining divisions of the Kiev Rada defended themselves in the Pechersky section. Yesterday, February 8, at 10 P.M. we received from Kiev, from Commander-in-Chief Muraviev, the official report of the capture of the Pechersky section, the flight of the remaining Rada, the seizing of all government institutions, and the liberation of Chudnovsky, Egoriev, Boyarsky, etc. On the request of the soldiers, Muraviev asked for the appointment of Egoriev as Commander of the Southwestern Front. The request was granted. All that took place yesterday, in twenty-four hours. On February 8 nothing was left of the Rada except a sad recollection. As you can see the delegation of the Kiev Rada now in Brest represents an empty spot. Stalin.

Ioffe, getting the wire back:

I am continuing. We refuted the report of Krylenko's capture and the victory of the Rada but the Germans seem to believe the Ukrainians. The purpose is evident. [American Military Intelligence translation.]

From that hour on into the next day corroborative dispatches of the fall of Kiev poured in on Trotsky—from Chicherin, from Petrov, and from Axelrod of the *Izvestia*, all relaying messages from Kiev and from Kharkov. They served no purpose. So cluttered did the wires become that telegrams written the evening of the ninth were not put on the wire until the early hours of the morning. Three messages, two of them written February 9 but all bearing the wire date February 10, told the final story. Two of them were bulletins from staff members, the third was from Trotsky. They were:

Jan. 28 [New Style, Feb. 10]. Tonight, Jan. 27 [Feb. 9] a separate peace has been signed between the quadruple alliance and the Ukrainian representatives of the Kiev Rada. (Signed) Samoilo. [Gen. Samoilo, military adviser.]

Jan. 28 [Feb. 10]. The separate negotiations of the delegates of the Kiev Rada with the Austro-Germans resulted in a treacherous separate peace. For their promise of bread the Ukrainian *bourgeoisie* received from Austro-Germany a large part of Poland, not only the Polish districts of the Cholm government, but also a part of Lublinsky and Sedlezky. The boundary line is to pass through the following points: Tarnogrood, Bilgorai, Krasnostav, Medsirjeche, Melnik, Brest-Litovsk. Peace with the Rada was signed yesterday. (Signed) Bobinsky.

The third, from Trotsky.

Jan. 28 [Feb. 10]. To Lenin and Stalin, Smolny. Rush. [Note: Trotsky wrote the message during the night of February 9–10, as the report of a part of the day's stenographic report of the session showed, incidentally the only stenographic report sent by wire in the last days, others going laggardly by couriers.]

Today Kuhlman and Czernin summed up all the disputes up to this time and proposed to decide definitely the fundamental questions tomorrow. Beginning tomorrow morning a purely military commission will go in session to examine the new boundary from a strategic point of view and to report its findings to the political commission which meets at 5:30 P.M. and is to decide the question definitely. The Austrians signed a peace treaty with the Kiev Rada today at 2 A.M., in spite of our protest that we will not recognize such a peace. So, I repeat, a definite decision will be reached tomorrow evening. Trotsky. [American Military Intelligence translation.]

The epitomized report of the open session of the Peace Conference on February 9 contained salient statements by Von Kuhlman, Czernin, and Trotsky:

Von Kuhlman: "Negotiations have been interrupted twice—I will not blame any one because negotiations so far have met with no success."

Czernin then stated that for weeks a fruitless discussion had been going on about the Russian western boundary—Courland, Lithuania, and Finland.

Trotsky: "We have no objections to Poland, Lithuania, etc. becoming republics, but while the German and Austrian armies remain there those two nations reserve the right to bind these people by military and other agreements so that the new boundary is not between Russia and Poland, etc. but between Russia and Germany and Austria.

"At the very moment when the Ukraine was coming into the Russian Federation the opposing side hastened to recognize the Ukraine. In its struggle for authority in the Ukraine the Rada tried by force and in concurrence with the Central Powers to snatch the Ukrainian people from the Russian Federal Republic. We notified the Central Powers officially of the fall of the Ukrainian Rada. [Note: The first seizure, coinciding with Trotsky's return to Brest.] Nevertheless the negotiations with a non-existing government continued. We therefore declare that treaty, as far as the Ukrainian people and the whole of Russia is concerned, is void."

Von Kuhlman: "Since the former speaker declared that the decision of boundaries demands the participation of military experts, I would suggest that the question be referred to a special sub-committee."

Czernin: "In regard to the existence of the Rada: We recognize the authority of the Rada, therefore as far as we are concerned, it does exist." [Note: Czernin spoke at more length but only enlarged on his challenge.]

Trotsky asked what the Central Powers considered as the boundary between the Ukraine and Austria.

He was told that reply could not be given until the military subcommittee reported, and the session adjourned.

The account of the last session of the Peace Conference on February 10, courier-brought to the Bolshevik press, fitted adequately to preceding events. It should do so. The stage was set for a declaration for which Trotsky desired world publicity.

Von Kuhlman opened the session with an acid comment accepting a proposal of Trotsky's that three memoranda about nationalistic questions be entered on the record "although these memoranda are absolutely unknown to the Quadruple Alliance and we agree only on the insistence of the president of the Russian delegation." The memoranda were protests from the Bolshevik organization in the Baltic provinces and one from Kharkov claiming rights of self-determination for the Bolshevik Ukraine. They were not identified by Von Kuhlman.

Harshly and without sign of courtesy—an element now laid aside—Von Kuhlman continued:

"Before passing on to the order of the day I would like to dispose of certain incidents. I call upon General Hoffman."

Gen. Hoffman: "I beg to state that according to information received here the Russian troops are not leaving Finland, despite Russian assertions, but are being re-inforced. Such transfers of troops are in violation of the armistice. Therefore I am bound to protest."

Trotsky: "As far as I am aware the number of Russian troops in Finland has been greatly reduced since the armistice. I undertake to prove this to General Hoffman."

Trotsky spoke truthfully, to the best of my knowledge. General Hoffman left the subject.

Gen. Hoffman: "I am charged also to submit another matter. According to information reaching me from Petrograd, the Russian Superior Command has issued an order, intended for circulation among German troops, for the troops to rise against Generals and officers. I ask the president of the Russian delegation if he is aware of this order and to explain the position of the Russian Government."

Trotsky: "I do not know anything about this order. I do not know whether it exists."

He retorted with a charge that the Germans had spread

false news of the arrest of General Krylenko. General Hoffman, having thrown his irritating darts, was through. Von Kuhlman called for the order of the day.

Von Kuhlman: "I would like, as far as the allied Powers are concerned, in view of the seriousness of the day's session, to refrain from polemics. I would like, if the president of the Russian delegation agrees, to ask the president of the sub-commission formed for the study of territorial questions, to make a report."

The subcommission reported tersely that it had been obliged to adjourn without agreement.

Von Kuhlman: "I think it was not included in our plans to give this technical sub-commission the final decision of the questions, and therefore I would like to ask the president of the Russian delegation if he has any explanation which would lead to a satisfactory solution of this question."

Trotsky, prepared for the crisis, read his reply:

The task of the sub-commission, as we understood it, was to answer the question in what measure the proposed new boundary line is capable of safeguarding the Russian people's right to self-determination. We have considered the statements of our representatives on this commission and think the hour for a decision has struck.

The nations are impatiently awaiting the results of the peace negotiations in Brest-Litovsk. The nations are asking themselves the question: Will there come an end to this unprecedented self-extermination of humanity? The war has long ceased among all belligerents to be a defensive war, if it ever had that character. When Great Britain is taking possession of African colonies and of Bagdad and Jerusalem, it is not a defensive war. When Germany is occupying Belgium, Serbia, Poland, Rumania, and is seizing the Mohnsund islands, it is not a defensive war. It is a war for dividing up the world.

We do not want to participate any longer in this purely imperialistic war, where the ambitions of the wealthy classes are being achieved at the price of human blood. Ours is an attitude of irreconcilability toward the imperialism of both camps, and we shall not any longer shed the blood of our soldiers in defense of the interests of one camp or the other. Looking forward to the day, which we hope is not far off, when the oppressed working classes of all countries will take power into their hands as the working people of Russia have done, we are leading our army and our people out of the war.

Our soldier-ploughman must return to his field to till the land that has been taken from the land-owner and given to the peasant. Our soldier-workman must return to the work-shop to produce not weapons of destruction but weapons of constructive work, building up with the ploughman a new socialist economic life.

We are leaving the war. We are advising all nations of this fact. We are issuing an order for complete demobilization of all armies now confronting the troops of Germany, Austro-Hungary, Turkey and Bulgaria. We are waiting and holding firm faith that other nations will follow our example.

At the same time we are announcing that the terms proposed to us by the Governments of Germany and Austro-Hungary are in basic contradiction of the interests of all nations. These terms are repudiated by the working people of all countries, including Austro-Hungary and Germany. The nations of Poland, the Ukraine, Lithuania, Courland and Esthonia consider that these terms do violence to their national will. For the Russian people these terms constitute a constant menace.

Looking forward to the day when the working people of all countries will establish standards of peaceful international life and the friendly coöperation of nations, we refuse to sanction terms which German and Austro-Hungarian imperialism is attempting to write with the sword upon the body of living nations.

We cannot affix the signature of the Russian Revolution to terms which carry oppression, grief and embitterment to millions of human beings. The Governments of Germany and Austro-Hungary desire to rule over land and nations by virtue of military might. Let them do their work in the open. We cannot sanctify outrages.

We are leaving the war but we are constrained to refuse to sign the peace treaty. In this connection I am handing to the united delegations the following written and signed statement.

And this the statement:

In the name of the People's Commissars, the Government of the Russian Federal Republic hereby informs the Governments of countries which are in a state of belligerency with us, which are allied to us, and which are neutral, that Russia, while refusing to sign a peace of annexation, proclaims terminated, on her part, the state of war with Germany, Austro-Hungary, Turkey, and Bulgaria. Simultaneously an order for the complete demobilization on all lines of the front is being issued to the Russian troops. Brest-Litovsk, Feb. 10, 1918. (Signatures) L. Trotsky, President of the Russian Peace Delegation, People's Commissar for Foreign Affairs; Bitzenko, Member of the Delegation; B. Karelin, Ioffe, Pokrovsky; V. Medvedev, President of the All-Ukrainian Central Executive Committee; Shakrai, People's Secretary for Military Affairs, Ukrainian Republic; Karakhan, Secretary of the Delegation.

Trotsky, flushed by the heat of his rhetoric, was picturesquely effective in his chosen scene, as all onlookers agreed. It was climax, arranged for and reached. Were succeeding events not so ludicrously anticlimactic one might regard the words as resounding rather than pompous, the pledges as brave tokens rather than as florid boasts. But the punishing fact was that the treaty he said Russia would not sign was the one— much hardened for added rebellion—that Russia, three weeks later, crawled on its knees to sign.

After brief furor, set aside for Radek's lively and imaginative relation, the delegations of the Central Powers—on the continued authority of the public records of the Bolsheviks— began at once a cool stripping of Trotsky words in search of the reality of Trotsky meaning. They pointed it out, too: the open gate for military advance.

The record:

Von Kuhlman: "Without conference the delegations of the Quadruple Alliance cannot define their attitude toward the extremely important statement of the president of the Russian delegation, but in order to have before us the intentions of the Russian Government, I wish to ask the president a few questions.

"From my understanding, the essential part is the announcement by the Russian Government of its intention to immediately issue an order for the demobilization of the Russian army, at the same time refusing to sign agreements of any kind with our delegations. If I am right in my analysis, the nations of the Quadruple Alliance are at present in a state of war with Russia, with military actions suspended on the basis of the still existing armistice. With failure of agreement the armistice would lapse automatically and hostilities be renewed. If my memory does not deceive me, the armistice agreement anticipates the conclusion of peace as its final meaning. If a peace treaty is not signed the armistice agreement, therefore, would be deprived of its very meaning, and the state of war between the nations would be renewed with the expiration of the time limit set in the agreement.

"The fact that one of the parties to the agreement is demobilizing its army does not alter the military situation in any practical or legal way. I desire to state that the existence of legal and of commercial relations between nations is the very essence of the state of peace. Therefore I would ask the president of the Russian delegation to make a statement upon these questions:

"First: How is it to be declared that the state of war between the nations is ended?

"Second: Where and how is the external line of frontier to be drawn, as this constitutes a necessity for the resumption of consular, economic, and legal relations?

"Third: Is the Government of the People's Commissars prepared to renew commercial and legal relations in the manner which an ending of war and the resumption of peace would take for granted?"

Trotsky made a poor business of replying to these hard-headed inquiries, though his pose was debonair. He said:

There is little that I can add to what has been said in our statement. As far as the practical difficulties are concerned, I could not propose any legal formula for them. We have not been able to find a formula to characterize the relationship between ourselves and the Central Empires, owing to the radical divergence of our original viewpoints. If I understand the president of the German delegation correctly, he wishes to state the theory that the search for the missing formula for the practical state of affairs can be carried on further with the aid of guns. I do not think so. To whatever misuse the term "defensive war" may have been subjected in this war, no one in the world would say that the renewal of hostilities by Germany and Austro-Hungary would be in defense of their fatherland. I profoundly believe that the people of these nations would not tolerate such action. If this fundamental fact is perceived, practical difficulties will find a solution one way or another.

Trotsky's sole defense to the charge of making a gift of Russia to Germany was set forth in the assertion of his "profound" belief that the German and Austrian people would not permit an invasion of a defenseless Russia. To credit it, Trotsky must be removed from an intellectual pedestal and deposited among the children whose delight is in fairy tales.

Von Kuhlman went through the motions of suggesting a final plenary session at which the delegations of the Central Powers would define an attitude. The life of the Commission, he added, was ended.

Trotsky remarked that his Commission did not have further power of action, and that a plenary session would be useless, since further communications from the German and Austrian delegations could be sent as readily to the Russian Government itself, which alone now had authority to reply.

Von Kuhlman asked curtly what were the mediums for exchange of opinions, and Trotsky answered that there was direct wire and wireless, and in Petrograd a German delegation with like connection with Berlin.

On this low note ended the Peace Conference of Brest-Litovsk.

There was innuendo in Trotsky's reference to Count Mirbach's Commission at Petrograd or reply to innuendo, as was shown in one of Trotsky's last messages from Brest-Litovsk:

The Germans here complain as if their delegation (in Petrograd) is deprived of means of communicating with Berlin. This is evidently a misunderstanding. At any rate I request that you overcome all difficulties if there are such. Likewise I request that Chicherin be immediately informed that in case the members of the Austro-German delegation desire to leave Petrograd full coöperation must be given them. The Germans here appear to entertain some sort of silly apprehension on that account. I request that you inform me at once of all measures taken. [American Military Intelligence translation.]

While the message hinted that Trotsky was wondering if he was to be regarded as a hostage, he and his delegation were not impeded in their rapid departure from Brest.

Radek came back with Trotsky, brimful of incident of the last day and of other days of the Peace Conference. Evidently I missed him, for I did not list myself in the group before which he talked, but after his three listeners had made laughing report to me of the occurrence, I logged their summary.

So the last view of the performance at Brest-Litovsk was Radek's, colored by him:

Feb. 13 [Balance of entry]: Radek entertains Gumberg, Ransome, and Fleurot with stunning word picture of Brest. A kidding carnival. The finale: Czernin's morning whisper to Trotsky, "What will help you? An ultimatum?" Trotsky's luring response, "I don't know. You might try it." They do try it. Listen smilingly to Trotsky's beginning. Still smile when he concluded. Absolute dumbness with which they received the order read separately by Trotsky—no peace, no war, demobilization, etc. Only one exclamation from an Austrian, "Wunderbar!" They can't grasp it. Try to hold Russians with the statement they must communicate with Berlin—to dissuade them from taking train. No train. Demand for it. Departure. Questions prior, "Can we send Ambassador? Can we trade? Don't you know there is no precedent in history? We find only one case, between the Scythians and the Persians." Trotsky: "We are as wild as the Scythians. We have nothing to add to the statement. Figure out yourselves what it means."

Radek also related incidents of earlier sessions of the Conference and of other by-scenes in which he himself figured. On the way to Brest-Litovsk in German territory, he said that Trotsky was hailed by Russian prisoners of war: "Don't make peace! Fight ten years! The Germans are brutes!" At one conference he said that he called Kuhlman a Jesuit and queried General Hoffman, "Getting messages from Kiev? From the Rada man in the next room?" American cigars had been sent to him from Petrograd. He said that he smoked them among the Germans, who whispered, "From America—America has bought the Russians." He added that he helped the impression along by sending messages to Lenin to make "bluff deals with the Americans" and that he told the Germans that America had bid for a food and products monopoly. If he sent the messages as wires I did not come upon them in any transcripts. The Bronsky project, however, was in the formula Radek outlined.

"The kidders of the world and the world for game," my Log of his narrative continued. "Germans are stupid. Are we, too?"

Radek also had views of the future; as recorded in the Log:

His guess at what Germany may do—take Petrograd to stamp out hornet's nest—into Ukraine for food—or decide not to fight as they do not have to. Evident belief that Austria's food necessity will drive it into the Ukraine. Believes Austria will blow up inside of three months as hunger pinches. Germany not so bad off. Incidental good food for delegation. Strike movement over-played in Russian newspapers. Strike has end. Revolution has not. Pamphlets secretly printed in Germany itself and 10,000 distributed. How Russia will fight. Demobilization already so complete that word did not add much. Guerrilla warfare. Machine gun nests for Petrograd. Government if necessary to Moscow.

Radek offset his penchant for pointing up the dramatic ele-ments of a tale by the shrewdness of his observations. He was unduly optimistic about a collapse for Austria and truthful about the failure of the strike movement in Germany. What he knew, Trotsky knew. Trotsky, therefore, was not the victim of infantile illusion when he proclaimed a faith that the German people would rise in revolt if the German army marched into Russia. He knew the German people would not do so. He was gulling not himself but the Russian people.

One phase of the last days at Brest-Litovsk never had public explanation. There was a three-day gap in the sessions of the Peace Conference—between February 5 and February 8. The cause, however, may have been simple and reasonable. A courier, I believe, took to Petrograd the draft of the treaty the Germans had offered the Russians and recess was taken to allow time for consideration of the document there. Corrobora-tion of the consideration of the offered treaty, in Petrograd, appeared in a telegram from Chicherin to Trotsky on Feb-ruary 9:

This evening a commission of representatives of the various provinces began the consideration of the plan of the treaty re-ceived from you both concerning commercial relations and the future economic agreement in general. We fail to understand why the plan is entitled "Between Germany and Russia" without men-tioning the others. It appears to us that the unrestricted admis-sion of consuls without any clause that the Government may not permit the appointment of consuls in any [particular] city is risky. Such clauses have heretofore always been incorporated in all consular treaties. No government has been tied down to re-ceive foreign consuls at any place desired.

And again the same day Chicherin telegraphed:

In my opinion there are demands which cannot be met, for in-stance, Section 6, part 2, article 3, in which the victors demand colossal indemnity for everything. [American Military Intelligence translation, both telegrams.]

The military demands, defining territorial and frontier lines, on which the Peace Conference shattered itself in the final session, of February 10, were not set forth in the draft of the commercial treaty. The military subcommission did not sit until the night of February 9. Formal Petrograd opinion of the commercial draft had not been reached when the Peace Conference dissolved.

CHAPTER XXII

*February 14—February 21, 1918. "No Peace,
No War!" Is War.*

TROTSKY went before the Central Executive Committee on February 14 and made his public report of the death of the Peace Conference. The presence of outside observers was invited. So Trotsky was talking the last time I set eyes on him. In spite of the dire tidings he bore, his speech was aggressive and his bearing high.

I logged that night under date of February 14, though I wrote at three o'clock on the morning of the fifteenth:

Feb. 14. (Thursday) Trotsky's speech—reiteration "Will fight for no imperialists—will not deal with allies." "Will hold Social-Democrats of Germany responsible before the world if Germany takes offensive against Russia." And in reply to debate his account of private talk with Czernin warning him that if Austria took advantage of peace bargain with defunct Rada to enter Ukraine, Bolsheviks "from heads of Government down to the last individual will fight and shed their blood in defense of Revolution." Czernin's careful public statement next day that Ukraine would be regarded as neutral. Resolution for each Soviet to help raise Red Army.

Tea 2 A.M. in room. Vaskov's statement that Lenin's idea was to sign any separate peace: "It is only for a little time"—and that "No Peace, No War!" idea was Trotsky's accepted by Lenin. Paragraph as read by Trotsky was adopted by Council before he went down. Revert to Trotsky at Soviet Convention— "Would have made separate peace if could have done it with dignity."

Vaskov, as I have said, was a Bolshevik politician whom I liked for himself. He knew a fact when he met it and his hostility to Germany was not assumed.

Trotsky, in the body of his speech, made a general apology for Russia's defeat at Brest-Litovsk, a defeat that he did not deny. He said that the major force of Germany displayed itself at the council table as well as in war. Germany, he said, was superior in organized state and industrial power to England or to France, and of might immensely greater than Russia.

"In a war," he said, "the weakest always has to pay, and Russia has proved to be the weakest of all the Great Powers."

That weakness, he continued, could not be concealed any- where, much less at a peace conference between the strongest and the weakest. For the first time, he conceded that he never had expected other than a separate peace, since the keeping of further company with the Allies, even for peace negotia- tions, would have implied continuance of war beside them until the moment of peace. "By this continuance of war," he said, "we would have weakened more and more our positions in any peace conferences."

A fallacious argument, as the outcome of war proved, but a casuistry hidden from his hearers by his assumption that the capitalistic Allies in victory would strip a socialistic Russia as the easiest way of recouping their losses.

He reached thus the text of World Revolution as the abiding hope of Russia and of Revolution in Austria and Germany as present aid. Yet of Germany he spoke more cautiously, stating that the strikes there were ending, and that they indeed, he feared, had led the German peace delegates to harden the Rus- sian terms, which was his way of saying that the Germans had demanded that Russians halt Bolshevik propaganda in Ger- many.

Again, too, he referred, as he had done before the Soviet convention, to the money indemnity Germany had demanded of Russia. Not shown openly in the later Brest-Litovsk treaty, but hidden as prisoner cost, industrial damages, and among the "separate agreements" the existence of which was recorded in that document, the amount ultimately levied was considered to be six billion rubles gold. Trotsky had named a higher sum before the Soviet. Now he named a lower one. He said:

That concealed contribution of which we spoke at the Third Soviet Convention, and which we estimated to reach the sum of eight or ten billions, was reduced to three billions.

He dwelt lengthily upon the "treacherous rôle of the Rada" and presented a measured argument in support of his course in "taking Russia out of the war," claiming to find much encouragement in the attitude of German officers and soldiers at Brest-Litovsk, who told him, he said, that "they were not bandits and could not be thrown against Russia."

Again he restrained himself, hastening to add that a German offensive must not, however, be considered impossible.

Thence to bombastic peroration:

If we have to face tacit understandings between the Imperialists of the Central Powers and even perhaps between them and the Allied Powers, if we have to face a plot of World Imperialism against the Russian Revolution, we have by our tactics in Brest-Litovsk maintained and reaffirmed the bonds with our natural allies, the workmen of France, England, Germany, Austria, and America. The protest of the Allied Ambassadors against the annulment of foreign debts is closing a ring of World Imperialism about us. But the World Revolution, the rising of the proletariat of Western Europe and of America will destroy this plot. We have done everything to bring nearer the hour of liberating social Revolution.

Trotsky won the approval of the Council for the course of the Russian Peace Delegation at Brest-Litovsk. It was voted in formal resolution. Another resolution called upon all the Soviets throughout Russia to begin immediately the creation of the "Red Army of Peasants and Workmen."

Trotsky's comment on the action of the Allied Ambassadors anent the decree of debt repudiation followed upon a meeting of the diplomats at the American Embassy on February 12, when it was decided to present a joint note to the Russian Foreign Office stating that the Governments that made the loans would not recognize the repudiation. A note to that effect greeted Trotsky on his arrival from Brest-Litovsk.

Foreign loans had been repudiated on February 3, the diplomatic representatives had notified their home offices, and waited for instructions, acting on their receipt. All that the protest did was to give Trotsky a new chance for oratorical attack.

It was difficult to tell how Petrograd took the Trotsky attitude, save that it was received without visible emotion. War might be over but there was no realization of it, and no jubilation over a proclaimed peace. The dwellers of the city perhaps were too dulled by cold and hunger to notice more than the physical sensations of the hour. The Bolshevik newspapers were noisy as usual in assuring the public that the party feats at Brest-Litovsk were masterly, and in volume drowned out questioning voices. In all the clamor Lenin was silent, although the one positive action of the period between February 13 and February 18 was his—that of countermanding one half of the Trotsky design, the demobilization of the army. The life of the Trotsky formula—to be exact—was three days. Unfortunately, except in the Ukraine and in the region of the Don there was not much army left. At the front, no army.

One public philippic only was hurled against the Bolsheviks, that of Vladimir Lebedev, a doughty person unknown to me. The *Volia Naroda* printed the article, without new arrest of its staff. Perhaps the Bolsheviks regarded a single example of explosive speech as a safety valve. Wrote Lebedev:

It happened. The "Council of People's Commissars" has summarized all its activities in an act of the greatest treachery the world has ever witnessed.

Russia is betrayed. The Russian Revolution is betrayed. Brest-Litovsk proved the burial ground for all that was splendid and bright in a movement which could have lighted the world.

The "Council of People's Commissars" began with treason against the Allies. Instead of a general and democratic peace it preferred a separate peace in obedience to the most evil desires of the German Imperialists. Having broken Russia into fragments, having thrust these fragments into deathly struggle with each other, Smolny has disarmed the front. It has done everything that human ingenuity could do to make the Russian Revolution defenceless before its most terrible enemy. It has made the gesture of opening the doors and not signing the terms demanded by the German and Austrian generals who have been spitting in their faces for three months. As if the lack of the signatures of these renegades changed the act of treachery with which they have betrayed Russia!

The plans of "holy war" if the Germans refuse a "just" peace are just lies. Peace has not come and will not come. There is not even a separate peace. The occupation of Russia by German troops is the specter facing the land.

The angry last paragraph was prophecy fulfilled. The "Russian Revolution" of the writer's meaning was that of March, 1917, which overthrew the Tsar and established popu-

lar rule. None aided Lebedev in an effort to rouse a mass movement. The masses were sodden. And this fatal inertia lost
them Russia, lost them their leaders. At Novocherkassk in this
week, General Kaledin, Ataman of the Cossacks, unable to raise
a fighting spirit in those about him, walked from the Council
Chamber and shot himself to death. The fatalistic defect, too,
was in him. Had he been supported a week longer, had he been
patient to strive a week longer, he might have seen opportunity in the new chaos coming.

The text of President Wilson's address of February 11, delivered before Congress, arrived over the Alexandrovsk cable
on February 15. The wires by way of Finland had ceased to
operate for through traffic. The speech was of hardly less value
in Russia than its Fourteen Points predecessor, of which it was
a development. A stern attack on Germany on openings provided by Count von Hertling's twisting reply to the Fourteen
Points Speech, it was an adroit invitation to Austria to advance
farther in the direction of negotiations for a general peace
along the road indicated by Count Czernin, who had said that
the President had furnished "a basis for a more detailed discussion of the purposes of the two Governments."

For this reason I stressed a circulation in Austrian areas
adjacent to the Ukraine, and among the former Austrian and
Hungarian prisoners who still remained in Russia in large
numbers. Printing was concentrated, therefore, on German and
Magyar versions, although the Russian form was not overlooked. Fortunately the speech was inherently so interesting to
Russia, that the translation we quickly made for press copy
received practically a universal newspaper distribution, doing
away with any necessity of billboard presentation. For continued use the Russian version was printed in a more permanent leaflet form.

The fast, precise way in which the office machinery put this
speech through its various processes was a joy to me. We had
learned much since December.

Two days more passed without serious public reverberations.
Hunger was everywhere.

On Sunday, February 17, I logged:

No bread for two days. Women in furs selling papers on street to

get money for food. Radek [has] statement in *Pravda* that proletariat intends to take everything from *bourgeois*. *Izvestia* for
unknown reason threatens the Embassies. Finland appeals for
food to Russia and America and promises to shut off goods to
Germany. Bridge with Chinese Ambassador and Governor [Am-
bassador Francis]. Cookies and nuts.

People starve quietly. Food riots, from my observations,
were manifestations of the panic of those who feared a foodless
future and were not yet at a peak of hunger. When that time
came, energy for outbreak was gone. Petrograd, as a whole,
lay nerveless, if not stoical.

A single flare of civilian violence, on the night of February
15 at the Nicholas Railway station, was the plundering of a
food train less by citizenry than by the "bag-men" or food
peddlers. A crowd of six or seven hundred persons overcame the
train guards and sacked the cars, which chiefly contained flour
and potatoes. Soldiers and Red Guards finally surrounded the
station, fired on or over the crowd, seemingly without casualties, and arrested two hundred persons, who were released the
next day, as they had thrown away whatever evidence might
have been used against them. A more serious conflict was between a body of Red Guards and a company of soldiers, the
latter "on the authority of their starving regiment" seeking to
seize a food depot previously confiscated by the Red Guards
at the Alexandro-Nevsky monastery. The Red Guards beat off
the attack after an hour's stiff firing.

An Extraordinary Commission for Food Supply—there always was an Extraordinary Commission to deal with ordinary
needs—was formed to meet the crisis, and Trotsky was placed
at its head. The first action was issuance of a ponderous resolution, ordering the Railroad Committees to "struggle with their
utmost energy against the transport of foodstuffs in bags by
individuals as this is malignant speculation," thus depriving
the city even of this trickle of food. Only the *bourgeois*, it was
alleged, would have money to buy from the "bag-men." Let the
bourgeois starve.

Good Bolsheviks would be rationed. The trouble with this
plan was that there was nothing to ration. The city went bread-
less for two days until a modicum of flour was supplied to the
bakers by the arrival of military convoyed trains from the in-

terior. Moscow, although nearer a supply area, was reported
to be in straits equal to those of Petrograd.

Trotsky stormed around the town, scolding his fellows for
lack of foresight in not stocking Petrograd for an emergency,
discharging the idlers from the food organization, appearing
at ration stations early in the morning and running them for
a few hours, commandeering private supplies, and sending
soldiers and sailors forth anew to prod the country districts.
One morning, finding the door of a ration station locked, he
broke the fastening away with an ax.

Such vigor was bound to bring a tidal improvement, and it
did—though the flow was not to the *bourgeoisie*. A reduced
bread ration began to be issued, one-eighth of a pound, and
then one-fourth of a pound, supposedly for a day but in practice for two days, often three. February 15, 16, and 17 pro-
gressively were the hungriest days of the winter for Petrograd Bolsheviks. For their opponents all days were hungry.

At the Embassy, in this period, we had for discussion the
renewed threats against the Embassies, allusion to the continued hostility of the Allies and a sneer at their representatives in Russia, intimating that they should be treated as
enemies. On its surface it might be aftermath to the protest
of the diplomats against repudiation. Not serious, we Americans thought. At the Ambassador's bridge table we chatted
lightly on the theme. The Chinese Ambassador, whom I had
the good luck to have for a partner, seemed to pay attention
only to his winning game. Perceiving that he was a smart
bridge player, I was content to play a supporting hand. The
Ambassador was inspired by the poker value of his own hands,
and too often took the bid from his orthodox partner, Colonel
Ruggles. We let the Ambassador pay in food and drink. Then
the Chinese Ambassador made his single political comment. He
expected to leave Petrograd soon, he said. Wire communication was bad—he believed he would make his report in person.
China also was an Ally. So he knew more than we and was
passing warning in a quiet, oriental fashion. His lone remark
left us thoughtful, indeed.

But what did the Chinese Ambassador know? It was a fact
that Lenin and Smolny had known since the morning of that
day, the seventeenth, that Germany had denounced the armi-

stice and that a state of war would begin at noon, the eighteenth. That information, however, they had kept well to themselves and their advisers while they made effort to renew talking contact with the German Government. They were too late. Perhaps the Chinese Ambassador was sensitive to atmosphere. The coincidence of his words and the alarm, however, was uncanny.

Not until four o'clock on the afternoon of Monday, February 18, with war four hours old and the march of the German army begun, was Petrograd aware of the risen peril.

Eight hours later, on war's inception and spread, my Log read:

Four, afternoon, news Germans had declared armistice ended noon today and were advancing. During evening Dvinsk announced taken. Reval reported taken, but not verified. Advance believed to be on Narva-Pskov-Dvinsk-Minsk line. Petrograd can be taken from Narva whenever desired. Surprise of Radek and Trotsky who had not believed German soldiers would come. Latter's indignant protest to Hoffman. Government will stay and fight. With what?

Radek intimated later that his "surprise" was assumed for his public face because he had taken his stand with the "war faction" in the party debates. Trotsky was committed to his attitude.

That Smolny had been earlier informed of war outbreak was not much longer concealed. The circumstances were that General Samoilo, military member of the staff of the Peace Delegation, who had remained at Brest-Litovsk for purposes of official contact, telegraphed the night of February 16, the message not coming through until the early hours of the following morning:

At 7:30 tonight I was officially notified by Gen. Hoffman that the armistice concluded with the Russian Republic terminates at 12 noon Feb. 18, and that the state of war resumes. On the morning of Feb. 17 I shall depart with the Commission under me for Baranovichi and Minsk.

Lenin received the message first and called Trotsky into his office. Lenin's remark, Trotsky wrote,[1] was: "There is nothing

1 *Lenin*, p. 112.

for us to do but sign the old conditions if the Germans still agree to them."

While the Council was sitting upon that question of surrender, Trotsky telegraphed Berlin for an explanation (which never was given):

The Government of the German Empire, Berlin: Today, Feb. 17, we have received from Gen. Samoilo a direct communication stating that beginning with noon, Feb. 18, the state of war is resumed. The Government of the Russian Republic presumes that the telegram received was not sent by the signer but has the character of a provocation, considering that—should even the possibility of the termination of the armistice on the part of Germany be admitted—a notice to this effect must be served, according to the armistice terms, not two days, but seven days before the expiration of the armistice agreement. We request an explanation of the misunderstanding, by wireless. People's Commissar for Public Affairs, L. Trotsky.

The Germans said nothing and moved troops menacingly toward strategic points on a wide front. The threat against Petrograd was one of railroads, possibilities of other advance being negligible at that season of the year. The first report we got was that the Russians were retreating without destroying railroad tracks. The threat from Minsk might be against the Ukraine and Kiev. Activities, however, we guessed, would be more at the north, with Dvinsk the first objective and Pskov the second. Rumor followed of another column heard from toward Reval on the Gulf of Finland itself. Narva would be the probable objective.

The railroad from Narva and the line from Pskov met at Gatchina, south of Petrograd. When Gatchina fell, so would Petrograd. Between the four o'clock flash that the armistice was denounced and a midnight summary of developments, at a gathering in my rooms, our world had changed so completely that we already were getting adjusted to it. We had become slaves to maps and hung upon bulletins. As yet, however, our interest was that of onlookers. There was comfortable distance on the map between Petrograd and any German area.

For my own night's work, I turned to draft a reply to a cable just received from Chairman Creel asking for a survey of committee work and outline for the future. The inquiry was apropos indeed, more so than Washington could have conceived. The message, coded and sent the following day, in large part was:

As to future situation, if Petrograd not taken by Germans publicity work can go on with great ultimate after-war advantage to the United States. An All-Russian distribution machine for pamphlets is already nearly built on a large scale. Now on press an excellent pamphlet which Bullard has just finished writing— *Letters to a Russian Friend*. News pamphlets and pamphlet editions various Wilson speeches all feeding out in increased volume. A Petrograd printing plant that compares with the best in America relies almost solely upon our work and helps enthusiastically. On Bullard's pamphlets red, white and blue bands will appear.

Can add to report on Jan. 8 speech that the German version did get over the German line and parts of Austrian line—the whole allotment. Speech of Feb. 11 is being translated into Hungarian and German and the chief effort will be to get it into Austria. A soldier organization will do the work and plan is worked out. Distribution should start in week, fortunes of war permitting.

The cable service has got its roots down and I am beginning to be pleased with its work at both ends. Compub cable brought the only copy of President's last speech into Russia. Newspaper presentation sufficient to obviate necessity bill posting this city. Except for German and Austrian distribution I am letting Compub do this message job without help from me, as a test.

Therefore the general outlook is attractive until you put it to test of immediate war utility in a country distracted by civil war and warred on from without by a country which it may fight defensively but not with any intent of helping the Allies. These are wild internationalists who not only in the beginning but until lately were willing, for their own ends of Revolution, to have German support. Germany thought she could direct the storm but the storm had no such intention. No other country which gives kindness or aid will fare better. Anything short of military aid will be accepted and will not count in the balance against the intended program of agitation in the United States and among *Entente* nations. So on strict basis, war utility is lacking, for what the Bolsheviks will do they will do anyhow.

But indirectly America gains by having America all the time presented, and the President's influence in the crucial time of future general peace making grows largely through a continued Russian drive. My recommendation is that the news and circulation plan go ahead to the end of the war, or until Russia is at actual peace.

I probably have disappointed you on meetings and oratory. You cannot appreciate how useless they would have been until I tell you face to face. I would have liked to start outspoken government-owned newspaper but both mechanical power and men were lacking. For instance it has taken a week to get permit for stringing one electric wire for projecting machine. To get cash money from bank takes me three days. In such absolutely unexampled disorganization of all business life it was sounder to let newspapers themselves be the disseminators. Later Bullard will try out a cartoon poster idea. Forward him cartoons and posters. With film publicity I have preparation and no films. Neither Bernstein nor Mott party came through Finland.

Supposed from outside you knew as well as we that for nearly a month we have been cut off from world except by cable. Government ice-breaker carried out Madame Kollontai and body of world revolutionists day or so ago but Finnish war blocks travel. No couriers. Will come out earliest moment I can.

Any day Germany can unmake most of plans we have made. She declared armistice ended at noon today and is already advancing toward Dvinsk and Reval. In case advance is beyond Reval we shall know that in three to five days additional Petrograd will fall. We will not be here then. If Government survives the internal shock it will go to Moscow, also the Embassies. In that contingency will send Bullard and group to Moscow, and will go myself if I cannot get out to the north. Do not worry if silence falls. We shall be safe. Give my love to family.

Things may go on as usual if the Germans do not advance beyond Reval but I think I see the Bolsheviks going out and worse and faster peace makers coming in. We will keep going as though the future were serene. Good luck.

In twenty-four hours I was converted away from the major assertion in the last paragraph, and recorded my enlightenment in a trailing message. The cable:

Feb. 20. I expressed opinion in cablegram Feb. 19 that another party might beat the Bolsheviks to a worse and faster peace. I made a mistake. Today the Bolsheviks tried to take lead themselves by complete surrender to the separate peace terms of Germany. May be too late to save them anyway. Dvinsk has fallen.

Germans are still advancing. There are some indications the Pskov line has been passed.

Lenin had pushed Trotsky and his gestures to one side and taken command.

The period between February 18 and February 21 did not divide itself into days but was fused. Adjournments of the Central Executive Committee, the Council, and the strictly party meeting of the Bolsheviks were only for irregular sleep and food. All were at the Tauride Palace, now equipped with a wireless station. With the passage of the hours the suspense hung not upon surrender but acceptance of surrender. With good reason, the Bolshevik leaders feared that the Germans intended to give them an object lesson.

Lenin's insistence upon surrender won him an early victory. Before midnight of February 18 the Council had agreed with him on action and during the night of February 18–19 the following message was put on the air for Berlin:

The Government of the German Empire, Berlin: The Council of People's Commissars protests against the launching of troops by the German Government against the Russian Soviet Republic, which declared the state of war ended and began to demobilize its army on all fronts. The Workmen's and Peasants' Government could not have expected such a step if for no other reason than that none of the parties to the armistice have been served with the seven day notice of termination stipulated in the agreement of December 15, 1917.

The Council of People's Commissars considers itself, under the circumstances which have arisen, constrained to sign a peace upon the terms which were proposed by the Delegations of the Quadruple Alliance in Brest-Litovsk. The Council of People's Commissars makes the announcement that an answer to the definite peace terms proposed by the German Government will be given without delay. The Council of People's Commissars. President of the C.P.C., V. Ulianov (Lenin). People's Commissar for Foreign Affairs, L. Trotsky.

The German Government replied curtly the evening of the nineteenth:

Put your offer in writing and send it to our representatives at Dvinsk.

A courier was started for Dvinsk on the morning of the twentieth bearing at least the written equivalent of the second paragraph of the wireless message—the surrender.

It is probable that other messages passed between Berlin and the Tauride Palace. Circumstantial report was given me the night of the nineteenth that Germany had demanded the occupation of a list of border cities but verification was not possible. If such a demand was made it was conceded.

But the German advance was not halted.

In the Log the war phases of the days were:

Feb. 19—Bolsheviks give up and offer accept German peace terms —complete surrender by Lenin and Trotsky. Central Council at Tauride, closed session on Germany's reply—purported—asking occupation of certain cities as guarantee, and sending delegation to Dvinsk. Will do anything demanded, am sure.

Bullard has good plan of German bill-posting President's second message (Fourteen Points Speech) in Petrograd if Germans come. Plan to distribute third message Austrian and German front ahead their advance.

Ambassador called at my room. Group discussed report that Germans might by railroad lines reach Petrograd in day or so. Riggs of Col. Ruggles' staff, earlier had considered this unlikely. Went to Embassy at 10:30. Urged staff to plan to get Ambassador away. Even separate peace should not keep him.

Feb. 20—Word of Trotsky's secret resignation. Only nine Commissars present when peace acceptance voted. Trotsky and Lenin both voted for it. Twenty-one speakers still to talk at Bolshevik fraction (party) meeting at one A.M. so meeting adjourned to 5. Still talking this midnight, Radek leading forces for war. Courier sent to Dvinsk but no delegation. Lettish soldiers in Petrograd furious and call for war. Lenin addresses them and says he will go to Dvinsk. Hot air. Commissars debating at night meeting. Will they talk until the Germans come?

There was soon report of German terms so much worse than those of the treaty Trotsky had refused to sign at Brest-Litovsk that all of the Bolshevik leaders except Lenin were appalled. The war talkers stiffened. The cry of a "Holy War" was heard. Lenin's very control seemed threatened on the twenty-first. He appeared for a matter of hours to bow and to agree to fight.

The Germans let the Bolsheviks wrangle over the new terms and let their troops march deeper into Russia.

Dvinsk already was theirs. Riezhitsa on the road to Pskov was taken. Minsk was occupied, and Polotsk. Movement of troops to cut off Reval was well forward. Russian Staff Headquarters at Mogilev were abandoned. The war was less than three days old.

CHAPTER XXIII

*February 21—February 26, 1918. The Hard Hand
of Lenin.*

PUBLICLY the Bolsheviks maintained that they veered
again to a program of "Holy War" because the Germans did not answer their proclamation of willingness
to surrender on the basis of the Brest-Litovsk terms. In reality
they were debating among themselves the freshly punitive demands, doubtful whether they could accede to them and survive. Germany now had demanded that they recognize the
Ukraine as a separate Government and depart from it. Germany had ordered them to abandon their Red brethren in Finland. More territory than originally asked was to be taken
from them in the Baltic west. Were they left so maimed that
the Don country would quickly fall away to interior enemies?
Had disaster so encompassed them that they might as well
now fight in desperation as be dispersed later? These were the
questions they asked each other. For a time only Lenin and a
diminished cohort that would follow him in all weathers asserted that the answers to the questions could be safely, "No!"

Meantime the public pose was put on display on February
21 in an appeal to "The Working People of All Russia."

Omitting preliminary protest much in the style of the introduction to the message of wireless surrender, the statement
ran:

The Hohenzollern and Hapsburg Governments launched an offensive of their troops against Revolutionary Russia. The scattered
remnants of our troops retreated, almost without offering resistance. The enemy's troops have occupied Dvinsk, Venden,
Lutzk, and their further advance threatens to cut off the most
important lines of traffic and starve the centers of the Revolution.

Taking into consideration the frame of mind of our exhausted
army as well as the state of the entire country, the Council of
People's Commissars made another attempt to stop the invasion
by expressing its readiness to sign the peace terms offered us. We
took this most trying step—even at the price of the greatest concessions—in order to save the country from final prostration and

the Revolution from perdition. . . . Once the German labor class proved too weak to stop the criminal purpose of its militarists, we had no other choice but to accept the terms of German Imperialism—until the coming of European Revolution will abolish them.

At present we do not know what the answer of the German Government will be. It is not in a hurry to give an answer, as it apparently wants to gain possession of the greatest possible number of important positions in our territory. We still hold the profound conviction that the German labor class will rise against the attempts of the ruling class to smother the Revolution, but we cannot foresee with certainty when this will happen. We are waiting for the German terms to be submitted, and are ready to make the greatest sacrifices to save our exhausted people from the appalling consequences of the war, and to enter upon the road of socialist development.

At the same time it is our duty to warn you, Workmen, Peasants, and Soldiers that the German Imperialists may stop short of nothing in their desire to break the Soviet Power, to take the land away from the peasants, and to restore the rule of landowners, bankers, and monarchy. We want peace, we stand ready to make even a hard peace, but we must also stand ready to offer resistance should the German counter-revolution finally determine to hang a noose around our neck.

The Council of People's Commissars appeals to all local Soviets to apply all efforts to the recreation of an army. All demoralizing elements, hooligans, and cowards, must be ruthlessly expelled from the army and in the event of their struggle, they must be effaced from the surface of the earth. . . . The *bourgeoisie,* which under the Tsar and Kerensky escaped the hardships of war, must be brought to the performance of its duty by the most energetic and ruthless measures. Strictest discipline must be established in the ranks of the army and in the entire country. In Petrograd it is necessary to maintain order with an iron hand.

Lenin, even when he seemed to waver, possessed a source of unrevealed strength. He was aware that, whatever the amount of castigation, Germany would prefer that he continue to rule Russia, since to destroy him would be to destroy also the utility of Bolshevism as an agitational weapon against the Allies, and in their countries. He had no fear that German armies would expel him. His sole danger lay in the success of interior rebellion which might oblige the Germans to abandon him. In his appeal he railed, therefore, less against the Germans, at whom he only shrugged his shoulders as the possessors of power they likely would use, than against the *bourgeoisie* of Russia against whom he invoked "the most energetic and ruthless measures."

This part of the pronouncement was the only one operative in Petrograd. "*Bourgeois*" squads were gathered and with Red Guards over them sent to the outskirts, nominally to dig trenches which probably were not dug in the frozen ground, but at any rate to be given menial work under brutal keepers. Opposition, it could be said, was put in prison or held as hostage.

Over Petrograd as chief keeper of a less awesome form of order was set William Shatov of New York, though I would not call him so if I did not have white paper in front of me. Bill Shatov he was and should be—an anarchist in New York and a chief of police in Bolshevik Petrograd. He still called himself an anarchist, and the Bolsheviks recognized such a party, and Bill Shatov as a leader of it, and took them both within the ranks. I will aver, too, and meet with no contradiction anywhere, that Police Chief Shatov kept order in that city of mounting panic in the last week of February, 1918. He did not bother the *bourgeoisie*, leaving that persecution to Lenin's henchmen, and he did not trouble himself with the ins and outs of Red politics. He just kept order. One cast of his drag-net and the streets of Petrograd were free of hooligans, who as in every period of excitement had begun to stage holdups and to loot shops and houses. I walked and drove miles nightly through diverse parts of the city throughout the week, often alone, and never was suspiciously accosted.

Of the events of February 21, including an appearance of "about face" to war on the part of Lenin, I logged:

Thursday. Good dinner at Military Mission. Evening at Ambassador's. Train to go Saturday, but Bullard, Malcolm Davis, and I will stick until the job is done. Front windows as greetings if Germans come. Radek wins his fight and Council of Commissars forced to reverse itself again and decide to fight, Lenin yielding. Why? That is aside from opportunism of still holding leadership that must otherwise have been lost.

The last comment was obscure, and reflected late flying gossip of a break between Trotsky and Lenin, with each struggling for tactical party advantages. I do not believe there was a break. Lenin's method as a politician was to concede until he was ready to overwhelm. He lacked two days of being ready. My question of "Why?" was more pertinent. I was convinced that he intended to make the peace, and that the Germans would accept it. I could not understand why he delayed, and did not until I realized how completely his concern was politics and not war. His views will come, shortly, from his own lips.

At the Embassy it was decided that the Ambassador should go into interior Russia for safety, and not to Moscow, which might follow Petrograd in fall. Vologda, on the Siberian road, a juncture point from Moscow, was chosen. The front window greeting meant for Germans was of posters and of Wilson speeches. I had just taken new quarters for the cable division in the Martin Building on the Nevsky Prospect, an American style business building with broad expanse of plate glass windows for display.

It was arranged Friday that the Ambassador should go out with seventy persons and that with him would go forty Chinese of the Chinese Ambassador's retinue, and about the same number of Japanese. Consul Tredwell secured the train. The tentative date of departure was moved forward to Sunday night.

From the Log of Saturday, February 23:

Episode of General invited to Smolny from Peter and Paul prison to tell Lenin how to defend Petrograd. Tea, advice, and back to prison. His request for "Leave of absence next time."

On again peace. Germany's destructive offer. Lenin's *Evening Pravda* statement that he favored any peace. Evidently he knew substance of terms before. Probability of acceptance. Night meeting of Central Council. Dinner at Military Mission. Evening with Ambassador. Bridge while Bolsheviks burned.

Lenin, about ready to coerce the Council of Commissars and assured of success, had set about the winning of the Bolshevik public to his views. To no other public did he pay attention except in the way of abuse. Simultaneously, the German terms for peace, admitted now to have been received on February 21, two days before, were made public.

Money terms of indemnity were not stated in the German clauses, though it was possible to indicate where part of them were "concealed." Nor was it certain that supplemental penalties were not assessed in another stipulation. However, the terms disclosed were punitive and were harshly phrased. The communication:

Answer of the German Government to the application of the Russian Government, Feb. 19, 1918. Germany is willing to continue peace negotiations and conclude peace on the following conditions:

1. Germany and Russia declare the state of war between them ended. Both nations are convinced that in the future they will live on friendly terms with each other.

2. Countries west of the line indicated to the Russian representatives at Brest, formerly belonging to Russia, will no longer be under the protection of Russia. In the Dvinsk district this line must be moved toward the eastern frontier of Courland. The said countries will be under no obligation to Russia, which renounces every kind of interference in the internal affairs of these countries. Germany is ready after the conclusion of peace and the full demobilization of the Russian army to evacuate the territory east of the line in question, with the exceptions noted Paragraph Three.

3. Lifland and Estland are to be cleared immediately of Russian troops and Red Guards, and German police substituted for the Red Guards until such time as the reconstruction of the country guarantees safety and governmental order. All inhabitants arrested on political grounds must be immediately released.

4. Russia must conclude peace immediately with the Ukrainian People's Republic. Ukraine and Finland must be cleared immediately of Russian troops and Red Guards.

5. Russia will do everything within its power to secure for Turkey the return of her east Catholic provinces and the recognition of the abolition of Turkish capitulation.

6. (a) Full demobilization of the Russian army, including the battalions newly formed by the present Government must take place immediately.

(b) Russian warships in the Black Sea, Baltic Sea, and the Arctic Ocean must be immediately brought to Russian ports and be interned until the conclusion of general peace negotiations, or be dismantled. Warships of the Entente under Russian control must be treated as Russian ships.

(c) Commercial navigation in the Black Sea and Baltic Sea must begin at once, in accord with the agreement in the armistice; the removal of mines must begin at once; the blockade of the Arctic Ocean will continue until the conclusion of general peace.

7. The Russian-German commercial treaty of 1904 will be put in force as stated in Paragraph 7, No. 2-a, of the peace as concluded with the Ukraine except in regard to Sec. II. Nos. 3, *3*, of the special privileges concerning Asiatic countries; further- more the first part of the concluded protocol will be put in force. To this must be added the guarantee of export of ores free of duty; the immediate inauguration of negotiations for a new com- mercial treaty; guarantee of favored nation rights to the end of 1925 even to the completion of the *provisorum;* and lastly the affirmation of Nos. 3 4a, 1 and 5 of the peace agreement with the Ukraine.

8. The legal relations—political—will be regulated according to the decision of the first reading of the German-Russian legal convention. Where decisions have not been reached, the reim- bursements of the losses of civilians will be according to the Ger- man proposals, the reimbursement for expenses for the prisoners of war will be according to the Russian proposals. Russia must accept and assist the German Commission on prisoners of war, civilian losses and refugees.

9. Russia obligates herself to stop all kinds of government or government-assisted agitation or propaganda against the gov- ernments of the Quadruple Alliance, including the territory oc- cupied by the Central Powers.

10. The above-mentioned terms must be accepted within forty- eight hours. The Russian plenipotentiaries must immediately go to Brest-Litovsk and there during three days sign the peace agreement, which is to be ratified within two weeks.

Von Kuhlman signed the ultimatum.

Payment of indemnities could be hidden either in clauses 7 or 8, the easiest lurking place being under the description of "reimbursement for civilian losses."

Inland seas controlled by Germany and Turkey were to be freed of mines, the Arctic Ocean was to remain mined and blockaded against the Allies.

The penalties incurred by Trotsky's "pedagogical demon- stration" were:

1. Forced acceptance of peace with the Ukraine and withdrawal of Bolshevik troops from that province, leaving the thousands of the slain as the only positive relic of the vaunted Red victory at Kiev.

2. A German police protectorate over Livonia and Estonia.

3. The advancement eastward of the frontier line in the Dvinsk section.

4. An increase in indemnity, difficult of estimate, but large.

Lenin's prepared brief in support of the acceptance of the terms was released in the evening edition of the *Pravda* the same day, February 23. Among its disclosures was admission that the leader had made the same arguments in party conference on January 21, prior to the All-Russian Convention, prior to Trotsky's gesture.

I kept the full statement; and the digest, following, was made with careful purpose of presenting all of Lenin's points, and in his own language. Arguments necessarily were condensed. The numerical arrangement of clauses was his. Wrote Lenin, in introduction, verbatim:

The German answer, as the readers can see, tenders us even harder terms than those of Brest-Litovsk. Nevertheless I am absolutely convinced that only intoxication of revolutionary phrase is capable of driving anyone to refuse to sign these terms. For this reason in my articles in the *Pravda* under the signature of "Karpov" I attacked the "itching disease" of revolutionary phrase, seeing in it the greatest menace to our party and consequently to the Revolution. [Note: In the "Karpov" articles Lenin described "the revolutionary phrase" as "the repetition of revolutionary watch-words without the reckoning with objective circumstances."]

Until now I have sought to impress upon the party my views of the emptiness of the revolutionary phrase. Now I must present them in the open. For, alas, the worst of my suppositions has come true.

On January 8, 1918 [January 21, New Style] I read at a meeting of about sixty of the most prominent party workers in Petrograd my "Thesis on the Question of Immediate Conclusion of a Separate or Annexationist Peace." In this thesis, clause 13, I declared war on the revolutionary phrase. I said that the policy of renunciation of the proposed peace would correspond perhaps to the longings of man for the ideal but would not take into account the reality of class forces and the material factors in the moment of incipient socialist Revolution through which we are now passing.

In clause 17 I wrote that should we refuse to sign the proposed peace "crushing defeats will make Russia conclude a still less advantageous peace."

Worse than that happened, for our retreating army, in a state of demobilization, entirely refuses to fight.

Only an unrestrained phrase can drive Russia under such circumstances into a war at the present moment, and I personally, of course, would not remain for a second either in the Government or in the Central Committee of our party should the policy of the phrase get the upper hand.

Now the bitter truth has evidenced itself with such terrible clearness that it is impossible not to see it. The entire *bourgeoisie* of Russia is rejoicing and triumphant on account of the advent of the Germans. Only the blind or those who are intoxicated by the phrase can blind themselves to the fact that the policy of revolutionary war (without an army) is throwing water upon the mill wheel of our *bourgeoisie*. In Dvinsk the Russian officers already are walking about in shoulder straps. In Riezhitza the *bourgeois* received the Germans with joy. In Petrograd, on the Nevsky and in the *bourgeois* newspapers, the enthusiasm over the imminent overthrow of the Soviet power by the Germans is hardly repressed.

Let everyone know it: whoever is against immediate although extremely hard peace, is ruining the Soviet power. We are constrained to go through a hard peace. It will not end until Revolution in Germany and in Europe. We shall set out to create a Revolutionary army, not by phrases and exclamations (as it was created by those who since January 7 [January 20, N.S.] have done nothing) but through organized work, through deeds.

The clauses of the thesis, a digest:

1. The position of the Russian (Bolshevik) Revolution at the present moment (January 21, 1918) is such that almost all workmen and the majority of the peasants are supporting the Soviet Power.

2. At the same time the civil war has been necessitated by the frenzied opposition of the property classes, which are aware that the struggle for the preservation of private ownership of land has not yet reached its apex. Soviet victory in this war is guar-

anteed, but unavoidably some time will elapse, unavoidably a considerable exertion of force will be necessary, unavoidably a certain period of disintegration and chaos will ensue until the resistance of the *bourgeoisie* is overcome.

3. Moreover this resistance in its least militant forms, such as sabotage, bribery, infiltration of the agents of the *bourgeoisie* into socialist ranks to frustrate our efforts, will be stubborn and prolonged. On the other hand without victory over this passive resistance, the success of the socialist Revolution will be impossible.

4. The task of organization for the socialist transformation is one of tremendous difficulty and will take much time.

5. These factors taken together demand a certain interim, several months at least, during which the socialist Government must have its hands free, first for the conquest of the *bourgeoisie* of its own country, and then for the consolidation of intensive organization abroad.

6. The status of the socialist Revolution in Russia must serve as the basis for the determination of the international tasks. Undoubtedly the socialist Revolution in Europe must and will come. All our hopes for the final victory of socialism are based on this certitude. Our propaganda activities in general must be intensified. But it would be a mistake for the socialist Government in Russia to rely upon a German or a European Revolution in a stated time, six months or any short period.

7. The peace negotiations at Brest-Litovsk have made it quite clear at the present time, January 7/20, that the military party has the upper hand in the German Government, and in essentials already has presented an ultimatum to Russia—its formal presentation may be expected any day. This ultimatum will lead either to a continuation of the war or to an annexationist peace, that is, a peace in which we return all territory occupied by us, while the Germans keep all territory occupied by them, and also impose upon us a contribution covered up under the guise of maintenance of prisoners of war—an indemnity amounting approximately to three billion rubles, with instalment payments extending over several years.

8. The socialist Government of Russia is confronted with the condition of accepting this annexationist peace at once or of waging revolutionary war at once.

9. In considering the arguments for a revolutionary war we come, first of all, upon the inference that a separate peace would be practically an agreement with the German imperialists—"an

imperialist deal"—and that consequently such a peace would be a complete break with the principles of proletarian internationalism. But this argument is manifestly wrong. Workmen who lose a strike and sign disadvantageous terms and resume work, do not betray socialism. Whoever calls a war with German imperialism a defensive and just war is actually receiving support from the Anglo-French imperialism. But he who agrees to sign peace terms disadvantageous to a weak nation and advantageous to the imperialists of one group is not betraying socialism in the smallest degree.

10. Another argument for immediate war pleads that by concluding peace we are practically becoming agents of German imperialism, as we are releasing troops from our front and are returning millions of prisoners of war, etc. But this argument is also manifestly wrong, as a revolutionary war at the present moment would practically make us agents of the Anglo-French imperialism. The right inference to be drawn is that since a socialist government has obtained a victory in one country, it is necessary to determine all questions not from the viewpoint of any imperialism but exclusively from the viewpoint of the welfare and the stabilization of the socialist Revolution achieved. In other words: the principle is not of determining which of two imperialist groups it is more advantageous to help but of solidifying the socialist Revolution and holding out in one country until other countries join in Revolution.

11. We are told that the German Social Democratic opponents of war are asking us not to yield to German imperialism. Should the German radical socialists propose to us to delay the peace for a certain time, guaranteeing within the interval a revolutionary movement in Germany, then the question would have a different meaning. But the German radical socialists not only do not say this but say that "nothing positive can be promised with regard to German Revolution."

12. We are told that we have directly promised revolutionary war in a number of statements and that the conclusion of a separate peace would be a betrayal of our word. This is wrong. We have spoken about the necessity of "preparing and waging" a revolutionary war. We have spoken about it to combat abstract pacifism, the theory of the complete repudiation of "defense of country" in an epoch of imperialism, but we have not assumed an obligation to start a revolutionary war without calculating the possibilities of waging it. Even now we must unquestionably prepare a revolutionary war. But the question of waging it must be

determined by concrete conditions and by the interests of the socialist Revolution.

13. Summing up the arguments for an immediate revolutionary war, the conclusion must be reached that such a policy would correspond perhaps to the longings of a man for the effective, the resplendent, and the ideal, but would not take at all into consideration the reality of class forces and the material factors of the moment of incipient socialist Revolution through which we are passing.

14. There can be no doubt that our army, now, in the next few weeks and probably for months to come, will be absolutely unable to check the German advance. In the first place the majority of the soldiers are weary and exhausted and there are no reserves. In the second place there is complete disorganization of food supply, and the lack of horses dooms our artillery. In the third place it is impossible to defend the coast line between Riga and Reval, giving the enemy opportunity to conquer the remaining portions of Livonia and Estonia, and to encircle our troops from the rear and take Petrograd. [Note: Lenin himself shattered the organizations that fed the army.]

15. There is no doubt that the majority of the peasants would prefer an annexationist peace to an immediate revolutionary war. Moreover, with the army completely democratized, it would be venturesome to wage war against the will of the majority of the soldiers. For the creation of a socialist army months would be necessary.

16. The poorest peasantry in Russia is in a position to support the socialist Revolution but it is not in a position to support a serious revolutionary war. It would be a fateful mistake to ignore this concrete co-relation of class forces.

17. The matter of revolutionary war appears consequently in the following aspect:

Should a German Revolution break out within the next three or four months, then perhaps the tactics of an immediate revolutionary war would not be dangerous to our socialist Revolution.

Should the German Revolution fail to break out, the continuation of the war infallibly will result in such crushing defeats that Russia will be forced to conclude an even more disadvantageous peace, and a peace which will not be concluded by a socialist Government—e.g., by a bloc of the *bourgeois* Rada with the Chernovists or some such combination—as the peasants' army, after the first defeats will overthrow the workmen's socialist Government.

18. Considering this state of affairs, the fate of the socialist Revolution, already begun, ought not to be staked on the card of the chance of German Revolution. We have no right to take such risks.

19. Moreover, the German Revolution, on foundations of its own, will not be embarrassed should we conclude a separate peace. The position of imperial Germany remains extremely difficult. The war with England and America will be protracted. The example of the socialist Republic of Russia will be a living symbol before the nations and the propaganda of Revolution inherent in this symbol will be gigantic.

20. By concluding a separate peace we are freeing ourselves— in the degree possible for the present moment—from both belligerent imperialist groups. We will use this period to stabilize the socialist Revolution. A reorganization of Russia on the basis of the dictatorship of the proletariat, nationalization of banks and of industry, of barter exchange between the towns and leagues of small farmers, is economically possible if a few months of peaceful work can be secured. Such reorganization will make socialism invincible in Russia and in the entire world, creating a foundation for a powerful Red Army.

21. An actual revolutionary war at the present moment would be a war of the socialist Republic against all *bourgeois* parties, with the distinctly expressed purpose of overthrowing the *bourgeoisie* in other countries. Nevertheless we know that at the present moment we cannot set ourselves this purpose. We should be fighting for the liberation of Poland, Lithuania, and Courland. But not a single Marxian could deny that the interests of socialism must be placed above the interests of the right of nations to self-determination. Our socialist Republic is continuing to do everything it can for the realization of the right of self-determination for Finland, the Ukraine, etc. But if the concrete situation has shaped itself so that the existence of the Socialist Republic is placed in jeopardy, then of course the interests of the Socialist Republic are the higher.

Conceding Lenin his premises of brigandage and murderous civil war in Russia, the steps of his thesis held a road of logic. The summary of the whole twenty-one points was that he had so disorganized Russia, its army, its industry, its food supply, that it lay defenseless before Germany and therefore, to be left free to carry on further work of disintegration and to complete the "conquest of the *bourgeoisie*," it must submit to any terms of German peace.

A clever German, desirous of ridding his country of the incubus of eastern war, had he been able to appear before Lenin's audience of doctrinaires rabid for test of theories, and of politicians ravenous for a deeper draft of the hardly sipped sweets of absolute power, could have done no better than to have made Lenin's address.

Lenin read the thesis to his colleagues the first time on January 21, less than a week after he had exclaimed to me against the imputation, self-described, that he had been a German spy. I have recorded agreement with him on the feebleness and inadequacy of such a term. Lenin regarded himself as a realist. Let him so be weighed. Regardless of any issue of what support he received from Germany, or manner or time of any aid, his actions advantaged Germany, and at timely moments. However contentiously, Lenin and the German militarists in outcome shared Russia. Lenin had realm for the human experimental laboratory of his dreams, the military empire had new strength of released armies, rich territory, and an accessible granary.

One joy the thesis had for me—the clause in which Lenin stripped pacifism of its false face, lampooning its theory of repudiation of national defense in an era of war.

The most curious clause in the list, in the afterview, was the one (No. 5) which named a few months as time enough for the domestic victory of his theories and for much "intensive organization abroad"—that is, advance toward World Revolution.

At council at the Military Mission on the night of February 23, with both the German terms and the foreword of Lenin's argument before us (the thesis itself was not printed until the following day), we had no doubt the war was ending. Just where it would end was another matter. To make the lesson good, the Germans might wish to have an army parading in Petrograd when the peace was signed. Their progress toward the city was methodical and not seriously opposed. We did not believe, however, that the purpose was to occupy Petrograd permanently, since with that course would come the responsibility of feeding the city. Menace, said the military men, Colonel Ruggles and Major Riggs, was better than capture.

Playing bridge with the Ambassador in the evening, those present relished the harassment of the Bolsheviks. They, not we, were burning. Whether Petrograd stood or not, they had had enough of alarms in that exposed position. Off to safer Moscow they were to go. Smolny's day was ending.

The Ambassador had found that he could not be ready for departure on Sunday, as he had first planned, and it had been concluded that there was no danger for him in a day or so of delay. But go he must. There was no use taking a risk that might tempt the German Government or a German commander to add an American Ambassador to their list of prisoner exhibits.

Through the night the Bolsheviks scorched and writhed in the fire Lenin had built under them, and in the morning they obeyed their master. I logged:

Feb. 24—(Sunday) German peace accepted and radio sent 5 A.M. Vote in Bolshevik caucus: 26 for war, 72 for peace, 12 not voting. In Council: 85 for war, 116 for peace, 26 not voting. Bolsheviks [Note: in Council after caucus] voted solid party line for acceptance except Rosanov and Bukharin. Lenin spoke fifteen minutes, almost carelessly, wholly sardonically. Gumberg and Ransome got into meeting on my pass. Find Gumberg and Vaskov at noon at breakfast. Latter's dejected but frank talk on Lenin's philosophy and Lenin as boss. His attitude on agitation. Socialist army. Am convinced Germany vetoed its formation. The assumption otherwise vain.

Opera in the evening, "Pagliacci," and Chekov's "The Wedding." Performance of the first good, without distinction. Latter's music by Russian, Alexandrovsky, apt.

Vaskov had voted for war in the party caucus, and at the bidding of that caucus had voted for peace in Council. He said that Radek had done the same. Trotsky had figured less prominently than usual and had answered obediently to party orders. It was understood that his feelings would be spared by not including him in the makeshift delegation which would speed to Brest-Litovsk in accord with German command.

Of Lenin's surface philosophy, Vaskov could not tell more

than Lenin himself had told, but what he explained about Lenin's attitude on agitation was of great import. Lenin had argued that the proper after-peace policy of the Bolsheviks would be to refrain from communistic agitation in the Central Empires and to pursue such agitation in the countries of the Allies. As in his thesis, he maintained that Bolshevism, to get a free hand in Russia, must buy its peace from Germany on any terms, and that cessation from agitation in Germany was one of those terms. While as for the Allies, they were the capitalistic and militaristic enemies of Soviet socialism, and the campaign of agitation should proceed against them.

The concrete deduction was that for the future of the World War, Russia was a working ally of Germany.

Germany had indeed vetoed the formation of a Russian Red Army. One clause in the German terms I had not read closely enough, or I need not have speculated.

I wrote that night a message, coded and sent the next day, not to the Committee on Public Information but to the State Department, with request to pass to the General Staff:

I have positive information that Lenin takes the stand that there should be no agitation against German militarism but that agitation should be continued against "the militarism" of the nations at war with Germany. He will use every influence to have the new peace treaty terms obeyed in all particulars of non-interference with Germany.

In the hurry of the day either I failed to keep a copy of this dispatch or later lost it, for it was not in my files when I sought it. But the Military Intelligence Department at Washington used the cable as text for analysis of Russian conditions and so preserved the record.

To Creel of the Committee I cabled separately:

Feb. 25. Acceptance of German peace by Bolsheviks brings situation where Washington should express view on scope of continued activities of news organization. My judgment is that it should go ahead as it is until funds now in Russia are exhausted. Ruble funds now here cannot be taken out of country, so should be spent here to best advantage. Unless President speaks very frequently money will last several months. He averages two hundred thousand rubles a speech, printing and distribution, and is worth the money. For effect on stout little band of workers here wish you would cable me few words Bullard could pass to them indicating that they are serving by doing the job at hand. No one of our group has left. They are Graham Taylor, Malcolm Davis, William Adams Brown, Jr., Guy Smith, and Read Lewis.

Two days earlier I sent Creel a cable belonging also in this group:

Feb. 23. First two hundred thousand of German version President's Feb. 11 speech moving toward German line in packages carried by individual distributors. Balance German and first of Hungarian will be started within three or four days. Looks tonight as if peace parleys more likely than continued German advance but for contingency of German entry plans made to transfer part equipment to Vologda on Embassy train. In same contingency Moscow office will go with Summers to Samara. Bullard has developed finely practical plan of greeting Germans if they ever arrive Petrograd with bill posted copies President's messages of Jan. 8 and Feb. 11. Copies are ready. Bill posters keen for job. Germany's new and increased peace demands received tonight.

No reply to the message asking decision on Russian work ever reached me, and I followed the course outlined.

Pskov was announced taken on February 25, Monday, and this was the first day approaching panic in the city. In the buzz and whirl rumor took the place of news. A peace delegation was reported gone to Brest-Litovsk, its recall was bruited, its sending was denied. As a matter of fact a nondescript delegation had left Petrograd but touch with it was lost soon afterward. The only certainty was that the Germans still were coming on toward the city. Fear that the Moscow line would be cut in an encircling movement caused the railroad station to that capital to be rushed. Vainly so, for the Bolshevik guards turned the crowd back to the control offices. None could leave Petrograd without papers of exit. Even panic was used as a weapon against the *bourgeoisie*. Many who sought papers were arrested. Crowds milled around the billboards waiting the posting of the newspapers.

The most encouraging of the verifiable reports was that Reval had not yet been occupied by the Germans. A direct wire still operated. Field Marshal Eichhorn, however, was advancing along the coast of the Gulf of Riga, and was at the straits between the Mohnsund Islands and the mainland. Lemsal and Venden had been taken. Count Mirbach, who on his departure from Petrograd had taken command of a German force moving into Estonia, issued a proclamation, intercepted by the Petrograd wireless, as he intended it to be, threatening reprisals if harm came to "Germans or to Estonians or Letts under German protection should they be arrested by Red Guards or their property taken."

Of the war aspect I entered in the nightly Log:

How much does German theatrical desire figure? Alarm at 1:30 (morning of 26th) of Germans at Dno, toward Moscow line. Consul Tredwell (after report) calls Ambassador from my room.

This particular report, fortunately, was without substance. The Embassy had no fresh alarm to speed its going. The Log of two days told the succinct story of departure.

Feb. 26. (Tuesday) Getaway day for Embassy and Red Cross and Consulate; Passport and Military Missions. A busy round of calls. Gumberg and Ransome say good-bye. Thacher also, but not Robins. They are off at midnight to Vologda. Last talk with Ambassador in the afternoon.

Feb. 27. They got away at 2 A.M. Peaceful day. Signs of fighting spirit of the people rather than the Government. Marseillaise played by soldier bands. Red Guards at hotel, searching for guns apparently.

In that last talk with the Ambassador he told me he had been asked to warn me that Trotsky was aware of the inquiry I was making in the matter of the German relations with the Bolsheviks, and to advise me to halt it. Such advice, he said, he could not give, but about the warning he felt concern. I asked him to name his informant and he did so. I considered the warning a bluff, designed to frighten me. Trotsky could have no knowledge except through persons I did not believe would care to put me in peril.

Sorry as I was to part with the Ambassador, it was a relief to have him safely gone. The departure of the Red Cross unit was a surprise to me, the impending event unknown until Thacher, the evening of February 25, informed me and returned funds I had intrusted to the keeping of his Treasurer's chest.

CHAPTER XXIV

February 27—March 3, 1918. Search and Foray.
The Historical Sequels.

1.

ALTHOUGH restricted at intervals by other activities, the inquiry to which the Ambassador referred at our final Petrograd meeting had advanced steadily since inception, and from about mid-February in an organized fashion.

After a period of observation I had decided to ask to be taken more directly into the confidence of two groups which, I had surmised, either might be separate from each other, or be in contact. The group in charge of the invasion of the telegraph wires I knew to be military and naval. The other group, attacking the files at Smolny, had Eugene Semenov as outside representative, and it might be as leader. For a while I could not tell. From British Intelligence Officer Boyce, I had the knowledge that the wire watchers knew and trusted Semenov. I suspected he was in their ranks as well. I needed to know more about him.

By this time, too, the matter, in my concern, had resolved itself into the question whether representatives of the German General Staff were giving current orders to Smolny, and, if they were, the measure of the obedience they were receiving. The files of Smolny should hold the answer. The difficulty of ascertainment lay in the haphazard manner in which the search for information was being conducted. It occurred to me that this was a condition that might be remedied.

In my association with the general run of Bolsheviks I had acquired contempt for their casualness, slothfulness, and incompetence. Any sustained adventure against them, it appeared to me, had a chance of success. They had, too, the Russian weakness for bureaucratic detail; for notations on correspondence; for the passing of letters from desk to desk; for "secret" files. Studied scrutiny of their files of correspondence seemed not impossible. But without a general plan, the utility could be slight.

With this opinion I sent for Semenov, and when I had him

in a room alone with me and Bullard I told him that I knew he was in contact with two groups of anti-Bolshevik workers and that I believed they had a common leader, whom I would like to meet. He appeared to have some fear of me, for reasons I did not understand until later, but he has stated that I convinced him of sincerity. It turned out that my analysis was not exact, and that the two groups were in large degree independent. Semenov, however, was in both of them and could be regarded as the head of one of them, a capacity in which our relations continued.

Shortly afterward he took me to the commander of the wire group, Colonel Samsonov, whose name I did not write down anywhere until I was assured he was safely out of Russia, a year later. This dynamo of a man, debonair, resourceful, and reliant, was the one I sought henceforth when I desired others to be inspired beyond my ability to lift them forward. He never failed me.

To the two men I outlined a simple procedure, which they agreed was practical. It was to bring me each day, in so far as possible, a list of the communications passing through the hands of the watchers at Smolny, and allow me to indicate the ones worth the trouble of taking from the files, photographing at night, and returning to the files the next day. Until late in February this was the method followed.

Not until the Bolsheviks prepared to evacuate Smolny for the Kremlin at Moscow, and packed to go, was a time opportune for taking from the files the originals of some of the material already photographed, and as many other originals as possible. To have taken them earlier would have been to risk the disruption of the service.

Meantime it was shown that German orders were passing continually both to Lenin and Trotsky, some of them sinister with projects for agents-agitators in Allied countries. The contents of these orders I cabled to the State Department as fast as they came into my possession. So we were informed of the purpose of the Germans to use Russia as a base for the export of plotters to our Pacific coast, and of the German hope of a Pacific submarine base on Russian territory.

During this period I shared with Boyce the almost daily portion of information, but the retreat of the Embassies from

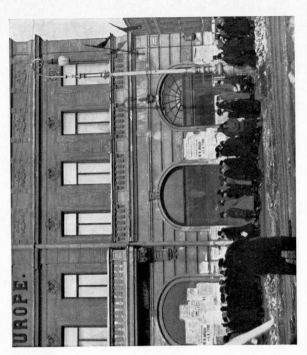

Petrograd was a paradise for bill-posters. This scene shows the Nevsky side of the Hotel d'Europe. Photograph taken on March 1, 1918.

Railway station scene of flight from Petrograd in the panic week, the last days of February, 1918. The passenger overflow has taken to the tops of freight cars.

SCENES IN PETROGRAD

Petrograd broke our association. He and the British consular group left for Vologda the same night our Embassy departed, February 26.

Preparations for raid did not begin until February 27, and it was not made until the night of March 2. The project was my idea. It was not received with any cries of enthusiasm at the outset, but when Semenov realized that miracles need not be invoked, when Colonel Samsonov supported the plan with vigor, and finally when the workers in Smolny advised of its practicality and themselves suggested technique, a fury for accomplishment swept through the band. In the last two days I had to urge patience, a waiting for the actual time when papers would be boxed at Smolny for shipment to Moscow. Emotions were dangerous, the more so I understood that in spite of efforts at control and of the necessity for playing a daily part with Bolshevik officials, my own feelings had risen toward rage.

In the face of German attack on Russia, German officers were demanding of Lenin that he offer no actual defense to that attack, and Lenin and Trotsky were sharing in an ordered harrying of an Allied Ambassador. The developments from the passage of four of these epistles from February 23 to February 27 were an integral part of the experiences of my last days in Russia.

Within a reasonable period after its receipt at Smolny, a copy of the following letter was in my hands:

Feb. 23, 1918. To the Commissar of Foreign Affairs [Note: Trotsky]: According to my personal conversation with the Chairman of the Council of People's Commissars [Note: Lenin], it has been decided to delay the departure of the Italian Embassy from Petrograd and, as far as possible, to search the Embassy baggage. Of this decision I count it my duty to inform you. For the Head of the Bureau, R. Bauer. Adjutant, Henrich.*

"Bauer" was listed in my working notes as the cipher signature of the German who also went by the name of Major Bayermeister, and as one of the superiors of the German advisory group. A Russian notation on the letter was "To be given to Blagonravov," my acquaintance, the Commissar of Martial Law.

* Document No. 26, "The German-Bolshevik Conspiracy," Appendix, pp. 471–472.

Hurried inquiry showed that the Italian Embassy was packing and had not yet been molested. Since there was no indication that the arrest of the Italian Ambassador was intended, I concluded to let the incident be a prime test of the accuracy of the Smolny service and sent no warning.

When the Ambassador was ready to depart two or three days later, he was allowed to enter the train with his suite and possessions, and then the train was held twenty-four hours at the station and every piece of baggage searched. Release of the train and safe departure of the Embassy followed. What, if anything, the search got, was not ascertained.

The Bolsheviks, as usual, made a jest of the performance. Petrov at the Foreign Office told me, March 2, that the Italians had given "a diplomatic passport to the embassy cook," hence the fuss.

Whatever the Italian Ambassador was supposed to have in the way of papers was wanted badly. In the interval when he was getting ready to leave, his automobile was held up at night almost in front of the Hotel d'Europe, and the public sensation was blamed upon robbers.

In my possession, however, was a copy of the following report:

Petrograd, Feb. 24, 1918. To the People's Commissar of Foreign Affairs. Our agents investigating the Italian Embassy, I. E. Maerov, Imenitsky, and Urov, followed up the Ambassador and conducted a search of him in the street, with a confiscation. Documents regarding relations with German diplomats and the special papers of the Ambassador to the Allied Ambassadors, mentioned by you, were not found. In order to mask the attack several articles listed in the protocol furnished by Comrade Imenitsky were taken from the Ambassador.*

The signature was "Mitopovich, Commissar." Jewelry and a gold pen were the minor valuables taken to simulate robbery.

Two current demands of the Germans upon Lenin were harshly clear. The first:

Feb. 26, 1918. To the Chairman of the Council of People's Commissars: This division of the staff has the honor to request data of the attitude of the detachments being sent to Pskov and to

---

* Portion of Document No. 27, "The German-Bolshevik Conspiracy," Appendix, p. 472.

caution against most disastrous results if these detachments carry on patriotic propaganda and agitations against the German army. Head of the Russian Division General Staff, O. Rausch. Adjutant, U. Wolff.*

At the top of the letter was the written comment, "Urgent. Chairman of the People's Commissars asks Volodarsky to communicate this to agitation department. Skripnik." Volodarsky, later to be assassinated, was of the body of Bolsheviks who had lived in New York. His duties of the moment were agitational. Skripnik was a government secretary reporting directly to Lenin. The detachments being sent to Pskov at this time were composed of Red Guards and of the recruits of the new Red Army. Pskov was taken by the Germans without a fight.

The second order, from another German bureau:

Feb. 27, 1918, to the President of the Council of People's Commissars: Not having received an exact answer to my question of the 25th of February, I now have the honor a second time to request you to inform me in the shortest possible time the numbers and kinds of forces sent to Narva and Pskov.

At the same time, at the orders of the representatives of our General Staff, I once more remind you of the desirability of naming Gen. Parsky to the post of commander-in-chief of the Russian armed forces, in place of Gen. Bonch-Bruevich, whose actions do not meet the approval of the German High Command. Since the attack on the lives and property of the German land-holders in Estonia and Livonia, which, according to our information, was carried out with the knowledge of Gen. Bonch-Bruevich, and his nationalistic actions in Orel, his continuance in the position of General is no longer desirable. Head of the Bureau: Agasfer.†

Across this letter was written, "Send to Trotsky and Podvoisky. N.G." The initials I regarded as those of Gorbunov, a Council secretary. Podvoisky was Commissar of War. In my working list "Agasfer" was placed as the cipher signature of Major Luberts, named as the chief of the Petrograd Intelligence Bureau of the German General Staff unit in Petrograd, the head of which was listed as Major Rausch, referred to in the letter as the representative of "our General Staff."

Up to the time I left Petrograd I was unable to learn

* Document No. 30, "The German-Bolshevik Conspiracy," Appendix, pp. 473–474.

† Document No. 31, "The German-Bolshevik Conspiracy," Appendix, p. 474.

whether the order in respect to General Parsky had been obeyed. In June, however, Joseph Shaplen of the United Press Association found General Parsky at the post, interviewed him, and sent me a copy of the script. Near the close of the talk, Parsky for no reason apparent in the questioning, naïvely volunteered his explanation for having surrendered the city of Riga to the Germans without adequate defense, in the early autumn of 1917, prior to the Bolshevik Revolution.

"When I commanded the 12th Army," he said, "I undertook the evacuation of Riga contrary to the orders of General Klembovsky, and made no mistake. Due to this action the enemy captured only 7,500 prisoners of the entire 12th Army. I am proud that I succeeded in rescuing the 12th Army."

Parsky was indeed a Russian general of whom Germany could approve.

These letters, convincing to me of the Bolshevik purpose of surrender to the Germans, of their measure of sullen obedience to them, and of the German intention of accepting that surrender after a certain amount of punishment given, were among the strongest of the reasons for urging forward a raid on the Smolny archives. Photographs of the four letters I had, but since they were of the current hour I hungered for the original orders. I may add that three of the four were secured.

Plans for the venture were completed on March 2. Only the event impended. On Sunday morning, March 3, I went to Smolny to say goodbye to scene and persons, and to cast my eyes around for signs. The latter I thought I found. Several large pine boxes of document files, with sides broken, lay on the snow in the courtyard. Workmen were beginning to nail on new strips. A little accident, it was explained—a group of guards had tossed the boxes around too carelessly. I hoped the cause was otherwise, but had to chafe the day through until meeting time set for late evening. That night I had in my hands rather more than half of the letters I had listed as desirable, a percentage I thought excellent.

Others, to be quoted, have written more fully than I about the foray, the preceding campaign, and the material results.

The Log of March 3 had the entry: "Last visit Smolny. Wind-up. Another air-raid. Where heard of it."

Some time subsequently I set down an outline of the event,

and in 1924, at the request of Northwestern University for an epitome of war work, included an account of the episode. Writing without comparison of notes, however, I placed the date of delivery of the final material to me as March 2 instead of March 3. From the epitome:

Cool men did this work. At even a hint of suspicion their lives were gone. My only part in this final raid was to induce the men to map out the details of a practical plan, and to raise their ardor to carry it out. They were patriots, bitter against Bolshevism. At the last meeting I gave them individually enough rubles—a moderate number of dollars in American valuation—to give each a means of flight or hiding, and the organization scattered widely. At a later period some members of the body were able to reassemble and it is a matter of State Department record that a new liaison was established with an American consul in a border territory and that useful intelligence continued to be furnished Washington long after every American was out of Russia.

It is my experience that the element of drama is not apt to be present in the crises where literature and the natural human desire alike expect it, but the Germans were good enough on the night of the band's last meeting to supply that high light. The last of their air-plane shells dropped a block or so away while we were bending over a table strewn with papers. The area was close built with the block-deep type of Petrograd apartment houses, densely populated, and I have the notion that all the women within half a mile yelled in unison. As far as I could learn the shell killed no one; and the hard-boiled conspirators only shook their heads in irritation at the noise.

Arthur Bullard was with me. The apartment was that of one of the members of the group, and was in the Tauride district. All told we numbered nine or ten persons. For two hours we sat around a large table, listing, checking, and reading. Everyone was exuberant and some of the members of the Russian party were inclined to eloquence. One wanted a pause to toast the "historical occasion." I thought history could take care of itself and that we had best do the same for ourselves. When the detail work was done, Bullard and I clasped each man by the hand, thanked him, and wished him safety and whatever good luck there could be in a clouded land. It was farewell. No man of this band ever was taken by the Bolsheviks.

A mile and a half of streets, lonely and deserted in the after-midnight hours—we trusted—lay between the apartment and the Military Mission on the Fuhrstatskaya which I had lately taken for headquarters. Bullard and I walked the distance, choosing the middle of the streets for pathway, the letters in our inner pockets. We did not meet a person on the way.

Semenov was not able to get out of the Bolshevik area of Russia until the following winter, when he reached Archangel, then under Allied protection. There, before the American Consul, Leslie A. Davis, he made the following affidavit, forwarded in duplicate to the State Department and to me:

Consulate of the United States of America, Archangel, Russia.

Eugenie Petrovitch Semenov, being duly sworn deposes and says:

1. That the originals and photographs of the documents which were published in America in a pamphlet entitled, "The German-Bolshevik Conspiracy" issued by the Committee on Public Information, and other documents were delivered to Edgar Sisson, Special Representative in Russia of the Committee on Public Information in the winter of 1917–18, by me or in my presence by the persons who with me organized the means of securing the said documents.

2. That these persons whose identity it is not yet possible to reveal for reasons connected with their personal safety, maintained connection with the departments of the Bolshevik Government personally and through officers and employes of such departments who had continued their work in them after the accession of the Bolsheviks to power, or who had entered their service for the purpose of securing evidence as to the true character of the Bolshevik leaders and their Government.

3. That some of these persons were connected with the Military and Naval staffs and had the right of entering without hindrance the Staff offices, the Bolshevik departments at Smolny, and the Commissariat for Foreign Affairs.

4. That as a member of the group which was engaged in this work, and my partnership in organizing its details, and my personal daily intercourse with the men who were carrying it on and who were employed in the Government as already stated, I was familiar with the facts as to the actual securing of these original documents and photographs.

5. That after the documents referred to and similar ones had been received at the Commissariat for Foreign Affairs, Smolny, or the offices of the Military and Naval Staffs, and had been laid

before the appropriate Commissar or Bolshevik official, they were forwarded to be filed with the current or secret papers of that department, and that during this process they passed through the hands of the aforesaid officers and employes who were collaborating with me and the other persons in charge of the business of detection, and that such officers and employes made lists of such documents and noted their contents and gave such lists and information to me and that I and my associates marked on these lists the documents we desired to take.

6. That Mr. Sisson went over some of these lists with me and helped to designate the particular documents desired.

7. That the originals of such documents were photographed by the said officers and employes and our agents at the first opportunity; that as after the documents had first been filed they might be wanted by the Bolshevik officials or commissars in connection with the current work or for their information, they were removed from the files only for a few hours, photographed in the same building and replaced in the files; that in some cases the documents were taken out of Smolny altogether and retained for a day or two before they were returned; that in several cases the documents at Smolny were photographed in the same room where the daily work of the office was carried on; that in one instance one of our agents went to Smolny and together with one of our agents who was employed there photographed certain of the documents in the very room in which Commissar Uritsky was at the time, and that when the latter asked what they were doing, they replied that it was urgent work necessary in the course of the office.

8. That later when the original documents were not likely to be needed in the current work, and when the Commissars and officials were likely to have forgotten them, some of them were taken from the files and transferred to my personal association and that of my associates.

9. That many of the original documents that were given to Mr. Sisson were secured in February, 1918, at the time when the Bolshevik Government was preparing to evacuate Petrograd and remove to Moscow, as a result of the confusion and panic that then existed; that the officers and employes who were acting as our agents were among those who packed the files of the various departments at Smolny and they knew the particular boxes in which the desired documents, especially those from the German General Staff and the Nachrichten Bureau, had been placed; that they led the sailors who were on guard at Smolny to believe that these

cases contained gold which was being secretly removed to Moscow; that the sailors broke into these cases, searched for gold, and not finding it, left them open in the yard at Smolny; that our agents removed from the boxes as many of the documents as they had time for before the breaking into of the boxes was discovered; that our agents were not able to seize some of the originals because part of the current files were suddenly removed from Smolny to the office of the Commissariat for Foreign Affairs, and thence transferred to Moscow before they were accessible to us.

10. That after the incident just described and the partial removal of the files to Moscow, our agents continued to carry on the same processes of detection, photographing, and seizure.

(Signature) EUGENIE PETROVITCH SEMENOV.

Subscribed and Sworn To before
Me in Duplicate Original
This 21st Day of February, 1919.
(Signature) LESLIE A. DAVIS
Consul of the United States of America.

2.

BY order of President Wilson my official report, made to him May 9, 1918, was given to the public four months later. Its publication, in daily instalments, began in the newspapers of the United States on Sunday, September 15, 1918, and continued throughout the week.

It caused a furor, mainly of approval, but in some quarters a fury of assault. Only one attack, however, was of consequence, and that was less on account of the attacker than of the vehicle he found for utterance, the staid *New York Evening Post*. The spokesman, Santeri Nuorteva, who described himself as representative of the "Finnish Information Bureau," charged that the documents were "brazen forgeries."

Brought to Washington and examined by me, on September 23, he admitted that he had no personal knowledge upon which to base any such accusation, and conceded that he never had met two of the three American Red Cross men who, he had stated publicly, would corroborate his "facts." These two, Col. William Boyce Thompson and "Mayor T. Thatcher," by whom he meant Maj. Thomas D. Thacher, denied acquaintance with Nuorteva or any ability to "corroborate." He had got his "information," he said, from Raymond Robins, at a meeting in New York City in August. Robins, found by an Associated Press correspondent in company with Colonel Thompson at Globe, Arizona, on September 23, said he was "under instructions from the State Department and could not make any statement at this time." The actions of Robins I have already discussed.

I asked Nuorteva how he got his article to the *New York Evening Post*. He answered:

"I sent it to Mr. Henry Alsberg. He is the editor. I sent it under his name, because I have met him."

He had sent other copies of the article, he said, likewise by mail from Fitchburg, Massachusetts, to the *Boston Globe* and the *Springfield Republican*. Neither of these papers published it.

What Mr. Alsberg's exact place on the editorial staff of the *New York Evening Post* was, I do not know. The newspaper was without personal ownership supervision at the time. It had just passed, on September 1, 1918, into the hands of Thomas W. Lamont of the banking house of J. P. Morgan & Co.; but he had not taken active control, I was informed directly in January, 1931, and had made neither changes of staff nor suggestions of editorial policy. He was under stress of war responsibilities, preparing to leave soon for Europe.

Nuorteva stated in identification of himself: "I represent the Finnish Government. It is in Moscow."

To the question, "Between the Russian Soviet Government and the Government of the United States, which do you choose?" he replied: "I represent the Socialists in Russia and Finland. My prime allegiance is to them."

To the further question, "If the Russian Soviet Government were in a state of war with the United States, would you choose the Russian Soviet Government?" he answered: "I believe so."

Our troops were in Siberia and Archangel or *en route* but a formal state of war did not exist. Although not a citizen of the United States, Nuorteva technically was not an enemy alien. After his statement was taken, I ordered his release.

Meantime, after the *Evening Post* had followed its publication of the Nuorteva allegation with the complaint that the documents in my report had not been submitted in facsimile to the newspapers or to the scrutiny of an authoritative historical body, Chairman George Creel of the Committee on Public Information turned the originals and all material listed in that report over to the National Board of Historical Service, for examination. That body selected a committee of which Professor J. Franklin Jameson, the historian, was chairman. I appeared for questioning and testimony before the committee, which also called in various historians for consultation, among them the late Professor Archibald Cary Coolidge of Harvard University.

The committee's report summarized into the statement, for the main body of my material: "We have no hesitation in declaring that we see no reason to doubt the genuineness or authenticity of these fifty-three documents."

There could be no clear verdict on the mimeographed copies in the "Appendix to the Report" (Documents No. 54–68) as I had myself pointed out in the introduction to that Appendix, when recording them for comparison. I was convinced, however, of their interlacing fact value, and was pleased when Professor Miliukov later vouched for this group and accounted for the source. This group had been Nuorteva's target.

The committee also made critical although not hostile analysis of several documents containing inclosures. The covering documents themselves, however, showing that the German representatives wished to get custody of the inclosures, were all that had concern for me.

The committee likewise answered in detail other criticisms made by the *Evening Post*.

After receipt of the verdict of the historians, the Committee on Public Information republished my report as a government pamphlet, with facsimiles of many of the originals, and with the full report of the committee of historians included.*

Nuorteva, after the War, was associated with Ludwig C. A. K. Martens, who called himself the "Soviet Ambassador" and was the organizer of the Russian buying bureau from which the present Amtorg Trading Company finally emerged. In this period Nuorteva signed himself "Secretary of the Russian Soviet Government Bureau."

He became involved in factional strife in the local Communist party, being censured in one noisy convention for mak-

* See Appendix, pp. 459–488.

ing "reckless charges" against a fellow Bolshevik. In July, 1920, he left the country, carrying a "passport" signed by Martens. He cited the paper in England as ground for diplomatic courtesy, but the British police arrested him as an undesirable visitor and ordered his deportation. Barred as an alien from return to the United States, he asked and secured deportation to Russia, which may have been his goal when he left New York.

He was well received in Moscow, in any event, and given a post in the Russian Foreign Office. Moscow, however, was for him not the looked-for paradise. In May, 1921, he was arrested for some undefined offense and placed in prison, where he was kept until late in January, 1922. On release he disappeared from view—at least from mine.

3.

ONE copy of Semenov's affidavit of February, 1919, took quiet place in my files, there to remain until I began to arrange the material for *One Hundred Red Days*. The attested duplicate went to the State Department archives.

Semenov wrote later, however, for publication in Paris, which he reached in 1921. There he met Professor Paul Miliukov, former Duma leader and Minister of the Russian Cabinet of the First Revolution, who was conducting a Russian language newspaper, *Posliednia Novosti* ("The Latest News"). Comparison of experience between the two exiles led most interestingly to the disclosure of the history of the group of documents I had printed as an Appendix to my report, the ones that started me on quest of evidence of German control of the Bolshevik leaders.

Although they were of different political parties, Professor Miliukov opened to Semenov the pages of his newspaper, the most influential of organs of the exiles in western Europe, and himself wrote a commendatory introductory article.

Semenov analyzed many of the separate documents of my report, citing objective corroborative detail not now essential, and also included the substance of the affidavit. Other portions of his narrative were more personal, either to him or to me, and of the latter some were novel and a few acrid. His feelings were understandable.

When copies of the newspapers containing the articles reached the United States, I asked an able translator, Leo Pasvolsky, to prepare the English version; and, at the request of the State Department, I annotated the translation for its files, retaining a copy. Quotations used are from this copy. The articles began in the *Posliednia Novosti*, April 5, 1921, and continued for several days, under the heading, "German Money to Lenin."

Wrote Semenov in his own introduction:

The future historian of the Bolshevist coup d'etat, or the reporting member of a Reichstag Commission, if it is ever created at the demand of Edouard Bernstein, to investigate the "transfer of money to Lenin by the German General Staff" will have to acquaint itself with three series of documents.

First series: The documents which, as originals or copies, must exist in the various Bureaus, Sections, and Departments of the German General Staff (the Central Abtheilung, Nachrichten Bureau, Section R. or M.R., or at the General Staff of the Navy).

Second series: Documents in the archives of the Imperial Bank and its correspondents and agents abroad (for instance, in Stockholm).

Third series: All the exposures published in such important papers as those in Copenhagen, in which the Parvus activities were brought to light; the *Vorwaerts, Berliner Tageblatt*, and others; and particularly an American pamphlet which appeared in October, 1918, published by the United States Committee on Public Information under the title, "The German-Bolshevik Conspiracy." This pamphlet at the time of its publication occasioned much discussion. It represented the first occasion on which charges against Lenin and Company were systematized and supported by documentary evidence. The Committee of the Government of the United States consisting of the Secretaries of State, War, and Navy, with George Creel as Chairman, which published the documents, before reissuing them as a pamphlet, submitted them for verification to the Advisory Board of the National Board of Historical Service consisting of Professors Schaeffer, Ford, Franklin Jameson, and Samuel Harper. This Board appointed a special committee to investigate the authenticity of the documents and the charges against them which began to appear in America as well as in Europe, as early as 1918.

The committee in its report of October 26, 1918, affirmed the "authenticity or genuineness" of fifty-three documents, and, with

corrections, reservations, interpretations, and explanations, of the
genuineness of the rest—about twenty documents. Thus the documents submitted to the committee by Edgar Sisson, special agent
of the United States Government in Russia, winter of 1917–18,
in their overwhelming majority—53 out of 70—were found to be
authentic and genuine.*

The responsibility for the genuineness of these documents rests
upon me personally. Over fifty of them I handed to Mr. Sisson
during February, 1918, when he came to me with a recommendation from the American Ambassador, Mr. D. Francis. . . .

It was arranged between Edgar Sisson and myself that the
documents furnished him by us would be translated and circulated in three languages: Russian, English, and French.

Mr. Sisson and his assistant left me on March 3, 1918, and I
waited for news of the publication of the documents first in Petrograd, then in Murmansk, and afterward in Archangel, where
I learned finally that the documents were published in the United
States and were the subject of animated discussions not only in
the Allied countries but also in Germany, where such a serious
organ as the *Berliner Tageblatt* in an article bearing so authoritative a signature as that of Mr. Vorst, recognized the credit-
ability of the disclosures in the Sisson pamphlet.

Now along comes Edouard Bernstein and raises again, this time
not merely in the press but in Parliament as well, the question of
Lenin's treason and of the fifty million rubles in gold paid out to
him. I therefore deem it my duty to write to Edouard Bernstein
that I am at his service for every possible evidence I can furnish
as to the treason of Lenin and Company. It is of no little interest
to note right here that his charges coincide with a certain document published in Edgar Sisson's pamphlet—Document No. 8
[which asserted the transfer of credit for 50,000,000 rubles gold
from Germany through Stockholm to Russia in January, 1918
for support of Red Guards and agitators].

When Semenov concluded a detailed analysis and the ac-

* Note: The reference concerning reservations is to the collection of documents the translations of which were set forth, as co-related but unproved
material, in the Appendix to my report. Professor Miliukov in his introduction supplies the link that turns the Appendix set to prime evidence: "This
commission—Committee of the National Board of Historical Service—after
careful study and scrutiny of the documents declared them genuine, *making
reservations only concerning our Novocherkassk series since the documents of
that series were known only in the translations, which might contain errors
and inaccuracies.*" E. S., May 14, 1921.

count covered by his affidavit, he headed a chapter, "The Rôle of Mr. Sisson," and continued:

I was informed that the government agent heading the Committee on Public Information came to Russia in order to gather data and prepare everything for the recognition of the Bolsheviks. Therefore I strictly refused in the beginning to have anything to do with the American Government.*

But Mr. Sisson entreated me continuously to give him the documents containing proof about Lenin and his group's work with the Germans. He showed me a few photographs—our photographs which were given to him by one of the Allied Missions. "Give me," he said, "the documents about which the Ambassador is talking. You will be doing an important historical work."†

After a long conversation I asked permission to give him my decision in twenty-four hours. Next day our conversation continued. When I was convinced that everything was not lost at Washington, I agreed to give Mr. Sisson all I had at the time. We spoke in detail about the military organization and about the telegraph tapes. I never told anyone about the telegraphic strips which confirmed objectively the contents of our documents, except the officers in one of the Allied Groups [Note: the British] who were working with the military organization. The strips were our military secret and the existence of organization securing them by tapping the direct wire from Brest-Litovsk to Petrograd was unknown both to our friends in the "Red" camp and to my nearest colleague. Sisson was the first one to whom I said anything about the telegraphic strips. His soul of a newspaper man and an

* Note: This is my first knowledge that a slander so useful to the Bolsheviks was ever circulated in Petrograd concerning me, but it follows the cynical Bolshevik advertising formula so well that I am not surprised. Russian internal depression and the Russian proneness to accept the worst as an act of fate were played upon by the Bolsheviks from the very beginning as instruments for the retention of power. For this reason every foreign representative or unofficial visitor has been valuable to them, enabling them to proclaim—whether falsely or truly—that here comes an intermediary from the "foreign imperialists" negotiating recognition. Imagine the moral effect of this upon a population steeped in melancholy, shut off by Bolshevik act from any but Bolshevik "news," and this "news" flared forth in Bolshevik headlines. An H. G. Wells, a foreign mission of any sort, give added length to the Bolshevik *régime.*

If the Bolsheviks proclaimed that my rôle was that of a trafficker for recognition, that advertisement must have added greatly to the shock of their later disillusion. E. S., May 26, 1921.

† Note: Not accurate as a quotation, but difference is immaterial. E. S., May 26, 1921.

agent was all astir. He jumped with joy, notwithstanding his American seriousness and his cold blood. The next interview I set for a time when the member of the military organization would come to see me with a new telegraph tape.*

When Edgar Sisson received the documents and tapes, the first from my colleague, the second from the member of the military mission, he was so content that he declared, "I have nothing further to do here; I am going back." On March 3, 1918 he departed, but from Petrograd he sent several coded despatches and I am told these despatches stopped recognition of the Bolsheviks by Washington.†

At all of my conversations with Sisson, his assistant, Bullard, was present.

I turned over to Mr. Sisson about fifty documents,‡ the last information tapes, manuscripts characterizing the chief Bolshevik leaders, and if I am not mistaken, a voluminous manuscript with

---

* Note: It is not strange that Mr. Semenov should be puzzled and in general error concerning the route of the inquiry that led to him. He assumes that the Ambassador directed me to him. One development at the Embassy did trace back to him. (The Ioffe letter.) Another development at a different source traced back to him—connection with the wire group indicated at the British Consulate. The crossing of these two lines in one person interested me deeply. My conclusion was that he was in the confidence of two divergent groups, and I set out to trace him down in the person. The matter proved to be one of some difficulty but eventually I got him in a room and asked him directly if he did not have entry to the military group that was tapping the Petrograd–Brest-Litovsk wires. The inquiry, coming from a person in whom he had no reason for particular confidence, and whom he even suspected—as he now discloses—of being friendly to the Bolsheviks, was alarming. But perhaps my cold manner, of which he does not quite approve, helped to convince him of my sincerity. At any rate he came through with an affirmative which I considered courageous under the circumstances, and then I asked him to take me to the leader of the military group. It took a day or so, as I recall, to work it all out. I was convinced that these two groups between them could go a step beyond the photo-making operation and in the excitement of the approaching transfer of Bolshevik headquarters from Petrograd to Moscow, raid the Smolny files for original documents. The conclusion proved to be correct—and workable. E. S., May 26, 1921.

† Note: I left March 4, 1918—Monday—after the public announcement of the signing of the Brest-Litovsk peace, but saw Semenov for the last time on March 3. E. S., March 21, 1921.

‡ Note: Semenov's reference to documents in the above paragraph is to the originals taken at Smolny. The leader of the Smolny group handed them to me with some formality. The telegraph tapes from the wire group were current messages, not the telegraph material of the Brest-Litovsk Peace Conference, which, unknown to Semenov, I already possessed. None of my cables contained mention of Bolshevik recognition, an issue long discounted negatively. E. S., Oct. 3, 1929.

a register of German firms and agents spying in the world. About the last register I am not quite sure. It must be remembered under what circumstances we had to work at that time, how dangerous it was to meet, to keep and to deliver the manuscripts and documents. It may be that I gave the list to another mission from which Sisson should have received it.*

The persons who took particular pains to discredit our documents were Col. Robins and the Consul General at Moscow of one of the Allied Powers who insisted to his Government upon the necessity of recognizing the Bolsheviks and of fighting together with them against the Germans. Unless I am mistaken I saw Col. Robins once at the Nikolaiev Station, when he was going somewhere, at the time when the Bolsheviks already were in power and I exchanged a few words with him in the presence of Ambassador Francis. I never had any dealings with him.

Soon after that I found that Col. Robins was in favor of the recognition of the Soviet Government and that he was trying to influence President Wilson to do that. I was also informed that Col. Robins was hoping to "push aside" Mr. Francis and to take his place as the Ambassador to the Council of People's Commissars.†

During all that time, which was so difficult and grievous for him the American Ambassador remained extraordinarily calm and collected. Only when he found himself in Archangel, again an influential Ambassador and the dean of the diplomatic corps, in communicating to me the contents of a telegram he had received from Lansing in which he asked whether I would consent to come to the United States in connection with the documents, he said to me, "I always shared your view and I believed in the documents which prove the Bolshevik treason. But Col. Robins was against me and at the beginning Sisson also. Later on Sisson came over to my side."‡

The Ambassador's correctness of behavior may be seen also from the fact that, exclusively in the interests of the cause, he

* Note: Mr. Semenov is mistaken about this list. I did not get it. E. S., May 26, 1921.

† Note (not in State Department notations): Colonel Robins had no access to President Wilson. He tried to influence the Ambassador, and, through him, the State Department. On his return to the United States he sought to obtain an interview with the President. His request was refused. E. S., Oct. 3, 1929.

‡ Note: I doubt if Semenov caught the Ambassador accurately on the comment referring to me, but the reference is personal and therefore immaterial. The Ambassador gave me support and confidence, and that is the material thing. E. S., May 14, 1921.

sent to me Edgar Sisson, who had come to Petrograd on a special mission. We members of the organization did not receive a kopek out of the sums which were received for the purpose of obtaining the documents, sums which were expected to be added to a fund the division of which we fixed in such a way that each one of the workers could have about five·thousand rubles in case he had to flee.

My feelings for Semenov I expressed in a letter to the translator, Leo Pasvolsky.

July 8, 1921.

DEAR MR. PASVOLSKY:

A person gets curious reactions when he reads what some one else writes about him. But no matter what comments may do to his pet vanities, there is no doubt but what the gain is (or ought to be) for his soul.

Now I never have thought of myself as being "cold-blooded." Yet the big bearded Russian Semenov, my associate during an intense, strenuous three weeks in which we got almost as much action as sometimes gets crammed into a life-time, writes me down in the light of his impressions as a "cold-blooded" person.

But as I look back dispassionately I can see that he may have had his justification. He saw the outside and objectively was the recipient of the intensity given to the drive for facts and more facts, proof and more proof. Everything centered at the last on the raid on Smolny for the originals of certain orders already located, and the plans were made as if for battle. In some emergencies it is necessary to lose something of human kindness and to regard human beings as checkers on the board.

But if I drove him with a certain relentlessness, I also yelled encouragement. He was a stake horse and responded because he had class. I have a fondness for him, trust he has forgiven me for my driving tactics, and am sure that if we ever meet again he will change his mind about the temperature of my heart.

Pictorially Semenov is a big chap, full beard and hair that a few years ago must have been dark brown. The upper face had, when I knew him, the distinctive Russian winter pallor. In blood I think he is partly French, though his appearance gives no clue. I noticed that he was equally the master of French and Russian, both for speaking and writing.

Professionally he is a writing man, and a journalist of parts. He must also have strong art instincts, for his daughter is a clever sculptress, who has exhibited both in Paris and Petrograd.

I saw many samples of her work in her studio in her father's residence, and they were good.

When Semenov and his family reached Archangel in safety I was relieved of a great weight, and I was positively light hearted when a few months later word came to me that the resourceful leader of the military wire-tapping group, who gave so much aid both to Semenov and to me, also had succeeded in escaping from Russia.

To the best of my knowledge all the members both of the civil and the military groups evaded the clutches of the Bolsheviks, although Admiral Stchastny, who was executed by Trotsky, appears to have been the victim of events subsequent to, but growing out of, the enterprise.

Professor Paul Miliukov's comprehensive article prefatory to Semenov's account was printed in *Posliednia Novosti* on April 3, 1921. It was, in translation:

At the end of December, 1917, the Headquarters of the Volunteer Army at Novocherkassk received from Petrograd by special courier a series of documents, complementing those which were published in the days of the Bolshevik uprising in July and exposing the sources from which Lenin's "enterprise" was subsidized, and the channels by which the subsidies of the German "heavy industry" passed into the pockets of Lenin, Trotsky, and their colleagues. The references on the documents left no room for doubt of their origin. They represented data gathered by the agents of the Allied Military Intelligence. The documents had all internal indications of authenticity. They were at that time published in the Novocherkassk and Rostov press, and the writer of this wrote a pamphlet as a commentary to the documents. This pamphlet was never published, however, because the Bolsheviks seized Rostov before it was ready for the press.

In the early part of 1919, after I had gone abroad, I learned that the collection of documents was not limited to the packages we received at Novocherkassk. Edgar Sisson, special agent of the Committee on Public Information for the United States, was collecting them in Russia throughout the winter of 1917–18. The documents known to me contained data covering the period prior to the Bolshevik coup d'etat (they were published in America as an Appendix to the Sisson documents under Numbers 54 to 68, unfortunately omitting the major part of the footnotes found in the Novocherkassk copies which threw light upon their origin). The documents later collected by Sisson referred to the period of the open collaboration of the Bolsheviks with the Germans, after the October coup d'etat.

When the documents of the last series began to appear in America, they aroused a veritable storm. Public opinion in general was disposed to discredit in advance all statements concerning the "bribery" in precisely the same manner as the complaints concerning the Bolshevik "atrocities." The campaign against the Sisson documents fell on favorable soil. Soon there became established in certain circles the opinion that the Sisson documents are forgeries and, consequently, of no value.

The American Committee referred the question to a special commission which included such a well known professor of history as Franklin Jameson, and such an excellent specialist on Russia as Samuel Harper.

This Commission, after careful study and scrutiny of the documents, rehabilitated their authenticity and declared them genuine, making reservations only concerning our Novocherkassk series, since the documents in that series were known only in the translations, which might contain errors and inaccuracies. Some reservations were also made about two German documents, Nos. 56 and 68 [Note: Both also in the Novocherkassk series. E.S.]. With this approbation of the Commission, the documents were (re-)published in America under the title "The German-Bolshevik Conspiracy" by the Committee on Public Information, War Information Series No. 20, October 1918.

But the accusation of "forgery" did not pass unnoticed. People feared to refer to the Sisson documents for data, and the proof of the Bolshevik bribery contained in them was gradually forgotten. Personally, when I first acquainted myself with them, I had no doubt about the genuineness. But the charge of falsification had in time an effect even upon me. For my own satisfaction I found the following explanation:

The person who furnished Sisson with his documents really had access to Bolshevik institutions and really supplied him with valuable documents. But since money was paid for these documents,* and, most probably, fairly large sums, the procurers of the documents, might possibly when short of genuine documents, have delivered falsified ones, which they could fabricate with the aid of the knowledge and the official

* Note: No large amount of money was spent on this operation. It was necessary to safeguard the lives of the Semenov and the military groups by affording them means of escape should suspicion attach to them following my departure. An amount was set aside for this purpose. But the cost of this phase of the investigation was less than seventy-five hundred dollars. E. S., May 14, 1921.

blanks which they had obtained. In this way the whole series was ruined.

This explanation I also introduced into the text of my *History of the Second Revolution*.

The charges made by Edouard Bernstein and his demand for a Reichstag investigation reawakened the interest in the authenticity of the documents. The exact figure of the bribe mentioned by Bernstein is confirmed by one of Sisson's documents. So the testimony, not merely of a witness, but an active agent in supplying these documents to Sisson, assumes an exceptional importance.

This testimony was fortunately secured by the *Posliednia Novosti*. It appears that Sisson's intermediary was the well-known contributor to the *Vechernoe Vremya*, E. P. Semenov. Mr. Semenov is not of our camp, but his articles, which we shall begin publishing in the *Posliednia Novosti* on the 5th of April, will have all the weight and value of testimony bound to figure as one of the most important pieces of evidence before the Reichstag Commission, if such a Commission is ever created.

These articles of Semenov place the question upon an entirely new plane. His conclusions coincide with my own convictions in the matter. The documents are genuine. Most of them, at the least. Were this testimony known earlier there would have been no need for any other proofs that Lenin received German money. Of course, now, when the part that Germany played in the Bolshevik coup d'etat is no longer doubted by anyone, the timely interest in our documents has lost its acuteness. But Lenin has not been overthrown as yet and as far as the masses that have been deceived by him are concerned, an acquaintance with these documents may produce upon them an impression similar to that which the publication of data much less effective in content, in July, 1917, produced upon the garrison of Petrograd. From this point of view Semenov's disclosures are undoubtedly of highest political value.

At any rate they are invaluable to the historian, who again acquires the right of making use of the once suspected documents —the internal evidences of the genuineness of which was never a matter of doubt to me, personally, even before.

(Signature) PAUL MILIUKOV.

4.

PROFESSOR VOSS, who wrote under the name of Hans Vorst and had unusual standing in Germany as an authority on Russian affairs, made his statement—to which Semenov made introductory reference—in the *Berliner Tageblatt* (March 31, 1919). Translation of his analysis of my report follows:

The public still remembers the sensational return of Lenin and some of his German comrades to Russia via Germany and Sweden after the Entente had refused them permission to pass through their territory. This fact alone proves that German Imperialism was ready to support Russian Bolshevism and that the leaders of the Russian Revolution did not hesitate to avail themselves of the assistance of the German authorities. The only question remaining was as to what extent this help was granted. The press of Russia and the Allied countries asserted that the Bolshevik leaders had been supplied by Germany with large sums of money for propaganda purposes but these assertions could not be substantiated and were strenuously denied by the Bolsheviks.

However, the fact that Lenin had been allowed to pass through Germany made it obvious that there existed secret relations between the Bolsheviks and German Imperialism and we pointed out, as far as the censor would allow us to do so, the short-sightedness of this policy and the danger it held for Europe. At a later date we criticised German Imperialism for forcing upon Russia a peace of dictation, the peace of Brest-Litovsk, which of all the Russian parties the Bolsheviks alone, and that merely for party-political reasons, were willing to sign. From this moment on there existed a situation during which German Imperialism had an interest in keeping Bolshevism in Russia in power. From the anti-Bolshevik side it was said that within the actual territory of the Soviet Republic, Bolshevik rule found every possible support German militarism could lend, and these statements were accompanied by the most surprising details, seemingly so incredible that they failed to carry weight.

But there have recently been published, first in the United States and now in Switzerland, a number of documents which seem to furnish evidence of what before had been thought unbelievable. Edgar Sisson, who was active in Russia during the winter of 1917–18, came into the possession of these documents. Some of them were published in obviously faulty German translation* and quite a number of them in Russian facsimile. It is impossible in the space of a newspaper article to undertake a thorough textual

---

* Professor Voss saw a German translation version, *Der Freie Verlag* edition, translated and published in Switzerland. In translation of Russian material into English and from English into German, word nicety was bound to suffer.

criticism of the material, which is unequal in value, as the editor himself admits. [Note: In regard to the Appendix series, not the Report.] It is even questionable whether some of the documents he considers genuine are so—we refer to Nos. 5, 6, 10, 11, and 35. [Note: Nos. 5 and 6 related to personnel, and that personnel was used. Nos. 10 and 11 were economic, one of them a circular dealing with post-war trade intentions in an unpleasant punitive way. No. 35 was a project for the assassination of General Kaledin, which Professor Voss may not have wanted to believe.]

The conclusions at which Mr. Sisson arrives are in many instances exaggerated, or at least open to question. *But by far the larger part of the collection bears, we are sorry to say, the stamp of authenticity on the face of them.*

In the first place the documents are to prove that in March, 1917, credits were assigned by the German Imperial Bank in neutral countries to Lenin, Zinoviev, Kamenev, Trotsky, and others for the purpose of peace propaganda in Russia; that the Council of People's Commissars, immediately after the October Revolution, speedily removed from the archives the proofs which the Government of Kerensky had in hand; and the German General Staff aided the Council of People's Commissars in obliterating the traces of this murky transaction. Even after the Bolshevik October Revolution the game is carried on; on January 8, 1918, the representative of the German Imperial Bank, von Schanz very confidentially tells the People's Commissar for Foreign Affairs—it was Trotsky—that 50,000,000 rubles in gold have been placed at the disposal of the People's Commissars. The Russian Government had been given this credit to pay the expenses of supporting the Red Guard and the agitators in the country. The Imperial Government thinks it necessary to draw the attention of the Soviet to the desirability of increasing their propaganda in the country as the hostile attitude of Southern Russia and Siberia toward the existing Russian Government disquiets the German Government.

Thus it is made to appear that in those first months when the Soviet Government was fighting so hard for its existence, the German Government interfered in internal Russian politics in favor of the Soviets, giving powerful financial assistance and solicitous counsel to Bolshevik rule. According to information of the Counter-Espionage Bureau of the Russian Army Headquarters of January 16, 1918, addressed to the Council of People's Commissars, one hundred German officers and two hundred and fifty sergeants departed for the Russian interior.

But let that be enough. Owing to this active support by the German Government, the Council of People's Commissars got into such dependence on the German authorities as hardly could be believed until now. I have indeed my doubts as to the genuineness of documents No. 5 and 6 in which conferences are mentioned which are said to have taken place between Lenin and his companions and the representatives of the German General Staff as early as spring and July, 1917, at Stockholm and Kronstadt, conferences at which at the outset, in case the Bolshevik movement should prove victorious, a coöperation between the German General Staff and the Bolshevik Government is said to have been agreed upon.

But it is nevertheless a fact that, immediately after the October Revolution the German General Staff already had its branch at Petrograd, which transmitted its desires to the People's Commissars—very far reaching desires which were almost always obligingly granted; that the German General Staff and the Bolsheviki Government coöperated peacefully in the peace propaganda in the Entente countries; that the Soviet Government furnished passports to agents of the German General Staff for their activities in Entente countries; that it removed from the Russian archives, at the demand of the German General Staff documents discrediting German politics.

If Mr. Sisson finally reaches the conclusion, however, that Lenin and Trotsky have been *merely* German agents, he certainly goes too far. As the German military men have served Bolshevism in order to obtain their aims, so Lenin and Trotsky have served German Imperialism to gain their ends—the World Revolution.

With Professor Voss's conclusion as to the status of Lenin and Trotsky I am in agreement.

Edward Bernstein, upon whose efforts for official investigation both Semenov and Professor Miliukov commented, was not able to force a Reichstag inquiry and eventually was stilled, but not before he had made public and pertinent accusations against the former Imperial Government of Germany and against Lenin. Under the heading, "A Dark Chapter," he wrote in the *Vorwaerts* on January 14, 1921:

Lenin and associates have in truth received great sums from Imperial Germany. I learned of this as early as the end of December, 1917. I asked a friend to quiz a certain person who in consequence of his connection with official places was bound to be

well informed and received an answer which proved this a fact. I
only did not learn how large these sums were and who were the
middlemen. Now I have learned from a dependable source that the
sums paid to these Russians were almost unbelievably high—
surely more than fifty millions of gold marks. . . . The military
man who mentioned the matter to me added that a prominent
member of the Parliament of a power allied with Germany had
told him that this financing of the Bolshevist propagandists was
a "master-piece of Germany." . . . The financial action has the
greatest similarity with the "reptile funds" of Bismarck.

Retorting to attacks, Bernstein on January 25, 1921, declared:

In communistic and nationalistic papers appears the assertion
that my report concerning the large sums of money which Lenin
and his associates received from Imperial Germany in 1917 were
based only on the publications of the Entente governments of the
fifty-seven documents concerning "The German-Bolshevik Conspiracy" published by the investigation Committee of the United
States in Washington—the so-called Sisson documents. This is a
mistaken view. The publication of the Washington Information
Bureau appeared in the summer of 1918, but my own information
reaches back to the end of 1917.

Immense sums, of course, were necessary for the agitational
campaign of Lenin and Trotsky throughout the summer of
1917, and in the autumn for inauguration of their insurrection,
and there could be but one source. The significance of the
50,000,000 ruble credit is that it was the last visible credit. It
was, moreover, a ruble and not a mark credit. While in point
of time the fund to which Bernstein had clue could have been
the same, it could also have been an earlier advance.

Vital circumstances afforded a background at that particular time for just such a transaction as that defined by the German who signed himself Von Schanz in Petrograd. The date of
the memorandum itself, January 8, 1918 (January 21, New
Style), was memorable. This was the date on which Lenin read
to the inner sixty of the Bolshevik party his Thesis of Twenty-
one Arguments why Russia should make any kind of peace,
even a disgraceful one, with Germany. He would have known
of the credit before Trotsky, just returning from Brest-
Litovsk to attend the All-Russian Convention, would have re-

ceived his memorandum. Importantly, too, the Bolsheviks had just suppressed the Constituent Assembly, and for the first time had assured a control warranting new and large financial support in their campaign against Alexeiev and Kaledin on the Don. The Germans, too, were anxious to have a clear route through Siberia to the Pacific Ocean.

When the document relating the credit was published in 1918 criticism was made that the Reichsbank was in no position to transfer such a sum in gold and could not do so secretly. Removal of reserves from Berlin vaults need not be implied. Germany intrenched itself with credit and reserves with its own industrial firms in neutral countries, Sweden being gateway to Russia. Nor would gold itself necessarily be transferred to Russia. Credit, Von Schanz stated, was extended for 50,000,000 gold.

It is demonstrable that the Bolshevik Government was in funds very shortly after January 21, although Germany, if it discovered the plan for expenditure, could not have been expected to appreciate the joke. For the Council of Commissars secretly voted 20,000,000 rubles to be expended in revolutionary agitation against and in Austria under a plan worked out by Dr. Albert Menzikovsky, who was placed at the head of the agitational unit. Menzikovsky was voted the money the last week in January, but on February 9, when disaster began to overtake the Brest-Litovsk Conference, he was still in Petrograd telegraphing complaints of obstacles to Trotsky and thereby recording the project. The enterprise apparently was then dropped, and the Germans may have been smart enough to get the money diverted to agitation elsewhere than against them. The Brest-Litovsk peace interdicted Bolshevik propaganda in Germany and Austria.

The sum of 20,000,000 rubles was also voted publicly the last week of January for the creation of a Red Army.

5.

ALTHOUGH the Reichstag hushed up investigation into the relations of the late Imperial Government with the Russian Bolsheviks, the flow of German admissions of political and military war-dealings continued.

General Ludendorff admitted, in the spring of 1921, the

responsibility of the Imperial German Government for the embodiment and material support of Lenin and Russian Bolshevism. The article by him, to that effect, was printed in the *Militär-Wochenblatt* ("Army Weekly"), February 26, 1921, and in the United States in the magazine *The Living Age*, April 30, 1921. Quoting the English version of the latter:

The (First) Revolution had so weakened the Russian Army that the German General Staff considered it feasible to shatter it by a vigorous offensive. Unhappily we had very inadequate forces at our disposal. At the same time, the more complete and decisive Russia's collapse the better for us. The Revolution in Russia afforded us an opportunity, first to compel that country to make peace, and second to start a successful offensive in the West.

By sending Lenin to Sweden the Chancellor believed he could speed up the Russian Revolution and greatly strengthen the peace currents already known to exist in the Russian army and nation. For the German General Staff the main thing was to render Russia's army machine impotent as speedily as possible.

We did not know who advised the Imperial Chancellor to help Lenin reach Sweden. We assumed at Headquarters that the Social Democrats had recommended it. Up to this time the German General Staff knew nothing whatever about Lenin, not even his name. But its assumption as to what he could accomplish was subsequently confirmed.

Ernest Drahn says in his book *Underground Literature in Revolutionary Germany during the World War:*

After Russia had put a *bourgeois* cabinet in power and the new cabinet showed no disposition to make a separate peace with Germany, we gladly welcomed the proposal of a former Bolshevik who had subsequently become a war profiteer [Note: Parvus, known also as Helphant, Helphand, and Parvus Helphant. E. S.] to ship the Bolsheviks who were living in Switzerland back to Russia.

Albrecht Wirth writes in his *History of the Russian Empire from 400 B.C. to 1920 A.D.:*

But Kerensky himself showed that he was an ardent Chauvinist and he eagerly revived the military spirit. . . . Just at this time Count Brockdorff-Rantzau, our Ambassador at Copenhagen, had gathered about him a company of all sorts and conditions of men as was his wont—and was openly promoting Revolution in Russia through the agency of Parvus Helphant, an extraordinarily shrewd Eastern Jew, who chanced upon the happy thought of driving out the devil with Beelzebub or, in other words, destroying the Revolution by Anarchy.

With this plan in his mind he urged that Lenin and Trotsky be sent to Russia to put the Bolsheviks in power.

I believe the principal parties in the scheme to send the Bolsheviks back to Russia are indicated here. It fell to the General Staff to provide military permits at the instance of the Imperial Chancellor, for Lenin and his associates. So far as we were concerned we were merely obeying a law of necessity, imposed upon us by the military situation.

The German attacks in the summer and autumn of 1917 shattered Russia's peace resistance, but peace negotiations did not begin until Lenin had seized the Government. The assumptions which induced the General Staff to assent to passing the Bolsheviki through Germany were proved correct by that event. We got peace with Russia, although it was not a perfect peace; and we thus secured a free hand for the Western offensive.

I wrote in my *War Memoirs:* "In sending Lenin to Russia our Government assumed a special responsibility. From the military point of view the measure was justified. Russia must fall. It was for our Government to see we did not fall." [Note: Before Bolshevik propaganda.]

So Germany acted perfectly right from the military standpoint in providing Lenin with money. A nation must fight the minds and the spirit of its enemies at the same time that it fights them with weapons. Money is important in such a campaign. We were defeated by the millions piled upon millions which the Entente and the Americans spent prodigally for that purpose.

Less than a month before General Ludendorff conceded the complicity of the German General Staff, General Hoffman gave Ellis Loring Dresel, American post-war Commissioner to Germany, his "word of honor" that he knew nothing of the passage of Lenin across Germany, adding, more ambiguously, that he was "clearly convinced the matter was not handled by the General Staff." He intimated however, reported Dresel to the State Department,

that it is possible both Philip Scheidemann [recently Chancellor] and Helphand (Parvus) had had a finger in the transaction. Parvus had been an instructor of Lenin and Trotsky in Geneva, he understood. He believed, however, that it was more probable that Erzberger was responsible for the whole matter. The General made it clear that, had he known of it, he would not have disapproved of their trip.

So, between them, they involved most of the true actors in the conspiracy. Parvus, who was again with Lenin in Petrograd in January, 1918, and Brockdorff-Rantzau, the German delegate to Paris who refused to sign the Versailles Peace Treaty and who later succeeded Count Mirbach as Ambassador to the Soviet Government after the latter's assassination, may be accepted as the originators of the plan of poisoning the first Russian Revolution by the infusion of Bolshevism. In general, the Imperial Government organized the adventure with the aid of German diplomatic officials in Switzerland. Scheidemann and Erzberger aided actively. The German General Staff was a party to the affair from the first and—as I have shown—an active military instrument in Russia after the Bolshevik Revolution.

The scenes attendant upon the distillation of the brew in Switzerland were for consideration apart; so also the post-armistice uses to which Germany put the potion in effort to lighten the penalty of war-defeat. I spent the winter of 1918–19 in France, Switzerland, Czechoslovakia, and Austria observing current phenomena and studying sources.

CHAPTER XXV

February 28 (Retrospect)—March 4, 1918. The Brest-Litovsk Peace. The Hundredth Day.

1.

FOR the course of events apart from the foray and its sequels, let us return to Thursday, February 28, 1918— the scene Petrograd in its last days as Bolshevik capital. From the Log of that day:

Ups and downs of rumor. Night report of Germans at Luga. Doubt it, but if so we may be caught. Will have to risk it. Fine cartoon of Hungarian edition printed. Austrians help in plan for distribution.

Reports of the day had seemed to show that the German advance was slowing down, and the night rumor was disconcerting, as we had decided that the fall of Luga must be signal for departure if we hoped to get away easily. Arrangement for that possible event had been placed in the hands of Malcolm Davis, and each of us carried a copy of his methodical instructions for rendezvous at an address on the Ligovskaya, to proceed to a place where sledges and fresh horses and drivers were kept waiting. Route was to be toward Lake Ladoga. Neither Bullard nor I, however, could convince ourselves that the Germans really intended to burden themselves with Petrograd. The peril, however, might be in sally, capture, and short occupation.

Fortunately we had our own scouting organization, enabling us to discount wild accounts in the badly served press. One of our men was at Luga itself and others toward threatened points of the so-called front, and we also had men posted at the railroad stations to question all arriving groups. None of our men verified the capture of Luga, and our doubts were reasonable. Delay of a few days in any German action now was all that I asked.

Routine department work went forward as if nothing mattered. Graham R. Taylor was jubilant over the gold lettering, *Americanskoe Buro Pechati* ("American Press Bureau") shining above the Nevsky and busied himself with detailed installation of telephone equipment, not knowing whether a call might ever be made over the lines by our own forces.

Arthur Bullard was ready for a cartoon campaign to complement the news and pamphlet service. He had found a Russian artist of talent, and the subject of the first cartoon was the German invasion of Russia. The German military hand was shown thrusting a bayonet through the palm of a prostrate Russian, who had dropped a banner upon which the German had planted his boot. Nothing about the cartoon was left doubtful. The word "Germany" appeared on the soldier's gauntlet. The word *Svoboda* ("Freedom") was inscribed upon the fallen banner. So the challenge was to Bolsheviks as well as Germans. If the former let that cartoon appear the act was hostile to Germany. If they prevented us from using it, the act was friendly to the German invader. A nice test, it seemed to us.

The Hotel d'Europe no longer was tenable, servants few and food less, and I moved on March 1 to the Military Mission, where there was cook and larder. Also it was essential that the few Americans be close together. Nearly all but Stephens of the National City Bank and his clerks, William Brown, Malcolm Davis, and Arno Dosch-Fleurot of the *New York World*, and Brackett Lewis of the Y.M.C.A., were under one roof at the Military Mission. They were Arthur Bullard, Graham Taylor, Guy Croswell Smith, Capt. John Hamilton Prince, and Lieutenant Bukovsky. Other members of the group had been sent to Vologda to open an office there. The Press Association correspondents also had accompanied the Ambassador.

The two young officers, Captain Prince and Lieutenant Bukovsky, had been left behind by Colonel Ruggles of the Military Mission, with instructions to keep in communication with the new embassy headquarters at Vologda as long as possible. Captain Prince, who looked like a New Englander, was the son of an American father, born in Russia of a Russian mother. Lieutenant Bukovsky was a sturdy young Polish-American from Chicago. Both at home in the Russian language, they were of the greatest possible use in our emergencies. If flight from Petrograd became necessary they would go with us.

AMERICAN PRESS BUREAU, PETROGRAD

Central office, on the Nevsky, the new headquarters opened the last week in February, 1918, after a winter spent in offices at 4 Gorokhovaya. Left to right: Arthur Bullard, William Adams Brown, Jr., Graham R. Taylor, Jr., Malcolm W. Davis.

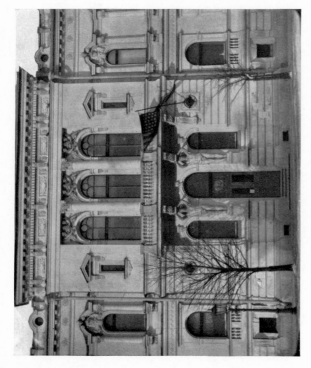

HEADQUARTERS, AMERICAN MILITARY MISSION TO RUSSIA

On the Fuhrstatskaya, not far from the American Embassy. After the departure of Embassy and Mission, the American group left in Petrograd centered here.

That evening at dinner one other was present for the last time—Capt. Lee Hagood, also of the Military Mission, about to seek exit by way of Finland. My Russian acquaintance, Adam, who was to go with the Captain to the border station of Beloöstrov, also was a guest. Adam I had not seen for many weeks. His wife, he said, was safe in the interior. I told him I hoped to attempt the Finnish route in a few days, barring German entrance, and he kindly offered to accompany me to the border when the time came. We had quite a celebration, having found flour, corn meal, and a variety of canned goods at the Mission. Our quarters were grandiose without being wholly comfortable. The house itself was the property of a wealthy Russian who kept a suite of rooms for himself and his family on an upper floor, well content to have the protection of the American flag above the building. The commodious salon had become a staff office, lined with desks, and the dining-room had become the living center. Heat was the lack but food went far to take its place.

Hagood's departure seemed good opportunity for removing some of my earlier photographic records outside of Russia, and when I explained the need, Hagood said he was willing to take the risk. The package was small and I did not believe he would be searched. To avoid that danger the suggestion was made that he drop the package on the floor of his compartment when he went into the control station, a newspaper tossed over it. I said I would take the material off his hands in Helsingfors in a week's time, if no accidents intervened. Otherwise he would make delivery to the State Department. The plan worked smoothly, although Helsingfors proved to be the limit of Hagood's journey.

Panic came to Petrograd Saturday, March 2. From the day's Log:

Cry of alarm in morning papers. Delegation returning, peace supposedly unsigned. Not until evening was it known that peace on horrible terms had been signed. Message relating to the affair both ludicrous and disgraceful. Scenes of the day—women with guns, not one but many, old and young. Tea and damnation. Poster blocked by Smolny. Warsaw station bombed.

This was Petrograd's worst day since revolutionary conflict

had raged in its streets, and in the degree of threat of foreign conquest the worst in all its history. By all visual evidence the city was about to be captured by the Germans. German planes had flown over the city for several days, low enough to make out their insignia, although their purpose apparently was observation. But on March 2 and again on the night of March 3, they dropped bombs upon the defenseless city, not a measured bombardment, yet aimed at particular targets, the thronged railroad stations noticeably. How many bombs were dropped altogether I did not know. Two I heard, and there were assertions that the total was five or six. Lives were reported lost at the Warsaw Station. I was unable to verify. The action of bombing was itself atrocious since the German military commanders should have known on Saturday that peace was being signed, and had no excuse whatsoever for not having on Sunday the knowledge of the formally accepted pact. In accord with the policy of "frightfulness" they wanted Petrograd to remember hours of dread and panic.

They did not quite succeed, being balked by the quality of fatalism in the Russian spirit. I moved about the city during the day without being hampered by any wildness of mobs. The Bolshevik populace, men and women, took arms, but not a rifle was served out to a *bourgeois* resident. The women seemed delighted to be considered as warriors. Their familiarity with their weapons was slight and soldiers and civilians alike willingly made lanes for them as they marched up and down the city blocks. There was not the least semblance of military order anywhere in the city.

A part of the afternoon I spent with Petrov in the Foreign Office, accounting for and checking out Americans. Stephens was ready to start his men and his securities for Vologda, and considerable red tape had to be cut to get the passports of the bank personnel *viséed* in a body and to secure the other certificates needful. Petrov, however, was in a good frame of mind and hurried matters along. His attitude, moreover, was not that of a man who expected an enemy force to rout him out. From which I drew the fair augury that peace was near. He claimed, however, to have no exact information, and was lightly insulting in his comments about the flights of the different Embassies.

The last of the Embassies of the *Entente* had now gone, *Chargé* Lindley having taken the British staff into Finland the night of February 28–March 1, closely trailed by the train carrying Ambassador Noulens of France and his *cortège*. Just a matter of hours separated the departure of these two trains. The first got through the civil war barrier in Finland. The second did not. On one of these nights, February 28, March 1, or March 2, I went to the British Embassy and witnessed the spectacle of the burning of such records of the Embassy as could not be easily transported, a lurid courtyard scene, men feeding sheaf on sheaf of papers into the flames. The men doing the work were several young officers left behind by the Military Mission. They had a railroad car ready to be attached to the last train that might leave Petrograd. An interchange of arrangements was made with them, they to hold railroad space if we could go by rail, our party to hold sledge space for them if railroad exit was barred.

The building of the American Embassy had been transferred meantime to the care of the neutral Norwegian Ministry, and the flag of Norway floated from the staff above it.

"Tea and damnation" certainly expressed the feelings of all of us on Saturday afternoon. We cursed the peace, although it brought us physical safety.

In the evening, also, Bullard brought account of new troubles of our own. Our presses printing the anti-German cartoon had been stopped during the afternoon by direct order from Smolny. Bullard had hastened out to the Bolshevik center to ask explanation and to seek removal of the ban. He was greeted with smiles and shoulder-shruggings and the placid statement that the cartoon was not "permissible." Were we stopped utterly? No, the ban only was on the cartoon. To save other work, the cartoon plates were lifted from the presses. But watch over us was haphazard. Graham Taylor the same day was able to get printed in the Bolshevik press cables from America protesting against the impending peace. Such were the anomalies of the Russian hour.

A bare bulletin from a lesser member of the Peace Delegation, the gist of which was that the surrender had been accepted, was the first word that crisis of war was flitting. Sokolnikov, the head of the delegation, was not heard from, and indeed official announcement of peace was not made until Monday, March 4. Such parts of the city as heard the Saturday night report received it skeptically, pointing to the German plane, hovering whitely in the dusk. The bombing of the Warsaw Station came during the evening and was taken as a material denial of the peace of words.

Oral assent to the forced treaty, however, was given at Brest-Litovsk on the afternoon of Saturday, and the treaty was executed on Sunday morning, March 3. There was no debate. The Russians, ushered into German, Austrian, Bulgarian, and Turkish presence in the way that prisoners would be lined up in court, asked what the terms were. They were read to them, and again, like prisoners receiving sentence, they were asked if they had anything to say. Sokolnikov, as spokesman, said they had nothing of argument to offer and would sign the treaty as presented to them. In the morning they signed.

The members of the Russian delegation were Gregory Sokolnikov, L. Karakhan, George Chicherin, and Gregory Petrovsky.

The signatories for Germany were Foreign Secretary Von Kuhlman, Dr. Von Rosenberg, Major General Hoffman, and Captain Horn; for Austro-Hungary, Count Czernin, Foreign Secretary, Privy Councilor Von Kapos-Mere, and General Von Bacsany; for Bulgaria, Andrea Toschev, Ambassador to Vienna, Col. Peter Gantschev, and Dr. Theodore Anastassov; for Turkey, Ibrahim Hakki Pasha and Zekki Pasha.

The treaty, complete in its public form:

Article I. Germany, Austria-Hungary, Bulgaria and Turkey on the one side and Russia on the other declare that the state of war between them is ended. They are resolved to henceforth live in peace and friendship with one another.

Article II. The contracting parties will refrain from every agitation against the government or the political and military institutions of the other party. This obligation holds also, in so far as it is incumbent upon Russia, for those districts occupied by the Powers of the Quadruple Alliance.

Article III. Those districts lying west of the line agreed upon by the contracting parties and formerly belonging to Russia shall no longer be subject to Russian sovereignty. The line agreed upon is clear from the map attached as an essential part to this treaty

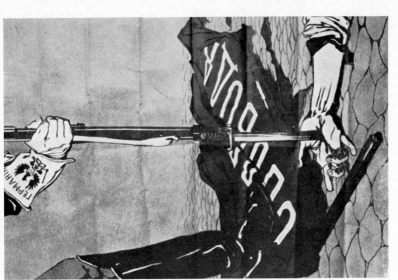

A SUPPRESSED POSTER

This poster was banned by the Bolsheviks on March 2, 1918, by an order from Smolny Institute. *Svoboda*, the Russian word for liberty, appears on the red flag. The German bayonet pierces the hand of the Russian people from whom the banner has been torn.

AMERICAN EMBASSY BUILDING

Fuhrstatskaya 34, Petrograd. Showing the Norwegian flag flying after the building was intrusted to the Norwegian Minister upon the departure of Ambassador Francis and his staff on February 26, 1918. The second floor bow windows looked out from his office.

of peace. (Enclosure I.)* The exact establishment of this line will be insured by a German-Russian Commission. No obligation whatsoever toward Russia shall accrue to those said districts from their former appertainance to Russia. Russia renounces any and all interference in the internal conditions and relations of these districts. Germany and Austro-Hungary intend to determine the future fate of these districts in concurrence with their inhabitants.

Article IV. Germany is ready, as soon as general peace has been concluded and the Russian demobilization has been completely carried out, to evacuate that territory East of the line designated in Article III, in so far as Article IV does not otherwise determine.

Russia will do everything in its power to secure the immediate evacuation of the East Anatolian Provinces and their legal return to Turkey.

The districts Erdehan, Kars, and Batum will be likewise evacuated by Russian troops without delay. Russia will not interfere in the reformation of the internal and external legal relations of these districts, but will leave it to the inhabitants of these districts to carry out this reformation in concurrence with the neighboring states, especially Turkey.

Article V. Russia will without delay carry out the complete demobilization of its army, including those divisions newly formed by the present Government. Furthermore, Russia will either transfer its war vessels to Russian harbors and leave them there until the general conclusion of peace or immediately disarm them. War vessels of countries still remaining in a state of war with the Powers of the Quadruple Alliance will, in so far as they are within Russian jurisdiction, be treated as Russian vessels.

The closed war zone in the Arctic Ocean shall remain in effect until the general conclusion of peace. In the Baltic Sea and in the Black Sea as far as the Russian power extends the removal of mines will be immediately begun. Commercial navigation upon those parts of these seas is free and will be resumed at once. Mixed commissions will be appointed for the establishment of more definite determinations and especially for the announcement of safe courses for merchant ships. The courses of navigation are to be kept permanently free from floating mines.

Article VI. Russia binds itself to immediately conclude peace with the Republic of the People of Ukraine and to recognize the treaty of peace between this state and the Powers of the Quad-

* Facsimile of the map not made public.

ruple Alliance. Ukrainian territory will be evacuated without delay by the Russian troops and the Russian Red Guard. Russia will cease all agitation or propaganda against the Government or the public institutions of the Republic of the People of Ukraine.

Esthonia and Livonia shall likewise be evacuated by the Russian troops and the Russian Red Guard without delay. The Eastern boundary of Esthonia runs in general along the Narva River, the Eastern boundary of Livonia runs in general through Lake Petpus and Lake Pskof to its Southeastern corner, then over Lake Luban in the direction of Livenhof on the Dvina. Esthonia and Livonia will be occupied by a German police force until security has been guaranteed by the institutions of the country itself, and the public order has been restored. Russia will free at once all the inhabitants of Esthonia and Livonia who have been imprisoned or carried away, and guarantees the safe return of all such inhabitants of Esthonia and Livonia.

Finland and the Aland Islands shall be immediately evacuated by the Russian troops and the Russian Red Guard, and the harbors of Finland by the Russian fleet and the Russian naval forces. As long as the ice shall prevent the transfer of Russian war vessels to Russian harbors, small commands only shall remain upon these war vessels. Russia will cease all agitation and propaganda against the Government or the public institutions of Finland.

The fortifications established upon the Aland Islands shall be removed as soon as possible. An especial agreement between Germany, Finland, Russia, and Sweden shall be made concerning the non-fortifying of these islands as well as their disposition otherwise in military respect and with respect to navigation. The contracting parties agree that at the express wish of Germany other countries bordering upon the Baltic Sea may also be included in this matter.

Article VII. Assuming the fact that Persia and Afghanistan are free and independent countries, the contracting parties bind themselves to respect the political and economic independence and the territorial integrity of these countries.

Article VIII. The prisoners of war taken by both sides shall be dismissed to their homes. The regulation of questions shall ensue through separate agreements provided for in Article XII.*

Article IX. The contracting parties mutually renounce compensation of their war expenses, that is, the national expendi-

* Inclosures and separate agreements not made public.

tures for the conduct of the war; as well as compensation for war damages, that is, such damages which they and their subjects have suffered in the war zones through military measures, including all requisitions made in hostile country.

Article X. The diplomatic and consular relations between the contracting parties shall be resumed immediately after the ratification of the treaty of peace. Especial agreements reserve the mutual right of acceptance of the consuls of both parties.

Article XI. The economic relations between the Powers of the Quadruple Alliance and Russia are based upon provisions contained in Enclosures 2 to 5,* Enclosure 2 being for the German-Russian, Enclosure 3 for the Austro-Hungarian-Russian, Enclosure 4 for the Bulgarian-Russian, and Enclosure 5 for the Turkish-Russian relations.

Article XII. The restoration of public and private legal relations, the exchange of prisoners of war and civilian prisoners, the question of amnesty, as well as the question of the treatment of merchant ships shall be regulated by *separate agreements with Russia,* which form an essential part of the present treaty of peace and which shall, as far as feasible, come into force simultaneously with this treaty.

Article XIII. In the interpretation of this treaty the German and Russian text shall be authoritative for the relations between Germany and Russia, the Hungarian and Russian text for the relations between Austro-Hungary and Russia, the Bulgarian and Russian text for the relations between Bulgaria and Russia, and the Turkish and Russian text for the relations between Turkey and Russia.

Article XIV. The present treaty of peace shall be ratified; the documents of ratification shall be exchanged in Berlin as soon as practicable. The Russian Government pledges itself to undertake, at the wish of one of the Powers of the Quadruple Alliance, the exchange of documents of ratification within two weeks. The treaty of peace, unless its articles, its enclosures or the supplemental agreements otherwise determine, comes into force with its ratification.

In witness whereof the plenipotentiaries have with their own hands signed this treaty.

Executed in five-fold original in Brest-Litovsk the third of March, 1918.

The text of the treaty, in translation, was that received by the State Department at Washington. The treaty became pub-

* *Ibid.*

lic soon after it was made. In Petrograd it was published on March 6.

Territorial seizures were plain in the document itself. Penalties added to the treaty first offered Trotsky at Brest-Litovsk were the forced acceptance of the German treaty with the Ukraine, allowance of a German protectorate over Livonia and Estonia, abandonment of Red revolutionary effort in Finland, and cession of the oil regions of Batum.

Money indemnities intended to reach the sum of six billion marks or about two and a half billion rubles, were hidden in Article XII and the included separate agreements, in the guise of German property confiscated in the Revolution, German civilian war losses in various categories, and inflated costs of prisoner maintenance. How many of these pertinent agreements were reached between Count Mirbach and Lenin at Petrograd, rather than submitted at the winter sessions of the Peace Delegations at Brest-Litovsk, was problematical. Perhaps all of them were arrived at thus. At any rate Count Mirbach was appointed German Ambassador to Russia because of his familiarity with all these economic stipulations. Deliveries of goods, either in addition to money assessment or in equivalent, were nominated also in the separate agreements, the proof being that such deliveries were at once begun.

The amount of the money indemnity was admitted in the supplemental treaties which Russia signed with Germany in August, 1918—treaties of military alliance, defensive and offensive.

So the "Peace Projects" of Lenin and Trotsky came to a logical apex.

Tragedy and farce, the story of Brest-Litovsk was ended.

2.

ARNO DOSCH-FLEUROT was with me on final trip to Smolny Sunday morning. We called on "Chief of Police" Bill Shatov, who, now that Petrograd was freed of the threat of Germans, looked for a shortened and a serene term of office. Order, he assured us, would be kept as long as he was boss, and we believed him.

I looked my last on the halls of Smolny, first seat of Bolshevik power in Russia, now about to become a memory to Bolsheviks themselves. Here Trotsky had strutted and here Lenin had spun. Here I had listened to the drone of monotone oratory and to more New Yorkese vernacular than I ever had thought could be exported to one spot.

Odd, twisted, jangled Smolny, a bedlam that Hogarth should have lived to draw. One might with smiling patience penetrate most of its recesses except the interlacing maze that concealed Lenin. Of an evening while Trotsky was trying to spellbind the Germans at Brest-Litovsk I have sat on his high desk, drumming my heels on the side while I listened to the gossip budget of one of his messengers, just arrived, and wondered what was going on in the minds of the big, solemn-faced girl, Sholopina, and her bustling but not very busy staff. Trotsky had one trick of the time-saving executive. Chairs were few. Callers in delegations had to stand.

Whether Trotsky and Lenin already were on their way to Moscow I did not take the trouble to make Sunday morning inquiry. But they, too, were done with Smolny. Moscow was to be the scene of the ratification of the "Peace."

For us Petrograd no longer was a city that must be abandoned. Sledge plans could be discarded. The exiled officials at Vologda might return if they cared to. News and printing work could continue. We would not have the favors the Germans would receive and our status might be precarious, but it was tenable. Utility remained the sole issue. And, with the Bolshevik headship moving to Moscow, the utility of Petrograd as a center was vanishing. I gave the orders Monday, March 4, for a measured removal to Moscow, a transfer that would not be complete for several weeks, until printing jobs in Petrograd were finished.

The last of my days in Petrograd had come. My course henceforth led elsewhere. Two essential tasks remained for the day's doing. One was to report to Washington the fact situation of German purpose for Petrograd and Russia. In the message I reiterated the warning I had sent on February 25 that Lenin would construe the terms of peace in such wise that he would be military supporter of Germany, refraining from revolutionary agitation against the Central Empires and stimulating it against the Allies; and permitting Germany the use of Arctic and Siberian bases. The Germans, I continued, would leave Petrograd in the possession of Russians as long as they deemed the Russian attitude satisfactory. The city was in fact a hostage for Bolshevik good behavior, as it could be taken any time, a situation, too, that accounted for the decision of the Bolsheviks not to allow the "Peace" to interrupt the trek of the Government to Moscow. The Russian status, I concluded, permitted the Germans to launch a western offensive any day henceforth they willed.

The difficulty was to get the message through. The code room force was gone to Vologda. We had codes but we judged the old ones to be useless, probably already decipherable in the Bolshevik telegraph rooms through which the message would go. We had, however, one unused code and in this code Captain Prince and I laboriously incased the dispatch, addressing it to the State Department with inner direction to the General Staff, and routing it over the single land wire leading to the Alexandrovsk cable. I did not keep a copy of the cable, destroying also the sheets on which we wrote the intermediate steps of code transfer.

I did not know for weeks whether or not the cable went to destination. But when I reached Christiania a "Thank You" message came from Washington, stating also that the cable came through three days after its date.

The second need of the day was to assure safe transfer out of Russia of the material taken in the Smolny raid and of other data not intrusted to Captain Hagood. Failure could not be risked and a device was necessary. In my belief the credit for the plan finally adopted belonged to Lieutenant Bukovsky, but many years afterward I learned that the accident of a pleasant remark by the Norwegian Minister, who had become the custodian of the American Embassy property, led him to make a report of the circumstance; and so decision followed.

Both Bukovsky and Malcolm Davis already knew of the problem facing us; and Davis, who spoke Russian, had volunteered to play the rôle of provision carrier to Americans isolated in Finland and precede me across the border that very day, a parcel of papers bound at the small of his back.

The Lieutenant and Davis started together in the morning for the Finland Station, stopping on the way at the Norwegian

Ministry on the former's errand to see whether he could have a letter included with the Norwegian courier mail. As he came out he told Davis, who had not entered with him, that the Minister had said that the official pouch was at our disposal. The two talked over the new possibilities, and agreed that it was Lieutenant Bukovsky's duty to report back to me at the Military Mission. He did.

The opportunity to return some of their own coin to the Germans was apparent. We all remembered the *spurlos versenkt* incident. The question was whether Lieutenant Bukovsky could "carry off" the scene of returning immediately to the Norwegian Minister to ask the advantage of his offer. Bukovsky was sure that he could act at ease.

So everything I wanted to send out was put in one package, sealed with embassy seals and directed to the American Minister at Christiania, with an inner wrapper addressed to me, carrying also the instruction to hold the parcel for my arrival. Lieutenant Bukovsky was sent to the Norwegian Minister to ask of him the courtesy of forwarding the package by the courier we knew he was sending that day, and performed the mission with aplomb.

One rite remained, waiting on mutual promise. I went to say goodbye to my dapper friend, Colonel Samsonov. With gay snap of fingers at all Bolsheviks, he did me the honor to dress in his officer's uniform for the occasion. The winter sun shone through the windows of his apartment and shot flashes of light from the metal ware of his equipment. Trim and erect he stood in salute, and then we laid hands together in greeting and farewell.

The sun was setting and the spires of Peter and Paul and the Admiralty agleam as we drove toward the Finland station across the Neva. Miserable Petrograd was roofed with beauty for a passing hour, its final scene for me.

Bullard and Taylor, Prince and Bukovsky grouped around me in the train compartment. We talked lightly, but my heart was heavy. From Bullard particularly I hated to part. The winter had welded us close, and I feared, too, what Russia might yet hold for him. Yet I had reliance, too. He was careful, reflective, and wise, and a man of action, withal.

Adam was also there, getting his soft-spoken way with

guards and trainmen. The train finally moved, as even Russian trains will, and Adam and I were off. One barrier lay ahead, the Beloöstrov control station at the Finnish border, which we reached in the middle of the evening. In spite of precautions several troublesome papers, besides telegraph texts received from Colonel Samsonov that afternoon, had not been included in the Christiania package. On a personal search I was vulnerable. My exit documents, however, were exceptional. Petrov had seen to that, and I believed I would be treated with respect. So it proved. The examination of passport and attendant stamped orders was rapid and routine.

If I had not seen other persons roughly treated in the control room, I would have thought that border passage was an easy matter. The chief victim was a young nonofficial Englishman, whom I had known slightly as the correspondent for a London newspaper. He had missed the embassy train and was trying to catch up with it, having heard definitely, he told me later, that the train was blocked in Finland. For some reason unknown, he said, to him, he was suspect. He was gone through thoroughly, a process with which I could not interfere. When nothing incriminating was found on him or in his luggage, however, Adam was able to reach him with word to place his bags in my compartment on the train.

There we put him in the inside corner and waited for the last ordeal, passage of Red Guards through the train. In preparation for that Adam chalked the Russian for "official compartment" on the door of the car, with the word "Amerikansky" prominent. Then when the guards came, I closed myself in and with signs indicated the Englishman as included in the diplomatic protection, holding my *laissez-passer* outfit where the stamps could be seen. Adam, who had wished me well, did his duty of debate in the corridor, and we were left in peace. The gracious Adam went away with the Guards as the train started. At Terioki, with Finnish Red Guards, the scene was repeated successfully.

At three o'clock in the morning at a junction, the pleasant and now serene young Englishman left me, to take train for Tammerfors. If I could have gone with him instead of being obliged to meet Captain Hagood at Helsingfors, I would have been in Stockholm in eight days. For *Chargé* Lindley got a flag of truce for the passage of his train on March 7. Yet at the end of such swift travel I would have found myself in an agony of unrest. For the Norwegian courier, my parcel bearer, intending passage from Abo, was blocked at Helsingfors. Fate guided me usefully to his side.

My hope was that the errand to Helsingfors might be completed in time to enable me to join the British train before it left Tammerfors. Or, if that route closed, and the Germans refrained briefly from taking the Aland Islands route from Abo by sledge over the ice to the islands seemed possible. Between the islands and the Swedish coast was open water, boats plying irregularly.

Dosch-Fleurot, going out the same day, concluded that neither prospect was inviting or certain, and elected to put his chances on a sledge sally around Lake Ladoga and northward until he should pass in Russian territory to the east of the mid-Finland battle zone, thence into White Finland until he should intercept the railroad line to Torneo. That journey had adventurous lure but would take three weeks or a month. If luck were with me I might be in Stockholm in a week. I chose Finland. Yet he was the faster traveler. Torneo proved to be the one way out. When in my season I reached there, I read his name on the control records as having passed the border some days before, and in Stockholm he came down the hotel steps to welcome me. He had experienced cold and travel fatigue, but had met no other obstacles.

That night on the train, my useful portable typewriter left behind for office use, I placed note paper on a portfolio and scrawled with fountain pen:

March 4. Getaway day. Report German plan for Petrograd. Farewell call on the dapper man. Beautiful sunset scene over the Neva on sleigh route. My kind escort to Bieloöstrov. Comfortable exit after all. Leave permits for balance of party to go.

AFTER THE HUNDRED DAYS

CHAPTER XXVI

The Escape from Finland.

IN Helsingfors, at a clean, cheery hotel, I sat before a small table facing a sunny window in the late morning of March 5 and looked at the first egg I had seen since early November. Much as I hungered for it, I let my eyes have the first feast. Then I tapped the end of the shell above the egg-cup until I had opening for the tiny spoon, and dusted salt and pepper into the soft content while I gravely stirred the spoon. Not a sensation did I intend to miss. Twenty minutes I took for the eating of the egg, savoring each sip. Out of Russia, I was rid of Russian Bolshevism. So at least ran my jubilant thought.

A few hours later I began to suspect otherwise. Helsingfors was a brisk, western European city, orderly of aspect. Yet its civilization, too, hung in balance, barbaric threat hovering close. The city was under Finnish Bolshevik control. The difference between Petrograd and Helsingfors was that the Finnish brothers were so little sure of themselves that they had as yet done little in the way of economic confiscations. The wheels of industry had stopped, but the Bolsheviks had not had time to put the theories of destruction into practice, all of their energies given to the defense of their long battle line to the north, against which the White army of General Mannerheim was pressing harder day by day. Meantime the *bourgeois* population of southern Finland lived in dread of massacre, a death that came to many.

Hunting up Captain Hagood, I got humorous, acid, and genuine welcome from him, with the information that after one visit from Red Guards, the intended severity of whose search he had mitigated at the cost of half a bottle of good brandy, he had hastened to place in the safe at the Consulate the package of photographs I had intrusted to him. They had been lying, he said, in the top of an opened bag when the Red Guards paid their visit. He had dragged the brandy bottle from the same bag and shoved the photographs farther inside. No damage had been done except to his nerves. The Red

Guards, it seemed, had adopted the pleasant Petrograd custom of darting around the hotels. The implied suggestion was good. I said I would also pay a call on the Consul and leave some keepsakes with him until I was ready to leave Helsingfors.

Just how soon that would be became at once problematical. Hagood had found no exit, having just been warned away from Abo. His news was that a German fleet was due at the Aland Islands. He had about made up his mind to return to Petrograd, and indeed did so a few days later, thereby deferring by several months his arrival in the United States.

Even then I could have reached the British Embassy train, but before the day was over as I checked up the foreigners at the different hotels I found that the Norwegian courier was among them. Within sight of him I determined to stay. In disarrangement of my plans all my eggs were in one basket and I with them.

I wondered that night if I could get contact again with headquarters in Petrograd. The next morning I found I could do so—easily, by long-distance telephone. For three days I had communication at will with the office. Then on the fourth day, the wires either were cut or ordered out of service. But the time had been long enough for my purposes. I had found out what was going on in Petrograd, had learned that our last hope of films was lost, the delayed Bernstein having arrived without them, and had ordered Guy Croswell Smith to join me at Helsingfors, having decided to transfer him to Stockholm. Also, Bullard reported, Robins had returned to Petrograd for a day, and then gone again to Vologda. He had inquired about me.

In Finland conditions continued to grow worse. On the seventh, German craft lay off the Aland Islands. On that day, also, the British Embassy party of about forty persons was allowed to pass the lines at Tammerfors. According to the Allied plan this was to be the first of a succession of parties to pass through. But on March 8 all permits, either for passage on from, or to, Tammerfors itself, were revoked. We were told that the order was given because a Red Guard soldier accompanying the British flag-bearing party had been fired on and wounded by the Whites. This was obviously an excuse as the flag-bearing party had gone a day ahead of the main party, which still had been allowed to proceed unhindered. In the days following, in fact during the entire period of our restraint, we were told by various Red leaders that they had no objection to our departure, but that their subordinates accused all foreigners of being spies who would bear information of military value to their White Guard enemies.

We also were told that the foreign parties were so large that they were a nuisance near the front lines, and that the operations could not be halted for the several days that would be required to get them through the lines. The French, the Italian, and the Belgian Embassy parties all were ordered back from Tammerfors to a junction point, Toyola, in the rear. Here at Toyola they remained on their trains for three weeks, then gave up the effort at advance and returned to Russia, finally getting out during the summer by way of Archangel. More than five hundred persons were on the combined trains. Their plight at Toyola was most uncomfortable and their food slight.

Smith joined me on March 10. He brought word that for some reason the Bolsheviks had halted at the border and searched in defiance of diplomatic immunity the Norwegian courier next in order of departure after the one already under my eye in Helsingfors. The excuse given was that the courier was suspected of carrying gold coin, which was proscribed. The Bolsheviks found no gold. I trusted for more disturbances of civil war and hoped that amid them one courier and I were well lost. That day I enrolled the courier as member of the American party and charged Smith with the oversight of him and his baggage. Neither one or the other was out of our sight in the weeks following, and his courier sacks were our particular charge. We carried them when we hired others to tote our own goods. The courier, a good-natured country boy, was delighted with our attentions, even if he never understood them.

One party and one party only—twelve Americans, a Norwegian courier, a Rumanian *attaché*, and the odd refugee family of a naturalized Russian-American—got through the war lines after the gates shut down behind the British Embassy train.

In Washington, May 27, 1918, I wrote in report to Chairman George Creel:

This is the story of the escape of the American party. It comprised all of the Americans in Finland except American Consul Haynes and Vice-Consul Waldo at Helsingfors, who in event of German occupation were protected by agreement made with Germany through Sweden.

The attention of the world was so engaged with the affairs of the Great War that it overlooked the territorially small but cruel war which broke out in Finland in the last days of January. It was, like that of Russia, a war of proletarian Revolutionists against the *Bourgeois*. Unlike that of Russia it was a real war. Both sides had external aid. The Reds had artillery, rifles and ammunition in abundance from Russia. The Whites had supplies from Sweden and additions of men, guns, and ammunition from Germany, which returned to Finland a body of young Finnish officers who had been serving in the German army. The White Guards soon controlled northern Finland down to a line beginning at Mentuolota and Bjorneborg on the Baltic Sea, paralleling to Tammerfors the line of railroad connecting these points and then dipping to the eastward until it approached within a few miles of Viborg, the big industrial city of southeastern Finland. From this point adjacent to Viborg the line continued to the Russian border near the north of Lake Ladoga. The through railroad line from Torneo at the topmost point of Finland to Petrograd was cut some thirty kilometers above Tammerfors, and this thrifty manufacturing city became the strategic point of contention between the two armies. Each line was strongly held.

During the month of February occasional parties were allowed, under flag of truce, to pass between the lines. Moreover during February several boat loads of refugees, largely Swedish, were taken by Swedish craft from Mentuolota. These facts, which were well-known in Petrograd, accounted for the influx of foreigners into Finland when the general evacuation of Petrograd began before the German advance.

The Americans came into Finland at varying times, several of them as early as the middle of February. When the trap was sprung they were scattered between Helsingfors and Tammerfors. In the first ten days of March they gradually located each other. Conferring by wire, they determined tb concentrate at some spot remote from the congested points where other foreigners were being held. Bjorneborg was chosen as the rendezvous. At Helsingfors were Frederic A. Corse and family; W. T. Bull, a Californian who had been selling wooden legs to Russian crippled soldiers; Smith, myself, and John J. Tyer, the last named a South

THE AMERICAN PARTY AT WHITE HEADQUARTERS AHLAINEN, FINLAND

Photograph taken on March 25, 1918, the morning after passage through the Red lines. Front, left to right: Captain and Mrs. Norman Stines, sister of Mrs. Corse, Captain Walter V. Crosley, U.S.N., Mrs. Corse, Mrs. Crosley, Mr. Sisson, Guy Croswell Smith. Rear, left to right: John J. Tyer, Hilma Ronti, W. T. Bull, Rumanian *Attaché* Guranesco, Finnish Commander Talvela, Frederic A. Corse.

Carolinian who for seven years had been the head of the British-American Tobacco Company in Finland and now must become a refugee. At Tammerfors were Captain Walter Crosley, United States Naval Attaché at Petrograd, and his wife; Captain Norman Stines, of the United States Military Mission, and his wife; and Roger Simmons, government forestry expert. At Abo were two other Americans, Major Harry Emery of the United States Military Mission (Professor Emery of Yale), and his wife. Major Emery and his wife were the only ones not destined to reach the rendezvous. Although counselled by Mr. Corse, who went to Abo for that purpose, that the Aland Islands were about to be captured, Major Emery persisted in attempting that route. The Germans got to the Islands first. He was taken prisoner and transported to Danzig. [Note: He was released or exchanged in the late summer.] His wife was allowed to go to Stockholm.

Upon us at Helsingfors fell the task of securing permits for travel in interior Finland and of impressing the Red rulers with the necessity of giving us a chance to make our own arrangements to be at a place accessible for rescue by sea or for parleying with the Whites for flag of truce between the fronts. Our first attempt to secure permission to leave Helsingfors was met by refusal from Sorola, the Red Foreign Minister. After consultation we resorted to subterfuge and sent Consul Haynes to tell the Foreign Office that we were confident it would be only a matter of a few days after our arrival at Mentuolota, the port of Bjorneborg, before a ship would come from Sweden for us. We stated we had asked for a ship. This was true. Consul Haynes sent the cable to Minister Morris at Stockholm, and I cabled guardedly to the Minister suggesting that he give us every hope possible, believing he would get an idea of our project and not send a discouraging reply.

Vice-Consul Waldo returned energetically to the attack on the Foreign Office on this new line of campaign, and on March 11 we had the permit for departure from Helsingfors. On the list covered by the permit I had placed the names of Americans in Tammerfors as well as those in Helsingfors, and also the name of the Norwegian courier. Hagood also was listed in the event that he should change his mind and take chances with us instead of returning to Russia. Tyer was left off because he had papers of his own and was to remain briefly in Helsingfors for a communication post, to follow us on signal. Consul Haynes also placed the name of an unknown "American and family" on the list. The name was Szwerdovsk, and to my inquiry he replied that he had been pestered by a naturalized American, and that he wished I would help him out by taking the family along. As the permit had secured us a special train, the request seemed reasonable. Not until later did I recognize a handicap. I continued in my report:

We left Helsingfors on Tuesday morning, March 12, without any regret. It is a bright, American appearing city, of essentially modern appearance, but the cloud of civil war hung low over it. The partially dismantled Russian fleet lay in the snug harbor, some ships flying the red flag of Russian Socialism and some the black flag of Russian Anarchy. Between the twenty thousand Russian sailors and the Finnish Red Guards there was continual minor but turbulent warfare. The sailors were under orders from Russia to abandon their ships and return by rail to Petrograd.* They wished to go carrying their arms. The Red Guards needed the rifles in Finland and disarmed them whenever they had the force. Sometimes a departing body would yield up its arms and sometimes show sufficient fight to keep them. The retention, however, was only temporary as they were universally disarmed by large Red Guard bodies beyond Viborg, distant a night's journey from Helsingfors.

The Finnish Red Guards also in these latter days disliked the sailors for the amount of food they ate. Their committees attempted to ration the sailors but after one experience did not visit any more of the ships. That visit ended by their being thrown from the ship's deck to the very hard ice below. The result of this mutual ill-feeling was that the streets of Helsingfors were a fighting ground each night. The sailors would land with a machine gun and throw streams of bullets up the streets leading from the harbor front. The Red Guards would shelter themselves on the roofs and try their luck at picking off sailors with rifles. The fatalities on neither side were proportionate to the noise. Residents of the town had one obvious rule for safety—to keep off the streets after dark. They did.

* Despite these orders the heroic Admiral Stchastny saved the fleet from the Germans, running the ships out of harbor with skeleton crews as the ice broke up and bringing them safe to Kronstadt. He was shot at Moscow by order of Trotsky, in June, ostensibly on a charge of conspiracy unrelated to the salvaging of the fleet. Appendix, pp. 433–444.

There was chance, too, each night that the British submarines, several of which were in the harbor, would be blown up. This was to be the last act of the British officers in command of them. The submarines were blown up while we were still in Finland, two weeks after we left Helsingfors.

Our train (consisting of engine, baggage car and two second class coaches) reached Tammerfors in the middle of the afternoon. Captain Crosley was on the platform but he told us that the Tammerfors group would not be allowed to join us. He knew no reason for the decision and hoped he might be able to change it in a few days. We told him we would go to Bjorneborg and wait for him.

We reached Bjorneborg at nine o'clock at night, after a journey begun at eight o'clock in the morning. There we were told that we could not go to Mentuolota as that village was without food, and that we would be allowed to stay in Bjorneborg only twenty-four hours. We slept on that cheerful information and then set to work in the morning to make it untruthful. Luck and a bright faced Red Guard whom we had brought with us as an escort from Helsingfors were both on our side.

Eric Mellin, the Red Guard, had been in the United States. We had all taken pains to make Eric like us. I had straightened him out on a bit of American geography. He had a dentist brother in Virginia, Minn. He did not know what *Minn.* was or where, but believed it was some little distance from Washington. I came from Minnesota myself and told him in as much detail as I could imagine what sort of a town Virginia was, giving it a fine reputation. His own knowledge was confined to New York City. He wished he was back there. We all wished we were there with him. We told him that our chances of getting there depended upon him, and that naturally his chances of having friends when he should return to the United States would be increased if we were there ahead of him. He saw the point clearly, and when he started for Red Guard headquarters he told us he was going to convince the people there that we should be allowed to stay at Bjorneborg.

We never knew what story he told but had the impression that he may have exaggerated our importance to suit his argumentative needs. He delivered. He brought us back word that we could stay in Bjorneborg "until a boat came for us." We were not sure but what this was a right to a life-time residence, for we received telegraphic word from Tyer that day that no boat was coming. Minister Morris had not comprehended my cautionary telegram.

Since our stay in Bjorneborg was apt to be indefinite, Smith and I moved to the Otavo hotel during the day, Wednesday, as a test of what liberty of action the party could have. When we were not interfered with, the other Americans—Corse, his wife and sister-in-law, and Bull—and the Norwegian courier followed us to the hotel the next day. The cars we left to the naturalized Russian-American and his wife and babies.

He had lived as a shoemaker in Chicago for ten years prior to 1914, when he had started out to return to Russian Poland. Journeying by a devious northern route he had gotten no further than Archangel, where he had married a young peasant woman. Finding Russian conditions uncongenial after the Bolshevik Revolution he had decided to return to the United States by way of Petrograd and Finland. At the Russian frontier he had been searched and ten thousand rubles taken from him. He had been allowed to keep five hundred rubles and five hundred more had been secreted in the diaper of the youngest baby. So in war time he was seeking to reach the United States on the equivalent of less than a hundred dollars. Nor did he do so badly on the first stages. We kept him in food on one of our cars, which we never used again, and he lived comfortably. Whatever may have happened to him afterward, his capital was intact when we delivered him and his brood in Stockholm. For reward those of us who desired to learned from him some new curses for Bolsheviks and how to spit and swear at the same time.

On Friday, March 15, Minister Morris wired us that Emery was taken on the Aland Islands and warned us against any effort whatsoever to cross by sea. We replied with a request that he send a Legation Attaché via Torneo to the White Guard Headquarters in the north of Finland to try to arrange for a flag of truce. He wired back affirmatively. One of the peculiarities of our situation was that while we were not allowed to use the telephone we were able to telegraph freely up to two days before we left town, when the telegraph office was seized by soldiers and we were warned to keep a block away from it. Nothing came of the endeavor to get White Headquarters to order a flag of truce for us. The first news Lieutenant Thorling, Assistant Military Attaché, had of us at Sunioki, the Headquarters town, was when we telephoned from Christinastadt that we had gotten through.

Our whole party finally got together on Saturday, March 16, when Captain Crosley and his wife, Captain Stines and his wife, and Roger Simmons were permitted to come from Tammerfors. They had made an attempt the day before but had been almost forcibly taken from the train after they and their baggage were on. They were given no reason for the discourteous act. Then they were told the next morning they could come and they made haste to do so.

With them came Alexander Guranesco, the Secretary of the Rumanian Legation. He had been held in Finland since January 29, when Minister Diamandi, with a Rumanian colony of three hundred women and children, had been driven out of Petrograd on ten hours' notice. When the Minister and his staff had been allowed to proceed, Guranesco had been left behind, presumably to look after the balance of the refugees. There was considerable mystery about the circumstances which led to the Red Guard permission for him to join our party. We were not inclined to delve too much, however, for on translating his pass we found that it read that he was to be allowed "to pass through the lines with the American party." This gave us the first definite intimation that if we had patience we would be able to get through.

There were several Rumanian families in lodgings at Bjorneborg but Guranesco made no effort to have us add them to our party. These Rumanians quite naturally suspected us of coming to Bjorneborg with a definite project in mind and they hung persistently about us. We would have liked to have helped them and could not, though we were truthful in telling them from day to day that we had no encouragement. We did not. Instead we did have hope and determination, but neither of these qualities did we feel justified in sharing with them. When finally we did leave the town, we went in early morning, and I often have regretted the disappointment which must have submerged these unfortunate folks when they came to the hotel that day and found us gone.

The last member of Captain Crosley's group was the most important of all—Miss Hilma Ronti. She was a Finnish girl whom Captain Crosley had hired in Tammerfors as an interpreter. Miss Ronti had lived in New York for seven years, and her appearance was rather of Broadway than of interior Finland. She spoke Finnish, Swedish, English, and German. She had returned from New York within the year. Captain Crosley on first coming to Tammerfors, a fortnight earlier, had arrived late in the evening, had been told there was no hotel space, and he and his wife were going from house to house seeking shelter.

They came to a house over which hung an American flag. On entering they found themselves not in a residence but in the office of a Finnish firm, kept open and lighted so that the flag would show at night. Miss Ronti was at a desk. She had put the flag out to keep the Reds off the premises. She got space in a hospital that night for the wayfarers, and the next day took service with the Captain. We were quick to recognize that Miss Ronti would be as much of an asset at Bjorneborg as she had been at Tammerfors. She was both energetic and diplomatic and would not take NO from her countrymen when she wanted them to say YES.

We judged it best to make no move for several days until Miss Ronti had familiarized herself with affairs of the town. In the meantime we were fairly comfortable on hotel rations and on purchases we were able to make. The bread ration, though confined to a thin slice for a meal, was of better quality than we had known in Petrograd—that is, it contained less sawdust and more grain, though it did have some content of wood-shavings. There were eggs, however—one a day. In a shop, too, we discovered a number of cans of fruit—Russian compote, one of our reliances during the winter. We bought the stock of the place. So with eggs, bread, and canned fruit we thought we were in luck.

In Guy Smith, too, were the talents of a good chef. In our rooms were porcelain stoves, wonders of radiation, able to turn a few sticks of wood into heat lasting through a night or a day. By the time we retired at night the wood was turned to ash, the bricks and the tiles of the ceiling high stoves had stored heat for hours ahead, and the fire box itself was a slow oven. Smith had an idea. He took hard Finnish crackers which we sometimes could get in place of bread, poured fruit juice from a compote can over them, added whatever of odds and ends he could get from the table, put everything into a tin pan, and the pan upon the ashes. In the morning we had a tasty dish. Soon others patterned after him. One day we found a small quantity of dried prunes in the village. And so prunes were added to the recipe.

The mornings we spent in getting physically fit for extra hardships that might be ahead, walking from five to seven miles up and down a half mile tree lined avenue that must have been delightful in spring and summer and that even was attractive under covering of ice and snow. Of late afternoons some of us played bridge, imparting to me the knowledge that I was not on the card plane of the Army and the Navy.

Nor did we lack for some excitement during the week, for we could hear the heavy guns on the battle-line about twelve miles away. More than ever, too, we realized the brutality of the conflict. The night we entered the town the Red Guards took the proprietor of a factory in an adjacent town and shot him and twelve of his office employes on the charge of having given information to the Whites. He was buried in the town cemetery during the week. Bodies of Red Guards, also, were brought in day by day from the front. They were buried in red coffins, one above the other in a single large grave, which was continually being widened in preparation for the bodies to come. The Reds said the Whites were taking no prisoners, killing every Red that fell into their hands. The Reds, for their part, were retaliating.

Minister Morris gave us a glum day, March 19th, by wiring us that the best thing we could do would be to return to Petrograd and start again by sledge around Lake Ladoga. And within a few hours Consul Haynes wired us to go to Viborg and attempt a sally directly north. Neither project was practicable. I wired Minister Morris: "Route around Lake Ladoga not possible. We are at best practical place. Suggest you send Haynes cable worded so he can use it to bring further pressure on authorities, pointing out that extension their courtesy is to United States Government." And to Tyer, in whose energy I had much confidence, I wired at Helsingfors: "Am putting my dependence upon you to get party through. There is no hope from Stockholm."

Yet it was the girl, Hilma Ronti, who extricated us.

We made ready to center appeal upon the local Red Guard commander, Salminen. Like us he had been living at the Otava Hotel. We judged that he had no black marks against us, although the hotel proprietor had come to us in a panic one night to ask us to curtail an effort at self-entertainment. We had dug up the only phonograph in town and were running off some badly battered records, several of them of American dance tunes that had been up-to-date before the World War began. We liked them but the Rumanian said they were too noisy. So we played a melancholy Continental air for his benefit, and it was this that brought the landlord to the door. He said the Red Guards were gathering outside in the street and that if we desired to protect his life as well as our own we should stop at once. On observation from the window the Red Guard seemed to consist of half a dozen persons who rather liked the music, but the hotel-keeper was badly scared and we shut off the instrument.

Our move was to be an official visit to Salminen by Captain Crosley, as party leader, with Miss Ronti as spokesman and advocate for the request that we be allowed to go to the front line at its Baltic extremity and there hoist an American flag and flag of truce in effort to attract favorable attention and reciprocation of truce from the White forces opposite. Miss Ronti asked and secured an appointment for the afternoon of March 21. Capt. Crosley was not optimistic. So many of his requests had been refused at Tammerfors that he expected another denial. He dug up his uniform cap, however, and put on a good navy front.

In an hour the pair were back, jubilant. The Commandant had said that we might start in two days, on condition that we should receive word from Minister Morris that word of our coming had reached the White Guards. We wired Stockholm at once, and to Tyer at Helsingfors to join us. But no replies ever came for the conclusive reason that the telegraph office was raided and closed two hours after our messages were sent. Tyer, however, had received his signal and joined us the next night. He brought word that the British had blown up their submarines, and that five hundred White adherents had escaped to Reval, across the gulf, by a bold and clever ruse. An ice-breaker anchored at the lower end of the harbor had received Red orders to move to berth nearer shore. The captain got up steam, but ran his ship to the outside of a little island in the bay. There, in the darkness, the Whites boarded the vessel, and the captain headed outward instead of inward and broke way through the ice, across the forty-mile channel. Several hundred other Whites attempted to cross the ice on foot, but most of them were hunted down and killed the next day.

Friday, March 22, was a day of preparations, ending in huge disappointment. At six o'clock in the evening we were told that we could not leave. One excuse given was that we had received no reply from Stockholm. Another was that no horses were available. We learned that Sorola, the Foreign Minister, was in town. We were not allowed to see him. Particularly were we disturbed by the knowledge that the excuse of absence of reply from Stockholm was a mask, since the telegraph office had been dismantled on orders.

But we knew that our only chance was to keep on asking, and on Saturday afternoon Captain Crosley and Miss Ronti went again to Salminen. Captain Crosley said afterwards that the intelligent and attractive girl beat the Commandant down with superior armament. She won a chance for us, though the Commandant thought he was granting little. We could go to the front, but were warned of failure and of grave consequences.

"The Whites will fire on you," Salminen said, "and you will have to come back. Then we will send you back behind the lines, for Bjorneborg will be put under martial law Sunday morning and all foreigners will be expelled."

He agreed to hold our railroad cars for us until twenty-four hours after we left Mentuolota.

We prepared that night for quick movement in the morning.

We had bought white sheets to serve as white flags and had had a carpenter make poles both for the white flags and for the American flags belonging to the party. One of these American flags was a handsome silk banner sent from the United States to Petrograd as a gift to the Minister of Finance, Shingarev. It reached there after the Bolshevik Revolution when Shingarev already was in Peter and Paul prison, and Mr. Corse became the custodian of the banner. It was deemed fitting that the flag meant for the martyr should add further to its history by leading us out of Red Finland.

We put Bjorneborg behind us on the morning of Sunday, March 24, in the cars that had brought us from Helsingfors, covering the twenty versts to the wateredge town of Mentuolota in an hour. There our cars were switched onto a siding at the very edge of the frozen bay. We could look across to a little island, five miles away, the extreme left flank of the Red line. Three miles beyond this island, was another island, unseen, held by the Whites, the right extremity of their line.

A sledge was already waiting. We took the flag poles from the baggage car and nailed the flags to the poles, two white flags and two American flags. Tyer spoke Swedish fluently. It was decided that he should go as the second interpreter. Miss Ronti was to be the Finnish interpreter. Captain Crosley searched through his baggage until he found his uniform coat, which had been misplaced. He changed in the baggage car. Within fifteen minutes our truce sledge was on its way.

It reached the Red field headquarters on the island in little more than half an hour. The Commandant there was a young laborer named Aloranta. He was as confident as Salminen had been that the Whites would pay no attention to a flag of truce. But he was willing to make the effort, and went with our flag-bearers to a natural rocky fort on the top of the highest hill on the island far-shore. There the flags were set up and anchored. Captain Aloranta ordered the Red fire along the mile of front to cease. White Guard firing continued for an hour, first intensified by the appearance of the flags, then desultory as if the White officers were puzzled.

Captain Crosley reasoned correctly that they would suspect at first a ruse, and also that it would take some time for them to identify the American flag. At the end of an hour the firing stopped, Captain Crosley stood up on the hill, took one American flag and walked down to the ice. No shot was fired. Mr. Tyer, with a white flag, and Miss Ronti joined him and they started to walk across the ice. They found the going too difficult as there were several inches of snow and water on the ice, which had been thawing for a week. They signalled back to the shore for a sledge and Captain Aloranta drove it out himself, a brave action as he was not guarded by the flags and was recognized through glasses as the Red leader.

The flag-bearers entered the sledge and drove toward the White line, Capt. Aloranta walking back to his line. As the sledge neared the opposite shore, the occupants received the command, in English, to "Halt." The order was by Lieut. Charles F. Diehl, recently of the Swedish Army, who had joined the White Guard forces at this point only a few days before. He spoke accentless English. All of his dealings with us in the next twenty-four hours were courteous and kind. He took Captain Crosley, Mr. Tyer, and Miss Ronti to the headquarters of the sector, three miles away, and secured formal permission there for the party to cross and for Captain Crosley and Mr. Tyer to return to us. But Miss Ronti, as a Finn, was detained.

Captain Crosley and Mr. Tyer returned to the Mentuolota side at four o'clock in the afternoon. The Reds sent twelve sledges from the island in half an hour's time, and as fast as each sledge could be loaded with baggage it was started across the ice, the party distributed where space offered. The group was re-united at Red field headquarters at five-thirty o'clock, and Captain Aloranta mounted his horse and led the way to the front line. Our flags had been left flying on the hill when the bearers returned. Captain Aloranta insisted on taking an American flag and carrying it outward on the ice. One white flag we left on the hill. At a point halfway between the two lines Captain Aloranta planted the American flag on the ice. His sledges drew up rapidly, their occupants alighted, the baggage was dumped and the drivers departed, lashing their horses to a run. Captain Aloranta saluted and walked his mount away. We remained on the ice for an hour before the Whites sent their sledges out for us. We had arrived earlier than anticipated.

When we saw the first of the sledges start out from the shore we let the women of the party walk toward them. The thermometer had fallen sharply and a biting wind was blowing from the north. We also had another reason for getting the women away from the scene. One hundred yards to our right were black spots upon the ice. The men knew that these were the bodies of Red soldiers who had been shot while on scout several nights before. The Reds had asked us to secure permission for them to remove the bodies,

Flags calling to the Finnish White line from the Finnish Red line
on March 24, 1918. American flag bearer, Captain Walter V. Crosley, U.S.N. Flag-of-truce bearer, John J. Tyer.

On the Baltic Sea midway between the Red and the White lines,
evening of March 24, 1918. The women had been sent on ahead to
the White line. Left to right: Mr. Sisson, Rumanian *Attaché* Guranesco, Guy Croswell Smith, Frederic A. Corse, Captain Walter V.
Crosley, Captain Norman Stines.

BETWEEN THE WHITE AND RED LINES

stating that their hospital flag had been shot at every time they made the effort. This request was made of the first Swedish officer, an under-lieutenant, who drove up to us. He gave immediate assent and expressed surprise that the bodies had been left there so long.

We had time to send back word to the Reds and while we were still on the ice Captain Aloranta ran his horse the mile and a half from shore to where the bodies lay. A sledge followed and in our sight the bodies were loaded and taken away. The Reds drove off cheering us, with their caps swinging in the air. We gave them a parting yell. We had had a hard time within their lines but they had treated us right on this, our last day with them.

The last of our sledges passed within the White Guard lines before eight o'clock in the evening, and in half an hour's further ride we crossed from the island to the mainland to the White field headquarters in the little town of Ahlainen.

We had come through without loss of one of our hundred odd pieces of baggage. We were hospitably received and had a progressive dinner—tea, bread and butter at the headquarters, a large farm-house; and soup and meat at another house a quarter of a mile away. We were divided up around the village for the night. Five of us slept at the house of the Lutheran minister, which was turned over to us. We found the rooms prepared for guests, fires lighted and every attention paid to our comfort. In the morning coffee and bread were served to us and we were told that a complete breakfast waited us at headquarters.

Lieut. Diehl there, while we were chatting after breakfast, told us that one of his raiding parties, composed of four or five youngsters, had gone on skis during the night to a Red outpost toward Bjorneborg, had bombed it, destroying the house and apparently killing all within—thirty or forty soldiers. They had returned with the loss of only one member, and were then around us.

One of the boys, round-faced and cheerful, made himself uncannily interesting to us by the story of another action of his. He related in detail to Miss Ronti, who translated, that while the bodies we had seen had been lying on the ice, he had crawled out to them for two consecutive nights to try to arrange two of them so that they would stand upright, leaning against each other. He said that in the pocket of one he had found a cup and in the pocket of another a spoon; and that he had sought to make one dead hand hold the cup and a hand of the other body the spoon, so that the spoon would seem to be dipping into the cup. The Reds had told us the day before that the bodies were moved nightly.

This young devil had served one year in the German army as a Finnish volunteer and had returned to Finland when the Civil War broke out. His misplaced sense of humor seemed wholly ingenuous.

It will be observed that brutality on one side seemed to be balanced by brutality on the other. During the whole time I was in Finland I could not see that one side was more merciful than the other, or more terrible.

I do not know whether Lieut. Diehl knew of the boy's action. He did not hear the recital to us.

Lieut. Diehl also showed us maps indicating that Tammerfors was nearly surrounded. "It will fall in a week," he said. Tammerfors held out one week longer than his estimate. The Reds of south Finland were doomed.

Our breakfast was good in quality and kind. We had been told in Red Finland that we would starve in White Finland. Instead we found more food than we had seen for months—good bread, butter, milk, eggs and coffee.

At Ahlainen we were ninety kilometers from the nearest rail-point, the city of Christinastadt, straight up the coast of Finland. We already had travelled about twenty kilometers. Lieut. Diehl told us that sledges had been ordered from another village and would arrive before noon. They came, thirteen of them, drawn by sturdy Finnish ponies. The day was sharply cold, but most of us were well acclimated.

Lieut. Diehl, his Commander, a good-looking Finn, Captain Paavo Talvela, who could not speak English, and the headquarters' staff, turned out to see us off. As we swung out of the big barn-yard, Lieut. Diehl and the Commander both took off their caps and called for a cheer for "the Americans and America." It was given with a right good will. We returned the salute with another cheer. So, within the short period of sixteen hours we were cheered both by the Reds and the Whites. It was one of the rare experiences of War. It gave us, too, a feeling of sadness that these two sides were engaged in the destruction of each other, to the disaster of Finland and the gain of Germany.

Our cavalcade proceeded without halt for six hours, skirting the shore of the Baltic Sea, going from island to island and from peninsula to peninsula, sometimes touching the mainland, sometimes far out on the bays. We passed through only one town. The last two hours were ones of endurance, but we knew we could reach Christinastadt the same night if we could make the first stretch to Sideby, about fifty kilometers, by six o'clock. We did.

THE WHITE COMMANDERS

Lieutenant Charles F. Diehl (left), volunteer, late of the Swedish army, who welcomed us into the White lines, and Captain Paavo Talvela (right), in command at Ahlainen. The "S" on Captain Talvela's sleeve stands for Suomi (Finland).

HILMA RONTI

The Finnish girl who helped extricate the American party from the Red area of Finland. This and the accompanying picture taken on March 25, 1918, at Ahlainen, Finland.

And we were refreshed there in the village parsonage with a hot meal. A new relay of sledges was in readiness, and in an hour we were off again. This time we took the sea entirely, cutting forty kilometers across the gulf to Christinastadt. On the way across I chanced to express to Smith, who was riding with me, a wonder as to what lights on shore might be. The answer, the name of the fishing village, came in English from the driver's seat in front. Our reinsman was formerly of Portland, Oregon, who had come to his Finnish home on a visit and had been caught there by war. He meant, too, to get back to the United States.

We made a fast trip, the first of our sledges reaching Christinastadt shortly after ten o'clock. Our baggage was up by midnight. Again we were distributed around the town in different private houses for the night. Finnish hospitality girt us about. That, too, in spite of German presence near.

Christinastadt was a divisional headquarters, and the only hotel, where we took our meals, housed a part of the general staff. It did not take us long to discover that the personnel of this staff was German in its sympathy and included German officers. Thirty young Jaeger officers, over from Germany within the preceding two or three weeks, had a long table in the dining-room with us. They were of Finnish or Swedish birth for the most part, but were German trained and had been serving in the German army, some of them for three years. Now they were Finnish volunteers, aiding General Mannerheim in drilling his troops. The atmosphere of that dining-room was frigid. Each group ignored the other.

The elder officers at the headquarters, however, were not only courteous but friendly, and at once gave us passes to continue our journey. We still had several hundred miles to go to Torneo, at the top of Finland, but we could do it by rail.

We left Christinastadt in the afternoon of March 26 for Sunioki, seventy miles away, travelling on a passenger train at ease. We reached Sunioki at ten o'clock at night and there got into first actual touch with Western Europe, being met at the station by Lieut. Thorling of the Stockholm Legation, whose job of rescuing us we had made unnecessary. He had a dinner waiting for us in the station hotel and got rooms for us in the village. We made an early start next day with a six o'clock breakfast. Lieut. Thorling did not accompany us, being delayed a day by the formalities of getting his own passport viséed.

We reached Torneo, the Finnish frontier, a distance of 290 miles, at midnight March 27, and spent the rest of the night in the cars, uncomfortable in body and content in mind.

Our baggage was put through the customs on both the Finnish and the Swedish side without inspection. The rivalry between the two frontiers seemed to be as to which could show us the more courtesy.

Miss Ronti had been allowed to come with us to Torneo. There we left her. At Stockholm we learned that she returned in safety to her relatives. [Note: She later came again to the United States, as a member of the staff of the Finnish Consulate.]

In the Swedish town of Haparanda, at noon March 28, we dined—and drank to our luck. By the kindness of Minister Morris a special car for us was ready to be hitched to the night train. We concluded our journey of escape from Finland with our arrival in Stockholm on Saturday afternoon, March 30, 1918.

For some of the party the time from Petrograd had been more than six weeks. For me it had been twenty-six days.

CHAPTER XXVII

In the War Month of April, 1918.

ONE duty remained for Smith and me that night before we began to celebrate. We took our Norwegian courier to the railroad station and put him on a train for Christiania. Then to the Grand Hotel for bath and the first dressing for dinner in months. With Dosch-Fleurot and a circle of refurbished refugees that grew and grew we basked in the moist warmth in the area circling the dome-inclosed tropical garden, sipped our coffee, and twirled lovingly the goblets in which according to Swedish custom brandy is served in order to diffuse the aroma of the few mouthfuls of liquor at the bottom of the glasses.

As I entered the anteroom at the Legation the next morning I walked squarely into my old courier friend, Sergeant Joe Franklin.

He took me by the shoulders, stood me off and looked at me.

"Boy," he said, "you're all drawn up. Haven't you been eating?"

I wasn't much more than ten years younger than he, I was hard with intense and prolonged exertion of body and mind, I had been on a sparse diet but it had served, I felt fit even if I did look pinched, and until I heard his worried voice I supposed I had not changed since he saw me last in Petrograd, more than two months before. After Stockholm was cut off from Petrograd he had been running between that capital and London.

"It's all right, Joe," I answered. "I'm going to let you take me back to London."

"That's what you are," he said.

At that, I wasn't so sure about it. I would have to go on to Christiania, return once more to Stockholm, and finally head out through Christiania, Bergen, and the North Sea.

Lingering only at Stockholm for advisory contact with Washington, for cable to my family—which Minister Morris very thoughtfully had relieved of its long anxiety as soon as he knew our party had reached Sunioki—and for hearty thanks to the Minister for his many and continued efforts in our behalf, I hastened to Christiania, taking Captain Stines with me as a Russian translator.

The material the Norwegian courier had carried awaited me in Minister Schmedeman's office. Many of the letters in the packet had not had a written translation. Fortunately Captain Stines was an adept in the Russian language. There in two days and two nights, broken only for four or five hours of sleep and recesses for food, I wrote the full report for the President, and a cable epitome of three hundred words. The latter was coded and sent April 3.

Returning then to Stockholm for the conveniences of the larger staff and better equipment there, I had copies of the report made, and photostats also of all letters and photographs, filing one set with the Legation. The report itself was not forwarded by courier mail as I would travel as fast as a courier. Boats ran from Bergen irregularly. I would be advised of the next to go.

For a week I was free in Stockholm for other matters. The film situation interested me. While I had been in Christiania, Guy Croswell Smith had been making survey. He reported that Germany was launching an enlarged film propaganda drive, trusting principally to a theater it had secured in Stockholm and intending to get other theaters in other cities. The method seemed to me to be weak in that all films would be propaganda, with entertainment feature lacking.

American entertainment films, on the other hand, already were favorites in Sweden. Where they were shown the houses were packed and there were many houses. So it seemed feasible to restrict the German films to a very limited area and to use the American commercial films as a medium for influencing the users of them to include also on their programs a percentage of films presenting the American side of war affairs. Film houses not willing, would not get the entertainment films, and would lose patronage.

Success of the plan came down to willingness of the American film industry to participate, and its ability also to supply in conjunction with the Government the varied war films necessary. I learned, by cable, that export *liaison* was in process of formation in the United States between the film producers and the Committee on Public Information. Balancing organization abroad was the essential. So we began to build it then and there. Smith was placed in charge of operations in Sweden, Denmark, and Norway. In three months he reported the success of the campaign. German films were throttled. So, later, in Holland also. Every agency of the American Government and of the film producers collaborated in this endeavor. The Trading with the Enemy regulations were invoked usefully.

That week in Stockholm was black week otherwise. The German drive was at its height, and seemed to be sweeping to Paris and the sea. Berlin papers, early in our hands, carried daily maps of new territory won and were filled with claims of victory. We had only the belief that Providence would not permit the Germans to win, and to that we clung stoutly. These were the gloomiest days of the war. The Allied cause was near to being flouted in the neutral countries. Stockholm cheered each new German advance.

The journey was resumed. Franklin met me at Christiania on April 13, and we two who had left London together in early November headed toward the city, again in company, in latter April. On this passage of the North Sea no destroyers could be spared to escort the dispatch boat. So the fast craft ran in the night from Bergen to Lerwick in the Shetland Islands, lay the day there in harbor, and in the night sped again for Aberdeen, sliding inside the breakwater at dawn.

In London I reported to Ambassador Walter Hines Page. That fine man greeted me as a father might a son. He opened his arms and folded me in. His words, "My boy!" were the most treasured acknowledgment I ever received. I had stood considerable and believed I had become impassive. But I had not.

The Ambassador desired that my full report be cabled to Washington, but Secretary Lansing decided otherwise and ordered that I was to bring it with me. Copy and photostats were filed with the Ambassador.

After analyzing all data, I reached a conclusion and took a step that had an enduring bearing on the after-Russian situation. It was apparent to me that the intent of the Bolsheviks was to keep Ambassador Francis—and the Allied nationals— in Russia as long as possible, practically as hostages, and to

make a public show of their helplessness, thus exploiting before
the Russian masses their ability to insult with impunity the
representatives of powerful peoples. It was an advertising
method potent toward consolidating internal power, aimed to
impress the fatalistic Russian millions with the sense of helplessness under rulers strong enough seemingly to defy the great
nations of the world. The ultimate movement in such a game
could be expected to be the expulsion or imprisonment of all
Allied nationals after the Bolsheviks grew tired of the play, or
—not unlikely—at the instigation of Germany. If one saw the
game, one might as well participate in it with a counter-move,
I reasoned.

As such a move, I cabled to Washington, April 22:

Please instruct Bullard that he and his American men are ordered
out of Bolshevik area of Russia by two weeks from date. He will
know how to take cover. Keep up cable service as camouflage.
Russian staff can keep it going until it can be transferred to safe
base. In my judgment Red Cross unit should be at once recalled
and Embassy likewise for same reasons of safety but recognize
that Washington, lacking the complete knowledge of my reasons,
is apt to take this as an exaggerated opinion.

This cable I sent by embassy code, with the request that it
be recoded and sent *via* Alexandrovsk to Ambassador Francis
at Vologda for delivery to Bullard. The purpose was, first, to
give the State Department a chance to read and to exercise,
if it desired, a veto power. If sent, the remaining purpose would
be achieved automatically. Not only my men would go but the
Ambassador, in a reasonable time, would follow—either going
to Archangel or through Siberia. The Ambassador, I was quite
sure, would grasp the meaning.

Bullard, naturally, would hate to receive the order. But he
would obey. He did, and without destroying the organization.
One man, Read Lewis, was attached to the Consulate at Moscow, to remain for a few additional weeks. He kept the Moscow
office in operation until the consular staff itself went out by
way of Finland in the late summer, and himself proceeded by
boat around the north coast of the Scandinavian peninsula to
Archangel, where under the protection of the for-a-time independent government of Chaikovsky, he continued work until

the late winter of 1919. Even after he was gone from Moscow, the Russian Lebedev, son-in-law of Prince Kropotkin, kept the distributing machinery going until one day in the autumn the Bolsheviks seized office and plant.

Bullard and Graham Taylor got to Archangel and shipped nominally as British sailors out of that port for England, so avoiding passport difficulties. Malcolm Davis and William Adams Brown, Jr., had moved on into Siberia and Asia, and went on a mission with dispatches from the American Consul at Irkutsk, across Mongolia, reporting finally by cable from Peking, China.

By that time back in Washington, I cabled the latter two to go to Harbin and open offices of the Committee on Public Information there, awaiting the coming of Bullard and an enlarged group for penetration back into Siberia toward Russia with Admiral Kolchak's forces. Bullard came to the United States; and thirty days later, in the mid-summer of 1918, reinforced, and with additional equipment including moving picture machines and films, sailed from Seattle for Tokyo and Vladivostok. The Russian Division had been moved nearly around the world to new bases in Siberia. Its vanguard advanced nearly to the Ural Mountains, behind the lines of the troops of the Kolchak government. Some of the men were so deep in Siberia when demobilization came that they could not get back to the United States until June, 1919.

Bullard himself, transferred in November for duty at the Paris Peace Conference, suffered an attack of mastoiditis on board ship in the Pacific, was taken ashore at San Francisco for operation barely in time to save his life, and did not leave the hospital for many weeks. His premature death in September, 1929, when he was only forty-nine years old, must be held due, in no small degree, to his bountiful expenditure of vitality in war service.

Before September, 1918, all American nationals, officials included, were out of Russia save one—Consul Roger Tredwell, victim of mishap before he could get away from Tiflis, and held in jail for several months.

The British were slow to believe the handwriting on the wall, and several hundred of their nationals were locked up for a winter of starvation when the Bolsheviks slammed shut the doors of Russia in the early autumn. The maneuver that I believed I could foresee had become a fact.

While I remained in London, the British nation was facing its sternest trials of war—and its head was highest. Boulogne and the sea coast, and Paris itself might be lost; long-range guns might smite its coasts and London and its cities be more mercilessly bombed. But the War itself would not be lost. The problem of transferring troops from northern to southern France was being squarely faced. New regiments were going to the front—boys this time. They seemed so young. They smiled and waved their hands as they marched through the lined streets. One could wave back but could not smile. Yet death were better than vassalage.

I thought of Russian soldier-prisoners in Poland who had cried to the perfidious Trotsky:

"Fight ten years! Never give up!"

I wondered if American soldiers would come in time. Without them the War would not be won, despite British valor, despite French steadfastness. An army of ours was in France, but not large enough for this crisis. This offensive the European Allies must stop—this offensive that the Russian debacle, that Lenin and Trotsky, had made possible. If it were stopped, our soldiers would be bulwark for the next. And what was the news of America? Great armies being welded together. Shipyards a-hum. But those ships would be launched too late. English transports in the meantime. Everything a question. Everything in the future.

Nothing more to learn until I should be home again. Perhaps there was doubt there. And perhaps also hunger—the same hunger under which all Europe was wasting. The England accustomed to full fare was of the past. Bread cards seemed near. Sugar was for the sick, the wounded, and the soldiers. For sweetening I carried in England a phial of saccharine tablets in my pocket. I had lived in darkness for five months. I seemed to have emerged less into dawn than into new descending dusk. Perhaps civilization was falling to pieces before my eyes. I could not conceive that there remained on earth a land of health and plenty, to which the War itself was hardly more than a rugged incident. Nor could awakening come at once.

Taken in October, 1917.

Taken at Stockholm, Sweden, in April, 1918, soon after return from Russia.

Егоръ Г Сиссонъ

Европейская гостиница
Петроградъ

Mr Edgar G Sisson

Washington D C
U S A

Russian face of Author's card. Lower left reads: Hotel d'Europe, Petrograd.

English reverse of Author's Russian card.

PASSPORT PHOTOGRAPHS OF AUTHOR

The larder of the old *New York*, to bear me home again, was teemingly stocked, but I reasoned that military and naval men would be better fed than most. And I asked no questions, for I would have disbelieved all answers.

Instead I began to conceal a private sugar stock. I told my steward to be lavish with the lump sugar when he brought my morning coffee to my berth. One lump went into the coffee, the rest into a paper sack. Each time I left the table I carried three or four lumps of sugar in my hands. The hoard grew.

Three days we lay at the mouth of the Mersey River while a flotilla gathered. The ships were to go out together under convoy, the *New York* on the left flank, the splendid *Justicia*—its first voyage—at the right, half a dozen vessels between. The destroyers, half a dozen also, ringed the fleet, and the voyage began. For a night and a day the destroyers circled, and then, in an evening hour, were gone. The fleet scattered, each vessel for itself, anxious to lose all its companions.

The *New York* was first into New York Harbor, the morning of May 6. The *Justicia* crossed and returned safely, its only round trip. Once more it came westward, and once more it started homeward, to be riven and sunk by a pack of German submarines off the coast of north Ireland.

My wife had come from Washington to meet me. Hardly had we greeted each other before I thrust gleefully into her hands a bulging paper sack.

"What's that?" she asked.

"Sugar!" I cried. "Sugar! I saved it all the way over."

She thought I had gone mad.

"Do you mean that everyone has sugar here?" I asked, understanding slowly that the gift I had thought so precious was meaningless to her.

She said that everyone had sugar, and all else of food.

Then I knew the War would be won.

I set about convincing her that I was sane.

Memory had ceased, however, to perform one of its lesser duties. For many weeks I could not recall the names of persons I knew well, and had to school myself to wait until they or someone else should speak the name. So I concluded that the brain at its need crowds out the unnecessary to make room for the necessary. To this day I have forgotten scarce a Russian name and not many Russian occurrences. The hundred days were graven deep.

On the night of May 9, 1918, my Russian report was in the hands of President Wilson.

APPENDIX

TROTSKY'S EXECUTION OF ADMIRAL STCHASTNY

TROTSKY demanded and got the life of Admiral Stchastny, savior of the Russian fleet. Stchastny was shot at Moscow in the early morning of June 22, 1918. At the short, misnamed trial June 20, Trotsky, appearing against him, was the only witness heard. The defendant was refused the right of calling the roster of witnesses submitted by him to the Bolshevik Tribunal, and his attorney was not allowed to plead for him.

One chain of circumstances tended to show that the sailor's major "crime" was that instead of destroying the Russian fleet in the harbor of Helsingfors or of letting it fall into the hands of the Germans when their fleet approached the city in March, 1918, he took advantage of the break-up of ice and ran the fleet to safety at Kronstadt while the ice-barrier still impeded the pursuit by the Germans. With the ships in haven, Stchastny at a later date also demurred to an instruction from Trotsky for arrangements to blow up the ships, the Admiral explaining that the vessels no longer were in danger of German seizure.

After the "Peace of Brest-Litovsk" the fleet was regarded by the Bolshevik leaders—and not without cause—as more of a menace than a protection to them; and the Germans could not regard it otherwise than as a potential threat until the ships were disarmed, if not seized or destroyed.

The later revolt of the Navy* disclosed how well grounded were the fears of Lenin and Trotsky.

The time had come, in March, 1918, when the Bolshevik leaders no longer wished to rely upon the Army and the Navy which had given them earlier support. History contained too many instances where the makers of rulers had unmade them also. The Army they could demobilize, and did. The Navy was more difficult. The ships were both fort and home. The Navy was more loyal to itself. In spite of all efforts to the contrary its feelings, too, were more nationalistic. It might hoist Red or Black flags but it regarded itself still as Russian. It believed itself also to be an essential part of Bolshevik power and rule, and was jealous of its prerogatives, as it viewed them. The dissolution of the fleet as a fighting unit, mandatory in the Brest-Litovsk treaty, sat ill on the Navy. To it Stchastny became a hero for his feat of the rescue of the ships, officer though he was, with overlords of Commissars. And these

* In the spring of 1921.

also sought his advice. The situation bothered Moscow. Finally against Lenin and Trotsky was the steady pressure of Germany to secure complete obedience to the Peace terms concerning the Navy.

Large as were these reasons, in Moscow regard, for circumscribing the Navy and shearing Stchastny of influence, it is my opinion, nevertheless, that these purposes would have been accomplished without taking Stchastny's life except for one detached action by him. Stchastny was no man to become involved in the intricate politics of such an hour. He saw only with a professional eye, and the study of the fatal course he trod disclosed how simple and trusting and honest he was. He took, in my belief and I will show my reasons, his own death warrant to Trotsky and delivered it, or was ready to deliver it, into Trotsky's hands, believing he was giving a superior officer statements which should be investigated and which coincided with his own suspicions that Germany intended to crush Russia into subserviency under the guise of Peace. Once he spoke to Trotsky, I conclude that his removal was determined upon. Stchastny had come unwittingly, even without action of his own, into possession of material implying a strange relationship between the German General Staff and Lenin. One of the prime charges brought against him in prosecution was that he:

"Kept in his possession and distributed forged documents with the purpose of discrediting the Soviet Government."

The papers, it was said, were "found" on him.

What were the "forged" documents and how did he get them?

A letter, according to statement made to United States Consul DeWitt C. Poole, who conducted at Moscow an inquiry for his Government, came to Admiral Stchastny by mail, and in it four papers, declared without explanation to be from the archives of the Soviet Government. The first of the documents was signed "R. Bauer," its date March 30, 1918, and itself an avowed protest of the German General Staff against the appointment as Chief Commissar of the Baltic fleet of one Blohin, as being "defensively" minded. The letter was addressed to the "President of the Soviet of People's Commissars," who was Lenin. Two of the other documents were similar German protests against sailor actions "harmful to Germany," one of them asking that the recreant sailors be sent "far into Russia." The fourth was the complaint of a Russian counter-espionage bureau that its reports of activities of German spies in the Russian fleet had not resulted in ordered action against the spies.

Admiral Stchastny, according to research statement, found on investigation that the sailors named had been sent into interior Russia, and that they had been killed there, presumably in various fighting. The Admiral's feelings were recorded as such that when an officer, "Bauer," sought to call on him aboard ship he refused audience. When summoned to Moscow, the Admiral took copies of these documents along and carried them when he went to Trotsky. His only precaution was to place record of script and contents in the hands of his friend and attorney, Vladimir Zhdanov, before he went to Trotsky.

Papers in my Government Report bore also the signature "R. Bauer." I had left Petrograd March 4 and this Bauer letter was of nearly a month's later date. Nor have I now knowledge of the identity of the person who sent Admiral Stchastny the letter of inclosures.

Intelligence channel, however, between Russia and the United States was not closed. Robert Imbrie, sent by Ambassador Francis from Vologda to be acting Consul at Petrograd after the Brest-Litovsk peace reopened the city, became the active intelligence officer, and continued in that capacity after Americans left Russia, going then to the border city of Viborg, in Finland. His work, so far as I know, never has received public credit, and certainly not its deserts. Nor have I felt that his death, in Teheran, July 18, 1924, was free from mystery. He was killed, supposedly by accidental violence, in a street riot which suddenly flared up around him without understood cause. Teheran at that time was a center for a Bolshevik group plotting Asiatic turmoil. The Persian Government, because the death was in its territory, paid indemnity to Imbrie's widow and the international episode was officially closed.

I was protected from the Bolsheviks by the publication of my Report. To have harmed me afterward would have been a silly form of confession. Imbrie, however, never had that protection. He remained on distant service. He had, too, a dashing, adventurous disposition, and scorned precautions.

One of Imbrie's expresses was a file of letters, archive marked, some of them in time sequence to my material. One period covered was late March, 1918. When for purposes of research comparison in the State Department at Washington, the date and Bureau file number of the "Bauer" letter sent to Admiral Stchastny was checked with the March letters of the State Department collection, they matched. That is, in the latter series was vacant place for the March 30 letter sent to Stchastny. As recorded in analysis: "One of the Department's documents is No. 1325 and dated March 28, 1918. Another is 1340, dated March 31, 1918, while the one above set forth (the letter Stchastny received) fits in exactly between these two, being No. 1333 and dated March 30, 1918."

Documents 1325 and 1340 both bore the signature "R. Bauer," with usual Bureau markings, and the latter like the Stchastny letter, dealt with the attitude of the "defense group" of sailors in the Baltic fleet. Both Documents No. 1325 and No. 1340 were directed to Lenin.

When this discovery was made, which was not until 1920, I wrote to Allan Carter of the Russian Division of the State Department, with whom I had been in collaboration in final analysis and notation of the Department series:

"It is as if Providence had stepped in two years afterward to write into history the direct and simple record that Trotsky, even though he killed Admiral Stchastny to hide his own and the German guilt, failed wholly."

In the compilation of the direct record of the Stchastny execution and the charges brought against him, Imbrie had no part. Consul Poole was not able to send cipher report of the Admiral's death until June 29, 1918, when he cabled:

The former commander of the Baltic fleet, Admiral Stchastny, was shot June 22 at Moscow by order of the supreme revolutionary tribunal. He was afforded no proper means of presenting his defense and other circumstances of the case strongly suggest German instigation.

When the Baltic fleet was threatened in March by German advance he was given command and, despite serious hindrances, removed all the important units from Helsingfors to Kronstadt—168 vessels. Subsequently he endeavored to send the destroyer flotilla into Lake Ladoga, and in general he consistently labored to withhold Russian naval vessels and material from Germany.

On May 26 Stchastny was ordered to Moscow and arrested, following a brief interview with Trotsky during which the latter behaved very violently. His trial took place at noon June 20. Before the trial two Social Revolutionary members of the Tribunal were excluded and two Bolsheviks substituted for them. The accused was refused a copy of the charges against him and none of his witnesses was allowed to testify. The sole witness actually called was Trotsky, who concluded his testimony as follows: "Comrades, you have before you a very dangerous counter-revolutionary, whom I think should be punished without mercy." The Tribunal forthwith condemned Stchastny and the execution was carried out the same night.

The charges were seven in number, intending to show that the accused was plotting against the Bolshevik Government. All but the following two were trivial in character and refuted by his record: First, disclosure of a secret telegram respecting preparations to destroy vessels and forts; second, keeping in his possession and distributing "forged" documents with the purpose of discrediting the Soviet Government.

The supposed secret telegram was one sent to Stchastny on May 21 by Trotsky, in open language. The alleged "forged documents" are four in number and include three communications of the German Information Bureau which were found in the possession of the accused at the time of his arrest. These documents are similar to some of those already in the possession of the Department. They are signed "Bauer."

Consul Poole continued with brief account of contents of the letters, which he said came from Stchastny's counsel, and concluded:

"The execution of Stchastny is causing widespread comment and even unrest, especially in the Baltic fleet."

Consul Poole forwarded to the American Ministry at Stockholm as soon as possible a detailed Memorandum, including interview with Admiral Stchastny's counsel, Vladimir Zhdanov, the communication reaching Washington in the autumn of 1918. It follows:

Memorandum, June 24, 1918. This morning I had an interview with Vladimir Anatolievich Zhdanov, the late Admiral Stchastny's advocate in the latter's recent trial.

The following was the summary of charges against Stchastny, as put by the Tribunal, Krylenko and Trotsky:

1. Raised objections to the appointment of Commissars by the Council of People's Commissars.
2. Insisted on the old system according to which Commissars were elected by the crews of the ships.
3. Did not induce Zeleny to take measures to establish the demarkation line.
4. Disclosed the secret telegrams regarding preparations to destroy vessels and forts.
5. Detained in Petrograd the destroyer flotilla.
6. Did not execute the order dismissing Lisanevich and Zaseneuk.
7. Kept in his possession and distributed forged documents with the purpose of discrediting the Soviet Government.
8. All the above was done with the intention of preparing a plot against the Government.

Before the Revolution Stchastny was Commander of a destroyer. During the Revolution he became Officer in the Staff Command of the Baltic fleet. In March he was appointed by Raskolnikov (member College of Fleet Commissars) Admiral in command of the Baltic fleet.

His appointment took place in the days when the fleet was greatly endangered by advancing Finns and Germans.

Stchastny successfully led out of Helsingfors and delivered at Kronstadt all of the important ships of the fleet, in all 168 ships. Two of the three German dreadnaughts that ventured after the escaping fleet struck mines.

After the Peace Treaty was signed at Brest,* the fleet was ordered to demobilize. Crews were declared free from compulsory service, and were from now on employed on a free-employment basis. Many new men were thus taken, most of whom were Finns. Stchastny reported repeatedly that he had suspicion that the newly employed crews were under outside influence. No notice was taken of these reports. Stchastny's suspicions were later proved by the treachery of the crews of two ice-breakers, who gave them over to the Germans. Stchastny opened way out for his fleet with but one ice-breaker.

On arrival at Kronstadt, Stchastny suggested to Trotsky and received the latter's approval, to take part of the fleet, namely the destroyer flotilla, into Lake Ladoga. Stchastny was of the opinion that the fleet was in danger even in Kronstadt, and all the ships before leaving Helsingfors were mined and prepared for immediate explosion in case of any danger from the Germans. This was done by Stchastny's order, of which Trotsky was aware.

Stchastny left behind in Helsingfors his assistant, Admiral Zeleny, and instructed him to start diplomatic negotiations with the German Commandant respecting forts, ammunition and the smaller vessels still in Helsingfors. On receipt of an order from Trotsky to demand from the Germans establishment of a demarkation line in the Finnish bay and to defend this line with floating mines, Stchastny expressed the opinion that it was premature and that the establishment of such a line would definitely give over to the Germans all that was left of Helsingfors. Nevertheless Stchastny telegraphed Trotsky's order to Zeleny on April 28, and receiving no reply repeated it on April 29, May 1, 2 and 3. Zeleny replied on the 5th saying he did not think it possible to get the Germans to agree to the establishment of a demarkation line. On the 6th Stchastny ordered Zeleny to put the demand before the Germans and received a reply on the 7th saying the Germans refused to give him an answer to his demand. At the trial Trotsky stated that only a few days ago the Germans agreed to appoint a place where a Commission called to establish the demarkation line was to assemble. [Count No. 3 against Stchastny was that he did not induce Zeleny to take measures to establish a demarkation line.]

In the beginning of May the destroyer flotilla as stated above started to Lake Ladoga. Hindrances of the strangest nature and delays were met with at every step. The flotilla was stopped at every bridge, as

---

* Stchastny saved the fleet after the Peace Treaty was signed. That was a cause of German rage against him. Germany had hoped to get 168 ships. The fleet was in Helsingfors Harbor when I left the city March 12.

none was opened. In many cases days passed before it could be arranged for the bridge to open. The crew of the tug-boats, which towed the ships, refused to work more than eight hours a day, so that the flotilla had to be at a stand-still sixteen hours out of twenty-four. When the flotilla had passed the bridges and it was possible to go under steam, no naphtha was available, although Stchastny telegraphed for it continuously. The naphtha arrived only on May 24. The crew of the flotilla became dissatisfied with this state of affairs and adopted a resolution in which it expressed its disgust with the Government of the Petrograd Commune and declared for the overthrow of the Commune, to be succeeded by a dictatorship of the Commandant of the Baltic fleet. For this purpose the crew demanded the calling of a conference of representatives of the different vessels, which should elect the new Commandant. The propaganda campaign which preceded this resolution was headed by two sailors, Lisanevich and Zaseneuk.

At this time, the beginning of May, a Conference of the sailors of the Baltic fleet was called in Petrograd. Stchastny prepared a report on the general situation which he intended reading at the Conference. The Council of the Conference advised Stchastny not to deliver his report at the sitting of the Conference, but make it known only to the members of the Council of the Conference.

On the 14th of May the Council of People's Commissars appointed a new Commissar of the Baltic fleet, Flerovsky. The former Commissar, Blohin, elected by the Sailors' Council, was dismissed. The Council of People's Commissars informed Trotsky of this new appointment May 16. Trotsky never informed the Commandant of the Baltic fleet that Flerovsky was to take the place of Blohin, and therefore everybody in the fleet, including Stchastny, regarded Blohin as Commissar and refused to deal with the other man.

On May 13 the Sailors' Conference passed a resolution to expel the sailors Lisanevich and Zaseneuk from the fleet on account of their counter-revolutionary conduct. This resolution was sent to Stchastny by Saks, member of the College of Fleet Commissars for information, but no orders to dismiss the two sailors were ever given to Stchastny. To dismiss them without an order Stchastny had no right. On May 18 Saks again writes to Stchastny and in the name of the College reprimands him for not having yet dismissed the sailors, and also orders Stchastny to publish a special order re the dismissal, as worked out in the College in Petrograd. Stchastny in reply asked that the text of the (first) order be forwarded to him, as it never was sent to him.

On May 3 Trotsky sent Stchastny a secret wire *en claire* (on the open wire, not coded) saying that in case the fleet in Kronstadt should be endangered by the Germans, it should be blown up and that all measures for the explosion should be prepared at once. Stchastny, having received information that the German battleships had left Helsingfors for Germany wired the fact to Trotsky, stating that there was no danger now for the fleet in Kronstadt. In reply to this wire Stchastny received a telegram from Trotsky dated May 21, reading as follows:

"People's Commissar Trotsky has sent the following to No. 803/Op: 'It is very probable that the departure of German officers and the transferring to Finland of all matters respecting the fleet is a threat of an attack on our fleet, ostensibly in the name of Finland. It is necessary, therefore, to take all proper measures of precaution. Have all necessary preparatory measures been taken to destroy the vessels in case of acute emergency? Have the money deposits been made in the bank in the name of those sailors who have been charged with the destruction of the vessels? It is necessary that all this be verified in the most accurate way. Trotsky.' Informing you of the above, I beg you to advise immediately whether lists of persons charged with the destruction of vessels have been prepared. The lists are necessary, as it is the intention to give money rewards for successful fulfillment. I request Namorsi (cableword for Chief of Navy Forces—Stchastny) to immediately give his conclusion, after consulting L. Goncharov, respecting method of paying such rewards, their distribution and conditions, for the submission of the project to the College and the Supreme War Council. Berens, assistant to the Flag-Captain, Bery, of the Operative Department."

As the giving of rewards involved a sum of *several million rubles,* Stchastny had to consult on this matter with the Council of Commissars of the Baltic Fleet. Had he done otherwise, apart from the impossibility of obtaining such a sum of money, it would have been against the law. The Council of (Fleet) Commissars was against giving money rewards to sailors for a work it was their duty to perform. The Head Commissar of the fleet even said: "Our sailors never will agree to sell themselves for money." The Council decided to send a delegation to Trotsky to ask for explanations.

The crews of the ships became restless and expressed the view that *Trotsky intended to destroy the fleet purposely,* as there was no evidence of immediate danger. Trotsky's order to blow up the ships seemed mysterious, as it was well known that all ships were ready to be exploded, from the day the fleet left Helsingfors.

On May 7 Trotsky sent Admiral Altfater to Petrograd to investigate the question of the demarkation line and the preparedness of the fleet for self-destruction. Altfater reported everything to Trotsky, and said that all was done with the exception of the money deposits in the bank. The latter could not be done in view of the opposition of the (Fleet) Council to this undertaking.

On May 25 Stchastny handed in his resignation. On the 26th he received a telegram saying that his request was not granted and ordering him to come to Moscow. Stchastny at once left for Moscow, taking along with him all materials and also copies of four documents, which, according to his words, he received by post. These documents were of the following nature.

Document No. 1 (Translation)

"*Intelligence Bureau*
"*Section M*
"*No. 1333.*
"*March 30, 1918.*
"*To the President of the Council of People's Commissars.*

"The General Staff has intrusted the Intelligence Bureau to express its satisfaction with the already decided upon dismissal of the Chief Commissar of the Baltic Fleet Izmailov. On the other hand, the election in his place of the sailor Blohin is met by the General Staff with disapproval, in view of Blohin being enlisted in the Defensive Group of the ex-Navy Commissar Dybenko.

"For the Chief of the Bureau
"(Signed) R. BAUER,
Adjutant."

[In hand-writing] "Invite Comrade Raskolnikov for consultation.

"(Signed) M. SKRYPNIK."

Document No. 2. The Intelligence Bureau informs the President of the Council of People's Commissars of the activities of the Defensive Group of sailors, harmful to Germany, and requests that these sailors be taken far into Russia.

Document No. 3. Similar to No. 2.

Document No. 4. From the Russian Reconnoissance Bureau (Counter-espionage) advising that it repeatedly informed of activity of German spies in the Baltic Fleet, but that no measures against them have been taken.

Upon receiving these documents, Stchastny made an inquiry into the statements therein. The inquiry gave the following results: Lieutenant R. Bauer called on Stchastny one day, but the latter refused to see him. It proved on investigation that all sailors mentioned in documents No. 2 and 3 were sent far into Russia and that all of them were killed on different occasions. Kingissen, appointed investigator in Stchastny's case told the former [Zhdanov] that he was informed that four such documents were missing from the archives.

On arriving in Moscow, Stchastny was received by Trotsky and arrested by him after a short conversation.

Proceeding of the Supreme Revolutionary Tribunal:

After the investigation was finished, the Tribunal resolved to call the following persons as witnesses: Trotsky, Raskolnikov, Blohin, Duzhik, Saks, and Flerovsky. This resolution was taken late at night on June 18. None of the witnesses [Note: Other than Trotsky] was informed. Mr. Zhdanov requested that the following be called as witnesses: Commissars of the Baltic Fleet Stary, Spilevsky, Minaev and Vladimirov; Commanders Zarubaev, Altfater, Yakimov, and Zeleny. The Tribunal refused to summon witnesses living in Moscow but agreed to summon those living in Petrograd and Kronstadt.* This decision

* Distant witnesses, who would not reach Moscow until the trial was over.

was announced to Mr. Zhdanov at 12 noon, June 19. The trial was to take place on the following day at 12. A second lawyer was also refused to Stchastny, as well as his request to receive a copy of the proceedings of the investigation.

Of all witnesses, only Trotsky appeared.

When Zhdanov asked the chairman of the Tribunal, Medvedev, what was the reason of such injustice, Medvedev replied, "We were tried under still worse conditions."

The Supreme Revolutionary Tribunal has two Left Social Revolutionary members. All the rest are Bolsheviks. These two (S.R.) members were not invited to attend the trial, and two Bolsheviks were substituted for them.

Little space was given in the Bolshevik press to Stchastny's trial or execution. The charges against him were not printed.

Spiridonova's Left Social Revolutionary party, however, raised a clamor, although it was as much against the exclusion of their members from the Tribunal as it was over Stchastny's fate, which, nevertheless, was deplored. The Socialist Lefts were against the death penalty "by court sentence." The *Svoboda Rossii* ("Freedom of Russia"), Left Social Revolutionary organ, of June 23, 1918, contained the following article, specific charges against Stchastny lacking, the paper apparently having no knowledge of them:

THE EXECUTION OF STCHASTNY

The former commander of the Baltic fleet, Stchastny, was sentenced to death yesterday by the Supreme Tribunal and was shot at 6 A.M.

Both before the trial and during the trial, in the course of five days, Stchastny was kept under strict guard in the building of the Court Institutions under the direct supervision of the commander of the Tribunal.

At 10 o'clock in the morning he was taken from the building and removed to an unknown place.

Yesterday the counsel for the defense, Zhdanov, inquired of the President of the Tribunal, Medvedev, concerning Stchastny's fate, and Medvedev replied that the verdict already had been carried out. Medvedev gave similar information to Stchastny's relatives. The request of Stchastny's relatives for his body had been refused.

The execution of Stchastny is the main topic of political conversation and serves as a subject of heated debate in the party groups. Prominent Bolshevik leaders declare that they are very much affected by what has taken place but that there could not have been any other outcome.

"The Revolution," they say, "has a right to punish ruthlessly its open enemies who attempt to translate into action their hatred toward the Soviet regime. Therefore, all the protest that capital punishment does not exist in Russia and that there has not been any decree of the Council of People's Commissars concerning its re-establishment, got colored by narrow doctrinairism and a lack of desire to realize that the Revolution has a right to self-defense."

"The Social Revolutionaries of the Left," some of the Bolshevik leaders point out, "committed a grave error at yesterday's session of the Central Executive Committee. They insisted on abrogation of the verdict, for which there were no grounds, instead of demanding an alleviation of the culprit's fate in view of his purely technical services as the Commander of the fleet."

"Then why did you do this?" replied the Social Revolutionaries of the Left.

Among the Socialist Revolutionaries of the Left and the Socialist Opposition General the verdict in the Stchastny case arouses great agitation and protest. An interesting question that is being raised is concerned with the possible attitude toward the event on the part of Generals who are now in the service of the Soviet authorities. There are many reports to the effect that the attitude toward the verdict among the sailors, with whom Stchastny was very popular, and among the workmen, is distinctly negative.

The members of the Left, as has been stated, protested against the sentence of death pronounced by the Supreme Tribunal. Our correspondent has interviewed the leader of the group, Karelin, who said:

"The members of our party did not participate in the opening of the session of the Tribunal as they did not receive the proper notification. When we protested against this, we were told that notice was published in the newspapers. We consider the sentence itself inadmissible because the death penalty was abolished at the Second Congress of the Soviets. No one, not even the Central Executive Committee, has the right to re-establish the death penalty until the convocation of the Fifth Congress, which will meet June 28. Our party has raised the question concerning the abrogation of the sentence in Stchastny's case by the presidium of the Central Executive Committee, but our suggestion was not accepted. We have considered it necessary to recall representatives of our party. In the future we shall continue against capital punishment by court sentence in every way possible."

Spiridonova's attack on Lenin, Trotsky, and Count Mirbach in the Soviet Congress was made on July 4, 1918, ten days later. Stchastny's execution had its part in the break between the Bolsheviks and the Left Social Revolutionaries; the last party allies of the Bolsheviks with whom now they were obliged, if not ready, to dispense.

The veteran Socialist L. Martov, once the friend of Lenin, sent to John Spargo in the United States his opinion of the trial. He said:

Captain Stchastny was accused of conspiring against Soviet power. He denied the charge. He asked the Tribunal to hear witnesses, including Bolshevist Commissars, who had been appointed to watch him. The Tribunal refused to hear witnesses. . . . But the witness for the prosecution was heard. This witness was Trotsky, who as Commissar for War and Navy, had arrested Stchastny. At the hearing of the case by the Tribunal Trotsky acted not as witness but as prosecutor. As a prosecutor he declared, "This man is guilty; you must condemn him!" And Trotsky did it after having gagged the prisoner by refusing to call in witnesses who might refute the accusations against him.

It was not a trial; it was a farce. There was no jury. The judges were officials dependent upon the authorities, receiving their salaries from the hands of Trotsky and other People's Commissars. And this mockery of a court passed the death sentence. . . .

Under Nicholas Romanoff one could sometimes stop the carrying out of a monstrously cruel sentence and pull the victim out of the executioner's hands.

Under Vladimir Ulianov (Lenin) this is impossible.

The Bolshevik leaders slept peacefully when, under cover of the night, the first victim of their Tribunal was stealthily being killed.

No one knew who murdered Stchastny or how he was murdered. No one knows whether Trotsky himself came to the place of execution to watch and direct it.

In the name of Socialism, in thy name, O Proletariat, blind madmen staged this appalling farce of cold-blooded murder![1]

[1] John Spargo, *The Greatest Failure in History.*

THE GERMAN INTELLIGENCE OFFICER
RUDOLPH BAUER

THE keen and active German who went variously under the names of Bauer, Bayermeister, and Bayer, all longer forms of the cipher name Ber, while not the chief of the German military advisory group in Russia, appeared in almost every spot where energy of operation was desired. In my working notes he was listed as second in command of the Nachrichten (Intelligence) Bureau, Section M/R of the German General Staff. In Document No. 5 of my Government Report he was named as Major Bayermeister, cipher signature Ber. His chief, nominal or otherwise, was listed as Major Luberts. Whether Bauer took the name Rudolph for euphony or whether it was his own never was disclosed. I have considerable reason to believe that he was a member of a well-known family of Baltic Germans, long resident in the German settled area of Russia. It might be that the name I could add was his true name. He has delighted me always, however, as a person of aliases and as far as I am concerned he can remain behind them. When my report was published in 1918, the German Government put forward the well-known staff officer, Col. Max Bauer, to deny that he was Bauer of Russia. This he could very well do as he was not the Bauer—or ever named as such.

The last recorded appearance of Bauer, as far as my knowledge goes, was in the Transcaucasus, 1918 and 1921. Rear Admiral Mark L. Bristol, United States High Commissioner in the Near East, sent on January 31, 1921, the following "Memorandum from a reliable source in Tiflis, regarding Bauer, who is expected to arrive shortly in that city to serve with the local German Mission":

Tiflis Jan. 7, 1921. Memorandum for Admiral in re Rudolph Bauer.

1. Rudolph Bauer first came to the Transcaucasus with the German military force that occupied Georgia in 1918 during the summer.

2. He was appointed as German Political Agent at the Turkish Military Headquarters, Batum, the Turks being then in occupation at that port.

3. During the German Occupation, June–November, 1918, he travelled extensively throughout the Transcaucasus.

4. After the German and Turkish armistices, and before British troops came to Batum, he left this country, going to Germany. His movements between that time and the present have not been obtainable at this end.

5. He is expected to return to Tiflis during the present month (January, 1921). A new German Mission is being installed here, one Ulrich Rauscher* succeeding Von Dreuffel as its head. Rauscher and some of his suite arrived here Jan. 4, and were received by representatives of the Georgian Government.

6. During the past two months two letters have been addressed to Bauer in Germany from the Von Dreuffel Mission.

7. Bauer's return to the Transcaucasus in connection with the installation of a new German Mission is significant. It is likely to preface increased German activity in this part of the world.

8. The reappearance of Bauer in Georgia should also be considered in the light of the threatened Russian Bolshevik occupation of Tiflis and Georgia, which in some responsible quarters is considered only a matter of time. The alliance between German military agents and the militarized Moscow Government is well known, as is also the economic and financial aid given by Germans to the Bolsheviks.

* Ulrich Rauscher, who became German Minister to Poland in 1922, following a year of service in Georgia, died in Germany December 18, 1930. Early in the World War he was attached to the press section of the German Government, in Belgium first.

SIDE LIGHT FROM HUNGARY ON GERMAN-BOLSHEVIK RELATIONS AND THE BREST-LITOVSK TREATY

Dispatch of Commissioner U. Grant Smith, American Commissioner, Budapest, February 27, 1920, to State Department, Washington (Extract):

After the fall of the Kerensky Government, the German and Austro-Hungarian military authorities deliberately sent their emissaries, not only to Soviet Russia but likewise to the Ukraine, Poland, and the Baltic provinces. They helped to organize the local governments, and encouraged them to fight indiscriminately against their neighbors. Officers of my acquaintance have told me of their personal activities in this regard, and not one single person who was in an official position here, including Admiral Horthy, has attempted to deny that the whole affair was organized and directed by the respective war offices of the Central Empires.

Germany felt confident of ability to control her own people while chaos might reign beyond her borders; and that terrorism could be overthrown and the dictatorship of the proletariat could be replaced by Governments which could best serve her ends. The German military party deliberately furnished the agitators with practically unlimited funds to carry on their propaganda, first in Russia, and later in other countries of the Entente.

An old acquaintance, an Austro-Hungarian officer, in describing his adventures since last we met in January, 1917, said that he had been in Russia, and had seen a great deal of Bolshevism; that they together with the Germans were supporting the anti-Bolshevist Government in the Ukraine on the one hand while on the other hand they were aiding the Bolshevist Government elsewhere. I remarked, "Then you were playing both ends against the middle," to which he smilingly assented.

He also introduced the subject of the Brest-Litovsk Peace negotiations and fully confirmed my oft-expressed conviction that the Soviet delegates acted according to instructions from the Central Powers, and that the entire affair was staged for the purpose of giving an aspect of legality to the *soi disant* treaties negotiated at that time.

When faced with these facts, when I expressed a desire to inflict punishment on an old acquaintance who had participated in the Brest-Litovsk comedy, an acquaintance who for many years had been a subordinate official in the Foreign Office at Vienna exclaimed with a look of shame, "Yes! Those stupid military politics."

It is known and, in fact, admitted by everyone here that the Russian Soviet army is at present largely commanded by former officers from the Central Empires. The question naturally arises then to what extent they are simply soldiers of fortune who are seeking a livelihood, or are pursuing a plan for the eventual conquest of Russia.

I venture to suggest, therefore, that before any measures are taken to strengthen the resistance of these (former Central Empire) countries which are really responsible for the state of affairs which exist at present in the world, that their present rulers and public should be made to thoroughly understand their responsibility with regard to the propagation of Bolshevism, and that convincing proof should be forthcoming of their absolute sincerity, and that they are not playing the double game as they undoubtedly did in the last days of the War and the early days under the Armistice. In other words, are they sincere in their fight against Bolshevism, or is it simply a ruse in order to obtain the means of strengthening their armed forces while the agents of the Military Party operate in Russia?

COLONEL KALPASHNIKOV'S LETTER TO
COLONEL ANDERSON

Dec. 19, 1917.

Col. Anderson, Jassy.

At least ten days prior to the arrival of Major Perkins here I had thirty-five cars entirely loaded and ready for shipment. Even before Verblunsky went to Rumania we asked for the co-operation of Mr. Iokinsky in the matter of cars and were informed that they could be had at any time.

Knowing that the American Red Cross Mission to Russia has also sent some supplies I went to the Hotel d'Europe and proposed to take some of their cars. From this day on, all our misfortunes began and if we should be blocked up here altogether then (to) Col. Robins and his assistants our gratitude will be due [Note: We can thank them] for having prevented by all legitimate and illegitimate means the Rumanian Mission from getting the automobiles.

At first I was informed that Wardwell had formed a regular train, taking upon himself all responsibility for delivery when I was told that no special formalities were required. I was informed that the American Red Cross Mission to Russia wants to be fair and honest with regard to Smolny, and to the Maximalists, who gave them a special "laissez passer."

I was extremely surprised at hearing all this, but told them it was all right. The next day I was engaged with serious matters, and later on Wardwell in conversation with me began to question me as though I was some criminal capable of embarking on all kinds of questionable things. He wanted to find out from me the names and the general description of my assistants and chauffeurs. When I asked him right out what the strange conversation signifies, he told me that Col. Robins suspects me of the desire of joining, with the automobiles, troops fighting against the Maximalists.

Also this was very inconvenient for me, but as I desired to join you at any rate and as soon as possible, I announced to him immediately that instead of thirty-five Russian chauffeurs, I should take only eight mechanics. Even after this statement, repeating every minute "We must be honest with the Bolsheviks," he tried to insist that I should send this dangerous army of ten unarmed Russians by special train.

Your telegrams have probably been delayed somewhere as I received them only a day ahead of the arrival of Major Perkins. [Note: They were delivered to him, then, on Dec. 15. E. S.] Considering the present state of affairs, Major Perkins decided to send you only ten Fords and one Talbot motor truck and to make the rest ready for shipment as soon as the horizon would clear up.

Robins, in an intensely disagreeable conversation told Perkins he was not going to send his automobiles because this contravenes the desires of Smolny, and attempted to convince him that Col. Verblunsky is on the verge of being arrested by the Maximalists and that I myself am in his, Robins', opinion, a suspicious person. He informed him of a few more details referring to me with animosity as if to a dangerous Counter-Revolutionist.

All this was set forth in a written statement which Perkins as an honest man, signed and delivered to me. At the same time Perkins asked me to do everything possible to ship the necessary automobiles to you. Owing to this I had to hold back not only automobiles but many other supplies received for the American Red Cross in accordance with your telegram.

Now I wish to make the following definite statement: I consider Col. Robins as a man who has been playing a false game and acting not only against me but also against the interests of the American Mission to Rumania in an entirely ungentlemanly and revolting way. And when Perkins asked for the straight evidence against me, and my work neither Robins or Wardwell could say anything except—"We are suspecting—we must be honest in regard to Smolny."

I personally consider this campaign an unworthy "bluff," unbecoming a representative of the United States.

If this statement regarding the possibility of an arrest of Verblunsky, and perhaps also myself, is correct (these times anybody may be arrested) this would accentuate the close friendship of the Maximalists with Col. Robins. I would even go further. There is a certain affinity in their views, because the Maximalists are not such gentlemen that they would give away their secrets to the first comer who would knock at their door, especially if he is a foreigner.

Formally the Maximalists did not know even about the existence of my automobiles and if they issued to me a certificate for their safety this was only due to a paper from the Embassy requesting this.

Now it is possible that after the "mess" caused by Robins that these automobiles can be seized. Eleven automobiles could have been shipped today by the Rumanians (who wanted to do this) but for the interference of the American Mission to Russia, continuing its policy of preventing by all possible means their shipment.

When the first train of thirty-five cars was loaded the Russian Red Cross turned it over to me as your official representative and all expenditures which may be caused on account of the delay of the shipment will have to be covered by the Mission to Rumania. I discussed all details of the financial aspect of the matter with Major Perkins who gave his consent in principle, and with the next courier I shall render you an itemized account.

I am entertaining great hopes of defeating the enemy and to deliver not only the automobiles but also everything else you have ordered in your telegrams.

Your last telegram inquires concerning one hundred [?] rubber gloves. I am sending you three hundred because Wardwell insists on the absolute necessity of having one thousand pairs, and for the purpose of getting even three hundred I had to call on several stores not only in Petrograd but Moscow as well.

Since I left you I have been working very hard and never expected surprises of this kind from your compatriots in the American Mission in Russia. But knowing your views and the great work you are doing for Rumania, I decided to continue energetically the work which you desire me to do for you.

Trusting that this letter will find you in good health, I remain, dear Colonel,

Yours respectfully,
A. KALPASHNIKOV.

MEMORANDUM OF INTERVIEWS
WITH MAJOR PERKINS

"Memorandum of Interviews with Major Perkins," compiled by American Red Cross staff at Petrograd, Dec. 18, 1917, as follows:

Major Perkins arrived at the Hotel d'Europe, Dec. 16, 1917 at 10:30 o'clock in the morning. He was met by Majors Wardwell and Thacher; and a short interview lasting not more than 10 minutes took place between Majors Wardwell, Thacher, Perkins and Col. Robins. In this interview, Major Perkins, when informed that a train load of supplies was ready to be immediately dispatched to Rumania, replied that no supplies whatsoever should be shipped to Rumania [General supplies independent of Kalpashnikov's motor car train load]. He stated that Rumania was out of the war and that the American Red Cross would not render any further relief, preferring to use the supplies elsewhere. Col. Robins asked Major Perkins if he had definite instructions from Col. Anderson to this effect, and Major Perkins replied that he had. Col. Robins then stated that the train would be held and that if Col. Anderson so ordered no supplies would be sent to Rumania.

Immediately instructions were given by Col. Robins to hold the train; and these instructions were promptly carried out.

Nothing further was seen of Major Perkins by any member of the Russian Mission until about 6:30 P.M. on Sunday when he called on Major Thacher who was shortly joined by Col. Robins and later by Major Wardwell.

Before Col. Robins came into the room, however, Major Thacher explained to Major Perkins that the supplies which had been purchased had been largely paid for with funds of the Rumanian Government; the balance being paid for by part of the proceeds of the One Million Dollar credit authorized by the American Red Cross in Washington, but that such expenditures as had been made from the proceeds of this credit were covered by an obligation of the Rumanian Government to repay the same from the proceeds of any loan which might be made by the United States to the Government of Rumania; that consequently the question involved was whether or not the American Red Cross should assist in any way in the shipment of the supplies which belonged to the Rumanian Government, and would in any event have to be shipped to Rumania.

Major Perkins agreed that the supplies whether paid for with funds of the Rumanian Government or by advances of the American Red Cross, should be regarded as belonging to the Rumanian Government; but stated that whether or not it should eventually be considered advisable for the American Red Cross to assist in the shipment of these supplies, it was impossible to consider shipping them at the present time because they could not be delivered at destination. In response Major Thacher stated his belief that the supplies could be delivered if promptly shipped but Major Perkins was equally positive in the belief that it would be unwise to attempt to ship the supplies at once.

Col. Robins then joined the conference and Major Perkins proceeded to give a careful statement of the situation as he understood it to be in Rumania, leading up to the conclusion that Rumania had finished fighting and had but a single choice to make—between a separate peace with Germany and a return to Bucharest with German aid or a retirement from Rumania into Bessarabia. While Major Perkins stated that this choice was still open, he expressed the opinion that Rumania would be forced by the circumstances into making a separate peace with Germany which would be quite acceptable to the upper-class Rumanians.

After this discussion of the general situation Major Perkins positively stated that in view of the fact that all fighting had ceased there would be no need whatsoever for any motor cars in Rumania; that more than enough cars of every conceivable purpose had been released from active service on the front, and that consequently none of the cars loaded on the Red Cross train should be shipped. This was agreed to by Col. Robins and it was definitely decided not to ship any motor cars.

In the course of the discussion Major Perkins stated that Col. Anderson was planning to leave Rumania and move his entire unit to the British front in Mesopotamia; that the plan discussed before he left Jassy involved the sending of Col. Kalpashnikov's motor cars to Rostov-on-Don so that they might be transported from there to Mesopotamia, but that in view of the disorders at Rostov he would advise against shipping any motor cars to Rostov at the present time, stating that it was impossible to think of doing such a thing.

The question whether the American Red Cross should assist in the transportation of the supplies purchased by it for the Rumanian Government, either with the funds of that Government or by making advances to it, was then discussed. Major Perkins was still of the opinion that no shipment could be made at the present time. He mentioned the fact that the railroads of Southern Russia were entirely dependent upon coal supplies from the region of the Don and stated his opinion to be that all railroads probably would be tied up. When asked what prejudice there could possibly be to the American Red Cross in endeavoring to the extent of its ability to assist the Rumanian Government in making shipments he said it was against the tenets of the Red Cross to handle any supplies which were to be sold at more than their cost price; that, in his judgment these supplies, if handed over to the Rumanians, would be sold at more than cost and that to assist in the transportation might be a breach of this rule. On this point Major Perkins was answered by Major Wardwell that he had the personal assurance from the Rumanian Minister in Petrograd, which he had promised to reduce to writing, that none of the supplies to be transported would be sold at more than cost. In the same connection Major Perkins stated that the Rumanians could not be trusted to distribute the supplies if delivered in Rumania, and in view of Col. Anderson's contemplated departure very little good would be accomplished by assisting the Rumanian authorities in getting the supplies there.

The conclusion of this discussion was that Major Perkins stated that in so far as the transportation of these supplies—not including the automobiles—was concerned, he desired to consider the matter over night and would confer with us at 10 o'clock the following morning. In leaving, Major Perkins stated to Major Wardwell and Major Thacher that the sole question to be discussed the following morning was whether or not we should assist in the transportation of supplies belonging to the Rumanian Government and again stated that the question of automobiles was decided.

The next day, Monday, Dec. 17th, Major Perkins called on Majors Wardwell and Thacher at about 10:30 A.M.; stated that he had decided that the supplies purchased by the Rumanian Government should go forward, and that he desired that about twelve motor cars with certain supplies and gasoline and extra parts, etc., should also be transported. A tentative conclusion was reached but upon communication with Col. Robins the latter stated to Majors Wardwell and Thacher that the situation in the Ukraine was most critical, that an open break between the de facto Russian Government and the Ukrainian Rada was quite probable and that in view of this situation which might result immediately in civil war he regarded it as impossible to ship with the other supplies any motor cars whatsoever; that the shipment of such supplies would endanger the successful transportation of the clothing and clothing material needed by the civil populace of Rumania.

Major Wardwell immediately endeavored to communicate with Major Perkins and Col. Kalpashnikov in order to advise them of the situation and of Col. Robins' conclusion that the automobiles should not be shipped, and made repeated attempts to communicate with either or both of them during the day. Finally about 5:30 P.M. Major Perkins came to the office of the American Red Cross in the Hotel d'Europe and there met Major Wardwell. Major Wardwell explained to him Col. Robins' decision that no motor cars should be moved.

Major Perkins immediately insisted upon the moving of these motors, explaining that in his judgment they would be useful and necessary for the removal of Col. Anderson and his staff from Rumania if that should become necessary, and requesting also that the Russian mechanics and chauffeurs—ten or twelve in number—should be allowed to accompany them on the ground that the Rumanian chauffeurs did not operate the Ford car satisfactorily; that Col. Kalpashnikov and his assistant, Col. Verblunsky, would not accompany the cars.

Major Wardwell explained to Major Perkins that in the judgment of Col. Robins and himself the attempt to transport motor cars through the Ukraine would seriously endanger, if not render impossible, the transportation of the other supplies needed by the civilian population in Rumania; that the only question was whether the motor cars should be transported with the Red Cross train, and that the Russian Mission would not attempt to prevent Col. Kalpashnikov from transporting his cars to Rumania as had been originally planned by Col. Anderson; that the Russian Mission had merely offered to assist Col. Kalpashnikov when it became evident that Col. Kalpashnikov was unwilling to assume the responsibility for the transportation of his cars under present conditions and with no more protection than he was able to afford.

Major Perkins nevertheless urged the movement of the motor cars and mechanics and chauffeurs, and at this point Major Wardwell said the matter ought to be taken up with Col. Robins, and thereupon asked Col. Robins to come in.

On Col. Robins' arrival he advised that the situation in the Ukraine would not permit the shipment of the automobiles, and that an attempt to ship them would seriously endanger the transportation of the other supplies for Rumania.

Major Perkins objected, stating his wishes in regard to the motor cars in substantially the same words used with Major Wardwell, and criticized the conduct of the Russian Mission, charging that it had continuously blocked the efforts of the Rumanian Mission to render relief in Rumania. He said that when the Russian Mission had not blocked, it had interfered with and delayed their plans and that if it had not been for the Russian Mission the motor cars would have already been in Rumania; that he was expressing not only his own opinion but the opinion of Col. Anderson; that we had treated the Rumanian Mission as a mere appendage of the Russian Mission.

Col. Robins simply stated to Major Perkins that he was sorry that that was his feeling; that he could not agree with him, and that nevertheless the motor cars could not be moved.

Col. Robins then left the room and within ten minutes thereafter received direct instructions from the Russian de facto government that the transportation of the entire train was refused and would be prohibited because a definite break between the Ukrainian Rada and the Russian de facto government had occurred. Col. Robins immediately advised Major Perkins of these instructions.

On the following day, Tuesday, Dec. 18th, Col. Robins had an interview with the representatives of the Russian de facto government as the result of which he received written instructions authorizing the dispatch of the train of cars containing clothing and other materials for civilian relief, but that no motor cars could be transported.

The statement ended with the indorsement: "Dec. 18, 1917. To the extent of my knowledge the foregoing statement is correct. (Signed) Raymond Robins, Thomas D. Thacher, Allen Wardwell."

FACSIMILE REPRODUCTION OF THE RE-
PORT, "THE GERMAN-BOLSHEVIK
CONSPIRACY"

IN THE PAMPHLET FORM OF ITS ISSUE BY
THE COMMITTEE ON PUBLIC INFORMATION
OF THE UNITED STATES GOVERNMENT IN OC-
TOBER, 1918, ONE MONTH AFTER ITS PUBLICA-
TION IN DAILY NEWSPAPER INSTALMENTS,
FIVE MONTHS AFTER ITS SUBMISSION IN
MANUSCRIPT FORM ON MAY 9 TO PRESIDENT
WILSON

The GERMAN-BOLSHEVIK
CONSPIRACY

ISSUED BY

THE COMMITTEE ON PUBLIC INFORMATION
GEORGE CREEL, Chairman

CONTENTS

The German-Bolshevik Conspiracy

INTRODUCTION

The Committee on Public Information publishes herewith a series of communications between the German Imperial Government and the Russian Bolshevik Government, and between the Bolsheviks themselves, and also the report thereon made to George Creel by Edgar Sisson, the committee's special representative in Russia during the winter of 1917-18. There is also included, in Part II, a report by a committee appointed by the National Board for Historical Service to examine into the genuineness of these documents.

The documents show that the present heads of the Bolshevik Government—Lenin and Trotsky and their associates—are German agents.

They show that the Bolshevik revolution was arranged for by the German Great General Staff, and financed by the German Imperial Bank and other German financial institutions.

They show that the treaty of Brest-Litovsk was a betrayal of the Russian people by the German agents, Lenin and Trotsky; that a German-picked commander was chosen to "defend" Petrograd against the Germans; that German officers have been secretly received by the Bolshevik Government as military advisers, as spies upon the embassies of Russia's allies, as officers in the Russian army, and as directors of the Bolshevik military, foreign, and domestic policy. They show, in short, that the present Bolshevik Government is not a Russian government at all, but a German government acting solely in the interests of Germany and betraying the Russian people, as it betrays Russia's natural allies, for the benefit of the Imperial German Government alone.

Russian Workmen Betrayed

And they show also that the Bolshevik leaders, for the same German Imperial ends, have equally betrayed the working classes of Russia whom they pretend to represent.

The documents are some 70 in number. Many are originals, annotated by Bolshevik officials. The balance of the others are photographs of originals, showing annotations. And they corroborate a third set of typewritten circulars (see Appendix later) of which only two originals are possessed in any form, but all of which fit into the whole pattern of German intrigue and German guilt.

The first document is a photograph of a report made to the Bolshevik leaders by two of their assistants, informing them that, in accordance with their instructions, there had been removed from the archives of the Russian Ministry of Justice, the order of the German Imperial Bank "allowing money to Comrades Lenin, Trotsky, 'and others' for the propaganda of peace in Russia"; and that, at the same time, "all the books" of a bank in Stockholm had been "audited" to conceal the payment of money to Lenin, Trotsky, and their associates, by order of the German Imperial Bank.

This report is indorsed, in Lenin's initials, "V. U." [Vladimir Ulianoff, his real name], for deposit in "the secret department" of the Bolshevik files. And the authenticity of the report is supported by Document No. 2, which is the original of a report sent by a German General Staff representative to the Bolshevik leaders, warning them that he has just arrested an agent who had in his possession the original order of the German Imperial Bank referred to in Document No. 1, and pointing out that evidently "at the proper time steps were not taken to destroy the above-mentioned documents."

Protocol Signed by Leaders

Document No. 3 is the original protocol signed by several Bolshevik leaders and dated November 2, 1917 (Russian calendar), showing that "on instructions of the representatives of the German General Staff in Petrograd" and "with the consent of the Council of People's Commissars," of which Trotsky and Lenin were the heads, two incriminating German circulars had also been "taken from the Department of Counter Espionage of the Petrograd district" and given to the Intelligence Bureau of the German General Staff in Petrograd. On the bottom of the protocol the German adjutant acknowledges receipt of the two incriminating circulars with his cipher signature.

These two circulars apparently had been obtained early in the war by some Russian agent in Germany and transmitted to Russia. The German General Staff evidently wished to get them back in order to remove evidence. By the order of the German General Staff and with the "consent" of Lenin and Trotsky they are turned over to the Germans. Why? Because they fit in with other information of Germany's war plans and preparations before August, 1914. Indeed, several weeks before the assassination of the Austrian Archduke, which was made the pretext for war.

And Lenin and Trotsky surrender them in conformity with a working agreement between the Bolshevik leaders and the German General Staff, of which agreement a photograph is included in the series as Document No. 5.

This is dated October 25, 1917. It is from a division of the German General Staff. It is addressed to the Government of the People's Commissars, of which Lenin and Trotsky were the heads. It begins: "In accordance with the agreement which took place in Kronstadt, in July of the present year, between officials of our General Staff and leaders of the Russian revolutionary army and democracy, Messrs. Lenin and Trotsky, Raskolnikov, and Dybenko, the Russian Division of our General Staff operating in Finland is ordering to Petrograd officers for the disposal of the Intelligence Bureau of the staff." Among the officers named are Maj. Luberts and, Lieut. Hartwig, whose cipher signature, Henrich, is given as it appears on the receipt for the two circulars accompanying Document No. 3. And an indorsement on this letter (No. 5) from the German General Staff records that the German officers assigned to Petrograd had appeared "before the military revolutionary committee" and had "agreed on conditions with regard to their mutual activities."

Mutual Activities Shown

What their "mutual activities" were to be is sufficiently indicated by Document No. 7, which is a photograph of a letter signed in cipher by this Maj. Luberts and his adjutant, Lieut. Hartwig. They notify the Bolshevik leaders, on January 12, 1918 (Russian calendar), that "by order of the German General Staff" the German Intelligence Bureau "has reported the names and the characteristics of the main candidates for reëlection" to the Russian Bolshevik "Central Executive Committee," and "the General Staff orders us to insist on the election of the following persons." They add a list of Russian leaders satisfactory to the German General Staff. The list is headed by Trotsky and Lenin. They were elected, and the rest of the present Bolshevik executive committee were chosen from the same German list.

Document No. 8 gives evidence of the *quid pro quo*. It is a photograph of a letter from the representative of the German Imperial Bank to the Bolshevik Commissar of Foreign Affairs. It is marked "Very secret" and dated January 8, 1918. It says: "Notification has to-day been received by me from Stockholm that 50,000,000 roubles of gold has been transferred to be put at the disposal of the People's Commissars," which is the title of the Bolshevik leaders. "This credit," the letter continues, "has been supplied to the Russian Government in order to cover the cost of the keep of the Red Guards [the Bolshevik revolutionary troops] and agitators in the country. The Imperial Government considers it appropriate to remind the Council of People's Commissars of the necessity of increasing their propaganda in the country, as the antagonistic attitude of the south of Russia and Siberia to the existing Government in Russia is troubling the German Government."

War Materials at Vladivostok

Four days later the same representative of the German Imperial Bank sent another 5,000,000 roubles to the same address to provide for the sending of a Russian revolutionary leader to Vladivostok, to get possession of the "Japanese and American war materials" at that port, and if necessary to destroy them. A photograph of his letter is given as Document No. 9.

There were earlier payments, but probably none later than these. None was necessary. By this time the loot of an empire lay open to the Bolsheviks—and to the Germans.

Most significant of all are two photographs of further communications from the German Imperial Bank, given as Documents Nos. 10 and 11. One is a letter addressed to the Chairman of the Council of People's Commissars, and the other is the "resolution of a conference of representatives of the German commercial banks" received by the Chairman of the Bolshevik Central Executive Committee and indorsed by his secretary. Together they give a complete synopsis of the terms on which Germany intends to have control of all Russian industries.

For five years from the signing of peace, English, French, and American capital in Russia is to be "banished" and "not to be allowed in the following industries: coal, metallurgical, machine building, oil, chemical, and pharmaceutical." These industries are to be developed under the control of a "supreme advisory organ consisting of 10 Russian specialists, 10 from the German industrial organizations and the German and Austrian banks." Germany and Austria are to "enjoy the unlimited privilege of sending into Russia mechanics and qualified workmen." "Other foreign mechanics and workmen . . . are not to be allowed to enter at all" for five years after the conclusion of peace between Russia and Germany. "Private banks in Russia arise only with the consent" of the Union of German and Austrian banks. And so forth.

Conspiracy is Indorsed

And this conspiracy between German Imperial capitalism and the pretended Russian Reds is indorsed by a Bolshevik leader, with the recommendation that it should be "taken under advisement" and "the ground prepared in the Council of the Workmen's and Soldiers' Deputies, in case the Council of People's Commissars will not accept these requests."

Various details of the conspiracy between the Bolshevik leaders and the German General Staff are exposed in documents Nos. 16 to 29. These are photographs of letters which passed between the Bolshevik leaders and the German General Staff, or the German officers in Russia. Document No. 21 shows that on November 1, 1917, when Russia was still regarded as an ally of Great Britain, France, and America, the German General Staff was having "the honor to request" the Bolshevik leaders to inform it "at the earliest possible moment" concerning "the quantity and storage place of the supplies which have been received from America, England, and France, and also the units which are keeping guard over the military stores."

Document 18 shows the German General Staff requiring the Bolshevik leaders to send "agitators to the camps of the Russian prisoners of war in Germany," in order that they might procure spies to work among the English and French troops and to further "peace propaganda." And this is proposed by the German General Staff as being "according to the negotiations between the Russian and German peace delegations at Brest-Litovsk."

In Document 22 the Bolshevik leaders and the Germans are arranging to send "agents-agitators, and agents-destructors" out of Vladivostok "to ports of the United States, Japan, and British colonies in Eastern Asia."

Passports for Germans

In Document 16 Trotsky is providing fraudulent passports for German officers who are going to England, France, and America, as spies and enemy agents. And Document 17 shows Trotsky indorsing a similar proposal: "To be urgently executed. L. T."

Three German submarines are to be sent to the Pacific on the trans-Siberian railway by orders of the German High Command in Document No. 23. Lists of German and Russian spies watching the British, French, and American embassies in Petrograd are given in Document No. 25. And, finally, in Document No. 15 the Bolshevik leaders are warned that information concerning "the connection of the German Government with the Bolshevik workers" has leaked out and that Russian troops are hearing of it.

Letters are given to show how the Bolshevik leaders and the German officers arranged for the assassination of Russian Nationalist leaders (Documents 35, 39, and 52), for the destruction of the Polish legionaries in the Russian army (Documents 40 to 42), for the disorganization of the Roumanian army and the de-

posing of the Roumanian king (Document No. 37), for the substitution of officers satisfactory to Germany in command of Russian troops instead of patriotic Russian generals (Documents 31 and 32), for the suppression of patriotic agitation among the Russian soldiers (Documents 13 and 14), for an attack upon the Italian ambassador in Petrograd and the theft of his papers (Documents 26 and 27), and for the employment of German soldiers in Russian uniforms against the Russian national armies in the South (Document 35).

Several of the letters are indorsed by Trotsky. Even standing alone, they are complete proof that the Bolshevik leaders were ruling as German agents in Russia, and obeying German orders to act against all Germany's enemies and even against Russia itself.

Acted as German Agents

Moreover, these Bolshevik leaders acted as German agents by suppressing their own socialist revolution in the Russian provinces where their doctrines interfered with German plans of annexation. Document 46 is the original letter from the Petrograd Intelligence Bureau of the German General Staff addressed to the Bolshevik Commissar of Foreign Affairs. It reads: "According to instructions of the representative of our General Staff, I have the honor once more to insist that you recall from Esthonia, Lithuania, and Courland all agitators of the Central Executive Committee of the Council of Workmen's and Soldiers' Deputies." And in Document 47 the General Staff orders the Bolsheviki to cease the agitation in Esthonia which had "finally led to the local German landlords being declared outlawed," and to "take immediate steps for the restoring of the rights of the above-mentioned German landlords."

Another group of letters (Nos. 33 to 36) shows how the Germans cheated the Bolshevik leaders in their dealings with the Ukraine and made a separate German peace with the anti-Bolshevik leaders in that Russian province. And another group shows the Germans assisting both sides of the civil war in Finland (Documents 38, 43, and 53).

The documents, as they follow, are given in the main in the report form in which they were transmitted by Mr. Sisson to Mr. Creel, chairman of the committee, with some later data added and carefully indicated. For instance, Mr. Sisson did not learn until several weeks after he had left Russia that the German order (which he possessed) naming the Russian who was to "defend" Petrograd had been obeyed.

In preparing this material for publication as a pamphlet advantage has been taken of the opportunity to improve in some mooted points the form in which the documents and translations are presented.

PART I
The German-Bolshevik Conspiracy
A REPORT BY
E D G A R   S I S S O N
Special Representative in Russia of the Committee on Public Information in the Winter of 1917-18

CHAPTER I.
THE BASIC CONSPIRACY

Three groups of documents are subjected to internal analysis in the material that follows. One group consists of originals, one group consists of photographs of documents believed still to be in the file rooms of the Russian Bolsheviki, and the third (Appendix I) of typewritten circulars that have not been traced to their originals except perhaps in the case of two of the number. The chief importance of the third group is that its appearance inspired the efforts that led to the uncovering of the other groups. And they fit into the fabric of the whole.

The first set of these appendix circulars came into my hands on February 2, in Petrograd. An additional set appeared the following day at an office where I frequently called. A third appeared in another quarter a day afterwards. One set was in Russian and two in English. On February 5 I held all three sets. A possible explanation for their appearance at this time and their intent is given in Appendix I.

By themselves they were plausible but not substantiated. Having first performed the obvious duty of analyzing them for surface values and transmitting them and the analyses to Washington, I turned, therefore, to the task of further investigations.

It is not yet possible to name those who helped, but in three weeks' time the judgment of facts became apparent.

The text of the documents discloses both the methods and the effects of the German conspiracy not alone against Russia but the world. With each document is the indication of whether it is an original or photograph. With each document is an interpretative note.

DOCUMENT NO. 1

People's Commissary for Foreign Affairs.
(Very Secret)
Petrograd, November 16, 1917.
To the Chairman of the Council of
People's Commissars:

In accordance with the resolution passed by the conference of People's Commissars, Comrades Lenin, Trotsky, Podvoisky, Dybenko, and Volodarsky, the following has been executed by us:

1. In the archives of the Ministry of Justice from the dossier *re* "treason" of Comrades Lenin, Zinovieff, Koslovsky, Kollontai and others, has been removed the order of the German Imperial Bank, No. 7433, of the second of March, 1917, for allowing money to Comrades Lenin, Zinovieff, Kameneff, Trotsky, Sumenson, Koslovsky and others for the propaganda of peace in Russia.

2. There have been audited all the books of the Nia Bank at Stockholm containing the accounts of Comrades Lenin, Trotsky, Zinovieff, and others, which were opened by the order of the German Imperial Bank No. 2754. These books have been delivered to Comrade Müller, who was sent from Berlin.

Authorized by the Commissar for Foreign Affairs.
E. POLIVANOFF.
F. ZALKIND.

NOTE.—*The Russian Council of People's Commissars was dominated by the president, Vladimir Ulianov (Lenin); the then foreign minister, Leon Trotsky, now war minister; and the ambassador to Germany, A. Joffe. The marginal indorsement in writing is: "To the secret department. B. U." This is the fashion in which Lenin is accustomed to initial himself. The English equivalent would be V. U., for Vladimir Ultanov. So, even if there existed no further record of German Imperial Bank order No. 7433, here would be the proof of its contents, and here is the link connecting Lenin directly with his action and his guilt. The content matter of the circular exists, however, and herewith follows:*

Order of the 2d of March, 1917, of the Imperial Bank for the representatives of all German banks in Sweden:

Notice is hereby given that requisition for money for the purpose of peace propaganda in Russia will be received through Finland. These requisitions will emanate from the following: Lenin, Zinovieff, Kameneff, Trotsky, Sumenson, Koslovsky, Kollontai, Sivers, and Merkalin, accounts for whom have been opened in accordance with our order No. 2754 in the agencies of private German businesses in Sweden, Norway, and Switzerland. All these requests should

bear one of the two following signatures: Dirshau or Milkenberg. With either of these signatures the requests of the above-mentioned persons should be complied with without delay.—7433, IMPERIAL BANK.

I have not a copy of this circular nor a photograph of it, but Document No. 2, next in order, proves its authenticity at once curiously and absolutely. Particular interest attaches to this circular because of Bolshevik public denial of its existence. It was one of several German circulars published in Paris in the "Petit Parisien" last winter. The Petrograd Bolshevik papers proclaimed it a falsehood. Zalkind, whose signature appears not only here but on the protocol (Document No. 3), was an assistant foreign minister. He was sent in February on a mission outside of Russia. He was in Christiania in April when I was there.

Have photograph of the letter.

DOCUMENT NO. 2

G[reat] G[eneral] S[taff], . Intelligence [Nachrichten] Bureau, Section A, No. 292.

(Secret)
February 12, 1918.
To the Chairman of the Council of People's Commissars:

The Intelligence Bureau has the honor to inform you that there

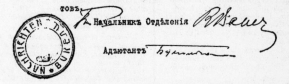

G. G.-S.
NACHRICHTEN-BUREAU.

Section *R.*

№ 72

12 Февраля 1918 г.

Г. Предсѣдателю Совѣта Народныхъ Комиссаровъ.

№ 1845. Секретно.

Развѣдочное Отдѣленіе имѣетъ честь сообщить, что найденные у арестованнаго кап. Коншина два германскихъ документа съ помѣтками и штемпелями Петербургскаго Охраннаго Отдѣленія, представляютъ собою подлинные приказы Имперскаго Банка за № 7433 отъ 2 Марта 1817 года объ открытіи счетовъ г.г. Ленину, Суменсонъ, Ковловскому, Трошкому и другимъ дѣятелямъ на пропаганду мира, по ордеру Имперскаго Банка за № 2754.

Это открытіе доказываетъ, что не были своевременно приняты мѣры для уничтоженія означенныхъ документовъ.

Начальникъ Отдѣленія

Адъютантъ

Facsimile of Document Number 2

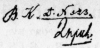

ПРОТОКОЛЪ

Сей протоколъ составленъ нами 2 Ноября 1917 года въ двухъ экземплярахъ въ томъ, что нами съ согласія Совѣта Народныхъ Комиссаровъ изъ дѣлъ Контръ-Развѣдочнаго Отдѣленія Петроградскаго Округа и бывш. Департамента Полиціи, по порученію Представителей Германскаго Генеральнаго Штаба въ Петроградѣ изъяты:

1. Циркуляръ Германскаго Генеральнаго Штаба за № 421 отъ 9 Іюня 1914 г. о немедленной мобилизаціи всѣхъ промышленныхъ предпріятій въ Германіи и

2. Циркуляръ Генеральнаго Штаба Флота Открытаго Моря за № 93 отъ 28 Ноября 1914 г. о посылкѣ во враждебныя страны спеціальныхъ агентовъ для истребленія боевыхъ запасовъ и матеріаловъ.

Означенные циркуляры переданы подъ росписку въ Развѣдочное Отдѣленіе Германскаго Штаба въ Петроградѣ

Уполномоченные Совѣта Народныхъ Комиссаровъ

Означенные въ настоящемъ протоколѣ циркуляры № № 421 и 93, а также одинъ экземпляръ этого протокола получены 3 Ноября 1917 г. Развѣдочнымъ Отдѣломъ Г.Г.Ш. въ Петербургѣ.

Адъютантъ

Document Number 3—Facsimile of Protocol

were found on the arrested Capt. Konshin two German documents with notations and stamps of the Petersburg secret police [Okhrana] which show themselves to be the original orders of the Imperial Bank, No. 7433, March 2, 1917, concerning the opening of accounts for Messrs. Lenin, Sumenson, Koslovsky, Trotsky, and other active workers on the peace propaganda, by order No. 2754 of the Imperial Bank.

These discoveries show that at the proper time steps were not taken to destroy the above-mentioned documents.

For the head of the Bureau:
       R. BAUER.
Adjutant: BUKHOLM.

NOTE.—*Observe the thoughtfulness with which Bauer, a careful man, set down ex-*

actly what was in the document, thereby permitting the contents to rise again from the ashes to which perhaps he committed the damaging paper. He admits that the documents found were truthful originals. The world will thank him and Germany will not.

I have the original letter. It bears marginal indorsements: "Referred to the Commission for Combating Counter Revolution. Demanded documents. M. Skripnik"; and an illegible comment by N. Gorbunoff, Lenin's other Government secretary. The letter is directed to Lenin. Did Skripnik get the documents? I do not know.

The letter is remarkable otherwise, for the arrested Capt. Konshin mentioned is a German officer, Lieut. Otto, who appears elsewhere as an agent in the German double-crossing intrigue in the Ukraine. What was behind the mystery of his arrest? What was his fate?

NOTE (Oct. 1, 1918).—*The order of the second of March, 1917, as pointed out in the note to Document 1, has had publicity since last winter, and naturally has been*

subject to the attack of the defenders of Lenin and Trotsky. The effort at confusion, however, is of the straw-man variety. If this date were in the Western European calendar, it would precede the March Revolution. So the defenders of Lenin and Trotsky have argued against the letter that it must have been written by a Counter-Revolutionary Russian who FORGOT the 13 days' difference in time between the Russian and the European calendar. Curiously, the persons who make this contention overlook the reverse of such an argument—that the order was written by a German who KNEW AND USED the Russian calendar. He ought in common sense to have used it, as the letter was written to state when orders for money from Russians would be honored.

The Germans who maneuvered in Russia were letter perfect in Russian form (See Document 5, "who use the Russian language perfectly and who are acquainted with Russian conditions.")

But the date, March 2, may be either German or Russian, for any important bearing it has on the documents. If German, it was written before the March Revolution, but in preparation for getting into it as soon as it started. Many persons, both in Russia and in Germany, knew of an impending effort at Revolution. What more natural on Berlin's part than to desire to get its "agents-disturbers" there? And if they were at that moment widely scattered over the world, the more reason to begin quickly to call them in.

DOCUMENT NO. 3

V. K. [Military Commissariat] D. No. 323—two inclosures.

PROTOCOL

This protocol, drawn up by us on the 2d of November, 1917, in duplicate, declares that we have taken with the consent of the Council of People's Commissars from the papers of the Department of Counter Espionage of the Petrograd district and the former Department of Police [Okhrana], on instructions of the representatives of the German General Staff in Petrograd:

1. Circular of the German General Staff No. 421, dated June 9, 1914, concerning the immediate mobilization of all industrial enterprises in Germany, and

2. Circular No. 93, dated November 28, 1914, of the General Staff of the High Sea Fleet, concerning the sending into enemy countries of special agents for the destruction of war supplies and materials.

The above noted circulars were given over under signed receipt into the Intelligence Bureau of the German Staff in Petrograd.

Authorized by the Council of People's Commissars.

      F. ZALKIND.
      E. POLIVANOFF.
(Illegible, but may be Mekhanoshin.)
      A. JOFFE.

The Circulars No. 421 and No. 93 mentioned in this protocol and also one copy of this protocol were received on the 3d of November, 1917, by the Intelligence Bureau of the G[reat] G[eneral] S[taff] in Petersburg.
Adjutant: HENRICH.

R. GENERALSTAB.
CENTRAL ABTHEILUNG.

Section M.

№ — —
Berlin.

CIRCULAR

vom 9 Juni 1914

an Bezirkscommendanten.

Nach 24 Stunden vom Empfang des vorliegenden Circulars alle Besitzer der Industrie-
unternehmungen telegraphisch zu benachrichtigen die Packete mit mobilisations—gewerbli-
chen graphischen Darstellungen und Plänen zu eröffnen, die im Circular der Komission
von Graf Waldersee und Caprivi vom 27 Juni 1887 angewiesen sind.

№ 421 Der Mobilisationsabtheilung.

Document No. 3—Facsimile of June 9 Circular

NOTE.—*The circulars inclosed are
printed in German, and are as follows:*

Gr[eat] General Staff, Central Division,
Section M, No. —, Berlin.
CIRCULAR OF JUNE 9, 1914, TO DISTRICT
COMMANDERS:

Within 24 hours of the receipt of this
circular you are to inform all industrial
concerns by wire that the documents
with industrial mobilization plans and
with registration forms be opened, such
as are referred to in the circular of the
Commission of Count Waldersee and
Caprivi, of June 27, 1887.
No. 421, Mobilization Division.

G[eneral] S[taff] of the High Sea Fleet,
No. 93.
CIRCULAR OF NOVEMBER 28, 1914, TO
MARINE AGENCIES AND NAVAL
SOCIETIES:

You are ordered to mobilize immediately all destruction agents and
observers in those commercial and
military ports where munitions are
being loaded on ships going to England,
France, Canada, the United States of
North America, and Russia, where
there are storehouses of such munitions, and where fighting units are stationed. It is necessary to hire through
third parties who stand in no relation
to the official representatives of Germany agents for arranging explosions
on ships bound for enemy countries,
and for arranging delays, embroilments,
and difficulties during the loading, dispatching, and unloading of ships. For
this purpose we are especially recommending to your attention loaders'
gangs, among whom there are many
anarchists and escaped criminals, and
that you get in touch with German and
neutral shipping offices as a means of
observing agents of enemy countries
who are receiving and shipping the
munitions.

Funds required for the hiring and
bribing of persons necessary for the
designated purpose will be placed at
your disposal at your request.
Intelligence Bureau of the General
Staff of the High Sea Fleet.
KOENIG.

NOTE.—*Both the circulars bear the penciled notation that "one copy has been given
to the German Intelligence Bureau" at
Petrograd. The German intent here was to
remove from the records of the old Russian
Government the evidence, first, that Germany
was beginning in June, 1914, its active
preparations for the war that surprised the
world in August, 1914, and second, to remove the evidence of its responsibility for
incendiarism and explosions in the United
States, a country with which Germany was
then at peace. The result was to give new
evidence of the truth of the charges. The
evident mixture of bad and good German
in these circulars seems to me evidence of
an attempt to provide an alibi against the
almost inevitable day when the circulars
would be revealed. (See also page 30.)
Have original of protocol and have the
printed circulars.*

DOCUMENT NO. 4

G. G.-S., Intelligence Bureau, Section R,
No. 35.

January 17, 1918.
TO THE COMMISSARIAT OF FOREIGN
AFFAIRS:

The Bureau has received exact information that the leaders of the
socialist party now ruling in Russia,

G. S. der HOCHSEEFLOTTE.

№ 93.

CIRCULAR

vom 28 November 1914

den Marineagenturen und den Flottenvereinen.

Es wird Ihnen vorgeschriben sofort alle Agenten-Beobachter und Agenten—Vertilger
in diesen Handels und Militar-Häfen zu mobilisieren, wo Schiffe zur Lieferung der Kriegsam-
munition nach England, Frankreich, Kanada, Vereinigte Staaten der Nord-Amerika und
Russland aufgeladen sein können, wo Niederlagen für solche Ammunition sich vorfinden und
auch wo Marine-Kriegseinheiten stehen.

Es ist durchaus nothwendig durch dritte in keiner Verbindung zu officielen Vertreten
Deutschlands stehende Personen Agenten zu erwerben, um Explosionen auf in feindliche
Länder sich begebenden Schiffen zu veranstalten, um Verspätigungen, Verwierungen sowie
Missverständnisse bei Beladung, Absendung und Ausladung der Schiffe zu bewirken.

Zu diesen Zweck empfehlen wir Ihrer Aufmerksamkeit ganz besonders Ladungs-Verei-
nigungen (Artelen), unter welchen viele Anarchisten und entlaufene Verbrecher sich finden, ferner deutsche und neutrale Transport-Comptoirs und auch Agenten feindlicher Länder
bei Empfang und Absendung des Kriegsmaterials.

Die dazu nöthigen Geldsummen werden laut Ihrer Aufforderung zur Verfugung gestellt, um das unentbehrliche Personal zur Erreichung des angegebenen Zweekes zu miethen
und zu bestechen.

Nachrichten-Bureau des Gen. Stabes der Hochseeflotte.

Koenig.

Document No. 3—Facsimile of November 28 Circular

through Messrs. Fuerstenberg and Radek, are in correspondence with Messrs. Scheidemann and Parvus regarding the destruction of the traces of the business relations of the party with the Imperial Government. We also know that this correspondence was caused by the demand of leading groups of German socialists, who saw in the said communications a danger to the cause of world socialism. By order of the staff, I have the honor to request the submitting of this question to special discussion in the presence of the representative of our staff and Mr. von Schoenemann.

For the head of the department:

R. BAUER.
Adjutant: [Illegible.]

NOTE.—The world penalty, therefore, was apparent to some Germans. Of the personalities named in the letter, Scheidemann, the leader of the German Government-supporting wing of the Socialist party. is the most notable. Once before he has been named in relation to the "business relations" of the Russian Bolsheviki with the Imperial Government, writing a letter from Copenhagen in 1917, to a "Mr. Olberg" in which he stated that 150,000 kroners had been placed at Olberg's disposal at Fuerstenberg's office through the Nia Bank. (See Appendix, later.) Now Fuerstenberg by this time, January, in Petrograd at Smolny, is trying to help Scheidemann in covering up old trails. Radek is a clever Polish-Austrian Jew who came from Switzerland with Lenin. He and Trotsky between them staged the public play-acting at Brest-Litovsk. Von Schoenemann was the accredited German representative to the Bolshevik foreign office. He is named later in Document No. 5. Parvus is a handler of German propaganda money, with headquarters at Copenhagen, and is credited with being the directing force behind Joffe. (For Parvus, see "New Europe," January 31, 1918, pp. 94-95.) Have photograph of this letter.

DOCUMENT NO. 5

Gr[eat] General Staff, Central Division, Section M, No. (blank), Berlin.

October 25, 1917.

To THE GOVERNMENT OF PEOPLE'S COMMISSARS:

In accordance with the agreement which took place in Kronstadt, in July of the present year, between officials of our General Staff and leaders of the Russian revolutionary army and democracy, Messrs. Lenin, Trotsky, Raskolnikov, and Dybenko, the Russian Division of our General Staff operating in Finland is ordering to Petrograd officers for the disposal of the Intelligence Bureau of the staff. At the head of the Petrograd Bureau will be the following officers, who use the Russian language perfectly and who are acquainted with Russian conditions:

Maj. Luberts, cipher signature Agasfer.
Maj. von Boelke, cipher signature Schott.
Maj. Bayermeister, cipher signature Ber.
Lieut. Hartwig, cipher signature Henrich.

The Intelligence Bureau, in accordance with the agreement with Messrs. Lenin, Trotsky, and Zinovieff, will have the surveillance of the foreign

embassies and military missions and of the counter revolutionary movement, and also will perform the espionage and counter espionage work on the internal fronts, for which purpose agents will be assigned to the various cities.

Coincidently, it is announced that at the disposal of the Government of People's Commissars are assigned consultants to the Ministry of Foreign Affairs, Mr. von Schoenemann, and to the Ministry of Finance, Mr. von Toll.

Chief of the Russian Division, German General Staff: O. RAUSCH.
Adjutant: U. WOLFF.

(*And below on the same letter:*)

TO THE COMMISSARIAT OF FOREIGN AFFAIRS:

The officers indicated in this paper have been before the military revolutionary committee and have agreed on conditions with Muravieff, Boie, and Danishevski with regard to their mutual activities. They have all come under the direction of the committee. The consultants will appear as called for.

Chairman Military Revolutionary Committee, Council of Workers' and Soldiers' Deputies: A. JOFFE.
Secretary: P. KRUSHAVITCH.

October 27, 1917.

NOTE.—Here is the working compact. If Rausch was then in Berlin he presumably came immediately afterwards to Petrograd. It is more probable that the letter was written in Finland than Berlin. In some other letterheads on which Berlin is printed the word is run through with a pen. Stationery was hard to get in Petrograd. Maj. Luberts became the head of the Intelligence Bureau (Nachrichten Bureau). Kronstadt was the midsummer headquarters of Lenin. Raskolnikoff will be referred to in connection with the project to sell the Russian fleet to Germany. Dybenko was the commissar of the fleet, the naval minister, a driving man and keen witted. Zinovieff is the president of the Petrograd Soviet, during the winter the most powerful of the local bodies of the Russian Soviets. He is Jewish and well educated. Joffe, in the letter of Bolshevik acceptance of the German compact, again stands forth for what he is, the spokesman, after Lenin, in all matters of supreme importance to Germany.

Have photograph of the joint letter.

DOCUMENT NO. 6

Gr[eat] General Staff, Central Division, No. 813.

November 19, 1917.

To THE COUNCIL OF PEOPLE'S COMMISSARS:

This is to advise you that the following persons have been put at the disposal of the Russian Government as military advisers: Maj. Erich, Maj. Bode, Maj. Sass, Maj. Zimmerman, Maj. Anders, Lieut. Haase, Lieut. Klein, Lieut. Breitz.

These officers will choose a cadre of the most suitable officers from the list of our prisoners, who will likewise be at the disposal of the Russian

Government, as was agreed at the conference in Stockholm when Lenin, Zinovieff, and others were traveling through to Russia.

Head of the Russian Section, German General Staff: O. RAUSCH.
Adjutant: U. WOLFF.

NOTE.—Maj. Anders took the Russian name Rubakov and Maj. Erich the Russian name Egorov. Lenin and Zinovieff passed through Germany and Stockholm together. Have photograph of letter

---

DOCUMENT NO. 7

G. G.-S., Intelligence Bureau, Section R, No. 27.

(*Confidential*)

January 12, 1918.

To THE COMMISSAR OF FOREIGN AFFAIRS:

By the order of the local department of the German General Staff, the Intelligence Department has reported the names and the characteristics of the main candidates for the reëlection of the Central Executive Committee. The General Staff orders us to insist on the election of the following persons: Trotsky, Lenin, Zinovieff, Kameneff, Joffe, Sverdlov, Lunacharsky, Kollontai, Fabrizius, Martov, Steklov, Golman, Frunze, Lander, Milk, Preobrajenski, Sollers, Studer, Golberg, Avanesov, Volodarsky, Raskolnikov, Stuchka, Peters, and Neubut. Please inform the president of the council of the General Staff's wish.

Head of the Bureau: AGASFER.
Adjutant: HENRICH.

NOTE.—The indorsements are: "Copy handed to chairman Council Workmen's and Soldiers' Deputies, No. 956." "Deliver to Comrade Zinovieff and to secret department. M.Ov——(?)" January 12(Russian calendar) fell in the week of the All-Russian Soviet convention in Petrograd, the week after the forcible dissolution of the Constituent Assembly. The election came at the end of the week and was a perfunctory re-election of practically the whole former executive committee of commissars. Lacking the exact list, I nevertheless can state that the present executive committee was drafted from this group. The name there surprising to me is that of Martov, the head of a supposedly separate faction.

Martov is an able writer, was associated with Trotsky in his Paris journalistic venture, but was supposed to have split with him in Russia. The evidence that he is still agreeable to Germany is pertinent. Madame Kollontai, the only woman on this list, was the Commissar of Public Welfare. She was sent abroad for foreign propaganda in February, but did not get beyond Scandinavia and later returned to Russia. Kameneff, who went out of Russia with Kollontai, also sought to return, but was arrested by the Finnish White Guards (not the Germans) on the Aland Islands, and his release was the subject of negotiations. He is Trotsky's brother-in-law. Sverdlov was temporary chairman of the All-Russian Soviet. Lunacharsky is Commissar of Education. Steklov is editor of the official paper "Isvestia." Volodarsky, who has lived in the United States, was in close confidence with Lenin. He was killed in Moscow the last week in June. Agasfer, who delivered the order in behalf of Rausch, is Maj. Luberts. Have photograph of letter.

CHAPTER II.
RÔLE OF THE REICHSBANK

The following documents show in detail how the German Government financed the Russian Bolshevik revolution through the German Imperial Bank.

They show what rewards the German financial and industrial interests demanded in return for the German support of the Bolsheviki. And they show how the Bolshevik leaders betrayed their own followers and abandoned the preaching of their social revolution wherever the Germans ordered that it should be abandoned.

DOCUMENT NO. 8

Imperial Bank [Reichsbank], No. 2.
(*Very Secret*)
January 8, 1918.
To the People's Commissar of Foreign Affairs:

Notification has to-day been received by me from Stockholm that 50,000,000 roubles of gold has been transferred to be put at the disposal of the representatives of the People's Commissars. This credit has been supplied to the Russian Government in order to cover the cost of the keep of the Red Guards and agitators in the country. The Imperial Government considers it appropriate to remind the Council of People's Commissars of the necessity of increasing their propaganda in the country, as the antagonistic attitude of the south of Russia and Siberia to the existing Government in Russia is troubling the German Government. It is of great importance to send experienced men everywhere in order to set up a uniform government.

Representative of the Imperial Bank:

G. von Schanz.

Note.—*Members of the Red Guard were paid from 12 to 16 roubles a day, whereas soldiers were paid hardly that number of kopecks. This letter shows where the money came from. The Bolshevik Government also required factory owners to pay regular wages to their workers while the latter served in the Red Guard. The notation on letter indicates that it was referred to Menshinski, the financial minister, whose expert councillor was the German, von Toll. Menshinski personally conducted the wrecking of the Russian banks, a maneuver that deprived all opponents of Bolshevikism of their financial means of warfare. It was a classic job of destruction, done in the name of reconstruction.
Have photograph of this letter.*

DOCUMENT NO. 9

Imperial Bank, No. 8, Berlin.
(*Very Secret*)
January 12, 1918.
To the Commissar of Foreign Affairs:

I am instructed to convey the agreement of the Imperial Bank to the issue out of the credit of the General Staff of 5,000,000 roubles for the dispatch of the assistant naval commissar, Kudriashoff, to the Far East.

On arrival at Vladivostok he should visit the retired officer of the Russian Fleet, Mr. Panoff, and instruct Butten-

hoff and Staufacher, who are known to Panoff, to come to see him. Both the mentioned agents will bring with them Messrs. Edward Shindler, William Keberlein, and Paul Diese [or Deze]. With these persons it is necessary to think out a plan for carrying out the Japanese and American war materials from Vladivostok to the west. If this is not possible then they must instruct Diese [or Deze] and his agents to destroy the stores. Shindler must acquaint Kudriashoff with the Chinese agents at Nikolsk. These persons should receive the agreed amounts and should be dispatched to China to carry on an agitation against Japan.

Representative of the Imperial Bank:

G. von Schanz.

Note.—*If this plan was developed to a climax it was not by Kudriashoff. He was killed on his passage through Siberia two or three weeks later and it was reported that a great sum of money was taken from his body by his murderers, who were said to be two Cossacks. Most of the German agents named in this letter were still active in Siberia in the spring, as shown by Document No. 29.
Have photograph of this letter.*

DOCUMENT NO. 10

Imperial Bank, No. 5.
January 11, 1918.
To the Chairman of the Council of People's Commissars:

My Dear Mr. Chairman: The industrial and commercial organizations in Germany interested in trade relations with Russia have addressed themselves to me in a letter, including several guiding indications. Permit me to bring them to your attention.

1. The conflict of the Russian revolution with the Russian capitalists absolutely does not interest German manufacturing circles, in so far as the question does not concern industry as such. You can destroy the Russian capitalists as far as you please, but it would by no means be possible to permit the destruction of Russian enterprises. Such a situation would produce a constant ferment in the country, supported by famine of materials and, in consequence of that, of products also. The English, American, and French capitalists take advantage of this disorder and understand how to establish here corps of their commercial agents. It is necessary to remember that German industry in the first years after the general peace will not be in a position to satisfy the purchasing demand of the Russian market, having broad similar parallel tasks in the Near East, in Persia, in China, and in Africa.

2. It is essential, therefore, to conduct a canvass and gather statistical information with regard to the condition of industry, and, in view of the absence of money in Russia, to address in business conversations whichever is desired of the groups of German commercial banks.

3. Trade with Germany may be in the first period almost exclusively exchange for wheat and for any remaining products to receive household necessities. Everything which exceeds the limits of such trade should be paid for in advance to the amount of 75 per cent of the market value, with the payment of the remaining quarter in a six months' period. In

place of such an arrangement, probably, it would seem to be possible to permit, privately, the taking of German dividend shares on the Russian financial market, or solidly guaranteed industrial and railroad loans.

In view of the indicated interest of German manufacturers and merchants to trade relations in Russia, I cordially beg you, Mr. Chairman, to inform me of the views of the Government regarding the questions touched upon, and to receive the assurances of my sincere respect.

Representative of the Imperial Bank and Stock Exchange in Berlin:

G. von Schantz.

Note.—*The engaging attitude of the German manufacturers toward Russian capitalists is the feature of this letter, apart from the cordial and evidently understanding expressions of the representative of the German Imperial Bank to that opposed enemy of the capitalists of all nations, Lenin. The letter was sent to the secret department by Secretary Skripnik. Perhaps some day von Schanz will disclose Lenin's answer.
Have photograph of letter.*

DOCUMENT NO. 11

Imperial Bank, No. 12378.
[Printed circular in Russian]

RESOLUTION

of a conference of representatives of the German commercial banks convened on proposal of the German delegation at Petrograd by the management of the Imperial Bank, to discuss the resolutions of the Rhine-Westphalian Industrial Syndicate and Handelstag.

Berlin, December 28, 1917.

1. All loans are canceled the bonds of which are in the hands of German, Austrian, Bulgarian, and Turkish holders, but payment must be realized by the Russian treasury in the course of a 12-months' term after the conclusion of separate peace.

2. The purchase is permitted of all Russian securities and dividend-bearing paper by the representatives of the German banks at the rate of the day on the open market.

3. After the conclusion of separate peace, on the expiration of 90 days, there are reestablished all the shares of private railway companies, metallurgical industries, oil companies, and chemical pharmaceutical works.

Note.—The rating of such papers will be made by the German and Austrian stock exchanges.

4. There are banished and for five years from date of signing peace are not to be allowed English, French, and American capitals in the following industries: Coal, metallurgical, machine building, oil, chemical, and pharmaceutical.

5. In the question of development in Russia of coal, oil, and metallurgical branches of industry there is to be established a supreme advisory organ consisting of 10 Russian specialists, 10 from the German industrial organizations and the German and Austrian banks.

6. The Russian Government must not interfere in the region of questions connected with the transfer to the benefit of Germany of two mining districts in Poland—Dombroski and

G. G.-S.

NACHRICHTEN-BUREAU.

Section *18*

№ *20*

•25 Февраля 1918 г.

Господину Предсѣдателю Совѣта Народныхъ Комиссаровъ.

Послѣ совѣщанія съ Народнымъ Комиссаромъ г. Троцкимъ, имѣю честь просить срочно извѣстить руководителей Контръ-Развѣдки при Ставкѣ-Комиссаровъ Фейерабенда и Кальмановича, чтобы они работали по-прежнему въ полной независимости и тайнѣ отъ оффиціальнаго Штаба Ставки и Генеральнаго Штаба въ Петербургѣ и особенно ген. Бончъ-Бруевича и Контръ-Развѣдки Сѣвернаго Фронта, сносясь лишь съ Народнымъ Комиссаромъ прап. Крыленко.

Начальникъ Отдѣленія **R. Bauer**

Адъютантъ

Передать въ Комис по дол. дѣлам
Секретарь А. Скрипникъ

Facsimile Document Number 12

Olkishski—and to Austria of the oil region in Galicia. The transfer of the latter will be only in the form of limitations of the right of making claims, land allotments, and application of capital for the production and refining of oil.

7. Germany and Austria enjoy the unlimited privilege of sending into Russia mechanics and qualified workmen.

8. Other foreign mechanics and workmen during five years after the conclusion of peace between Russia and Germany are not to be allowed to enter at all.

9. The statistical department of producing and manufacturing industries with the corresponding Government organ must be controlled by German specialists.

10. Private banks in Russia arise only with the consent and according to the plan of the Union of German and Austrian Banks, whereby the rating of the stocks of the banks on all exchanges of the New and Old World will be handled by the group of the Deutsche Bank.

11. At the ports of Petrograd, Archangel, Odessa, Vladivostok, and Batum will be established, under the leadership of specialists from Germany, special statistical economic committees.

As regards the tariff, railway and shipping rate policies to regulate the Russo-German-Austrian trade relations, this part of the economical treaty will be discussed by the special Tariff Council of the Handelstag.

Signed:

Chairman: VON GRENNER.

Secretary: BERENBLUET.

NOTE.—*The penned indorsement on the photographed copy of the resolution is:*

"Chairman of the Central Executive Committee: Commissar Menshinsky requests that this resolution should be taken under advisement, and to prepare the ground in the Council of the Workmen's and Soldiers' Deputies, in case the Council of People's Commissars will not accept these requests. Secretary D. Khaskin." Menshinsky is Minister of Finance. All of these terms, wholly punitive to American, English, and French capital, could lurk in the secret section in the present German-Russian treaty. I do not know *the fate of the resolution on this, its early winter appearance.*

Have besides the notated photograph a printed copy of this circular.

DOCUMENT NO. 12

G[reat] G[eneral] S[taff]. Intelligence Bureau, Section N, No. 780.

Feb. 25, 1918.

(Secret)

TO THE CHAIRMAN OF THE COUNCIL OF PEOPLE'S COMMISSARS:

After conferring with the People's Commissar Trotsky, I have the honor to ask you urgently to inform the directors of the Counter Espionage at Army Headquarters [Stafka], Commissars Feierabend and Kalmanovich, that they should work as formerly in complete independence and without the knowledge of the official staff at Army Headquarters and the General Staff in Petersburg, and particularly Gen. Bonch-Bruevich and the secret service of the northern front, communicating only with the People's Commissar Lieut. Krilenko.

For the head of the Bureau:

R. BAUER.

Adjutant: BUKHOLM.

NOTE.—*Across the letter is written: "Inform Mosholov. N. G." (Gorbunoff's initials). In the margin is written: "Passed on to the Commissar of War. M. Skripnik." The significance of this letter is that it is to Lenin; that the two chief secretaries of himself and the council passed it on for action; and that Trotsky and Lenin on February 27 were continuing to hamper the Russian commander at a moment when the German army was threatening Petrograd. Mosholov was one of the commissars on the staff of Krilenko, the commissar representing the Council of Commissars in the command of the Russian military forces. His achievements as a disorganizer were notable. This letter indicates that he had the confidence of Germany.*

Have original letter

В.Секретно.

G. G.-S.

NACHRICHTEN-BUREAU.

Section *N*

№ *773*

25 Февраля 1918 г.

Г. Предсѣдателю Совѣта Народныхъ Комиссаровъ.

Въ Комис. по дол. дѣл. и др. свѣд. черед
А. Скрипникъ

По донесеніямъ нашей тайной агентуры, въ-отрядахъ, дѣйствующихъ противъ Германскихъ войскъ и противъ Австро-Украинскаго корпуса, наблюдается пропаганда національного возстанія и борьбы съ Нѣмцами и ихъ союзниками-Украинцами. Прошу сообщить, что предпринято Правительствомъ для прекращенія этой вредной агитаціи.

Начальникъ Отдѣленія **R. Bauer**

Адъютантъ Геприн

Facsimile Document Number 13

DOCUMENT NO. 13

G[reat] G[eneral] S[taff], Intelligence Bureau, Section R, No. 733.

February 25, 1918.

(Very Secret)

To the Chairman of the Council of People's Commissars:

According to reports of our secret agency in the detachments operating against the German troops and against the Austrian Ukrainian corps, there has been observed propaganda for a national rising and a struggle with the Germans and their allies, the Ukrainians. I ask you to inform me what has been done by the Government to stop this harmful agitation.

For the head of the Bureau:
R. BAUER.
Adjutant: HENRICH.

NOTE.—Across the top is written: "Urgent. To the Commissars of War and Special Staff. M. Skripnik." The last sentence is underscored, and in the margin appears a question mark, initialed "L. T." The first is Lenin's order through the secretary, and the second may possibly be taken as Trotsky's opposition to any action. The loss of the Ukraine by counter German intrigue was a sore point in prestige with him. But his essential obedience to Germany was not lessened.
Have original letter.

DOCUMENT NO. 14

G. G.-S., Intelligence Bureau, Section R. No. 278/611.

To the People's Commissar of Foreign Affairs:
February 7, 1918.

According to information of the Intelligence Bureau it has been ascertained that the promise given personally by you, Mr. Commissar, in Brest-Litovsk, not to circulate socialistic agitational literature among the German troops is not being fulfilled. I ask you to inform me what steps will be taken in this matter.

For the head of the Bureau:
R. BAUER.
Adjutant. HENRICH.

NOTE.—Brusque words to the foreign minister of the Soviet Government of Workmen, Soldiers, and Sailors of the Russian Republic, delivered not by an equal in official rank, but by the deputy of a German major at the head of an intelligence department of the German Government. Did Trotsky resent or deny the imputation? Instead he wrote with his own hand in the margin: "I ask to discuss it. L. T." Thus he admits that he did give the promise at Brest-Litovsk. The question raised concerns only the measure of obedience to be required.
Have original letter.

DOCUMENT NO. 15

Counter Espionage at Army Headquarters [Stavka], No. 311, special section.

To the Chairman of the Council of People's Commissars:
January 29, 1918.

The Counter Espionage at the Army Headquarters advises that at the front is being spread by unknown agitators the following counter revolutionary literature·

1. The text of circulars of various German Government institutions with proofs of the connection of the German Government with the Bolshevik workers before the passing of the Government into their hands. These leaflets have reached also the German commanders.

The Supreme Commander has received a demand from Gen. Hoffman to stop this dangerous agitation by all means possible.

2. A stenographic report of the conversation of Gen. Hoffman with Comrade Trotsky, whereby it was supposedly proposed to the latter to make peace on conditions of considerable concessions on the part of the Central Empires, but on the obligation of the Russian delegation to stop the socialization of the life of the state. Comrade Trotsky supposedly offered the termination of war without peace and the demobilization of our army. When Gen. Hoffman announced that the Germans would continue the advance, Trotsky supposedly replied: "Then under the pressure of force we shall be forced to make peace and fulfill all demands:"

This document has created indignation among the troops. Against the Council of People's Commissars are heard cruel accusations.

Commissar: S. KALMANOVICH.

NOTE.—This letter is a warning of the slow rising but coming storm that will sweep these boldest pirates of history from the country they have temporarily stolen. To get a real understanding of the meaning of the second, and important, section of the letter, it must be pointed out that until February 1, the Russian calendar was 13 days behind the Western European calendar. The real date of this letter, therefore, is February 10. This is the date Trotsky's "No peace; no war" pronouncement was made at Brest-Lit-ovsk. The news of it did not reach even Petrograd until the next day. Yet on that day printed circulars were being distributed at the front stating that Trotsky had agreed to do the very thing he did do, and giving an augury of events that did take place a week later when Germany did begin its advance and when the Bolsheviks did fulfill all demands. The fact is that simple truth was being told. Nor is the means by which it was secured at all obscure. A few daring and skillful Russians had found a means to get information from Brest-Litovsk.

The circulars referred to in the first

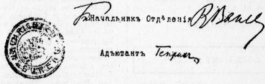

G. G.-S.
NACHRICHTEN-BUREAU.

Господину Народному Комиссару по Иностранным Дѣламъ.

Section *R*

№ 278/611

7.Февраля.1918 г.

До свѣдѣнія Развѣдочнаго Отдѣленія дошло, что данное Вами лично, Господинъ Комиссаръ, въ Брестъ-Литовскѣ обѣщаніе не распространять въ германскихъ войскахъ соціалистической агитаціонной литературы не исполняется. Прошу сообщить, какія будутъ по этому поводу приняты мѣры.

Б.Начальникъ Отдѣленія

Адъютантъ

Facsimile Document Number 14

paragraph are of course those already familiar to Washington from February dispatches.

The following naive comment adds to the attractiveness of the letter: "The Committee for Combating the Counter Revolution states that these circulars were sent from the Don, and the stenographic report was seized in transmission from Kieff. Its origin is undoubtedly Austrian or from the Rada.—M. Skripnik."
Have photograph of letter.

CHAPTER III.

THE GERMAN-BOLSHEVIK PLOT AGAINST THE ALLIES

The following documents, with Mr. Sisson's interpretative notes, expose the German-Bolshevik plot against the Allies.

DOCUMENT NO. 16

Counter Espionage at Army Headquarters, No. 215.

January 21, 1918.

To the Commissariat of Foreign Affairs:

We hereby advise you of the arrival in Mogilev of the following German officers, who are being ordered to England, France, and America:

Zanwald, von Weine, Pabst, Mayer, Gruenwaldt, and Baron Schilling. They have been granted passports, sent here by Commissar Trotsky.

Von Weine, with a Danish passport in the name of Hansen, a merchant of Copenhagen, is to proceed to England.

Baron Schilling is ordered to the United States of America with a Norwegian passport in the name of Dr. Joseph Brun.

Gruenwaldt has instructions to proceed to France with a Russian passport in the name of the Lett, Ivan Kalnin.

The remaining persons are to make a journey through Finland and Sweden, supplied with papers from the German staff, in order to follow up the counter revolutionary work of countries allied to us.

Chief of Counter Espionage:

FEIERABEND.

Commissar: VUZNETORFF.

NOTE.—*A young German who said he was a deserting officer and that his name was Mayer, sought the aid of the Embassy, the military mission, and myself in getting to America. He was a good-looking young Prussian, had lived in New York, spoke English with very little accent, and claimed to have been converted to the President's views on peace requisites. He said he had walked across the lines as a deserter because he could stand no more of German war, and that he wanted to go to the United States to talk and write against Germany. I was not receptive. He said he was a lieutenant. There is no record at our military control office in Christiania of a passport to Dr. Joseph Brun.*

Have photograph of letter

DOCUMENT NO. 17

Commissar for Combating the Counter Revolution and Pogroms, No. 32. Petrograd.

January 5, 1918.

TO THE PEOPLE'S COMMISSARIAT FOR FOREIGN AFFAIRS:

The plenipotentiary Commissar for Combating the Counter Revolution, Comrade Antonoff, requests the commissariat for foreign affairs to issue passports for going to Denmark to the following comrades, who are going to the allied countries to conduct peace propaganda:

To England are going: Comrades Adolf Pavlovich Ribba, Ilia Julievich Uritski, Vladislav Antonovich Dashkevich.

To France: Rimma Lvovna Orlova, Vladimir Konstantinovich Schneur.

To America: Isai Borisovich Kahn, Mark Vlasievich Gritsker, Sofia Arturovna Mack.

All the named comrades will visit at Copenhagen the premises of the staff where they will receive neutral passports for the trip to the named countries. At the disposal of the dispatched will be placed the necessary means for combating in the press with the imperialists of England, France, and the United States. Their confidential addresses will be transmitted to you later on the arrival of the

named comrades at the places of their destination.

Authorized commissars

A. SHILINSKI.

F. ZUBERT.

NOTE.—*Trotsky indorsed this note: "To be urgently executed. L. T."*

The plan of peace propaganda campaign in the allied countries is plainly outlined. These Bolshevik-German agents will preach international Bolshevism and will charge the countries at war with Germany with the very imperialistic offenses of which Germany is guilty. This also was the method used in Russia by the Bolshevik-German press in attacking the United States, England, and France. In the formula of the propaganda, imperialism relates not only to territory but to business enterprise. The agents listed above likely sought entrance under different names. They and the centers from which they work should be recognized, however, by their words and their works. The commissars who sign are members of the commission for Combating the Counter Revolution.

Have photograph of letter.

DOCUMENT NO. 18

G[reat] General Staff, Central Division, Section M, No. 951.

December 20, 1917.

TO THE COMMISSARIAT OF FOREIGN AFFAIRS:

According to the negotiations between the Russian and German peace delegations at Brest-Litovsk, the Russian Division of the German General Staff have the honor to request the hastening of the departure of agitators to the camps of Russian prisoners of war in Germany, for the recruiting of volunteers who will be sent to the English and French troops for the purpose of observation and peace propaganda.

Simultaneously, the staff requests the following sailors to be sent to Germany: Shishko, Kirshu, Matviev, and Dratchuk. They will receive special instructions when traveling through Brest-Litovsk.

Chief of the Russian Division, German General Staff· O. RAUSCH.

Adjutant: U. WOLFF.

NOTE.—*This request was referred to the Commissariats on Military and Naval Affairs.*

A marginal question asked by E. P. (probably Polivanoff): "[Is] Dratchuk at Black Sea?" He was at Sevastopol and may not have been sent. The others went, visited the camps for war prisoners in Germany, and then returned to Russia. Shishko in February was Commissar of the Naval College in Petrograd.

Have photograph of letter.

DOCUMENT NO. 19

Counter Espionage at Army Headquarters, No. —.

January 16, 1918.

TO THE COUNCIL OF PEOPLE'S COMMISSARS:

I hereby bring to the notice of the Council of People's Commissaries that through our front, on the personal permission of the Supreme Commander, have passed 100 German officers, 250 non-commissioned officers, who proceeded to our internal fronts; part of the German

officers have gone to the front in the Don region, part to the front against Dutoff, and part to Eastern Siberia and the Trans-Baikal for the surveillance, and if it shall be possible, to oppose the Japanese occupationary detachment and the counter revolutionary Trans-Baikal Cossack officers.

Counter Espionage Official:

P. ARKHIPOV.

NOTE.—*An odd comment gives interest to this letter. It is this: "An accusation or a silly accusal for personal benefit? Communicate [to] Comrade Krilenko," signed "N. G."*

Have photograph of letter.

DOCUMENT NO. 20

Counter Espionage at Army Headquarters, No. 52.

Jan. 8, 1918.

TO THE COUNCIL OF PEOPLE'S COMMISSARS:

The Supreme Commander Krilenko has received an offer from the Supreme Commander of the German army to send to the disposal of the German staff ten reliable officers of the revolutionary army. The said persons must arrive at Warsaw, where they will receive their further instructions. The aim of the trip is to visit the camps of our prisoners of war on the propaganda of peace ideas. The staff points out the desirability of sending Dzevaltovsky, Simashko, Saharoff, and Volodarsky.

For the Chief of the Counter Espionage: S. KALMANOVICH.

For the Commissar: ALEXIEFF.

NOTE.—*Dzevaltovsky was an officer of the Life Guards Grenadier Regiment, and an agitator who aroused the soldiers at the time of the ill-fated June advance. Volodarsky has been referred to previously. He was assassinated in late June at Moscow. Kalmanovich was a Commissar on the staff of Krilenko, the talking man who was assigned to disorganize the army. In actual army rank Krilenko was a sublieutenant.*

Have photograph of letter

DOCUMENT NO. 21

Gr. General Staff, Central Division, Section M, No. 750.

Berlin, November 1, 1917.

TO THE COUNCIL OF PEOPLE'S COMMISSARS:

In accordance with an inquiry from the German General Headquarters, I have the honor to request you to inform me at the earliest possible moment the exact quantity of ammunition at the following places: Petrograd, Archangel, Kazan, Tiflis.

It is necessary also to state the quantity and storage place of the supplies which have been received from America, England, and France, and also the units which are keeping guard over the military stores.

Head of Division: O. RAUSCH.

Adjutant: U. WOLFF.

NOTE.—*This is a request made upon a country which America, England, and France still regarded at that date as an ally.*

Have photograph of letter.

DOCUMENT NO. 22

G[eneral] S[taff] of the High Sea Fleet,
No. 79.
Jan. 10, 1918.
(Very Secret)

To THE COUNCIL OF PEOPLE'S COM-
MISSARS:

The Petersburg representative of
the Supreme Sea Command has received by wireless from Kiel orders
to propose to the Council of People's
Commissars to place at the disposal
of our agents at Vladivostok—But-
tenhof, Staufacher, and Franz Walden—several steamships. On these
ships must be loaded the goods indicated by our named agents and also

G. G.-S.
NACHRICHTEN-BUREAU..

Section ....*R*....

№....7..*5*..

23 Февраля 1918 г.

Facsimile Document Number 26

persons indicated by them, and be
sent as directed to ports of the United
States, Japan, and British colonies in
Eastern Asia. In case of absence of
free tonnage in Pacific ports, it is necessary to charter ships sailing under a
foreign flag. The object of sending the
ships is to carry to enemy countries
agents-agitators, and agents-destructors. All the expenses and risk the
Petrograd agency of the Supreme
Naval Command takes for account
of the naval operations fund.

Capt. Lieut. RUDOLPH MILLER.

NOTE.—*The indorsement of Lenin's secretary Skripnik is: "Reported." The active Vladivostok agents have been referred
to previously. The threat of the arrival
of German agents through Pacific ports is
apparent.
Have photograph of letter.*

DOCUMENT NO. 23

G[eneral] S[taff] of the High Sea Fleet,
No. 85.
Jan. 14, 1918.
(Very Secret)

To THE COUNCIL OF PEOPLE'S COM-
MISSARS:

According to instructions of the German High Sea Command, transmit-

ted to-day to me by radio A, I apply
to the Russian Government with a
proposal to take measures to deliver
to the Pacific by railway three of our
submarines, disassembled. On the
conclusion of peace negotiations and
the conclusion of peace between Russia and Germany this transporting
must be begun immediately, whereby
on the conclusion of the war the
transported vessels will remain at the
disposal of the Russian Government.

Capt. Lieut.:   RUD. MILLER.

NOTE.—*The letter is indorsed: "Reported. Secretary Skripnik." The transporting,
according to the categorical demand, was
to begin immediately after peace was
signed. These are the only two communications of Capt. Miller that appear.
Have photograph of letter.*

DOCUMENT NO. 24

Commissar for Combating the Counter
Revolution and Progroms, No. 445/63.
Petrograd, Jan. 21, 1918.

To THE COMMISSAR OF WAR, SKLIAN-
SKY:

Our agency on the Furhstatskaya
informs us that two people not seen
before have been noticed to visit the
American Embassy three times.

Maj. Luberts begs to point out to
Commissioner Podvoisky the necessity of keeping a watch over the
movements of these two persons. I
ask your instructions.

Commissar: A. KOZMIN.

NOTE.—*Maj. Luberts believed in identi-
fying visitors to the American Embassy.
Podvoisky was the Minister of War.
Have photograph of letter.*

DOCUMENT NO. 25

G. G.-S., Intelligence Bureau, Section R,
No. 168.
Dec. 17, 1917.
(Very Secret)

To THE COMMISSAR ON FOREIGN AF-
FAIRS:

At the request of the Commission

on Combating the Counter Revolution
of December 17, the Intelligence Bureau has the honor to forward a list
of men watching the missions of the
countries allied to Russia:

The British Embassy is watched by
German scouts Luze, Telman, Possel,
Franz, and Gezel; Russian agents
Ovisannikov, Gluschenko, and Balia-
sin.

The French Embassy is watched by
German scouts Silvester, Butz, Fol-
hagen; Russian agents Balashev,
Turin, Gavrilov, Sadavnokov, and
Shilo.

The U. S. A. Embassy is watched
by German scouts Strom, Buchholtz,
Fasnacht, Todner; Russian agents
Spitzberg, Sokolnizky, Turasov, and
Vavilov.

The Roumanian mission is watched
by German scouts Suttner, Baider,
Wolf; Russian agents Kuhl, Nikitin,
Zolotov, and Arkipov.

The Italian Embassy is watched
by Austrian scouts Kuhlder, von Geze,
Goin, and Burmeister; Russian agents
Salov, Alekseievsky, and Kuzmin.

These agents must fulfill all in-
structions of the Commission for
Combating the Counter Revolution,
Sabotage, Looting, etc.

Head of Bureau: AGASFER.
Adjutant: E. RANTZ.

NOTE.—*The German Maj. Luberts
(Agasfer, see Document No. 5), therefore
was the keeper of Ambassadorial hostages
of the allied countries in Russia throughout the winter. The names listed above
were unidentifiable in the establishments
of at least the British and the American
Embassies. All may have been outside
watchers. The method of outside surveillance is shown in Document No. 27.
Have photograph of letter.*

DOCUMENT NO. 26

G. G.-S., Intelligence Bureau, Section R,
No. 715.
(Personal)
Feb. 23, 1918.

To THE COMMISSAR OF FOREIGN AF-
FAIRS:

According to my personal conversation with the chairman of the Council of People's Commissars, it has
been decided to delay the departure
of the Italian Embassy from Petersburg and, as far as possible, to search
the Embassy baggage. Of this decision I count it my duty to inform
you.

For the head of the Bureau:
R. BAUER.
Adjutant: HENRICH.

NOTE.—*Across the top of letter is written by Trotsky, "Instruct," and signed
with the initials, L. T. It is here set
forth laconically that a German officer of
the General Staff and Lenin in conference
ordered the search of the baggage of the
ambassador of a country friendly to Russia and at war with Germany; and that
Trotsky gave the instructions for carrying out the order. A clerk's note at the
bottom is additionally specific: "To be
given to Blagonravoff." The last named
was the Commissar of Martial Law in
Petrograd. The Italian Embassy train
was delayed for more than 24 hours when
it sought to depart, some days later.
Petroff, assistant foreign minister, told
me on March 2 with a great show of indignation, that "The Italians had given
a diplomatic passport to the embassy
cook." So, he said, it was right to search*

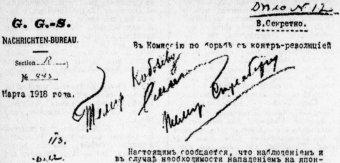

G. G.-S.

NACHRICHTEN-BUREAU.

Section ___*12*___

№ *843*

Марта 1918 года.

Дѣло № 12

В. Секретно.

Въ Комиссію по борьбѣ съ контръ-революціей

Настоящимъ сообщается, что наблюденіемъ и въ случаѣ необходимости нападеніемъ на японскихъ, американскихъ и русскихъ офицеровъ, командующихъ оккупаціоннымъ корпусомъ въ Восточной Сибири, завѣдуютъ наши агенты Штауфахеръ, Кригеръ, Гизе, Вальдейнъ, Буттенгофъ, Латтанъ и Скрибановичъ, къ коимъ и надлежитъ обращаться какъ комиссару Кобозеву, такъ и командированнымъ Комиссіей лицамъ. Адреса агентовъ указаны въ спискѣ № 3.

Начальникъ *[signature]*

Адъютантъ *[signature]*

Facsimile Document Number 29

---

the train. *If they had better luck than they did when they held up and searched the Italian ambassador in his automobile almost in front of the Hotel Europe, I did not hear of it. Document 27 tells of that robbery.*

Have original letter, No. 26.

DOCUMENT NO. 27

Commissar on Combating the Counter Revolution and Pogroms, No. 71.

Petrograd, Feb. 24, 1918.

(Specially Secret—Personal)

TO THE PEOPLE'S COMMISSAR ON FOREIGN AFFAIRS:

Our agents investigating the Italian Embassy, I. E. Maerov, Imenitski, and Urov, followed up the ambassador and conducted a search of him in the street, with a confiscation. Documents regarding relations with German diplomats and the special papers of the ambassador to the allied ambassadors, mentioned by you, were not found In order to mask the attack several articles listed in the protocol furnished by Comrade Imenitski were taken from the ambassador.

The watch on the British and American ambassadors and the Serbian minister has been intensified. The supplementary observation point on the British Embassy has been estab-

---

lished in the Marble Palace—Lieut. Bekker and a member of the central executive committee of the Council of Workmen's and Soldiers' Deputies, Frunze.

On the French Embassy, on the French Quay, house No. 8, Comrade Peters, member of the central executive committee of the council of Workmen's and Soldiers' Deputies, supplementary.

On the North American Embassy observation has been established at Furhstatskaya Street, house No. 23, apartments Nos. 1 and 4. In the latter Comrades Goldberg and Spitzberg are carrying on the observation very successfully. Telephones have been installed in the above-mentioned places. General management of the surveillance has been intrusted to Alfred von Geigendorf.

Commissar: MITOPOVICH.

For Secretary: R. BAETSKI.

NOTE.—*Most of the names in this letter including the signatures at end, are unfamiliar. Peters, placed in charge of French observation, is a Lettish sailor, active and able, a former resident of England. The robbery of the Italian ambassador took place late in the evening on a highly frequented central street and was a day's sensation. The observation point on the American Embassy was a yellow apartment house almost opposite the entrance. After I got the information I tested the watch and always saw a head or hand retreating from a window. But I doubt if the watchers profited much by studying the visitors to the embassy.*

Have photograph of letter.

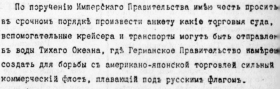

GR. GENERALSTAB.

CENTRAL ABTHEILUNG.

Section M.

24 Февраля 1918 г.

№ *339*

Довѣрительно.

Господину Народному Комиссару по Иностраннымъ Дѣламъ.

По порученію Имперскаго Правительства имѣю честь просить въ срочномъ порядкѣ произвести анкету какія торговыя суда, вспомогательные крейсера и транспорты могутъ быть отправлены въ воды Тихаго Океана, гдѣ Германское Правительство намѣрено создать для борьбы съ американо-японской торговлей сильный коммерческій флотъ, плавающій подъ русскимъ флагомъ.

Вмѣстѣ съ тѣмъ довожу до Вашего свѣдѣнія, что въ Балтійскомъ Флотѣ Ваши матросы распродаютъ съ военныхъ кораблей катера, мелкіе механизмы, мѣдныя и бронзовыя части машинъ и проч. Не было-ли бы посему своевременнымъ поднять вопросъ о продажѣ Германіи этихъ расхищаемыхъ и разоряемыхъ военныхъ кораблей.

Рѣшеніе Правительства благоволите мнѣ сообщить.

Начальникъ Русскаго Отдѣла Германскаго Генеральнаго Штаба *[signature]*

Адъютантъ *[signature]*

Facsimile Document Number 28

DOCUMENT NO. 28

Gr. General Staff, Central Division, Section M, No. 389.
(*Confidential*)

February 24, 1918.

To the People's Commissar of Foreign Affairs:

According to instructions of the Imperial Government, I have the honor to ask you to make in the shortest possible time an investigation as to what commercial boats, auxiliary cruisers, and transports may be sent into the waters of the Pacific Ocean, where the German Government intends to form, for the purpose of opposing the American-Japanese trade, a powerful commercial fleet flying the Russian flag.

graph as indicating the use against America to which Germany intends to put Russia is self-evident. The ludicrous picture painted in the second paragraph at once intensifies the shame of the ending of the fine new Russian Navy and discloses the German hope of securing and refitting the vessels.
Have original letter.

DOCUMENT NO. 29

G. `G.-S., Intelligence Bureau, Section R, No. 883.
(*Very Secret*)

March 9, 1918.

To the Commission for Combating the Counter Revolution:

It is herewith communicated that for watching, and if necessary attacking, the Japanese, American, and Rus-

Секретно.
- - - - - - - - -

GR. GENERALSTAB.
CENTRL ABTHEILUNG.

Section M./K
25.Февраля 1918 г.
№ 403
Berlin

Господину Предсѣдателю Совѣта Народныхъ Коммиссаровъ.

Отдѣленіе Штаба имѣетъ честь просить свѣдѣній о настроеніи направляемыхъ къ Пскову отрядовъ и предостерегаетъ отъ возможныхъ печальныхъ послѣдствій, если въ этихъ отрядахъ будетъ вестись патріотическая пропаганда и агитація противъ Германской Арміи.

Начальникъ Русскаго Отдѣла
Германскаго Генеральнаго Штаба

Адъютантъ

Facsimile Document Number 30

At the same time I call to your attention the data that in your Baltic fleet your sailors are selling from the war ships the launches, small fittings, copper, and bronze parts of machines, etc. Would it not be the proper time to raise the question of selling to Germany these war vessels which are being stripped and disarmed?

Be so kind as to communicate the decision of the Government.

Head of the Russian Division of the German General Staff: O. Rausch.
Adjutant: U. Wolff.

Note.—*Opposite first paragraph is the notation: "Ask Lomof. Markin." Latter was one of Trotsky's secretaries. Opposite paragraph second, Markin makes notation, "Refer to Raskolnikoff." Latter is a commissar on this Naval General Staff, who conducted conferences with German officers in Kronstadt in March, April, and July, 1917, and an active aid to Dybenko in stirring up the Russian fleet to revolt. Do not know who Lomof is. The importance of the first para-*

sian officers who may command the expeditionary forces in eastern Siberia, our agents Staufacher, Krieger, Geze, Walden, Buttenhoff, Dattan, and Skribanovich take charge, and to whom it is necessary that either Commissar Kobozeff or any of those named by the commission must apply. The addresses of the agents are shown in list No. 3

Head: R. Bauer.
Adjutant: M. K——.(?)

Note.—*Comments to "Telegraph Kobozeff" and "Telegraph Streaberg," with an illegible signature, appear on letter, and below it is the order: "Give the list," initialed "D. Z.," corresponding with the signing habit of Dzerzhinski, chairman of the Commission for Combating the Counter Revolution. Below this order appears the list of addresses, as follows.*

Report according to list No. 3.
1. Staufacher Vladivostok, Panoff's house.

2. R. Krieger, Nikolsk, Ussurisky.
3. A. Geze, Irkutsk, drug store, Zhinzheroff.
4. F. Walden, Vladivostok, his own house.
5. Buttenhoff, Khabarovsk, firm Kunst & Albers.
6. Dattan, Tomsk, Nechayevskaya Street (Initial A.)
7. [Brothers or Baron] Kuzberg, Harbin, offices of the Chinese-Eastern Railway.
8. Skribanovich (initial G.), Blagoveschensk, house of Kunst & Albers.
9. Panoff, Vladivostok, his own house.

This letter was sent me after I left Petrograd and reached me April 5. It is important not only for content, indicating as it does the names and addresses of agents-destructors who are called upon for increasing activity against the United States and Japan to make the Pacific Ocean a new area of terror, but showing that the German General Staff was continuing after the Brest-Litovsk "peace" to work actively with the Russian Bolshevik Government.
Have original letter.

CHAPTER IV.

THE PLOT FOR A SHAMEFUL PEACE

Germany made its Russian peace with its own puppet government, the misnamed Council of People's Commissars, the president of which is Vladimir Ulianov (Lenin), the foreign minister of which was Leon Trotsky, and the ambassador of which to Germany is A. Joffe. Germany made this peace harder upon the Russian people as punishment to the ambition of its tools in seeking to become too powerful, and in hoping for a little while not only that Russia would be delivered over to them, but that they could double-cross their masters by turning a simulated German revolution into a real one.

But their craftiness was a toy in the hands of rough German force. Germany was actually double-crossing them by negotiating with the Ukranian Rada at the moment they dreamed they were tricking Germany.

Germany, however, did not discard the Bolshevik leaders, recognizing their further use in the German world campaign for internal disorganizations in the nations with which it wars, but confined them to the limited inland province which Great Russia proper has now become.

Lenin, according to statements made public as soon as Trotsky's spectacular device of "No peace—No war" failed, always was for peace on any German terms. He dominated the situation thereafter and conceded everything that Germany asked. Nor did Trotsky cease to continue to obey the German orders delivered to him both by Gen. Hoffman at Brest-Litovsk, and at Petrograd directly by the Russian Division of the German General Staff, which was seated in Petrograd itself from November, 1917, and which was still there in full operation when I left, Monday, March 4, the day that Petrograd received notification that peace had been signed at Brest-Litovsk by the Russian and German delegations.

Trotsky, therefore, rests rightly under the accusation of having staged his theatrical scene as a climax to the Russian disorganization desired by Germany. The actual order he gave was for the immediate demobilization of the Russian army, leaving the German army unopposed.

The actual effect of the work of the Bolshevik leaders, moreover, was to enable Germany to combine its former army of the Russian front with its western army, for the launching of its March offensive in France. Such has been the fruition of Russia's German-directed Bolshevikism.

The following documents tell the story of the betrayal of Russia to a shameful and ruinous peace.

DOCUMENT NO. 30

G[reat] General Staff, Central Division Section M/R, No. 408.

(Secret)

February 26, 1918.

To the Chairman of the Council of People's Commissars:

This Division of the Staff has the honor to request data of the attitude of the detachments being sent to Pskoff and to guard against all possible disastrous results if in these detachments any will carry on patriotic propaganda and agitations against the German army.

Head of the Russian Division German General Staff: O. Rausch.
Adjutant: U. Wolff.

Note.—*The chairman of the Council of People's Commissars is Lenin. At the top of this letter is the written comment: "Urgent. Chairman of the Council of People's Commissars asks Volodarsky to communicate this to the agitation department. Secretary Skripnik." Skripnik is the first secretary of the Government, personally reporting to Lenin. A second notation in margin is: "Central Executive Committee No. 823 to report," signed with illegible initials. The detachments being sent to Pskoff at this time were composed of Red Guards and of the recruits of the new Red Army. Pskoff was taken by the Germans without a fight.*

Have original letter.

DOCUMENT NO. 31

G. G.-S., Intelligence Bureau, Section R, No. 750.

(Very Secret)

February 27, 1918.

To the President of the Council of People's Commissars:

Not having received an exact answer to my question of the 25th of February, I now have the honor a second time to request you to inform me in the shortest possible time the numbers and kind of forces sent to Pskoff and Narva.

At the same time, at the orders of the representative of our General Staff, I once more remind you of the desirability of naming Gen. Parski to

---

the post of commander in chief of the Russian armed forces, in place of Gen. Bonch-Bruevich, whose actions do not meet the approval of the German High Command. Since the attacks on the lives and property of the German landowners in Esthonia and Livonia, which, according to our information, were carried out with the knowledge of Gen. Bonch-Bruevich, and his nationalistic actions in Orel, his continuance in the position of general is no longer desirable.

Head of the Bureau:

Agasfer.

Note.—*Across the letter is written "Send to Trotsky and Podvoisky. N. G." (Gorbunov's initials, chief secretary of the Council of Peop'e's Commissars.) Observe the mandatory nature of the whole letter and particularly of the first paragraph. Agasfer, as has been shown, is the cipher signature of Maj. Luberts, head of the Petrograd Intelligence Bureau of the German General Staff, the chief branch of the Russian Division of the German General Staff, the head of which is Maj. Rausch, referred to in this letter as the representative of "our General Staff." Apparently both Luberts and Rausch wrote a warning against sending any patriots to the defending forces, and seemingly the Bolshevik effort at obedience as indicated in document No. 30 was not fast enough to suit the German martinets. Podvoisky was minister of war. Gen. Parski was appointed to the com-*

---

mand of the Petrograd district, and as late as June 14 still held the post. He formerly was in command of the city of Riga, which was surrendered to the Germans without adequate defense in the early autumn of 1917. Have original letter.*

DOCUMENT NO. 32

G. G.-S., Intelligence Bureau, Section R, No. 272/600.

(Very Secret)

February 6, 1918.

To the People's Commissar of Foreign Affairs:

I ask you to immediately give the Turkish subject, Carp C. Missirof, a Russian passport in place of the one taken from him in 1912 on the basis of the inclosed national passport.

Agent C. Missirof is to be sent to the staff of the Russian High Command, where, according to the previous discussion between Gen. Hoffman and Commissars Trotsky and Joffe, he will keep watch on the activity of the head of the staff, Gen. Bonch-Bruevich, in the capacity of assistant to the Commissars Kalmanovich and Feierabend.

For the head of the Bureau:

R. Bauer.
Adjutant: Bukholm.

G. G.-S.

NACHRICHTEN-BUREAU.

Section *R.*

№ *750*

27 Февраля 1918 г.

В. Секретно.

Г. Предсѣдателю Совѣта Народныхъ Комиссаровъ.

Настоящимъ, не получивъ точнаго отвѣта на мой запросъ отъ 25 февраля, имѣю честь вторично просить въ срочномъ порядкѣ сообщить мнѣ количество и качество силъ направляемыхъ къ Пскову и Нарвѣ.

Одновременно, по порученію Представителя нашего Генеральнаго Штаба, еще разъ напоминаю о желательности назначенія ген. Паржескаго на постъ Верховнаго Главнокомандующаго русскими вооруженными силами, вмѣсто ген. Бончъ-Бруевича, дѣятельность котораго не встрѣчаетъ сочувствія Германскаго Верховнаго Командованія. Теперь-же, послѣ покушеній на жизнь и имущество нѣмецкихъ землевладѣльцевъ въ Эстляндіи и Лифляндіи, что, по нашимъ свѣдѣніямъ, произошло съ вѣдома ген. Бончъ-Бруевича и націоналистической дѣятельности его въ Орлѣ, пребываніе генерала на его посту нежелательно.

Начальникъ Отдѣленія

Адъютантъ

Facsimile Document Number 31

NOTE.—*Here we have the behind-the-scene disclosure of the real relations between Trotsky and Gen. Hoffman at Brest-Litovsk, stripping the mask from the public pose. Trotsky got his orders in this case and he carried them out. Across the top of this letter, too, he has written his own conviction, "Ask Joffe. L. T.," while Joffe, whose rôle seems to be that of the mouthpiece of Germany, has written in the margin, "According to agreement this must be done. A. Joffe." Thereby he becomes a witness for the agreement itself—that pledge between himself, Trotsky, and the military chief of the German Government at the Brest-Litovsk conference, to betray the commander of the Russian army when he should attempt to defend Russia against Germany. A further marginal note states that the passport was given February 7, under the Russian name, P. L. Ilin.*

Have original letter and the surrendered passport. Kalmanovich and Feierabend were Commissars of Counter Espionage.

THE UKRAINIAN DOUBLE-CROSS

How the Bolsheviki themselves were double-crossed in the Ukraine; how the Germans toyed with their puppets to disorganize Russia, with disclosures of plans for assassination of loyal Russian leaders, are shown in the following documents and Mr. Sisson's accompanying notes.

DOCUMENT NO. 33

Counter Espionage at Army Headquarters, No. 63.

January 10, 1918.

TO THE COMMISSION FOR COMBATING THE COUNTER REVOLUTION:

The Commissar on Combating the Counter Revolution in a cipher telegram, No. 235, demanded the sending of special agents to Kieff and Novocherkask.

There have been sent Comrades Vlasenko, Gavrilchuk, and Korablev, who have more than once very successfully performed information service. The commissar in his cipher telegram indicates that the German and Austrian agents assigned from Petrograd, Lieuts'. Otto, Kremer, Blum, and Vasilko, are playing a double rôle, reporting on what is happening at Petrograd, and they carry on an intensive agitation in favor of a separate peace of the Ukraine with the Central Powers, and for the restoring of order. Their work is having success.

To Siberia have been ordered Comrades Trefilev and Shepshelevich, in connection with your report of the purchase and export of gold by Austrian prisoners in Siberia.

Director of Counter Espionage:

FEIERABEND.

Secretary: N. DRACHEFF

NOTE.—*So stands disclosed the manner in which Germany set about to double-cross the Bolshevik servants who in success had become at times uppish in bargaining with their masters. It was not a part of the German program to create in Russia a power which it could not at any time control, or, if need be, overturn. Its plan here had the additional advantage of not only disciplining the Petrograd Bolsheviks but also of disunifying Russia still further. It worked out to a separate peace with Ukraine and a separate peace with Great Russia. Lieut. Otto is the Konshin afterwards arrested for some unknown betrayal. See Document No. 2.*

Have photograph of letter.

DOCUMENT NO. 34

Counter Espionage at Army Headquarters, No. 511.

January 30, 1918.

TO THE COMMISSION FOR COMBATING COUNTER REVOLUTION:

You are informed that the German and Austrian officers located at Kieff now have private meetings with members of the deposed Rada. They insistently inform us of the inevitable signing and ratification of peace treaties both between the Ukraine and the Central Powers and between Roumania and Austria and Germany.

Director of Counter Espionage:

FEIERABEND.

Commissar: O. KALMANOVICH.

NOTE.—*Corroborative of the preceding document. The separate peace with the Ukraine already had been signed.*

Have photograph of letter.

DOCUMENT NO. 35

G. G.-S. Intelligence Bureau, Section R, No. 181.

(*Very Urgent*)

December 9, 1917.

TO THE PEOPLE'S COMMISSAR OF FOREIGN AFFAIRS:

In accordance with your request, the Intelligence Bureau on November 29 sent to Rostof Maj. von Boehlke, who arranged there a survey over the forces of the Don Troop Government. The major also organized a detachment of prisoners of war, who took part in the battles. In this case, the prisoners of war, in accordance with the directions given by the July conference at Kronstadt, participated in by Messrs. Lenin, Zinovieff, Kameneff, Raskolnikoff, Dybenko, Shisko, Antonoff, Krilenko, Volodarsky, and Podvoisky, were dressed in Russian army and navy uniforms. Maj. von Boehlke took part in commanding, but the conflicting orders of the official commander Arnautoff, and the talentless activity of the scout Tulak, paralyzed the plans of our officer.

The agents sent by order from Petrograd to kill Gens. Kaledin, Bogaevsky, and Alexieff were cowardly and nonenterprising people. Agents passed through to Karauloff. The communications of Gen. Kaledin with the Americans and English are beyond doubt, but they limit themselves entirely to financial assistance. Maj. von Boehlke, with the passport of the Finn, Uno Muuri, returned to Petrograd and will make a report today at the office of the chairman of the council at 10 p. m.

For the head of the Bureau:

R. BAUER.

Adjutant: M. K.——(?).

NOTE.—*This is a cold-blooded disclosure of a German-Bolshevik plan for the assassination of Kaledin and Alexieff, as well as proof of a condition often denied by Smolny during the winter—that German prisoners were being armed as Russian soldiers in the struggle against the Russian nationalists on the Don. The letter also contains the most complete list of the participants in the July conspiracy conference at Kronstadt. The marginal comment opposite the assassination paragraph, "Who sent them?" is in an unknown handwriting. Maj. von Boehlke is a German*

officer referred to in Document No. 5. His cipher signature is Schott.

Have photograph of letter.

DOCUMENT NO. 36

G. G.-S., Intelligence Bureau, Section R, No. 136.

(*Very Secret*)

November 28, 1917.

TO THE COUNCIL OF PEOPLE'S COMMISSARS:

In accordance with your request, the Intelligence Bureau of the General Staff informs the Council of People's Commissars that the Ukrainian Commission at the Austrian High Command, in which participate the empowered representatives of the German Staff, has worked out a plan of the activities of the revolutionaries known to the Council of People's Commissars and the Central Executive Committee of the Council of Workmen's and Soldiers' Deputies—Chudovsky, Boyarsky, Gubarsky, and Piatakov—who are under the full direction of the Austro-Hungarian High Command.

The commander in chief of the Russian army has been made acquainted by Schott with plans of the Austro-German High Command and will cooperate with him.

Head of Bureau: AGASFER.

NOTE.—*At this early time there was harmony all around on the Ukraine program, Germans, Austrians, and the Commissars in complete brotherhood. Schott is Maj. von Boehlke and Agasfer is Maj. Luberts.*

Have photograph of letter.

CHAPTER V.

TROTSKY AND ROUMANIA

The machinations of Trotsky, inspired by the German Gen. Hoffman, for the disruption of Roumania are disclosed in the following:

DOCUMENT NO. 37

Counter Espionage at Army Headquarters, No. 20.

January 2, 1918.

TO THE COMMISSION ON COMBATING COUNTER REVOLUTION:

Commander in chief Krilenko has requested the Counter Espionage at the Army Headquarters to inform you that it is necessary to order the following persons to the Roumanian front immediately: From Petrograd, Commissar Kuhl, Socialist Rakovsky, Sailor Gnieshin; and from the front the chief of staff of the Red Guard, Durasov. These persons should be supplied with literature and with financial resources for agitation. To them is committed the task of taking all measures for the deposing of the Roumanian king and the removal of counter revolutionary Roumanian officers.

Director of Counter Espionage:

FEIERABEND.

Secretary: N. DRACHEV.

NOTE.—*This marks the continuance of large-scale work to disorganize the Roumanian army. That it advances disappointingly to Germany is evidenced by vengeful steps taken by Gen. Hoffman and Trotsky from Brest-Litovsk, when in the middle of January*

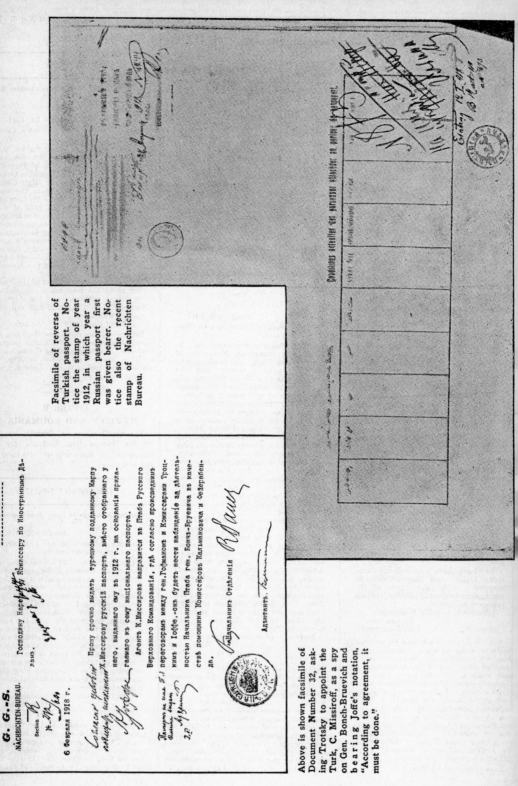

Facsimile of reverse of Turkish passport. Notice the stamp of year 1912, in which year a Russian passport first was given bearer. Notice also the recent stamp of Nachrichten Bureau.

Above is shown facsimile of Document Number 32, asking Trotsky to appoint the Turk, C. Missiroff, as a spy on Gen. Bonch-Bruevich and bearing Joffe's notation, "According to agreement, it must be done."

Facsimile of face of Turkish passport surrendered by Missiroff. Notice that the passport was given him by Turkey in 1911. Letter No. 32 indicates that he had a previous Russian passport delivered to him in 1912, on basis of Turkish passport.

(*western calendar*) Trotsky, at the request of Gen. Hoffman, ordered the arrest in Petrograd of the Roumanian minister Diamandi. (See Document 37A.)

At about the same time the Roumanian public gold reserves in custody within the Kremlin walls at Moscow were seized by the Russian Government. Diamandi was released from arrest at the demand of the united diplomatic delegations at Petrograd, but his humiliations continued, and on January 28 he was immediately ordered from Petrograd, being given less than 10 hours to prepare for the departure of a party that contained many women and children. Ambassador Francis sought in vain of Zalkind, who was acting as Foreign Minister in the absence of Trotsky again at Brest, for an extension of the time of departures. The Roumanian party was thrown pell-mell on a train at midnight. It was delayed in Finland on one excuse and another, not immediately apparent, but in three weeks the minister, leaving behind a large part of his people, was allowed to proceed to Torneo. By good luck he reached there the day after the Red Guard lost Torneo to the White Guard. That day saved his life, for on the person of Svetlitzsky, a Russian commissar who joined him in mid-Finland and accompanied him to Torneo, was found an order to Timofeyeff, the commissar at Torneo, to shoot him. Svetlitzsky was shot instead. When I passed through Torneo the control officer talked frankly about the details, expressing the opinion that the shooting might have been a mistake, as it was not shown that Svetlitzsky was aware of the contents of the letter. Svetlitzsky, however, was an important person in Petrograd, close to Trotsky. Our American party brought Guranesco, the first secretary of the Roumanian delegation, out of Finland through the lines with us. He had been in Red Finland seven weeks. Behind us at Bjorneburg we left several families of Roumanians who had departed from Petrograd with the minister. We would have liked to have brought them through the lines of the two armies, but our venture was too desperate to permit unauthorized additions to the party.

The marginal notation on this letter is "Execute," initialed "Ch," the sign manual of Chicherin, the returned exile from England, at that time Assistant Commissar of Foreign Affairs, now Minister of Foreign Affairs. Have photograph of letter.

DOCUMENT 37A*

* The contents of this letter, written by Joffe, were telegraphed to Washington in February, and photographic copy of letter forwarded by Ambassador Francis to State Department.

No. 771, Affair of Peace Delegation

(*Confidential*)

Brest-Litovsk, December 31, 1917.

To THE COUNCIL OF PEOPLE's COMMISSARS:

Comrade L. Trotsky has charged me to bring to the knowledge of the Council of People's Commissars the motives for his telegraphic proposal to arrest the Roumanian diplomatic representatives in Petersburg.

Gen. Hoffman, referring to the conference which had taken place in Brest-Litovsk between the members of the German and Austro-Hungarian delegations on December 29, presented to the Russian delegation in the name of the German and Austrian Chief Command (a deciphered radio-telegram was exhibited in this connection) a *confidential demand* concerning the immediate incitement of the Roumanian army to recognize the necessity of an armistice and adopting the terms of a democratic peace pointed out by the Russian delegates. The implacability of the staff and the whole commanding force of the Roumanian army, with regard to which the Chief Command of the German army has received the most exact agency information, spoils the excellent impression produced in Germany and on all the fronts by the Russian peace propositions, which has made it possible to again *stimulate the popular feeling against England, France, and America and can bring about an undesirable and dangerous aggravation of the peace question, up to the German army going over to the attack on our front and an open annexation of the territories occupied in Russia.*

The general expressed his opinion that against peace might be the Cossacks, some Ukranian regiments, and the Caucasian army, in which case they will also doubtless be joined by the Roumanian armies, which, according to the information in possession of the German staff, enters into the calculations of Kaledin and Alexieff. It is greatly in the interests of the German and Austrian delegations that complete harmony should prevail on the entire Russian front as regards the conclusion of an armistice and adopting the terms of a separate peace between Russian and Germany, seeing that in this event the German and Austrian Chief Command will propose to Roumania their terms of peace, and will be in a position to take up their operative actions on the western front on a very large scale; at the same time Gen. Hoffman, in the course of a conversation with Comr. Trotsky, twice hinted at the necessity of immediately beginning these war operations.

When Comr. Trotsky declared that at the disposal of the council's power there are no means of influencing the Roumanian staff, Gen. Hoffman pointed out the necessity of sending trustworthy agents to the Roumanian army, and the possibility of arresting the Roumanian mission in Petersburg, and repressive measures against the Roumanian king and the Roumanian commanding forces.

After this interview Comr. L. Trotsky by cable proposed to arrest the Roumanian mission in Petersburg with all its members. This report is being sent by special courier—Comrade I. G. Brossoff, *who has to personally transmit to Commissar Podvoisky some information of a secret character regarding the sending to the Roumanian army of those persons whose names Comr. Brossoff will give.* All these persons will be paid out of the cash of the "German Naphtha - Industrial Bank," which has bought near Boreslav the business of the joint-stock company of Fanto & Co. The chief direction of those agents has been intrusted, according to Gen. Hoffman's indication, to a certain Wolf Vonigel, who is keeping a watch over the military agents of the countries allied with us. As regards the English and American diplomatic representatives, *Gen. Hoffman has expressed the agreement of the German staff to the measures adopted by Comr. Trotsky and Comr. Lazimiroff with regard to watching over their activity.*

Member of the delegation:

A. JOFFE.

[*Marginal Notations*]

Comr. Shitkevitch: Take copies and send to the Commiss. for Foreign Affairs, personally to Comr. Zalkind. [*Passages printed above in italics marked:*] To Sanders.

Reported January 4, regarding the arrest of Diamandi and others.

M. SHITKEVITCH.

January 5, 1918.—To the Chancery: Send an urgent telegram to Trotsky about the arrest of the Roumanian minister.—SAVELIEFF.

NOTE (as cabled Feb. 9).—*The date is January 13, western calendar, the eve of the Russian New Year. The Roumanian minister was arrested that night in Petrograd, and only released on the united demand of all embassies and legations in Petrograd. Since then he has been sent out of Russia. The letter shows that Trotsky took Gen. Hoffman's personal demand as an order for action. Most important of all, however, it strips the mask from the Lenin and Trotsky public protestations that they have sought to prevent the peace negotiations with Germany from turning to the military advantage of Germany against the United States, England, and France. The aim here disclosed is instead to aid Germany in stimulating feeling against England, France, and the United States, in enabling Germany to prepare for an offensive on the western front. A German bank is named as paymaster for Bolshevik agitators among the Roumanian soldiers. Is "Wolf Vonigel," the field director, the Wolf von Igel of American notoriety? The similarity in name is striking. Finally, Gen. Hoffman and the German staff is satisfied with Trotsky's watch over the American and English diplomats. Joffe, who signs the letter, is a member of the Russian Peace Commission. Since this letter was written Zalkind has gone to Switzerland on a special mission.*

NOTE.—(July 6, 1918). *He did not reach there, being unable to pass through England, and in April was in Christiana.*

DOCUMENT NO. 38

Commission for Combating the Counter Revolution and Pogroms, No. —

Petrograd, Dec. 14, 1917.

MAJOR VON BOEHLKE:

ESTEEMED COMRADE: I bring to your notice that our Finnish comrades, Hakhia, Pukko, and Enrot have advised the Commissar for Combating the Counter Revolution of the following facts:

1. Between the English officers and the Finnish bourgeois organizations there are connections which cause us serious apprehension.

2. In Finland have been installed two wireless stations which are used by unknown persons who communicate in cipher.

3. Between Gen. Kaledin and the American mission there is an undoubted communication, of which we have received exact information from your source, and, therefore, a most careful supervision of the American Embassy is necessary.

These reports must be established exactly. Our agents are helpless. Please excuse that I write on the official letter heads, but I hasten to do this, sitting here at the commission at an extraordinary meeting. Ready to service.

F. ZALKIND.

NOTE.—*The written comment at the top of the letter is: "Commissar for Foreign Affairs. I request exact instructions. Schott." It is von Boehlke's question, signed with his cipher name. (See document 5.) The letter may imply that von*

Boehlke had, in the opinion of his good friend Zalkind, a means of internal observation at the American Embassy. Have photograph of letter.

DOCUMENT NO. 39

Counter Espionage at the Army Headquarters, No. 268.

(Very Secret)

January 25, 1918.

To the Commission on Combating the Counter Revolution:

The 23d of January at the Army Headquarters [Stavka] there took place a conference at which there participated Maj. von Boehlke, assigned from Petrograd. It was decided, upon the insistence of the German consultants, to send to the internal fronts the following persons, furnishing them all powers for dealing with individual counter revolutionaries:

To the Don: Zhikhorev, Rudnev, Krogultz, and Ernest Delgau.

To the Caucasus Front: Vassili Dumbadze, Prince Machabelli, Sevastianov, and Ter-Baburin.

To the 1st Polish Corps of Gen. Dovbor-Menitsky are assigned Dembitski, Stetkus, Zhimiitis, and Gisman.

Be so good as to take all measures for the quick assignment and the adequate furnishing of the assigned persons with money, reserve passports, and other documents.

Senior officer: PETER MIRONOV.

NOTE.—*This is an assassination order against individuals. It was not successful against the Polish general. Dembadze and Prince Machabelli were German spies implicated in the Sukhomlinoff affair and sentenced to prison, but afterwards liberated by the Bolsheviks. Lieut. Col. Dembitski was a Bolshevik Polish officer. Baburin was an assistant chief of staff under Krilenko. The letter is indorsed: "Comrade Lunacharsky. Go and report to Comrade Zinovieff," signature illegible. Have photograph of letter.*

DOCUMENT NO. 40

Counter Espionage at the Army Headquarters, No. 51/572.

January 19, 1918.

To the Commission for Combating the Counter Revolution:

There have been received two notes addressed to the Supreme Commander from the staffs of the Austrian and German High Commands. These notes inform the Army Headquarters [Stavka] that the organizer of the volunteer army in the Don region, Gen. Alexieff, is in written communication with the officer personnel of the Polish legions at the front, with the view of getting the help of Polish officers in the counter revolution. This information has been received by the Austrian agents from the Polish Bolshevik Comrade Zhuk, who played a large part at Rostov during the November and December battles. On the other side, the representative of the German Government, Count Lerchenfeldt, reports of the rapidly growing movement in Poland in favor of the bourgeois estate owners' imperialistic plan to defend with arms the greatest possible independence of Poland, with the broadening of its fron-

tiers at the expense of Lithuania, White Russia, and Galicia.

This movement is actively supported by the popular democratic party in Warsaw, as well as Petrograd, by military organizations guided by the counter revolutionary estate owners and the bourgeois Polish clergy.

The situation which has arisen was discussed on the 16th of January at the Stavka in the presence of Maj. von Boehlke, sent by the Petrograd branch of the German Intelligence Bureau, and it was there decided:

1. To take the most decisive measures, up to shooting *en masse*, against the Polish troops which have submitted to the counter revolutionary and imperialistic propaganda.

2. To arrest Gen. Dovbor-Menitsky.

3. To arrange a surveillance of the commanding personnel.

4. Send agitators to the Polish legions to consult regarding this the Polish revolutionary organizations known to the committee.

5. On learning of the counter revolutionary activity of Polish officers to immediately arrest them and send them to the Stavka at the disposal of the Counter Espionage.

6. To arrest the emissaries of Gen. Alexieff, Staff Capt. Shuravsky, and Capt. Rushitsky.

7. To request the Commission for Combating the Counter Revolution, in agreement with the German Intelligence Bureau at Petrograd, to arrange a surveillance and observation of the following institutions and persons:

(a) The military committee.

(b) The Society of Friends of the Polish Soldier.

(c) Inter-Party Union.

(d) The Union of Polish Invalids.

(e) Members of the Polish Group of the former state Duma and council.

(f) The chairman, Lednitsky, and the members of the former Committee for the Liquidation of Affairs of the Kingdom of Poland.

(g) Boleslav Jalovtski.

(h) Vladislav Grabski.

(i) Stanislav Shuritski.

(j) Roman Catholic Polish clergy.

(k) The Polish Treasury through which, according to agency reports, the governments of countries allied with Russia intend, with the assistance of the New York National City Bank, to supply with monetary resources the counter revolutionary camp.

(l) It is necessary to verify the private reports of several Lithuanian revolutionaries that among the Church Benevolent Funds, which are at the disposal of the Polish clergy, are the capitals of private persons who hid their money from requisition for the benefit of the state.

In case of establishment of any connection with the counter revolution, the guilty Polish institutions are to be liquidated, their leaders and also persons connected with the counter revolutionary activity are to be arrested, and sent to the disposal of the Stavka.

Chief of the Counter Espionage:

FEIERABEND.

Commissar: KALMANOVICH.

NOTE.—*Again Germany, through Count Lerchenfeldt, was intriguing on both sides. Chiefly, however, the significance of the letter is in the thoroughness of the outlined German plan to crush the threat of armed opposition from the Polish legions of the Russian army. The troops were fired upon, as indicated. The preceding document really follows this in natural sequence. The next two further elucidate the situation for the benefit of the Poles of the outside world.*

Have photograph of letter.

DOCUMENT NO. 41

Counter Espionage at the Army Headquarters, No. 461.

January 28, 1918.

To the Commission for Combating the Counter Revolution:

The Special Constituent Commission on the conflict with the Polish counter revolutionary troops has begun its activity. All the conduct of its affairs has been located at the Counter Espionage at the Army Headquarters [Stavka], where is being collected all information on the counter revolution on the external and internal fronts. At the commission have arrived members of the Commission for Combating the Counter Revolution, E. Miekonoshin, I. Zenzinov, Zhilinski, and from Sevastopol Comrade Tiurin. To a conference were called agents announcing their wish to be sent for conflict with the bourgeois Polish officers: Lieut. Col. Dembitski, Boleslav Yakimovich, Roman Strievsky, Joseph Yasenovsky, and Mikhail Adamovich. All those agents are under obligation to carry the affair to the point of open insubordination of the soldiers against the officers and the arrest of the latter.

For emergency the commander in chief ordered to assign Nakhim Sher and Ilya Razymov for the destruction of the counter revolutionary ringleaders among the Polish troops, and the commission recognized the possibility of declaring all Polish troops outside the law, when that measure should present itself as imperative.

From Peterburg, observers announced that the Polish organizations are displaying great reserve and caution in mutual relations. There has been established, however, an unquestionable contact between the High Military Council located in Peterburg and the Polish officers and soldiers of the bourgeois estate-owning class with the counter revolutionary Polish troops. On this matter in the Commissariat on Military Affairs, there took place on January 22 a conference of Comrades Podvoisky, Kedrov, Boretzkov, Dybenko, and Kovalsky. The Commissar on Naval Affairs announced that the sailors Trushin, Markin, Peinkaitis, and Schultz demand the dismissal of the Polish troops, and threaten, in case it is refused, assaults on the Polish legionaries in Peterburg. The commander-in-chief suggests that it might be possible to direct the rage of the sailors mentioned, and of their group, to the front against the counter revolutionary Polish troops.

At the present time our agitation among the Polish troops is being car-

Above is shown facsimile of reverse of Nevalainen's Finnish passport, which he surrendered in receipt for Russian passport.

Below is shown facsimile of Letter Number 43, ordering issuance of new passport to the Finn, Nevalainen.

Facsimile of front of Finnish passport surrendered by Nevalainen in order to receive
the Russian passport referred to in Document Number 43.

ried on in very active fashion and there is great hope for the disorganization of the Polish legionaries.

Chief of Counter Espionage:

FEIERABEND.

Secretary: Iv. ALEXIEFF.

NOTE.—*Have photograph of letter.*

DOCUMENT NO. 42

Counter Espionage at the Army Headquarters, No. 21.

January 28, 1918.

TO THE COMMISSION FOR COMBATING THE COUNTER REVOLUTION:

At the request of the commander in chief, in answer to your inquiry, I inform you, supplementary to the dispatch, that the funds sent with Maj. Bayermeister have been received here. Among the troops acting on the front against the counter revolutionaries have been prepared several battalions for conflict with the Poles and Roumanians. We will pay 12 roubles a day, with an increased food ration. From the hired sections sent against the legionaries have been formed two companies, one from the best shots for the shooting of officer-regiments, the other of Lithuanians and Letts for the spoiling of food reserves in Vitebsk, Minsk, and Mogilev governments, in the places where the Polish troops are situated. Various local peasants have also agreed to attack the regiments and exterminate them.

Commissar: G. MOSHOLOV.
Secretary: Iv. ALEXIEFF.

NOTE.—*These two documents show that the policy against these patriotic soldiers was one of merciless extermination, financed by German money, handed out by a German officer. Bayermeister is named in Document No. 5.
Have photograph of letter.*

CHAPTER VI.

THE COMPLETE SURRENDER

The following documents show the complete surrender of the Bolshevik leaders to their German masters:

DOCUMENT NO. 43

G[reat] General Staff, Central Division, Section M-R, No. 411.

February 26, 1918.

(Very Secret)

TO THE COUNCIL OF PEOPLE'S COMMISSARS:

According to instructions from the High Command of the German Army, I have the honor to remind you that the withdrawing and disarming of the Russian Red Guard from Finland must be commenced immediately. It is known to the staff that the chief opponent of this step is the head of the Finnish Red Guard, Yarvo Haapalainen, who has a great influence on the Russian *tovarische* [comrades] I request you to assign for this struggle with Haapalainen our agent, Walter Nevalainen (Nevalaiselle), bearer

---

of Finnish passport 3681, and supply him with a passport and passes.

Head of the Division:

O. RAUSCH.

Adjutant: U. WOLFF.

NOTE.—*Written at the top of the letter and signed N. G., the initials of Lenin's secretary, N. Gorbunov, is the order: "Send to the Commissar of Foreign Affairs and execute." In the margin is written "Passport 211—No. 392," but unfortunately the name under which the new passport was given is not mentioned. This order explains the withdrawal of the Russian Red Guard from Finland in early March and the abandonment of the Finnish Red Guard to its fate. The latter, however, took care of the disarming both of Russian soldiers and sailors as they left Finland, for the Finns needed guns and ammunition. The Russians sometimes fought but were surrounded and disarmed. In Helsingfors while I was there in March the Red Guard and the sailors were fighting each other nightly with rifles and machine guns. One of two Finnish Red Guard leaders almost surely is Nevalainen, but under the circumstances I do not care to speculate.*

*The order to hold all foreign embassies in Red Finland was given coincidently with the appearance of one of them upon the scene. The excuse offered was that foreigners were carrying information to the White Guard. Simultaneously influence was exerted in the White Guard to increase difficulties in passage between the lines. It is reasonable to place the obstacles to passage created on both sides of the Finnish line to German effort, for German aid was being given the White Guard openly at the moment it was intriguing in the inner councils of the Red Guard. The American party cornered in Finland escaped only by persistence and good fortune. The British Embassy party was passed through the day before the closing order came. The French and Italian Embassies were obliged after a month of vain effort to return to Russia.
Have original letter and the surrendered passport.*

DOCUMENT NO. 44

G. G.-S., Intelligence Bureau, Section R, No. 283.

February 7, 1918.

TO THE COMMISSAR OF FOREIGN AFFAIRS:

We are told that secret service agents attached to the Army Headquarters [Stavka] are following Maj. Erich, who has been ordered to Kieff. I ask you to take urgent measures to remove the surveillance of the above-named officer.

Head of the Bureau: AGASFER.
Adjutant: BUKHOLM.

NOTE.—*Chicherin, assistant foreign minister, initials a marginal comment, "Talk it over." This note marks the period of acute irritation over the Ukraine between Bolsheviks and Germans. Agasfer is Maj. Luberts.
Have original letter.*

DOCUMENT NO. 45

G. G.-S., Intelligence Bureau, Section R, No. 228.

February 4, 1918.

TO THE COMMISSAR OF FOREIGN AFFAIRS:

By instructions of the representative of our staff I have the honor to

---

ask you immediately to recall from the Ukrainian front the agitators Bryansky, Wolf, Drabkin, and Pittsker. Their activity has been recognized as dangerous by the German General Staff.

Head of the Bureau:

AGASFER.

Adjutant: HENRICH.

NOTE.—*An exchange of courtesies of the same period as Document No. 44. Chicherin has notated it, "Discuss."
Have original letter, and also photo secured earlier.*

DOCUMENT NO. 46

G. G.-S., Intelligence Bureau, Section R, No. 238.

February 3, 1918.

TO THE COMMISSAR OF FOREIGN AFFAIRS:

According to instructions of the representative of our General Staff, I have the honor once more to insist that you recall from Estonia, Lithuania, and Courland all agitators of the Central Executive Committee of the Council of Workmen's and Soldiers' Deputies.

Head of the Bureau: AGASFER.
Adjutant: BUKHOLM.

NOTE.—*Another instance of the time when Germany was using an iron hand of discipline, clearing of agitators the Provinces it already had announced its intention of seizing for its own. The letter was referred by Markin, one of Trotsky's secretaries, to Volodarsky, who seems to have been in charge of the proletarian agitation in these Provinces.
Have original letter, and also photo secured earlier.*

DOCUMENT NO. 47

G. G.-S., Intelligence Bureau, Section R, No. 317.

TO THE COUNCIL OF PEOPLE'S COMMISSARS:

The Intelligence Bureau has received precise information that the agitators of the Petrograd Council of Workmen's and Soldiers' Deputies, Volodarski, Brosoff, and Guschin, have completely changed the character of the Esthonia socialists' activity, which finally led to the local German landlords being declared outlawed. By order of the General Staff I ask you to take immediate steps for the restoring of the rights of the above-mentioned German landlords and the recalling of the agitators.

For the head of the Bureau:

R. BAUER.

Adjutant.   E. RATITZ.

NOTE.—*This order for the release of the German landlords was at once obeyed, and the act of surrender, evidently at the direct order of Lenin, to whom this letter is addressed, marked the end of the incipient rebellion of the Bolshevik leaders against their German masters.
Have photograph of letter*

VARIED ACTIVITIES

The following documents show various miscellaneous activities, including measures for the assassination of counter revolutionaries:

DOCUMENT NO. 48

Counter Espionage at the Army Headquarters, No. —

January 22, 1918.

To THE COUNCIL OF PEOPLE'S COMMISSARS:

By our agents it has been established that connections between the Poles, the Don, and French officers, and also probably the diplomatic representatives of the allied powers, are maintained by means of Russian officers traveling under the guise of sack speculators. In view of this we request you to take measures for the strict surveillance of the latter.

Commissar: KALMANOVICH.

NOTE.—*The indorsement on this is by Gorbunoff, "Copy to inform Podvoisky and Dzerzhinsky." The former was War Minister, the latter chairman of the Commission for Combating the Counter Revolution. Sack speculators were food peddlers who went into the provinces and brought food to the cities for profitable sale. Soldiers practically had a monopoly of the trade.*
Have photograph of letter.

DOCUMENT NO. 49

G[reat] General Staff, Intelligence Bureau, Section R, No. 151.

December 4, 1917.

To THE COMMISSARIAT OF MILITARY AFFAIRS:

Herewith the Intelligence Bureau has the honor to transmit a list of the persons of Russian origin who are in the service of the German Intelligence Department:

Sakharoff, officer First Infantry Reserve Regiment; Ensign Ter-Arytiuniantz, Zanko, Yarchuk, Golovin, Zhuk, Ilinsky, Cherniavsky, Capt. Postinkov, Schneier, Sailors Trushin and Gavrilov. All the persons mentioned are on the permanent staff of the Intelligence Bureau of the German General Staff.

Head of the Bureau:
                    AGASFER.
Adjutant.   HENRICH.

NOTE.—*Have photograph of letter.*

DOCUMENT NO. 50

G[reat] General Staff, Central Division, Section M, No. 22.

January 14, 1918.

(Very Confidential)

To THE CHAIRMAN OF THE PEOPLE'S COUNCIL OF COMMISSARS:

The Russian Division of the German General Staff has received an urgent report from our agents at Novocher-

---

kash and Rostoff that the friction which has arisen between Gen. Alexieff and Gen. Kaledin, after which the volunteer corps of Gen. Alexieff began the movement to the north, is a tactical step to have a base in the rear. In this way the army of Gen. Alexieff will have a reliable rear base, protected by Cossack troops, for supplying the army, and a base in case of an overwhelming movement on the part of the enemy. The communications of Gen. Alexieff with the Polish troops have been proved by new reports of the Polish Bolshevik commissars, Zhuk and Dembitski.

Chief of the Division of General Staff: O. RAUSCH.
Chief Adjutant: R. KRIEGER.

NOTE.—*Important as showing that the German had a real fear of the military possibilities in the Alexieff-Kaledin movement. The suicide of Gen. Kaledin at a moment of depression, following betrayals that undoubtedly were carefully plotted, was tragically a part of the great national tragedy.*
Have photograph of letter.

DOCUMENT NO. 51

Counter Espionage at the Army Headquarters, No. 263/79.

January 23, 1918.

To THE COMMISSARIAT OF FOREIGN AFFAIRS:

To your inquiry regarding those agents who might be able to give an exact report of the sentiment of the troops and population in the Provinces, I transmit to you a short list of the Russo-German agents-informers: In Voronezh, S. Sirtzoff; in Rostoff, Globoff and Melikoff; in Tiflis, Enskidze and Gavriloff; in Kazan, Pfaltz; in Samara, Oaipoff and Voenig; in Omsk, Blagovenschensky and Sipko; in Tomsk, Dattan, Tarasoff, and Rodionoff; in Irkutsk, Zhinzherova and Geze; in Vladivostok, Buttenhoff, Pannoff, and Erlanger.

Chief of Counter Espionage:
                    FEIERABEND.
Commissar: KALMANOVICH.

NOTE.—*Apart from the list of agents this letter has interest from the comment: "To the company of Comrade Bonch-Bruevich and Secret Department." The signature is illegible.*
Have photograph of letter.

DOCUMENT NO. 52

Counter Espionage at the Army Headquarters, No. 395.

January 21, 1918.

To THE COMMISSION FOR COMBATING THE COUNTER REVOLUTION:

The agents of the Counter Espionage at the Stavka [Army Headquarters] have established that the anarchists Stepan Kriloff, Fedor Kutzi, and Albert Bremsen, at Helsingfors, and also Nahim Arshavsky, Ruphim Levin, and Mikhail Shatiloff

---

had during the recent days a conference with the chief of staff of the Petrograd army district Shpilko. After Comrade Shpilko transmitted to the anarchists the offer of Comrade Antonoff and Comrade Bersin to recruit agents for the destruction of several counter revolutionists, the latter expressed their willingness and immediately began the recruiting. To Kieff are assigned the following, who have been hired at Helsingfors: S. Smirnoff and Rigamann; and to Odessa, Brack and Schulkovich.

For the Chief of the Counter Espionage.

Commissar: C. MOSHLOV.

NOTE.—*This is an assassination compact between Bolsheviks and anarchists. Antonoff, if one of the chief Bolshevik military leaders, is credited with the taking of Petrograd, and was in charge of the operations against Alexieff and Kaledin. The list of anarchists include several notorious characters.*
Have photograph of letter.

DOCUMENT NO. 53

Counter Espionage at the Army Headquarters, No. 471.

January 27, 1918.

To THE COMMISSION FOR COMBATING THE COUNTER REVOLUTION:

By us here there has been received a report from Finland, from Grishin and Rakhi, of the counter revolutionary activity of the lawyer, Jonas Kastren. This Kastren, in the years 1914-15 recruited on German funds Finnish volunteer regiments and sent them to Germany. For facilitating the work of recruiting he represented himself as a Socialist-Maximalist, and promised support to the Workers' Red Guard. In his office in Stockholm many of our comrades found a cordial reception and material support. Kastren furnished to Russia German money for the propaganda of Bolshevism in Russia. He had already established in 1916 a division of the German General Staff in Helsingfors. Now he, together with Svinhuvud, Ernroth, and Nandelschtedt, is on the side of the White Guards and is aiding them with money, supplies, and arms. We are informed that Kastren works both with German and English money. It is necessary immediately to cut short the work of Jonas Kastren and his group. The commander in chief advises to call to Petersburg the Finnish comrades, Rakhi and Pukho, or order Grishin to Helsingfors.

Commissar: A. SIVKO.
Secretary: IV. ALEXIEFF.

NOTE.—*Kastren was still alive when I spent a week in Helsingfors in March, but he added to his chances of longevity by fleeing in early February to the White Guards headquarters at Vasa. The order for his removal came too late. Again we see Germany playing with both sides in Finland at the same time.*
Have photograph of letter.

APPENDIXES TO THE REPORT

APPENDIX I
DOCUMENTS CIRCULATED BY ANTI-BOLSHEVIKI IN RUSSIA

This appendix is of circulars of which (except in two cases noted) I have neither originals nor authenticated copies. A number of sets of them were put out in Russian text in Petrograd and in other parts of Russia in the winter (1917-18) by the opponents of the Bolsheviki. The circulars were declared to be copies of documents taken from the Counter Espionage Bureau of the Kerensky Government, supplemented by some earlier material from the same bureau when it was under the Imperial Government. The opportunity for securing them could easily have been afforded to the agents and employees of the Bureau, for most of the employees walked out when the Bolsheviki grasped the Government, and could have taken freely of the contents of their departments.

Some of the documents were included in the publication made in Paris, hitherto referred to.

I have not relied on them as proof, but they fit to other fabrics of proof, and in the light of it are more valuable for themselves than they were when they stood alone.

Two of the documents among these circulars are the circular of industrial mobilization of June 9, 1914, and the "destruction agents" circular of November 28, 1914. (See Document 3 of my Report.) This group of circulars came into my hands the first week in February, 1918, in an English version with the unknown translator's notes and a few days later two other sets, one in English and one in Russian, reached me. I prepared a digest of the set and Ambassador Francis cabled the message in code to the State Department February 9. It was nearly four weeks later before I secured the matter referred to in my Report as "Originals" and all the photographs listed in my Report. Two of these originals were of circulars I had seen in copy form four weeks earlier. That summarizes the case of the circulars of the appendix considered as evidence.

EDGAR SISSON.

Analysis of German conspiracy matter, with notes as prepared by me and cabled State Department in Ambassador Francis's code February 9, 1918, and with some added notes, as indicated.*

DOCUMENT NO. 54

Circular February 18, 1914.—From the Ministry [of Finance] to all groups of German banks and, by agreement with the Austro-Hungarian Government, the Oesterreichische-Kreditanstalt:"

The managements of all German banks which are transacting business

* The text which is presented in this publication is in the main that of the translation into English, by an unknown translator, which was cabled to the State Department. For convenience this is called version A. A second translation into English differing in extent and phraseology from the former is styled version B. The mimeographed set of these circulars in Russian, which Mr. Sisson secured, is referred to as version C; it agrees in the main with B so far as the latter extends. Version B does not include Documents 61 to 68 inclusive. Passages printed in italics in the text are in version A but not in B and C; passages in brackets are in B and C but are omitted in version A.

abroad and, by agreement with the Austro-Hungarian Government, the Oesterreichische - Kreditanstalt Bank, are hereby advised that the Imperial Government has deemed it to be of extreme necessity to ask the management of all institutions of credit to establish with all possible dispatch agencies in Luleo, Haparanda, and Varde, on the frontier of Finland, and in Bergen and Amsterdam. The establishment of such agencies for a more effective observation of the financial interests of German shareholders of Russian, French, and English concerns may become a necessity under certain circumstances, which would alter the situation of the industrial and financial market.

Moreover, the managements of banking institutions are urged emphatically to make provisions for very close and absolutely secret relations being established with Finnish and American banks. In this direction the ministry begs to recommend the [extremely active] Swedish Nia Banken in Stockholm, *the banking office of Furstenberg*, the commercial company, Waldemar Hansen, in Copenhagen, as concerns which are maintaining lively relations with Russia.—(Signature) No. 373. In charge of Division for Foreign Operations.

NOTE.—*This is the outline of the basic financial structure begun in February, 1914, five months before war was launched, and still in operation. Notice the reappearance in subsequent Lenin messages of towns Luleo and Varde. Likewise the reference to American bank*. *Olaf Ashberg, one of the heads of the Nia-Banken, came to Petrograd a month ago (January, 1918) and on the way boasted that Nia-Banken was the Bolshevik bank. He was overheard by one of our own group. He secured from Smolny permit for export several hundred thousand gallons of oil, opened at Hotel d'Europe headquarters where both Mirbach and Kaiserling of German commissions have been entertained, negotiated with State bank February 1 contract for buying cash roubles and establishing foreign credit for Russian Government. Furstenberg is now at Smolny using the name Ganetzky, is one of the inner group, and is likely soon to be placed in charge of State bank. Ashberg now in Stockholm, but returning.*

DOCUMENT NO. 55

Circular, November 2, 1914.—From the General Staff to all military attachés [agents] in the countries adjacent to Russia, France, Italy, and Norway.

In all branches of German banks in Sweden, Norway, Switzerland, [China,] and the United States special war credits have been opened for subsidiary war requirements. The General Staff is authorizing you to avail yourself in unlimited amounts of these credits for the destruction of the enemy's factories, plants, and the most important military and civil structures. Simultaneously with the instigation of strikes it is necessary to make provision for the damaging of motors, of mechanisms, with the destruction of vessels [carrying] military supplies to enemy countries] setting incendiary fires to stocks of raw materials and finished

products, deprivation of large towns of their electric energy, stocks of fuel and provisions. Special agents, detailed to be at your disposal, will deliver to you explosive and incendiary devices, and a list of such persons in the country under your observation who will assume the duty of agents of destruction.—(Signed) Dr. [E.] FISCHER, General Army Councilor.

NOTE (Oct. 10, 1918).—*Of the typewritten versions of this letter in my possession, one is dated June 9, 1914, and two are dated Nov. 2, 1914. The latter is the more likely date, and the chances are that June 9 is a typographical error. No evidence value has been placed on this circular, as the introduction to this chapter carefully points out.*

The case of the next circular, however, No. 56, of the date June 9, is different. Here the date is right, and has the corroborative support of Document No. 3.

DOCUMENT NO. 56

Circular, June 9, 1914.—General Staff to all [district] intendencies:

Within 24 hours after receipt of this circular you are to inform all industrial concerns by telegraph that the documents with industrial mobilization plans and with registration forms be opened, such as are referred to in the circular of the Commission of Count Waldersee and Count Caprivi, of June 27, 1887.—No. 421 RE MOBILIZATION.

[*Versions B and C read:* Within 24 hours of receipt of this circular notify by telegraph all owners of industrial enterprises to open packets with industrial mobilization statistics (or specifications) and plans, as stated in the circular, etc. Both versions B and C add the note: This circular was seized in the correspondence of Major Epeling with Consul Count Lerchenfeldt.]

NOTE.—*This is the content of circular of which I have original German printed circular in the form in which it is reproduced in my report in connection with Document No. 3. E. S., July 6, 1918.*

DOCUMENT NO. 57

Circular, November 2, 1914.—From the Imperial Bank to the representatives of the Nia-Banken and the agents of the Diskonto Gesellschaft and of the Deutsche-Bank:

At the present time there have been concluded conversations between the authorized agents of the Imperial Bank and the Russian revolutionaries, Messrs. Zinovieff [*here and below version A has* Zenzinoff] and Lunacharsky. Both the mentioned persons addressed themselves to several financial men, who for their part addressed themselves to our representatives. We are ready to support the agitation and propaganda projected by them in Russia on the [one] absolute condition that the agitation and propaganda noted [planned] by the above-mentioned Messrs. Zinovieff and Lunacharsky will touch the active armies at the front. In case the agents of the Imperial Bank should address themselves to your banks we beg you to open them the necessary credit which will be covered completely as soon as you make demand on Berlin.—(Signed) RISSER.

[*Addition as part of document*]: Zinovieff and Lunacharsky got in touch with Imperial Bank of Germany through the bankers, D. Rubenstein, Max Warburg, and Parvus. Zinovieff addressed himself to Rubenstein and Lunacharsky through Altvater to Warburg, through whom he found support in Parvus.

NOTE. — *Lunacharsky is the present People's Commissioner of Education. Parvus and Warburg both figure in the Lenin and Trotsky documents. Parvus is an agent at Copenhagen (see "New Europe," January 31, 1918, pp. 94-95). Warburg is believed to have been lately in Petrograd.*

DOCUMENT NO. 58

Circular, November 28, 1914.— From Naval General Staff to the naval attachés [*Version C reads* agents]:

You are ordered to mobilize immediately all destruction agents and observers [agents-observers and agents-destroyers] in those commercial and military ports where munitions are being loaded [may be loaded] on ships going to England, France, Canada, the United States of North America, and Russia, where there are storehouses of such munitions and where [naval] fighting units are stationed. It is necessary to hire through third parties who stand in no relationship to the official representatives of Germany, agents for arranging explosives [explosions] on ships bound for enemy countries, and for arranging delays, embroilments, and confusions during the loading, dispatching, and unloading of ships. For this purpose we are specially recommending for your attention loaders' gangs, amongst whom there are many anarchists and escaped criminals [and that you get in touch with*] German and neutral [shipping] offices, and [as a means of observing*] agents of enemy countries who are receiving and shipping the munitions. Funds required for the hiring and bribing of persons necessary for the designated purpose will be placed at your disposal at your request.—(Signed) No. 93. Secret Service Division of the Naval Staff. KOENIG.

[*Original translator's comment (as part of document):*] The above document was among the documents seized during the investigation of the fire of the storehouses of the firm of Iversen, and among the documents of Consul Gering and Vice Consul Gerold.

* In the German circular (see Document No. 3) but omitted in versions A, B, and C.

NOTE.—*This is an English translation, by an unknown translator, of circular of which I have German printed circular in form in which it is reproduced in connection with Document No. 3. See my Report, Document No. 3.—E. S., July 6, 1918.*

DOCUMENT NO. 59

Circular, January 15, 1915, from the General Staff to the military attachés [agents] in the United States: Inclosed you will find [*original translator's note:* or, we are sending you] the circular of November 2, 1914, for your guidance and its application in the territory of the United States. In this connection your attention is called to the possibility of hiring destruction agents among members of anarchist [labor] organizations.—(Signed) General Army Councilor, Dr. [E.] FISCHER.

[*Original translator's comment (as part of document):*] This circular is recited in the letter of Dr. Klassen to the board of the Pan-German League in Stockholm, which was intercepted in Stockholm.

NOTES (By Edgar Sisson, July 6, 1918).— *The date of November 2 appears in typed version as I have seen it, but probably this is error, as instruction is a direct sequel to document of November 28 (No. 3). (Later.)— Nov. 2 is right. Nov. 28 was to naval agents. This is to military agents.—E. S.*

DOCUMENT NO. 60

Circular, February 23, 1915.—Press Division of the Ministry of Foreign Affairs to all ambassadors, ministers, and consular officials in neutral countries:

You are hereby advised that in the country to which you are accredited special offices are established for the organization of propaganda in the countries of the coalition of powers which is in a state of belligerency with Germany. [*Versions B and C read:* in countries at war with German coalition]. The propaganda will be connected with the stirring up of social unrest and strikes resulting from it; of revolutionary outbreaks; of separatism among the component parts of the state; of civil war; and will also comprise agitation against [in favor of] disarmament and the discontinuation of the war butchery. You are requested to coöperate with and to favor in every way the managers of said offices. These persons will present to you proper certificates [credentials].

(Signed) BARTHELM.

[*Original translator's comment (as part of document):*] According to reliable information to this category of persons belonged: Prince Hohenlohe, Björnson, Epeling [Eveling], Karsberg [Kerberg], Sukennikoff, Parvus, Furstenberg (Ganetsky), Ripke, and probably Kelyshko [Kolishko].

NOTE.—*Here is the exact German formula for the incitement of war "from the rear"— strikes, efforts at revolution, the use of humanitarian appeals to weaken the arm of its foes.*

DOCUMENT NO. 61

Circular, October 14, 1916.—From president of Kirdorff's Rhenish-Westphalian Industrial Syndicate to the central office of Nia-Banken in Stockholm, to Sevnsen-Baltzer, representative of the Diskonto-Gesellschaft in Stockholm, and to Mr. Kirch [Kriek], representative of Deutsche Bank in Switzerland:

The Rhenish-Westphalian Industrial Coal Syndicate charges you with the management of the account of which you have been apprised for the support of Russian emigrants desirous of conducting propaganda amongst Russian prisoners of war and the Russian army.—(Signed) KIRDORFF.

NOTE.—*This document already figures in the archives of several Governments, having been intercepted in the correspondence of Prince von Buelow. It has new and direct pertinency on the Lenin-Trotsky data which follows herewith.*

DOCUMENT NO. 62

COPENHAGEN, June 18, 1917.
Mr. RUFFNER [RUFFER], Helsingfors.

DEAR SIR: Please be advised that from the Disconto-Gesellschaft account 315,000 marks have been transferred to Mr. Lenin's account in Kronstadt, as per order of the Syndicate. Kindly acknowledge receipt: Nilandeway 98, Copenhagen, W. Hansen & Co.—SVENSEN.

NOTE.—*Kronstadt, the navy base, was the nerve center from which Lenin's activities radiated during the summer, both before and after he fled Petrograd. He was not always there but it was the Bolshevik domain. The sailors were and still are his first dependence. Hansen & Co. are named in Document No. 54.*

DOCUMENT NO. 63

GENEVA, June 16, 1917.
Mr. FURSTENBERG, Stockholm: Please note that at the request of Mr. Katz, francs 32,000 [$2,000] have been paid for the publication of Maximalist-Socialist pamphlets. Advise by telegram addressed to Decker of the receipt of the consignment of pamphlets, number of bill of lading, and date of arrival. — (Signed) KRIEK, Deutsche Bank.

NOTE.—*Furstenberg is named in Document No. 54 and is Ganetsky in Petrograd.*

DOCUMENT NO. 64

STOCKHOLM, September 21, 1917.
Mr. RAPHAEL SCHOLAN [SCHAUMANN], Haparanda.

DEAR COMRADE: The office of the banking house M. Warburg has opened in accordance with telegram from president of Rhenish-Westphalian Syndicate an account for the undertaking of Comrade Trotsky. The attorney [agent] purchased arms and has organized their transportation and delivery up to Luleo and Varde. Name to the office of Essen & Son in Luleo, receivers, and a person authorized to receive the money demanded by Comrade Trotsky.—J. FURSTENBERG.

NOTE.—*This is the first reference to Trotsky, and connects him with Banker Warburg and Furstenberg. Luleo and Varde are Swedish towns, the former near to Haparanda, which is on the border of Sweden and Finland.*

DOCUMENT NO. 65

STOCKHOLM, September 12, 1917.
Mr. FARSEN, Kronstadt (via Helsingfors): Carried out your commissions; passports and the indicated sum of 207,000 marks as per order of your Mr. Lenin have been handed to persons mentioned in your letter. The selection found the approval of his excellency, the ambassador. Confirm the arrival of said persons and the receipt of their counter receipts —SVENSON.

NOTE.—*See Document No. 61. Lenin had received more than half a million marks at this date. (See also Document No. 68).*

DOCUMENT NO. 66

LULEO, October 2, 1917

Mr. ANTONOV, Haparanda: Comrade Trotsky's request has been carried out. From the account of the Syndicate and the ministry [*Original translator's note:* probably Ministry of Foreign Affairs in Berlin, press division] 400,000 kroners have been taken and remitted to Comrade Sonia, who will call on you with this letter, and will hand you the said sum of money.—J. FURSTENBERG.

NOTE.—*Antonov is the chief military leader of the Bolsheviki. He was in command of the forces that took Petrograd. He now is in the field against Kaledin and Alexieff. At the date of this letter Trotsky already was at the head of the Petrograd Soviet and the Bolsheviki revolution was only a month away.*

DOCUMENT NO. 67

BERLIN [COPENHAGEN], August 25, 1917.

Mr. OLBERG: Your desire considered together with the intentions of the Party. [*Version C reads:* Your wish, based on your correspondence with M. Gorky, falls in entirely with the aims of the Party.] By agreement with the persons known to you 150,000 kroners are transferred to be at your disposal at Furstenberg's office, through Nia-Banken. Kindly advise *Vorwärts* about everything that is being written by the newspaper [of M. Gorky] about present events.—SCHEIDEMANN.

NOTE.—*This letter from Scheidemann, the German Socialist leader, links him with Furstenberg-Ganetsky, with the Nia-Banken, and with the subsidy of the Russian revolution. "Vorwärts" refers to Scheidemann's organ at Berlin. Scheidemann's rôles both as German peace propagandist and as German strike queller are illumined by this letter.*

NOTE (Sept. 12, 1918).—*Gorky did support the Bolsheviks before they came into power, but almost immediately afterward turned against them.—E. S.*

DOCUMENT NO. 68

BERLIN, July 14, 1917.

Mr. MIR [MOR], Stockholm: We are transferring to your name through Mr. I. Ruchvergen 180,000 marks [. Of this sum Engineer Steinberg will transmit 140,000 marks to Lenin] for the expense of your [his] journey to Finland. The balance will be at your disposal for agitation against England and France. The letters of Malianik and Stocklov, which were sent [by you] were received and will be considered.—PARVUS.

NOTE.—*Lenin was in hiding in July. Report placed him, among other places, in Stockholm. Notice that the agitation is to be against England and France. It took the form from the opening days of the Bolshevik revolution of attacks upon them as "imperialistic nations." Parvus is the Copenhagen agent already referred to.—E. S., July 6, 1918.*

APPENDIX II

ILLUSTRATING THE "OFFENSE TACTICS" OF THE BOLSHEVIK LEADERS AGAINST GREAT BRITAIN AND THE UNITED STATES. —A CONVERSATION BY TELEGRAPH BETWEEN CHICHERIN AT PETROGRAD (WHO IS SPEAKING) AND TROTSKY AT BREST-LITOVSK, IN FIRST WEEK IN FEBRUARY, 1918, A FEW DAYS BEFORE TROTSKY MADE HIS "NO PEACE—NO WAR" GESTURE, WITH ITS PRACTICAL ASPECT OF DEMOBILIZING THE ARMY AND OPENING RUSSIA'S UNARMED BREAST TO GERMANY.

With reference to the allies the situation is evidently favorable. Separate peace will not cause a rupture. England has reconciled herself to this in advance. The recognition of us is a matter of the near future. England and America are playing up to us separately. A few days ago there appeared a so-called head of a commercial mission, Lockhart, with a letter from Litvinoff stating that the bearer is an honest man who indeed fairly sympathizes with us. Indeed, he is a subtle, alert Englishman; expresses very liberal views; runs down his Government. He is a type of the diplomat of the new school. At present he is not an official representative, but *de facto* he is an envoy, having been sent by the war cabinet. After our recognition he will obtain an official position with us. He promises all kinds of favors from England.

He explained that if we should not spoil the situation our recognition is a question of the near future, but something would have to be ceded on our part. He said that no government could tolerate intervention in its internal affairs. If we are going to raise the British people, if our agents in England will attempt to cause strikes, England will not tolerate this. It proved later that this had reference to Petroff's mission. Concerning the latter specially Lockhart said that his appointment would be difficult for England to swallow, and should he be arrested in England or not be allowed to land we would probably reply by reprisals, and thus the whole business would be spoiled. He begged that we postpone this matter for 10 or 12 days.

Simultaneously Ransome tried to persuade Petroff not to go to England. His journey in case of a conflict would put the question of a revolution in England on edge, which would be exceedingly risky. We discussed this question and decided that our strength was in attack, and that whatever would happen it would be the worse for Lloyd George & Co., and the revolution would be the gainer. We sent Petroff's passport to be viséed. Lockhart came running to us. I arranged for an interview with Petroff. Lockhart stated that the question had been referred for decision to London. We said that Russia represented a part of the world's revolutionary movement and that in this was its strength. We and our comrades in England would proclaim that this is not a concrete organization of strikes. We explained the aim of Petroff's mission—*i.e.*, the clearing up of misunderstandings between two nations. He will appeal to all organs of the British nation. This has also been sent by radio.

Lockhart stated that he was very well impressed and promised to telegraph advising that the visé should be granted. We await further developments. He stated that according to English information the German troops on the eastern front were so badly infected by our propaganda that no second course of barrack regime could cure them. He said that our method of fighting militarism was the most effective. We listened to this and laughed up our sleeves.

NOTE.—*There in the last sentence we have it. The Bolshevik plot in Russia could be placarded a cynical farce, if it were not a world tragedy. This appendix is from an intercepted dispatch which came into the possession of Mr. Sisson.*

PART II

I. LETTER OF MR. CREEL TO NATIONAL BOARD FOR HISTORICAL SERVICE

COMMITTEE ON PUBLIC INFORMATION,
WASHINGTON, D. C.

October 18, 1918.

PROFESSOR JOSEPH SCHAEFER, Vice--Chairman National Board for Historical Service, 1133 Woodward Building, Washington, D. C.

DEAR SIR:—Professor Ford tells me that the Directors of the National Board for Historical Service are meeting this afternoon at four o'clock; and I have asked him to take up with you the matter of considering the documents recently released for publication by the Committee on Public Information for the purpose of showing the intimate and continued connection of Lenin and Trotsky and their immediate associates with the German Government.

When only the opening installments of the series of seven had been published, the question of authenticity was raised by the New York *Evening Post*. The rest of the press of America, virtually without exception, accepted the fact of publication as evidence of the genuineness of the documents; and even the continued attempts of th3 New York *Evening Post* to rally the forces of doubt failed absolutely, only two men with any pretension of historical knowledge joining in any degree with the *Post*.

As a matter of course, the Committee on Public Information was committed from the first to a policy of absolute openness with regard to these documents. While never submitted to any unofficial body for purposes of investigation, it is nevertheless the fact that they have been gone over time and again by various agencies of the Government, and were not released for publication by this Committee until express sanction had been received from the highest authorities of the Government.

It was our idea from the first, and it is our idea now, to make pamphlet presentation of the documents, together with facsimile reproductions of all the more important originals. This task, attended by many mechanical difficulties, has just been completed.

The situation that now faces us is this: The documents were given to the press with the good faith of the Government behind them, and our promise is out to present them in pamphlet form with the photographic reproductions of originals. We cannot, in any manner, afford to appear dilatory or evasive, nor do we desire to publish the pamphlet without taking cognizance of the charges that have been made.

What I would like to do is to present the documents to a Committee, to be appointed by you, together with the charges that have been made, and to have these charges considered carefully with a view to determining their truth or falsity. If you will undertake this task, I would not desire to place any time limit upon you in any degree, but it is still the case that time is the very essence of the matter, for publication has been promised, and is waited for daily. May I suggest, therefore, that you appoint an authoritative committee, small in numbers, and that this committee assemble at once here in Washington where the necessary material is available for their information?

Believe me,

Very truly,

GEORGE CREEL,
Chairman.

The committee as appointed by the Executive Committee of the National Board for Historical Service, in response to the above request, consisted of Dr. J. Franklin Jameson, editor of the "American Historical Review" and Director of the Department of Historical Research of the Carnegie Institution of Washington; and Dr. Samuel N. Harper, Professor of Russian Language and Institutions in the University of Chicago.

II. REPORT OF THE SPECIAL COMMITTEE ON THE GENUINENESS OF THE DOCUMENTS

NATIONAL BOARD FOR HISTORICAL SERVICE.
WASHINGTON, D. C.:

October 26, 1918.

GEORGE CREEL, ESQ., Chairman of the Committee on Public Information, Washington, D. C.:

DEAR SIR:—By your letter of October 18, addressed to the vice-chairman of the National Board for Historical Service, you have asked that body to appoint a committee to examine, in respect to their genuineness, the series of documents purporting to show the relations between the Russian Bolshevist leaders and the German Government, which were released for publication in the September newspapers by the Committee on Public Information. You have asked that such committee should take into careful consideration the arguments against the genuineness of those documents put forward in the columns of the New York *Evening Post*, with a view to determine the validity or invalidity of those arguments. The undersigned were on October 19 appointed by the Board named to serve as a committee, and were requested by you to report their findings with the utmost frankness, regardless of any positions already publicly taken by you or by the Government. In pursuance of these instructions we beg leave to submit the following report.

As a basis for our work you have laid before us proof-sheets of a pamphlet edition of these documents, entitled *The German-Bolshevik Conspiracy*, and containing facsimiles of some sixteen of the documents in question, translations of documents numbered from 1 to 68, and of a few other documents subjoined to them, and comments and notes by Mr. Edgar Sisson, who procured the documents and edited them for the first or newspaper publication. The translations thus laid before us are those which appeared in the newspapers, and the documents bear the same numbers, by which, accordingly, we shall refer to them in this report. Mr. Sisson's comments include some additional notes, of October date, correcting and enlarging his previous comments in the light of information subsequently received.

Concerning the translations, though in strictness our function is limited to examination of originals, we will take the liberty to say that the versions put forth for publication in the newspapers are marked by grave imperfections. These imperfections we understand to have arisen naturally from the fact that Mr. Sisson, under the circumstances in which he worked in Petrograd and at other successive places, was obliged to have his translations made by several different hands. Whether the resulting unevenness and other imperfections should be removed before publication of the translations in a more permanent form, is a matter which we, of course, leave to your discretion; but we are obliged to allude to them because they have laid the documents open

---

at certain points, some of which will be mentioned later, to suspicions which the originals of those passages nowise warrant.

Upon Mr. Sisson's inferences from his documents we do not understand that we are expected to comment, nor do we desire to express, or to be influenced by, any opinion respecting the conduct of Bolshevist leaders or German officials; our present duty, as we conceive it, is confined merely to examination into the genuineness of a specific series of documents.

You have also laid before us the original documents in sixteen cases, and in the other cases the photographs, on which all the translations from No. 1 to No. 53 were based, and also the mimeographed texts in Russian from which were made the translations from No. 54 to No. 68. Mr. Sisson has detailed to us, with all apparent candor, the history of his reception of the documents, and has permitted us to question him at great length as to these transactions and as to various points relative to the papers. Several officials of the Government in Washington have obliged us by contributing other pertinent and valuable information.

In presenting the results of our investigations, we find it desirable to distinguish the documents into three groups: first, and much the largest, (I) those presented to us in Russian originals or photographs—four-fifths of the whole set; (II) the two documents presented to us in circulars printed in German; (III) those documents for which no originals or photographs are presented, but the translations of which rest solely on mimeographed texts in Russian, purporting to represent originals in or from Russian archives.

In other words, our first group (I) consists of the documents bearing the numbers 1 to 53, inclusive. Our second group (II) consists of the two documents which appear translated in the newspaper publication as annexes to document No. 3. They also appear, with facsimiles, after No. 3 in the proposed pamphlet; and they are identical with Nos. 56 and 58 in the appendix. Our third group (III) embraces all the documents of Appendix I (Nos. 54 to 68, inclusive) except Nos. 56 and 58. We comment upon these groups separately.

I. The originals and photographs composing what we have called the first group are all in the Russian language. They are typewritten (save one which is printed) on letter-heads of the Petrograd bureau of the German General Staff, of the Counter-Espionage at the Stavka (army headquarters), or of other offices in Russia, German or Russian. They are dated according to the Russian calendar ("Old Style"), up to February, 1918, when the Bolshevist Government made the change to "New Style." We have subjected them with great care to all the applicable tests to which historical students are accustomed to subject documents of the kind, and to as many others as we could devise and use, consistently with the need of making a reasonably early report. Besides studying whatever internal evidences could be derived from the papers themselves, we have, so far as we could, compared their versions of what went on with the actual facts. Upon the basis of these investigations, we have no hesitation in declaring that we see no reason to doubt the genuineness or authenticity of these fifty-three documents.

II. The two documents of our second group seem to us to call for a special, a less confident, and a less simple verdict. Printed in German, they purport to be official German orders of the year 1914,—the one addressed on June 9 of that year, seven weeks before the outbreak of the war, by the

General Staff of the German Army to district commandants, enjoining them to cause German industrial establishments to open their instructions respecting industrial mobilization; the other, dated November 28, 1914, addressed by the General Staff of the High Sea Fleet to maritime agencies and naval societies, and calling on them to mobilize destructive agents in foreign harbors, with a view to thwarting shipments of munitions to "England, France, Canada, the United States, and Russia." The problem of their genuineness must be considered in connection with Documents Nos. 56 and 58 in the Appendix, which are nearly identical with them, differing in sense only as Russian translations might easily differ from German originals.

The errors of typography, of spelling, and even of grammar, in these German circulars, make it impossible to accept them as original prints of the General Staffs named. Certain peculiarities of expression tend in the same direction. In the naval circular the explanation, in parenthesis, of the German word *Vereinigungen* by the Russicism *Artelen* (Russian word with German plural ending) makes it impossible to think of the document as one printed by the German Naval Staff for use indifferently in *all* the various countries in which there were German maritime agencies and naval societies. Furthermore, the reference to the United States is puzzling. On the other hand, Document No. 3, a protocol which presents exceptional evidences of genuineness, records the transfer from Russian archives, into the hands of German military officials in Petrograd, of two documents which it not only designates by date and number but describes; and date, number, and description correspond to those of the two papers in question. There is other evidence in Washington of the existence of two such circulars, said to be of the dates named, in Petrograd archives in 1915. Attention should also be called to the manuscript annotations on the circulars, plainly visible in the facsimiles. On both appears, in blue pencil, a note which, properly translated, reads: "One copy given to the Nachrichten-Bureau.—Archive." That is to say, one printed copy has been handed over, in accordance with the formal record made in Document No. 3, to the Military Intelligence Bureau of the German General Staff (a bureau which then or soon after was housed under the same roof with the Bolshevist Government, in the Smolny Institute), while this present printed copy is to be put in the Russian archives. The circular dated June 9 bears also the annotation in red ink, "To the protocol [of] Nov. 2, 1917," confirming the connection asserted.

We do not think these two printed circulars to be simply forgeries. We do not think them to be, in their present shape, documents on whose entire text historians or publicists can safely rely as genuine. If we were to hazard a conjecture, it would be that they are derived, perhaps at one or two removes, from actual documents, which may have been copied in manuscript and at a later time reproduced in print. In any case, they have no relation to the Bolshevist officials, except indirectly through their

connection with Document No. 3, which, with or without them, shows the Petrograd office of the German General Staff desirous of withdrawing certain papers from the Russian archives, and the Bolshevist Government complying with its desires.

III. For the documents of our third group, apart from Nos. 56 and 58, we have only the Russian mimeographed texts. The originals of nearly all of them would have been written in German. We have seen neither originals nor photographs, nor has Mr. Sisson, who rightly relegates these documents to an appendix, and expresses less confidence in their evidential value than in that of his main series, Nos. 1 to 53. With such insufficient means of testing their genuineness as can be afforded by Russian translations, we can make no confident declaration. Thrown back on internal evidence alone, we can only say that we see in these texts nothing that positively excludes the notion of their being genuine, little in any of them that makes it doubtful, though guarantees of their having been accurately copied, and accurately translated into Russian, are obviously lacking.

We should say the same (except that its original is not German) of the telegraphic conversation between Chicherin and Trotsky, which Mr. Sisson prints as Appendix II. The letter of Joffe, on the other hand, dated December 31, 1917, which he prints just after his No. 37,* stands on as strong a basis as documents Nos. 1 to 53, for Mr. Sisson had at one time a photograph of it, derived in the same manner as his other photographs.

As to the Reichsbank order of March 2, 1917, printed by him as an annex to Document No. 1, the text there presented does not purport to represent more than its general substance. The reader is not asked to rely on its accuracy and completeness, and we should not wish to do so.

It remains to consider the specific criticisms, as to genuineness of the documents, advanced by the New York *Evening Post* and its correspondents. Most of them fall away when it is known that the main series of documents, Nos. 1 to 53, are written in Russian and dated in accordance with the calendar currently used in Petrograd, and when it is considered that, as is well known, the Bolshevist *coup d'état* was expected in that city for some time before it took place.

Thus, the *Evening Post* (of September 16, 17, 18, 21, 1918) repeatedly scouts document No. 5, dated in the newspaper publication "October, 1917," and document No. 21, dated November 1, 1917,—letters addressed by the Petrograd bureau of the German General Staff to the Bolshevist Government—on the ground that on those dates, in the Berlin calendar, there was no Bolshevist Government, the Bolshevist *coup* having been delivered on November 7 of that calendar. But these documents are not of Berlin, though they are typewritten on letter-heads bearing that name in print,

---

* Printed as Document No. 37A in this pamphlet edition. It should be noted also that the "telegraphic conversation" referred to is taken from an intercepted dispatch which came directly into Mr. Sisson's hands. This, perhaps, was not made clear to the committee.

in the one case crossed out with the pen, in the other case not. Document No. 5 seems to have been written in Finland. We have been able to make out, in the photograph, the day-date in its heading. It is 25 October, *i.e.*, November 7 of New Style; and the Bolshevist acknowledgment at the bottom bears the date, not given in the newspaper publication, "27.X.1917," *i.e.*, November 9 of New Style. In other words, more cannot be said than that the German General Staff, not unaware of preparations of which all the world was aware in Petrograd, was prompt in action. It is a slight but significant touch that Colonel Rausch, writing from Finland on the day when the expected outbreak occurred, styles the new organization "Government (*Pravitelstvo*) of People's Commissaries" instead of "Council (*Soviet*) of People's Commissaries," the designation actually adopted.

The *Post's* criticism (September 16) of Document No. 2 on the ground of its mention of the "Petersburg Secret Police" (*Okhrana*), assumed by the writer to have been destroyed on March 10 or 11, seems to us to have no conclusive weight. The old Okhrana was abolished by the revolution, but the revolutionary Government itself had of course its secret service, to which a German might continue to apply the old name.

A correspondent of the *Post*, Mr. E. J. Omeltchenko, in its issue of October 4, rightly finds it singular that Dr. von Schanz, in Documents Nos. 8 and 9, should be represented as signing himself on January 8, "Representative of the Imperial Bank," and on January 12, "President of the Imperial Bank." It should be explained that the Russian word used is the same in both cases, *Predstavitel*, but that the translator of No. 9 wrongly translated it "President," while the translator of No. 8 translated it rightly, "Representative."

Mr. Omeltchenko also, with reference to Document No. 8, prints figures of the gold reserves of the Reichsbank and of the Bank of Sweden, November, 1917, to January, 1918, in the belief that, if the Reichsbank had at the beginning of January given the Bolshevist officials a credit in Sweden of 50,000,000 roubles gold, these figures would show the fact. We are informed on high financial authority that the Reichsbank would be able to effect such a transaction by means much less easily traced. Mr. Omeltchenko questions the need of the transaction, but the insecurity and unsettled conditions prevailing within the boundaries of the old Russian empire might easily account for the desire of the Bolsheviki to establish a large gold credit abroad without the necessity of actually exporting gold.

Professor Edward S. Corwin, in the same issue of the *Evening Post*, rightly criticises the date June 9, 1914, for Document No. 55. Its proper date appears to be November 2, 1914. The mimeographed Russian text bears that date. A translator, probably by confusion with No. 56, gave it the June date.

Respectfully submitted,

J. Franklin Jameson.
Samuel N. Harper.

INDEX

DATE DUE

JAN 30 '64			
APR 20 '64			
MAY 6 '66			
MAY 18			
GAYLORD			